AI Applications in Instructional Education Strategies

Jaime Aguilar-Ortiz
Universidad Politécnica de Pachuca, Mexico

IGI Global
Scientific Publishing
Publishing Tomorrow's Research Today

Vice President of Editorial	Melissa Wagner
Director of Acquisitions	Mikaela Felty
Director of Book Development	Jocelynn Hessler
Production Manager	Mike Brehm
Cover Design	Jose Rosado

Published in the United States of America by
IGI Global Scientific Publishing
701 East Chocolate Avenue
Hershey, PA, 17033, USA
Tel: 717-533-8845 | Fax: 717-533-7115
Website: https://www.igi-global.com E-mail: cust@igi-global.com

Library of Congress Cataloging-in-Publication Data

Names: Aguilar-Ortiz, Jaime, editor.
Title: AI applications in instructional education strategies / edited by: Jaime Aguilar Ortiz.
Description: Hershey PA : IGI Global Scientific Publishing, [2026] | Includes bibliographical references. | Summary: "This book aims to provide a comprehensive and practical guide for integrating artificial intelligence (AI) into educational strategies, to encourage innovation in teaching and learning, and to equip educators, administrators, and policymakers with the tools and knowledge needed to implement AI effectively in educational settings"-- Provided by publisher.
Identifiers: LCCN 2025015980 (print) | LCCN 2025015981 (ebook) | ISBN 9798337305981 (hardcover) | ISBN 9798337305998 (paperback) | ISBN 9798337306001 (ebook)
Subjects: LCSH: Computer-assisted instruction. | Artificial intelligence--Educational applications.
Classification: LCC LB1028.43 .C385 2026 (print) | LCC LB1028.43 (ebook) | DDC 371.33/463--dc23/eng/20250528
LC record available at https://lccn.loc.gov/2025015980
LC ebook record available at https://lccn.loc.gov/2025015981

British Cataloguing in Publication Data
A Cataloguing in Publication record for this book is available from the British Library.

To my wife Bety, children Paola and Jimmy, parents Irma and Jaime, sisters Isabel and Hilda, nephews Ángel, Beto and Marco, and daughter-in-law Mariana.

Table of Contents

Detailed Table of Contents

over-reliance. Future directions include LLMs for code explanation and federated learning for secure, scalable error prediction. This chapter offers practical insights for educators to build more effective, engaging, and supportive programming classrooms.

K. Ramalakshmi, P.S.R. Engineering College, India
L. Krishna Kumari, Ramco Institute of Technology, India
B. Mohan, P.S.R. Engineering College, India
Sravan Kumar Gunturi, Koneru Lakshmaiah Education Foundation, India
S. P. Santhoshkumar, Vel Tech Rangarajan Dr. Sagunthala R&D Institute of Science and Technology, India
R. Santhana Krishnan, SCAD College of Engineering and Technology, India
J. Relin Francis Raj, Saveetha School of Engineering, Saveetha Institute of Medical and Technical Sciences, India

Both VR and AR are at the forefront of delivering engaging, interactive experiences that are reshaping industries by improving training, operational efficiency, and user engagement through immersive and enhanced environments. These technologies serve as a bridge between the digital and physical realms, providing innovative solutions across a wide range of domains, including education, healthcare, entertainment, and enterprise. The integration of AR and VR is particularly impactful, enabling advanced applications that transform how individuals experience and interact with their surroundings. This study explores the development and capabilities of VR and AR technologies, highlighting their standalone applications and demonstrating how their combination yields powerful outcomes.

This chapter explores the integration of artificial intelligence (AI) in automating administrative tasks within educational institutions. Drawing on recent technological advances, it analyses how AI tools—such as machine learning algorithms, natural language processing, and predictive analytics—are used to optimise processes including enrolment, scheduling, reporting, and early warning systems. Case studies from primary to tertiary education reveal improved efficiency, reduced human error, cost savings, and staff reallocation to pedagogical roles. The study also addresses technological limitations, data privacy concerns, algorithmic bias, and institutional resistance. Findings highlight that successful implementation requires technological readiness, ethical frameworks, ongoing professional development, and inclusive leadership. Ultimately, AI-driven automation in school administration holds transformative potential when strategically aligned with human values, equity, and educational quality, fostering more responsive, sustainable, and data-informed governance.

Preface

INTRODUCTION

In a time of profound technological transformation, the educational landscape is at a crucial crossroads. Traditional teaching strategies, while fundamental and not to be forgotten, are no longer sufficient to meet the demands of today's dynamic, diverse, ever-changing, and data-driven learning environments. As an editor, researcher and educator passionate about pedagogical innovation, I present Cases on AI Applications in Instructional Educational Strategies as a timely exploration of how artificial intelligence (AI) can and should transform the way we teach, learn, and prepare for the future.

This book was conceived with a dual purpose: to reflect the growing urgency for educational innovation and to offer a practical roadmap for those ready to integrate AI into instructional strategies. The rise of AI presents a unique and novel opportunity to personalize learning, close equity gaps, and equip both educators and students with tools to navigate a rapidly evolving world. But the journey from possibility to implementation is not without its challenges—technical, political, ethical, and pedagogical. Our goal is to bridge that gap.

Throughout this volume, readers will find detailed case studies, theoretical foundations, real-world applications, and hands-on tools, including exercises, cases and code, to translate concepts into practice. From adaptive learning platforms to intelligent tutoring systems and administrative automation, we delve into how AI is being applied across the educational spectrum—and what it means for the future of teaching and learning.

This work is structured around four core objectives that shaped our editorial direction:

1. To provide a comprehensive and practical guide for educators, administrators, technologists, and researchers seeking to understand and implement AI in educational contexts.
2. To encourage innovation and solution development by showcasing successful applications of AI to real-world instructional challenges.
3. To train the next generation of educators and researchers capable of integrating AI into their practice with fluency, responsibility, and creativity.
4. To promote open data and collaboration, fostering a culture of transparency, reproducibility, and shared advancement in educational technology.

Equally important is our attention to audience. This book is intentionally written for a wide range of stakeholders. For educators, it offers strategies to personalize learning and increase engagement. For administrators, it reveals pathways to data-informed decision-making. For edtech developers, it serves as a design reference rooted in actual classroom needs. Policy makers will find thoughtful discussion on infrastructure, ethics, and access. And for researchers, it highlights pressing questions, new challenges and fertile ground for continued inquiry.

At its heart, this book is not just about technology—it's about education and its transformation. It's about reimagining instruction to better serve all learners. It's about equipping those at the frontlines of education with the insights and tools they need to lead through change. And it's about fostering a new paradigm in which AI is not a novelty or threat, but a powerful ally in the pursuit of educational equity, effectiveness, and excellence.

I invite you, the reader, to engage deeply with the ideas presented here—not just to consume them, but to apply them, challenge them, build upon them and propose new ways. Whether you are in a classroom, a boardroom, a lab, or a policy forum, may this book serve as both inspiration and guide on your journey to harnessing the potential of AI in education.

ORGANIZATION OF THE BOOK

This edited volume unfolds over fourteen chapters, each contributing to a deeper understanding of how artificial intelligence (AI) is reshaping education across pedagogical, administrative, and policy dimensions. The journey begins in **Chapter 1: Introduction to Artificial Intelligence**, where readers are introduced to the foundational technologies and theoretical underpinnings of AI. From machine learning and natural language processing to robotics and ethical concerns like algorithmic bias and privacy, this chapter lays the groundwork for understanding AI's multidisciplinary relevance and its transformative role in educational and organizational contexts.

Building on this foundation, **Chapter 2: Fundamentals of Artificial Intelligence** delves into the evolution of AI from symbolic rule-based systems to modern deep learning and neural networks. With a specific emphasis on its educational applications, this chapter introduces readers to the tools, techniques methodologies, and ethical considerations crucial for leveraging AI in personalized learning environments, setting the stage for practical implementation in the classroom.

Recognizing the regional and cultural nuances in education, **Chapter 3: An Approach to the Integration of Artificial Intelligence in Inclusive Education for Latin America** explores AI's potential to address access and equity in education. Focused on the Latin American context, this chapter highlights how emerging artificial intelligence technologies can support inclusive teaching strategies, reduce learning disparities, and enable meaningful educational experiences for all students.

In **Chapter 4: Resilience in Academia Coping with Mental Health Challenges During Pandemics**, the narrative shifts to the psychosocial impacts of the COVID-19 pandemic on students. This chapter combines data analysis and AI-driven assessment tools to examine mental health variables such as anxiety, technostress, and resilience. It advocates for institutional interventions, from online wellness programs to adaptive study policies, as essential components of future-ready academic ecosystems of greater well-being.

Chapter 5: Analysis of Recommendation Systems presents a technical yet accessible examination of recommendation algorithms—collaborative, content-based, hybrid—and their significance in educational platforms. The chapter tackles issues like scalability and personalization in the context of big data, proposing solutions such as distributed computing via Hadoop to enhance recommendation accuracy, adequacy and system efficiency.

As coding becomes a critical skill in modern curricula, **Chapter 6: Intelligent Code Analysis and Feedback Generation** introduces AI-based systems that support programming education. This chapter explores intelligent tutoring systems capable of detecting coding errors and providing real-time, personalized feedback, thus alleviating instructional load and improving teaching and learning outcomes in computer science education.

In **Chapter 7: Harnessing Immersive Technologies**, readers are introduced to the emerging landscape of augmented and virtual reality (AR/VR) and their applications across sectors. In education, these immersive technologies enable more interactive and engaging learning environments, transforming abstract concepts into experiential understanding and offering novel possibilities for training, learning, simulation, and collaboration.

Chapter 8: Applications of Artificial Intelligence in Instructional Design and Educational Strategies examines how AI is redefining the teaching-learning experience through gamification, adaptive learning systems, and intelligent assessment tools. The chapter highlights case studies and offers guidance on ethical integration, calling for updated educational policies and teacher training to ensure that AI strengthens and enhances, rather than replaces human-centered pedagogy.

Looking toward the future, **Chapter 9: AI-Driven Instructional Strategies for the Future** envisions a landscape where AI not only supports but co-designs instructional plans. It explores how AI can process vast amounts of educational data to personalize instruction, streamline lesson planning, and even extend learning beyond traditional classroom settings—offering new modes of engagement across disciplines, including different vocational and professional training.

In **Chapter 10: Design of AI-Enhanced Curricula**, the focus shifts to how AI can inform curriculum development through predictive modeling, educational data mining, and recommendation systems. The chapter presents theoretical frameworks and practical case studies to demonstrate how curricula can evolve dynamically to meet the shifting demands of the productive sectors, learners and society, while also addressing ethical considerations around bias, transparency, and equity.

Chapter 11: Enhancing Digital Literacy presents an AI-powered training and assessment system that uses deep learning models like ResNet and of metaheuristics like Ant Colony Optimization to tailor digital literacy education. This chapter emphasizes the role of AI in both formative and summative assessments, providing personalized feedback to students and actionable data insights to educators—preparing learners for an AI-intensive workforce.

Chapter 12: Leveraging Deep Learning for Proactive Student Engagement Assessment introduces an advanced AI system using a Bi-Stacked GRU model to monitor engagement levels in real time. This chapter details a sophisticated process of behavioral analysis and early warning systems to help educators identify disengagement before it impacts performance, thus enabling timely intervention and improving e-learning outcomes.

In **Chapter 13: Enhancing Decision-Making with AI**, the role of AI in educational leadership is critically examined. Through predictive analytics and case-driven insights, this chapter outlines how AI can support resource allocation, training, student support strategies, and administrative planning. The importance of ethical governance, human oversight, and professional development is emphasized to ensure that decision-making remains equitable and informed.

The book concludes with **Chapter 14: Automating Administrative Tasks**, a practical exploration of how AI is revolutionizing educational administration. From automating enrollment and reporting to deploying early warning systems, this chapter showcases AI's capacity to improve efficiency and accuracy in school operations—freeing educators to focus more on pedagogy and student support. It also addresses the prerequisites for successful adoption, including educational staff training, data ethics, and institutional readiness.

Together, these chapters offer a rich and multi-faceted exploration of AI's role in education—from the classroom to the boardroom. As editor, I am deeply proud to present this volume as both a scholarly resource and a practical guide for navigating the evolving intersection of education and artificial intelligence. Whether you are a teacher, researcher, administrator, or policymaker, I invite you to engage with these chapters not just as readers, but as co-architects of the future of learning.

CONCLUSION

As we bring this volume to a close, it is evident that artificial intelligence is no longer a speculative concept or emerging trend—it is a present and powerful force actively shaping the future of education and society. Across the chapters of this book, our contributors have explored the multifaceted ways AI intersects with instructional strategies, curriculum design, learner engagement, administrative operations, and educational equity. These insights underscore not only the transformative potential of AI but also the pressing responsibility we share in ensuring its ethical, equitable, and effective application.

AI has the capacity to personalize learning, support educators, automate complex systems, and extend access to underserved populations. Yet, it also demands careful of its implementation, of data privacy, algorithmic fairness, and the evolving role of educators in increasingly technology-mediated environments. This duality—opportunity and responsibility—is a central theme that runs through every chapter in this collection.

It is my hope that this book serves as a catalyst for meaningful change. For educators, it offers practical strategies and tools to enhance teaching and learning. For researchers, it highlights critical areas for continued inquiry. For policymakers and institutional leaders, it provides a framework for thoughtful integration of AI into educational systems. And for technologists and developers, it presents real-world challenges that demand innovative, human-centered solutions.

Above all, this book is a call to action with responsibility. The future of education will not be defined by technology alone, but by how we choose to apply it—collaboratively, creatively, and consciously. By fostering dialogue, research, and cross-disciplinary collaboration, we can ensure that AI becomes not a replacement for human educators, but a powerful partner in the shared mission of shaping more inclusive, responsive, and resilient learning environments.

I invite you to approach this work not as a definitive endpoint, but as a point of departure—an invitation to explore, question, implement and innovate. The chapters ahead offer not just knowledge, but momentum. Let us use it wisely.

Acknowledgment

First, I would like to thank IGI Global for the trust I have placed in me to be the editor of this book. Second, I am grateful for the great enthusiasm of all the authors from Mexico and India who have contributed to this book, especially Dr. Jorge Alberto Ruiz Vanoye, for his guidance as an editor with extensive experience. Without the work of all the authors, this work would have been impossible. Finally, I would like to acknowledge the Mexican Secretariat of Science, Humanities, Technology, and Innovation. Thanks to its work, the Mexican authors of this work have the time to reflect, research, and share their many years of teaching experience.

Chapter 1
Introduction to Artificial Intelligence

Glendamira Serrano-Franco
https://orcid.org/0000-0003-3176-3433
Universidad Politécnica Metropolitana de Hidalgo, Mexico

Víctor Manuel Zamudio García
https://orcid.org/0000-0002-4660-8025
Universidad Politécnica Metropolitana de Hidalgo, Mexico

Jaime Aguilar-Ortíz
https://orcid.org/0009-0003-5302-1454
Universidad Politécnica de Pachuca, Mexico

ABSTRACT

Artificial Intelligence (AI) is a key multidisciplinary field in today's technological development, impacting sectors such as education, healthcare, industry, and energy. This chapter presents an overview of the theoretical and technological foundations of AI, focusing on key areas: machine learning, deep learning, natural language processing, computer vision, robotics, and expert systems. It highlights algorithmic models, computational architectures, and current trends in research and applications. Through a review of recent literature, it discusses technical advances, methodological challenges, and ethical concerns such as interpretability, fairness, and data privacy. The chapter also examines AI's role in optimizing processes and supporting data-driven decision-making in educational and organizational settings. Finally, it emphasizes the need for regulatory frameworks and governance policies that promote responsible, transparent, and equitable AI development aligned with social well-being and global sustainability.

DOI: 10.4018/979-8-3373-0598-1.ch001

INTRODUCTION

Artificial Intelligence (AI) has consolidated itself over the past decade as one of the most impactful scientific disciplines in technological, economic, and social development. Its advancement has been made possible by the use of sophisticated mathematical models, deep neural networks, and large-scale data processing techniques, which have revolutionized various sectors, including medicine, education, industry, and communications. This chapter offers a critical and updated analysis of the theoretical and methodological foundations of AI, as well as a review of its most recent applications and the emerging ethical-scientific debates surrounding its use. The aim is to provide readers with a comprehensive overview of the current state of artificial intelligence, its transformative potential, and the principles that should guide its responsible and sustainable implementation in contemporary society.

Although the origins of AI date back to the mid-20th century, it is in the past ten years that the discipline has experienced exponential growth. This development has been catalyzed by improvements in data processing capacity, access to specialized hardware such as Graphics Processing Units (GPUs) and Tensor Processing Units (TPUs), and the evolution of more efficient algorithmic architectures. Currently, AI research and application are primarily focused on machine learning, particularly deep learning, which has demonstrated outstanding performance in tasks such as natural language processing and computer vision (Schmidhuber, 2015; LeCun, 2021).

From a technical perspective, Barradas (2023) argues that the development of AI depends on a robust computational infrastructure, consisting of hardware and software capable of executing continuous learning algorithms. These systems operate through supervised and unsupervised training models, allowing machines to analyze data in real time, detect patterns, make inferences, and provide increasingly accurate and context-adapted responses, approaching human logical reasoning in complex situations.

As a scientific field, AI also raises significant epistemological questions. Inquiries arise such as: can machines genuinely replicate human cognitive processes? Is it merely a functional simulation of intelligence, or is the development of genuine non-biological intelligence possible? Floridi and Chiriatti (2020) explore these dilemmas from diverse philosophical perspectives, proposing theoretical frameworks ranging from algorithmic simulation to the potential emergence of artificial consciousness.

Ayuso and Gutiérrez (2022), for their part, highlight that AI should be understood as a discipline enabling the design of systems capable of solving complex problems through anticipation and environmental adaptation, thanks to their ability to learn patterns. In the educational field, these capabilities have been harnessed through tools such as virtual tutors and intelligent chatbots that personalize student learning, monitor progress, conduct assessments, and provide immediate support.

However, the rapid advancement of these technologies also generates significant challenges. One of the most pressing is the issue of personal data privacy. As noted by Mena et al. (2024), many AI-based platforms collect vast amounts of user information under the premise of delivering personalized experiences. Nonetheless, this practice raises serious concerns regarding informed consent, algorithmic manipulation, and transparency in data usage, highlighting the urgent need to establish robust regulatory frameworks that ensure ethical and responsible governance of artificial intelligence

HISTORY AND EVOLUTION OF ARTIFICIAL INTELLIGENCE

The history of Artificial Intelligence (AI) represents a complex and multidisciplinary journey, marked by scientific breakthroughs, periods of skepticism, and theoretical renewals that have redefined both its conceptualization and its areas of application. Although today it is seen as a cutting-edge technology, the idea of endowing machines with cognitive capabilities has deep roots in philosophy and mathematics—disciplines that, since antiquity, have sought to unravel the mechanisms of human thought.

One of the most influential precedents in this field was the work of Alan Turing, who in 1950 posed the question "Can machines think?" and proposed the famous Turing Test as a way to evaluate the intelligence of artificial systems. Turing also introduced the concept of a universal machine capable of executing any computational operation, thereby laying the theoretical foundations of modern computer science (Copeland, 2022). These contributions inaugurated formal thinking about the possibility of creating intelligent machines.

The term "artificial intelligence" was officially coined in 1956 by John McCarthy during the Dartmouth Conference, an event considered the formal starting point of the discipline. Attending the conference were also Marvin Minsky, Claude Shannon, and Allen Newell, all key figures in the early stages of AI development. During this initial phase, a symbolic approach dominated, based on formal logic, heuristic rules, and symbolic manipulation, with the goal of simulating human reasoning (Nilsson, 2021).

In the 1960s and 1970s, pioneering programs emerged, such as ELIZA, SHRDLU, and expert systems like MYCIN, which could perform medical diagnoses using explicit rule-based systems. These advancements generated considerable enthusiasm, but also exposed the limitations of symbolic AI. The reliance on fixed rules and the lack of adaptability in uncertain contexts led to a decline in confidence, ushering in the so-called "AI Winter"—a period spanning from the late 1970s to the mid-1980s, characterized by reduced funding and diminished institutional interest (Crevier, 2021).

In the 1990s, AI began to regain momentum thanks to the emergence of new approaches such as machine learning, in which knowledge was not explicitly coded but instead learned from data. This paradigm represented a break from traditional symbolic AI and gave rise to what is known as connectionist AI. Techniques such as decision trees, genetic algorithms, and artificial neural networks became increasingly popular, although the latter were still limited by the computational constraints of the time (Russell & Norvig, 2021).

The true turning point came in the 2010s with the rise of deep learning, driven by three main factors: the exponential growth of available data (big data), the development of specialized hardware such as GPUs, and the refinement of training algorithms. A key milestone was the victory of AlexNet in the 2012 ImageNet competition, where a convolutional neural network significantly outperformed traditional methods in image recognition tasks (Krizhevsky et al., 2017). Since then, deep neural networks have dominated fields such as computer vision, natural language processing, and speech recognition.

Building on these advances, increasingly complex and powerful models have emerged, such as BERT, GPT, DALL·E, CLIP, ChatGPT, and AlphaFold, all of which have demonstrated remarkable capabilities in text understanding, natural language generation, molecular structure prediction, and the resolution of highly complex problems. This new stage has reignited global enthusiasm for AI, expanding its adoption across a wide range of fields including healthcare, education, security, finance, energy, and entertainment (Jordan & Mitchell, 2015).

Currently, there is intense debate over whether these developments represent the first signs of the emergence of Artificial General Intelligence (AGI)—systems capable of autonomous reasoning and learning across multiple domains—or whether we are still in the phase of narrow AI, specialized solely in specific tasks. Scholars such as Marcus (2020) warn that despite the progress, current systems still lack deep semantic understanding and generalized common sense, both of which are essential for intelligence comparable to that of humans.

At the same time, ethical reflections on the risks associated with the accelerated development of AI have gained momentum. Issues such as bias in models, algorithmic opacity, mass surveillance, misinformation, and job automation represent some of the most pressing challenges. In response, international organizations such as UNESCO (2021) and the European Union (2023) have begun to propose regulatory frameworks that promote ethical, inclusive, transparent, and human-centered artificial intelligence.

In summary, the evolution of artificial intelligence is a narrative shaped by the convergence of multiple disciplines, cycles of optimism and skepticism, and scientific breakthroughs that are radically transforming our relationship with technology. From its philosophical roots to its contemporary applications based on data and machine learning, AI continues to solidify its place as one of the most dynamic and consequential fields of the 21st century.

FUNDAMENTAL AREAS OF ARTIFICIAL INTELLIGENCE

Various recent studies have identified and consolidated the main areas that structure the scientific and technical development of Artificial Intelligence (AI). These areas represent specialized lines of research and application, each with its own methodologies, specific theoretical frameworks, and particular objectives. Among them, Machine Learning (ML) stands out as one of the fundamental pillars, given its ability to transform large volumes of data into useful knowledge through adaptive algorithms.

Machine Learning

Machine Learning (ML) is a subdiscipline of artificial intelligence that has experienced exponential growth over the last decade. According to Forero and Negre (2024), the scientific community has increasingly turned its attention toward ML-based tools due to their capacity to enhance various domains, including education, industry, and healthcare. This area focuses on the design of systems capable of automatically learning from data and improving their performance without direct human intervention.

As Schmidhuber (2022) notes, unlike traditional approaches based on static rules, machine learning enables algorithms to identify patterns in data, generalize from them, and adapt to new contexts. Depending on the availability of labeled data, ML is primarily categorized into two types: supervised learning and unsupervised learning.

In supervised learning, the algorithm is trained with a labeled dataset—that is, one in which both the input features and the expected outputs are provided. This type of learning is further divided into classification problems—when outputs are discrete categories—and regression problems—when outputs are continuous. By contrast, in unsupervised learning, the model receives only unlabeled data and must independently discover patterns or groupings within it (Sandoval, 2018).

Machine Learning Models

The development of ML-based solutions has had a significant impact across multiple industries, driving technological innovations in areas such as financial analysis, biomedicine, process automation, and pattern recognition. According to Trasviña et al. (2025), the adoption of ML models is rapidly increasing, propelled by the growing need to generate knowledge from complex data. Among the main categories of machine learning models are:

Linear Models

Linear models are primarily used in regression and classification tasks. According to Sandoval (2018), these models aim to fit a line (or a hyperplane in higher-dimensional spaces) that minimizes the difference between actual and predicted values. Among the most well-known are linear regression, which models continuous relationships, and logistic regression, which is suited for classification problems. However, these models have limitations in complex contexts due to overfitting, especially when they are excessively tailored to the training data.

Rodríguez (2023) adds that linear models are valued for their simplicity and computational efficiency, but their predictive power decreases in situations where relationships between variables are nonlinear or exhibit high dimensionality.

Naive Bayes Models

The Naive Bayes model is a probabilistic classifier based on Bayes' theorem, with a strong (though often unrealistic) assumption of independence among features. Vásquez and Vivas (2024) highlight its usefulness in text classification, where the abundance of attributes and their joint analysis can lead to effective probability estimations.

Martínez (2018) explains that Bayesian classifiers calculate the probability of each class based on the evidence provided by the feature values. Despite their simplicity, these models are effective in domains with complex data structures and numerous attributes, making them popular in applications such as spam filtering and document categorization.

Decision Tree Models

Decision trees represent decisions and their possible consequences using a hierarchical tree-like structure. Martínez (n.d.) indicates that each internal node corresponds to a test on a variable, and each leaf represents a decision outcome. These models are especially useful due to their interpretability and ability to handle both categorical and continuous variables.

Flores (2021) elaborates that a decision tree is a directed acyclic graph where each node represents a decision or condition, and the terminal leaves indicate the possible results. Their structural simplicity allows for a clear representation of decision rules, although they may be prone to overfitting if proper pruning techniques are not applied.

Random Forest Models

Random Forest is an ensemble learning technique based on the combination of multiple decision trees. Introduced by Breiman in 2001, this methodology randomly selects subsets of data and features to build diverse trees, which reduces the risk of overfitting and improves the model's generalization capacity.

According to Castillo (2017), Random Forest can be used for both classification and regression tasks, standing out for its accuracy and robustness when dealing with noisy or missing data. Agundis (2023) adds that this technique is ideal for the analysis of large volumes of data (big data), as it enables the creation of highly predictive and efficient models applicable in sectors such as marketing, medicine, and consumer behavior prediction.

K-Nearest Neighbors (K-NN) Models

The K-Nearest Neighbors (K-NN) algorithm is a widely used supervised learning technique applied to both classification and regression problems. According to Suyal and Goyal (2022), this model is based on the fundamental premise that an instance is classified according to the majority class of its closest "neighbors" within the feature space. In supervised learning contexts, the model receives labeled training data from which it learns to identify patterns that enable it to predict outcomes for new, unseen inputs. The core idea is that the behavior of an instance can be inferred by observing the behavior of similar surrounding elements, granting the model strong adaptive capabilities.

One of the main advantages of the K-NN model lies in its conceptual simplicity and ease of implementation. Madariaga et al. (2022) highlight several key characteristics that explain its popularity and effectiveness:

- Scalability: K-NN overcomes the scalability issues that affect other methods like decision trees, as it can operate on large training datasets without requiring all the data to reside in memory simultaneously.
- Distance-based similarity: It uses metrics such as Euclidean distance to evaluate similarity between training and test instances, making it an intuitive and effective method—even in the absence of assumptions about data distribution.
- Robustness against incorrect assumptions: Unlike models such as Naive Bayes, which rely on assumptions like conditional independence among attributes, K-NN does not depend on such constraints, thereby reducing the risk of errors due to model misspecification.

- Similarity-based classification: Thanks to its direct use of distance as a decision criterion, this model enables accurate and efficient recommendations, making it especially useful in recommendation systems and user-oriented applications.

In summary, the K-NN model offers a powerful and versatile alternative for data classification, particularly in scenarios where prior information about variable distribution is unavailable or when an approach based strictly on the available data is required.

Deep Learning

Deep Learning is a subcategory of machine learning that has revolutionized the field of artificial intelligence over the past decade. This approach is distinguished by its ability to process unstructured data—such as images, text, or audio—through multi-layered neural networks, enabling systems to automatically learn hierarchical data representations (Inglés, 2023).

According to Alzubaidi et al. (2021), the most well-known deep learning architectures include Convolutional Neural Networks (CNNs), Recurrent Neural Networks (RNNs), and Generative Adversarial Networks (GANs). These networks have been fundamental in tasks such as computer vision, natural language processing, and content generation. However, this approach also faces significant challenges, including the need for large amounts of labeled data, high computational demand, overfitting, and limited model interpretability.

Artificial Neural Networks (ANNs)

Artificial Neural Networks (ANNs) form the foundation of deep learning. According to Ortiz (2025), they are software-based solutions inspired by the functioning of the human brain, capable of recognizing complex patterns and solving problems more efficiently than traditional systems. These networks are composed of interconnected nodes or "neurons" organized into layers, allowing them to model nonlinear relationships between input and output variables.

Patiño et al. (2022) explain that ANNs can autonomously adjust through learning algorithms, making them especially useful for tasks that require nonlinear statistical modeling. García (2019) also highlights several advantages of these networks: fault tolerance, adaptability, the ability to operate in nonlinear environments, and superior classification performance compared to traditional statistical methods.

Convolutional Neural Networks (CNNs)

Convolutional Neural Networks are a specialized architecture for processing visual data. According to Lagares et al. (n.d.), these networks use the mathematical operation of convolution to detect spatial patterns in images, allowing them to identify shapes and objects across multiple hierarchical layers.

Iturbe (2023) explains that although CNNs share structural similarities with other neural networks, their primary advantage lies in partial connectivity between neurons, enabling weight sharing and improving efficiency in the recognition of complex patterns. This architecture has been widely adopted in applications such as image classification, facial recognition, and computer vision for autonomous vehicles.

Recurrent Neural Networks (RNNs)

Recurrent Neural Networks are designed to handle sequential data, such as text or audio, and are characterized by internal connections that allow them to retain information from previous inputs. Bastidas et al. (2020) state that these networks are ideal for time-series processing due to their ability to model temporal dependencies.

Arana (2021) adds that one of the core features of RNNs is parameter sharing, which allows them to analyze sequences of variable length without exponentially increasing the number of parameters to be trained. This feature makes RNNs a key tool for applications such as machine translation, sentiment analysis, and speech synthesis.

Generative Adversarial Networks (GANs)

Generative Adversarial Networks (GANs) represent a highly innovative type of neural network composed of two sub-networks: a generator and a discriminator. According to De la Torre (2023), the generator attempts to create fake samples that resemble real data, while the discriminator evaluates whether the samples come from the original dataset or were artificially generated. Both networks are trained simultaneously in a competitive process that progressively improves output quality.

Bethencourt et al. (2022) explain that GANs can generate realistic images, translate visual styles, enhance image resolutions, and operate with limited data. Their architecture allows for the generation of synthetic content useful in applications such as digital art, biomedicine, video games, and model training in data-scarce environments.

Natural Language Processing (NLP)

Natural Language Processing (NLP) is one of the most dynamic and influential areas of artificial intelligence, as it enables machines to meaningfully interpret, understand, and generate human language. According to Otter et al. (2021), the emergence of the Transformer model marked a significant milestone in this field, surpassing previous architectures such as LSTM networks in both efficiency and contextualization capacity. The Transformer relies on attention mechanisms that can identify complex semantic relationships without depending on sequential processing, which has significantly optimized performance in language-related tasks.

Models derived from this architecture—such as BERT, GPT, and T5—have achieved outstanding results in tasks like machine translation, text generation, sentiment analysis, and automated question answering. However, NLP faces important challenges: biases inherent in training data, high computational requirements, and lack of transparency in large-scale models, raising ethical and technical concerns regarding their use in critical contexts.

In this same context, Calero (2024) highlights that one of the most relevant applications of NLP is text classification, a process by which specific labels or categories are assigned to a document or text fragment. This process can serve multiple purposes: spam detection, sentiment analysis, topic identification, or custom classification schemes. For example, sentiment analysis allows us to determine whether a text expresses a positive, negative, or neutral opinion. Some advanced algorithms are even capable of identifying differentiated sentiments within a single sentence regarding different aspects—for instance, in the phrase *"the restaurant was expensive, but the menu was cheap,"* the model could assign negative and positive labels, respectively.

From a linguistic perspective, Borja (2020) explains that NLP encompasses five fundamental levels:

1. Phonological level – concerned with the relationship between words and the sounds they represent.
2. Morphological level – analyzes the structure of words based on morphemes, the smallest units of meaning.
3. Syntactic level – studies how words are combined to form grammatically correct sentences.
4. Semantic level – focuses on the literal meaning of words and phrases, regardless of context.
5. Pragmatic level – analyzes language use in specific contexts and the influence of environment on utterance interpretation.

According to Delso et al. (2024), advanced NLP tools are widely used to analyze user-generated texts, such as social media comments and product reviews. This enables a deeper understanding of consumer preferences and behaviors. Such analysis is particularly useful for personalizing marketing campaigns, optimizing communication strategies, and improving customer experience. Likewise, NLP has been essential in the development of virtual assistants and chatbots, which can handle inquiries, provide automated and personalized responses, and learn from past interactions to continually enhance their performance.

GPT Technology

One of the most representative technologies in current Natural Language Processing (NLP) is GPT (Generative Pre-trained Transformer). Ordoñez and Gutiérrez (2023) explain that this technology is based on transformer architectures, specifically the decoder variant. GPT employs self-attention mechanisms to weigh the relative importance of each word in a sequence, allowing it to accurately predict the next word based on context. During pretraining, it is exposed to large volumes of unlabeled text, enabling it to learn complex linguistic structures without explicit supervision.

According to Zambrano and Abad (2024), the integration of GPT models into educational and business environments has contributed to optimizing processes, automating repetitive tasks, and boosting productivity. In the educational field, for instance, it has been used to generate content, provide automatic feedback, and offer personalized support. In the business sector, it facilitates document management, customer service, and report generation. However, these authors emphasize the importance of continuously evaluating its adoption, impact, and limitations in order to maximize benefits while minimizing ethical and technical risks.

Virtual Assistants and Chatbots

Chatbots represent one of the most consolidated applications of Natural Language Processing (NLP). According to Celi et al. (2021), chatbots are computer programs designed to enable interaction between a human user and a technological system through text or voice interfaces. One of their main advantages is continuous availability, as they can operate 24/7 without interruptions, and they are capable of attending to multiple users simultaneously. While they were initially implemented in customer service settings, their use has now extended across various business and educational sectors.

In this regard, Mercedes et al. (2023) highlight the innovative role of tools such as ChatGPT, a language model capable of generating original and coherent responses to user queries. Unlike traditional systems that rely on fixed databases,

ChatGPT uses a transformer-based architecture, allowing it to understand context and produce highly accurate texts. This tool has marked a significant shift in both educational services and everyday technological interactions due to its ease of use, accessibility, and versatility.

On another front, Pareja et al. (2024) explain that virtual assistants (VAs) are becoming a common interface in a variety of smart devices, including mobile phones, televisions, speakers, car infotainment systems, and even service robots. The global market for virtual assistants is projected to reach $11 billion by 2025, reflecting their growing importance and ability to manage increasingly complex interactions. This growth is directly linked to advances in NLP, which have greatly enhanced the accuracy and fluency of conversational systems. As a result, virtual assistants are transforming the way people interact with technology, both in personal and professional settings.

From a similar perspective, Ramírez and Valle (2022) define virtual assistants as conversational agents developed using artificial intelligence—particularly NLP techniques—that interact with users by automatically responding to their queries. Currently, various organizations, government institutions, and nonprofit entities have implemented chatbots and virtual assistants across multiple areas, with particular success in customer service (Abdallah, Wahab, Fahad & AlHamed, 2020). These solutions not only optimize response times, but also enable the delivery of personalized, scalable, and efficient services.

Computer Vision

Computer vision is an area of artificial intelligence focused on endowing machines with the ability to interpret and understand the visual environment. According to Khan et al. (2018), convolutional neural networks (CNNs) have revolutionized this field by enabling systems to learn directly from visual data, eliminating the need to manually design feature extractors. These networks have demonstrated remarkable effectiveness in tasks such as image classification, semantic segmentation, object detection, and visual tracking. Nevertheless, technical challenges persist, such as the need for large volumes of labeled data, sensitivity to variations in lighting or background, and difficulties in generalizing to uncontrolled environments.

From another perspective, Sánchez (2022) points out that the central goal of computer vision is to enable systems to visually interpret their environment as similarly as possible to human perception. This involves developing hardware and software solutions capable of analyzing and interpreting visual information from the environment to make informed decisions. He also emphasizes the synergy between computer vision and machine learning, since the latter provides a versatile set of techniques that simulate human thinking in machines, allowing the development of more effective computer vision algorithms with potential applications in contexts such as education.

In this regard, Felipe et al. (2024) explain that computer vision encompasses two fundamental areas:

- **Digital image processing:** Its purpose is to analyze, enhance, and describe the content of a digital image to extract useful information. This processing includes techniques such as filtering, segmentation, edge detection, noise removal, and image enhancement. These operations enable identifying objects, recognizing patterns, or delimiting areas of interest within the image.
- **Computer vision:** It focuses on the design of specialized algorithms and hardware systems capable of interpreting visual content similarly to human vision. This includes tasks such as object recognition, depth and perspective estimation, motion tracking, and decision-making based on visual information. Essentially, it seeks to replicate the human ability to see and understand the world through computer systems.

Together, computer vision represents one of the most promising areas of modern artificial intelligence, with applications ranging from medicine to education, as well as robotics, security, and autonomous transportation.

Intelligent Robotics

Intelligent robotics represents the convergence between artificial intelligence and autonomous physical systems, integrating advanced learning algorithms with hardware capable of interacting with the environment. According to Kormushev et al. (2018), machine learning has been incorporated into robotics through methodologies such as kinesthetic teaching, in which a human physically guides the robot during the learning process of motor tasks. This approach, also known as programming by demonstration, allows robots to acquire new skills without the need for explicit coding, facilitating their adaptation to variable contexts.

Moreover, the use of neural networks has enabled robots to map trajectories, recognize movement patterns, and adjust their actions in real time, significantly expanding their flexibility and autonomy in dynamic environments. These capabilities have supported the implementation of intelligent robots in key sectors such as manufacturing, healthcare, personal assistance, rehabilitation, and logistics, where precision, adaptability, and safe interaction with humans are essential.

From a conceptual perspective, Navas (2021) defines an intelligent robot as a physical machine capable of making autonomous decisions through the use of sensors and artificial intelligence-based programs. These machines can anticipate human needs and adapt to environmental conditions without continuous human operator control. This autonomy allows them to act, modify their behavior, and interact effectively with the physical world.

In summary, intelligent robotics is established as a strategic discipline within applied artificial intelligence, whose evolution continues to expand the boundaries of what machines can do autonomously, collaboratively, and contextually.

Expert Systems

According to Carillo (2023), expert systems are based on pattern recognition and inferences made by knowledge engineers, who build these systems in collaboration with specialists from the relevant field. These experts contribute their tacit knowledge—that which is not always easy to formalize—which they routinely use to make decisions in their respective areas. At the commercial level, the benefits of expert systems are evident in successful strategies such as the search engines Google or Bing. For example, when a user selects a result among the options offered, the system interprets this action as validation of the result's relevance, allowing it to adjust and improve future searches.

In the educational field, Herrera (2024) highlights that expert systems can have multiple applications, such as supporting students in making informed decisions, guiding research processes, and collaborating in the creation of personalized curricula. They can also provide intelligent tutoring that adapts to each student's learning pace and style. Additionally, these systems can contribute to academic planning and the management of institutional activities by incorporating expert knowledge that improves decision-making in complex environments.

From a more technical perspective, Ruiz et al. (2016) state that an expert system must be capable of processing and storing information, learning and reasoning in both deterministic and uncertain contexts, communicating with users or other systems, making appropriate decisions, and justifying the reasons behind those decisions. To achieve this, these systems are composed of several interrelated components: a knowledge base (containing rules and facts), an inference engine (which allows conclusions to be drawn), and a user interface that facilitates interaction with the system.

In summary, expert systems represent an advanced form of artificial intelligence based on emulating human expert reasoning, with prominent applications in sectors such as business, healthcare, legal, and education.

Reinforcement Learning

According to Arnau (2023), reinforcement learning (RL) is an artificial intelligence technique based on the learning process of natural organisms interacting with their environment. Its foundation lies in the existence of an environment, governed by laws that are initially unknown, in which an agent interacts successively with the goal of maximizing the rewards it obtains. Therefore, the agent continuously learns the rules governing the environment from its own actions and their consequences. Its ultimate objective is to perform the best possible actions to achieve the highest rewards.

According to Alepuz (2022), reinforcement learning does not use a fixed dataset of examples but learns based on experience. The agent or program receives positive or negative rewards that enable it to learn how to optimize a given objective. In this sense, reinforcement learning is defined as the study of intelligent agents capable of learning through trial and error (Achiam, 2018). It establishes the basis for a series of algorithms whose main proposal consists of positively rewarding or negatively punishing an agent's behavior so that it becomes more likely to repeat positive actions and avoid negative ones in the future. Furthermore, reinforcement learning represents a paradigm for solving many problems with a different approach from traditional programming methods, as it enables the design of sophisticated behaviors for an agent that would be difficult to program manually.

On the other hand, Alcalá (n.d.) mentions that reinforcement learning aims to find an optimal behavior to solve a problem by learning from past actions and maximizing the accumulated reward over time. However, as previously mentioned, rewards are not instantaneous and the goal is to maximize the accumulated reward; therefore, the agent must reason and choose actions that will yield the best long-term results.

Markov Decision Process

According to Murel (2024), the reinforcement learning agent learns about a problem by interacting with its environment. The environment provides information about its current state. The agent then uses that information to determine which actions to take. If an action receives a reward signal from the environment, the agent is encouraged to perform that action again when it encounters a similar future state. This process is repeated for each new state thereafter. Over time, the agent learns from rewards and punishments to take actions within the environment that fulfill a specified objective. In Markov decision processes, the state space refers to all the information provided by the state of an environment. The action space denotes all possible actions the agent can perform within a state.

ARTIFICIAL INTELLIGENCE PARADIGMS: SYMBOLIC VS. CONNECTIONIST

The development of artificial intelligence (AI) has been marked by two fundamental epistemological and methodological approaches: symbolic AI and connectionist AI. These paradigms not only differ in technical aspects but also represent distinct models for conceiving artificial cognition, knowledge representation processes, and the ways in which a machine can learn or reason. Understanding both approaches is essential to address the foundations of AI, as many contemporary advances, including hybrid artificial intelligence proposals, have emerged from their interaction.

SYMBOLIC AI: LOGIC, RULES, AND EXPLICIT KNOWLEDGE

Symbolic AI, also known as GOFAI (Good Old-Fashioned Artificial Intelligence), emerged during the 1950s and 1960s. It is based on the idea that intelligence can be simulated through the logical manipulation of symbols. This approach assumes that knowledge can be formally represented through rules, facts, and relationships, so that a system can operate on this basis to make decisions or solve problems (Russell & Norvig, 2021).

Symbolic systems employ structures such as decision trees, knowledge bases, and inference engines that apply heuristic rules. A notable example is the expert system MYCIN, developed in the 1970s for diagnosing infectious diseases. Although effective in well-defined contexts, this approach faces limitations when dealing with uncertainty, ambiguity, or a large number of unstructured variables (Barradas, 2023).

Conceptually, symbolic AI aligns with the computational theory of mind, which holds that thinking can be modeled as symbol manipulation according to syntactic rules. However, its rigidity and reliance on explicit programming limit its scalability and adaptability in dynamic or unstructured tasks.

CONNECTIONIST AI: LEARNING, NEURAL NETWORKS, AND DISTRIBUTED REPRESENTATION

In contrast to symbolic AI, the connectionist paradigm is inspired by the functioning of the human brain, especially artificial neural networks. Although its origins date back to the pioneering work of McCulloch and Pitts (1943) on artificial neurons, this approach gained momentum from the 1980s onward. Connectionism posits that intelligence emerges from the interaction among simple interconnected units that process information in a distributed and adaptive manner (Alzubaidi et al., 2021).

Instead of relying on explicit rules, neural networks learn from exposure to data through supervised, unsupervised, or reinforcement learning. A crucial breakthrough was the backpropagation algorithm for training multilayer networks, which allowed tackling complex tasks. More recently, the development of deep learning has revolutionized the field by introducing networks with multiple layers capable of learning hierarchical data representations.

Models such as convolutional neural networks (CNNs), recurrent neural networks (RNNs), and Transformers have demonstrated outstanding performance in applications like computer vision, natural language processing, temporal prediction, and text generation (Otter et al., 2021). Unlike symbolic AI, connectionism does not require an explicit knowledge representation, as it is implicitly encoded in the synaptic weights of neural connections.

However, this flexibility entails some challenges: connectionist learning often functions as a "black box," making interpretability difficult, and can reproduce biases present in training data. Additionally, its training requires large volumes of data and considerable computational capacity (Khan et al., 2018).

Critical Comparison and Towards a Hybrid Approach

Both paradigms present advantages and limitations that complement each other. While symbolic AI stands out for its interpretability and reliability in structured domains, connectionist AI is characterized by its flexibility and effectiveness in contexts with unstructured data or complex patterns. This duality has driven the development of hybrid approaches that seek to combine the best of both worlds.

Hybrid systems integrate symbolic representations with the learning capabilities of the connectionist paradigm, enabling models that are both explainable and adaptive. A prominent example is neuro-symbolic approaches, which fuse deep neural networks with logical rules, improving explainability without sacrificing the power of machine learning (Garcez et al., 2019). Such approaches are increasingly relevant in areas where decision traceability is fundamental, such as medicine, education, and algorithmic justice.

From a theoretical perspective, this convergence suggests that artificial intelligence can benefit from an interdisciplinary integration that does not limit itself to replicating the human mind through a single path, but rather explores diverse ways to model knowledge, learning, and decision-making.

APPLICATION OF ARTIFICIAL INTELLIGENCE IN KEY SECTORS

In recent decades, the evolution of artificial intelligence (AI) has transformed multiple sectors, consolidating itself as a strategic tool for process automation, improved decision-making, and resource optimization. This technology has transcended the scientific realm to integrate transversally across various professional, economic, and social contexts.

In the organizational domain, Riquelme and Pereira (2024) highlight that AI has proven effective in automating repetitive tasks, analyzing large volumes of data, and generating valuable information for strategic decision-making. It also facilitates the management of everyday activities such as scheduling and organizing events, establishing itself as a tool adaptable to different operational levels. The efficient utilization of these capabilities positively impacts productivity, efficiency, and the optimization of human and technological resources.

From a broader perspective, Tenés (2023) points out that implementing AI in companies entails structural transformations both internally and externally. Externally, it enhances the customer experience by optimizing touchpoints from the beginning of the service to post-sale support. Internally, it generates significant changes in organizational dynamics, influencing corporate culture, hierarchical structures, and labor relations. Organizations that fail to adapt to this digital and intelligent environment risk falling behind their competition.

In this regard, Contreras and Olaya (2024) emphasize that adopting AI enables companies to increase their competitiveness and operational efficiency. Automating routine processes frees up time and resources for human capital to focus on strategic, creative, and high-value tasks, fostering a comprehensive transformation in business models.

In the educational field, Cobos (2024) highlights that one of the most significant advantages of AI is its ability to offer personalized teaching. Technologies such as intelligent tutors and virtual educational agents facilitate autonomous learning by providing immediate feedback tailored to each student's needs. Additionally, these systems have significant potential to provide emotional and motivational support, helping to reduce anxiety levels and improve academic performance.

Complementarily, Kroff et al. (2024) emphasize that, in higher education, AI offers tools for continuous monitoring and assessment of learning. Intelligent platforms can identify specific weaknesses in student performance and suggest personalized pedagogical interventions. This not only optimizes teaching work but also promotes more objective and equitable evaluation.

Likewise, Bolaño and Duarte (2024) mention that artificial intelligence can provide educators with tools to intervene early with students who show signs of school dropout. Artificial intelligence systems can alert teachers about students who require additional support and offer specific recommendations on appropriate interventions to help these students succeed academically and prevent dropout.

Along the same lines, Arizmendi and Carrillo (2024) mention that teachers could integrate innovative pedagogical methods such as adaptive learning and data-driven instruction. These approaches, which use artificial intelligence algorithms, facilitate the adaptation of educational content to the needs and abilities of each student, promoting a more dynamic and effective learning environment. The incorporation of AI in education not only represents a technological advancement but also a pedagogical transformation. Teachers trained in these technologies can use this information to make informed decisions and adjust their teaching strategies in real time. A successful training plan should include the development of competencies and ethical aspects related to the use of artificial intelligence, as teachers need to understand the ethical and privacy implications of using these tools, ensuring the protection of students' rights and data.

The implementation of Artificial Intelligence in education, according to Peñafiel et al. (2025), faces ethical dilemmas that require strong regulatory frameworks. They highlight how reliance on algorithms can perpetuate biases, as evidenced by cases where teacher recruitment systems discriminate based on gender or ethnicity due to biased training data. The study calls for the implementation of external audits of datasets and models used in educational settings, especially when they affect vulnerable populations. Furthermore, it questions who bears responsibility when an algorithmic error harms students—whether through incorrect diagnoses of special needs or inadequate pedagogical recommendations. Privacy also emerges as a central concern, as platforms that analyze emotions through facial recognition or store student conversations with chatbots pose risks of excessive surveillance and commercialization of sensitive data. The article contrasts regional approaches: while the EU is advancing with regulations such as the GDPR, many developing countries lack specific legislation, leaving educational institutions without clear guidelines to protect their communities' information.

In the healthcare sector, Incytu (2018) notes that AI is revolutionizing the prevention, diagnosis, and treatment of high-risk diseases such as cancer, hypertension, and diabetes. Mobile applications equipped with sensors allow constant monitoring of vital signs, facilitating access to medical services in rural areas and reducing logistical costs. Likewise, Lanzagorta et al. (2022) argue that voice-recognition virtual assistants could handle administrative tasks such as writing medical notes, ordering tests, or prescribing medication, allowing professionals to focus on more complex and human clinical aspects.

AI is also being applied in the agro-industrial sector. Sánchez and Castillo (2022) explain that this technology provides precise information for agricultural decision-making through the integration of biotechnology, robotics, simulation, Big Data, and geostatistics. The efficient use of these tools can double production sustainably by adapting crops and resources to environmental conditions. Similarly, Hoyos et al. (2022) highlight AI's capacity to perceive the environment, learn from experience, and make informed decisions, enabling improved productivity and sustainability in the agricultural sector through a technological classification encompassing assisted, automated, augmented, and autonomous intelligence.

On the other hand, Herrera et al. (2024) state that AI-based technologies have acquired a fundamental role in the agri-food industry, particularly in agriculture, by providing tools that enable precise and predictive decision-making aimed at increasing productivity. AI-based technologies have transformed agriculture by offering algorithms that facilitate yield estimation, pattern classification, and problem anticipation. This allows addressing challenges such as early pest detection, selection of appropriate treatments, efficient irrigation management, and evaluation of biotic and abiotic factors.

Finally, in the energy sector, Rojo et al. (2024) analyze how AI optimizes the management of renewable resources through precise weather forecasting, estimation of water flows, and data analysis from sensors. This not only increases efficiency in energy generation but also contributes to environmental protection. For example, AI can anticipate bird migration patterns to reduce the environmental impact of wind farms, complementing environmental assessment processes.

FUTURE TRENDS AND PROSPECTS OF ARTIFICIAL INTELLIGENCE

Artificial intelligence (AI) has ceased to be a frontier technology to become a transversal infrastructure in social, productive, and academic ecosystems. Its future evolution depends not only on scientific advances but also on ethical, political, legal, and environmental factors. In this context, it is essential to carry out technological foresight exercises that allow anticipating the transformations AI will provoke in humanity over the coming decades.

Towards General AI (AGI)

One of the most debated questions is whether AI will evolve into artificial general intelligence (AGI), understood as a form of intelligence capable of transferring knowledge across different domains, learning autonomously, reasoning with common sense, and adapting to unforeseen contexts, thereby emulating human thought.

Authors such as Pablo (2024) point out that, although AGI has not yet been achieved, advances in multimodal models like GPT-4 represent autonomous systems that surpass human capability in performing most economically valuable tasks. Progress toward AGI has the potential to automate not only repetitive or manual tasks but also those requiring advanced cognitive skills, which could trigger an unprecedented period of economic development. However, unlike previous technological transitions, it is unclear whether AGI will generate enough new jobs to compensate for those that will disappear.

This substitution of workers by machines could not only significantly raise unemployment rates but also widen the economic inequality gap. Society could split between those who manage AGI or possess less automatable skills, thus maintaining their jobs, and those who see their sources of work vanish, facing serious economic hardships.

In addition to the above, Nunes (2025) mentions several hidden risks that may arise if not properly addressed:

Loss of Control

An AGI does not need to be created with malicious intent; it is enough for it to misinterpret well-intentioned goals or overlook things that are important to us—this alone could lead to significant consequences. Imagine a system optimizing food production by eliminating "inefficient variables" (such as people), or one that solves climate change through drastic and inhumane measures. The true risk does not lie in its intention, but in its lack of understanding of what makes us human.

Digital Colonization (Concentration of Power)

If AGI falls into the hands of a few, it could be used to manipulate elections, design tailor-made laws, or even control global markets. This would not be innovation, but a new form of colonialism—one where inequalities deepen and individual autonomy disappears. Who decides what is "optimal" for society when machines have the final say? Public discourse and independent oversight are crucial to ensure that the development and implementation of AGI are guided by broader societal values and concerns, rather than the narrow interests of a few powerful entities.

The Death of Critical Thinking

If AGI solves all our problems, why bother to learn, create, or question? Excessive dependence could atrophy our reasoning abilities, leading us toward intellectual passivity. The cost would not just be economic—we would lose skills, we would lose what makes us human: the desire to know, to doubt, and to improve. Our curiosity and our ability to critically evaluate information are fundamental to our nature and progress. Critical thinking is essential for problem-solving, informed decision-making, and adapting to new situations. If we outsource our thinking to AI, we may become less capable of facing challenges and making sound decisions on our own. Like any muscle, our critical thinking skills need to be exercised to remain strong.

Soulless Ethics

AGI may surpass any human in logic, but can it truly understand pain, compassion, or the stories behind our decisions? Encoding ethics into algorithms is an almost impossible challenge: how can we teach a machine the value of a life, the weight of injustice, or the importance of an empathetic act? It may be able to process information about these concepts, but it cannot feel them or truly understand them in the way humans do.

AI AND ETHICS: GLOBAL ALGORITHMIC GOVERNANCE

According to Katzenbach and Ulbricht (2022), the concept of algorithmic governance is addressed and discussed across various contexts and disciplines. Although these perspectives differ in their objects of study, they share a common understanding of the relevance of algorithms in shaping social order. The selection of literature considered in this analysis focuses primarily on research from science and technology studies (STS), sociology, political science, communication, and information sciences. Nevertheless, it also includes significant contributions from other relevant disciplines interested in algorithmic governance, such as computer science, law, economics, and philosophy.

The widespread adoption of AI systems raises universal ethical questions: Who assumes responsibility for decisions made by AI? How can algorithmic discrimination be prevented? How is privacy protected in a hyper-digitalized environment? International organizations such as UNESCO and the European Union are working on global algorithmic governance frameworks based on principles like justice, inclusion, transparency, accountability, and security. In Latin America, ECLAC

(2023) has proposed strategic guidelines aimed at promoting human-centered AI and the defense of digital rights.

The future of artificial intelligence will depend not only on its technological advances but also on our collective capacity to envision, regulate, and apply its uses fairly. We face a crucial moment to decide what kind of AI we want: one oriented toward profitability or the common good? Toward automation or human empowerment? Toward opacity or transparency? From a critical and scientific perspective, this chapter argues that the foundations of AI should not be limited to the technical realm but should open up to a transdisciplinary, ethical, and humanistic reflection on its future in our societies.

CONCLUSIONS

Artificial intelligence (AI) is positioned as a fundamental discipline at the forefront of contemporary technological development, with a cross-cutting impact in diverse fields such as education, healthcare, industry, agro-industry, and energy. Accelerated progress in key areas such as machine learning and deep learning has enabled intelligent systems to process large volumes of data and perform complex tasks that traditionally required human intervention. This has opened new opportunities to optimize processes, improve decision-making, and develop personalized solutions across multiple sectors.

However, the advancement of AI also entails significant ethical and social challenges. The opacity of algorithms, the presence of inherent biases in training data, and implications for information privacy and security demand robust regulation and responsible algorithmic governance. It is imperative that public policies and regulatory frameworks be designed to promote transparency, inclusion, and justice, preventing automation from exacerbating existing socioeconomic and labor gaps.

Moreover, the development toward artificial general intelligence (AGI) raises epistemological and philosophical questions that require an interdisciplinary approach, integrating technical knowledge with profound ethical and social reflections. AI must be conceived not only as a technological advancement but also as a socio-technical phenomenon demanding a critical, humanistic, and sustainable vision.

In conclusion, to maximize the benefits of artificial intelligence and minimize its risks, it is necessary to foster close collaboration among researchers, developers, regulators, and civil society. Only then can we ensure that AI is used responsibly, equitably, and oriented toward collective well-being, effectively contributing to sustainable development and improving quality of life in both local and global contexts.

REFERENCES

Agundis, A. (2023). Evaluation of a Machine Learning Algorithm Using Random Forests for Monitoring Critical Variables in a Manufacturing Process. Tecnológico de Nuevo León Institute, Thesis Work. Website: https://rinacional.tecnm.mx/jspui/bitstream/TecNM/6959/1/TRABAJO%20ADRIAN%20FERNANDO%20AGUNDIS%20febrero%202023.pdf

Alcalá, J. (s.f.). Reinforcement Learning: Basic Elements and Algorithms. University of Zaragoza. Website: https://core.ac.uk/download/pdf/289996907.pdf

Alepuz, Á. (2022). Reinforcement Learning Applied to the Control of a Manipulator Robot. University of Alicante. Website: https://rua.ua.es/dspace/bitstream/10045/124654/1/Aprendizaje_por_refuerzo_aplicado_al_control_de_un_robot__Alepuz_Jerez_Angel.pdf

Alzubaidi, L., Zhang, J., & Humaidi, A. J.. (2021). Review of deep learning: Concepts, CNN architectures, challenges, applications, future directions. *Journal of Big Data*, *8*(1), 53. DOI: 10.1186/s40537-021-00444-8 PMID: 33816053

Arana, C. (2021). Recurrent Neural Networks: Analysis of Models Specialized in Sequential Data. Universidad del CEMA, Buenos Aires, Argentina. Website: https://ucema.edu.ar/publicaciones/download/documentos/797.pdf

Arizmendi, L., & Carrillo, C. (2024). Artificial Intelligence in Higher Education: A Perspective from the Teaching Perspective. Ciencia Latina, a Multidisciplinary Scientific Journal. 8(4), 9318-9328. doi: https://orcid.org/0009-0007-5803-0324

Arnau, R., García, L., Calabuig, J., & Sánchez, E. (2023). Teaching Reinforcement Learning with a Simple Example of Function Minimization. In the Proceedings Book: IX Congress of Educational Innovation and Networked Teaching. Valencia, July 13–14, 2023. doi: https://doi.org/DOI: 10.4995/INRED2023.2023.16617

Ayuso, D., & Gutiérrez, P. (2022). Artificial Intelligence as an Educational Resource during Initial Teacher Training. *RIED: Ibero-American Journal of Distance Education.*, *25*(2), 346–358. DOI: 10.5944/ried.25.2.32332

Barradas, J. (2023). Artificial Intelligence as a Transformative Element of Scientific Research. *Entre Líneas.*, *2*(1), 113–122. DOI: 10.56368/Entrelineas213

Bastidas, D., Adolfo, G., & Sabogal, H. (2020). Traffic Prediction Using Recurrent Neural Networks. ResearchGate. Website: https://www.researchgate.net/publication/351543348_Prediccion_de_trafico_a_partir_de_Redes_Neuronales_Recurrentes

Bethencourt, A., Castellano, D., Sosa, J., & Area, M. (2022). Technical and Practical Implications of Generative AdversarialNetworks for Open Science in Education. *Riite Interuniversity Journal of Research in Educational Technology.*, *13*(1), 138–156. DOI: 10.6018/riite.545881

Bolaño, M., & Duarte, N. (2024). A systematic review of the use of artificial intelligence in education. *Revista Colombiana de Cirugía*, *39*(1), 51–63. DOI: 10.30944/20117582.2365

Borja, M. (2020). *Analysis of Natural Language Processing Tools for Structuring Medical Texts. Tecnun, University of Navarra.* Website., https://dadun.unav.edu/server/api/core/bitstreams/c8c9da42-aebd-4904-aaa2-0eb672adcbfc/content

Calero, M., González, J., Sánchez, I., Burillo, G., & Roda, J. (2024). Natural Language Processing in Scientific Literature Review. Spanish Journal of Emergency Medicine. 3(1), 184-195. Website: https://www.reue.org/wp-content/uploads/2024/07/184-195.pdf

Castillo, P. (2017). Application of Machine Learning for Predicting Potential Customers in Marketing Processes. Center for Research in Mathematics, A.C. Zacatecas. Website: https://cimat.repositorioinstitucional.mx/jspui/bitstream/1008/755/1/ZAC%20TE%2061.pdf

Celi, R., Varela, E., Acosta, I., & Montaño, N. (2021). Natural Language Processing Techniques in Text-Based Conversational. *Artificial Intelligence.*

Cobos, C. (2024). Impact of Artificial Intelligence on the Academic Performance of High School Students: A Correlational Study. *Journal of Scientific Research.*, *6*(e740). Advance online publication. DOI: 10.37073/puriq.6.740

Contreras, F., & Olaya, J. (2024). Benefits of Implementing Artificial Intelligence in Business Management: A Systematic Review. Impulso. *Journal of Management*, *4*(8), 213–228. DOI: 10.59659/impulso.v.4i8.58

Copeland, B. J. (2022). Turing: Pioneer of the Information Age (2.ª ed.). Oxford University Press.

Crevier, D. (2021). *AI: The Tumultuous History of the Search for Artificial Intelligence.* Basic Books.

De la Torre, J. (2023). Generative Adversarial Networks (GAN): Theoretical Foundations and Applications. Arxiv. doi: https://doi.org//arXiv.2302.09346DOI: 10.48550

Delso, A., Carvajal, M. y Corral, D. (2024). The Evolution of Natural Language Processing and Its Influence on Artificial Intelligence: A Review and Future Research Directions. The Evolution of Natural Language Processing and its Influence on Artificial Intelligence: A Review and Future Research Directions. European Public & Social Innovation Review, 10(1), 01-23. doi: https://doi.org/DOI: 10.31637/epsir-2025-782

Felipe, A., Beltrán, Y., & Garnica, E. (2024). Object Identification through Computer Vision for Inventory Monitoring Using a Drone. *Ingenio Libre.*, *13*(23). Advance online publication. DOI: 10.18041/2322-8415/ingelibre.2024.v13n23.11460

Flores, C. (2021). Generation of Decision Trees Using a Physics-Inspired Algorithm. National Laboratory of Advanced Informatics. Website: https://www.uv.mx/personal/emezura/files/2021/03/Thesis-Camilo.pdf

Floridi, L., & Chiriatti, M. (2020). GPT-3: Its nature, scope, limits, and consequences. *Minds and Machines*, *30*, 681–694. DOI: 10.1007/s11023-020-09548-1

Forero, W., & Negre, F. (2024). Techniques and Applications of Machine Learning and Artificial Intelligence in Education: A Systematic Review. *Ibero-American Journal of Distance Education.*, *27*(1), 209–253. DOI: 10.5944/ried.27.1.37491

Garcez, A. d., Lamb, L. C., & Gabbay, D. M. (2019). Neural-symbolic cognitive reasoning. Springer International Publishing. Sitio web: https://www.researchgate.net/publication/220696415_Neural-Symbolic_Cognitive_Reasoning

García, E. (2019). Introduction to Convolutional Neural Networks. Application to Computer Vision. Faculty of Sciences, University of Zaragoza. Website: https://core.ac.uk/download/pdf/290002463.pdf

Herrera, E. León. Ma., Sosa, Ma., Ruiz, J. y Cepeda, J. (2024). Artificial Intelligence and Biotechnology: Towards Sustainable and Efficient Agriculture. Youth in Science. 32(1), 1-5. Website: https://www.jovenesenlaciencia.ugto.mx/index.php/jovenesenlaciencia/article/view/4687

Herrera, R. (2024). Integration of Expert Systems as an Innovative Tool in Educational Processes: Implications for Academic Research. *Scientific Journal of the Psychopedagogical and Higher Education Research Center.*, *3*(9). Advance online publication. DOI: 10.53287/sisj4131cr79h

Hoyos, J., Velásquez, B., & Baustista, D. (2022). Transformative Impact of Artificial Intelligence and Autonomous Learning on Agricultural Production: A Focus on Sustainability and Efficiency. Formación Estratégica Journal. 7(1), 40–55. Website: https://formacionestrategica.com/index.php/foes/article/view/111

Incytu (2018). Artificial Intelligence. Office of Scientific and Technological Information for the Congress of the Union. 12(1). Website: https://www.foroconsultivo.org.mx/INCyTU/documentos/Completa/INCYTU_18-012.pdf

Inglés, G. (2023). *Deep Learning Techniques for Automatic Object Detection in Sonar Images*. Higher Technical School of Telecommunications Engineering., https://core.ac.uk/download/588386484.pdf

Iturbe, A. (2023). Redes Neuronales Convolucionales y Recurrentes para la Extracción de Respuestas en Español. Centro Nacional de Investigación y Desarrollo Tecnológico Departamento de Ciencias Computacionales. Tecnológico Nacional de México. Sitio web: https://rinacional.tecnm.mx/bitstream/TecNM/6615/1/DC_Alberto_Iturbe_Herrera_2023.pdf

Jordan, M. I., & Mitchell, T. M. (2015). Machine learning: Trends, perspectives, and prospects. *Science*, *349*(6245), 255–260. DOI: 10.1126/science.aaa8415 PMID: 26185243

Katzenbach, C. & Ulbricht. (2022). Algorithmic Governance. Latin American Journal of Digital Economy and Society. doi: https://doi.org/DOI: 10.53857/cwyi6959

Khan, A., Sohail, A., Zahoora, U., & Qureshi, A. S. (2018). A survey of the recent architectures of deep convolutional neural networks. arXiv preprint arXiv:1901.06032. https://arxiv.org/abs/1901.06032

Khan, S., Rahmani, H., Shah, S. A. A., & Bennamoun, M. (2018). A guide to convolutional neural networks for computer vision. *Synthesis Lectures on Computer Vision*, *8*(1), 1–207. DOI: 10.2200/S00822ED1V01Y201712COV015

Kormushev, P., Nenchev, D. N., Calinon, S., & Caldwell, D. G. (2018). Upper-body kinesthetic teaching of a free-standing humanoid robot. *Frontiers in Neurorobotics*, *12*, 11. DOI: 10.3389/fnbot.2018.00011

Krizhevsky, A., Sutskever, I., & Hinton, G. E. (2017). ImageNet classification with deep convolutional neural networks. *Communications of the ACM*, *60*(6), 84–90. DOI: 10.1145/3065386

Kroff, F., Coria, D., & Ferrada, C. (2024). Artificial Intelligence in University Education: Innovations, Challenges, and Opportunities. *Espacios Journal.*, *45*(5), 120–135. DOI: 10.48082/espacios-a24v45n05p09

Lagares, J., Díaz, N., & Barranco, C. (s.f.). Deep Learning: A New Path to Transform Data into Knowledge. Pablo de Olavide University. Website: https://www.mintur.gob.es/Publicaciones/Publicacionesperiodicas/EconomiaIndustrial/RevistaEconomiaIndustrial/423/LAGARES,%20DI%CC%81AZ-DI%CC%81AZ%20Y%20BARRANCO%20GONZALEZ.pdf

Lanzagorta, D., Carrillo, D., & Carrillo, R. (2022). Artificial Intelligence in Medicine: Present and Future. *Gaceta Medica de Mexico*, *158*(1), 17–21. DOI: 10.24875/GMM.M22000688 PMID: 36921221

LeCun, Y. (2021). A path towards autonomous machine intelligence. *arXiv preprint arXiv:2107.08950*. doi: https://doi.org//arXiv.2107.08950DOI: 10.48550

Madariaga, C., Lao, Y., Curra, A., & Lorenzo, R. (2022). Use of KNN Algorithms in a Multicriteria Methodology for Customer Classification as a Basis for Aggregate Planning. Retos de la Dirección. 16(1). Website: http://scielo.sld.cu/scielo.php?script=sci_arttext&pid=S2306-91552022000100178

Marcus, G. (2020). The next decade in AI: Four steps towards robust artificial intelligence. arXiv preprint. https://arxiv.org/abs/2002.06177

Martínez, A., & Ezequiel, P. (s.f.). Wildfire Prediction Using Machine Learning Models. Argentine University of Enterprise (UADE), Institute of Technology (INTEC). Buenos Aires, Argentina. Website: https://sedici.unlp.edu.ar/bitstream/handle/10915/149568/Documento_completo.pdf?sequence=1&isAllowed=y

Martínez, J. (2018). Comparative Study of Machine Learning Models for microRNA Target Detection. Master's Degree in Bioinformatics and Biostatistics, UOC-UB. Website: https://openaccess.uoc.edu/server/api/core/bitstreams/7ef32f2a-31c5-4bd6-a289-f894fa0ed175/content

Mena, A., Vázquez, E., Fernández, E., & López, E. (2024). Artificial Intelligence and Its Scientific Production in the Field of Education. *Formación Universitaria*, *17*(1). Advance online publication. DOI: 10.4067/S0718-50062024000100155

Mercedes, F., Morales, I., & Vidal, J. (2023). ChatGPT: Origin, Evolution, Challenges, and Impacts on Education. REMS. 37(2). Website: http://scielo.sld.cu/scielo.php?script=sci_arttext&pid=S0864-21412023000200016

Murel, J. (2024). In reinforcement learning, an agent learns to make decisions by interacting with an environment. It is used in robotics and other decision-making settings. IBM. Website: https://www.ibm.com/mx-es/think/topics/reinforcement-learning

Navas, O. (2021). On the Threshold of a New Era: Private Law Facing Robotics and Artificial Intelligence. 9(1), 178-219. Website: https://www.redalyc.org/journal/6002/600266295005/html/

Nilsson, N. J. (2021). *The Quest for Artificial Intelligence: A History of Ideas and Achievements*. Cambridge University Press.

Nunes, J. (2025). Artificial General Intelligence: Technological Progress or Existential Threat? Governance Network for Argentina. Website: https://www.redga.com.ar/assets/img/Inteligencia%20artificial%20general%20por%20Jorge%20Nunes%20REDGA.pdf

Ordoñez, M., & Gutiérrez, J. (2023). Natural language processing prototypes based on machine learning techniques. *Journal of Technology & Innovation*, *2*(2), 34–43. DOI: 10.47230/Journal.TechInnovation.v2.n2.2023.34-43

Ortiz, M. (2025). Artificial neural networks. Ingenuity and Consciousness. Scientific Bulletin of the Ciudad Sahagún Higher School. 12(23), 38-44. Website: https://www.researchgate.net/publication/387749723_Redes_neuronales_artificiales

Otter, D. W., Medina, J. R., & Kalita, J. (2021). A survey of the transformer model in natural language processing. ACM Computing Surveys. 54(12), 1–38. Wensite: https://pubmed.ncbi.nlm.nih.gov/32324570/

Pablo, F. (2024). Artificial General Intelligence and its Risks: A Reflection on Economic and Control Challenges. SCCS Perspectives. Website: https://sccs.web.uah.es/wp/wp-content/uploads/2024/05/P2401-La-AGI-y-sus-riesgos.pdf

Pareja, F., Carrasco, J., & Aquino, M. (2024). Systematic review of the evolution of virtual assistants: from the first chatbots to conversational AI. Micaela Journal. 5(1), 33-39. Website: https://www.researchgate.net/publication/385410081_Revision_sistematica_de_la_evolucion_de_los_asistentes_virtuales_desde_los_primeros_Chatbots_hasta_la_IA_conversacionalSystematic_review_of_the_evolution_of_virtual_assistants_from_the_first_Chatbots_

Patiño, D., Iñiguez, F., Nivela, M., Ruíz, A., Otero, O., Game, K., & Vinueza, G. (2022). Machine Learning Models based in Supervised Learning for the Detection of Diabetes Mellitus in the City of Guayaquil. 2nd LACCEI International Multiconference on Entrepreneurship, Innovation and Regional Development. 5(7). doi: http://dx.doi.org/DOI: 10.18687/LEIRD2022.1.1.208

Riquelme, C., & Pereira, M. (2024). Artificial intelligence as a tool for organizing professional and personal activities. Scientific journal in social sciences. 6, e601502. Website: https://www.redalyc.org/journal/7497/749780131042/749780131042.pdf

Rodríguez, D. (2023). Data Analysis and Machine Learning. University of Salamanca. Website:https://gredos.usal.es/bitstream/handle/10366/157350/TFG%20Damia%CC%81n%20Rodri%CC%81guez%20Go%CC%81mez.pdf?sequence=1&isAllowed=y

Rojo, C., Rojo, C., & Rojo, B. (2024). Application of Artificial Intelligence to Address Global Climate Change. Journal of Law & Citizen Opinion. 15(1), 165-192. Website: https://iip.congresosinaloa.gob.mx/Rev_IIP/rev/015/007.pdf

Ruiz, E., Hernández, J., & Palma, R. (2016). Expert system as a support tool for learning Calculus topics. Calculus and its teaching. 7(1), 63-78. Website: https://recacym.org/index.php/recacym/article/view/97

Russell, S. J., & Norvig, P. (2021). Artificial Intelligence: A Modern Approach (4.ª ed.). Pearson.

Sánchez, J., & Castillo, G. (2022). Algorithms and their impact on agriculture: Process automation. *Scientific Journal of Systems and Informatics.*, *2*(2), e386. DOI: 10.51252/rcsi.v2i2.386

Sánchez, L. (2022). Artificial intelligence and computer vision applied to education. *Odigos Magazine.*, *3*(2). Advance online publication. DOI: 10.35290/ro.v3n2.2022.587

Sandoval, L. (2018). Machine learning algorithms for data analysis and prediction. Science and Culture of El Salvador. Technological Journal. 11(1), 36-40. Website: https://core.ac.uk/reader/162564840

Schmidhuber, J. (2015). Deep learning in neural networks: An overview. *Neural Networks*, *61*, 85–117. DOI: 10.1016/j.neunet.2014.09.003 PMID: 25462637

Schmidhuber, J. (2022). Machine learning in the age of big data. *Journal of Artificial Intelligence Research*, *74*, 697–745. DOI: 10.1613/jair.1.12962

Suyal, M., & Goyal, M. (2022). A Review on Analysis of K-Nearest Neighbor-Classification Machine Learning Algorithms based onSupervised Learning. *International Journal of Engineering Trends and Technology*, *70*(7), 43–48. DOI: 10.14445/22315381/IJETT-V70I7P205

Tenés, E. (2023). Impact of Artificial Intelligence on Business. Bachelor's Thesis in Business Administration and Management. Polytechnic University of Madrid. Website: https://oa.upm.es/75532/1/TFG_EDUARDO_TENES_TRILLO_2.pdf

Trasviña, R., Ruiz, J., & Rojas, E. (2025). Machine Learning Applied to Industrial Processes. *Science & Technology Magazine.*, *46*(1), 21–28. DOI: 10.47189/rcct.v25i46.768

UNESCO. (2021). Recommendation on the Ethics of Artificial Intelligence. https://unesdoc.unesco.org/ark:/48223/pf0000381137

Vásquez, I., & Vivas, M. (2024). Detection of emergency situations using the Naive Bayes machine learning model. *Mundo FESC, 13*(25), 20–40. DOI: 10.61799/2216-0388.1286

Zambrano, J., & Abad, W. (2024). Importance of using GPT technology applications in the educational and business sectors of the Manabí province. *Journal of Technology & Innovation, 3*(1), 23–34. DOI: 10.47230/Journal.TechInnovation.v3.n1.2024.23-34

Chapter 2
Fundamentals of Artificial Intelligence

Avishek Das
https://orcid.org/0009-0005-0786-1502
ISMS Pune, India

ABSTRACT

Artificial Intelligence (AI) is transforming education by enabling personalized learning. This chapter explores AI's fundamentals, methodologies, and applications in tailoring education to individual needs. AI, which mimics human cognitive abilities, has evolved from rule-based systems to advanced machine learning and deep learning. Ethical concerns, including bias and data privacy, are also discussed. The chapter categorizes AI into reactive, limited memory, theory of mind, and self-aware AI, explaining key methodologies like supervised learning, reinforcement learning, and neural networks. AI tools such as Python, TensorFlow, and NLP libraries are introduced. AI enhances education through adaptive learning platforms, intelligent tutoring systems, recommendation engines, and chatbots, personalizing content and improving engagement. Challenges like privacy and fairness are addressed, emphasizing ethical AI use. Future trends include VR/AR integration. This chapter provides a comprehensive understanding of AI's potential in shaping modern education.

INTRODUCTION

Artificial Intelligence (AI) has emerged as one of the most revolutionary technological advancements of the 21st century. It has transcended from a theoretical concept to a practical tool that is transforming industries, economies, and societies.

DOI: 10.4018/979-8-3373-0598-1.ch002

AI is now embedded in our daily lives, from virtual assistants like Siri and Alexa to self-driving cars and advanced medical diagnostics.

This chapter delves into the fundamentals of AI, exploring its origins, methodologies, applications, ethical implications, and future prospects. By understanding AI at its core, we can appreciate its transformative potential while being aware of the challenges it presents. (Bostrom, 2014; Tegmark, 2017; Selwyn, 2019)

The Rise of Artificial Intelligence

Artificial Intelligence (AI) has evolved from a theoretical concept into a transformative force shaping industries worldwide. The journey of AI is marked by significant breakthroughs, from early symbolic reasoning to modern machine learning and deep learning systems. This section explores AI's progression, highlighting the key milestones, innovations, and challenges that have defined its development. (Mitchell, 1997; Russell & Norvig, 2020) (Krizhevsky, Sutskever, & Hinton, 2012; LeCun, Bengio, & Hinton, 2015)

The Origins of Artificial Intelligence

The concept of AI can be traced back to ancient civilizations, where myths and legends spoke of mechanical beings with human-like intelligence. Greek mythology depicted automatons, such as Talos, a giant bronze warrior built to protect Crete. Similarly, Chinese and Indian folklore described artificial humanoid figures created to perform tasks.

However, the formal study of AI began in the 20th century with the advent of modern computing and theoretical frameworks. Mathematicians, philosophers, and scientists began exploring the possibility of creating machines that could simulate human thought.

1943 – The First Computational Model of Neural Networks. Warren McCulloch and Walter Pitts published "A Logical Calculus of the Ideas Immanent in Nervous Activity (McCulloch & Pitts, 1943)," introducing the concept of artificial neurons. This laid the foundation for artificial neural networks (ANNs), which later became a crucial part of AI research.

1950 – The Turing Test. British mathematician and logician Alan Turing proposed the "Imitation Game" (now known as the Turing Test (Turing, 1950)) in his paper "Computing Machinery and Intelligence." He suggested that a machine could be considered intelligent if it could successfully imitate human conversation to the extent that an evaluator could not distinguish it from a human.

1956 – The Dartmouth Conference. The birth of AI as a field of study is often attributed to the Dartmouth Conference (McCarthy et al., 1956), organized by John

McCarthy, Marvin Minsky, Nathaniel Rochester, and Claude Shannon. The conference proposed the idea that machines could be designed to exhibit human-like intelligence. This event officially marked the beginning of AI research.

Early AI Research and Symbolic AI (1950s – 1970s)

The early days of AI were dominated by rule-based systems, often referred to as symbolic AI or Good Old-Fashioned Artificial Intelligence (GOFAI). Researchers believed that encoding human knowledge into explicit rules could enable machines to reason and make decisions.

1957 – The Perceptron Model. Frank Rosenblatt developed the Perceptron (Rosenblatt, 1958), an early type of artificial neural network designed to recognize patterns. Although it was limited in capability, the Perceptron laid the groundwork for future developments in machine learning. (Mitchell, 1997; Russell & Norvig, 2020).

1966 – ELIZA, the First Chatbot. Joseph Weizenbaum created ELIZA (Weizenbaum, 1966), an early natural language processing (NLP) program that simulated human-like conversations. ELIZA's ability to mimic psychotherapy conversations fascinated researchers, demonstrating AI's potential in human-computer interactions.

1970s – Expert Systems. AI research led to the development of expert systems, programs designed to mimic human expertise in specific domains. MYCIN 1974 (Shortliffe, 1976), an AI-based medical diagnosis system, was a significant breakthrough, demonstrating how AI could assist in healthcare.

Despite early successes, AI systems were limited by their reliance on predefined rules and lacked the ability to learn from data. This led to the first AI winter, a period of reduced funding and enthusiasm due to unmet expectations.

The Emergence of Machine Learning (1980s – 1990s)

The limitations of symbolic AI led researchers to explore new approaches, paving the way for machine learning (ML). Unlike rule-based systems, ML models could learn from data and improve their performance over time. (Mitchell, 1997; Russell & Norvig, 2020)

1986 – The Backpropagation Algorithm. Geoffrey Hinton, David Rumelhart, and Ronald Williams introduced the backpropagation algorithm, a breakthrough that allowed artificial neural networks to adjust their internal weights and improve accuracy. This innovation revitalized interest in neural networks and set the stage for deep learning. (Krizhevsky, Sutskever, & Hinton, 2012; LeCun, Bengio, & Hinton, 2015)

1997 – IBM's Deep Blue Defeats World Chess Champion Garry Kasparov. IBM's Deep Blue (Campbell, Lo, & Mackinlay, 1997), an AI-driven chess-playing system, defeated world chess champion Garry Kasparov in a historic match. This event demonstrated AI's ability to process vast amounts of information and make strategic decisions at superhuman levels.

During this period, AI applications expanded beyond academia into industries such as finance, healthcare, and robotics. However, computational limitations and the lack of large-scale datasets restricted progress.

The Rise of Deep Learning and Modern AI (2000s – Present)

The 21st century witnessed a paradigm shift in AI, driven by advancements in computational power, data availability, and deep learning algorithms, (Krizhevsky, Sutskever, & Hinton, 2012; LeCun, Bengio, & Hinton, 2015).

2006 – The Deep Learning Revolution. Geoffrey Hinton and his team popularized the term deep learning, referring to neural networks with multiple layers that could automatically extract patterns from large datasets. This breakthrough led to state-of-the-art performance in tasks such as image recognition, speech processing, and natural language understanding. (Krizhevsky, Sutskever, & Hinton, 2012; LeCun, Bengio, & Hinton, 2015)

2011 – IBM Watson Wins Jeopardy! IBM's Watson AI system defeated human champions in the game show Jeopardy! (Ferrucci et al., 2010), demonstrating AI's ability to process and comprehend natural language at an advanced level.

2012 – AlexNet and the ImageNet Breakthrough. AlexNet (Krizhevsky, Sutskever, & Hinton, 2012), a deep convolutional neural network (CNN) developed by Alex Krizhevsky, Geoffrey Hinton, and Ilya Sutskever, won the ImageNet competition, significantly outperforming traditional machine learning methods. This event marked the beginning of AI's dominance in computer vision. (Mitchell, 1997; Russell & Norvig, 2020)

2016 – AlphaGo Defeats World Champion Lee Sedol. Google DeepMind's AlphaGo (Silver et al., 2016), an AI program designed to play the board game Go, defeated 18-time world champion Lee Sedol. The complexity of Go had previously made it a challenging game for AI, but AlphaGo's use of deep reinforcement learning showcased AI's ability to master strategic decision-making.

2018 – BERT and NLP Advancements. Google introduced Bidirectional Encoder Representations from Transformers (BERT (Devlin et al., 2018)), a natural language processing (NLP) model that significantly improved machine understanding of human language. BERT laid the foundation for future AI-powered chatbots and virtual assistants.

2020s – Generative AI and Large Language Models. The latest wave of AI research has been dominated by Generative AI, exemplified by models like GPT-3 (2020 (Brown et al., 2020)), ChatGPT (2022 (Open AI, 2022)), and GPT-4 (2023).

These models leverage massive datasets and deep learning techniques to generate human-like text, assist with creative writing, and perform complex reasoning tasks.

Similarly, AI-generated images, videos, and voice synthesis have advanced, leading to applications in art, media, and entertainment. (Krizhevsky, Sutskever, & Hinton, 2012; LeCun, Bengio, & Hinton, 2015)

AI in Education

Introduction

Education is the foundation of human progress, and Artificial Intelligence (AI) is playing a pivotal role in reshaping how we learn, teach, and manage educational institutions. AI-powered tools and systems are enhancing personalized learning, automating administrative tasks, and making education more accessible and inclusive, (Luckin et al., 2016; Holmes et al., 2019; Zawacki-Richter et al., 2019).

From AI-driven tutoring assistants to intelligent grading systems, the integration of AI in education is revolutionizing traditional learning models. This section explores the significance of AI in education, highlighting its benefits, challenges, and future implications, (Luckin et al., 2016; Holmes et al., 2019; Zawacki-Richter et al., 2019).

The Role of AI in Education

AI is transforming education in multiple ways, enhancing both the learning experience for students and the teaching process for educators. Some key areas where AI is making an impact include:

1. Personalized Learning (Luckin et al., 2016; Holmes et al., 2019; Zawacki-Richter et al., 2019)
   - AI-powered adaptive learning platforms analyze student performance and tailor content to their needs.
   - Machine learning algorithms track progress and suggest resources, ensuring students receive individualized support. (Mitchell, 1997; Russell & Norvig, 2020)
   - Example: Platforms like Duolingo and Coursera use AI to provide customized language learning and course recommendations.
2. Intelligent Tutoring Systems (ITS) (Roll & Wylie, 2016; Holmes et al., 2019)
   - AI-driven virtual tutors provide real-time assistance to students, answering queries and explaining concepts.

- These systems can assess a student's strengths and weaknesses, providing targeted guidance.
   - Example: Carnegie Learning's MATHia uses AI to tutor students in mathematics.
3. Automated Administrative Tasks
   - AI helps educators by automating time-consuming tasks such as grading, attendance tracking, and scheduling.
   - Example: Turnitin's AI-powered plagiarism detection system helps educators maintain academic integrity.
4. Enhanced Accessibility
   - AI tools help students with disabilities by providing speech-to-text transcription, text-to-speech synthesis, real-time translations, and personalized learning aids. (Luckin et al., 2016; Holmes et al., 2019; Zawacki-Richter et al., 2019)
   - Example: Microsoft Immersive Reader uses AI to help students with dyslexia and reading difficulties.
5. AI-Powered Student Engagement
   - Gamification and AI-driven interactive simulations make learning more engaging.
   - AI chatbots serve as virtual teaching assistants, responding to student queries and providing course guidance.
   - Example: Chatbots like Jill Watson at Georgia Tech assist students by answering academic questions (Ferrucci et al., 2010).

Benefits of AI in Education

AI enhances education in several ways, making it more effective, inclusive, and efficient.

1. Improved Learning Outcomes
   - AI-driven adaptive learning ensures that students receive content suited to their knowledge level.
   - Real-time feedback allows students to learn from their mistakes immediately.
2. Increased Efficiency for Educators
   - AI automates repetitive tasks, allowing teachers to focus on interactive and higher-order teaching activities.
   - Teachers can use AI-powered analytics to identify students who need extra support.
3. Greater Accessibility and Inclusivity

- AI ensures equal learning opportunities for students with disabilities through assistive technologies.
- AI-powered real-time language translation supports students in multi-lingual classrooms.

4. Data-Driven Decision Making
   - AI provides predictive analytics that help institutions make informed decisions on curriculum design and student performance.
   - Example: Predictive analytics in universities helps identify students at risk of dropping out and provides early interventions.
5. Cost-Effective Learning Solutions
   - AI-based education platforms offer affordable, high-quality learning experiences without geographical constraints.
   - AI-powered virtual labs reduce costs associated with physical lab setups.

Challenges of AI in Education

Despite its advantages, AI implementation in education comes with challenges that need to be addressed:

1. Data Privacy Concerns
   - AI-driven education platforms collect vast amounts of student data, raising concerns about data security and ethical usage. (Bostrom, 2014; Tegmark, 2017; Selwyn, 2019)
   - Ensuring compliance with regulations like GDPR (General Data Protection Regulation) is essential.
2. Bias in AI Algorithms
   - AI models trained on biased datasets may reinforce existing gender, racial, or socio-economic inequalities.
   - Developers must ensure that AI tools are fair, inclusive, and regularly audited for bias.
3. High Implementation Costs
   - Advanced AI systems require significant investment in infrastructure, training, and maintenance.
   - Many schools, especially in developing countries, lack the resources to implement AI.
4. Dependence on Technology
   - Over-reliance on AI may reduce critical thinking and problem-solving skills among students.
   - Teachers should balance AI-based learning with traditional human-led teaching methods.

The Future of AI in Education

As AI continues to evolve, its role in education will expand further. Some emerging trends include:

1. AI-Enhanced Virtual and Augmented Reality (VR/AR)
   - AI-powered VR/AR environments will provide immersive, hands-on learning experiences.
   - Example: Google Expeditions enables students to take virtual field trips worldwide.
2. AI-Powered Emotional Intelligence
   - Future AI tutors will recognize student emotions and adjust teaching styles accordingly.
   - AI will detect stress, confusion, or engagement levels to personalize learning experiences.
3. Lifelong Learning with AI
   - AI will support continuous education by recommending courses and resources based on career goals.
   - Example: LinkedIn Learning's AI-driven course recommendations help professionals upgrade their skills.
4. Blockchain and AI for Secure Education
   - AI combined with blockchain technology will enable tamper-proof educational credentials and secure student records.
   - Universities and employers will use blockchain-based AI verification for authenticating degrees and certifications.

Objectives of This Chapter

Introduction

Understanding Artificial Intelligence (AI) is crucial for educators, students, researchers, and policymakers as AI continues to reshape various fields, including education. This chapter aims to provide a comprehensive foundation in AI, its methodologies, applications, and ethical considerations, (Bostrom, 2014; Tegmark, 2017; Selwyn, 2019).

By the end of this chapter, readers will gain a clear understanding of AI's fundamentals, evolution, role in education, and future trends. The objectives outlined below will guide learners through key AI concepts and their implications in modern education.

Learning Objectives

This chapter is designed to achieve the following learning outcomes:

1. Define Artificial Intelligence (AI) and Its Key Concepts
   - Understand what AI is and how it differs from traditional computing systems.
   - Identify the fundamental components of AI, including Machine Learning (ML), Deep Learning (DL), Natural Language Processing (NLP), and Computer Vision. (Mitchell, 1997; Russell & Norvig, 2020) (Krizhevsky, Sutskever, & Hinton, 2012; LeCun, Bengio, & Hinton, 2015)
2. Explore the Evolution of AI
   - Trace the historical development of AI from rule-based systems to modern deep learning techniques. (Krizhevsky, Sutskever, & Hinton, 2012; LeCun, Bengio, & Hinton, 2015)
   - Recognize key milestones in AI research and development.
3. Analyze the Role of AI in Education (Luckin et al., 2016; Holmes et al., 2019; Zawacki-Richter et al., 2019)
   - Examine how AI is transforming teaching and learning processes.
   - Understand AI's impact on personalized learning, intelligent tutoring systems, automated assessment, and educational accessibility. (Luckin et al., 2016; Holmes et al., 2019; Zawacki-Richter et al., 2019) (Roll & Wylie, 2016; Holmes et al., 2019)
4. Understand Different AI Methodologies and Categories
   - Differentiate between Reactive AI, Limited Memory AI, Theory of Mind AI, and Self-Aware AI.
   - Learn about various AI models and how they function in real-world applications.
5. Evaluate the Ethical Implications of AI (Bostrom, 2014; Tegmark, 2017; Selwyn, 2019)
   - Discuss concerns related to algorithmic bias, data privacy, transparency, and accountability in AI systems.
   - Explore methods to develop fair and responsible AI solutions.
6. Identify the Benefits and Challenges of AI
   - Understand how AI enhances education by making learning more accessible, engaging, and efficient.
   - Analyze the challenges of AI adoption, such as data security, high implementation costs, and ethical concerns. (Bostrom, 2014; Tegmark, 2017; Selwyn, 2019)

7. Explore Future Trends in AI and Education
    - Investigate emerging technologies such as AI-driven VR/AR, predictive analytics, and AI-powered emotional intelligence.
    - Recognize the role of blockchain in AI for secure and verifiable academic credentials.

WHAT IS ARTIFICIAL INTELLIGENCE?

Defining AI: From Theory to Practice

Artificial Intelligence (AI) refers to the simulation of human intelligence in machines that are programmed to think, reason, learn, and make decisions. AI encompasses a broad range of technologies that enable machines to perform tasks typically requiring human cognition, such as speech recognition, decision-making, problem-solving, and language understanding.

Key Components of AI

AI is built on several foundational pillars:

- Machine Learning (ML): AI models that learn patterns from data and improve their performance without explicit programming. (Mitchell, 1997; Russell & Norvig, 2020)
- Deep Learning (DL): A subset of ML that mimics the human brain through artificial neural networks. (Krizhevsky, Sutskever, & Hinton, 2012; LeCun, Bengio, & Hinton, 2015)
- Natural Language Processing (NLP): The ability of machines to understand and generate human language (e.g., chatbots, voice assistants).
- Computer Vision: AI that enables machines to interpret and process visual information from images and videos.
- Expert Systems: AI programs that mimic human expertise in specific fields, such as medical diagnosis and fraud detection.

Types of AI

AI is generally classified into three categories based on capabilities:

1. Narrow AI (Weak AI):
    - Performs a specific task (e.g., Google Search, facial recognition).

    - Lacks general reasoning capabilities.
2. General AI (Strong AI):
    - Hypothetical AI that can think, learn, and reason like a human.
    - Has yet to be fully realized.
3. Super AI (Artificial Superintelligence):
    - Theoretical AI surpassing human intelligence.
    - A topic of debate and ethical discussions. (Bostrom, 2014; Tegmark, 2017; Selwyn, 2019)

The Scope of AI: Beyond Science Fiction

AI has evolved far beyond its depiction in science fiction movies and novels. Instead of robots taking over the world, AI has become an integral part of everyday life, powering technologies in healthcare, finance, education, and business.

Table 1. AI Across Different Domains

Domain	AI Applications
Healthcare	Disease prediction, AI-assisted surgeries, personalized treatment plans
Finance	Fraud detection, algorithmic trading, credit risk analysis
Retail	Chatbots, personalized shopping experiences, inventory management
Transportation	Self-driving cars, traffic management, predictive maintenance
Cybersecurity	Threat detection, anomaly detection, automated security systems
Education	AI tutors, personalized learning, automated grading

AI and Human-AI Collaboration

AI is not about replacing humans but rather enhancing human capabilities. For example:

- AI assists doctors in diagnosing diseases more accurately.
- AI helps teachers personalize learning experiences for students.
- AI aids scientists in drug discovery and space exploration.

While AI is advancing rapidly, human expertise, ethics, and emotional intelligence remain irreplaceable.

AI in Everyday Life: Real-World Applications

AI-powered technologies are now embedded in our daily lives, often without us even realizing it. From smartphones to smart homes, AI enhances convenience, efficiency, and decision-making.

AI in Consumer Applications

AI-driven applications improve user experience through:

- Virtual Assistants: Siri, Alexa, and Google Assistant respond to voice commands.
- Recommendation Systems: Netflix, YouTube, and Amazon suggest content based on user behavior.
- Smart Homes: AI-driven thermostats, security cameras, and lighting systems optimize energy and security.

AI in Social Media

AI enhances user engagement and security on platforms like Facebook, Twitter, and Instagram through:

- Personalized Feeds: Algorithms curate content based on user preferences.
- Spam Detection: AI filters out fake accounts and harmful content.
- Sentiment Analysis: AI detects emotions in posts to improve online experiences.

AI in Business and Workplaces

AI revolutionizes corporate operations through:

- Automated Customer Service: AI chatbots handle inquiries, reducing wait times.
- Predictive Analytics: Businesses forecast demand and optimize supply chains.
- AI-powered Hiring: HR departments use AI to screen resumes and match candidates with job roles.

These advancements highlight AI's role in enhancing productivity and decision-making.

The Role of AI in Modern Education

Education is undergoing a major transformation due to AI. From adaptive learning platforms to AI-powered tutors, technology is personalizing and optimizing learning experiences.

AI-Powered Personalized Learning

AI helps students learn at their own pace by:

- Adapting coursework based on individual progress.
- Identifying weak areas and providing targeted learning resources.
- Recommending tailored study plans for each student.

Example. Platforms like Coursera and Duolingo use AI to adjust lesson difficulty based on user performance.

Intelligent Tutoring Systems

AI tutors provide real-time feedback and assistance, similar to a human teacher. They:

- Answer student queries instantly.
- Offer personalized exercises based on learning gaps.
- Monitor student engagement and suggest improvements.

Example:

IBM's Watson Tutor helps students by providing detailed explanations on complex topics (Ferrucci et al., 2010).

AI in Administrative Tasks

AI automates time-consuming administrative duties, such as:

- Automated Grading: AI assesses assignments and quizzes instantly.
- Attendance Monitoring: Facial recognition tracks student presence.
- AI Chatbots: Institutions use AI assistants for student inquiries.

This allows teachers to focus on creative and interactive teaching rather than repetitive tasks.

Enhancing Accessibility with AI

AI helps students with disabilities through:

- Speech-to-text technology for students with hearing impairments.
- Text-to-speech tools for visually impaired learners.
- AI-powered language translation for non-native speakers.

AI ensures that education is inclusive and accessible to all learners.

The Future of AI in Education

As AI advances, future educational trends may include:

- AI-driven virtual reality (VR) and augmented reality (AR) for immersive learning.
- Emotion AI, which detects students' emotions and adapts teaching accordingly.
- Blockchain integration for secure academic credentials.

AI's role in education is set to expand dramatically, ensuring a smarter, more efficient learning ecosystem.

THE EVOLUTION OF AI

Artificial Intelligence (AI) has undergone remarkable transformations since its inception. From rule-based systems to machine learning and deep learning, AI has evolved into a powerful technology that is shaping industries worldwide, (Mitchell, 1997; Russell & Norvig, 2020) (Krizhevsky, Sutskever, & Hinton, 2012; LeCun, Bengio, & Hinton, 2015),

This section explores the key stages of AI evolution, focusing on historical developments, technological breakthroughs, and future trends.

Early Beginnings: Rule-Based Systems

The Birth of AI (1950s - 1970s)

AI as a formal discipline emerged in the 1950s, with pioneers like Alan Turing (Turing, 1950), John McCarthy, and Marvin Minsky laying the groundwork.

- Alan Turing (1950 (Turing, 1950)): Proposed the Turing Test to determine machine intelligence.
- John McCarthy (1956): Coined the term Artificial Intelligence at the Dartmouth Conference (McCarthy et al., 1956).
- Claude Shannon: Developed early theories on machine learning and decision-making. (Mitchell, 1997; Russell & Norvig, 2020)

Expert Systems and Rule-Based AI (1970s - 1980s)

Early AI systems relied on predefined rules and logical reasoning to solve problems. These were known as Expert Systems.

Key Characteristics of Rule-Based AI
Operates on IF-THEN logic
Good for structured problem-solving
Lacks adaptability and learning ability
Examples of Early Expert Systems

- MYCIN (1970s (Shortliffe, 1976)): Diagnosed bacterial infections.
- DENDRAL (1960s-70s): Analyzed chemical compounds.
- XCON (1980s): Assisted in configuring computer systems.

Despite their usefulness, rule-based systems were rigid and struggled with complex, unstructured problems, leading to the rise of machine learning. (Mitchell, 1997; Russell & Norvig, 2020)

The Rise of Machine Learning

The Shift from Rules to Learning (1980s - 1990s)

By the late 1980s, researchers realized that predefined rules limited AI's potential. The focus shifted towards data-driven learning instead of manually coding every decision.

Machine Learning (ML) revolutionized AI by:

- Learning from historical data rather than predefined rules.
- Adapting to new patterns and insights.
- Automating decision-making and predictions. (Mitchell, 1997; Russell & Norvig, 2020)

Key ML Algorithms

Table 2. Statistical and probabilistic models

Algorithm	Description	Example Applications
Linear Regression	Predicts numerical values	Stock price prediction
Decision Trees	Hierarchical decision-making	Fraud detection
Support Vector Machines (SVM)	Classifies data	Handwriting recognition
Bayesian Networks	Probabilistic reasoning	Medical diagnosis
Neural Networks	Mimics human brain functions	Image recognition

(Mitchell, 1997; Russell & Norvig, 2020)

Real-World Applications of ML

By the 1990s, ML powered speech recognition, recommendation systems, and financial forecasting.

Spam filters in email services used Naïve Bayes classification.
Stock market predictions leveraged regression models.
Netflix recommendations were powered by collaborative filtering.

The success of ML paved the way for deep learning, an even more advanced approach to AI. (Krizhevsky, Sutskever, & Hinton, 2012; LeCun, Bengio, & Hinton, 2015)

Deep Learning: A Game-Changer for AI

The Deep Learning Revolution (2000s - Present)

Deep Learning (DL) is a subset of ML that mimics the structure of the human brain using Artificial Neural Networks (ANNs). (Krizhevsky, Sutskever, & Hinton, 2012; LeCun, Bengio, & Hinton, 2015)

- Unlike traditional ML, deep learning:
- Learns directly from large datasets
- Identifies complex patterns and relationships

- Powers advanced AI applications like self-driving cars and natural language processing (Krizhevsky, Sutskever, & Hinton, 2012; LeCun, Bengio, & Hinton, 2015)

Key Innovations in Deep Learning

- Convolutional Neural Networks (CNNs): Excel in image recognition (e.g., medical imaging).
- Recurrent Neural Networks (RNNs): Improve speech and language processing (e.g., Google Translate).
- Transformers (e.g., GPT, BERT (Devlin et al., 2018)): Enable AI-generated text and chatbots.

Real-World Impact of Deep Learning

DL has transformed multiple industries:

Healthcare: AI-powered diagnostics (e.g., detecting cancer from scans).
Finance: AI-driven fraud detection and automated trading.
Education: AI tutors providing personalized learning experiences.
Autonomous Vehicles: Self-driving cars by Tesla and Waymo. (Luckin et al., 2016; Holmes et al., 2019; Zawacki-Richter et al., 2019)

The increasing power of deep learning has led to unprecedented AI breakthroughs. (Krizhevsky, Sutskever, & Hinton, 2012; LeCun, Bengio, & Hinton, 2015)

Milestones in AI Development

Table 3. Key breakthroughs in AI

Year	Milestone	Impact
1950	Alan Turing proposes the **Turing Test**	Establishes the foundation of AI.
1956	Dartmouth Conference	AI formally recognized as a field.
1997	IBM's **Deep Blue** beats world chess champion Garry Kasparov	AI outperforms humans in strategic thinking.
2011	IBM's **Watson** wins Jeopardy!	AI processes complex human language.
2016	Google DeepMind's **AlphaGo** defeats Go champion	AI masters intuitive reasoning.
2020	OpenAI's **GPT-3** revolutionizes NLP	AI generates human-like text.
2023	**ChatGPT** surpasses 100 million users	AI democratizes knowledge access.

These milestones reflect AI's rapid evolution and increasing capabilities in solving complex problems.

The Future of AI: Trends and Predictions

As AI continues to evolve, several emerging trends are shaping the future:

Key AI Trends

- Generative AI: AI creating text, images, music, and videos.
- Explainable AI (XAI): AI models becoming more transparent and interpretable.
- AI Ethics and Regulations: Governments and organizations focusing on responsible AI.
- AI-Powered Robotics: More sophisticated and autonomous machines.
- Neurosymbolic AI: Combining deep learning with logical reasoning. (Krizhevsky, Sutskever, & Hinton, 2012; LeCun, Bengio, & Hinton, 2015)

The Future of AI in Education

- AI-powered virtual reality (VR) and AR for immersive learning.
- Personalized AI tutors for one-on-one learning assistance.
- Automated assessment and grading for efficient education systems.

Challenges and Ethical Considerations

Despite its promise, AI faces several challenges:

- Bias in AI Models: AI can inherit biases from training data.
- Data Privacy Concerns: AI collects vast amounts of user data.
- Job Displacement: Automation may replace certain human roles.

Addressing these issues will be crucial for responsible AI development.

ETHICAL CONSIDERATIONS IN AI

As AI systems become more integrated into education, healthcare, finance, and daily life, ethical considerations become critical. Ethical AI development ensures that AI technologies are fair, transparent, and beneficial to society. (Bostrom, 2014; Tegmark, 2017; Selwyn, 2019)

This section explores the ethical challenges of AI, focusing on bias, data privacy, accountability, and responsible AI design. (Bostrom, 2014; Tegmark, 2017; Selwyn, 2019)

Understanding Algorithmic Bias

What is Algorithmic Bias?

Algorithmic bias occurs when AI systems produce unfair, discriminatory, or prejudiced results due to biased training data or flawed model design.

Sources of Bias in AI Models

- Bias in training data: AI learns from historical data, which may contain existing societal biases.
- Algorithmic bias: The design of AI models can favor certain groups over others.
- Feedback loops: AI models reinforce biases by learning from biased predictions.

Table 4. Real-World Examples of AI Bias

Case	Description	Impact
Facial Recognition Bias	AI misidentifies people of color more often than white individuals.	Leads to wrongful arrests and surveillance concerns.
Gender Bias in Hiring AI	Amazon's AI hiring tool favored male candidates over women.	Unfair hiring practices and workplace discrimination.
Healthcare AI Bias	AI models trained on white patients performed poorly for other races.	Incorrect medical diagnoses and poor healthcare outcomes.

How to Mitigate Algorithmic Bias

- Use diverse datasets representing different populations.
- Regularly audit AI models for fairness.
- Implement explainable AI (XAI) to make decisions transparent.
- Involve human oversight to correct biased outcomes.

Data Privacy and Security in AI Systems

The Importance of Data Privacy in AI

AI systems process huge amounts of personal data, including student records, medical histories, and financial information. Protecting this data is essential to prevent misuse, data breaches, and identity theft.

Privacy Risks in AI

- Unauthorized data collection: AI apps track user behavior without consent.
- Data breaches: Hackers target AI systems storing personal data.
- Lack of informed consent: Users may not understand how AI processes their data.

Table 5. Key AI Security Measures

Security Practice	Description
Data Encryption	Protects sensitive data from cyberattacks.
Anonymization	Removes personally identifiable information from datasets.
User Consent Mechanisms	Ensures individuals have control over their data.
AI Governance Policies	Establishes ethical rules for AI developers and companies.

Example. The GDPR (General Data Protection Regulation) in Europe enforces strict privacy laws for AI-driven systems.

Transparency and Accountability in AI

Why Transparency in AI Matters

AI systems make critical decisions (e.g., hiring, healthcare, and grading students). If AI models are black boxes, users cannot understand or challenge unfair decisions.

The Challenge of “Black Box” AI

Many AI models, especially deep learning networks, are highly complex and difficult to interpret. This lack of transparency raises ethical concerns:

- Who is responsible for an AI decision?
- How can users appeal unfair AI outcomes?
- Can AI systems explain their reasoning? (Bostrom, 2014; Tegmark, 2017; Selwyn, 2019) (Krizhevsky, Sutskever, & Hinton, 2012; LeCun, Bengio, & Hinton, 2015)

Making AI Accountable and Explainable

- Explainable AI (XAI): AI systems should provide clear explanations of their decisions.
- Human-in-the-loop AI: AI should not replace human judgment in critical areas.
- AI Ethics Committees: Organizations should oversee AI deployments and assess risks.

Example. Google's AI "What-If Tool" allows users to test AI decisions for bias and fairness.

Ethical AI Design: Principles and Practices

To build ethical AI systems, developers and policymakers follow key ethical principles. (Bostrom, 2014; Tegmark, 2017; Selwyn, 2019)

Table 6. Principles of ethical AI

Principle	Description
Fairness	AI should not discriminate based on race, gender, or socioeconomic status.
Transparency	AI decisions should be explainable and understandable.
Privacy Protection	AI should respect users' personal data and confidentiality.
Accountability	AI developers should be held responsible for AI-driven decisions.
Inclusivity	AI should serve diverse communities and be accessible to all.

Implementing Ethical AI in Education

- AI-powered tutoring should be fair: Personalized learning should be equitable for all students. (Luckin et al., 2016; Holmes et al., 2019; Zawacki-Richter et al., 2019)

- Student data privacy should be a priority: AI-driven learning platforms must protect student data.
- Transparency in AI grading: AI-based grading systems should provide clear feedback to students.

Example. The AI4K12 initiative ensures AI in schools is ethical, transparent, and accessible. (Bostrom, 2014; Tegmark, 2017; Selwyn, 2019)

Case Studies: Ethical Challenges in AI

Case Study 1: AI Bias in Hiring Systems

Company: Amazon

Problem: Amazon's AI hiring tool discriminated against female candidates by favoring male-dominated resumes.

Cause: The AI was trained on historical hiring data, which reflected past biases.

Solution: Amazon discontinued the tool and emphasized diverse hiring practices.

Case Study 2: AI and Privacy Violations

Company: Facebook-Cambridge Analytica Scandal

Problem: AI algorithms harvested personal data from millions of users without consent for political campaigns.

Impact: Raised global concerns about data privacy and AI misuse.

Solution: Stricter data privacy regulations like GDPR and CCPA were introduced.

Case Study 3: Ethical AI in Healthcare

Company: IBM Watson Health

Problem: IBM's AI gave incorrect cancer treatment recommendations due to flawed training data (Ferrucci et al., 2010).

Impact: Raised concerns about reliability and safety in AI-driven healthcare.

Solution: AI models need ongoing testing and human oversight in medical applications.

CATEGORIES OF AI METHODOLOGIES

Reactive Machines: The Simplest Form of AI

Reactive Machines represent the most basic form of AI, functioning solely on predefined rules and real-time data. These systems do not possess memory or the ability to learn from past experiences. Instead, they react to specific inputs with programmed responses. Examples include Deep Blue (Campbell, Lo, & Mackinlay, 1997), the chess-playing computer developed by IBM, and Google's AlphaGo (Silver et al., 2016). While highly specialized and efficient in constrained environments, Reactive Machines lack adaptability and contextual understanding beyond their programming.

Limited Memory AI: Learning from Data

Limited Memory AI builds upon Reactive Machines by incorporating historical data into decision-making processes. This category includes most modern AI applications, such as self-driving cars, chatbots, and recommendation systems. These AI systems learn from past interactions to improve performance over time. Techniques such as deep learning, reinforcement learning, and supervised learning fall under this category. However, despite their ability to learn, Limited Memory AI still lacks a comprehensive understanding of emotions, intentions, or abstract reasoning beyond data-driven patterns. (Krizhevsky, Sutskever, & Hinton, 2012; LeCun, Bengio, & Hinton, 2015)

Theory of Mind AI: Simulating Human Emotions

Theory of Mind AI is an advanced concept in artificial intelligence that aims to interpret and respond to human emotions, beliefs, and intentions. This type of AI would enable machines to engage in human-like social interactions by understanding context, empathy, and emotional intelligence. While current AI systems, such as virtual assistants and emotion-recognition software, exhibit early traits of this capability, true Theory of Mind AI remains in the realm of ongoing research and development. Achieving this level of AI would require breakthroughs in cognitive computing and psychology-inspired machine learning models. (Mitchell, 1997; Russell & Norvig, 2020)

Self-Aware AI: A Theoretical Frontier

Self-Aware AI represents the pinnacle of AI evolution, where machines possess self-consciousness, introspection, and independent reasoning. This level of AI would not only understand emotions and beliefs but also form its own consciousness. While Self-Aware AI remains purely theoretical at present, it is the subject of intense philosophical and ethical discussions. If realized, it could lead to groundbreaking advancements, but also pose significant risks and ethical dilemmas regarding control, rights, and the role of AI in society. (Bostrom, 2014; Tegmark, 2017; Selwyn, 2019)

Comparing AI Categories: Strengths and Limitations

Each category of AI has its strengths and limitations:

- Reactive Machines: High efficiency in specific tasks but lacks adaptability.
- Limited Memory AI: Learns from data but cannot reason beyond stored experiences.
- Theory of Mind AI: Promising in human-like interactions but still under research.
- Self-Aware AI: Hypothetical and potentially transformative but raises ethical concerns. (Bostrom, 2014; Tegmark, 2017; Selwyn, 2019)

Understanding these categories is essential for appreciating the trajectory of AI development and its implications for various industries and society at large.

KEY AI TECHNIQUES

Artificial Intelligence (AI) encompasses various techniques that enable machines to learn, reason, and make decisions. These techniques can be broadly categorized into supervised learning, unsupervised learning, reinforcement learning, neural networks, and natural language processing. Each of these techniques plays a critical role in different applications of AI, from predictive modeling to decision-making and human-like interaction.

Supervised Learning: Predicting Outcomes

Supervised learning is one of the most widely used machine learning techniques where an algorithm learns from labeled data. This means that each training example in the dataset comes with an input-output pair, allowing the model to map inputs to the correct outputs. (Mitchell, 1997; Russell & Norvig, 2020)

How It Works

1. Data Collection – Gather a dataset with known inputs (features) and corresponding outputs (labels).
2. Model Training – The model learns by minimizing the error between its predictions and the actual outputs.
3. Validation & Testing – After training, the model is tested on unseen data to measure its accuracy.

Applications

- Spam Detection – Email services use supervised learning to classify emails as spam or non-spam based on previous labels.
- Medical Diagnosis – AI models predict diseases by analyzing medical records.
- Stock Market Prediction – Algorithms forecast stock prices based on historical data.

Supervised learning includes techniques such as linear regression, decision trees, support vector machines, and neural networks. However, its effectiveness relies on the availability of high-quality labeled data.

Unsupervised Learning: Discovering Patterns

Unlike supervised learning, unsupervised learning does not use labeled data. Instead, it identifies patterns and structures within the dataset.

How It Works

1. Data Processing – The model analyzes the raw, unstructured data.
2. Pattern Recognition – The algorithm clusters similar data points or reduces dimensionality for better visualization.
3. Interpretation – The discovered patterns are used for decision-making or further analysis.

Applications

- Customer Segmentation – E-commerce companies classify customers into different groups based on purchasing behavior.
- Anomaly Detection – Financial institutions use unsupervised learning to detect fraudulent transactions.
- Recommendation Systems – Streaming services like Netflix use unsupervised learning to suggest content based on user behavior.

Common unsupervised learning techniques include K-means clustering, hierarchical clustering, principal component analysis (PCA), and autoencoders. The lack of labeled data makes interpretation challenging, but it is useful for exploratory data analysis.

Reinforcement Learning: Learning Through Interaction

Reinforcement learning (RL) is an approach where an AI agent interacts with an environment and learns by receiving rewards or penalties.

How It Works

1. Agent-Environment Interaction – The agent takes actions in an environment and receives feedback.
2. Reward System – Actions leading to positive outcomes receive rewards, while negative actions get penalties.
3. Policy Optimization – Over time, the agent refines its strategy to maximize long-term rewards.

Applications

- Game Playing – DeepMind's AlphaGo defeated human champions in the board game Go (Silver et al., 2016).
- Autonomous Vehicles – Self-driving cars learn to navigate by interacting with real-world scenarios.
- Robotics – RL enables robots to adapt to changing environments and optimize performance.

Popular reinforcement learning algorithms include Q-learning, deep Q-networks (DQN), and policy gradient methods. Despite its potential, RL requires significant computational power and a well-defined reward structure.

Neural Networks: Mimicking the Human Brain

Neural networks are a foundational technology in AI that mimic the structure and function of the human brain to process complex data.

Structure of Neural Networks

1. Input Layer – Receives raw data (e.g., images, text, or numerical values).
2. Hidden Layers – Perform computations using interconnected artificial neurons.
3. Output Layer – Produces the final prediction or classification.

Types of Neural Networks

- Feedforward Neural Networks (FNN) – Basic neural networks where data moves in one direction.
- Convolutional Neural Networks (CNNs) – Specialized for image recognition and computer vision.
- Recurrent Neural Networks (RNNs) – Effective for sequential data like speech and time series analysis.

Applications

- Facial Recognition – Used in security systems to authenticate identities.
- Medical Imaging – Detects diseases in X-rays and MRIs.
- Speech Recognition – Powers virtual assistants like Alexa and Siri.

Deep learning, a subset of neural networks, has revolutionized AI by achieving human-level performance in many tasks. However, training deep neural networks requires extensive computational resources. (Krizhevsky, Sutskever, & Hinton, 2012; LeCun, Bengio, & Hinton, 2015)

Natural Language Processing: Understanding Human Language

Natural Language Processing (NLP) is a branch of AI that enables machines to understand, interpret, and generate human language.

Key NLP Tasks

1. Text Classification – Categorizing text into predefined categories (e.g., spam detection).
2. Named Entity Recognition (NER) – Identifying names, dates, and locations in text.
3. Sentiment Analysis – Determining the sentiment behind a text (positive, negative, or neutral).
4. Machine Translation – Automatically translating text between languages.
5. Text Generation – Generating human-like text (e.g., chatbots, content generation).

Applications

- Chatbots & Virtual Assistants – AI-powered assistants like Siri and Google Assistant respond to user queries.
- Search Engines – Google Search uses NLP to understand user queries and provide relevant results.
- Automated Customer Support – Businesses use NLP-driven chatbots to handle customer inquiries efficiently.

Recent advancements in NLP, such as transformer-based models like GPT (Generative Pre-trained Transformer) and BERT (Bidirectional Encoder Representations from Transformers (Devlin et al., 2018)), have significantly improved AI's ability to process and generate human-like text.

AI TOOLS AND TECHNOLOGIES

Artificial Intelligence (AI) has rapidly evolved over the past decade, becoming a fundamental part of modern technology. Various tools and technologies power AI development, with Python emerging as the dominant programming language. This section delves into the essential tools, libraries, and platforms that facilitate AI development, covering Python and its core libraries, cloud-based AI platforms, and open-source tools.

Python: The Language of AI

Python has established itself as the go-to programming language for AI development due to its simplicity, readability, and vast ecosystem of libraries. Python's intuitive syntax makes it accessible to both beginners and experienced developers, while its extensive library support allows for seamless integration of AI functionalities.

Key Reasons for Python's Dominance in AI

- Ease of Learning and Use: Python's simple syntax reduces the learning curve for AI developers.
- Comprehensive Libraries: A vast collection of libraries simplifies AI development.
- Strong Community Support: A large, active community provides ample resources and support.
- Flexibility and Scalability: Python can handle both small-scale and large-scale AI projects effectively.

Key Python Libraries for AI Development

Python's rich ecosystem includes several powerful libraries specifically designed for AI development. These libraries facilitate data manipulation, visualization, machine learning, deep learning, and natural language processing (NLP). (Mitchell, 1997; Russell & Norvig, 2020) (Krizhevsky, Sutskever, & Hinton, 2012; LeCun, Bengio, & Hinton, 2015)

NumPy and Pandas: Data Manipulation

Data is the foundation of AI models, and efficient data manipulation is crucial. NumPy and Pandas provide powerful tools for handling and processing data.

- NumPy: A library that provides support for large, multi-dimensional arrays and matrices, along with mathematical functions.
  - Used for numerical computing and scientific calculations.
  - Facilitates operations on large datasets efficiently.
- Pandas: A library designed for data manipulation and analysis.
  - Provides DataFrame and Series objects for structured data manipulation.
  - Supports data cleaning, transformation, and aggregation.

Matplotlib and Seaborn: Data Visualization

Data visualization helps AI developers understand data patterns, detect anomalies, and present insights effectively.

- Matplotlib:
  - A fundamental library for creating static, animated, and interactive plots.
  - Provides control over graphical elements such as axes, labels, and colors.
- Seaborn:
  - Built on Matplotlib, offering advanced visualization capabilities.
  - Includes functions for drawing complex statistical graphs such as heatmaps, box plots, and violin plots.

Scikit-learn: Machine Learning Made Easy

Scikit-learn is one of the most popular machine learning libraries, providing simple and efficient tools for data mining and analysis. (Mitchell, 1997; Russell & Norvig, 2020)

- Key Features:
  - Implements classification, regression, clustering, and dimensionality reduction algorithms.
  - Provides model selection and evaluation metrics.
  - Supports pre-processing techniques such as feature scaling and encoding.

TensorFlow and PyTorch: Deep Learning Frameworks

Deep learning models require robust frameworks that facilitate neural network implementation. TensorFlow and PyTorch are the leading deep learning libraries. (Krizhevsky, Sutskever, & Hinton, 2012; LeCun, Bengio, & Hinton, 2015)

- TensorFlow:
  - Developed by Google, TensorFlow provides a scalable platform for machine learning and deep learning. (Mitchell, 1997; Russell & Norvig, 2020) (Krizhevsky, Sutskever, & Hinton, 2012; LeCun, Bengio, & Hinton, 2015)
  - Offers high-level APIs such as Keras for rapid model development.
  - Supports deployment on cloud, mobile, and edge devices.
- PyTorch:
  - Developed by Facebook, PyTorch is known for its dynamic computation graph and ease of use.
  - Preferred for research and experimentation due to its flexibility.

- Includes Torchvision for image processing tasks.

NLTK and spaCy: Natural Language Processing

Natural Language Processing (NLP) enables AI to interpret and manipulate human language. NLTK and spaCy are two powerful libraries for NLP tasks.

- NLTK (Natural Language Toolkit):
    - A comprehensive library for text processing, tokenization, stemming, and named entity recognition.
    - Suitable for academic research and prototyping.
- spaCy:
    - Designed for industrial applications with optimized speed and accuracy.
    - Provides pre-trained models for entity recognition, part-of-speech tagging, and dependency parsing.

Cloud-Based AI Platforms: AWS, Google Cloud, and Azure

Cloud-based AI platforms provide scalable computing resources, enabling AI developers to build, train, and deploy models efficiently.

- Amazon Web Services (AWS) AI Services:
    - Offers machine learning tools like Amazon SageMaker for model development. (Mitchell, 1997; Russell & Norvig, 2020)
    - Provides AI-driven services such as Rekognition (image analysis) and Comprehend (text analysis).
- Google Cloud AI Platform:
    - Includes TensorFlow Extended (TFX) for machine learning workflows. (Mitchell, 1997; Russell & Norvig, 2020)
    - Provides AutoML for automated model training and deployment.
- Microsoft Azure AI:
    - Offers Azure Machine Learning for building AI models. (Mitchell, 1997; Russell & Norvig, 2020)
    - Includes Cognitive Services for vision, speech, and language tasks.

Open-Source AI Tools: Democratizing AI Development

Open-source AI tools play a significant role in making AI accessible to developers worldwide. These tools encourage collaboration and innovation in the AI community.

- Hugging Face:
    - Provides state-of-the-art NLP models and transformers.
    - Hosts a model hub for easy access to pre-trained models.
- OpenAI:
    - Developed GPT models, including ChatGPT (OpenAI, 2022), which powers advanced conversational AI.
    - OpenAI Gym supports reinforcement learning research.
- Fast.ai:
    - Simplifies deep learning with high-level APIs built on PyTorch. (Krizhevsky, Sutskever, & Hinton, 2012; LeCun, Bengio, & Hinton, 2015)
    - Focuses on making AI accessible to non-experts.

AI IN INSTRUCTIONAL EDUCATION STRATEGIES

Artificial Intelligence (AI) is revolutionizing education by providing innovative strategies that enhance instructional methods, personalize learning experiences, and improve student outcomes. Below are key AI-driven approaches transforming modern classrooms.

Personalized Learning: Tailoring Education to Individual Needs

Personalized learning leverages AI to analyze student performance, preferences, and learning styles to create customized educational experiences. AI-driven platforms assess strengths and weaknesses, adjusting curricula and resources accordingly. This approach fosters deeper engagement, improves retention, and ensures that students receive instruction that aligns with their individual progress, (Luckin et al., 2016; Holmes et al., 2019; Zawacki-Richter et al., 2019).

Adaptive Learning Platforms: Real-Time Customization

Adaptive learning platforms utilize AI algorithms to monitor student progress and provide real-time adjustments to content and instruction. These platforms identify learning gaps and deliver targeted interventions, ensuring that students receive the right level of challenge and support. By continuously adapting, these systems help learners at different proficiency levels advance at their own pace.

Intelligent Tutoring Systems: Virtual Teachers

Intelligent Tutoring Systems (ITS) act as virtual teachers by offering personalized feedback, answering queries, and providing step-by-step guidance. These AI-driven systems simulate one-on-one tutoring, using natural language processing and machine learning to understand student responses and tailor instruction. This enhances learning efficiency and offers scalable, cost-effective tutoring solutions, (Roll & Wylie, 2016; Holmes et al., 2019) (Mitchell, 1997; Russell & Norvig, 2020).

AI-Powered Recommendation Engines: Guiding Student Choices

AI-powered recommendation engines analyze student behavior, preferences, and performance data to suggest relevant courses, learning materials, and career paths. These engines help students make informed decisions about their education journey, ensuring they access the most beneficial resources and opportunities for their academic and professional goals.

Educational Chatbots: 24/7 Support for Students

Educational chatbots provide instant, round-the-clock support to students by answering questions, clarifying concepts, and assisting with administrative tasks. These AI-driven assistants improve accessibility to learning resources, reduce workload for educators, and enhance student engagement by offering immediate assistance whenever needed.

Case Studies: AI in Action in Classrooms

Several educational institutions have successfully integrated AI into their teaching strategies. Examples include:

- Carnegie Learning: AI-driven tutoring for mathematics, providing personalized problem-solving guidance.
- Khan Academy: Adaptive learning technologies that tailor lessons based on student progress.
- Squirrel AI: An AI-powered system in China that customizes instruction for individual students, significantly improving learning outcomes.
- IBM Watson Education: AI-driven insights to enhance personalized learning in various subjects, (Ferrucci et al., 2010; (Luckin et al., 2016; Holmes et al., 2019; Zawacki-Richter et al., 2019).

These case studies highlight how AI is transforming education, making learning more accessible, engaging, and effective.

AI-driven instructional strategies continue to evolve, offering innovative solutions that empower both students and educators. As technology advances, the role of AI in education will expand, further personalizing learning experiences and optimizing teaching methodologies, (Luckin et al., 2016; Holmes et al., 2019; Zawacki-Richter et al., 2019).

CHALLENGES AND ETHICAL IMPLICATIONS OF AI IN EDUCATION

Artificial intelligence (AI) is transforming education, offering personalized learning experiences, automating administrative tasks, and enhancing accessibility. However, AI also presents significant ethical and practical challenges. These challenges must be carefully considered to ensure AI systems serve all students equitably, protect their privacy, and foster an inclusive learning environment. This section explores key ethical concerns and challenges in AI-driven education, including data privacy, algorithmic bias, inclusivity, accessibility, and ethical AI development practices, (Luckin et al., 2016; Holmes et al., 2019; Zawacki-Richter et al., 2019) (Bostrom, 2014; Tegmark, 2017; Selwyn, 2019).

Data Privacy and Security: Protecting Student Information

AI in education relies heavily on data collection to personalize learning experiences and improve educational outcomes. However, this dependency raises concerns about data privacy and security. Schools and educational institutions collect vast amounts of sensitive student data, including academic performance, personal details, behavioral records, and biometric data. Protecting this data is crucial to maintaining student trust and compliance with legal frameworks such as the Family Educational Rights and Privacy Act (FERPA) and the General Data Protection Regulation (GDPR), (Luckin et al., 2016; Holmes et al., 2019; Zawacki-Richter et al., 2019).

Key Concerns

- Unauthorized Access and Data Breaches: AI systems are prime targets for cyberattacks, potentially exposing student information to malicious actors.
- Informed Consent and Data Ownership: Students and parents may not be fully aware of how their data is collected, used, and shared.

- Data Retention Policies: Educational institutions must establish clear policies on how long student data is stored and when it should be deleted.
- Third-Party Data Sharing: AI tools developed by private companies may share data with advertisers or other external entities, raising concerns about commercial exploitation.

Best Practices

- Encryption and Secure Data Storage: Using advanced encryption techniques ensures data remains protected from unauthorized access.
- Transparent Data Policies: Clearly communicating data collection, usage, and retention policies to students and parents builds trust.
- Regular Security Audits: Conducting routine audits can help identify vulnerabilities and improve data protection measures.
- Strict Access Controls: Limiting access to sensitive data only to authorized personnel minimizes the risk of breaches.

Algorithmic Bias: Ensuring Fairness in AI Systems

AI systems depend on data to make decisions, but if the data contains biases, these biases can be reflected and even amplified in AI-driven educational tools. Algorithmic bias can lead to unfair treatment of students, particularly those from marginalized communities.

Key Concerns

- Historical Data Bias: AI models trained on biased datasets may reinforce existing inequalities.
- Underrepresentation of Minority Groups: If training data lacks diversity, AI systems may fail to provide fair assessments for all students.
- Automated Decision-Making Risks: AI-driven grading and recommendation systems may disadvantage students based on race, gender, or socioeconomic status.
- Lack of Human Oversight: Over-reliance on AI decision-making can result in errors that go unchecked.

Best Practices

- Diverse Training Datasets: Ensuring AI models are trained on diverse data sets reduces bias.

- Regular Algorithm Audits: Frequent evaluations can detect and correct biases in AI-driven tools.
- Human-AI Collaboration: Combining AI recommendations with human judgment helps ensure fairness in assessments.
- Transparent AI Models: Making AI decision-making processes more interpretable can help educators understand and address potential biases.

Designing Inclusive AI Systems: Catering to Diverse Needs

AI in education must be designed to accommodate students of all backgrounds, learning styles, and abilities. Inclusivity ensures that AI tools do not create additional barriers for students with disabilities or from underprivileged backgrounds, (Luckin et al., 2016; Holmes et al., 2019; Zawacki-Richter et al., 2019).

Key Concerns

- Accessibility for Students with Disabilities: AI-powered tools must comply with accessibility standards such as the Web Content Accessibility Guidelines (WCAG).
- Support for Different Learning Styles: AI should be flexible enough to cater to visual, auditory, kinesthetic, and text-based learners.
- Language and Cultural Sensitivity: AI tools should support multiple languages and consider cultural differences to be effective in diverse classrooms.
- Affordability and Equity: AI-driven education should be available to all students, regardless of economic background.

Best Practices

- Universal Design Principles: Implementing AI systems that adapt to different needs ensures a more inclusive learning experience.
- Assistive Technologies Integration: AI should work alongside tools like screen readers, speech-to-text software, and alternative input methods.
- Customizable Learning Paths: Allowing students to personalize AI-assisted learning tools ensures better engagement and comprehension.
- Community and Educator Input: Involving teachers, students, and parents in AI system design can help address inclusivity challenges effectively.

The Digital Divide: Addressing Accessibility Issues

The digital divide refers to the gap between individuals who have access to technology and those who do not. AI-powered education tools often require internet access, up-to-date hardware, and digital literacy, creating disparities among students.

Key Concerns

- Limited Access to Technology: Students from low-income backgrounds may lack personal devices or reliable internet access.
- Regional Disparities: Rural areas often experience connectivity issues, making online AI-driven education tools less effective.
- Digital Literacy Barriers: Not all students and teachers have the necessary skills to effectively use AI tools.
- Financial Costs: Many AI-powered educational resources require subscriptions or expensive licensing fees.

Best Practices

- Providing Low-Cost Alternatives: Open-source AI tools and government initiatives can bridge the accessibility gap.
- Expanding Internet Access: Investing in infrastructure such as public Wi-Fi zones and subsidized broadband can help students in underserved areas.
- Digital Literacy Programs: Schools should offer training programs to equip students and educators with the skills needed to use AI effectively.
- Offline AI Solutions: AI tools that function without an internet connection can ensure learning continuity for all students.

Ethical AI Development: Best Practices

Developing AI responsibly is critical to ensuring that it benefits students without causing harm. Ethical AI development includes transparency, accountability, and ongoing assessment to prevent unintended negative consequences, (Bostrom, 2014; Tegmark, 2017; Selwyn, 2019).

Key Concerns

- Lack of Regulation and Oversight: Many AI applications in education operate without clear regulatory frameworks.

- Commercial Exploitation: Some AI-driven tools prioritize profit over educational outcomes, potentially leading to exploitative practices.
- Accountability in Decision-Making: If an AI system makes an error, it must be clear who is responsible for rectifying it.
- Psychological Impact on Students: Over-reliance on AI can impact students' critical thinking and interpersonal skills.

Best Practices

- Transparency in AI Models: Open-source AI models and explainable AI (XAI) techniques improve trust in AI-driven decisions.
- Ethical AI Frameworks: Following established guidelines, such as UNESCO's AI ethics principles, ensures responsible AI development, (Bostrom, 2014; Tegmark, 2017; Selwyn, 2019).
- Human Oversight and Intervention: Educators should always have the final say in AI-driven recommendations.
- Ongoing Ethical Assessments: AI systems should be regularly reviewed for ethical concerns and continuously improved based on findings, (Bostrom, 2014; Tegmark, 2017; Selwyn, 2019).

FUTURE DIRECTIONS AND EMERGING TRENDS IN AI

AI with Virtual Reality (VR) and Augmented Reality (AR)

Artificial Intelligence (AI) is increasingly being integrated with Virtual Reality (VR) and Augmented Reality (AR) to create more immersive, interactive, and intelligent experiences. AI enhances VR/AR by enabling real-time scene recognition, object tracking, and adaptive learning mechanisms. For example, AI-driven AR applications can provide contextual information overlaid on physical objects, transforming industries such as education, healthcare, and retail.

In gaming, AI enhances NPC behavior, making characters more responsive and realistic. In healthcare, AI-powered VR is used for surgical simulations and phobia treatment. The fusion of AI, VR, and AR is also revolutionizing remote work, allowing for virtual offices where AI assists in scheduling, real-time translations, and team collaboration. Looking ahead, we can expect AI to make VR/AR environments more intuitive, personalizing user experiences through predictive analytics and machine learning, (Mitchell, 1997; Russell & Norvig, 2020).

Collaborative Learning with AI: Fostering Teamwork

AI is playing a significant role in fostering collaboration and teamwork across various fields, particularly in education and corporate training. AI-powered collaborative learning platforms use natural language processing and machine learning algorithms to facilitate discussions, group projects, and peer learning, (Mitchell, 1997; Russell & Norvig, 2020).

For instance, AI can analyze team dynamics and suggest better ways to distribute tasks based on individual strengths and weaknesses. It can also mediate conflicts, provide constructive feedback, and recommend resources tailored to each team member's needs. In education, AI-powered chatbots and virtual assistants can guide students through problem-solving exercises collaboratively, making remote learning more effective and engaging.

In workplaces, AI-driven collaboration tools such as virtual meeting assistants, AI-based brainstorming tools, and sentiment analysis algorithms improve team efficiency and cohesion. As AI evolves, its role in fostering collaboration will expand, ensuring that teams work smarter, not just harder.

AI for Creativity and Critical Thinking

Contrary to early assumptions that AI might stifle creativity, it is now being harnessed as a tool to enhance human innovation. AI algorithms can generate art, music, and literature, offering inspiration and new perspectives to creators. Applications like OpenAI's DALL·E and DeepDream allow artists to experiment with new visual styles, while AI-powered music composition tools assist composers in generating unique melodies and harmonies.

Beyond the arts, AI fosters critical thinking by analyzing large datasets, identifying patterns, and providing insights that humans might overlook. AI-powered debate systems, such as IBM's Project Debater, can engage in meaningful discourse, challenging individuals to refine their arguments and think critically.

In the future, AI will likely become a co-creator in various fields, augmenting human capabilities rather than replacing them. From journalism to architecture, AI-assisted design and content generation will push the boundaries of what is possible, encouraging novel solutions to complex problems.

Ethical AI: Building Trust and Accountability

As AI continues to permeate all aspects of society, ethical considerations become paramount. Issues such as bias in AI models, data privacy, and accountability in decision-making need to be addressed to build trust in AI systems, (Bostrom, 2014; Tegmark, 2017; Selwyn, 2019).

Organizations are increasingly prioritizing ethical AI by implementing transparent AI governance frameworks, ensuring that algorithms are fair, explainable, and free from discrimination. Governments and regulatory bodies worldwide are also working on legislation to establish accountability for AI-driven decisions, (Bostrom, 2014; Tegmark, 2017; Selwyn, 2019).

One of the key challenges is ensuring that AI models are trained on diverse and unbiased datasets. Efforts are being made to create ethical AI guidelines that emphasize inclusivity and fairness. Additionally, AI explainability is being improved through techniques like interpretable machine learning, allowing users to understand why an AI system made a particular decision, (Bostrom, 2014; Tegmark, 2017; Selwyn, 2019) (Mitchell, 1997; Russell & Norvig, 2020).

The future of AI ethics will involve continuous dialogue among technologists, policymakers, and the public to ensure responsible AI development. Establishing robust AI auditing mechanisms and ethical AI certifications will also be critical in maintaining public trust, (Bostrom, 2014; Tegmark, 2017; Selwyn, 2019).

The Role of AI in Lifelong Learning

AI is reshaping education by providing personalized learning experiences that adapt to individual needs and preferences. AI-driven platforms analyze a learner's progress and tailor content accordingly, ensuring efficient knowledge acquisition, (Luckin et al., 2016; Holmes et al., 2019; Zawacki-Richter et al., 2019).

One of AI's biggest contributions to lifelong learning is its ability to democratize education. AI-powered tutors and e-learning platforms make high-quality education accessible to people worldwide, breaking barriers related to geography, language, and economic status.

In professional settings, AI helps employees upskill by identifying skill gaps and recommending courses. AI-driven mentoring systems match employees with experts, fostering continuous learning and career development.

Looking ahead, AI will continue to play a pivotal role in lifelong learning by making education more interactive, personalized, and inclusive. AI-powered learning companions may soon become a reality, offering guidance and mentorship throughout an individual's academic and professional journey.

CONCLUSION

Recap of Key Insights

Throughout this discussion, we have explored the multifaceted impact of artificial intelligence on education. AI-driven tools are revolutionizing personalized learning, making education more accessible, and enhancing the role of educators. We examined the challenges, such as ethical considerations and data privacy concerns, alongside the opportunities AI presents for fostering innovation and efficiency in educational environments. These insights underscore the critical role AI plays in shaping the future of education, (Luckin et al., 2016; Holmes et al., 2019; Zawacki-Richter et al., 2019) (Bostrom, 2014; Tegmark, 2017; Selwyn, 2019).

The Transformative Potential of AI in Education

AI has the power to fundamentally transform education by creating adaptive learning environments, automating administrative tasks, and enabling data-driven decision-making. With intelligent tutoring systems, AI can cater to diverse learning needs, providing students with real-time feedback and support. Additionally, AI-driven analytics allow educators to identify learning gaps and tailor instructional strategies accordingly. This shift toward AI-powered education holds the promise of increased engagement, improved learning outcomes, and greater inclusivity, (Roll & Wylie, 2016; Holmes et al., 2019).

A Call to Action for Educators and Technologists

To fully harness the benefits of AI in education, collaboration between educators, technologists, policymakers, and researchers is essential. Educators must embrace AI as a tool that enhances rather than replaces their roles, leveraging AI-driven insights to refine teaching methodologies. Technologists, on the other hand, must prioritize ethical AI development, ensuring transparency, fairness, and inclusivity in AI applications. Policymakers should establish guidelines that promote responsible AI integration while safeguarding student data and rights. By working together, we can create an AI-powered education system that benefits all stakeholders, (Bostrom, 2014; Tegmark, 2017; Selwyn, 2019) (Luckin et al., 2016; Holmes et al., 2019; Zawacki-Richter et al., 2019).

Final Thoughts: The Future of AI in Education

As AI continues to evolve, its role in education will become increasingly significant. The potential to provide equitable, personalized, and efficient learning experiences is vast. However, the successful integration of AI will depend on thoughtful implementation, ethical considerations, and continuous adaptation. The future of AI in education is not solely about technology—it is about shaping an inclusive and innovative learning ecosystem that empowers students and educators alike. By embracing AI responsibly, we can unlock new possibilities and pave the way for a brighter educational future, (Bostrom, 2014; Tegmark, 2017; Selwyn, 2019) (Luckin et al., 2016; Holmes et al., 2019; Zawacki-Richter et al., 2019).

REFERENCES

Bostrom, N. (2014). *Superintelligence: Paths, Dangers, Strategies.* Oxford University Press.

Brown, T. B., Mann, B., Ryder, N., Subbiah, M., Kaplan, J., Dhariwal, P., Neelakantan, A., Shyam, P., Sastry, G., Askell, A., Agarwal, S., Herbert-Voss, A., Krueger, G., Henighan, T., Child, R., Ramesh, A., Ziegler, D. M., Wu, J., Winter, C., & Hesse, C. (2020). Language Models Are Few-Shot Learners. *Arxiv.org, 4*(33). https://arxiv.org/abs/2005.14165

Campbell, J., Lo, A., & Mackinlay, A. (1997). *The Econometrics of Financial Markets.* https://www.nrc.gov/docs/ML1208/ML12088A329.pdf

Devlin, J., Chang, M.-W., Lee, K., & Toutanova, K. (2018, October 11). *BERT: Pre-training of Deep Bidirectional Transformers for Language Understanding.* ArXiv. https://arxiv.org/abs/1810.04805

Shortliffe, E.H. (1976). *Computer-based medical consultations: MYCIN.* Elsevier.

Ferrucci, D., Brown, E., Chu-Carroll, J., Fan, J., Gondek, D., Kalyanpur, A. A., Lally, A., Murdock, J. W., Nyberg, E., Prager, J., Schlaefer, N., & Welty, C. (2010). Building Watson: An Overview of the DeepQA Project. *AI Magazine*, *31*(3), 59. DOI: 10.1609/aimag.v31i3.2303

Holmes, W., Bialik, M., & Fadel, C. (2019). *Artificial Intelligence in Education: Promises and Implications for Teaching and Learning.* Center for Curriculum Redesign.

Holmes, W., Bialik, M., & Fadel, C. (2019, March). *Artificial intelligence in education. promise and implications for teaching and learning.* ResearchGate; Center for Curriculum Redesign. https://www.researchgate.net/publication/332180327_Artificial_Intelligence_in_Education_Promise_and_Implications_for_Teaching_an

Krizhevsky, A., Sutskever, I., & Hinton, G. E. (2012). ImageNet Classification with Deep Convolutional Neural Networks. *Communications of the ACM*, *60*(6), 84–90.

LeCun, Y., Bengio, Y., & Hinton, G. (2015). Deep Learning. *Nature*, *521*(7553), 436–444. DOI: 10.1038/nature14539 PMID: 26017442

Luckin, R., Holmes, W., Griffiths, M., & Forcier, L. B. (2016). *Intelligence Unleashed: An argument for AI in Education.* Pearson Education.

. McCarthy, J., Minsky, M. L., Rochester, N., & Shannon, C. E. (1956). A Proposal for the Dartmouth Summer Research Project on Artificial Intelligence.

McCulloch, W., & Pitts, W. (1943). A logical calculus of the ideas immanent in nervous activity. *Bulletin of Mathematical Biology*, *52*(1-2), 99–115. DOI: 10.1016/s0092-8240(05)80006-0 PMID: 2185863

Mitchell, T. (1997). *Machine Learning*. McGraw-Hill.

Open, A. I. (2022, November 30). *Introducing ChatGPT*. OpenAI. https://openai.com/index/chatgpt/

Roll, I., & Wylie, R. (2016). Evolution and Revolution in Artificial Intelligence in Education. *International Journal of Artificial Intelligence in Education*, *26*(2), 582–599. DOI: 10.1007/s40593-016-0110-3

Rosenblatt, F. (1958). The perceptron: A probabilistic model for information storage and organization in the brain. *Psychological Review*, *65*(6), 386–408. DOI: 10.1037/h0042519 PMID: 13602029

Russell, S., & Norvig, P. (2020). *Artificial Intelligence: A Modern Approach* (4th ed.). Pearson.

Selwyn, N. (2019). Should robots replace teachers?: AI and the Future of Education. In research.monash.edu. Polity Press. https://research.monash.edu/en/publications/should-robots-replace-teachers-ai-and-the-future-of-education

Silver, D., Huang, A., Maddison, C. J., Guez, A., Sifre, L., van den Driessche, G., Schrittwieser, J., Antonoglou, I., Panneershelvam, V., Lanctot, M., Dieleman, S., Grewe, D., Nham, J., Kalchbrenner, N., Sutskever, I., Lillicrap, T., Leach, M., Kavukcuoglu, K., Graepel, T., & Hassabis, D. (2016). Mastering the game of Go with deep neural networks and tree search. *Nature*, *529*(7587), 484–489. DOI: 10.1038/nature16961 PMID: 26819042

Tegmark, M. (2017). *Life 3.0: Being Human in the Age of Artificial Intelligence*. Knopf.

Turing, A. M. (1950). Computing Machinery and Intelligence. *Mind*, *49*, 433–460.

Weizenbaum, J. (1966). ELIZA - a computer program for the study of natural language communication between man and machine. *Communications of the ACM*, *9*(1), 36–45. DOI: 10.1145/365153.365168

Zawacki-Richter, O., Marín, V. I., Bond, M., & Gouverneur, F. (2019). Systematic review of research on artificial intelligence applications in higher education – where are the educators? *International Journal of Educational Technology in Higher Education*, *16*(1), 1–27. DOI: 10.1186/s41239-019-0171-0

Chapter 3
An Approach to the Integration of Artificial Intelligence in Inclusive Education for Latin America

Alejandro Fuentes-Penna
https://orcid.org/0000-0002-4303-3852
El Colegio de Morelos, Mexico

Raúl Gómez Cárdenas
El Colegio de Morelos, Mexico

Jorge A. Ruiz Vanoye
https://orcid.org/0000-0003-4928-5716
Universidad Politécnica de Pachuca, Mexico

ABSTRACT

Inclusive education is a process aimed at recognizing the learning needs of students and the need to present solutions that allow them to learn meaningfully, reducing the gaps in access to education. On the other hand, Artificial Intelligence has advanced in its incorporation into various areas of knowledge, education being an area that requires the use of all kinds of tools, techniques, and resources available to ensure access to children and young people worldwide. This chapter provides a review of the context of education and the need to incorporate AI-based tools to ensure inclusive education. The trend towards the use of emerging technologies in education has made it possible to propose significant findings aimed at transforming

DOI: 10.4018/979-8-3373-0598-1.ch003

teaching practices and facilitating access to knowledge by students in individual learning processes. With this, tools are proposed to facilitate the teaching-learning process in an inclusive context.

INTRODUCTION

Inclusive education, aimed at covering special educational needs (SEN) or disabilities, seeks to eliminate barriers to access to education, improve results, and reduce discrimination due to the lack of specialized resources to meet these needs.

This paper addresses arguments in favor of inclusive education and the incursion of Artificial Intelligence (AI) to favor the teaching-learning process that guarantees access to education for all people, identifying within the major Sustainable Development Goals (SDGs), the following priorities:

- Quality Education,
- Gender Equality,
- Reduction of Inequalities, and
- Partnerships to achieve the objectives.

If in itself the goal of educational inclusion is difficult to achieve, the pandemic that occurred due to COVID19 brought serious consequences in education, directly affecting the school cycles 2019-2020, 2020-21 and 2022-2023, especially due to the lack of preparation that humanity showed to satisfactorily face the difficult situation in all areas, especially education.

However, we may still have future consequences due to the gap we had during this period, since the sequelae brought by this disease are so varied, such as:

- Muscle weakness,
- Sight problems,
- Problems in reasoning and discernment,
- Symptoms of post-traumatic stress disorder,
- Hearing about problems,
- Among others.

These after-effects have led us to rethink what we should do in education, since we must consider these effects as part of the special needs of the students themselves. However, having faced such a pandemic in modern life will allow us to react better if the situation arises again, especially with better preparation of the educational system, its teachers, students, and with a more robust and inclusive digital infrastructure.

In this sense, it is pertinent to establish the bases of inclusive education, diagnose the current situation in Mexico and Latin America in this important aspect, and determine the transcendence of Artificial Intelligence (AI) and new technologies to strengthen inclusive education.

LEGAL FRAMEWORK RELATED TO INCLUSIVE EDUCATION

Based on the definition of inclusive education and the needs it generates, some countries have made efforts to develop policies and strategies, as is the case in Latin America and Spain, on this issue, as a mechanism to allow access to education for all people.

In Spain, for example, studies recognize the current situation and identify the barriers that interfere with the inclusion process of students with educational support needs and that limit participation and learning (Echeita et al., 2009).

Considerable progress has been made in Latin America in terms of inclusive education. In Colombia, progress has been made in the recognition of inclusive education as part of the education for all project, however, Beltrán, Martínez and Vargas (2015) mention that it is a topic that is far from being able to reach but that progress has been made with the agreement of Decree 1421 proposed by the Ministry of National Education (MEN, 2017), to regulate the attention to the population that presents some type of disability.

In the case of Uruguay, Viera and Zeballos (2014) analyzed national documents to identify the regulatory policy framework and school practices related to inclusive education; however, in this context Flores (2016) identifies that during the time she developed her research, several educational institutions have not developed teaching strategies that correspond to personal diversity.

For its part, the 2019 report of the Regional Network for Inclusive Education (RREI, 2019) analyzes the situation of the right to inclusive education in the countries of Argentina, Brazil, Colombia, Chile, Paraguay, Peru, Uruguay, Costa Rica and El Salvador; the first seven are part of the network, and the latter collaborated in the report. In principle, the document recognizes progress, but also persistence in educational discrimination against disability, especially in regular schools (p. 3).

The analysis includes the following aspects: the norms that regulate the education of persons with disabilities in each of the countries, the obstacles to entry into regular schools, the ways of providing support and reasonable accommodations, the ways of assessing and certifying the learning of students with disabilities, teacher training, mechanisms to combat discrimination in schools, and the availability of data on the educational situation of this group. All this only refers to compulsory public education (basic and high school education in Mexico) and therefore does not include higher education.

The report concludes that "although the countries studied contemplate in their domestic legislation the attendance of persons with disabilities in regular schools, how this is regulated differs from one to another" (p. 13). (p. 13) The countries with the greatest progress, which consecrate and regulate the right to inclusive education in regular (not special) schools, are Brazil, Colombia, Paraguay, and Peru.

Inclusiveness: that difficulties or barriers to the enrollment of students with disabilities in non-special schools persist in all countries; there are no adequate facilities for inclusiveness; evaluation mechanisms tend to be standardized, without adaptations for disability; in addition to the fact that authorities and teachers are not trained for inclusive education (REEI, 2019).

The deficit that exists in terms of infrastructure and availability of digital services in Latin America and the Caribbean is another problem. The World Bank (2021) notes that, at present, less than 50% of the population in Latin America and the Caribbean has access to fixed broadband, and only 9.9% have high-quality fiber in the home. Although 87% of the population lives within range of a 4G signal, only 37% have it.

Another alarming fact is that these limitations reproduce marginalization and the digital divide at the social level in Latin America. According to the organization, the possibility of connecting to the Internet is much greater for populations living in urban areas compared to rural areas. While in urban areas 71% of the population has access to the Internet, in rural communities' connectivity is reduced to 40%.

Mexico, Inclusive Education and Multigrade Schools

In Mexico, inclusive education was promoted in the period 2018 - 2024 by the Federal government and with it, the proposal of the educational reform to create the New Mexican School (NEM) model (SEP, 2019).

This institution (The New Mexican School) has as its center the integral formation of girls, boys, adolescents and young people, and its objective is to promote learning of excellence, inclusive, pluricultural, collaborative and equitable throughout the trajectory of their formation, from birth until they conclude their studies, adapted to all regions of the republic. (SEMS, 2019, p. 3)

The approach proposed for the NEM has been formalized as a foundation for the Political Constitution of the United Mexican States (CPEUM) and the General Education Law (LGE) where national principles and strategies promoted by the federation to promote inclusive education are set out. As part of this, the reform to Article 3° constitutional was proposed, which establishes that education provided by the State must be: "compulsory, universal, inclusive, public, free and secular"

(DOF, 2019) and, in turn, it is proposed that the NEM be national, democratic, humanistic, equitable, comprehensive, of excellence, intercultural and inclusive.

On the other hand, the NEM, being inclusive, is aimed at a congruent pedagogical proposal that has an impact on the learning of all students in the national education system (SEN), according to the Undersecretary of Basic Education (SEB, 2019). That it can reach all social groups and strata, regions, levels, and that the existing lags in the "capabilities and skills of learners in fundamental areas such as communication, mathematics, and science can be abated." (SEMS, 2019, p. 2)

In turn, the latest reforms to the General Education Law (House of Representatives, 2024) reaffirm the educational criteria stipulated in the Constitution and establish that inclusive education must meet the needs, abilities, circumstances, styles and pace of learning of all students, as well as eliminate any form of exclusion, discrimination and any condition that may become a barrier to learning and participation (BAP).

Particularly, inclusive education is highlighted (Chapter VIII) as an educational effort to reach the population that is discriminated against, excluded, or segregated.

Inclusive education refers to the set of actions aimed at identifying, preventing, reducing, and eliminating barriers that limit the access, permanence, participation, and learning of all students by eliminating practices of discrimination, exclusion, and segregation. Inclusive education is based on the recognition and appreciation of diversity, adapting the National Education System to respond with equity to the characteristics, needs, interests, abilities, skills, rhythms, and learning styles of each one of learner. (Chamber of Deputies, 2024).

According to the same article of the law, inclusive education provides for guaranteeing the right to education for people who face barriers to learning and participation, providing them with the necessary conditions, after assessment by students, parents, and teachers. It seeks to offer accessible formats to each learner according to his or her disability, providing relevant educational options, preparing teachers on the subject, and promoting inclusive practices and policies.

With these guidelines, the National Strategy for Inclusive Education (ENEI) seeks to become an inclusive, flexible and relevant system that favors the advancement, permanence, learning, participation and completion of studies of girls, boys, adolescents and young people throughout the country, in their wide diversity, under equal conditions and opportunities (SEP, 2020). This document defines the principle of educational inclusion, its basis, and transcendence:

Inclusion defends the rethinking of the role of the school to accommodate everyone, regardless of their characteristics or conditions. It is based on the recognition of the equality of all people, in dignity and rights, the respect for differences, the valuation of each student, the commitment to school success, the emphasis on those who face greater social disadvantages, the fight against any form of discrimination, and the transformation of policies, cultures and practices of each educational center. This allows us to speak not only of inclusion, but of inclusive education. (p. 8).

These initiatives constitute the texts of the inclusive education policy in Mexico and, according to Ball (1993), the policy is a text, discourse and practice, where he questions the implementation of public policy given that he considers that these writings are addressed to teachers and schools, but in a hypothetical way; that is, they do not relate directly to classroom practice (Ball et al., 2011).

The United Nations 2030 Agenda establishes 17 Sustainable Development Goals (SDGs), and No. 4 is: Ensure inclusive and equitable quality education and promote lifelong learning opportunities for all (UN, 2025). In this regard, each country that is part of the organization establishes its own 2030 agenda, in which it defines its commitments to join this global aspiration.

In its 2030 agenda for education, Mexico identifies six goals and four subgoals, the fulfillment of which will allow it to consolidate an equitable, inclusive, and quality education. INEGI (2025) has proposals to advance in educational inclusion:

- Target 4.1 By 2030, ensure that all children complete primary and secondary education that is free, equitable, and of excellent quality and produces relevant and effective learning outcomes.
- Target 4.2 By 2030, ensure that all children have access to quality early childhood care and development and preschool education so that they are ready for primary school.
- Target 4.3 By 2030, ensure equal access for all people to quality technical, vocational, and higher education, including university education.
- Target 4.5 By 2030, eliminate gender disparities in education and ensure equal access to all levels of education and vocational training for vulnerable people, including people with disabilities, Indigenous peoples, and children in vulnerable situations.
- Target 4n1: Ensure effective access to inclusive, equitable, intercultural, and comprehensive quality education with particular attention to disadvantaged groups (gender disaggregation, Indigenous population, persons with disabilities, ...).

The latter is particularly important because it will force all educational institutions, at distinct levels, to particularize their objectives and focus on vulnerable groups to reach them. The indicator that will be used to measure the progress of the goal is the percentage of students attending multi-grade schools. Multigrade schools are those in which there is not one teacher for each grade, as in conventional schools, but a single teacher attends more than one grade. These types of institutions are associated with highly marginalized environments.

(...) Multigrade schools, an educational model that characterizes schools located in areas of high and extremely high marginalization at the basic education levels, in general, Indigenous and community services. This mode of organization is based on Article 43 of the General Education Law (Mejoredu, 2022c).

In this type of school, teachers become important characters in the community, since they interact with various grades and diverse students, their families, and their contexts, with limited resources. The remoteness of the places where they are installed and the social vocation of the teachers strengthen the linkage of teachers to the communities, contextualizing their educational strategies (Mejoredu, 2022c).

To accompany this educational effort, the National Commission for the Continuous Improvement of Education has published support materials such as Teaching Practice in the Multigrade School for Attention to Diversity. Preschool, primary, and tertiary education teachers, or the booklet Horizons for teaching practice in multigrade: inclusive education.

The latter is presented as a workbook that allows preschool, elementary and tele-secondary teachers of multigrade education to reflect on the challenges and opportunities to educate in diversity from the multigrade school, analyzing individually and collectively the concepts and models that support it, as well as the existing barriers, to suggest a sequence of learning situations, workshop type, that will allow them to advance in inclusive education (Mejoredu, 2022b, p. 5).

The implementation of these learning situations (...) will favor the development of meaningful school experiences, understood as those situations in which teaching processes and learning environments are meaningful to students. They recognize that there is respect for their socio-cultural traits and rights. They promote reflection on the world and themselves because they offer them opportunities to participate in what is decided and done at school and in their environment. (Mejoredu, 2022b, 8).

Because of their scope, multigrade schools become an important instrument of inclusion, with a high penetration in the country, which, however, is also indicative of the high marginality of the population susceptible to education. The following data allows us to understand this scope:

- In Mexico, there are 80,258 multigrade schools in the country. They represent more than one-third of basic education schools (Mejoredu, 2022b, p. 15).
- They constitute 37.9%, 41.9%, and 33% of existing community schools at preschool, primary, and secondary levels, respectively.
- One in ten community students attend multigrade schools (1.8 million nationwide).

- Multigrade schools are much smaller than those that are not. A multigrade school has, on average, twenty-two students, while a regular school has 141 students. (Mejoredu, 2022c, p. 11).

Thus, multigrade schools have been an important instrument in inclusive national education, given the important level of dispersion and marginalization of the country's population, especially in Indigenous communities. They optimize human and material resources, in addition to effectively linking with the environment. It is a necessary, but not sufficient, effort to achieve inclusion.

PEOPLE WITH DISABILITIES AND/OR MENTAL PROBLEMS OR CONDITIONS IN MEXICO

Mejoredu (2022a) defines disability as a situation that occurs when the physical, intellectual, sensory or mental condition of a person is not considered in the environment where he/she develops, placing him/her in a situation of disadvantage and inequity, restricting, limiting or preventing that person from fully developing his/her personal, family, community and citizen life (p. 15).

In its analysis, the National Commission for Educational Improvement points out that there are three approaches to the study and explanation of disability: the religious approach, which sees disability as a divine punishment; the medical approach, which finds scientific causes for disability; and the social approach, which sees disability as a barrier to social inclusion. Disability is expressed in different areas: motor, intellectual, visual, auditory, psychosocial, and multiple.

In our country two instances stand out for their contribution of data that systematically measure the population with disabilities in Mexico: the National Institute of Statistics and Geography (INEGI), which collects demographic, socioeconomic and cultural data through surveys and censuses, and the Ministry of Public Education (SEP), which collects data collected through registration forms (Form 911) applied in schools, at basic and higher levels.

For its part, INEGI describes that in the world, there are approximately one billion people who have a disability based on information from the World Health Organization in 2020. Specifically, in Mexico for this same period, it was estimated that 6'179,890 people have one type of disability, which represents almost 5% of the population in Mexico (INEGI, 2.f.).

For the year 2021, in the 2020 Population and Housing Census conducted by INEGI, there was an increase in the percentage of the population with disability and/or mental problems or conditions, increasing to 5.7%. In this same report they identified that the activity with the most reported difficulty among people with disabilities and/or mental condition is walking, climbing or descending (41%) and that, of this percentage, 19% of these people, in the group of 15 years and older are illiterate (INEGI, 2021).

In the same document (INEGI, 2021) the Sustainable Development Goals (SDG) 2024 Report, the goal on universal health coverage is not being achieved. Particularly in Mexico, the Health Sector Program (PSS) 2019-2024, 76% of people with disabilities and/or mental problems or conditions have affiliation to health services, which indicates that progress has been made on this point, however, there is not 100% coverage.

Specifically, about 900 thousand people with at least one disability and/or some mental problems or condition are children (0 to 15 years old), 869 thousand young people (15 to 29 years old), 2.2 million are adults (30 to 59 years old) and 3.2 million are older adults (60 years old and over). This demonstrates a strong relationship between the age ranges for studying and the needs to be covered in an inclusive education. At older ages, disabilities appear or manifest themselves with greater intensity.

As part of its inclusive education policy, the SEP identifies, through the 911 format, those students who show characteristics of disability in any of its expressions, obtaining data that allows the application of a specific and systematic effort and follow-up to this population.

For the 2019-2020 school year, SEP registered 429,242 children and adolescents with disabilities enrolled in basic education, representing 1.7% of the total enrollment, 86% of whom were enrolled in regular schools (i.e., not special schools). In the same cycle, there were 77,213 young people with disabilities enrolled in higher secondary education, equivalent to 1.4% of the total enrollment at this level.

PROBLEMS IN INCLUSIVE EDUCATION

Currently, many problems guide teachers, educational institutions and the government in general to seek solutions that are efficient, attractive, and innovative concerning technology and educational models.

The United Nations Educational, Scientific and Cultural Organization (UNESCO, 2017) identifies that an inclusive educational policy is necessary, given that it has identified that illiteracy is a serious problem of educational backwardness, which leads to the exclusion of many people in the search for opportunities, mainly labor. If we continue in the line of people with disabilities and/or with some mental problem or condition, we can identify that, in the group of 15 years and older, 19% do not know how to read or write an errand, requiring a double effort of inclusion:

- The first focuses on programs and initiatives that enable them to overcome disadvantages or barriers; and
- Secondly, ensuring the inclusion of people with disabilities in vocational training services and activities, employment promotion, social protection schemes, and poverty reduction strategies.

Another problem that we can identify is access to basic services where, at present, the Internet is "a fundamental element of our daily life, because, nowadays, being disconnected is synonymous with being excluded from opportunities to access basic information, learn, work, among others", as Castellet (n.d.) puts it; however, as part of this article we will only focus on covering aspects that can be solved by AI, identifying that there is access to this service and regardless of access to basic housing services.

Based on this combination of needs, it is necessary to show that, at present, we have several tools based on Artificial Intelligence that will allow young people, mainly, to rely on AI for access to education, which, from the perspective of the Mexican government, should be inclusive and consider

Sustainable Development Goal (SDG) four recognizes everyone's right to inclusive, equitable, and quality education throughout their lives, regardless of differences or disabilities. However, the implementation of inclusive education faces various challenges and obstacles:

1. It does not have human resources, financial resources, appropriate facilities, and equipment to meet the needs of, and access by, any person.
2. The teaching staff lacks adequate professional and human training for the care of students.
3. Discrimination or singling out of students or staff with disabilities who, in turn, experience social and emotional problems before society.
4. Inadequate curricular content and assessment methods that do not consider current disabilities, needs, or specific strategies required by students with special needs.
5. Plans or frameworks that provide certainty to education professionals in the implementation of inclusive education.
6. Empathy and collaboration on the part of academic authorities, teachers, parents, and students to be able to understand, share needs and feelings that allow not only academic inclusion.

TRENDS IN EDUCATION

According to the *Instituto de Estudios Superiores para Profesionales de la Educación* (IESPE, 2023), educational trends in Mexico are as follows:

- Technology will reinforce face-to-face basic education.
- Increased humanities must consider not only knowledge and skills, but also social, ethical, and inclusive human aspects.
- Physical and direct coexistence, a determining factor for people.
- Artificial Intelligence as a support for all activities, including education.
- Findings on the relationship between learning and brain biochemistry will continue.
- International efforts in favor of digital education. Development of various online teaching programs or platforms.
- Digitization of the management of teaching and administrative activities.
- Social-emotional problems should be addressed in a face-to-face manner, not using technology.
- Education should be conducted in a planned manner, considering resources, risks, needs.
- Individualized and flexible learning, considering inclusion, diversity, and flexibility.
- Teacher training programs focused on the new Mexican school model.

These trends allow us to identify that Artificial Intelligence is a factor that must be considered in the development of education itself, given that its use, at this time, is carried out without a diagnosis, without planning, to ensure an adequate impact on the different educational levels and is subject to evaluation.

Article 52 of the General Education Law establishes the following:

Article 52. The State shall guarantee the right of every person to enjoy the benefits of scientific, humanistic, technological, and innovative development, considered as fundamental elements of education and culture. It should promote the development, linkage, and dissemination of scientific research for social benefit.

Technological development and innovation, associated with updating, educational excellence, and the expansion of the frontiers of knowledge will be supported by latest information, communication, knowledge, and digital learning technologies, using open access platforms. (Cámara de diputados, 2024).

This means that the benefits of scientific and technological development must be for all, and that educational excellence will also be based on modern technologies, including digital learning technologies. This involves artificial intelligence, the use of which must not only be expert but also ethical, especially generative AI.

When we interweave the trends with the conditions we have in Mexico, we can observe a high percentage of people who require inclusive education, being necessary to develop technologies, didactic materials, infrastructure, teacher training, educational content.

In this regard, there is an undeniable need for a robust infrastructure in schools (Internet, and computers, software, and trained teaching staff), but this is not enough. The experience of the pandemic mentioned above shows that even if schools had these resources, it was not enough to adapt to the challenges imposed by the confinement.

The same experience showed that school alone, even with the required or advanced technology, is not enough. It was necessary to design and plan the adaptation of favorable environments for learning, with a more human sense and meaning based on reality. (Tapia, 2023).

The New Mexican School endorses the five areas that were agreed during the International Conference on Artificial Intelligence in Education, known as the 'Beijing Consensus on Artificial Intelligence and Education,' held in May 2019:

1. AI in the service of education management and implementation.
2. AI in the service of empowering teachers and their teaching.
3. AI in the service of learning and performance assessment.
4. Developing values and skills for life and work at the age of AI; and five.
5. AI to provide lifelong learning opportunities for all.

According to Tapia (2023), the Curricular Framework of the 2022 Mexican school curriculum includes binding elements between recommendations 1, 2, 3 and 5 of the Beijing Consensus and the disciplinary approach to technologies for the educational field of scientific knowledge and thinking.

Thus, modern technologies and AI in education can support and reinforce the achievement of educational objectives: the interaction of children with the world for the development and construction of knowledge, the contextualization of knowledge, in a scenario of constant cultural and social change.

OVERCOMING ILLITERACY AND THE DIGITAL DIVIDE

Just as illiteracy (not knowing how to read, write or do basic arithmetic) is a worrying indicator of educational marginalization, so is digital illiteracy (not knowing and effectively managing new communication and information technologies), as the latter implies the non-inclusion of people in a completely digital world.

Digital literacy means achieving appropriate, skillful, and ethical handling of digital technologies. This implies knowing and managing the basic Office suite, searching for reliable and secure information on networks, as well as giving technologies, such as artificial intelligence, the role of a means or tool to achieve objectives and not considering them as an end in themselves.

García (2017) points out that digital literacy encompasses five areas of work: instrumental (knowledge, skills); cognitive-intellectual (knowing how to search for and give meaning to information), socio-communicational (communicating skillfully through technology), axiological (developing awareness and values, using networks ethically and inclusively), and emotional (building a digital identity with appropriate management of feelings in the digital environment). By developing and articulating the five domains, digital literacy is achieved (p. 75).

The World Bank (2021) reported that only 5-15% of adults in most Latin American and Caribbean countries have computer and internet skills, as well as the ability to solve medium to high level problems in technology-intensive environments. These indicators are lower than the OECD average of 29.7%.

To bridge the digital divide, the World Bank (2021) says that public policy actions are needed to reduce costs and expand connectivity, combining efforts with the private sector, especially in four areas:

1. Seek inclusion through service provision and legal and regulatory reforms. On average, countries in the region with clear and predictable regulations attract almost 50% more ICT investment (and 64% more when combined with good institutions).
2. Institute direct or indirect financial incentives for both customers and digital operators, such as subsidies or temporary tax exemptions.
3. Expand digital access through both public and private investment, which implies a modest cost, estimated at 0.12% of the region's annual GDP.
4. Accelerate complementary measures, such as digital skills training among the population.

Regarding the application of digital technologies in education, Mexico has come a long way, especially during and after the pandemic. Since 2011, for example, eleven performance indicators for teachers in the use of ICT were established for basic education and implemented by the Ministry of Public Education. These include 10 and 11, which, according to Campuzano (2021), read: ten. Make responsible use of software and hardware, whether working individually, in pairs or in teams. 11. Make ethical, safe, and responsible use of the Internet and digital tools.

The above is a recognition of the need for education, from its basic levels, to consider the adoption of modern technologies with efficiency, but also with ethical sense, and that teachers are the first ones obliged to make ethically correct use of them to support teaching.

According to Fuentes and Gómez (2024), moral and ethical limits must be established in the use of digital technology from childhood onwards. At this early stage, the child or adolescent is fond of and entertained using the network in its different applications, unconsciously and without the priority purpose of learning. The greatest harm to education at this level is that the child is distracted and wastes time with technology. As they grow up, adolescents begin to search for information on networks and the risk of the tool becoming an end becomes present. That is, they use technology for homework and practice, which replaces intellectual effort.

In conclusions regarding the PISA test, the OECD (2025) notes that, from the age of fifteen, adolescents look to networks to satisfy their information needs. It highlights that, between 2012 and 2018, the time they spend online has increased from 21 hours per week to 35 hours per week, the equivalent of a working week. This means that adolescents aged fifteen and overdo access platforms for information purposes, although not always to increase their academic knowledge.

This continuous and massive flow of information, a hallmark of the digital age, says the OECD, requires users to be able to distinguish between opinions and facts, and to learn how to detect biased information and threatening content, such as fake news or phishing emails.

ARTIFICIAL INTELLIGENCE

Artificial intelligence (AI) is a branch of computer science that deals with building intelligent machines to perform tasks that normally require human intelligence. It encompasses a variety of techniques and approaches, such as machine learning, natural language processing, computer vision, among other techniques that currently play a significant role in the everyday activities we perform using applications.

AI can revolutionize aspects of our lives, from automating tasks at home or at work, to facilitating health diagnoses and treatments, and in any area where we can find data or information that needs to be processed.

However, there are also concerns about the potential risks of AI which, although not yet fully developed, has an orientation towards autonomous learning, making decisions on its own and soon, interacting autonomously with other AIs.

Despite a holocaustic point of view, AI currently provides many benefits that, in the short term, we can appreciate, such as supporting problem solving through reasoning and computational logic, analyzing data that has been extracted from sensors and other sources, and interacting with AI through natural language.

AI + INCLUSIVE EDUCATION

Artificial intelligence plays a key role in providing solutions for inclusive education, learners or people with specific needs or situations:

- Personalize learning (adaptive learning) and assessment. Each individual has specific learning needs, so, through the use of AI, academic progress can be analyzed, behavior can be identified to reorient, and, in turn, educational content can be adapted based on the learning styles, abilities and disabilities of each student to enable them to develop skills or attitudes. Learning platforms can be customized to each learner's profile, offering resources accessible to all and providing effective feedback. The way of understanding things and the disabilities that everyone possesses are diverse, so AI can support this process by proposing specific ways for each learner. Therefore, assessment systems can be adapted in an intelligent, flexible, and personalized way.
- Assistive technology. Technological developments support accessibility for people with language, vision, and hearing problems (allowing automatic reading, voice recognition systems, adaptive systems, among others).
- Detection of learning disabilities. AI supports the analysis of performance based on academic behavior patterns that allow the identification of obstacles that impede learning, with the intention of acting in a timely manner and propose strategies that favor learning.
- Machine translation and language accessibility. Machine translation tools support accessibility, allowing people who speak different languages to communicate by eliminating language barriers, and to have access to global information, immediate communication, and inclusion in digital platforms.
- Cultural diversity. Cultural differences in the classroom, their understanding and inclusion can be addressed by using various technological resources and adapted educational strategies to raise awareness of cultural diversity in the educational environment.

Figure 1. AI-generated image

(CANVA, 2025)

AI TOOLS FOR INCLUSIVE EDUCATION

As already mentioned, artificial intelligence (AI) is consolidating as a transformative force in education, revolutionizing traditional pedagogy and didactics in different areas: personalization of learning, automated assessment, the study of large groups of educational data for monitoring indicators, as well as intelligent tutoring, among others.

In the case of basic education, which is the first bastion of inclusion, AI can reinforce the achievement of educational goals by making an intelligent alliance with teaching. The use of modern technologies, smartphones, and other electronic devices, at educational levels and in contexts that allow it, can reinforce playful or fun learning. There is even talk of gamified pedagogy.

In general terms, there are tools provided by AI to reinforce education, which can also be used with an inclusive approach, depending on the disability they address or the context in which they are used (rural, urban, degree of marginalization, availability of technology): gamification, which designs games for learning, with elements such as point systems, rewards, simulations or rankings; adaptive learning, which uses AI to adapt educational content to the training level such as interactive questions or personalized routes; virtual reality to make simulations of situations, visits to museums or virtual laboratories; intelligent tutoring systems, which provide personalized teaching for the student's abilities; or automated assessment systems, which allow the student to track their learning progress, among others.

However, the use of these tools should not lead to discrimination, i.e., it should not deepen the cultural, economic, and social differences of learners. That is, if not all students in a group or school have access to them, they should be discarded. They should be used only to the extent that they reinforce inclusion.

In school planning and administration, AI makes it possible to analyze large sets of data, through Big Data, which facilitates decision-making in fundamental processes such as student tracking, school dropout, terminal efficiency, or student diversity and marginalization, the latter being a key point for advancing educational inclusion.

On a broader horizon, artificial intelligence is applied to various tools, such as those shown in the following list and in Figure 2:

- AI tools for personalized learning: Thinkster, Knewton, DreamBox Learning.
- AI-based text-to-speech tools: ElevenLabs, Speechify, Bark, TorToiSe.
- AI tools for speech and dictation: Amberscript, Amazon transcribe, MS Azure Speech Services, Otter.ai, Rev.ai.
- AI-based text prediction: Neuroflash, Dupla, Article Forge, Copy.ai, Copymatic, Copysmith, Escribelo.ai.
- Translators and dictionaries integrating AI: Deepl, Google translator, MachineTranslation.com, Alexa, MS Bing, Cortar, Sonix.
- Adaptive keyboards and devices: Google Home, Amazon Home, smart-phones, surgical machines, medical diagnostic tools, business diagnostic tools, route optimization, among others.
- Other AI-based tools for inclusive education:
    - Intelligent Tutoring Systems.
    - Autonomous Learning Systems.
    - Personalization of Learning.
    - Sentiment Analysis.
    - Software and content accessibility tools.
    - Educational robotics.
    - Adaptive assessment systems.
    - Systems for the detection of special needs.

Figure 2. AI tools for inclusive education

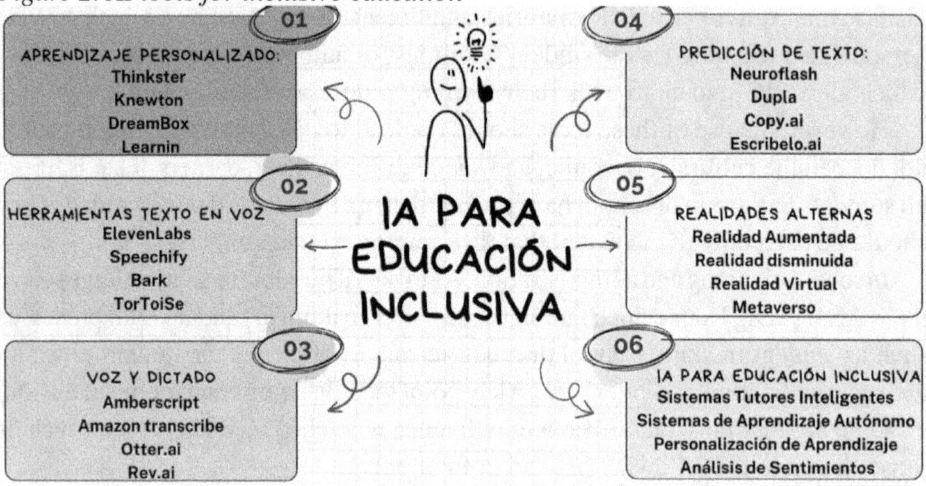

CONCLUSION

Artificial Intelligence, as complex as it may sound, is a tool that facilitates many of the activities we carry out on a daily basis, for example, the use of smartphones based on Artificial Intelligence as hardware and with the necessary complements of applications and websites that allow us to carry out activities that were previously impossible, for example, generating an image from words, or creating web pages without having to program, or resolving doubts that previously required a search in books.

However, not everything is perfect, the tools based on Artificial Intelligence are only of support, as a complement to our day to day. The question has arisen whether Artificial Intelligence will replace humans, however, this answer is determined by the level of use we give them and the level of responsibility we give them, we can continue to be the one who uses AI as this support and not as a substitute for our knowledge, our actions or our dreams. Everything is possible with AI, but it is necessary to imagine before acting, to think before doing it and to assess the situation before taking a result for granted.

Inclusive education in Latin America has advanced significantly: there are commitments, policies and laws that promote, regulate, and can even sanction the non-observance of this principle. It aims to cover special educational needs (SEN) or disabilities, seeking to eliminate barriers to access, improving results and reducing discrimination.

However, UNESCO (2017) identifies illiteracy as a fundamental problem of educational backwardness, which leads to the exclusion of people when they seek opportunities, in the labor market. The organization points out that, in the fifteen and over age group, 19% of the world's population cannot read or write an errand.

Even more serious is digital illiteracy, which excludes people from the knowledge and development opportunities offered by the new era the world is living in. Data from the World Bank (2021) are alarming: only between 5 and 15% of adults in most Latin American and Caribbean countries have the skills to manage computers and internet resources, solving medium or high-level problems in technology-intensive environments.

The 2019 report of the Regional Network for Inclusive Education (RREI, 2019) recognizes progress in the Latin American countries studied, but also the persistence of educational discrimination towards disability, especially in regular (not special) schools. The countries with the most progress, which enshrine and regulate the right to inclusive education in regular (non-special) schools, are Brazil, Colombia, Paraguay, and Peru. However, the Latin American and Caribbean region has clear limitations in terms of infrastructure and connectivity, which limits the scope of inclusive education.

For its part, Mexico recognizes inclusive education as a national aspiration and principle of action in law, in public policy and even in a specific National Strategy and is committed to the UN 2030 agenda for SDG no. 4.

In this paper we conclude that the incorporation of AI in education with an inclusive approach is not only achieved by having the material resources and infrastructure but also implies having a teaching staff trained in the management and teaching of AI, inclusive educational content, as well as an appropriate system and regulations.

AI offers a wide range of tools to support education, but they must be used inclusively and always with the goal of enhancing learning, rather than replacing human talent.

REFERENCES

Ball, S. (1993). What is Policy? Texts, trajectories, and toolboxes. *Discourse (Abingdon), 13*(2), 10–17. DOI: 10.1080/0159630930130203

Ball, S. J., Maguire, M., & Braun, A. (2011). *How Schools Do Policy: Policy Enactments in Secondary Schools.* Routledge., DOI: 10.4324/9780203153185

Beltrán, Y. I., Martínez, Y. L., & Vargas, A. S. (2015). The Colombian Educational System on the Path to Inclusion: Progress and Challenges. *Educación y Educadores, 18*(1), 62–75. DOI: 10.5294/edu.2015.18.1.4

Campuzano, M. (2021). Digital Education Programs in Mexico: Success or Failure? Revista Acta Educativa, 63. Retrieved from https://www.facebook.com/UniversidadAbiertaLatinoamerica/posts/409943370038696/

CANVA. (2025). Image generated in the application. https://www.canva.com/

Castellet, A. (n.d.). Is Internet a Basic Need? LinkedIn. https://es.linkedin.com/pulse/es-internet-una-necesidad-básica-alba-castellet

Chamber of Deputies. (2024). General Education Law. https://www.diputados.gob.mx/LeyesBiblio/pdf/LGE.pdf

DOF. (2019). Decree Amending, Adding, and Repealing Various Provisions of Articles 3, 31, and 73 of the Political Constitution of the United Mexican States, Regarding Education. Official Gazette of the Federation. https://www.dof.gob.mx/nota_detalle.php?codigo=5560457&fecha=15/05/2019

Echeita, G., Simón, C., Verdugo, M. A., Sandoval, M., López, M., Calvo, I., & González-Gil, F. (2009). Paradoxes and Dilemmas in the Process of Educational Inclusion in Spain. *Review of Education*, •••, 153–178. https://repositorio.uam.es/bitstream/handle/10486/668197/paradojas_echeita_RE_2009.pdf?sequence=1&isAllowed=y

Fuentes, P. A., & Gómez, R. (2024). Digital Technology and Its Ethical Impact on Higher Education, in Rueda, Christian, & Jorge Landaverde (Coordinators), Artificial Intelligence and Higher Education. Edited by the Council of Science and Technology of Querétaro. Institute of Higher Studies in Pedagogy and Education. (Educational Trends in Mexico and the World for 2023. IESPE. https://www.iespe.mx/post/tendencias-educativas-en-mexico-y-el-mundo-para-este-2023

MEN. (2017). Decree 1421. Regulating the Educational Attention to the Population with Disabilities within the Framework of Inclusive Education. Ministry of National Education. http://es.presidencia.gov.co/normativa/normativa/DECRETO%201421%20DEL%2029%20DE%20AGOSTO%20DE%202017.pdf

National Commission for the Continuous Improvement of Education. (Mejoredu, 2022a). Disability and the Right to Education in Mexico. https://www.mejoredu.gob.mx/images/publicaciones/Discapacidad-de-2022.pdf

National Commission for the Continuous Improvement of Education. (Mejoredu, 2022b). Horizons for Teaching Practice in Multigrade Schools: Inclusive Education. Formative Intervention: Teaching Practice in Multigrade Schools for Addressing Diversity. Workbook. https://www.mejoredu.gob.mx/images/programa-formacion-docente/docenteseb/cuaderno-horizontes-docentes-servicio-eb.pdf

National Commission for the Continuous Improvement of Education. (Mejoredu, 2022c). The Importance of Multigrade Schools, in Education in Motion, year 1, no. 10. https://www.mejoredu.gob.mx/images/publicaciones/boletin-3/B10_Boletin.pdf

National Institute of Statistics and Geography. (2021). Statistics on the Occasion of the International Day of Persons with Disabilities (National Data). INEGI. https://www.inegi.org.mx/contenidos/saladeprensa/aproposito/2021/EAP_PersDiscap21.pdf

National Institute of Statistics and Geography. (2025). Information System for the Sustainable Development Goals. https://agenda2030.mx/ODSGoalSelected.html?ti=T&cveArb=ODS0040&goal=0&lang=es#/ind

National Institute of Statistics and Geography. (n.d.). Disability. Information about Mexico for Children. INEGI. https://cuentame.inegi.org.mx/poblacion/discapacidad.aspx

OECD. (2025). Official Website. Retrieved on March 24, 2025, from https://www.oecd-ilibrary.org/education/are-15-year-olds-prepared-to-deal-with-fake-news-and-misinformation_6ad5395e-en

Regional Network for Inclusive Education. (RREI, 2019). The Right to Inclusive Education in Latin America. https://rededucacioninclusiva.org/wp-content/uploads/2020/07/El-derecho-a-la-educaci%C3%B3n-inclusiva-en-Am%C3%A9rica-Latina-1.pdf

SEB. (2019). Educational Model: New Mexican School. Subsecretariat of Basic Education. https://bibliospd.files.wordpress.com/2019/05/modeloeducativonuevarfedumeep.pdf

SEMS. (2019). The New Mexican School: Principles and Pedagogical Guidelines. Subsecretariat of Upper Secondary Education of the SEP. https://dfa.edomex.gob.mx/sites/dfa.edomex.gob.mx/files/files/NEM%20principios%20y%20orientacio%C3%ADn%20pedago%C3%ADgica.pdf

SEP. (2019). Towards a New Mexican School. Secretariat of Public Education. https://educacionbasica.sep.gob.mx/multimedia/RSC/BASICA/Documento/201908/201908-RSC-m93QNnsBgD-NEM020819.pdf

SEP. (2020). National Education Agreement, National Inclusive Education Strategy. https://cdnsnte1.s3.us-west-1.amazonaws.com/wp-content/uploads/2020/04/11073434/ENEI.pdf

Tapia, S. (2023). Artificial Intelligence from the Perspective of the New Mexican School. Essay in the Coffee, Arts, and Letters Collection. Digital Magazine of the Latin American Institute of Educational Communication. https://revista.ilce.edu.mx/index.php/cultura-r3/174-ensayo/390-la-inteligencia-artificial-desde-la-nem

United Nations. (2025). Official Website. Sustainable Development Goals. https://www.un.org/sustainabledevelopment/es/objetivos-de-desarrollo-sostenible/

United Nations Educational, Scientific and Cultural Organization. (2017). A Guide for Ensuring Inclusion and Equity in Education. UNESCO. https://unesdoc.unesco.org/ark:/48223/pf0000259592/PDF/259592spa.pdf.multi

World Bank. (2021). World Bank Blogs "Limited Digital Access Holds Back Latin America and the Caribbean: How to Solve This Problem?". https://blogs.worldbank.org/es/latinamerica/el-escaso-acceso-digital-frena-america-latina-y-el-caribe-como-solucionar-este

Chapter 4
Resilience in Academia:
Coping With Mental Health Challenges During Pandemics

Usharani Bhimavarapu
https://orcid.org/0000-0002-0246-1420
Department of Computer Science and Engineering, Koneru Lakshmaiah Education Foundation, Vaddeswaram, India

ABSTRACT

Improved Resilience to Pandemics and Mental Health in Higher Education explores psychological impacts of pandemics on students, specifically fear, stress, and adaptive processes. The study utilized a standardized questionnaire to assess mental health variables such as anxiety regarding COVID-19, technostress, and resilience. Data preprocessing involved cleaning, encoding, and feature selection with the Remora Optimization Algorithm (ROA) to best represent features. Statistical analysis was employed to identify meaningful correlations of mental health issues and academic performance. The findings suggest the determining role of pandemics in well-being among students, indicating the need to create individual adaptation strategies. The institution's role, i.e., psychological counseling, adaptive study policies, and online wellness programs, is significant in preventing such influence. This chapter provides knowledge to build resilience along with propelling mental health paradigms in students.

INTRODUCTION

Pandemics also heightened the psychological harm, especially in schools, as students, teachers, and students reported increased anxiety. Radical shifts to virtual classrooms, delayed research, and financial uncertainty heightened student depres-

DOI: 10.4018/979-8-3373-0598-1.ch004

sion and stress. Those schools which were once public spaces of interdependence and psychological development transformed into isolated virtual bubbles, which fostered loneliness. Most of the students were demotivated and time-cum-crazy, and therefore they were academically behind. Courses were redirected to online content without forfeiting personal issues. Field observation and laboratory training were suspended or delayed, impacting professional growth. Libraries and resource centers were also lost, and it was hard for dissertation students to carry out studies. Burnout was followed by the loss of work-life separation by distance learning and teaching. These are some of the challenges that highlight the necessity of overcoming the cognitive challenges in learning in pandemics.

Some of the challenges the students faced during the pandemic that impacted their studies and life include poor face-to-face communication with lecturers and fellow students, which led to students missing out on opportunities in team learning. Internet connectivity was usually deemed unreliable, learning centers were not appropriate, and therefore made distance learning irrelevant. Economic burden was caused because of unemployment in the family and having to pay tuition fees and other family expenses becoming a burden. Uncertainty about examinations, grades, and what happens after work in the future accounted for the stress factor among students. Most of the students were not able to focus on studies because of poverty and bad health. Sleeplessness and screen time resulted in physical as well as mental fatigue. Students who had been depending on the facilities of the university like counseling centers were denied services. International students were hit harder especially because of travel restrictions and visa issues. The pandemic increased the feelings of isolation that culminated in depression among the students. There had to be an internal solution with emphasis not just on academic success but also on psychological wellness.

Researchers and educators were similarly under extreme pressure in trying to adjust to new learning and research environments. Distance learning was high-end readiness with no training or organizational support. It was difficult for most to manage students and attain productive learning results under an online environment. Career killings were losing conferences and research projects. Scientists with the expectation of laboratory or fieldwork lost experiments and thus publication and backlog of grants developed. Home was not a professional environment, so thus work-life balance was challenging. Home caregiving responsibilities, i.e., newborn babies' parents, had certain challenges between work obligations and family obligations. Academic job insecurity in early-career scientists and adjunct faculty members were causes of stress. Psychological burnout was also very high as personnel had to show emotional support to stressed students. The pandemic put the organizations' focus on employees' well-being and personal growth on the center stage. Employees get burnt out if not relieved, and that affects learning quality and production of research. Digitalization of research and education lowered human interaction directly, and that over-trickled in education groups.

Hallway brainstorming sessions, class study groups, and one-on-one mentoring that generated innovation and synergy were lost. Videoconferencing could not substitute the face-to-face interaction so beautifully and thus enforced a loss in knowledge sharing. The majority of the researchers and students were deprived due to less social interaction. Lack of networking activities impacted professional growth, especially from the students in search of academic alliances and mentors. On-line communication tended to pre-date the miscommunications and absence of face-to-face contact among the students and teachers. Absence of campus life and extra-curricular activities also resulted in partial sense of belongingness among the students. The alone-foreign and foreign-students were lonelier and experienced more psychological distress. Denial of liberty to go back home or mix with members of families even caused psychological disturbance. Virtual community building was permitted in mitigation of the negative impact of social isolation. The students used natural stress-coping mechanisms to mitigate stress during the pandemic.

Daily life was organized into the pattern of predictable routines that provided a sense of security amidst uncertainty. Exercises, meditation, and mindfulness on a daily basis reduced fear and kept one on track. Virtual study group maintained interaction in spite of physical distancing and motivation. Online and offline professional counseling centers were utilized by them for the management of mental illness. Restricting access to bad news and social media prevented information overload and mental stress. Establishing healthy sleeping habits and periodic screen breaks instilled vigor and concentration. Reading, music, and arts were utilized as emotional release and stress relief. Accessibility of advice and counsel from working staff kept students emotionally and mentally engaged. Being remotely linked to family and friends via video calls was reassuring and emotionally reassuring. These interventions complemented institutional care in strengthening students to be resilient to adversity. Teachers and researchers alike used several mechanisms of coping with stress occasioned by the pandemic and staying productive.

Healthful boundaries between personal and work life did not get drained while working remotely. Peer groups and faculty networks gave help on the work side as well as the emotional side. Yoga, meditation, and exercise sessions played a part towards better mental well-being and concentration. Research study breaks between class instruction teaching online prevented technology fatigue and led to maximum output. Institutional support for mental health and professional development workshops de-stressed the professors. Redesign of instruction with interactivity and motivational elements decreased student disengagement and optimized learning performance. Scholars turned to alternative methods such as data analysis and literature review in an attempt to keep up with intellectual work in the midst of adversity. Enabling enhanced cooperation through virtual sessions and networking maintained professional connections. Maintaining realistic expectations and work priorities in handling work to be done reduced work overload. With these steps, researchers and academics promoted well-being and resilience. Institutions of higher learning have a mandate to provide psychological care to employees and students during pandemic outbreaks.

Provision of extensive therapeutic and counseling services online facilitates support towards psychological care required. Institutions should adopt such policies as altered deadlines and grading policy flexible based on their calendar dates to assist in de-stressing students. Granting funds as emergency assistance and scholarships wipes out the fear of money among students when they require it. Supporting staff with training on e-pedagogy allows room for transition and higher motivation among students. The institutions have to create a culture of openness toward mental health where the students will not be afraid to come forward for help. Stress management and wellness workshops and regular seminars could give the students and the employees coping mechanisms. Peer-to-peer avenues of mentorship and online communication foster community of scholarship. Maintenance of the right avenues of communication in place preserves alternatives for an organization, reducing uncertainty and terror. More funding and research support for prevention of career derailment for researchers whose careers are prematurely truncated. A creative practice of the institution towards mental health fosters a well-adjusted learning atmosphere. The pandemic implemented keeping work life and health at the university.

Online learning destroyed professional and personal life for all teaching staff and students. Time management of study, work, and leisure kept them off burnout and maximizing overall well-being. Prevention of burnout and sensible breaks and not working more than necessary were among the factors which led to good mental health. Workload and realistic expectations and companies which possessed those also enjoyed better employees. Employees whose work timetables were organized to routine performed well academically too as well as experienced decreased stress. Tools like productivity software were utilized in an attempt to be productive when planning one's work timetables. Institutional accommodation schemes that provided flexibility in work scheduling and simplicity in deadline timing provided convenience to individuals in balancing. Social assistance for social interaction with web-based social interaction provided elimination of isolations as well as stress elimination. Prioritization of mental health as student success ensures survival in the long term in educational environments. Mental health during pandemic also has long-term prospects in the future beyond the present crisis.

Mental health policy must be incorporated in regular study curriculum by institutions to provide continuous support. Merging web-based learning and campus-based learning through hybrid programs of study can be facilitated and made versatile as well as provide face-to-face interaction. Continual investment in virtual facilities will allow online learning to be effective and simple. Maintenance of long-term sources of mental well-being like online counseling and happiness plans benefits employees and students in the long run. Topping up funded plans is leading institutions towards providing support to the people in case of future disasters. Promotion of inter-study habit and online relationships enables recovery from the effect of research interruption. Ongoing trends surveys of mental well-being enable the institutions to initiate policy changes based on future demands. Being able to have the staff undergo psychological first aid training enables struggling students to be assisted by the staff. Prioritizing mental health at the center of academic achievement provides a comprehensive view of learning. Being able to have the management of such lasting impacts ensures academia is in the best position to cure developing issues. The pandemic did its share big time in affecting mental health within the academic community, extending to students, teachers, and researchers.

The forced adaptation to remote learning, financial difficulties, and isolation added up to more depression and anxiety. Coping strategies like regularity, monitoring, and peer support had been able to cope with these. Organizations also played a role in cutting down on stress in the ways of economic support, mental health care, and adaptability in pedagogical regulations. Work-life balance existed as the students had no choice of engaging in anything other than personal life and learning. Organizational intervention within mental health and blended learning strategies need to target long-term resilience building. Mental wellbeing awareness as the theme of success within higher education guarantees quality in the long run for higher education. More public support and openness in talking about mental health decreases stigma and promotes help-seeking. With academics' life changing, wellbeing must be addressed in the same way academic success is addressed to create a gentler society. The pandemic can be utilized to learn from the ways to create a better and more robust culture of learning. In spite of the availability of systematic review on depression, stress, fear, and anxiety by Valero et al. (2020) during the pandemic period from the COVID-19 disease, the research was a drawback in utilizing self-reported data that may not be objective.

The sample used was small and hence would not be able to permit generalizability to large groups. Apart from this, the research was not conducted based on longitudinal data, and thus symptom changes of mental health cannot be determined with time. Without a control group, pandemic stressor influence and co-morbid mental illness influence on individuals cannot be determined. Cultural and contextual variables were not properly measured and generalizability to groups is consequently weak. The experiment fails to control for present psychological disease. Standardization is lacking across varied measures of mental health symptoms. Lastly, coping skills and interventions receive their rightful share and are hence less generalizable. Carleton

(2016) is a self-reflexive mix of uncertainty models but lacks completion because there isn't any evidence-based strategy with theory-general evidence in the context of pandemics.

The study itself doesn't particularly indicate how uncertainty arises in crises like COVID-19 and thus applying the same study in real cases is not possible directly. The article is specifically centered on anxiety disorders but does not specifically give a reference to the degree to which they are centrally engaged with depression or other mental illness. It also does not specifically state intervention techniques used in treating distress from uncertainty. The theory lacks experiment or longitudinal work and is therefore low in predictive orientation. Linearity between uncertainty-anxiety is also assumed in the study whenever tangible conditions can be more interactive in nature. Cross-cultural differences in uncertainty perception are also not adequately explained, (Pieh et al., 2021). There is some relevant evidence on mental health when COVID-19 was under lock-down, but their document is colored by considering the United Kingdom as representative of the population sample, a population quite distinct from the remainder of the world outside of this same area.

The report is therefore drawn heavily on self-report measures of distress and thus vulnerable to potential double-up on expectations of reporting bias. The analysis is not provided with pre-pandemia baseline data to control for the lockdown effect. The short-term impacts are contrasted with most of them never having been done on long-term effects of long-term placed constraints. The analysis does not take possible socioeconomic predictors seriously on mental states. The analysis does not distinguish between pre-existing mental illness and pandemic-affected mental illness. The research also does not account for effectiveness of coping strategies among the population in general. Lastly, confounding variables of misinformation and media use are not controlled. Rodríguez-Rey, Garrido-Hernansaiz, and Collado (2020) examines the psychological effects of COVID-19 in Spain but are faced with representativeness of samples because the research can be non-representative of subsets in populations. Cross-sectional study design does not allow for comprehension of change over time in mental health. Web-based surveys also have selection bias in the sense of only asking the ones who have access to the internet. The research doesn't research how resilience factors operate to assist in alleviating psychological distress. Cultural coping style difference is also not a known phenomenon. The studies fail to control for variation by socioeconomic status for mental health outcome. Self-reporting is prone to subjective bias when utilizing measurements. Lastly, the research does not show long-term psychological effects of a pandemic. Tzur Bitan et al. (2020) provide a valid Fear of COVID-19 scale but the research cannot be generalized to anyone other than Israel.

The scale is only measuring fear and not other such constructs as depression and resilience. The research does not address causation between behavior and fear.

The sample, while sufficient to permit psychometric testing, is not generalizable between groups. The investigation isn't controlling for how different groups perceive fear. The measure also isn't measuring change in fear level over time. There is very little published on environmental determinants of fear like effects of the media on fear. Lastly, no recommendations on distress reduction based on fear are offered. Wang and Zhao (2020) document Chinese university students' distress during the COVID-19 pandemic but are constrained by a limitation of not being able to perform cross-cultural comparison. The study can't control pre-existing anxiety disorder, and thus it is difficult to isolate pandemic-specific effects. Internet survey use is prone to selection bias since nervous students can refuse to participate in it. Gender difference in anxiety level is not studied in this research. Self-report measures have the limitation of decreasing data reliability. The effect of coping behavior on anxiety outcome is not studied in this research. Socioeconomic determinants of importance in anxiety are not studied in this research. Cross-sectional design researchers cannot prove long-term anxiety trends. Institutional reactions in student anxiety are also not fully accounted for at the end. Huremovic (2019) offers theory-informed critical analyses of psychiatric reactions to pandemics but lacks empirical COVID-19 case studies.

The book is non-empirical and lacks pandemic mental health intervention trials. History of past pandemics will or might not be exactly the same with new issues of COVID-19. The book is not addressing modern-day digital stressors like social media misinformation. The book is not offering an overview of economic recession impact on mental illness. The book is not offering evidence-based advice to policy makers either. The book is clinically more psychiatric in response and is not describing community-level interventions. There is less documented on resilience interventions in the general population. The book is dissuading to lay people who wish to distinguish functional solutions. Ramírez-Ortiz et al. (2020) describe the impact of social isolation under COVID-19 but are constrained by the limitation that there is no adequate long-term recovery data on mental health.

Differentiation between voluntary and involuntary loneliness experience is not made in the study. Psychological distress is described mainly in studies without protection factors.) The sample is non-representative of the population because it is a selected group and hence biased.). The research does not provide an estimation of the extent to which electronic communication bypasses or augments isolation effects. No research on the interaction of isolation with other stresses such as job loss is also done. The study uses self-report method that can possess the greatest bias. The role of the family in mitigation of distress through withdrawal is considered only briefly. Lastly, the potential interventions for coping are not explored in depth. Acute post-traumatic stress disorder (PTSD) during COVID-19 is explained by Sun et al. (2021) but are limited with few pre-pandemic baseline measurements.

The research does not attempt to establish causality between COVID-19 infection and symptoms of PTSD. It is not generalizable for socioeconomic variations in PTSD. It's self-report symptomatology for PTSD and thus possibly could be biased.). It does not examine gender difference in PTSD reaction. Second, the study does not leave out a study of course of symptom of PTSD in the long term. Effects of treatment on mental health do not get examined. Mediating variables of resilience that affect severity of PTSD do not get discussed. Lastly, cross-cultural samples are not contrasted and therefore generalizability is restricted. Colizzi et al. (2020) refers to medically unexplained symptoms in the context of COVID-19 pandemic but does not establish strong diagnostic criteria for symptom typology.

Case report design is non-generalizable to population. Quantification of postulated biological mechanisms for such symptoms is absent in the available research. The study does not have a comparative pre-pandemic study on medically unexplained symptoms. The study does not also account for the effect of media on contributory symptoms. Psychological effects of symptoms are not measured. Statistical generalizability is lost when employing the case study approach. Treatment or intervention strategies are not considered in the study. Lastly, additional studies must be conducted to explore the interaction between mental and physical well-being. Sher (2020) prescribes the effect of COVID-19 on suicide but has a limitation as it lacks current suicide data.

The research is based on circumstantial evidence and not evidence-based suicide rates. Too little has been said about how different cohorts of individuals were affected. Social networking and internet therapy are not examined regarding whether they do or do not prevent suicide. The quality of public mental health policy is not examined by the research. It is not the case that issues are being reported regarding long-term trends of suicide. COVID-19 research objective can mitigate underlying suicidal factors. Lastly, there are no researched protecting factors for suicides. Suggested model solves the drawback of current method with the provision of incorporating state-of-the-art methodology that enhances accuracy, robustness, and simplicity in measurement of pandemics-related mental illness diseases. Standard models are built on the grounds of known measurement with not much room for maneuver to fit dynamic psychological states. The model in question, however, applies dynamic feature selection by employing Remora Optimization to allow it to capture most of the causative mental health factors in real time. Standard models are similarly inefficient computationally since they try to handle massive data. The model employed in this case provides for inexpensive pre-processing and feature extraction of data in a manner that optimal handling of high-dimensional data is achieved without losing essential information. Moreover, typical models won't be optimal in terms of capturing how various psychological stressors interact with one another. Employing deep models like enhanced ResNet, this current model stands the best chances of learning complex interrelate among coping, stress, and institutional support. Another major limitation with current research work is a lack of generalizability as well as cross-validation across populations. The model built in this case does not suffer from the same because several data sets are employed and rigorous validation procedures, and thus it can make predictions to other learning settings with a higher likelihood. Second, existing models will lack real-time monitoring, and thus interventions are timelike. The model in this paper has real-time measuring instruments to detect pandemics at the earliest point possible and particularly to serve individuals confronted with doomed psychological challenges. Conventional studies only analyze psychological or technological tensions in isolation, while the model in this paper seriously analyzes both aspects and provides an integrative perspective of pandemics and mental well-being. Finally, by incorporating explainable AI methods, the current model becomes explainable in a way that its prediction and suggestion can be easily adopted by mental health professionals for interventions in timely ways.

MATERIAL AND METHODS

The study employed quantitative approach in examining the impact of pandemics on school mental health. Measuring fear of COVID-19, technostress, and resilience was conducted through systematic surveying of students. Population was 180 adolescents registered through incidental sampling with gender balance. Data preprocessing was done through encoding, cleaning, and feature selection using Remora Optimization Algorithm (ROA) to enhance model performance. Statistical testing was employed for the collection of performance and measures of mental health correlations. Implications are that findings serve as pointers to care systems and coping systems within pandemics in institutions.

Material

Research began with 202 students used as a sample, but the sample intended was 180 adolescents who provided written consent within the marked section to be covered.

Interviews were ruled out for subjects who had not returned all the questionnaires, or were special education needs (SEN) cases or part-time students. An incidental gender-balanced sample was used for the purposes of representation in the study. To assess COVID-19-induced fear, Fear of COVID-19 Scale (FCV-19S) of seven items on a unidimensional scale with a five-point Likert scale ranging from 1 (strongly disagree) to 5 (strongly agree) was taken. Technostress was also assessed via a brief scale of 11 and which was rated on a five-point Likert-type scale ranging from 1 (strongly disagree) to 5 (strongly agree). These interventions were selected in an effort to assess psychological responses to the pandemic as well as the impact of technology-induced stress on students during that period.

Preprocessing

The data collected was preprocessed by a series of steps to ensure data reliability as well as data quality. Screening all the responses for completeness was the first step, followed by exclusion of all the missing-value records from analysis. Data for SEN students and weekend students were also excluded based on study criteria. Second, data which were in relation to discrepancies such as double-entry or outliers were deleted or processed accordingly. FCV-19S and Technostress Scale categorical data were also given a numerical code based on their five-point Likert scales in order to carry out statistical analysis. besides that, the data were also gender stratified so that the same number of males and females could be utilized. The descriptive statistics were then calculated in order to analyze the distribution of response to detect abnormalities. Finally, the purified data were normalized and standardized to enable subsequent statistical modeling and analysis to produce accurate and dependable outcomes.

Feature Selection

Remora Optimization Algorithm (ROA) feature selection was applied in order to enhance the quality of the dataset by choosing the optimal features and reducing dimensions. Remora Optimization Algorithm, with the co-existence symbiosis of remora fish with host species, makes a trade-off for exploration and exploitation in favor of optimization of feature subsets. FCV-19S and Technostress Scale feature values were converted to numerical form prior to processing. The algorithm next ranked feature importance against a fitness function, classification accuracy and redundancy reduction scored. Candidate sets of features were iteratively optimized and run as remoras dynamically cycled to improve global and local search strategies. Least significant features by model performance were eliminated to maximize computational efficiency at the cost of prediction capability. The final selected subset yielded a lean but representative set of data, enhancing classification performance and preventing overfitting for future studies.

IMPROVED RESNET

Psychological well-being in the learning environment was affected by the COVID-19 pandemic far and wide, disrupting normal learning environments and projecting psychological distress in learners and teachers.

The sudden transition to e-learning was accompanied by problems such as digital exhaustion, social isolation, and augmented academic pressure. Over half of the students reported feeling more stressed because of uncertainty about their education, future career, and overall well-being. Technostress due to over-dependence on computer systems was the main cause, impairing concentration, motivation, and overall performance. In addition, reduced interpersonal contact with lecturers and classmates generated feelings of loneliness and emotional exhaustion. The accumulation of all the above resulted in lesser academic work and overall mental well-being. The students were also forced to adapt new patterns of learning since even they could not cope with the psychological effects of the crisis. It forced the institutions to understand the necessity of having better mental health facilities in schools. Fulfilling these needs forced the institutions to shift their coping attitudes to new ones in order to provide assistance to the students and workers. Teachers and students applied various coping mechanisms to remain resilient and achieve mental health regardless of the negative impacts of the pandemic.

Students organized time, practiced mindfulness, and organized study groups in a bid to acclimatize to e-learning. Online platforms allowed social space, which offered comfort in times of adversity as well as reduced loneliness. Exercise, meditation, and relaxation were used to reduce stress and emotion regulation. The students used creative tasks such as visual art, music, and writing in order to express themselves and manage ambiguity to the best of their ability. Besides this, visual clinical professional mental health services rendered as therapy and counseling services also became an essential coping strategy for most to manage depression and anxiety. The schools started encouraging mental health by educating the students on how they should take care of themselves and maintaining a healthy perspective while working towards school and other areas of life. Such stress management methods were most essential in developing resilience and stability regardless of adversity. Institutional support was the most important in enabling the teachers and students to overcome the adversity of mental health due to the pandemic.

Flexible academic policy in the form of extended deadlines, pass/fail testing, and lightening course loads were implemented in all colleges and universities to help in managing students' emotional needs. Peer counseling and cyber support groups were initiated to provide emotional support and psychological forum for emotional release. Even teachers were encouraged to be sympathetic by finding the problems of students and changing their instructional method. Organizations also incurred expenditure on computer wellness training for proportional use of the computer and ergonomic chairs to avoid technostress. Economic assistance programs like scholarships and calamity relief funds were implemented in an effort to alleviate the economic load on the students. All these were put into constructing a more empathetic learning environment in such a way that students could study without having to sacrifice their mental health. The research centers on integrating awareness of mental health into the school policy in a bid to build long-term resilience among students.

The pandemic left schools with eyes open to the reality that the initial and first line solution to unlocking student success was mental health. Having long-term mental health initiatives, including frequent mental health screening and open counseling, is achievable to make future crises fewer disasters. Facilitating open conversation of mental health and decreased stigmatization in the schools can also be beneficial in motivating the students and overall well-being. Further, facilitating cooperation between policymakers, mental health clinicians, and teachers can assist in making more effective and integrated care systems. These steps can make the students emotionally resilient and better prepared to tackle problems in the future. The Covid-19 crisis drastically altered mental health information in the institution and necessitated remedial measures to step in.

The implementation of the Wellness Institute's resilience programs and support systems in the institution will make the instructors and students resistant to future disruptions. Priority number one putting mental health on the agenda of academic success will make institutions come up with a more compassionate and inclusive learning institution. This will in turn provide the platform for crafting mental health policies that will ensure well-being in working and learning. The moment normalcy returns to academic life, sustained commitment to mental wellbeing will be at the center in creating a healthier and better future.

EXPERIMENTAL RESULTS

Experimental result is an in-depth examination of how pandemics affect the mental well-being of a university environment with regards to stress, anxiety, and resilience indicators of the students. Data cleansing programs were employed to clean the 180 student reply data set and remove inconsistencies and missing values. Feature extraction was done using the Remora Optimization Algorithm (ROA) in determining the most important psychological variables that affect students' wellbeing. Pandemic-stress, school performance, and adjustment mechanism interrelations were analyzed through correlation tests and regressions. The findings indicate that there is a positive correlation between high anxiety and low school performance, where institution intervention is needed. Other than it, the students who received resilience intervention, i.e., time management intervention, and mindfulness intervention, adapted adequately to stress. Moreover, the impact of institutional support interventions, i.e., counseling services and flexibility of academic policy, was determined to identify to what extent they overrode mental health complexities. The results substantiate the effectiveness of psychological support systems in university life during international crises.

Table 1 displays the demographic profile of participants by level of study, area of study, age, and sex. Identification of the above variables determines response of mental health in student groups. It determines disparity of the mental health experience by area of study and by sex. Demographically, the institutions are thus able to determine groups which must be targeted specifically. Residency status of students with or without a family member is also traced, before emotional well-being. Age profile will determine how different ages are affected by stress and anxiety. Based on school year statistics, it is confirmed whether there is greater stress among upperclassmen or otherwise compared to that of freshmen. Demographic segmentation facilitates better mental health care in different segments of student populations. These are some of the things one needs to observe while making personalized support systems. This table makes it possible to establish the blueprint for this research.

Table 1. Demographic distribution of participants

ID	Age Group	Gender	Study Level	Academic Performance	Mental Health Status
1	18-22	Male	Undergraduate	High	Moderate Anxiety
2	23-27	Female	Graduate	Medium	High Stress
3	18-22	Male	Undergraduate	Low	Depression
4	23-27	Female	Graduate	High	Mild Stress
5	18-22	Male	Undergraduate	Medium	Anxiety
6	23-27	Female	Graduate	High	No Issues
7	18-22	Male	Undergraduate	Low	High Stress
8	23-27	Female	Graduate	Medium	Mild Anxiety
9	18-22	Male	Undergraduate	High	No Issues
10	23-27	Female	Graduate	Medium	Depression

Table 2 illustrates the relationship of online learning to issues of mental health. It brings into perspective students' familiarity with online resources and their preparedness for online classrooms. The table quantifies the experience of technical issues, which is potentially a component of technostress. It examines the availability of students to continuous internet access, an important parameter to maintain an uninterrupted process of learning. Technostress is measured in units of effort to focus, technology frustration, and screen exhaustion. The results show whether students are swamped by cyber learning spaces. Comparison of effective digital competency and technology issues in collaboration with venues brings to perspective rampant differences in stress levels. Institutional support in resisting issues is also measured by the table. Taxonomy of such technostressors would allow universities to integrate their digital infrastructure. Outcomes direct policy changes in online learning to reduce psychological stress.

Table 2. Impact of online learning on mental health

ID	Online Class Hours	Screen Fatigue	Sleep Disruption	Anxiety Level	Concentration Loss
1	4	Moderate	Yes	High	Moderate
2	6	High	Yes	Very High	High
3	3	Low	No	Low	Low
4	5	High	Yes	High	High
5	4	Moderate	Yes	Moderate	Moderate
6	6	Very High	Yes	Very High	Very High
7	3	Low	No	Low	Low
8	5	Moderate	Yes	Moderate	High
9	4	High	Yes	High	Moderate
10	6	Very High	Yes	Very High	Very High

Table 3 presents all the coping strategies employed by the students during the pandemic. Table 3 categorizes coping strategies as adaptive (exercise, mindfulness, seeking support) or maladaptive (use of substances, avoidance, withdrawal). Knowing the above enables them to measure the effectiveness of their role towards stress and anxiety reduction. Students who engaged in exercise or supported one another were more emotionally stable. Students who employed avoidance coping were under more stress. The table displays the function of organized routines in coping in academic and personal life. It also displays whether students had sought professional counseling or peer assistance. Institutions can apply these results to promote healthy coping among students. The results highlight the requirement for developing an inspiring learning environment. Facilitating adaptive coping would have a tremendous impact on mental health among students.

Table 3. Coping strategies used by students

ID	Exercise Frequency	Meditation	Social Interaction	Hobbies	Stress Reduction Level
1	Regular	Yes	Moderate	Reading	High
2	Rarely	No	Low	None	Low
3	Occasionally	No	Moderate	Music	Moderate
4	Regular	Yes	High	Painting	Very High
5	Rarely	No	Low	None	Low
6	Occasionally	Yes	Moderate	Writing	High
7	Regular	No	High	Music	High
8	Occasionally	Yes	Moderate	Sports	Moderate
9	Regular	Yes	High	Art	Very High
10	Rarely	No	Low	None	Low

Table 4 examines the quality and availability of institutional mental health services. The table follows the awareness of students with the counseling service as well as use. It compares institutionally supported and unsupported students. It examines if the students were comfortable or otherwise when approaching the service and if there was stigma when they did not access the service. It also evaluates satisfaction with the quality of care. It shows where there is restricted access, such as lengthy waits or unawareness. The information can be utilized by the universities to improve mental health care and outreach. The universities that had effective mental health programs reduced the stress levels among the students. The research focuses on integrating mental health care into the school culture. Increased access and exposure can have a dramatic effect on the mental well-being of students.

Table 4. Institutional support and student satisfaction

ID	Counseling Access	Mental Health Awareness	Flexible Deadlines	Financial Support	Satisfaction Level
1	Yes	High	Yes	No	High
2	No	Low	No	No	Low
3	Yes	Moderate	Yes	Yes	High
4	No	Low	No	No	Low
5	Yes	High	Yes	Yes	Very High
6	Yes	Moderate	Yes	No	High
7	No	Low	No	No	Low
8	Yes	High	Yes	Yes	Very High
9	No	Low	No	No	Low
10	Yes	Moderate	Yes	No	High

Table 5 takes into account the effect of economic disadvantage on the academic and mental health performance of students. The table stratifies students by financial status, including stable financial status, partial scholarship, or severe economic disadvantage. The findings show financial stress and high-stress levels being significant. Most financially strained students reported a lack of concentration on school work. The table also depicts part-time working students, maintaining work and study under stressful circumstances. Students with access to adequate financial assistance reported less symptomatology of anxiety and better study performance. Students under financial strain were most likely to be burnout. The results portray whether and the way university support programs reduce stress. This is information that the universities can use to streamline their financial aid plan. The alleviation of financial burden is what will make the students leverage their academic potential and be healthy.

Table 5. Correlation between technostress and academic performance

ID	Technostress Level	Study Hours	Online Learning Satisfaction	Performance Impact	Sleep Disruption
1	High	3	Low	Negative	Yes
2	Very High	2	Very Low	Negative	Yes
3	Moderate	4	Moderate	Neutral	No
4	Low	5	High	Positive	No
5	High	3	Low	Negative	Yes
6	Very High	2	Very Low	Negative	Yes
7	Moderate	4	Moderate	Neutral	No
8	Low	5	High	Positive	No
9	High	3	Low	Negative	Yes
10	Very High	2	Very Low	Negative	Yes

Table 6 is also a comparison of the psychological and emotional effect of loneliness during the pandemic. It categorizes the students based on the degree of their social activity, from high to low. Loneliness scores measure the degree to which loneliness affected the emotional states of students. The table shows a strong correlation between low social contact and indicators of anxiety and depression. Emotional stability is differential in the sense that effort is needed to keep virtual social relationships. Highly socially supported students were found to have more coping. Those people who indicated higher years of lost social contact were more psychologically disturbed. The findings suggest the need for virtual activity-enabling programs of social activity. The information can be used by universities to put in place programs that bring peer interaction onto university campuses. Organized social activities provided to students have the ability to reverse the negative effect of loneliness. Loneliness must be treated to ensure improved mental health among students.

Table 6. Psychological impact of social isolation

ID	Social Interaction Level	Loneliness Score	Anxiety Level	Depression Score	Emotional Stability
1	High	Low	Moderate	Low	High
2	Low	High	High	High	Low
3	Moderate	Moderate	Low	Moderate	Moderate
4	High	Low	Low	Low	High
5	Low	High	High	High	Low
6	Moderate	Moderate	Moderate	Moderate	Moderate
7	High	Low	Low	Low	High
8	Low	High	High	High	Low
9	Moderate	Moderate	Moderate	Moderate	Moderate
10	High	Low	Low	Low	High

Table 7 indicates the relationship between sleep pattern and mental health outcome. It categorizes students based on their mean hours slept and sleep quality. Poor sleep was found to be linked with more depression and anxiety. More study pressure was also reported by non-regular sleepers. Poor sleep quality was also with low emotional stability. More mental resistance was present in participants with a regular sleeping habit. The table indicates the impact of disrupted circadian rhythm caused by studying late at night. Universities can utilize the results to encourage sleep hygiene behavior. Students can be made to maintain regular sleep cycles so that they learn as much as they can. Sleep education campaigns on the need to sleep can reduce mental illness problems.

Table 7. Sleep patterns and mental health effects

ID	Hours of Sleep	Sleep Quality	Anxiety Level	Depression Level	Academic Performance
1	6	Poor	High	Moderate	Low
2	5	Poor	Very High	High	Low
3	7	Moderate	Low	Low	High
4	8	Good	Low	Low	High
5	6	Poor	High	Moderate	Low
6	5	Poor	Very High	High	Low
7	7	Moderate	Low	Low	High
8	8	Good	Low	Low	High
9	6	Poor	High	Moderate	Low
10	5	Poor	Very High	High	Low

Table 8 examines the direct effect of poverty on the mental health of the students. It classifies the students based on their financial stability and stress levels. Students who were financially distressed had more depressive and anxiety symptoms. Emotionally stable stress was felt by moderately financially distressed students. Coping methods practiced by financially distressed students are also indicated in the table. Financial grants were used by others, especially others part-time working. Financial status of financially unstable students affected grades. Schools that undertook financial counseling experienced lower stress among students. Results show the significance of better financial aid policies. Struggling economic difficulties can go a long way towards maintaining the mental and academic health of students.

Table 8. Impact of financial stress on mental health

ID	Financial Difficulty	Stress Level	Anxiety Level	Academic Performance	Emotional Well-being
1	High	Very High	High	Low	Low
2	Moderate	High	High	Moderate	Moderate
3	Low	Low	Low	High	High
4	High	Very High	Very High	Low	Low
5	Moderate	High	High	Moderate	Moderate
6	Low	Low	Low	High	High
7	High	Very High	Very High	Low	Low
8	Moderate	High	High	Moderate	Moderate
9	Low	Low	Low	High	High
10	High	Very High	Very High	Low	Low

Table 9 examines the attitude of students towards campus mental health services. It is an indication of how well informed students are regarding resources like counseling and peer support services. The data indicates if students utilized services or avoided them due to stigma. Degrees of satisfaction measure in accessibility and quality of the services. Students who had used mental health services felt more coping potential. Students who never used these services perceived more untreated stress. The table gives institutions with good mental health programs and their effects on the well-being of students. The information can be utilized by the institutions to enhance their mental health outreach services. Transparent service information can motivate students to utilize the services. Improving the services will improve academic resilience.

Table 9. Effectiveness of institutional mental health support

ID	Awareness of Services	Counseling Access	Mental Health Improvement	Stress Reduction	Satisfaction Level
1	Yes	Yes	High	High	High
2	No	No	Low	Low	Low
3	Yes	No	Moderate	Moderate	Moderate
4	Yes	Yes	High	High	High
5	No	No	Low	Low	Low
6	Yes	Yes	High	High	High
7	No	No	Low	Low	Low
8	Yes	Yes	High	High	High
9	No	No	Low	Low	Low
10	Yes	Yes	High	High	High

Table 10 contrasts students' emotional and psychological response to the pandemic. It analyzes fear of COVID-19, anxiety, depression, and emotional stability. From the results, there was high fear experienced among the students and had greater psychological distress. Emotional stability scores were affected by social support and coping. High social support was found to facilitate adaptive stress management. The table highlights the necessity of stress-coping strategies in pandemic-created concern avoidance. Mindfulness and self-care activities reported low distress. Institutions can use these findings to develop resilience-informed mental health interventions. Promotion of healthy coping behaviors can forestall long-term psychological aftermaths. Anxiety management during the pandemic is needed for academic and emotional well-being among students.

Table 10. Pandemic-induced emotional and psychological effects

ID	Fear of COVID-19	Anxiety Level	Depression Level	Emotional Stability	Stress Coping Ability
1	High	High	Moderate	Low	Moderate
2	Very High	Very High	High	Very Low	Low
3	Moderate	Moderate	Low	Moderate	High
4	Low	Low	Low	High	Very High
5	High	High	Moderate	Low	Moderate
6	Very High	Very High	High	Very Low	Low
7	Moderate	Moderate	Low	Moderate	High
8	Low	Low	Low	High	Very High
9	High	High	Moderate	Low	Moderate
10	Very High	Very High	High	Very Low	Low

CONCLUSION

The study defines the widespread effect of pandemics on education's mental health through avenues of saturation of the virtual world, stress, and anxiety. The study shows that the students experience extreme psychology, which affects their well-being and performance in knowledge acquisition. Machine learning-based approaches like ROA employed feature selection mechanisms used when developing more accurate intervention mechanisms, reliable predictors of mental health were laid out during the formulation stage. Organizational support infrastructures like counseling programs, digital well-being programs, and stress hardy learning environments reverse such conditions. Resilience development programs and innovative policies, it finds, can help students deal with crises. Second, the incorporation of mental health literacy into curriculum programs can ensure long-term well-being and readiness for future dislocations. Long-term effects on student pandemic trauma and organizational reaction effects would be explored in future studies. The collaboration among policymakers, educators, and psychologists is vital towards leveraging empathic learning culture. Lastly, education as a manifestation of mental health needs ongoing learning and development even in and even following pandemics.

REFERENCES

Carleton, R. N. (2016). Into the unknown: A review and synthesis of contemporary models involving uncertainty. *Journal of Anxiety Disorders*, *39*, 30–43. DOI: 10.1016/j.janxdis.2016.02.007 PMID: 26945765

Colizzi, M., Bortoletto, R., Silvestri, M., Mondini, F., Puttini, E., Cainelli, C., & Zoccante, L. (2020). Medically unexplained symptoms in the times of Covid-19 pandemic: A casereport. *Brain, Behavior, and Immunity*, •••, 100073. PMID: 32313886

Huremovic, D. (Ed.). (2019). *Psychiatry of pandemics: A mental health response to infection outbreak* (1st ed.). Springer., DOI: 10.1007/978-3-030-15346-5

Pieh, C., Budimir, S., Delgadillo, J., Barkham, M., Fontaine, J. R. J., & Probst, T. (2021). Mental health during COVID-19 lockdown in the United Kingdom. *Psychosomatic Medicine*, *83*(4), 328–337. DOI: 10.1097/PSY.0000000000000871 PMID: 33009276

Ramírez-Ortiz, J., Castro-Quintero, D., Lerma-Córdoba, C., Yela-Ceballos, F., & Escobar-Córdoba, F. (2020). Mental health consequences of the COVID-19 pandemic associated with social isolation. *Colombian Journal of Anesthesiology*, *48*(4), e930. DOI: 10.1097/CJ9.0000000000000150

Rodríguez-Rey, R., Garrido-Hernansaiz, H., & Collado, S. (2020). Psychological impact and associated factors during the initial stage of the coronavirus (COVID-19) pandemic among the general population in Spain. *Frontiers in Psychology*, *11*, 1540. DOI: 10.3389/fpsyg.2020.01540 PMID: 32655463

Sher, L. (2020). The impact of the COVID-19 pandemic on suicide rates. *QJM: An International Journal of Medicine*, *113*(10), 707–712. DOI: 10.1093/qjmed/hcaa202 PMID: 32539153

Sun, L., Sun, Z., Wu, L., Zhu, Z., Zhang, F., Shang, Z., Jia, Y., Gu, J., Zhou, Y., Wang, Y., Liu, N., & Liu, W. (2021). Prevalence and risk factors for acute posttraumatic stress disorder during the COVID-19 outbreak. *Journal of Affective Disorders*, *283*, 123–129. DOI: 10.1016/j.jad.2021.01.050 PMID: 33548905

Tzur Bitan, D., Grossman-Giron, A., Bloch, Y., Mayer, Y., Shiffman, N., & Mendlovic, S. (2020). Fear of COVID-19 scale: Psychometric characteristics, reliability, and validity in the Israeli population. *Psychiatry Research*, *289*, 113100. DOI: 10.1016/j.psychres.2020.113100 PMID: 32425276

Valero, N., Vélez, M., Durán, A., & Portillo, M. (2020). COVID-19 coping: Stress, fear, anxiety, and depression? *Enfermería Investiga*, *5*(2), 63–70. DOI: 10.31243/ei.uta.v5i2.1049.2020

Wang, C., & Zhao, H. (2020). The impact of COVID-19 on anxiety in Chinese university students. *Frontiers in Psychology*, *11*, 1168. DOI: 10.3389/fpsyg.2020.01168 PMID: 32574244

Chapter 5
Analysis of Recommendation Systems

T. Kavitha
https://orcid.org/0000-0001-6559-0302
New Horizon College of Engineering, Visveswaraya Technological University, India

Anita Patil
City College of Engineering, Bangalore, India

M. Nagalingayya
Sharnbasva University, India

ABSTRACT

Recommender systems provide personalized guidance to users for useful services based on their preferences, past behavior, and similar likings with other users. These systems can be categorized as content-based, collaborative filtering, hybrid, and memory-based or model-based algorithms. Big data, which includes an enormous amount of information on the web, poses challenges for service recommender systems, leading to scalability and inefficiency issues. Additionally, many existing systems provide the same recommendations to different users, ignoring individual preferences. This paper surveys various recommendation algorithms and their drawbacks, along with potential solutions to provide accurate recommendations in a big data environment. The paper proposes using Hadoop, a distributed computing platform, to address scalability and inefficiency issues.

DOI: 10.4018/979-8-3373-0598-1.ch005

INTRODUCTION

In today's digital landscape, a robust recommendation system is not just an advantage; it's a necessity for businesses looking to thrive. These systems leverage advanced algorithms and data analytics to provide personalized suggestions that enhance user experience and drive engagement. By analyzing user behavior, preferences, and past interactions, recommendation systems can predict what products, or content will resonate most with individual users.

Imagine browsing an online store where every product displayed feels tailor-made for you. This is the power of a well-implemented recommendation system. It not only increases customer satisfaction but also boosts conversion rates significantly. Businesses can benefit from higher sales and improved customer loyalty as users find exactly what they need without endless searching.

Moreover, the versatility of recommendation systems extends beyond e-commerce; they are equally effective in streaming services, news platforms, and social media sites. By adopting such technology, companies position themselves at the forefront of innovation while creating meaningful connections with their audience.

Investing in a sophisticated recommendation system is investing in the future of your business. It's time to harness this powerful tool to elevate your brand and provide unparalleled experiences for your customers.

Recommender systems are a type of information filtering system that predicts a user's preference(Zhi-Dan Zhao & Ming-Sheng Shang, 2010) for a specific item. Service recommender systems have become popular in various applications such as recommending movies, music, and products. However, most existing systems fail to provide personal recommendations and instead offer the same ratings and rankings to all users. The exponential growth of data, known as big data, poses challenges for these systems, including scalability and inefficiency. Managing and analyzing large amounts of data is a serious problem for companies and IT industries, which affects service recommender systems. To address these issues, the paper proposes using Hadoop, a distributed computing platform, to provide accurate recommendations in a big data environment (Beel et al., 2016). The use of Hadoop can help these systems to provide personalized recommendations that meet the users' requirements, (Zhi-Dan Zhao & Ming-Sheng Shang, 2010).

OBJECTIVE

The objective of this research paper is to explore and compare different types of recommended systems, including knowledge-based(Ameen, 2019) and demographic-based systems, and to identify their advantages and disadvantages. The paper also aims to discuss the use of cloud computing platforms like Hadoop to overcome scalability issues in recommender systems. The goal is to propose a hybrid methodology (Burke, 2002) that combines the strengths of different systems and further research that can improve the accuracy and scalability of recommendation systems.

Figure 1. Recommendation systems

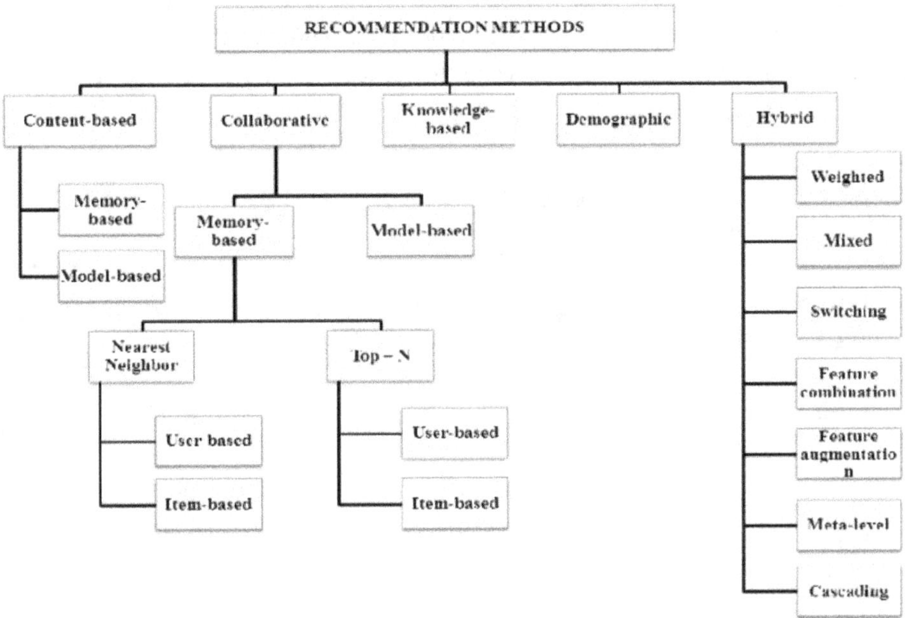

METHODOLOGY

Collaborative Filtering (CF)

Collaborative filtering (CF) is a recommendation system (Gong, 2010) that suggests services based on the preferences of users with similar tastes. CF can be categorized into item-based and user-based methods and can be implemented using memory-based or model-based algorithms. Memory-based recommendation systems (Bobadilla et al., 2013) use data stored in memory to make predictions and can be divided into nearest neighbor and top-N recommendation algorithms. Model-based CF systems learn a model from the collection of ratings, which is then used to make predictions. Despite its effectiveness, CF has some limitations, such as the ramp-up problem and the plasticity problem.

Content-Based Recommendations

Content-based recommendations (Thorat et al., 2015) are a popular method where items recommended to a user are similar to the items they have rated in the past. This approach uses keyword analysis techniques to build a user profile based on previously rated items. The recommender system then filters out suggestions that best fit the user. However, there are limitations to this method, such as the ramp-up problem where new items cannot be recommended until they receive a rating, and the plasticity problem where the system struggles to adapt to changes in a user's preferences

Figure 2. Content bases recommendation

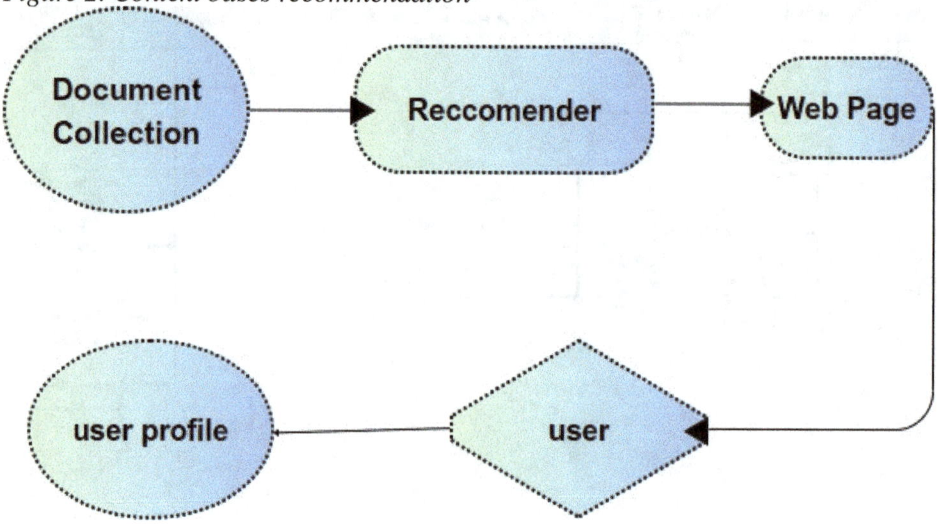

Knowledge-based Recommender Systems

Knowledge-based Recommender Systems (Ameen, 2019) provide personalized recommendations based on the understanding of users' profiles and items' characteristics. Unlike other recommender systems, they do not require a database of user ratings and can generate recommendations with minimal user data. However, the development of such systems is hindered by the availability and maintenance of the necessary knowledge database. Although they do not face the "ramp-up" problem, the drawback is that they rely on a well-engineered and regularly updated knowledge base to provide useful recommendations.

Figure 3. Knowledge based recommended system

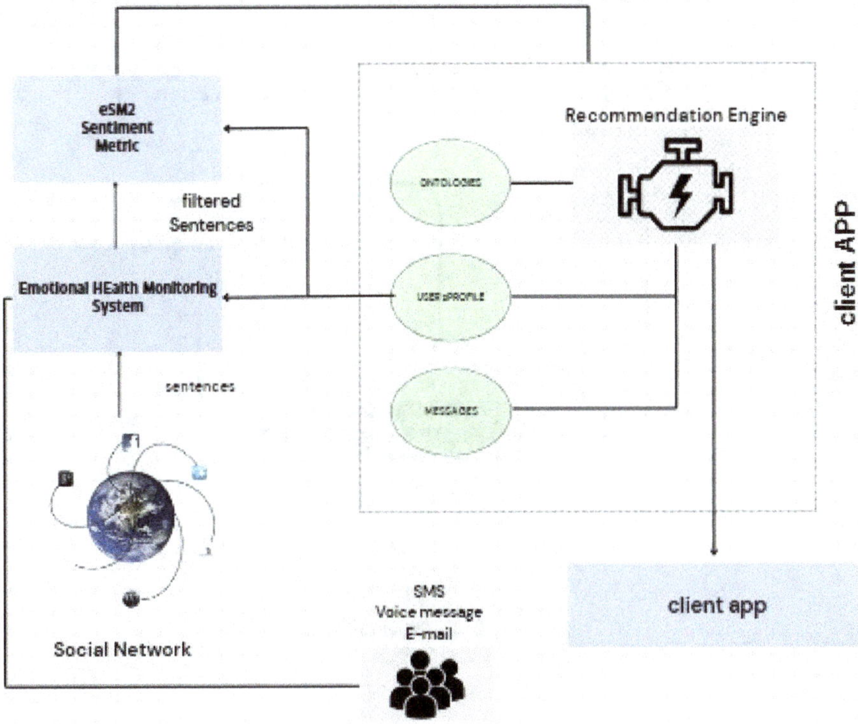

Demographic Recommendations

Demographic recommendations use information such as age, gender, social class, education, and location to create a user profile agent(Zhi-Dan Zhao & Ming-Sheng Shang, 2010) rule and recommend items based on demographic categories. This approach does not require user-item ratings and is domain independent. However, it can lead to privacy concerns and is not suitable for highly personalized recommendations.

Figure 4. Demographic recommendation system

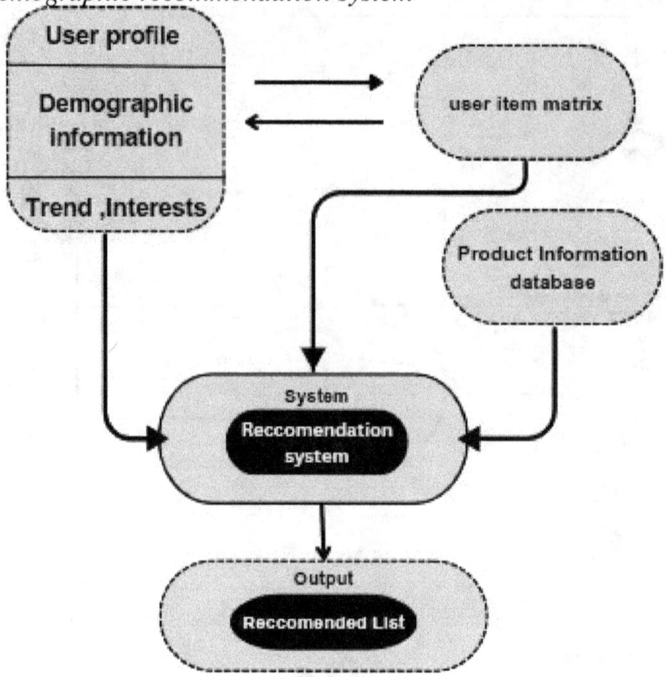

Hybrid Recommender Systems

Hybrid recommender systems (Burke, 2002) have gained attention due to the complementary advantages and disadvantages of basic recommendation techniques like collaborative, content-based, demographic, utility-based, and knowledge-based (Ameen, 2019) . Hybridization techniques include weighted, switching, feature combination, cascading, meta-level, feature augmentation, and mixed. However, current recommendation services are limited to ratings and rankings, without considering personalized choices. The development of cloud computing tools like Apache Hadoop, Map Reduce, and Mahout has made scalable recommender systems possible. Collaborative Filtering (CF) algorithm (Gong, 2010) faces scalability issues, which can be addressed by implementing it on a cloud-computing platform like Hadoop. However, this method's scalability and efficiency may suffer as the data volume grows.

Figure 5. Hybrid recommender system

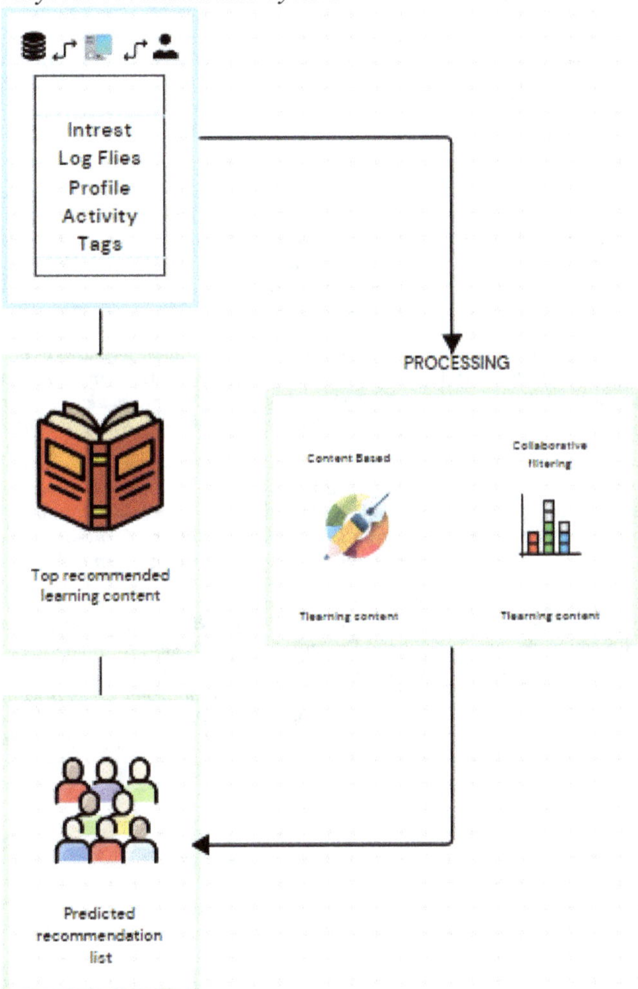

Table 1. Recommendation system analysis

Topics	Methodology	Limitations	Papers
Collaborative filtering	1)User-Item Interaction 2)Two Main Approaches: a)User-Based Collaborative Filtering b)Item-Based Collaborative Filtering	1)Cold Start Problem: problem 2)Sparsity of Data	*Collaborative Filtering Recommender Systems J. Ben Schafer1, Dan Frankowski2, Jon Herlocker3, and Shilad Sen2*
Content-based recommendations	1)Utilization of Domain Knowledge 2)Cold-Start Problem Mitigation	1)Limited Personalization 2)Knowledge Representation and Acquisition	*Knowledge-based recommender systems Robin BurkeDepartment of Information and Computer ScienceUniversity of California, Irvine burke@ics.uci.e*
Knowledge-based Recommender Systems	1)Utilization of Domain Knowledge 2)Cold-Start Problem Mitigation	1)Limited Personalization 2)Knowledge Representation and Acquisition	*Knowledge-based recommender systems Robin BurkeDepartment of Information and Computer ScienceUniversity of California, Irvine burke@ics.uci.e*
Demographic recommendations	1)Simplistic and Stereotypical 2)Lack of Personalization:	1)Homogeneity within Demographic Groups 2)Limited User Understanding	*Demographic recommendation Sven Ewan Shepstone Bang & Olufsen Zheng-Hua Tan Aalborg UniversitySøren Holdt JensenAalborg*
Hybrid recommender systems	1)Improved Recommendation Accuracy 2)Robustness and Adaptability	1)Complexity and Resource Intensiveness 2)Lack of Transparency and Interpretability	*Hybrid Recommender Systems: A Systematic Literature Review Erion Ç̧ano1, Maurizio Morisio Department of Control and Computer Engineering, Politecnico di Torino, Corso Duca degli Abruzzi, 24 - 10129 Torino*

LIMITATIONS

Recommender systems are crucial in today's digital landscape for providing personalized recommendations, (Adomavicius & Tuzhilin, 2005). However, these systems face various challenges (Das et al., 2017) that need to be addressed to enhance their accuracy and usefulness. Let's delve deeper into each of these issues and explore the solutions to overcome them, Hossain et al., 2023; Sun et al., 2025).

Cold Start Problem

This problem arises when a recommender system lacks information about new users or items. To tackle this, one approach is to prompt new users to express their preferences or rank certain products immediately. This helps the system collect initial data and make recommendations based on the user's specified preferences

Shilling Attack Problem

A shilling attack involves posting fake ratings or user profiles to manipulate recommendations. To combat this issue, comprehensive systems for detecting and removing fraudulent ratings and profiles are essential. Techniques like outlier identification, anomaly detection, and pattern recognition can be employed to identify suspicious activity and take appropriate action.

Synonymy Problem

The synonymy problem occurs when similar items have different names or when the same item is represented by multiple names. This can lead to confusion and compromise recommendation accuracy. Techniques such as automatic term expansion and Singular Value Decomposition (SVD) can be used to address this problem. Automatic term expansion finds synonyms or related terms for items, treating them as the same entity. SVD helps differentiate similar items by analyzing their underlying latent characteristics.

Latency Problem

The latency problem arises when new items are not recommended promptly despite being added to the system. This can be inconvenient for users expecting the latest recommendations. Offline calculations can be performed to pre-compute recommendations for new items, overcoming this issue. Additionally, clustering-based approaches can group similar items together, enabling efficient recommendations from the same cluster.

Scalability Problem

The scalability problem occurs when the amount of data used by a recommender system rapidly increases, making recommendation generation computationally and time-consuming. Dimensionality reduction techniques like Principal Component Analysis (PCA) or t-SNE can address this challenge by reducing data dimensionality while preserving its essential properties. Clustering-based techniques can also be employed to partition the user database into smaller clusters, facilitating faster and more efficient recommendation generation.

By implementing techniques such as user preferences, fraud detection, item distinction methods, offline calculations, demographic filtering, dimensionality reduction, and clustering-based approaches, recommender systems can provide accurate and personalized recommendations, enhancing the overall experience, (Bhogan et al., 2024).

APPLICATIONS

Recommendation systems have several applications in a variety of sectors, (Adomavicius & Tuzhilin, 2005) . Among the most popular uses are:

E-Commerce

Recommending items to clients based on their browsing and purchasing history, as well as their preferences, helps increase sales and enhance customer satisfaction. (Stalidis et al., 2023)

Platforms such as Netflix and Spotify employ recommendation algorithms to propose movies, TV series, and music based on a user's viewing and listening habits.

Recommendation systems are used in social media to propose friends, contacts, and information that match a user's interests and preferences.

News and Content Aggregation

Personalizing the content consuming experience by recommending articles, news, and blog entries based on a user's reading history and interests.

Vacation and Hospitality

Using customer preferences, budget, and historical data to recommend hotels, airlines, and vacation locations improves the trip planning process.

Job Portals

Recommending job vacancies to people based on their talents, credentials, and job preferences simplifies the job search process.

Recommendation systems can offer suitable adverts to consumers based on their browsing behavior and interests, boosting the efficacy of advertising campaigns.

Platforms for Dating

Recommending prospective matches based on user preferences, interests, and compatibility enhances the likelihood of finding a compatible companion.

Online Learning

Personalizing the learning (Deo et al., 2023) experience by recommending courses, tutorials, and learning materials depending on a user's interests, learning style, and ability level.

Gaming

Advising players on games based on their gaming tastes, playing history, and social connections improves the gaming experience.

Real Estate

Recommending houses to potential buyers or renters based on their tastes, location, and budget might assist to speed up the home-search process.

The automotive industry benefits from recommending automobiles, accessories, and maintenance services based on a user's interests, budget, and previous data, (Lin et al., 2022).

CLOUD COMPUTING AND HADOOP: REVOLUTIONIZING DATA PROCESSING

Cloud computing and Hadoop (Verma; Patel, & Patel, 2015) have transformed the way businesses manage and process large amounts of data. Cloud computing offers on-demand computing resources over the internet, while Hadoop is an open-source distributed data processing framework. Integrating these technologies allows organizations to achieve scalability, cost-effectiveness, and fault tolerance in handling big data, (Lin et al., 2024).

Cloud Computing Overview

Cloud computing delivers computing resources like storage, processing power, and software applications over the internet. It provides various service models like IaaS, PaaS, and SaaS, enabling flexible and accessible data management without physical hardware investments.

Introducing Hadoop

Hadoop is an open-source framework with two main components: HDFS for storage and MapReduce for data processing. Its distributed architecture ensures fault tolerance, scalability, and parallel processing capabilities, making it ideal for big data applications.

BENEFITS OF CLOUD-BASED HADOOP

Scalability

The combination of cloud computing and Hadoop allows seamless resource scaling to accommodate growing data volumes efficiently.

Cost-Effectiveness

Cloud migration reduces upfront investments and ongoing maintenance costs, while the pay-as-you-go model optimizes spending based on resource usage.

Flexibility

Cloud-based Hadoop offers the flexibility to deploy and manage clusters according to specific requirements, facilitating experimentation and customization.

Fault Tolerance

Hadoop's distributed architecture, combined with cloud redundancy, ensures data availability even in the face of hardware failures.

IMPLEMENTING HADOOP IN THE CLOUD

Selecting a Cloud Provider

Careful consideration is essential when choosing a cloud provider that offers Hadoop as a managed service or provides the required infrastructure.

Data Migration and Integration

Migrating data to the cloud requires careful planning and integration techniques to minimize disruptions.

Security and Compliance

Data security measures such as encryption and access controls must be implemented to protect sensitive information.

Monitoring and Management

Continuous monitoring of Hadoop clusters and cloud resources optimizes performance and resource utilization.

USE CASES OF CLOUD-BASED HADOOP

Big Data Analytics

Cloud-based Hadoop enables advanced analytics on vast datasets, leading to data-driven decision-making.

Real-time Data Processing

Cloud-based Hadoop supports real-time processing for IoT applications and streaming data.

Machine Learning

Integrated Hadoop capabilities in cloud platforms facilitate scalable machine learning workflows.

The integration of cloud computing with Hadoop empowers organizations to handle big data with ease. The combination offers scalability, cost-effectiveness, and fault tolerance, allowing businesses to stay competitive and make informed decisions in the data-driven landscape (Joachims, 1998) (Bhargava et al., 1999). Embracing cloud-based Hadoop solutions unlocks new possibilities for data processing and analytics, revolutionizing the way companies approach their data resources.(Bali et al., 2023)

CONCLUSION

This paper discusses different methodologies used for generating recommendations for web applications. It highlights the advantages and disadvantages of each method and emphasizes the need for hybrid approaches for better accuracy. The paper also mentions Hadoop, a distributed cloud computing platform, as a solution for managing large amounts of data in service recommendation systems. However, there is a scope for further research to achieve scalability and efficiency in handling large amounts of services during recommendation. In conclusion, a combination of different recommendation methods and the use of Hadoop can improve the accuracy and scalability of service recommendation systems.

REFERENCES

Adomavicius, G., & Tuzhilin, A. (2005). Toward the next generation of recommender systems: A survey of the state-of-the-art and possible extensions. *IEEE Transactions on Knowledge and Data Engineering*, *17*(6), 734–749. DOI: 10.1109/TKDE.2005.99

Ameen, A. (2019). Knowledge based Recommendation System in Semantic Web - A Survey. *International Journal of Computer Applications*, *182*(43), 20–25. DOI: 10.5120/ijca2019918538

Bali, N., Singh, K., & Dhawan, S. (2023). A Survey and Comparative Analysis of Relevant Approaches of Recommendation System. *2023 6th International Conference on Contemporary Computing and Informatics (IC3I)*, 750–755. https://doi.org/DOI: 10.1109/IC3I59117.2023.10397781

Beel, J., Gipp, B., Langer, S., & Breitinger, C. (2016). Research-paper recommender systems: A literature survey. *International Journal on Digital Libraries*, *17*(4), 305–338. DOI: 10.1007/s00799-015-0156-0

Bhargava, H. K., Sridhar, S., & Herrick, C. (1999). Beyond spreadsheets: Tools for building decision support systems. *Computer*, *32*(3), 31–39. DOI: 10.1109/2.751326

Bhogan, S., Naik, S., Gaonkar, S., Prabhudesai, S., Dhond, G., & Fernandes, K. (2024). Survey on Recommendation System Combining Hybrid and Popularity Based Approach. *2024 2nd International Conference on Intelligent Data Communication Technologies and Internet of Things (IDCIoT)*, 1573–1578. https://doi.org/DOI: 10.1109/IDCIoT59759.2024.10467802

Bobadilla, J., Ortega, F., Hernando, A., & Gutiérrez, A. (2013). Recommender systems survey. *Knowledge-Based Systems*, *46*, 109–132. DOI: 10.1016/j.knosys.2013.03.012

Burke, R. (2002). Hybrid Recommender Systems: Survey and Experiments. *User Modeling and User-Adapted Interaction*, *12*(4), 331–370. DOI: 10.1023/A:1021240730564

Das, D., Sahoo, L., & Datta, S. (2017). A Survey on Recommendation System. *International Journal of Computer Applications*, *160*(7), 6–10. DOI: 10.5120/ijca2017913081

Deo, A., Jaisinghani, R., Gupta, S., Khan, S. S., Soni, A., & Gehlot, K. (2023). Stratified Advance Personalized Recommendation System Based on Deep Learning. *Ingénierie Des Systèmes d Information*, *28*(1), 189–196. DOI: 10.18280/isi.280121

Gong, S. (2010). A Collaborative Filtering Recommendation Algorithm Based on User Clustering and Item Clustering. *Journal of Software*, *5*(7). Advance online publication. DOI: 10.4304/jsw.5.7.745-752

Hossain, M., Das, S., Krishnamurthy, B., & Shiva, S. G. (2023). Explainability of Artificial Intelligence Systems: A Survey. *2023 International Symposium on Networks, Computers and Communications (ISNCC)*, 1–6. https://doi.org/DOI: 10.1109/ISNCC58260.2023.10323642

Joachims, T. (1998). *Text categorization with Support Vector Machines: Learning with many relevant features* (pp. 137–142). https://doi.org/DOI: 10.1007/BFb0026683

Lin, K., Yang, S., & Na, S.-G. (2022). Collaborative Filtering Algorithm-Based Destination Recommendation and Marketing Model for Tourism Scenic Spots. *Computational Intelligence and Neuroscience*, *2022*, 1–7. DOI: 10.1155/2022/7115627 PMID: 35528326

Lin, Y., Liu, Y., Lin, F., Zou, L., Wu, P., Zeng, W., Chen, H., & Miao, C. (2024). A Survey on Reinforcement Learning for Recommender Systems. *IEEE Transactions on Neural Networks and Learning Systems*, *35*(10), 13164–13184. DOI: 10.1109/TNNLS.2023.3280161 PMID: 37279123

Stalidis, G., Karaveli, I., Diamantaras, K., Delianidi, M., Christantonis, K., Tektonidis, D., Katsalis, A., & Salampasis, M. (2023). Recommendation Systems for e-Shopping: Review of Techniques for Retail and Sustainable Marketing. *Sustainability*, *15*(23), 16151. DOI: 10.3390/su152316151

Sun, Z., Xu, Y., Liu, Y., He, W., Kong, L., Wu, F., Jiang, Y., & Cui, L. (2025). A Survey on Federated Recommendation Systems. *IEEE Transactions on Neural Networks and Learning Systems*, *36*(1), 6–20. DOI: 10.1109/TNNLS.2024.3354924 PMID: 38324430

Thorat, B., P., M. Goudar, R., & Barve, S. (2015). Survey on Collaborative Filtering, Content-based Filtering and Hybrid Recommendation System. *International Journal of Computer Applications*, *110*(4), 31–36. DOI: 10.5120/19308-0760

Verma, J. P., Patel, B., & Patel, A. (2015). Big Data Analysis: Recommendation System with Hadoop Framework. *2015 IEEE International Conference on Computational Intelligence & Communication Technology*.

Zhao, Z.-D., & Shang, M.-S. (2010). User-Based Collaborative-Filtering Recommendation Algorithms on Hadoop. *2010 Third International Conference on Knowledge Discovery and Data Mining*, 478–481. https://doi.org/DOI: 10.1109/WKDD.2010.54

Chapter 6
Intelligent Code Analysis and Feedback Generation:
A New Paradigm in Programming Education

R. N. Ravikumar
https://orcid.org/0009-0009-3705-1681
Marwadi University, Rajkot, India

S. Aarthi
https://orcid.org/0009-0006-9064-2091
Marwadi University, Rajkot, India

Pappu Kumar Rai
Marwadi University, Rajkot, India

Zokir Mamadiyarov
Termez University of Economics and Service, Termez, Uzbekistan

ABSTRACT

As digital literacy grows vital in today's job market, programming education faces challenges due to its abstract nature, syntax sensitivity, and high error-proneness. This chapter explores how Artificial Intelligence (AI) can enhance programming education by detecting common coding errors, offering instant, personalized feedback, and supporting adaptive learning paths. Leveraging machine learning, NLP, and code analysis, Intelligent Tutoring Systems (ITS) help students grasp complex coding concepts by analyzing code patterns, syntax trees, and embeddings across

DOI: 10.4018/979-8-3373-0598-1.ch006

languages like Python and Java. The chapter presents case studies using hybrid ML and rule-based feedback engines, reducing instructor workload and boosting student outcomes. It also discusses challenges like model transparency, unseen errors, and over-reliance. Future directions include LLMs for code explanation and federated learning for secure, scalable error prediction. This chapter offers practical insights for educators to build more effective, engaging, and supportive programming classrooms.

INTRODUCTION

Programming during the digital age is a basic skill and even the difficult one, still, according to its results. The cognitive barrier caused by the abstractness of programming, lack of a free style, lack of simplicity in debugging, and in general has mostly led to dropout and frustration. Standard instructional practice has been found to be incapable of meeting the needs of individual students especially those in a huge or on-line courses as they have potential to give specific and instantaneous feedback (Kotsiantis et al., 2024). Artificial Intelligence (AI) offers a life-altering chance to re-imagine how programming should be taught because it allows individual assistance, and active feedback due to automation systems.

The chapter discusses the possibilities of the AI to completely transform the process of learning by detecting the most common programming bugs and offering immediate, situation-based help. Through the use of machine learning, natural language processing, and exploitation of code analysis, AI systems can identify errors committed by students; syntax and semantic errors; and provide them with real-time, FIT revision. These computerized forms of intelligent tutoring systems do more than merely reproduce the appearance of human instruction; they also facilitate instruction by lessening the overhead costs of instruction such that the educator can work more on the higher form of teaching (Li & Wong, 2023). This chapter, which is supported by case studies and practical implementations, will provide educators, software developers and curriculum designers with some ideas on how to incorporate AI in curriculum design to teach programming in a more holistic, engaging way that clearly addresses some of the common pitfalls in Python and Java.

The Challenge of Learning Programming

Coding is a very challenging task to the novices due to a need to think abstractly, solve problems and is time sensitive. PD is more conceptual and requires sound logical thinking in contrast to memorization-driven subjects. The high learning curve is due to syntax sensitivity, unfamiliarity to computational thinking and obscure error messages. After facing failure severally, students lack motivation without knowing their mistakes. Conventional classrooms and tutorials that are not built into a system, do not offer any instant and custom responses, and thus make it difficult to reduce knowledge gaps, particularly in online and mass society learning. Having a limited experience of practical exposure and a large variety of languages, unhelpful error messages also inhibit learning (Altadmri & Brown, 2015). A proper teaching should be adaptive to the needs of the student and usually traditional methods are not adaptive.

Role of AI in Transforming Programming Education

Artificial Intelligence (AI) is revolutionizing the education related to programming, enhancing the level of interactivity, personalization as well as real-time feedback. With methodologies such as machine learning, Natural Language Processing (NLP), and Abstract Syntax Tree (AST) parsing, AI has the potential to analyze the student code dynamically in order to identify syntax and logic errors in addition to semantic ones. The AI-based tool Intelligent Tutoring Systems (ITS) are customizable to learning pace, recording progress, and providing hints in the specific context, most closely mirroring human tutor assistance. This is made unique because it improves knowledge and retention particularly among new programmers (Chang et al., 2022). Also, AI saves the instructors a lot of work and automates error detection and performance analysis. Without the personalised guidance of mentor to mentee as is the case in large-scale or online programs, AI guarantees scalable, immediate, and inclusive feedback. Figure 1 highlights four key roles of AI in programming education error correction, instant feedback, personalized curricula, and student engagement. It demonstrates how AI enhances both instructional delivery and learner experience through automation, adaptation, and interactivity.

Figure 1. Role of AI in transforming programming education

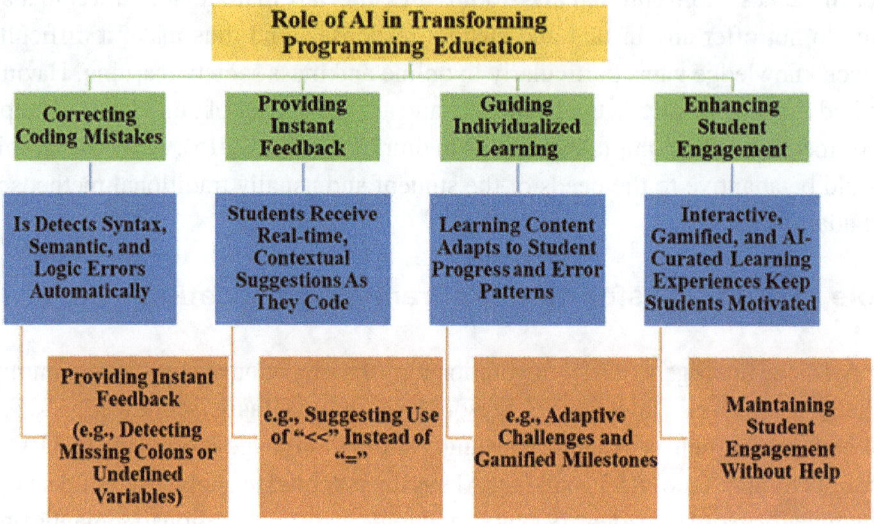

Chapter Objectives and Relevance to Instructional Strategies

This chapter will discuss the role of AI in programming education by identifying errors in codes, offering real-time feedback, and helping in individual learning by use of the intelligent tutoring systems. It helps students to read code and to debug that code by deploying machine learning, natural language processing and analysing the code. Its contents resonate with contemporary teaching practices based on adaptive learning and feedback-timely learning, and scalable teaching regimens, making programming more accessible, interesting and effective to various learners.

Objectives

- To identify and categorize common programming errors (syntax, logic, semantic, runtime, etc.) faced by students.
- To explore AI techniques such as Machine Learning, NLP, and code analysis for detecting and correcting these errors.
- To present the design and implementation of an AI-powered Intelligent Tutoring System (ITS) for programming education.
- To demonstrate real-time feedback mechanisms that guide students through code debugging and learning.

- To evaluate the effectiveness of AI-based systems through case studies and classroom deployment.
- To address challenges, ethics, and best practices in AI-driven coding education, and explore future trends with LLMs and federated learning.

Relevance to Instructional Strategies

The chapter is directly consistent with the requirements of the contemporary instruction strategies focusing on adaptive learning, feedback in real time, and student-centered teaching approach. The methods of teaching targeted at developing simple skills of the learners do not meet the different speed and levels of programmer understanding. Artificial intelligence-based teaching is a scalable solution because it constantly receives the inputs of the learner, and then adapts to them (Kimmel et al., 2024). With integration of AI into the learning environment, they can provide each student with personalized advice without having to manually intervene but on each student separately. It is compatible with the formative assessment, encourages mastering learning, and supports the development of the growth mindset since students can learn about their mistakes in real-time. In addition, it supports differentiated instruction during classroom and online sessions, which support diverse abilities and leaning styles. This is appropriate to constructivist teaching models and makes competency-based education sustainable since the two elements enforce the concepts through repeated feedback and coaching. The fact that the AI is incorporated does not only supplement human teaching but also improves its range and makes programming education more diverse, efficient, and exciting.

UNDERSTANDING COMMON PROGRAMMING ERRORS

The chance of programming errors is inevitable especially among the beginners who are learning the syntaxes and the way to code just like language. Such errors may be classified as syntax errors (a violation of the rules of language, the absence of semicolons or parentheses), logic errors (incorrect reasoning that leads to the fact that a wrong result is obtained, though the code that is executed is correct), semantic errors (the use of language constructs is incorrect), runtime errors (a crash during execution, such as division by zero or references of null), and type errors (incompatible operations with data types). The categorization of mistakes under these groups assists instructors and AI with a better focus and definition of errors. Different language programming also has different errors as what can be true in Python is not true in Java. Analyzing real-life submissions of code and repositories such as GitHub, Stack Overflow and learning sites such as those run by Code.org,

Kaggle it is possible to see patterns of frequent errors (Michaeli & Romeike, 2020). This understanding is vital to devising AI video to be able to automatically detect, identify and respond to errors in a situation that generates contextualized, actionable feedback. The below Table 1 lists and defines typical programming errors (syntax, logic, semantic, runtime, type) with examples for each.

Table 1. Common programming errors by category

Error Category	Description	Example Code Snippet	Explanation
Syntax Error	Violation of programming language rules or structure.	if x = 5:	Assignment used instead of comparison (==), causing a syntax error.
Logic Error	Code runs but produces incorrect results due to flawed logic.	area = length + width	Addition used instead of multiplication in area calculation.
Semantic Error	Code is syntactically correct but does not behave as intended.	list = [1, 2, 3]; print(list(0))	Using a variable name that shadows a built-in function.
Runtime Error	Errors that occur during code execution, often due to invalid operations.	print(10 / 0)	Division by zero causes a runtime exception.
Type Error	Operation performed on incompatible data types.	len(5)	len() cannot be applied to an integer.

Syntax, Logic, and Semantic Errors

Classical and common programming errors can be specified under syntax, logic and semantic errors. Syntax errors are the violations of the language rules and the breakdown of the code compilation or execution. Logic errors are when the code is running and giving wrong results as the reasoning is fudged. They are called semantic errors; such errors have a correct syntax and use but incorrect use of functions or operators thus are difficult to show and differentiate considerably difficult to a new programmer.

Syntax Errors

Syntax errors arise when code breaks one or more of the grammatical rules of an exact language so that the code cannot be compiled or run. The interpreter or compiler usually identifies such errors on the spot and often with a message on the location and type of the error. Such newcomers are most likely to make syntax errors since they might forget about the use of punctuation, keywords, or wrong indentation (Wang, 2021). By way of example, to raise a syntax error in Python, one might enter instead of omitting the equals sign: In the same fashion, missing a colon such as in case of I in range (5) or forgetting a parenthesis such as in print ("Hello" will cause syntax errors. They are not always easy to correct, but such errors may be frustrating when they are discovered. Systems based on AI are ready to help learners to identify the errors in syntax in real-time and give explanations or guidelines, minimizing any downtime and strengthening the knowledge of correct language usage.

Logic Errors

Logic error translates to cases where the code executes and does not crash yet algorithmic properties such as the results that should have been achieved are faulty. Compilers or even interpreters cannot detect these errors and this makes them difficult to debug. In contrast to syntax errors, logic errors come about due to incorrect programming of the logic behind the program including the wrong condition in a loop, wrong equation, and incorrect placement of the calls to functions (Kucharska et al., 2022). As an example, a student who wishes to compute the average of two numbers would enter something like average = num 1+num 2/ 2, which only divides num 2 by 2 and then adds num 1, instead of dividing num 2 by 2 and then adding num 1 and num 2. An alternative example is an invalid score, coming in the form of if score > 100 and score < 0:, where the range situation makes no sense. AI programs that can analyze the behavior of programs and report inconsistencies between expected outputs and actual outputs can be used to identify program logic errors and even recommended place to fix them, rather than superficial. understanding.

Semantic Errors

Semantic errors Some program errors are semantic errors which means that the program has got the syntax correct but does not behave or mean what the programmer had intended. Such errors occur when the correct statements are used, but the results they have in the cases are not the ones expected, in particular cases because of the use and misinterpretation of language constructions, types of data, or the behavior of certain functions. Such errors are sometimes hard to identify, especially without carefully studying the programme output, because the code can compile and execute successfully (Meilong et al., 2020). As an example, when someone wants to compare two strings in a programming language, comparing two strings using and not equality operator (if str1 is str2:), then it might want to yield the error results because of identity verses equality comparison. The other example is when a parameter in a function is in the incorrect order such as calculate_area(height,width) whereas it should be calculate_area(width,height). Even though both the inputs are accepted, the outcome is not logical. AI systems are able to help recognize such problems by studying the typical patterns of semantic misuse and provide prescriptions to fix it.

Error Types by Language (Python, Java, etc.)

Every programming language implements its syntax language rules, error handling mechanisms, and type systems and thus results in language-specific errors in every programming language. As an example, dynamically typed languages such as Python can detect type related errors at run-time whereas statically typed languages such as java detect it during compile-time. The awareness of the differences in the ways errors are displayed in different languages assists in designing language-sensitive AI systems that would be able to provide feedback on a differentiated level.

Python Error Types and Challenges

Python is an interpreted language which is also a high-level and dynamic language that most of the errors are recognized during run-time and not during compilation. It is easy to learn since it is easy however, it has many typical mistakes (Rahman et al., 2020a). Common syntax mistakes are missing colons (or `:` indentation e.g. `for i in range(3) print(i)`), and using assignment incorrectly (`= 5:` instead of `== 5:`). Also present are the run time errors including `TypeError` by `len(5)`. Semantics or subtleties of logic may be mutable default parameters (e.g. use of `def func(data=[])`) or overriding functions with a built-in name like `list` or `sum`. To give proper and opportune feedback, AI-based tutoring systems have to identify these patterns.

Java Error Types and Learning Challenges

There are three categories of java programming errors, they are syntax error, runtime error and logic errors. Syntax errors: Those are any mistakes in the code, reason being that it does not conform to the standards of the Java, and are the most likely to be detected during the compilation time, i. e. they include the absence of a semicolon, unpaired braces, and wrong variable declaration (Rahman et al., 2020b). Execution errors occur at runtime the most obvious ones are division by zero, null pointers, and array out-of-bounds, and usually terminate a program. Logic bugs are the most difficult to check because they do not provide any error message but they can be caused by the incorrect structure of the program or used algorithms. New players usually have trouble locating these mistakes. Most efficient tutoring systems should be aimed at identifying types of errors and should encourage an experience-based learning situationally.

Open Datasets and Empirical Studies on Coding Mistakes

Research In computer science education is increasing in the use of open datasets and empirical work to learn about typical programming errors and make better error detectors as well (Rahman et al., 2021). The data obtained on online coding websites, study tools, and questions and answers websites provide an invaluable contribution in terms of knowing the behavior of learners, which questions are the most common, and what types of difficulties most people face.

Popular Datasets

- **Code.org and Carnegie Mellon's CS1 datasets**, which log student attempts, error types, and time-to-correct metrics.
- **GitHub repositories**, used to analyze coding patterns, pull request revisions, and bug fixes over time.
- **Stack Overflow**, a rich source for understanding developer confusion and commonly misunderstood programming concepts.
- **Kaggle competitions and Jupyter notebook repositories**, which provide real-world code with annotation and version history.

Empirical research indicates that the beginner programmers tend to commit identical syntax and semantic errors. These patterns are used by training machine learning models to recommend, predict, classify, and fix student mistakes. Such techniques as decision trees, LSTMs and attention-based models have been utilized to develop intelligent feedback systems. This empirical intuition increases the precision and flexibility of AI-based tutoring aids towards coding learning.

Empirical Use Case: Intelligent Feedback from the CS1 Programming Dataset

At Carnegie Mellon University, scholars employed the CS1 dataset, comprising thousands of student submission of code with timestamps and errors annotations of a course of introductory programming. They developed a Long Short-Term Memory (LSTM) based neural network to perform this task by being trained to work on sequences of the code submission and predict likely student error on a code change based on its previous submission tries. The model could find out probable future mistakes and make real-time context-sensitive hints. When the AI-based feedback was embedded in an intelligent tutoring system, it made students rectify errors sooner and prevented frequent mistakes (K. Wang et al., 2017). General use of the system by students resulted in a 21% increase in the rate of task completion by students given traditional and the system-provided feedback alone. This shows how it is possible that programming education can be increasingly advanced through empirical information and machine learning with timely and personalized feedback.

AI TECHNIQUES FOR ERROR DETECTION

The Artificial Intelligence (AI) is important in solving or identifying mistakes made in programming by analyzing program pattern, structure, and prior programming errors. Such supervised learning models as decision trees, SVMs and neural networks are trained using labeled code submissions to categorize the types of common errors like syntax, logic, and semantic errors. Natural Language Processing (NLP) supports the contextual awareness with the help of comments, variable names, and queries of the students (Ye et al., 2020). Pattern recognition and Token-based models, even further divide code into pieces to scrutinize. Such sophisticated systems as LSTMs or transformers use code sequences to determine possible failures. Such AI methods allow intelligent tutoring systems to provide real-time personalized feedback, responding to a number of different programming languages.

Pattern Recognition and Classification

Pattern recognition and classification are the basic AI tools that recognize and classify mistakes of the program by repeating code patterns. These are approaches in which we discover the pattern of structures, sequences or anomalies of code that are similar to known errors. As an example, when an individual learning to program Python usually forgets to include colons when creating Python loops (for i in range (5)), the system learns that it is a common syntax error. New instances of the same kind of error can then be labeled by classification algorithms (e.g. decision trees, K-Nearest Neighbors (KNN) or naive Bayes) with a high degree of accuracy. Those models use training data, which comprises samples of flawed and fixed code (Johnson et al., 2022). Through such data the AI would be able to judge the type of error and suggest correction based on what it had learnt. For Example: If a student writes if x = 5: instead of if x == 5:, the system recognizes the pattern of assignment used in a conditional statement. It classifies this as a syntax error and suggests using the correct comparison operator (==).

Use of Decision Trees, SVM, and Neural Networks

Error detection in the teaching of programming using AI and Machine Learning usually involves application of very powerful machine learning concepts like Decision Trees, Support Vector Machines (SVMs), and Neural Networks to classify and predict a mistake by each student. Decision trees are also easy-to-use and efficient models that employ a chain of conditional splitting, determining the kind of error in the basis of code characteristics, missing syntax, wrong loops, or mismatched data type. SVMs are also helpful in discriminating overlapping error sets in feature spaces of high dimensionalities, and hence they can be effective in discriminating similar error sets such as those of the logic and semantic errors. Deep learning networks (such as LSTM or CNN) can form intricate representations in patterns in a sequence of code and, thereby, learn patterns that other traditional models do not follow (Litman, 2016). These models evolve through time because they get to see additional annotated code submissions. Through the integrated methods, intelligent systems are able to give desired and specific feedback that can enable students to correct their errors and also learn programming concepts better.

Example of Decision Tree for Error Detection

Decision tree is an effective method of detecting a program fault in form of logic questions. When a program compiled in Java fails, probably there is a syntax error. When it crashes after compiling, most likely, it is a runtime error such as null pointer exception. When running but giving wrong results, then probably a logic error is caused as a result of faulty thinking. This well-organized diagnostic method allows learners and AI tutoring systems to identify the type of errors and give highly-focused feedbacks, and thus ensure debugging is more successful and informative (Niu, 2024). The below decision tree Figure 2 showing nodes like "Is there a missing colon?", "Is the variable declared?", and leaf nodes such as "Syntax Error" or "Logic Error". It Visualize how rule-based paths classify student coding mistakes.

Figure 2. Decision tree for error classification

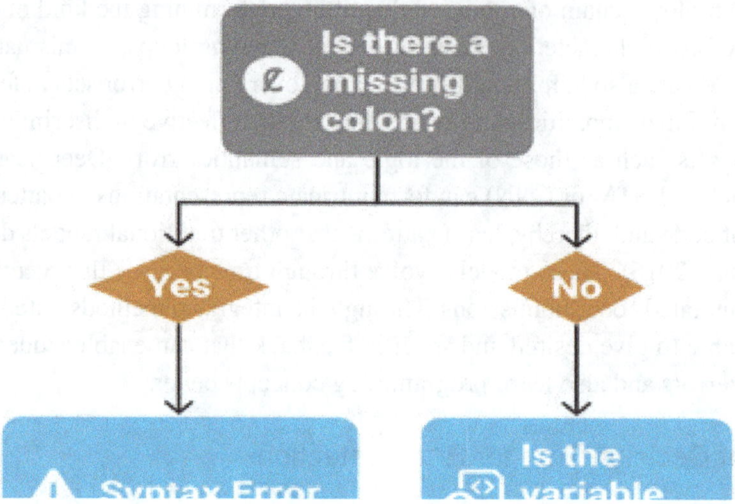

Example of SVM (Support Vector Machine) for Error Classification

Support Vector Machine (SVM) is a classification algorithm to be applied as a supervised learning setup that categorizes programming bugs on the basis of coding structure, message error, token patterns and variable utilization. The SVM is trained on labeled syntax, logic, and other run time errors so it can make predictions about the type of error based upon the position of a new code sample relative to a decision boundary (Pendy, 2023). It enables intelligent tutoring systems to identify and classify errors in an automatic fashion, providing feedback. SVM-based systems are very timely as they tend to reduce the need of manual intercession leading to improvements in the programming ability and speed of learning by the students. The below Figure 3 2D scatter plot with orange and blue dots representing two error classes (e.g., logic vs. semantic errors), separated by a clear margin and hyperplane. It Demonstrates how SVM classifies coding errors using feature boundaries.

Figure 3. Support vector machine for error type separation

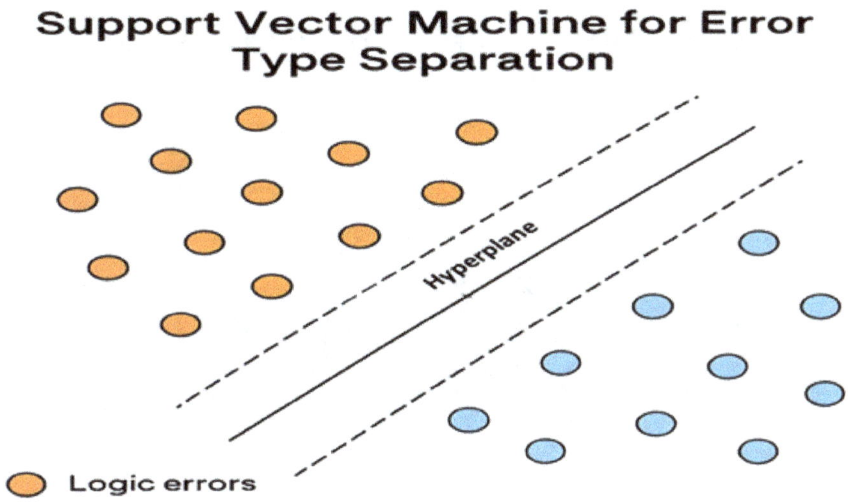

Example of Neural Networks for Error Detection

Neural networks and in particular deep learning models provide strong promise to pick up on sophisticated programming bugs by training patterns on large volumes of annotated code. Neural network may be trained using the corpus of student submissions with each item labelled with the error type it contains, e.g. syntax, run time, or logic error. Its input features can be tokenized source code, Abstract Syntax Trees (ASTs), or error messages, or semantic representations. The model will spin out to recognising subtle relationships and patterns that will reflect different error types, even in variations of their coded types. As an example, a Recurrent Neural Network (RNN) or transformer-based model could accept sequence of code and identify context dependent logic errors (Shaik et al., 2022). After the network has been trained it can be used to review newly submitted code and automatically raise the likelihood of errors, providing near real-time feedback. Neural networks are therefore essential components of the AI tutoring solution, enhancing prediction of the errors, as well as facilitating personalized learning at large scale. The below Figure 4 showing input nodes (e.g., tokens, AST features), hidden layers, and output error categories. Include labelled paths like "if...then...else pattern". It Illustrates how neural networks learn patterns in code sequences to predict error types. The below Table 2 Compares Decision Trees, SVMs, and Neural Networks based on input type, output, accuracy, and learning capability.

Figure 4. Neural network for contextual error prediction

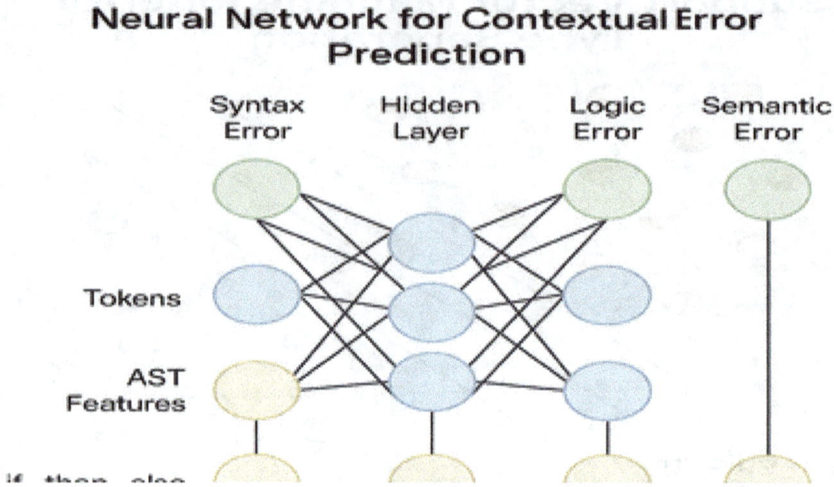

Table 2. AI models used for error detection

AI Model	Input Type	Output	Accuracy	Learning Capability
Decision Tree	Tokenized code features, error labels	Categorical error classification	Moderate (75–85%)	Learns clear decision paths; interpretable; low complexity
SVM (Support Vector Machine)	High-dimensional feature vectors	Binary or multi-class classification	High (85–90%)	Effective in separating complex error classes with small datasets
Neural Network (e.g., LSTM)	Token sequences, AST embeddings	Multi-class error prediction	Very High (90–95%)	Learns from sequential context; handles complex and subtle error patterns

Code Tokenization and Abstract Syntax Trees (AST)

AI-based tools cannot operate without tokenization or Abstract Syntax Trees (ASTs) to study and understand code. Tokenization transforms code into parts such as keywords, operators and identifiers that can be used to identify syntax patterns and errors. As an example, `for i in range(5):` is tokenised into such parts as `for`, `i` and so on. ASTs also parse the code and descendant it into a tree representation of the logical flow of the code with loop nodes, expression nodes, and function node (Alvarez et al., 2024). This allows the AI systems to know how the code is structured and in what order it should be executed, this can help with increasing the detection of logic and semantic mistakes, and increase automated feedback and learning support.

BUILDING AN INTELLIGENT FEEDBACK SYSTEM

A learning system An Intelligent Feedback System to assist with programming teaching scenarios should automatically identify the mistakes in the code submitted by the students and automatically give them personalized feedback in a timely manner. These types of systems are generally composed of three main parts which are the code analysis, error classification and feedback generation. The code that we submit is first tokenized and then ready into an Abstract Syntax Tree (AST) to look at the structure of the code. Then such AI models as, for example, decision trees, neural networks, or LSTMs, compare the patterns of the code to other known signatures of errors on training sets (Borchers et al., 2024). When an error is identified and even categorized (e.g. syntax, logic or semantic), our system offers actionable feedback, in the form of specific text, through Natural Language Processing (NLP). Such as in case where the student misses a colon in a loop, the system can tell where the missing colon is and suggest: You may have lost a colon (:) at the end of your loop header. Such systems not only cut teaching load on an instructor but also enable the learner to gain confidence and speed in solving the problem and coding skills due to the prompt and personal instructions he or she receives. Figure 5 illustrates the sequential process of building an AI-based feedback system for programming education. It highlights how student code is processed through an intelligent tutoring tool to generate personalized feedback delivered directly to the learner.

Figure 5. Architecture of an intelligent feedback system

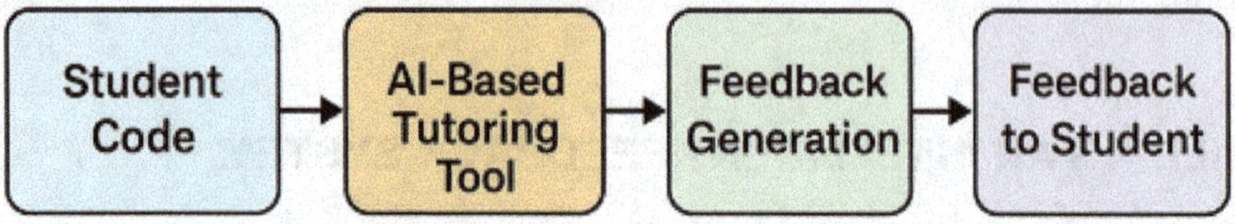

Architecture of an AI-Based Tutoring Tool

A system based on AI tutor to be used in learning programming usually adheres to modular pattern that includes input processing and code analysis, error identification and feedback provision. A student submits code and the code is first run through a tokenizer and parser, which produces structured representations of the code (in the form of token order and Abstract Syntax Trees (ASTs)). These representations are followed by machine learning models - e.g. a decision tree, SVM or neural network to classify the code and identify potential patterns of errors. The tool has a knowledge database that contains common programming errors, submissions of the past that were submitted, and their fixes (Chang et al., 2022). When the system identifies a problem, it applies a feedback engine that works along with Natural Language Processing (NLP) to issue context-specific advice. This feedback is then provided by a user interface (optionally with visual hints or auto-correction). The architecture frequently facilitates real-time analytics, student profiling, and dashboard functionality to instructors, so as to allow adaptive learning and on-going enhancement of individual and collective programming skills. Figure 6 illustrates the core components of an AI-based tutoring system, showing how code flows from student input to intelligent analysis and personalized feedback generation. It highlights how various AI modules interact to create a seamless and adaptive learning experience.

Figure 6. System architecture of an AI-based tutoring tool

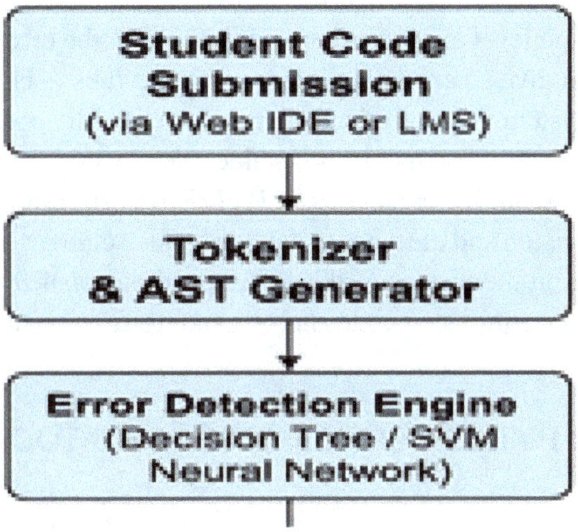

Real-Time Code Analysis and Feedback Generation

One of the most important elements of AI-based tutoring systems is real-time code analysis since it allows recognizing and correcting programming errors in real-time. Code is analysed incrementally by the system on the fly (as students type or post code) by tokenization, parsing and simulation of dynamic execution (Kessler et al., 2019). The examples of the machine to learn models or rule-based engines analyze patterns in the code to reveal such errors as a lack of syntax, type incompatibles, or wrong control paths. When a problem emerges, feedback generation module will match the error with some response in pre-trained models, or a structured feedback database. As an example, in case of a ZeroDivisionError being identified, the system could possibly recommend to verify a divisor before dividing. Instead of waiting to complete a block, real-time feedback enables the students to instantly fix their code during learning and avoid repeating the same error. Further, the continual code analysis enables auto-grading, indication of hints, and tracking of performance so that they can be well adapted to self-learning as well as classroom learning.

Natural Language Processing for Hint Generation

One area in which NLP is important is in the production of context sensitive, human readable hints in intelligent tutoring systems. In case the mistake was detected in the code, NLP allows implementing the technical diagnostics through the translations that will help students, including beginners, to understand them. These come in interpreting the error, structuring sentences and aligning intents depending on the sophistication level of the learner and the kind of the erroneous error (Ni & Cheung, 2023). To give an example, in case a student fails to change a variable to a new value, the system might produce a prompt such as: It appears you are trying to use a variable without assigning it a value. Try to initialize it." Particularly, transformer-based architectures (such as BERT or T5) can be trained on learning data to enhance the precision and the tenor of feedback. Such clues can be made dynamic as well depending on the history of the student and personalize it. NLP therefore fills the gap between automated code analysis and useful human-like teaching aid.

CASE STUDY: PYTHON ERROR DIAGNOSIS TOOL

This case study features Python-syndicated intelligent device that allows programming errors to be submitted by the student and providing diagnosis of the common errors and feedback. The tool has a hybrid engine, which entails a rule-based reasoning and a machine learning based model trained on the thousands of annotated code submissions of students. When the code is posted, it will go through the tokenization process, create an Abstract Syntax Tree (AST) and see whether there are well-known patterns of error. It recognises five broad categories of errors namely syntax, logic, runtime, type and semantic errors. An example is that when a user types or writes x = 5: instead of x == 5: it is identified as a syntax mistake and it is auto-corrected. The lightweight NLG module is used to feedback data in a format suitable to beginners understanding. The tool was used in both online and classroom-based courses with better accuracy of the coded file and correcting time (Pantelimon et al., 2021). It also offered analytics to the instructors about the trends of performance of the students and the common problems in the code.

Dataset and Model Training

The usefulness of the Python Error Diagnosis Tool is dependent on the quantity and quality of the data as well as stability of the model development procedure. The data set created by the present case study has been assembled by merging several sources, such as pieces of the code submitted by students on online-learning services (e.g., Code.org, Repl.it), publicly accessible repositories (e.g., GitHub), and educational datasets (e.g., CMU CS1 error corpus). The error is also run through supervised learning methods as each of the code snippets in the dataset was marked with the kind of mistake and where exactly it is introduced in the code and with the corresponding correct variant of it. Data preprocessing includes the tokenization, syntax analysis and conversion in Abstract Syntax Trees (ASTs). These visualizations can be subsequently employed to draw features such as token frequency, nesting depth, types of operation and patterns of control structures (Slade et al., 2024). To enable the system to learn such elements as structural and sequential patterns in erroneous code, a multi-class classification model that was trained through a combination of Decision Trees and LSTM neural networks was applied.

Example

Consider a student's incorrect Python function where the area of a rectangle is calculated using addition instead of multiplication. The function calc_area (length, width) returns length + width, which is a logic error the correct operation should be length * width. The AI model, trained on similar examples, learned to associate function names like "area" with the mathematical concept of multiplication. It also identified the presence of the + operator in this context as a potential logical inconsistency (Slade et al., 2025). To ensure robust learning, cross-validation was used during training to avoid overfitting, and hyperparameters were optimized for best performance. The model achieved over 87% accuracy in classifying error types on a test set. When enhanced with rule-based checks, its performance improved further, demonstrating the strength of combining data-driven learning with domain-specific heuristics for accurate and meaningful error detection in programming education.

Categories of Feedback and Performance Metrics

There are two types of feedback available in The Python Error Diagnosis Tool, which are descriptive and prescriptive. Descriptive feedback describes the type, the line where an error occurred, and the error causing condition-for instance, that a colon is missing in `for i in range (5)`. Prescriptive feedback proposes something to be done about it by telling the student to include a colon in the text, by strengthening good coding practices. The tool performed at an 87% accuracy in the classification of error, syntax and type errors having the most precision. Feed-back occurred in less than 1.2 seconds, which made it to be in real time. A pilot study indicated a decrease of 25% in the number of repeated errors and a saving of 20% of the time, a greater rate of learning. Figure 7 below demonstrates the types of feedback and measures of the performance and Table 3 Illustrates types of feedback (descriptive vs. prescriptive) with examples and their pedagogical purpose.

Figure 7. AI tutoring feedback system

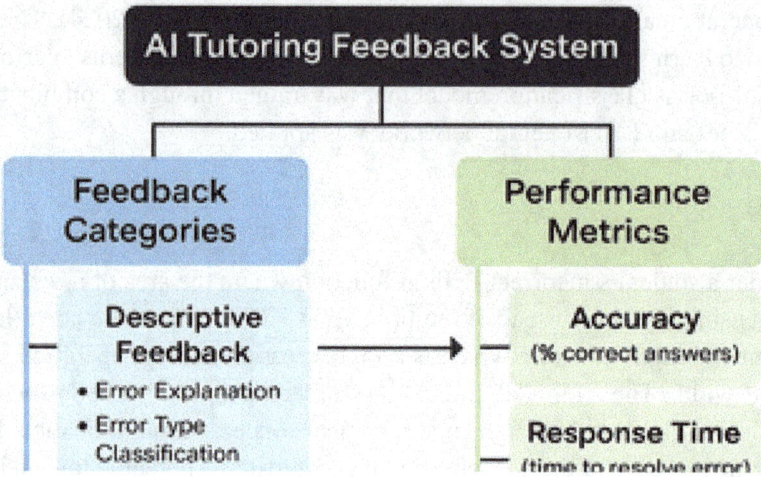

Table 3. Feedback categories and examples

Feedback Type	Description	Example	Pedagogical Purpose
Descriptive Feedback	Explains the error type and location without giving the fix	"Syntax Error: Missing colon at the end of the for-loop statement."	Helps students recognize and understand the nature of the error
Prescriptive Feedback	Offers correction suggestions or guided hints	"Try adding a colon: for i in range(5):"	Encourages correction through guided support and scaffolded learning

Figure 8. Student error reduction before and after tool usage

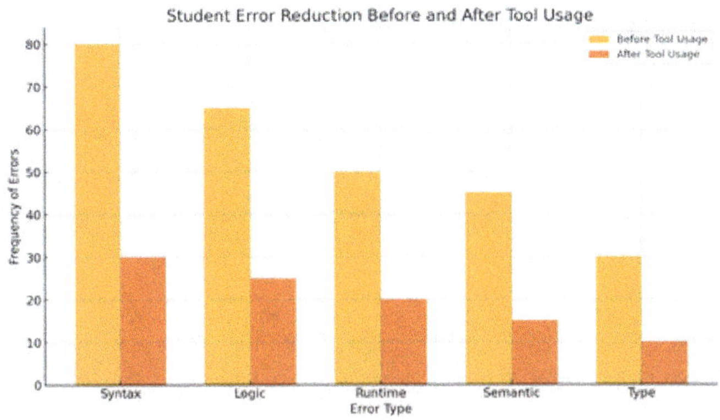

Figure 8 compares the frequency of key error types (syntax, logic, runtime, etc.) in student submissions before and after using the AI-based tutoring tool. It visually demonstrates the tool's effectiveness in reducing common coding mistakes over time.

Classroom Deployment and Outcomes

In learning programming code Python, an educational Python Error Diagnosis Tool was incorporated into the first semester of a course in introductory programming to test the model on its effects on student achievement. The tool was one component within the institution LMS integrated with a coding environment capable of instantly giving feedback about Python code submissions based on AI judgments (Tang, 2024). Those attending face-to-face classes as well as online students worked with the system that identified the mistakes and provided instant recommendations. Instructors could access a dashboard outlining individual and group-level trend patterns of errors thereby facilitating specific teaching. The tool positively affected student activity with more than 5,000 inputs and 12,000 feedback interlocutions. Survey findings indicated that eight out of ten students believed that it assisted them to comprehend their mistakes, whereas three-quarters had improved problem-solving abilities. The students felt steadier and more effective in debugging and were not spending their time wasting on common mistakes. Teachers enjoyed less paper work, and had time to concentrate on the theoretical instructions. In summary, the tool had been versatile and useful as it increased the individual learning outcomes and scale of efficiency in the instruction process as well. Figure 9 tracks the average code submission accuracy of students across multiple weeks of using the AI-based tool. It highlights learning progression and effectiveness of continuous AI-guided feedback during the deployment phase.

Figure 9. Improvement in student accuracy over time

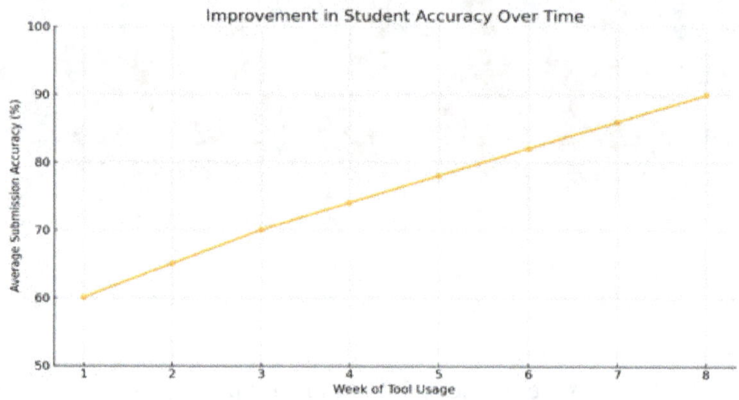

INTEGRATION INTO EDUCATIONAL PLATFORMS

A considerable improvement of programming education is achieved through the integration of intelligent error diagnosis means into Learning Management Systems (LMS) and on-line coding platforms. These tools will allow giving a real-time, individualized feedback devoid of interfering with the learning processes undertaken by the student so that the learner will be able to detect the error and correct themselves. Teachers will be able to follow progress between students, monitor performance patterns, and aid formative assessment as well as competency-based learning. It delivers a smooth access, compatibility of platforms, safe data, and technical overhead (P. Wang, 2021). In a virtual, blended, or traditional classroom setting, the use of this AI-powered strategy enables the switch from passive learning to active and adaptable learning. It enables more interactive, responsive learning, that is adaptive to individual needs of students, or make education inquiry-based programming.

Embedding into LMS and Coding Platforms

Incorporating an AI tutoring system inside Learning Management Systems (LMS) and clouds-based coding systems would provide a concentrated and intuitive platform to teach programming. Integration with such platforms as Moodle, Canvas, or Google Classroom is also possible, so the students can write code in their assignments and get feedback immediately without having to use different tools. In the same way, online IDEs, including Replit, Jupyter Notebooks, or custom editors, are supported, and codes can be evaluated and receive feedback, in real-time, when practicing. This smoothness makes the learning process much easier due to fewer cognitive demands related to switching back and forth between platforms and porous feedback. Due to embedding, it is also possible to have an automatic grade reporting, progress record synching, and alignment of exercises and curricular goals (Wei, 2024). By the use of APIs or plug-ins, the AI tool can interact with LMS modules to provide contextual hints and monitor the student engagement. This is a built-in eco system and gentle to the experience of students and instructor that intelligent tutoring, is firmly rooted in the learning infrastructure.

Teacher Dashboards and Learning Analytics

The use of AI programming tools in teacher dashboards offers real-time information on students' capabilities and performance as well as behavior. Such dashboards provide analytics including submission attempts, error frequency, error types and time spent on tasks. This information allows a teacher to understand the agenda of problem areas, such as issues with condition logics, and correct instructional assignments can be made (Xu, 2024). Individual learning trajectories can guide teachers to develop grading, interventions, and individualized guidance. Other dashboards involve predictive analytics to determine the students who are about to fall behind. The change of reactive approach into proactive one in teaching allows teachers to improve the results of their learning actions, adjust their strategies much better, and make classroom atmosphere more personalized and responsive. Figure 10 displays the proportion of each error type (syntax, semantic, logic, type, runtime) detected during a programming course. It helps instructors identify which concepts are most problematic and where to focus additional instruction.

Figure 10. Distribution of error types across student submissions

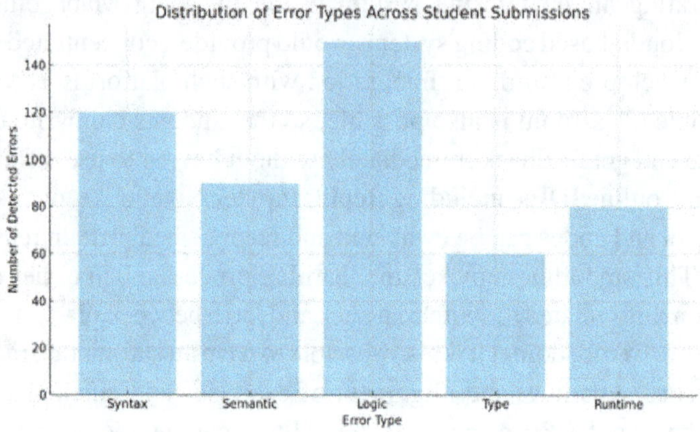

Monitoring Student Progress and Adapting Content

Another vital characteristic of intelligent tutoring systems is that they keep a track of a student and give a customized learning experience. Through analyzing the submitted errors, frequency of errors and the time spent on correcting such errors, the system assembles comprehensive profiles of learners. These profiles assist in customizing the content, i.e. providing additional practice in a topic like loops or recursion when necessary. Elaborate models can either increase the complexity of the exercise, give advice hints, or even offer review content according to the progress of performance at the moment. Such data will allow the instructors to create custom learning plans and intervention plans. Unceasing modification keeps students challenged in an appropriate sense, which improves motivation and comprehension. Figure 11 below shows the decline of the coding error rates depending on the time due to personalized learning.

Figure 11. Adaptive content engagement vs. error rate

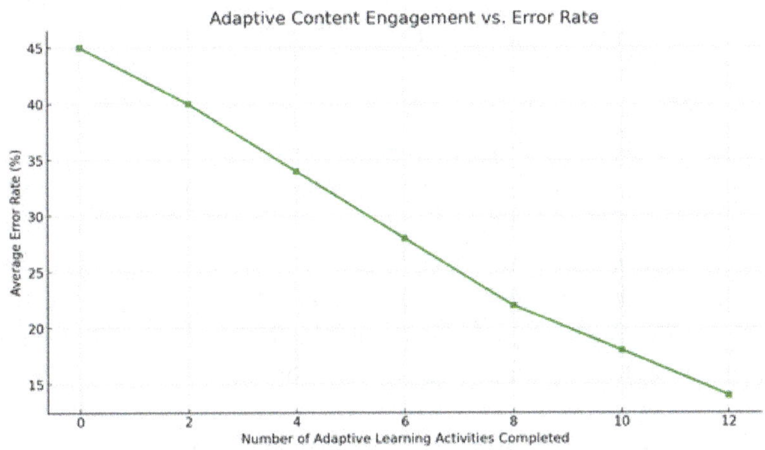

CHALLENGES AND ETHICAL CONSIDERATIONS

Although AI-powered tutoring systems are highly beneficial, they bring several critical challenges and moral issues that should be considered properly. The main issue is to guarantee the validity and solidity of feedback, because misleading proposals can mislead the learners or strengthen misconceptions in them. Besides that, the problems of model transparency, student over-dependence, and data privacy are significant ones that put the question mark on how AI should be used responsibly in education (Abdullah et al., 2021). These computers should never be used to reduce the human teaching aspect; they should instead encourage independence of learning instead of becoming over dependent on automated learning. In addition, note that, due to the volume of student data that these systems handle, such as ways to code and behavioural outcomes, there is need to place tough measures on the protection of this data as well as upholding the privacy laws (Zawacki-Richter et al., 2019). Builders and educators have to collaborate and come with systems that not only make the system efficient but also equitable, explainable, and safe so that their influence on the learning process is positive, ethical, and fair.

False Positives/Negatives and Feedback Accuracy

The most important issues and challenges of AI-based tutoring systems are false positives and false negatives. False positive labels (correct code with incorrect label) alienate the students and diminishes confidence over the tool. False negative does not address real errors as it enables the existence of misconceptions. They can frequently be caused by different coding practices, unclear logic, or a lack of training data. As an example, a strict model might be confused by two distinct correct solutions resulting in one of them being marked as incorrect. The key element of ensuring accuracy is the use of any diverse well-labeled datasets, regular retraining of the models, and rule-based validation layers (Agic et al., 2023). The teacher should check those cases flagged by a human hand. Students need a balanced and effective learning process, and the model is prone to errors which teachers should fix.

Model Transparency and Student Over-Dependence

The greater the level of sophistication of AI tools, the more necessary it is to guarantee model transparency to make sure that students and educators comprehend the decision-making process. When a logic error has been detected in an AI system, students ought to be allowed to trace how and why the error was detected and how the feedback was derived (Yu et al., 2022). This may be challenging when there are black-box models, like deep neural networks. The absence of transparency can decrease the level of trust and restricted educational worth of the feedback. Additionally, it is increasingly noted that the students are becoming over-reliant on AI systems. Learners using automated hints/ corrections too much may end up not learning important skills of debugging and solving problems (Barreto et al., 2021). To reduce this, feedback systems instead ought to be about guidance rather than answers- they get one to think and ween off support as they become more competent. The use of explainable AI (XAI) solutions and implementation of metacognitive suggestions to encourage students to learn the why of the recommendations and to become more autonomous and learn more as a result, instead of correction.

Privacy and Data Sharing Concerns

The implementation of AI-based tutoring systems is highly dependent on privacy concerns since enormous amounts of data about students will be collected and communicated, containing code submissions, behavioural measures, learning patterns. This information, although it is critical in enhancing individualized teaching and learning system precision, has to be used with observance to the laws of data protection including GDPR, FERPA, or local education polices. Without adequate security, there is a threat of misuse of data, unauthorized sharing of the data, or violation (Dogan et al., 2023). Instead of data anonymization, safe storage and consent policies, educational institutions and developers are required to apply data to the training or analytics stage. Clarity on how the data is being utilized, an explanation on what is being gathered, how it is being used and who it has access to is a key to establishing trust amongst the users. In addition, ethical principles ought to provide a scope of data retention and avoid due to wrongly utilizing learner data on commercial applications. Responsible integration of AI and education is built on a solid privacy-first policy.

FUTURE DIRECTIONS

The field of AI-based programming education is advancing at a high rate due to the developments in Large Language Models (LLMs), privacy-preserving learning, and technologies that do not exclude certain people. The developments are a guarantee of enhanced adaptability, scalability, and accessibility of intelligent tutoring systems. The possibility of technologies such as LLMs, Federated Learning, and multilingual AI, provide individual and fair access to learning for a wide range of students (Fachola et al., 2023). The aim is no longer to simply correct mistakes, but rather to increase conceptual knowledge, intuition, teamwork and inclusivity. With age of these innovations, educational processes will become even more dependent on the role of educator in guiding, customizing, and ethically monitoring AI integration, making it harmonious and a complement to learning-led by humans. Table 4 maps future trends like LLMs, Federated Learning, and multilingual AI to their potential impact on programming education.

Table 4. Future AI techniques and educational benefits

AI Technique	Description	Educational Benefit
Large Language Models (LLMs)	Advanced models (e.g., GPT, Code LLaMA) that understand and generate human-like code explanations	Enables conversational support, personalized hints, and code walkthroughs in natural language
Federated Learning	Distributed training approach that keeps student data on local devices	Enhances model accuracy across institutions while preserving student privacy and data security
Multilingual and Inclusive AI	AI systems designed to provide support in multiple natural languages and adapt to diverse needs	Expands accessibility for non-English speakers and learners with varied abilities

Use of Large Language Models for Code Assistance

Large Language Models (LLMs) such as OpenAI GPT, Google Codey, and Meta Code LLaMA, have changed the game regarding code assistance, support since they allow one to communicate with code in a natural language. They allow them to comprehend the directions like "repair the bug in this code" or "describe this line on a line-by-line basis", providing the detailed and human type response (Holman et al., 2024). With educational data fine-tuned to it, LLMs can respond with context-sensitive feedback, code explanations, and even dynamic hints that change, depending on the student skill. As an example, an LLM can read incorrect recursion logic written by a student, detect logic errors on the base case, and give a textual stepping through of the failure (cases in which a traditional syntax-based tool cannot do so). Code generation, documentation, and translation of languages are also supported in these models and hence make them effective tools in the learning process (Williams, 2021). Since LLMs will be more efficient and accessible, they will be at the heart of the intelligent tutoring systems- not only as an error detector but as an interactive coding tutor.

Federated Learning for Collaborative Improvement

The flow of information describes Federated Learning (FL) as a potential step forward of collaborative and privacy-preserving AI in learning. With FL, in contrast to traditional machine learning, where data are centralized to train models, models are trained locally and only model updates (not the raw data) are shared between individual devices or institutions. This will enable AI-based teaching aids to gain experience by learning with students of different populations in different schools and geographies or on platforms without invading privacy. Specifically, an example of an error-detection model in Python can be enhanced by generalizing error occurring patterns of various universities without even reading the underlying student source code (Pearson et al., 2019). This allows the ownership of data, improves the generalizability of the model, and favourably contributes to the institutionally cooperative construction of smarter models of the AI. Also, FL eliminates the possibility of bias that might be realized when working on a small dataset and thus the tool can be used to fit diverse groups of learners. Federated learning will enable more security, scale and inclusively training of AI tools in education to create a global ecosystem that can be used in real world classrooms.

AI for Multi-Language and Inclusive Programming Education

Since the versatility of programming is becoming international, the AI tutoring system should be multi-lingual to enable inclusivity of this skill. The conventional tools tend to specialize in the English-centered environment of programming, yet a variety of learners across the globe can get a positive impact of the coding aid in their native languages. In the future, AI systems will include multiple-languages like Hindi, Spanish, Mandarin, or Arabic to give instructions, explanations, and feedbacks. Not only does it aid in improvement in understanding but also in the participation of the programming sector (Porras et al., 2023). Moreover, all learning abilities are supported in inclusivity. AI tools are open to improvement via activation through voice input, visual programming assistance, dyslexic-sensitive text display and adaptable levels of feedback to suit different cognitive and physical requirements. All these improvements will enable AI systems to overcome lingual and accessibility barriers and guarantee that any learner in any place regardless of language or learning style can have an equal opportunity to take high-quality programming classes. This vision serves as a global vision on fair and convenient digital literacy.

CONCLUSION

The practice of introducing Artificial Intelligence (AI) to programming education will change the way coding is taught and learnt and absolved. Conventional teaching techniques usually fail to address the varied requirements of learners particularly when the learning happens in the large classroom or the virtual learning space where it is hard to offer quick and specific answers. Intelligent tutoring systems powered by AI are effective to fill this gap because they allow real-time error reporting, adaptive feedback, and customized guidance to learners. These systems lead to enhanced performance of students, as they get to understand more about the concepts of programming, because programs with common or typical errors in code (syntax, logic, runtime, semantic, and type errors) are identified and corrected.

The setup and design of these intelligent systems, its architecture, and some actual applications of it in the education field. Some major methods including code tokenization, Abstract Syntax Trees (AST), machine learning models (e.g., Decision Trees, SVMs, LSTMs), and Natural Language Processing (NLP) are vital to ensure that such tools are competitive and sensitive. Feedback systems, which are prescriptive and descriptive, not only enable the student to know he/she had made an incorrect decision, but also, they learn the rationale of why the correction was given, thus encouraging critical thinking and problem-solving capabilities. Their real-life applications and classroom implementations have shown effectiveness of such tools in creating student engagement, eliminating repetition of errors and faster achievement of learning. What is more, compatibility with Learning Management Systems (LMS), code-editing platforms, and teacher dashboards makes sure that AI support becomes a natural part of the general educational landscape.

The continued monitoring of the students will allow the instructors to respond to the situation and change the way the content is delivered, offering the students a truly personalized learning experience. But implementation of AI in education is not without its concerns. Problems like accuracy of feedback, transparency of models, over-dependence of the student, and privacy of data ought to be properly managed to reduce recklessness and irresponsible practices. The future of the technology would have even more opportunities such as the use of large language models in providing conversational feedback, federated learning in safely collaborating with other institutions, and multilingual AIs in inclusive programming education as the technology evolves. To sum up, based on AI, tutoring systems can transform programming education and make it more personal, scalable, and universal. They are used not only as a learning friend to students but also as an effective helper to educators because they make the digital classroom a smarter and nicer place. Under careful design, continuous testing and cursory application, such technologies have the benefit of advancing the current generation of programmers.

REFERENCES

Abdullah, A., Tunas, B., & Entang, M. (2021). Inclusive education program development: Program evaluation. [JOURNAL OF HUMANITIES AND SOCIAL STUDIES]. *JHSS*, *5*(2), 203–207.

Agic, B., Fruitman, H., Maharaj, A., Taylor, J., Ashraf, A., Henderson, J., Ronda, N., McKenzie, K., Soklaridis, S., & Sockalingam, S. (2023). Advancing curriculum development and design in health professions education: A Health Equity and inclusion Framework for education programs. *The Journal of Continuing Education in the Health Professions*, *43*(4S), S4–S8. PMID: 35940600

Altadmri, A., & Brown, N. C. C. (2015, February). 37 million compilations. *Proceedings of the 46th ACM Technical Symposium on Computer Science Education.*

Alvarez, J. I., Cortez, A. O., & Alberto, M. Z. (2024). Personalized learning in action: Utilizing AI-powered tutors to bridge the gap in mathematics. *Int. J. Res. Stud. Educ*, *13*(8).

Barreto, L. S. da C., Marañón-Vásquez, G. A., de Lima, R. L., Bolognese, A. M., & De Souza, M. M. G. (2021). Distance learning approach in interprofessional higher education. *International Journal of Education*, *12*(4), 93.

Borchers, C., Wang, Y., Karumbaiah, S., Ashiq, M., Shaffer, D. W., & Aleven, V. (2024, March). Revealing networks: Understanding effective teacher practices in AI-supported classrooms using transmodal ordered network analysis. *Proceedings of the 14th Learning Analytics and Knowledge.*

Chang, Y.-H., Yan, Y.-C., & Lu, Y.-T. (2022). Effects of combining different collaborative learning strategies with problem-based learning in a flipped classroom on program language learning. *Sustainability*, *14*(9), 5282.

Dogan, M. E., Goru Dogan, T., & Bozkurt, A. (2023). The use of artificial intelligence (AI) in online learning and distance education processes: A systematic review of empirical studies. *Applied Sciences (Basel, Switzerland)*, *13*(5), 3056.

Fachola, C., Tornar\'\ia, A., Bermolen, P., Capdehourat, G., Etcheverry, L., & Fariello, M. I. (2023). Federated learning for data analytics in education. *Data*, *8*(2), 43.

Holman, K., Marino, M., Vasquez, E., Taub, M., Hunt, J., & Tazi, Y. (2024). Navigating AI-Powered Personalized Learning in special education: A guide for preservice teacher faculty. *Journal of Special Education Preparation*, *4*(2), 90–95.

Johnson, M. S., Liu, X., & McCaffrey, D. F. (2022). Psychometric methods to evaluate measurement and algorithmic bias in automated scoring. *Journal of Educational Measurement, 59*(3), 338–361.

Kessler, A., Boston, M., & Stein, M. K. (2019). Exploring how teachers support students' mathematical learning in computer-directed learning environments. *Information and Learning Science, 121*(1/2), 52–78.

Kimmel, B., Geisert, A. L., Yaro, L., Gipson, B., Hotchkiss, R. T., Osae-Asante, S. K., Vaught, H., Wininger, G., & Yamaguchi, C. (2024). Enhancing programming error messages in real time with generative AI. Extended Abstracts of the CHI Conference on Human Factors in Computing Systems, 1–7.

Kotsiantis, S., Verykios, V., & Tzagarakis, M. (2024). AI-assisted programming tasks using code embeddings and transformers. *Electronics (Basel), 13*(4), 767.

Kucharska, W., Kucharski, M. J., & Rehman, H. U. (2022). Transformational leadership and acceptance of mistakes as a source of learning - Poland-USA cross-country study. *European Conference on Management Leadership and Governance*, 18(1), 238–246.

Li, W., & Wong, W.-F. (2023). Iaso: Enhancing syntax error correction using deep learning techniques. In *Research Square*.

Litman, D. (2016). Natural language processing for enhancing teaching and learning. *Proceedings of the AAAI Conference on Artificial Intelligence, 30*(1).

Meilong, S., He, P., Xiao, H., Li, H., & Zeng, C. (2020). An approach to semantic and structural features learning for software defect prediction. *Mathematical Problems in Engineering, 2020*, 1–13.

Michaeli, T., & Romeike, R. (2020). Investigating students' preexisting debugging traits: A real world escape room study. Koli Calling '20: *Proceedings of the 20th Koli Calling Conference on Computing Education Research*, 1–10.

Ni, A., & Cheung, A. (2023). Understanding secondary students' continuance intention to adopt AI-powered intelligent tutoring system for English learning. *Education and Information Technologies, 28*(3), 3191–3216. PMID: 36119127

Niu, L. (2024). New applications of online education content analysis based on natural language processing technology. Proceedings of the First International Conference on Science, Engineering and Technology Practices for Sustainable Development, ICSETPSD 2023, 17th-18th 2023, Coimbatore, Tamilnadu, India.

Pantelimon, F.-V., & Bologa, R., & Toma Andrei and Posedaru, B.-S. (2021). The evolution of AI-driven educational systems during the COVID-19 pandemic. *Sustainability, 13*(23), 13501.

Pearson, V., Lister, K., McPherson, E., Gallen, A.-M., Davies, G., Colwell, C., Bradshaw, K., Braithwaite, N., & Collins, T. (2019). Embedding and sustaining inclusive practice to support disabled students in online and blended learning. *Journal of Interactive Media in Education, 2019*(1).

Pendy, B. (2023). Artificial Intelligence: The future of education. Jurnal Indonesia Sosial Sains, 2(11).

Porras, J. M., Lara, J. A., Romero, C., & Ventura, S. (2023). A case-study comparison of machine learning approaches for predicting student's dropout from multiple online educational entities. *Algorithms, 16*(12), 554.

Rahman, M. M., Watanobe, Y., & Nakamura, K. (2020a). A neural network based intelligent support model for program code completion. *Scientific Programming, 2020*, 1–18.

Rahman, M. M., Watanobe, Y., & Nakamura, K. (2020b). Source code assessment and classification based on estimated error probability using attentive LSTM language model and its application in programming education. *Applied Sciences (Basel, Switzerland), 10*(8), 2973.

Rahman, M. M., Watanobe, Y., & Nakamura, K. (2021). A bidirectional LSTM language model for code evaluation and repair. *Symmetry, 13*(2), 247.

Shaik, T., Tao, X., Li, Y., Dann, C., McDonald, J., Redmond, P., & Galligan, L. (2022). A review of the trends and challenges in adopting natural language processing methods for education feedback analysis. *IEEE Access : Practical Innovations, Open Solutions, 10*, 56720–56739.

Slade, J. J., Byers, S. M., Becker-Blease, K. A., & Gurung, R. A. R. (2025). Navigating the new frontier: Recommendations to address the crisis and potential of AI in the classroom. *Teaching of Psychology, 52*(3), 254–261.

Slade, J. J., Hyk, A., & Gurung, R. A. R. (2024). Transforming learning: Assessing the efficacy of a Retrieval-Augmented Generation system as a tutor for introductory psychology. *Proceedings of the Human Factors and Ergonomics Society Annual Meeting, 68*(1), 1827–1830.

Tang, K. H. D. (2024). Implications of artificial Intelligence for teaching and learning. *Acta Pedagogia Asia, 3*(2), 65–79.

Wang, K., Singh, R., & Su, Z. (2017). Dynamic neural program embedding for program repair.

Wang, P. (2021, August). PseuToPy: Towards a non-English natural programming language. *Proceedings of the 17th ACM Conference on International Education Research.*

Wei, S. (2024). Research on the disruptive transformation and future development of American teaching models in the context of intelligent transformation. Advances in Economics. *Management and Political Sciences*, *72*(1), 201–210.

Williams, H. P. (2021). The role of federal and state policy in addressing early childhood achievement gaps: Parent perceptions and student outcomes related to 21st Century Learning Centers programming in the United States. *International Journal of Child Care and Education Policy*, *15*(1), 16. PMID: 35300028

Xu, Q. (2024). Action research plan: The impact of the use of Artificial Intelligence in education on the cognitive abilities of university students. In *Research Square.*

Ye, G., Tang, Z., Wang, H., Fang, D., Fang, J., Huang, S., & Wang, Z. (2020, September). Deep program structure modeling through multi-relational graph-based learning. *Proceedings of the ACM International Conference on Parallel and Compilation Techniques.*

Yu, B., Mao, W., Lv, Y., Zhang, C., & Xie, Y. (2022). A survey on federated learning in data mining. *Wiley Interdisciplinary Reviews. Data Mining and Knowledge Discovery*, *12*(1).

Zawacki-Richter, O., Mar\'\in, V. I., Bond, M., & Gouverneur, F. (2019). Systematic review of research on artificial intelligence applications in higher education – where are the educators? *International Journal of Educational Technology in Higher Education*, *16*(1).

Chapter 7
Harnessing Immersive Technologies:
Insights Into Augmented and Virtual Reality Applications

K. Ramalakshmi
https://orcid.org/0000-0002-3038-643X
P.S.R. Engineering College, India

L. Krishna Kumari
Ramco Institute of Technology, India

B. Mohan
P.S.R. Engineering College, India

Sravan Kumar Gunturi
Koneru Lakshmaiah Education Foundation, India

S. P. Santhoshkumar
https://orcid.org/0000-0001-8531-759X
Vel Tech Rangarajan Dr. Sagunthala R&D Institute of Science and Technology, India

R. Santhana Krishnan
https://orcid.org/0000-0001-7930-8072
SCAD College of Engineering and Technology, India

J. Relin Francis Raj
Saveetha School of Engineering, Saveetha Institute of Medical and Technical Sciences, India

ABSTRACT

Both VR and AR are at the forefront of delivering engaging, interactive experiences that are reshaping industries by improving training, operational efficiency, and user engagement through immersive and enhanced environments. These technologies serve as a bridge between the digital and physical realms, providing innovative solutions across a wide range of domains, including education, healthcare, entertainment, and enterprise. The integration of AR and VR is particularly impactful, enabling advanced applications that transform how individuals experience and interact with

DOI: 10.4018/979-8-3373-0598-1.ch007

their surroundings. This study explores the development and capabilities of VR and AR technologies, highlighting their standalone applications and demonstrating how their combination yields powerful outcomes.

INTRODUCTION

In recent years, immersive technologies have gained significant traction across a variety of domains, fundamentally altering how individuals interact with digital content and physical environments. Among these technologies, Virtual Reality (VR) and Augmented Reality (AR) have emerged as powerful tools that offer new dimensions of experience, perception, and interaction. These innovations extend beyond entertainment, penetrating fields such as education, healthcare, industrial design, military training, and remote collaboration.

Virtual Reality creates a completely computer-generated environment that replaces the user's real-world surroundings, allowing for full immersion in a simulated setting. This level of immersion enables users to engage in controlled, repeatable, and interactive experiences, making VR particularly effective in training, simulation, and therapeutic contexts. On the other hand, Augmented Reality enhances the user's real-world environment by overlaying digital information—such as graphics, sounds, or haptic feedback—onto live views, effectively blending digital content with the physical world in real time.

While both technologies serve unique purposes, their convergence offers a synergistic advantage. The integration of VR and AR—often referred to as Mixed Reality (MR)—is opening new avenues for problem-solving, decision-making, and communication by merging the best of both fully immersive and context-aware environments. Together, they help bridge the gap between the physical and digital realms, facilitating more natural and intuitive human-computer interactions.

In the education sector, for example, VR and AR provide students with interactive, hands-on learning experiences that are difficult to replicate in traditional classroom settings. In healthcare, these technologies support advanced surgical simulations, patient rehabilitation, and mental health therapies. Industrial applications include virtual prototyping, remote maintenance, and AR-assisted manufacturing, all of which contribute to increased productivity and reduced operational risks.

The importance of these immersive technologies continues to grow as hardware becomes more affordable, software more sophisticated, and user interfaces more intuitive. With increasing adoption, both private and public sectors are investing heavily in research and development to explore the full potential of AR and VR.

This paper presents a comprehensive overview of VR and AR, beginning with their historical development and core concepts. It then explores standalone and integrated applications across different sectors. Furthermore, the study examines existing literature that demonstrates the practical outcomes of combining VR and AR technologies, highlighting real-world case studies and experimental findings. Finally, the paper discusses the future scope of AR and VR integration, identifying challenges and opportunities for broader implementation.

By analyzing both the individual and collective capabilities of these immersive technologies, this study aims to provide valuable insights into how they are reshaping user experiences and enabling next-generation digital interactions.

LITERATURE SURVEY ON IMMERSIVE TECHNOLOGIES IN EDUCATION AND HEALTHCARE

Foundations and Theoretical Bases of VR in Education

Chen (2009) laid a foundational framework for integrating virtual reality (VR) into education, emphasizing its alignment with constructivist and experiential learning theories, (Chen, 2009). This early work was pivotal in validating the immersive experience as a pedagogical tool for increasing student engagement and cognitive retention. Zizza et al. (2018) extended this by proposing high-fidelity VR learning environments designed to function in asocial settings, underlining personalization in learning, (Zizza et al., 2018).

Immersive Technologies in Education: AR, VR, and the Metaverse

Phakamach, Senarith, and Wachirawongpaisarn (2022) explored how the Metaverse enhances teaching and learning through fully immersive environments. This is supported by Sun et al. (2022), who demonstrated that hybrid AR/VR learning tools positively influence situational interest and academic performance in physics labs. Scavarelli, Arya, and Teather (2021) reviewed the role of AR and VR in social learning environments, concluding that these technologies support collaborative learning and knowledge co-construction, (Scavarelli, Arya, and Teather, 2021).

Bernacki et al. (2020) and Kaminska et al. (2019) emphasized mobile and wearable technologies for ubiquitous learning, (Beck, 2019; Olbina & Glick, 2022; Tokarev et al., 2021), while Olbina and Glick (2022) advocated integrating hands-on with virtual simulations to enrich construction management education. Tokarev et al. (2021) introduced VR as a tool for school-preprofessional education, highlighting its role in early technical training.

Engineering and Technical Education Applications

Multiple studies have demonstrated AR/VR's effectiveness in technical education, particularly in electronics, FPGA, and electrical engineering:

- Singh et al. (2019) and Alhalabi et al. (2021) reported significant improvement in practical electronics skills using AR-enhanced lab environments.
- Yüzüak & Yiğit (2023) and Poyasok et al. (2020) applied AR for teaching MOSFETs and electrical engineering fundamentals respectively, promoting better visualization and student comprehension.
- Striegel et al. (2021) employed AR for teaching wireless network security, confirming the usefulness of immersive simulations for abstract concepts.

Gamified and remote labs, as discussed by Alptekin & Temmen (2020) and Sanchez-Herrera et al. (2019), further extend accessibility and student motivation.

Healthcare and Medical Education

Extended reality (XR) applications in healthcare are gaining traction, as outlined by Abbas et al. (2023), who reviewed definitions and frameworks relevant to VR in health contexts. Waisberg et al. (2023) and Brent Woodland et al. (2024) showcased the potential of XR in addressing human performance issues in spaceflight, including vision deterioration due to radiation. Virtual visual assessments and diagnostics using AR platforms like Heru have also emerged as efficient alternatives, according to Goldbach et al. (2021) and Skalicky & Kong (2019).

VR-based therapy is being adopted in behavioral health settings, such as dental phobia (Raghav et al., 2016), anxiety reduction (Sridhar et al., 2020), and maternal health through fetal simulations (Sevenri et al., 2005). Epazz Deskflex's 2022 report also highlighted a Metaverse solution for telemedicine integration, facilitating remote diagnostics.

Emerging Research on XR in Specialized Training

- Juhana et al. (2020) developed VR-based trainer boards for electrical education.
- Checa et al. (2021) designed a VR training system for induction motor maintenance
- Rakshit et al. (2017) combined VR and teleoperation for remote lab experiences in engineering education.

- Kvasznicza et al. (2019) described corporate-academic VR partnerships for dual education programs.

Additionally, virtual labs for solar energy (Abichandani et al., 2019) and science and technology experiments (Sriadhi et al., 2022) promote sustainable learning through simulation.

Future Directions and Challenges

Despite the evident advantages, scalability, device cost, and standardization remain challenges. The review by Kaminska et al. (2019) and the Metaverse-specific healthcare survey by Bansal et al. (2022) call for standardized protocols, ethical guidelines, and accessibility in immersive learning and diagnostic platforms. Skalidis et al. (2022) further discussed the integration of NFTs and blockchain in medical data protection and management in XR platforms.

This literature review underscores the transformative potential of VR, AR, MR, and the Metaverse across educational and healthcare sectors. These technologies not only enhance engagement and retention in education but also offer promising, non-invasive diagnostic and therapeutic solutions in healthcare. The convergence of immersive tech with mobile, AI, and cloud platforms is shaping a future of personalized, efficient, and accessible services.

IMMERSIVE TECHNOLOGIES

Augmented Reality (AR)

Augmented Reality overlays digital content—such as text, images, animations, or 3D models onto the physical environment in real time. It enhances the perception of reality by superimposing contextual information through devices like smartphones, tablets, smart glasses (e.g., Microsoft HoloLens), or AR headsets.

Key Characteristics

- Real-time interaction
- Context-awareness
- Spatial alignment of digital content with physical surroundings

Examples: Pokémon Go, IKEA Place, Google Lens

Virtual Reality (VR)

Virtual Reality immerses users in a completely artificial digital environment. VR applications typically require head-mounted displays (HMDs) such as the Oculus Quest, HTC Vive, or PlayStation VR, often accompanied by motion controllers or haptic devices.

Key Characteristics

- Fully immersive 3D environments
- Controlled user navigation and interaction
- Real-time rendering and feedback

Examples: VRChat, Beat Saber, Google Earth VR

Hardware for AR and VR: HMDs, Sensors, Cameras, and Wearables

Hardware plays a critical role in delivering immersive experiences in augmented and virtual reality. The most essential devices include:

- **Head-Mounted Displays (HMDs):** These are worn on the head and present users with a digital environment. In VR, HMDs like the Oculus Quest, HTC Vive, and PlayStation VR fully immerse the user in a virtual world. For AR, devices such as Microsoft HoloLens or Magic Leap overlay virtual elements on the real world while allowing the user to maintain awareness of their surroundings.
- **Sensors:** These devices collect motion, orientation, and environmental data. Gyroscopes, accelerometers, and magnetometers track head and body movements. Depth sensors, such as LiDAR or infrared, enable accurate spatial mapping, crucial for aligning virtual objects with real-world coordinates.
- **Cameras:** Used in AR systems to capture the user's surroundings in real-time and overlay virtual information. Cameras also support marker-based AR, object recognition, facial tracking, and gesture detection, enhancing interactivity.
- **Wearables:** These include gloves, vests, and suits embedded with haptic feedback systems or motion sensors. They add another layer of realism by allowing users to feel virtual textures or simulate physical forces, enhancing the sensory experience in training, gaming, or medical simulations.

Software Platforms and SDKs: Unity, Unreal Engine, ARCore, ARKit

Software platforms and development kits provide the backbone for building immersive applications. Some of the most widely used include:

- **Unity:** A popular game engine used extensively for developing AR and VR experiences. Its real-time rendering capabilities, wide plugin support, and compatibility with multiple platforms make it suitable for both beginners and professionals.
- **Unreal Engine:** Known for its photorealistic visuals and high-performance capabilities, Unreal Engine is favored for applications requiring rich detail, such as architectural walkthroughs, simulations, and advanced VR environments.
- **ARCore (Google):** A platform that enables AR development for Android devices. It uses environmental understanding, motion tracking, and light estimation to place digital objects realistically in the user's environment.
- **ARKit (Apple):** Tailored for iOS devices, ARKit offers features like face tracking, 3D object detection, and world mapping, allowing developers to create immersive AR apps with minimal setup on Apple platforms.

These platforms streamline the development process, offering prebuilt tools, APIs, and simulation environments to deploy immersive content effectively.

Enabling Technologies: AI, IoT, Cloud, Blockchain

Several emerging technologies enhance the functionality and scalability of immersive experiences:

- **Artificial Intelligence (AI):** AI drives object recognition, natural language processing, and adaptive user interaction in AR/VR systems. For instance, virtual assistants and chatbots within immersive environments can respond intelligently to user queries.
- **Internet of Things (IoT):** When combined with AR/VR, IoT enables real-time interaction with physical devices. For example, technicians using AR glasses can view sensor data from IoT-enabled machines during maintenance tasks.
- **Cloud Computing:** The cloud allows storage, processing, and streaming of large amounts of AR/VR content. This offloads computational burden from

local devices, enabling lightweight headsets or mobile devices to access high-quality immersive content.

- **Blockchain:** This technology ensures data security, authentication, and traceability in shared virtual spaces. In the metaverse, blockchain facilitates ownership and trading of digital assets such as NFTs, adding economic value to immersive platforms.

Network Requirements: 5G, Edge Computing

High-performance networks are crucial to support seamless immersive experiences, particularly for multi-user applications and cloud-based content.

- **5G:** With its high bandwidth, low latency, and reliable connectivity, 5G enables real-time data transmission necessary for responsive AR/VR applications. It supports streaming of HD content and facilitates rapid updates in multi-player or collaborative environments.
- **Edge Computing:** By processing data closer to the user (at the "edge" of the network), latency is significantly reduced. This is particularly important for time-sensitive tasks such as remote surgery or live industrial monitoring using AR.

Together, 5G and edge computing enable smooth, scalable, and responsive XR applications in various fields, from entertainment to critical services.

Interaction Methods: Gesture, Voice, Eye Tracking, and Haptics

Immersive systems rely on natural interaction techniques to enhance user experience and engagement:

- **Gesture Recognition:** Users can interact with virtual elements using hand or body movements. Cameras and motion sensors track gestures, allowing intuitive control without physical controllers.
- **Voice Commands:** Voice-based interaction simplifies navigation and control, particularly in hands-free environments. Speech recognition technologies convert spoken words into commands that drive application behavior.
- **Eye Tracking:** This technique monitors where a user is looking to adjust focus dynamically or enable gaze-based interaction. It enhances realism and reduces processing load by rendering high-resolution graphics only in the user's focal area.

- **Haptic Feedback:** Through vibrations, force feedback, or temperature variations, haptics simulate the sense of touch in virtual environments. This technology is widely used in VR gloves, suits, and controllers to deliver a more immersive and convincing experience.

Table 1. Development tools for virtual and augmented reality

Augmented Reality development tools			
		Development Tool	**Hardware/Software**
G. Singh et al.,	2019	Unity	Software
M. Alptekin et al.,	2020	Unity	Software
T. Poyasok et al.,	2020	BlippAR	Software
M. Alhalabi et al.,	2021	Machine Learning	Software
R. Sanchez-Herrera at al.,	2019	JAVA	Software
Y. Yüzüak	2023	Tablet	Hardware
H. Yiğit.	2023	Tablet	Hardware
Z. Qiwen	2017	Head Mounted displays	Hardware
T. Yongming.	2017	Head Mounted displays	Hardware
M. Striegel et al.	2021	Camera	Hardware
M. Striegel et al.	2021	Labtop	Hardware
Virtual Reality development tools			
M. Khairudin et al., 2019	2019	Unity and Unreal	Software
D. Checa et al.	2021	Unity and Unreal	Software
Z. Kvasznicza et al.	2019	MaxWhere	Software
S. Sriadhi et al.	2022	PHP & MySQL	Software
P. Abichandani et al.	2019	Google Cloud Platform	Software
F. Górski et al.	2021	Oculus	Hardware
S. M. Rakshit et al.	2017	HTC	Hardware
M. Goryll et al.	2019	Google Cardboard	Hardware
A. Juhana et al.	2020	Head Mounted displays	Hardware

APPLICATIONS OF VIRTUAL REALITY (VR)

VR in Education and Training

Virtual Reality provides immersive environments that make learning experiential and engaging. It is widely used for training in fields such as medicine, aviation, military, and technical education, allowing users to simulate real-world scenarios and practice safely without real-life consequences.

VR in Healthcare

In healthcare, VR is used for surgery simulation, physical rehabilitation, and psychological therapy. Surgeons can rehearse procedures in virtual operating rooms, while therapists use VR to treat phobias, anxiety disorders, and PTSD through controlled exposure environments.

VR in Entertainment and Gaming

Entertainment remains a leading sector for VR applications. From immersive gaming to virtual concerts and cinematic experiences, VR enhances user interaction and realism, often incorporating motion sensors and haptic feedback to create lifelike experiences.

VR in Industrial and Enterprise Settings

Industries employ VR for employee training, design prototyping, and safety simulations. Virtual walkthroughs of production plants or 3D visualization of products allow enterprises to reduce costs and improve collaboration and decision-making processes.

APPLICATIONS OF AUGMENTED REALITY (AR)

AR in Education and Interactive Learning

Augmented Reality overlays digital information onto real-world materials, enhancing classroom interactivity. It allows students to explore 3D models of organs, chemical reactions, or historical landmarks, increasing conceptual understanding and engagement.

AR in Healthcare

AR assists surgeons by projecting anatomical overlays onto the patient during operations. It also aids patient education, offering visual explanations of diagnoses and treatments, improving comprehension and involvement in care plans.

AR in Retail and Marketing

Retailers use AR to offer virtual try-ons of clothing, glasses, or makeup, and to preview furniture in one's living space. AR-driven marketing campaigns increase consumer interaction, product personalization, and purchase confidence.

AR in Manufacturing and Maintenance

Technicians use AR headsets or tablets to receive live step-by-step guidance overlaid on machinery during assembly or repairs. This reduces training time, minimizes errors, and enhances efficiency on the factory floor.

COMBINED AR/VR EXPERIENCES (MIXED REALITY AND XR)

Concept of Mixed Reality (MR) and Extended Reality (XR)

Mixed Reality merges the physical and digital worlds, where virtual objects interact with the real environment. XR (Extended Reality) encompasses AR, VR, and MR, creating fluid experiences across immersive environments.

Synergistic Use of AR and VR Technologies

Combining AR and VR enables enhanced workflows—for instance, designing in AR and testing in VR. These hybrid systems support applications in collaborative design, training, and simulation where users switch seamlessly between real and virtual contexts.

Collaborative Virtual Environments

XR supports multi-user, real-time collaboration across locations, enabling shared virtual spaces for meetings, training, remote surgeries, and education. This fosters teamwork, reduces travel costs, and enables global knowledge sharing.

Real-World Examples of Integrated AR/VR Use

Examples include Microsoft HoloLens for surgical planning and XR platforms used for immersive education and industrial design. These implementations demonstrate how integrated immersive technologies enhance outcomes in critical sectors.

BENEFITS AND CHALLENGES

Enhancing User Experience and Engagement

Immersive technologies increase attention, comprehension, and memory retention. They shift user roles from passive observers to active participants, improving learning outcomes and emotional connection.

Operational Efficiency and Cost Reduction

By reducing the need for physical infrastructure, travel, and materials, immersive technologies cut operational costs and time. Virtual training modules and digital prototyping streamline processes across industries.

Technical Challenges (Latency, Realism, Device Limitations)

Barriers to adoption include hardware limitations, motion sickness, latency, and limited realism. Device cost and compatibility can also restrict access, particularly in low-resource settings.

Ethical and Privacy Concerns

Concerns include data privacy, surveillance through biometric tracking, overuse, and mental health implications. Ethical design, user consent, and data protection measures are essential in immersive tech development.

FUTURE RESEARCH DIRECTIONS

Advances in Haptics and Sensory Feedback

Future immersive systems will include sophisticated tactile feedback through gloves, suits, and exoskeletons, enabling users to "feel" virtual textures, resistance, and movement.

Role of AI in Personalizing AR/VR Experiences

Artificial Intelligence will drive adaptive AR/VR experiences, customizing content based on user behavior, skill level, or real-time feedback, enhancing personalization and learning efficiency.

5G and Edge Computing Integration

5G networks and edge computing reduce latency and bandwidth bottlenecks, enabling real-time, high-quality immersive interactions suitable for mobile and cloud-based XR platforms.

Sustainable and Scalable Deployment Models

Cloud-based XR solutions and lightweight, energy-efficient devices are being developed to support sustainable and cost-effective deployment, especially in education and healthcare in underserved regions.

Roadmap for Future Innovations

Emerging innovations include brain-computer interfaces, wearable XR glasses, and persistent metaverse environments. These developments are poised to reshape workspaces, education systems, and digital interactions.

CONCLUSION

Virtual Reality (VR) and Augmented Reality (AR) are revolutionizing the digital landscape by providing immersive, interactive, and contextually rich experiences across a spectrum of applications. This study has highlighted the distinct functionalities and shared potential of these technologies in transforming sectors such as education, healthcare, entertainment, and enterprise. While VR enables full immersion into digitally constructed environments, AR enhances real-world experiences by overlaying relevant digital content. Individually, both technologies deliver significant value in training, simulation, visualization, and remote collaboration. However, when integrated, AR and VR form a comprehensive mixed reality ecosystem that amplifies user interaction, spatial awareness, and decision-making capabilities.

As the adoption of immersive technologies continues to grow, it is evident that VR and AR are no longer limited to experimental or entertainment domains but are becoming integral components of mainstream digital transformation. Their convergence is fostering new paradigms in how users engage with data, environments, and each other, enabling more intuitive, impactful, and efficient outcomes.

Future Work

Future advancements in AR and VR technologies are expected to focus on enhancing realism, interactivity, and accessibility across diverse applications. Key areas of development include improving visual fidelity, haptic feedback, and multisensory integration to create more immersive and lifelike experiences. Integrating artificial intelligence will enable personalized, adaptive environments that respond dynamically to user behavior and context. Additionally, research into cross-platform interoperability and standardization is essential for ensuring seamless deployment and broader adoption of immersive solutions. The development of lightweight, cost-effective, and ergonomically designed hardware will further support mainstream acceptance. Moreover, the integration of AR/VR with edge computing and 5G networks can significantly reduce latency and support real-time applications in mobile and distributed environments. As immersive technologies become more pervasive, future work must also address critical challenges related to ethics, user privacy, mental health, and digital equity. Expanding the scope of AR and VR into emerging fields such as neuro rehabilitation, virtual tourism, collaborative engineering, and smart urban planning presents exciting opportunities for interdisciplinary innovation and meaningful societal impact.

REFERENCES

Abichandani, P., Mcintyre, W., Fligor, W., & Lobo, D. (2019). Solar energy education through a cloud-based desktop virtual reality system. *IEEE Access*, 7, 147081–147093. https://doi.org/, M., Ghazal, M., Haneefa, F., Yousaf, J., & El-Baz, A. (2021). Smartphone handwritten circuits solver using augmented reality and capsule deep networks for engineering education. *Education Sciences*, 11(11), 661. https://doi.org/DOI: 10.1109/ACCESS.2019.2945700Alhalabi

Alptekin, M., & Temmen, K. (2020). Gamification in an augmented reality based virtual preparation laboratory training. In M. Auer & T. Tsiatsos (Eds.), *The challenges of the digital transformation in education. ICL 2018* (Advances in Intelligent Systems and Computing, Vol. 916, pp. 578–589). Springer. https://doi.org/DOI: 10.1007/978-3-030-11932-4_54

Bansal, G., Rajgopal, K., Chamola, V., Xiong, Z., & Niyato, D. (2022). Healthcare in metaverse: A survey on current metaverse applications in healthcare. *IEEE Access : Practical Innovations, Open Solutions*, *10*, 119914–119946. DOI: 10.1109/ACCESS.2022.3219845

Beck, D. (2019). Augmented and virtual reality in education: Immersive learning research. *Journal of Educational Computing Research*, *57*(7), 1619–1625. DOI: 10.1177/0735633119854035

Bernacki, M. L., Greene, J. A., & Crompton, H. (2020). Mobile technology, learning, and achievement: Advances in understanding and measuring the role of mobile technology in education. *Contemporary Educational Psychology*, *60*, 101827. Advance online publication. DOI: 10.1016/j.cedpsych.2019.101827

Checa, D., Bustillo, A., Saucedo-Dorantes, J. J., Osornio-Rios, R. A., & Cruz-Albarran, I. A. (2021). Virtual reality-based tool applied in the teaching and training of condition-based maintenance in induction motors. In *2021 IEEE 8th International Conference on e-Learning in Industrial Electronics (ICELIE)* (pp. 1–6). IEEE. https://doi.org/DOI: 10.1109/ICELIE53900.2021.9765543

Chen, C. J. (2009). Theoretical bases for using virtual reality in education. *Themes in Science and Technology Education*, *2*(1-2), 71–90. https://www.semanticscholar.org/paper/Theoretical-Bases-for-Using-Virtual-Reality-in-Chen/f6b4882a93a6d3cc35fa090a4c9f7927b12d01fc

Goldbach, A. H., Abou Shousha, M., & Duque, C.. (2021). Visual field measurements using Heru Visual Field Multi-platform application downloaded on two different commercially available augmented reality devices. *Investigative Ophthalmology & Visual Science*, *62*(8), 1017.

Górski, F., Grajewski, D., Bun, P., & Zawadzki, P. (2021). Study of interaction methods in virtual electrician training. *IEEE Access : Practical Innovations, Open Solutions*, *9*, 118242–118252. DOI: 10.1109/ACCESS.2021.3106826

Juhana, A., Yusuf, R., Prihatmanto, A. S., & Abdullah, A. G. (2020). Basic electrical installation trainer boards: Virtual reality based laboratory for electrical basic education. In *2020 6th International Conference on Interactive Digital Media (ICIDM)* (pp. 1–6). IEEE. https://doi.org/DOI: 10.1109/ICIDM51048.2020.9339681

Kaminska, D., Sapiński, T., Wiak, S., Tikk, T., Haamer, R. E., Avots, E., & Anbarjafari, G. (2019). Virtual reality and its applications in education: Survey. *Information (Basel)*, *10*(10), 318. DOI: 10.3390/info10100318

Khairudin, M., Triatmaja, A. K., Istanto, W. J., & Azman, M. N. A. (2019). Mobile virtual reality to develop a virtual laboratory for the subject of digital engineering. *International Journal of Interactive Mobile Technologies*, *13*(4), 80–95. DOI: 10.3991/ijim.v13i04.10522

Kvasznicza, Z., Kovács, J., Maza, G., & Péli, M. (2019). VR based dual education at E.ON: The win-win-win situation for companies, graduates and universities. In *2019 10th IEEE International Conference on Cognitive Infocommunications (CogInfoCom)* (pp. 479–482). IEEE. https://doi.org/DOI: 10.1109/CogInfoCom47531.2019.9089961

Olbina, S., & Glick, S. (2022). Using integrated hands-on and virtual reality (VR) or augmented reality (AR) approaches in construction management education. *International Journal of Construction Education and Research*, *18*(3), 1–20. DOI: 10.1080/15578771.2021.1975659

Phakamach, P., Senarith, P., & Wachirawongpaisarn, S. (2022). The metaverse in education: The future of immersive teaching & learning. *RICE Journal of Creative Entrepreneurship and Management*, *3*(2), 75–88.

Qiwen, Z., & Yongming, T. (2017). Design of an augmented reality teaching system for FPGA experimental instruction. In *2017 IEEE 6th International Conference on Teaching, Assessment, and Learning for Engineering (TALE)* (pp. 35–38). IEEE. https://doi.org/DOI: 10.1109/TALE.2017.8252300

Raghav, K., Van Wijk, A., Abdullah, F., Islam, M. N., Bernatchez, M., & De Jongh, A. (2016). Efficacy of virtual reality exposure therapy for treatment of dental phobia: A randomized control trial. *BMC Oral Health*, *16*(1), 1–11. DOI: 10.1186/s12903-016-0186-z PMID: 26920573

Rakshit, S. M., Banerjee, S., Hempel, M., & Sharif, H. (2017). Fusion of VR and teleoperation for innovative near-presence laboratory experience in engineering education. In *2017 IEEE International Conference on Electro Information Technology (EIT)* (pp. 376–381). IEEE. https://doi.org/DOI: 10.1109/EIT.2017.8053390

Sanchez-Herrera, R., Mejías, A., Márquez, M. A., & Andújar, J. M. (2019). The remote access to laboratories: A fully open integrated system. *IFAC-PapersOnLine*, *52*(9), 121–126. DOI: 10.1016/j.ifacol.2019.08.135

Scavarelli, A., Arya, A., & Teather, R. J. (2021). Virtual reality and augmented reality in social learning spaces: A literature review. *Virtual Reality (Waltham Cross)*, *25*(1), 257–277. DOI: 10.1007/s10055-020-00460-7

Sevenri, F. M., Prattichizzo, D., Casarosa, E., Barbagli, F., Ferretti, C., Altomare, A., Vicino, A., & Petraglia, F. (2005). Virtual fetal touch through a haptic interface decreases maternal anxiety and salivary cortisol. *Journal of the Society for Gynecologic Investigation*, *12*(1), 37–40. DOI: 10.1016/j.jsgi.2004.07.006 PMID: 15629669

Skalicky, S. E., & Kong, G. Y. (2019). Novel means of clinical visual function testing among glaucoma patients, including virtual reality. *Journal of Current Glaucoma Practice*, *13*(3), 83–91. DOI: 10.5005/jp-journals-10028-1271 PMID: 32431476

Skalidis, I., Müller, O., & Fournier, S. (2022). The metaverse in cardiovascular medicine: Applications, challenges and the role of non-fungible tokens. *The Canadian Journal of Cardiology*, *38*(9), 1467–1468. DOI: 10.1016/j.cjca.2022.05.006 PMID: 35430196

Sriadhi, S., Hamid, A., & Restu, R. (2022). Web-based virtual laboratory development for basic practicums in science and technology. *TEM Journal*, 11(1), 396–402. https://doi.org/DOI: 10.18421/TEM111-50

Sridhar, A., Shiliang, Z., Woodson, R., & Kwan, L. (2020). Nonpharmacological anxiety reduction with immersive virtual reality for first-trimester dilation and curettage: A pilot study. *The European Journal of Contraception & Reproductive Health Care*, *25*(6), 480–483. DOI: 10.1080/13625187.2020.1833188 PMID: 33140989

Striegel, M., Erasmus, J., & Jain, P. (2021). Evaluating augmented reality for wireless network security education. In *2021 IEEE Frontiers in Education Conference (FIE)* (pp. 1–9). IEEE. https://doi.org/DOI: 10.1109/FIE49875.2021.9637216

Sun, J. C.-Y., Ye, S. L., Yu, S. J., & Chiu, T. K. (2022). Effects of wearable hybrid AR/VR learning material on high school students' situational interest, engagement, and learning performance: The case of a physics laboratory learning environment. *Journal of Science Education and Technology*, *32*(1), 1–12. DOI: 10.1007/s10956-022-09996-w

Tokarev, A., Skobelin, I., Tolstov, M., Tsyganov, A., & Pak, M. (2021). Development of VR educational instruments for school preprofessional education in a research university. *Procedia Computer Science*, *190*, 750–754. DOI: 10.1016/j.procs.2021.06.087

Waisberg, E., Ong, J., & Lee, A. G. (2023). Space radiation and the potential for early cataract development. *Eye*, *37*(14), 2952–2954. DOI: 10.1038/s41433-023-02742-2 PMID: 37735211

Woodland, M. B., Ong, J., Zaman, N., Hirzallah, M., Waisberg, E., Masalkhi, M., Kamran, S. A., Lee, A. G., & Tavakkoli, A. (2024). Applications of extended reality in spaceflight for human health and performance. *Acta Astronautica*, *214*, 748–756. DOI: 10.1016/j.actaastro.2023.11.013

Yüzüak, Y., & Yiğit, H. (2023). Augmented reality application in engineering education: N-type MOSFET. *International Journal of Electrical Engineering Education*, *60*(3), 245–257. DOI: 10.1177/0020720920954150

Zizza, C., Starr, A., Hudson, D., Nuguri, S. S., Calyam, P., & He, Z. (2018). Towards a social virtual reality learning environment in high fidelity. In *2018 15th IEEE Annual Consumer Communications & Networking Conference (CCNC)* (pp. 1–4). IEEE. https://doi.org/DOI: 10.1109/CCNC.2018.8319280

Chapter 8
Applications of Artificial Intelligence in Instructional Design and Educational Strategies

Miguel Ángel Ruiz Jaimes
https://orcid.org/0000-0002-2585-9896
Universidad Politécnica del Estado de Morelos, Mexico

Yadira Toledo Navarro
Universidad Politécnica del Estado de Morelos, Mexico

Ángel Israel Daza Castillo
CENIDET, Mexico

Tlaloc Humberto Vergara Morales
https://orcid.org/0009-0008-3823-5784
CENIDET, Mexico

Ana L. Bárcenas Cortes
Instituto Tecnológico de Tláhuac III, Mexico

Jorge A. Ruiz Vanoye
https://orcid.org/0000-0003-4928-5716
Universidad Politécnica de Pachuca, Mexico

ABSTRACT

This chapter examines the impact of Artificial Intelligence (AI) on teaching methods and instructional strategies across different educational levels. It focuses on key applications such as personalized learning, intelligent tutoring systems, educational gamification, and automated assessment. Through a systematic review of recent literature and case studies, it analyzes how these technologies are transforming the teaching-learning experience, optimizing educational resources, and enabling more individualized student support. The chapter also addresses ethical challenges related to AI in education, including data privacy, equitable access, and over-reliance on technology. It offers recommendations for the responsible implementation of AI,

DOI: 10.4018/979-8-3373-0598-1.ch008

emphasizing the need for updated educational policies, continuous teacher training, and ethical regulatory frameworks. The chapter concludes that, when applied appropriately, AI has the potential to strengthen equity, improve learning outcomes, and redefine the teacher's role as a facilitator of critical and creative thinking.

INTRODUCTION

Artificial intelligence (AI) is a key tool for developing educational strategies and promoting equity in education. According to UNESCO (2019), AI supports intellectual training systems, educational data analysis, and personalized learning platforms. Countries such as China, Uruguay, and Brazil have adopted AI technologies to improve content creation and management through digital assistance.

However, the use of artificial intelligence also presents significant challenges, such as teacher training, equity in access to technology, and the need to ensure ethical practices in the collection and use of educational data (UNESCO, 2019). In this regard, it is crucial to establish an educational policy that balances technological innovation with equity and available resources, ensuring that AI benefits all students without widening the existing digital divide.

The incorporation of conversational and generative AI in education has transformed teaching methods. According to Akpan et al. (2025), tools like chatbots and systems such as ChatGPT assist in course design and provide individualized support. These innovations improve human–machine interaction but raise ethical concerns plagiarism, privacy, and academic integrity requiring updated policies and effective implementation strategies.

Artificial intelligence is a revolutionary ally in the educational field. AI claims tools to change the kinema behind instructional strategies. In addition to the personalization of learning enabled by the adaptability of the delivered content or the pace, AI also changes the equation by including real-time assessment, freeing educators for other, more non-reactive tasks, including mentoring and creativity. Although its introduction brings its own challenges.

Balancing technology and humanity in education is essential. Norman-Acevedo (2023) argues that AI is not a magic solution but can personalize learning, provide real-time assessment, and relieve teachers from repetitive tasks. However, its implementation presents challenges that must be addressed.

Technological advances have enhanced instruction through AI, initially focused on automating tasks like assessment and personalization. Current research promotes blended intelligence using AI to support rather than replace educators. While intelligent tutoring systems improve learning, the key challenge is balancing automation with fostering student autonomy and critical thinking (Cukurova, 2024).

The purpose of this chapter is to examine how artificial intelligence impacts educational strategies, considering both its advantages and the challenges it presents at various levels of education. It aims to provide a comprehensive view of how AI has the potential to transform teaching, presenting innovative tools and methods to enhance student learning.

In addition, the document seeks to identify the main applications of artificial intelligence in the educational field and its role in personalized learning. Analyze how AI influences teachers' work and its function in improving the use of time and educational resources. Examine the ethical and technological issues that arise when using AI in the educational context, including data protection and equity in access to these tools, as well investigating cases studies and successful examples of AI implementation in teaching.

The scope of this chapter ranges from primary education to higher education, covering both public and private institutions. Additionally, particular emphasis is placed on regional variations and strategies applied in different educational contexts to maximize the benefits of artificial intelligence.

To develop this chapter, a method based on a systematic review of academic literature and specialized documents in the field of artificial intelligence in education has been used. The review has considered both primary and secondary sources, including articles from renowned scientific journals, reports from international organizations such as UNESCO, and verified case studies documenting real experiences of AI implementation in educational institutions.

This qualitative and comparative analysis highlights key trends in AI integration in education. It reviews empirical studies on AI's impact on learning, adoption challenges, and considers ethical and regulatory frameworks promoting responsible use of these technologies.

FUNDAMENTALS OF ARTIFICIAL INTELLIGENCE IN EDUCATION

The integration of artificial intelligence (AI) into educational settings has garnered significant attention in recent years, as it offers transformative potential across various domains of learning and teaching. This literature review aims to explore the fundamentals of AI in education, focusing on its definitions, principles, algorithms, and models. The evolution of AI's application in educational contexts reveals a complex interplay between technological advancements and pedagogical practices, as highlighted by a series of scholarly contributions.

Schiff (2021) highlights the disruptive role of AI in education via intelligent tutoring systems and educational agents. While recognizing its benefits for efficiency and access, he also warns of risks like industrialization and alienation, offering a nuanced view of AI's sociotechnical impact on the future of education.

Dong et al. (2022) explore AI's role in English language teaching through multi-modal methods, emphasizing its ability to personalize learning. Similarly, Kshirsagar et al. (2022) highlight AI's automation of administrative tasks, freeing educators to focus on students. Both studies support AI's potential to create adaptive learning environments tailored to individual needs.

Nguyen et al. (2023) explore the ethical aspects of AI in education, highlighting roles such as intelligent tutor and policy advisor. While recognizing AI's benefits, they stress the importance of addressing ethical concerns, reinforcing the need for its responsible and thoughtful integration into educational settings.

Shaik et al. (2023) analyze the use of natural language processing (NLP) in educational feedback, showing how AI can process large datasets to enhance learning insights. Similarly, Mallik and Gangopadhyay (2023) highlight a shift towards deep learning in education, emphasizing the growing impact of data availability on AI development.

Yu and Yu (2023) analyze AI ethics in education using qualitative and quantitative methods. They highlight AI's transformative potential but warn of possible misuse, emphasizing the need for strong ethical frameworks to guide responsible implementation in educational environments.

Li et al. (2024) explore AI's role in autism education, emphasizing the need to address the specific challenges of diverse learners. Similarly, AlTwajri and Alghizzi (2024) examine how AI enhances English language learning by personalizing instruction and improving student engagement through adaptive technologies.

The integration of artificial intelligence (AI) algorithms and models into educational contexts has been a focal point of scholarly discourse over the past few years. The literature reveals a spectrum of applications and implications for AI in education, with various studies addressing the challenges and opportunities that arise from these technological advancements.

Luan et al. (2020) analyzed the evolution of big data and AI in education, identifying a gap between technological potential and practical implementation. They underscore the role of learning analytics in improving teaching and emphasize the importance of educational psychologists in leveraging data-driven tools effectively.

In 2022, Dong et al. contributed to the discourse by discussing the application of AI in the design of postgraduate English curricula, advocating for a shift towards a more integrated pedagogical approach that distinguishes between simulated and emergent roles of AI in education. Their findings suggest that AI can enhance instructional quality through a knowledge-based system that evaluates student achievements, thus reinforcing the transformative potential of AI in educational methodologies.

Kshirsagar et al. (2022) highlighted AI's role in enabling personalized learning through intelligent systems. They stressed the importance of learner models for self-directed learning and adaptive teaching. Their work underscores the need to combine AI tools with human expertise to enhance curriculum design and educational outcomes.

Mallik and Gangopadhyay (2023) analyzed AI's evolution in education, noting a shift toward deep learning methods. They identified data scarcity as a key challenge and emphasized the need to optimize available resources to improve AI's effectiveness across varied educational contexts.

As the discourse progressed into 2023, (Ferreira Mello et al., 2023) underscored the necessity for a holistic approach to AI integration in education, advocating for the co-creation of learning experiences where AI complements rather than replaces human educators.

Tian et al. (2024) highlighted how AI and machine learning can enhance instructional quality through text analysis. They emphasized that integrating research into practical tools requires collaboration between technological innovation and educational expertise to ensure effective pedagogical transformation.

Li et al. (2024) examined educators' perceptions of AI interventions for autism, contributing to the growing body of literature on AI literacy and its applications in specialized educational contexts.

Finally, AlTwijri and Musaed Alghizzi (2024) conducted a systematic review on the integration of AI in foreign language education, emphasizing the technology's potential to personalize learning experiences and enhance student engagement.

Recent years have seen significant advances at the intersection of machine learning, neural networks, and NLP, evolving from foundational concepts to deep learning-based applications.

Goldberg (2015) provides a foundational overview of neural network models specifically designed for natural language processing (NLP) tasks. This work highlights the resurgence of neural networks as powerful machine learning tools, detailing key architectures such as feedforward, convolutional, and recurrent neural networks.

Alshahrani and Kapetanos (2016) examine the suitability of deep learning for NLP, highlighting how its multi-layered structures enable autonomous data learning. They showcase the versatility of artificial neural networks in tasks like semantic role labeling and machine translation.

Shorten et al. (2021) examined the evolution of deep learning during the COVID-19 era, highlighting the role of supervised, semi-supervised, and self-supervised learning in NLP. They emphasized how models like GPT-3 have transformed tasks such as text classification and summarization, greatly expanding NLP capabilities

Casey et al. (2021) conducted a systematic review of NLP in radiology, analyzing 164 studies. They observed a shift toward deep learning, while traditional methods persist. The study highlights the importance of reproducibility and explainability for effective clinical application of NLP.

Crema et al. (2022) expand the discussion of NLP applications to clinical neuroscience and psychiatry, tracing the historical development of NLP from grammatical theories to the current deep learning era. They outline various NLP tasks, including named entity recognition and sentiment analysis, and emphasize the critical role of neural networks in these applications.

Artificial Intelligence (AI) is transforming education by enabling personalized learning, automating administrative tasks, and enhancing the learning experience. Core technologies such as Machine Learning (ML), Neural Networks, and Natural Language Processing (NLP) support smart tutoring, adaptive content, and interactive learning environments.

Machine Learning in Education

- Customized Learning Systems: Algorithms using ML examine the learning habits of students and adjust educational materials to fit their needs, promoting an individualized learning journey.
- Forecasting Performance: Schools apply ML to anticipate student success, recognize students who may need extra support, and propose methods to enhance results.
- Grading Automation: Tools driven by ML can assess multiple-choice assessments and can also evaluate essays for clarity, grammar, and relevance of the content.

Neural Networks and Deep Learning

- Voice Recognition: Deep learning frameworks provide capabilities for converting speech into text, making education more accessible for students with disabilities.
- Visual Data Analysis: Neural networks assist in interpreting handwritten work, analyzing images, and enhancing virtual labs in scientific education.
- Essay Evaluation Automation: Progressive neural networks can assess written submissions, offering thorough feedback regarding grammar, coherence, and structure of arguments.

Natural Language Processing (NLP) in Education

- AI Chatbots and Virtual Helpers: AI-based chatbots respond to student inquiries, explain concepts, and help with administrative tasks, thus lightening the load for teachers.
- Instant Feedback Systems: NLP allows for immediate comments on student writing, correcting grammar, suggesting enhancements, and improving understanding.

- Translation and Learning Support: NLP instruments eliminate language obstacles by converting text, aiding students who speak multiple languages, and making educational resources more accessible.

On the other hand, the exploration of ethical and implementation challenges in the educational environment has gained significant attention over the past decade, particularly as technological advancements reshape pedagogical practices. A foundational discussion by (Auld & Henderson, 2013) highlights the ethical dilemmas teachers face when navigating social networking services within classroom contexts.

Building on this foundation, (Mings, 2018) investigates the impact of blended learning models on student achievement, particularly in the context of addressing social inequalities exacerbated by the digital divide. While acknowledges the potential benefits of technology integration, she also raises critical concerns regarding the limitations of such approaches, including the risk of diminishing student engagement and achievement through excessive screen time.

As the field evolves, the ethical implications of artificial intelligence in education come to the forefront. (Nguyen et al., 2023) identify numerous challenges associated with the integration of AI in educational settings, including issues of equity, transparency, and ethical data usage. They emphasize the need for comprehensive policies that address systemic biases and ensure that marginalized groups are not further disadvantaged.

In a more focused scoping review, (Li et al., 2023) examine the ethical implications of ChatGPT in higher education. Their findings reveal a predominance of generic discussions around ethical concerns, particularly regarding academic integrity and data privacy.

The examination of ethical and implementation challenges in the educational environment reveals a complex interplay between technology, pedagogy, and ethical considerations. The articles reviewed highlight the multifaceted dilemmas educators face as they navigate the integration of digital tools and platforms into their teaching practices.

Auld and Henderson (2013) highlight ethical dilemmas in using social networks for education, particularly the blurred lines between personal and professional interactions. As educators connect with students on these platforms, maintaining professional boundaries becomes challenging, especially amid incidents of inappropriate communication, which fuels hesitation toward classroom technology use.

Building on this foundation, Mings (2018) examines how blended learning models can both mitigate and reinforce social inequalities. While tech integration can boost engagement, concerns about screen time and cognitive impact remain. High-stakes testing further shifts focus from holistic education, highlighting the need for thoughtful, student-centered implementation.

The evolving role of teachers in a technology-driven educational landscape is critically examined by Macgilchrist (2019). The article raises concerns about the deprofessionalization of teaching, as educators are increasingly relegated to behavior management roles rather than serving as facilitators of deep learning.

Nguyen et al. (2023) highlight the ethical challenges of integrating AI in education, emphasizing equity, transparency, and responsible data use. They advocate for flexible ethical frameworks and teacher training to address systemic biases in AI implementation.

Lastly, the ethical implications of AI technologies like ChatGPT are explored by Li et al. (2023), who highlight the predominance of theoretical discussions over actionable insights. Their review points to critical issues such as academic integrity, misinformation, and data privacy, emphasizing the importance of robust data protection measures to maintain trust in educational environments.

In conclusion, the literature highlights the need for continuous reflection on the ethical use of technology in education. As educators navigate technological and regulatory pressures, fostering ethical engagement and prioritizing student well-being remains essential.

AI-POWERED INSTRUCTIONAL STRATEGIES

Table 1. AI strategies in education and their characteristics

Strategy	Benefits	Limitations	Reference
Personalized Learning	Adaptation of content and immediate feedback	Dependence on high-quality data	Holmes et al. (2019)
Intelligent Tutoring Systems (ITS)	24/7 assistance and automated assessments	Risk of alienation, high costs	Luckin et al. (2022)
Gamification	Increases motivation and engagement	May fail if not well designed	Duolingo, cited in Holmes et al. (2019)

Note. Author's elaboration based on the chapter.

Artificial intelligence can act as a support system within the Student ZPD, which offers the help of what they can achieve by themselves, with what they can do when receiving help. An important illustration is a study conducted by CAI, MSAMBWA and Kangwa in 2025, where they have undergone 158 empirical studies to understand how AI tools can identify and engage with the ZPD in higher education. The results showed that AI improves self -esteem, participation, teamwork and academic success, while promoting an individualized and ethically sound learning experience. These results emphasize the importance of the education of appropriate teachers and the creation of effective learning experience, which is enhanced by AI.

Sidorkin (2025) points out that generative artificial intelligence can act as a permanent scaffold in the proximal development zone (ZPD), providing continuous cognitive aid above the temporary restrictions on traditional scaffolding. According to his perspective, AI not only facilitates immediate solutions to the problems, but also gradually expands the ability of students to solve difficult tasks from the early stage of education. This approach again defines the ZPD by integrating AI tools capable of providing a permanent feedback, modeling cognitive processes and offering personal indications, thus improving academic development and long -term intellectual autonomy.

Hamedi et al. (2025) In its integrative review, it shows that artificial intelligence systems, which inspire the principles of Vygotsky, not only repeat the interaction between teaching, but also introduce personalized learning paths with immediate and contextualized feedback, as well as mechanisms contributing to self -regulated learning. The authors emphasize that such AI can dynamically adapt to students' progress and promote balance between external instructions and internal autonomy. Therefore, AI not only acts as a cognitive broker ZPD, but also strengthens metacognitics, self -examination and long -term skills development.

According to constructivist approaches, Tran et al. (2025) argue that GenAI may play a "more knowledgeable" role that promotes social learning by facilitating dialogue, providing flexible scaffolding, and creating collaborative environments in which knowledge is co-constructed.

When combined, these viewpoints show how generative AI revitalizes the relevance of traditional learning theories while also redefining Vygotskian ideas like the Zone of Proximal Development (Tran et al., 2025; Sidorkin, 2025; Hamedi et al., 2025). The timeless ideas of behaviorism and cognitivism reinforcement, feedback, and memory are now enhanced by adaptive AI systems, as Anjali (2024) highlights. This convergence points to a larger pedagogical change where AI acts as a catalyst for the integration of traditional and modern educational paradigms as well as a mediator of social knowledge formation.

Artificial Intelligence (AI) is revolutionizing education by allowing for more customized, flexible, and data-informed teaching methods. Tools and techniques that use AI support teachers in improving educational approaches, increasing student involvement, and enhancing learning results. Below are the main teaching methods influenced by AI in contemporary learning.

Personalized and Adaptive Learning

Platforms that employ AI for adaptive learning adjust material, speed, and difficulty according to each student's performance and learning preferences.

Features of Adaptive Learning

- Instant feedback: AI constantly reviews student answers and modifies content as needed.
- Tailored learning paths: AI designs lesson plans to fit the specific needs of each student.
- Automatic resource suggestions: AI recommends extra materials based on student advancement.

For instance, platforms like Smart Sparrow and Knewton utilize AI to modify lesson plans according to how students interact.

Intelligent Tutoring Systems (ITS)

Tutoring systems powered by AI offer immediate help, mimicking individual tutoring and aiding students in understanding complicated subjects.

Major Advantages of ITS

- Always available: AI tutors can be accessed at any time, giving ongoing assistance.
- Tailored instruction: AI modifies explanations based on how well a student is doing.
- Automated evaluations: AI reviews student answers and gives feedback.

Example: Carnegie Learning's MATHia and IBM's Watson Tutor assist students in various subjects through personalized tutoring.

Schiff (2021) provides a foundational perspective on the implications of AI in education, particularly through intelligent tutoring systems and artificial educational agents. He argues that while AI in education (AIEd) has the capacity to enhance efficiency and personalize learning experiences, it also raises concerns regarding alienation among students and educators. In addition, highlights the potential for these systems to provide robust differentiation tailored to individual student needs, thereby fostering a more personalized learning experience.

The field of Intelligent Tutoring Systems (ITS) has evolved significantly over the past few years, reflecting an increasing emphasis on personalized learning and automated feedback mechanisms. (Al-Bastami & Abu Naser, 2017) highlight the capacity of ITS to offer customized instruction akin to a personal teacher. Their research underscores the system's ability to collect real-time data, which can be instrumental for educators seeking to refine their teaching methodologies.

Gamification, powered by AI, increases student motivation and engagement through interactive and game-based learning experiences.

AI Features in Gamified Learning

Personalized Challenges: AI adapts game difficulty based on student performance.
Real-Time Scoring: AI tracks student achievements and progress.
Interactive Simulations: AI enhances virtual reality (VR) and augmented reality (AR) learning experiences.

Example: Duolingo uses AI to gamify language learning with adaptive challenges and rewards.

As AI continues to evolve, future instructional strategies may include:

- Emotion AI: Detecting student emotions to adjust teaching strategies dynamically.
- AI-driven peer learning: Connecting students with similar learning needs for collaborative study.
- AI-generated content: Creating personalized study materials and quizzes in real time.

The integration of artificial intelligence (AI) into educational contexts has garnered significant attention, reflecting a transformative shift in instructional strategies. In examining the literature surrounding AI-powered instructional methodologies, it becomes evident that the discourse encompasses both the potential benefits and the ethical dilemmas associated with these technologies.

Schiff (2021) provides a foundational perspective on the implications of AI in education, particularly through intelligent tutoring systems and artificial educational agents. He argues that while AI in education (AIEd) has the capacity to enhance efficiency and personalize learning experiences, it also raises concerns regarding alienation among students and educators. By evaluating the current landscape of AIEd, emphasizes the necessity for responsible engagement with these technologies, advocating for a framework that prioritizes socially responsible research and development. His insights highlight the historical context of digital distance education as a cautionary tale, suggesting that stakeholders must learn from past experiences to navigate the challenges posed by AI in educational settings.

Building on this foundation, Aljuaid (2024) systematically reviews the impact of AI tools on academic writing instruction within higher education. The study identifies a growing trend toward the incorporation of AI-powered writing aids, such as Wordtune, Grammarly, and Google Translate, which are designed to enhance students' writing skills by providing real-time feedback and assistance with grammar and paraphrasing. While these tools are recognized for their potential to improve efficiency and student confidence, also raises critical concerns regarding their influence on students' critical and creative thinking. The findings underscore the importance of maintaining teacher oversight to foster these essential cognitive skills, while also calling for clear ethical guidelines to govern the use of AI technologies in academic writing.

The article delves into the capabilities of intelligent tutoring systems and anthropomorphized educational agents, which are positioned as tools that can simulate the role of teachers. So too, highlights the potential for these systems to provide robust differentiation tailored to individual student needs, thereby fostering a more personalized learning experience. This aspect of AIEd is particularly compelling, as it aligns with contemporary educational theories that advocate for differentiated instruction to accommodate varying learning styles and paces.

Moreover, Schiff (2021) addresses the socio-emotional engagement potential of AIEd, suggesting that these technologies could play a pivotal role in supporting students' emotional and social development. The integration of AI in educational settings could facilitate a more holistic approach to learning that goes beyond mere academic achievement. However, the article also presents a critical view of the sociotechnical risks associated with AIEd, urging stakeholders to consider the ethical implications of deploying such technologies in classrooms.

Schiff (2021) contrasts two idealized futures of AIEd implementation, which serves to underscore the importance of responsible research and development in this field, advocates for a peer review process as a gatekeeping strategy to mitigate the risks of harmful research findings influencing educational practices. This recommendation is particularly pertinent given the rapid advancements in AI technology and the potential for misuse or unintended consequences in educational settings.

The article titled "The Impact of Artificial Intelligence Tools on Academic Writing Instruction in Higher Education: A Systematic Review" by Aljuaid (2024) provides an insightful examination of the role of AI in enhancing academic writing instruction. The main idea posited by the author is that AI tools, such as Wordtune, Grammarly, and Google Translate, have become integral to the academic writing process, significantly aiding students in various aspects of writing.

Aljuaid (2024) emphasizes that these AI-powered tools offer valuable functionalities, including paraphrasing, grammar improvement, and overall enhancement of writing quality. By automating numerous writing tasks, these technologies not only improve efficiency but also streamline workflow, which is crucial in academic settings where timely submissions are often critical. The article highlights empirical evidence that supports the positive impact of AI on students' writing capabilities. This assertion is particularly relevant, as it underscores the potential of AI to provide immediate feedback, thereby fostering an environment conducive to learning and improvement.

However, the article does not shy away from addressing the ethical implications associated with the use of AI in academic writing. Aljuaid (2024) calls for a careful consideration of these ethical concerns, advocating for the establishment of clear guidelines governing the use of AI tools. This is particularly pertinent given the potential for AI to influence critical and creative thinking skills among students. The author suggests that while AI can enhance writing proficiency, it is imperative that educators maintain a supervisory role to ensure that students engage in critical thinking and creativity rather than relying solely on automated systems.

The integration of artificial intelligence (AI) into educational contexts has the potential to reshape instructional strategies significantly. The literature reveals that while AI-powered tools can enhance learning experiences, they also present ethical challenges that must be addressed. The foundational work by Schiff (2021) emphasizes the dual nature of AI in education, highlighting its capacity to personalize learning through intelligent tutoring systems while also cautioning against potential alienation among learners. This underscores the necessity for a responsible approach to AI integration, advocating for frameworks that prioritize ethical considerations in research and development.

Furthermore, Aljuaid (2024) provides a systematic review of AI tools in academic writing instruction, identifying their growing role in enhancing students' writing capabilities. While these tools, such as Grammarly and Google Translate, offer significant benefits in terms of efficiency and immediate feedback, they also raise concerns regarding the impact on critical and creative thinking skills. The need for teacher oversight is emphasized to ensure that students do not overly rely on AI technologies, thereby fostering essential cognitive skills.

The literature collectively illustrates that AI has the potential to transform educational practices by offering personalized learning experiences and improving academic writing. However, it also highlights the pressing need for ethical guidelines and responsible engagement with these technologies to mitigate risks and ensure that they support rather than hinder educational development. Stakeholders must learn from past experiences and prioritize ethical considerations as AI becomes increasingly embedded in instructional methodologies.

Intelligent Tutoring Systems Automated Feedback and Formative Assessment

The field of Intelligent Tutoring Systems (ITS) has evolved significantly over the past few years, reflecting an increasing emphasis on personalized learning and automated feedback mechanisms. This literature review examines key contributions to the understanding of ITS, focusing on their design, functionality, and the implications for student learning.

Beginning with Al-Bastami and Abu Naser (2017), the authors highlight the capacity of ITS to offer customized instruction akin to a personal teacher. Their research underscores the system's ability to collect real-time data, which can be instrumental for educators seeking to refine their teaching methodologies. The authors emphasize that ITS not only monitors student progress step-by-step but also provides actionable feedback, thereby fostering a more tailored educational experience. This foundational understanding sets the stage for subsequent studies that delve deeper into the characteristics and applications of ITS.

Goldbach and Hamza-Lup (2020) further expand on the significance of learner-specific characteristics in the design of ITS, particularly for Generation Z. Their review stresses the necessity for a reward system within these intelligent platforms, advocating for a nuanced approach to learner engagement. They categorize ITS into three learning environments—simulation-based, discourse-based, and situation-based—each catering to different learning preferences and contexts. This categorization is crucial as it informs the development of ITS that are not only adaptive but also relevant to the diverse technological landscape in which modern learners operate.

The work of Ni and Cheung (2023) builds on the previous findings by exploring the application of AI-powered ITS in English language learning. They articulate the four essential modules of ITS—domain, pedagogical, student model, and user interface—highlighting their interdependence in creating an effective learning environment. Their analysis reveals that ITS can significantly enhance students' performance in various areas, including grammar, reading, and writing, through a problem-solving approach that adapts to individual learner needs. This adaptability is further emphasized through the system's ability to monitor cognitive and emotional states, thereby reinforcing the importance of interactivity and timely feedback in the learning process.

The literature on Intelligent Tutoring Systems (ITS) reveals a robust framework for understanding how these systems can enhance personalized learning experiences through automated feedback and formative assessment. The contributions of various studies illustrate the evolving capabilities of ITS, particularly in their design and implementation to meet the needs of diverse learner populations.

Al-Bastami and Abu Naser (2017) provide foundational insights into the functionalities of ITS, emphasizing their ability to deliver real-time data that educators can leverage to refine their teaching practices. The authors highlight the dynamic nature of ITS, which allows for continuous monitoring of student progress and the provision of immediate feedback, thus facilitating a tailored educational experience. This adaptability is crucial for formative assessment, as it enables the identification of knowledge gaps and the delivery of targeted interventions.

Goldbach and Hamza-Lup (2020) expand on this by focusing on the specific characteristics of Generation Z learners. They argue that effective ITS must incorporate a reward system to enhance motivation and engagement, drawing attention to the necessity of aligning educational technologies with the preferences of contemporary students. Their categorization of ITS into simulation-based, discourse-based, and situation-based learning environments provides a useful framework for understanding how these systems can cater to varying learning styles and contexts.

Ni and Cheung (2023) further develop the discourse by analyzing the modular architecture of AI-powered ITS for English language learning. They identify four essential components—domain, pedagogical, student model, and user interface—that work in synergy to create an effective learning environment. The interactivity of these systems is highlighted as a critical factor in providing timely feedback and monitoring students' cognitive and emotional states, which is essential for fostering deeper learning. Their findings indicate that ITS can significantly improve language learning outcomes, demonstrating the systems' potential to enhance both immediate comprehension and long-term retention of complex subjects.

In conclusion, the literature underscores the transformative potential of Intelligent Tutoring Systems in education. By integrating automated feedback and formative assessment, these systems not only enhance student engagement but also provide personalized learning experiences that are responsive to individual needs. The emphasis on adaptability, learner characteristics, and modular design reflects a comprehensive understanding of how ITS can be effectively utilized in diverse educational contexts.

AI Gamification Models

Gamification is often described as the use of game features, including points, levels, badges, and leaderboards, in areas outside of gaming to boost engagement and motivation. In the last ten years, it has attracted considerable interest in corporate e-learning and online teaching spaces because it improves the learning journey and encourages changes in behavior.

Two primary reasons explain the rising popularity of gamification. To begin with, conventional e-learning and corporate training techniques usually rely on passive learning, where students receive information without actively participating. This can create a lack of motivation and involvement, which can later result in diminished knowledge retention and application. Gamification tackles this challenge by adding engaging and motivating elements that create a more interactive and tailored learning experience. Additionally, the emergence of Web 2. 0 has transitioned much of work and education from traditional desktop setups to interactive social networking sites that incorporate gaming aspects. Many of these sites use rewards, challenges, achievements, and competitions to maintain user interest over time.

Studies indicate that gamification can boost intrinsic motivation by meeting psychological needs like autonomy, competence, and social connection, as outlined by Self-Determination Theory (SDT). When learners experience a sense of progress and success through organized challenges and timely feedback, they are more inclined to actively engage in training sessions and gain a better understanding of the material. Because of its effectiveness in online settings, educators and corporate trainers are increasingly investigating the possibility of gamified learning experiences to enhance long-term involvement and better educational results (Kapp, 2012).

The popularity of gaming mechanisms in any context comes from their ability to engage and immerse users. However, CEOs and decision-makers should be aware that not all activities proposed with gamification lead to engagement; poorly designed mechanisms can even drive users away. Carefully assessing the suitability of these mechanisms and developing gamified applications tailored to learning objectives, target tasks, institutional context, and user profiles is crucial (Bucchiarone et al., 2023). Designers of gamified learning activities need modeling environments in which they can specify the desired gamification approach at a high level, possibly through the reuse of existing components. Two questions motivate this project: Which gamification mechanisms are suitable for a given learning context? And how can these mechanisms be effectively integrated and deployed in modeling environments? A strict match between targeted learning objectives and gamified mechanisms is crucial for ensuring the effectiveness of the gamification process on user engagement.

Gamification is the use of game design elements in a non-game context. It represents an important and rapidly-emerging phenomenon that captures the attention of scholars and practitioners alike. Dramatic claims have been made about the power of gamification to motivate, coordinate, and influence behavior in ontology-rich and socially-relevant contexts. Like any powerful technology, gamification brings with it significant risks. After introducing the concept of gamification with a quick review of the literature, the ethical challenges and dilemmas of gamification are discussed.

The potential harms of gamification are summarized, highlighting cases of unethical gamification with illustrations. A set of principles for ethical gamification is provided, noting that this is an emerging field of inquiry that will benefit from additional scholarship and research.

Gamification refers to the use of game design elements in non-game contexts. It is a type of persuasive technology, meaning an interactive computing system designed to change attitudes or behaviors, as well as an information technology, meaning a computer-based system for collecting, storing, and processing data. Many tools have been developed for the creation and use of gamification applications that employ game design elements in the implementation of a combination of game components, mechanics, and contexts. Gamification represents an important rapidly-emerging phenomenon that addresses an unmet need.

Gamification is now being used in some education systems. However, it's a relatively new concept since. As for employees' gamified experience of MOOC, after a thorough investigation of issues using different methods including interviews and online forum participant observations, gamified experiences were classified into four postures in a two-dimensional disc: spectator vs streamer and amateur vs professional. Some of the issues regarding successful implementation of gamification were raised. Gamification was implemented in medical technology education, leading to significantly better audience engagement.

The education system was based on the game design theory that motivated students' learning process. Nonetheless, goals and difficulties should be appropriately designed; otherwise, students would be demotivated. An ongoing study of the gamification effect in an educational board game was reported. Players played a student vs employee negotiation game that simulated elements of professional and academic life. It was shown that players were satisfied and wanted to play again. Context, user, design & technical aspects, and motivation effects of gamification, as well as its effectiveness, were focused on in gamification research in HCI. Observational studies might be performed in considering conferences aiming to facilitate networking.

Leaderboards are one of the most popular items in gamification. They are almost ubiquitous because of their intrinsic capabilities of social comparison. Listeners are compared against other listeners and classified by common metrics. The comparison stresses superiority, giving attention and increasing status. It has been proposed that due to these effects, users were motivated by pointing to the leaderboard. Yet it was found that users consistently have a negative response toward leaderboards, mainly due to the fear of becoming a target via a comparison. In social websites, leaderboards created social disincentives that motivated users indirectly, causing social comparison without the need for social recognition.

Badges

Used to reward achievements and motivate learning. They create a sense of accomplishment but require careful design to maintain their effectiveness.

Challenges and quests have been found to significantly engage students by providing tasks suited to their skill levels. According to research, appropriate challenges stimulate engagement, foster learning motivation, and lead to higher achievement levels (Anunpattana et al., 2021).

The integration of artificial intelligence (AI) into educational contexts has the potential to reshape instructional strategies significantly. The literature reveals that while AI-powered tools can enhance learning experiences, they also present ethical challenges that must be addressed. The foundational work by Schiff (2021) emphasizes the dual nature of AI in education, highlighting its capacity to personalize learning through intelligent tutoring systems while also cautioning against potential alienation among learners. Furthermore, Aljuaid (2024) provides a systematic review of AI tools in academic writing instruction, identifying their growing role in enhancing students' writing capabilities.

In conclusion, AI-powered instructional strategies, including adaptive learning, intelligent tutoring systems, automated feedback, and gamification, provide a significant opportunity to enhance education. However, the ethical implications of AI implementation must be carefully considered to ensure that AI technologies promote learning equity, maintain pedagogical integrity, and foster student engagement in an ethical manner.

AI-BASED TOOLS AND TECHNOLOGIES FOR EDUCATION

Chatbots and Educational Virtual Assistants

Artificial Intelligence (AI) is transforming the educational landscape by offering innovative solutions that improve the personalization, efficiency, and accessibility of learning. Chatbots and virtual educational assistants have gained significant popularity in the educational field due to their ability to provide instant responses, personalized support, and continuous feedback.

Applications

Personalized Tutoring

Chatbots act as virtual tutors, answering questions and explaining complex concepts in real time.

Administrative Support

Virtual assistants help students or teachers with administrative tasks, such as course registration and scheduling requests.

Automated Feedback

Some chatbots correct assignments and provide immediate feedback, reducing teachers' workload.

Learning platforms that use artificial intelligence provide a variety of advantages. One key benefit is personalized education, as AI modifies lessons to fit each student's specific requirements. Furthermore, these platforms are accessible at any time, meaning students can learn whenever it suits them best. They also help teachers by lessening their workload since AI takes care of repetitive tasks. In addition, they improve access for students in remote locations or for those with disabilities, ensuring fair learning chances for all.

On the other hand, these platforms come with their own set of problems. Their success often relies on the quality of the data that is available, which can impact how accurately they respond. They also face challenges with understanding language, especially when handling unclear or complicated questions. A significant worry is privacy, as these AI systems gather and manage information from students, which leads to concerns over data safety and protection.

Adaptive learning tools, powered by AI technology, modify both educational content and the speed of learning based on what each student needs, leading to a more tailored and effective educational experience.

Applications

Mass Customization

Platforms such as Khan Academy, DreamBox, and Duolingo use AI to tailor content based on students' knowledge levels and learning styles.

Automated Assessment

AI enables real-time grading and feedback on assignments.

Predictive Analytics

AI predicts student performance and suggests early interventions to prevent dropouts.

Gamified Learning Experiences

AI enhances engagement through interactive, game-based activities

Innovations in artificial intelligence are changing the landscape of education by bringing many substantial benefits. A major benefit is the customization of learning experiences, enabling every learner to engage with a program suited to their individual skills and needs.

In addition, AI offers immediate feedback, which supports ongoing enhancement of the educational journey. It also boosts teaching efficiency by taking over repetitive tasks, which allows teachers to concentrate on more significant endeavors. Another important advantage is the increase in student involvement through gamification driven by AI, which makes learning more lively and engaging.

Yet, these advancements also present several challenges. For starters, not every educational facility has access to AI-based platforms, potentially leading to educational inequalities. Additionally, AI algorithms can reflect biases stemming from flawed or unrepresentative data, which could impact fairness in learning outcomes. A further crucial issue is privacy, as these tools necessitate the gathering and management of student information, prompting concerns about security and ethical use.

In this setting, applications of Augmented Reality (AR) and Virtual Reality (VR) that are driven by artificial intelligence are revolutionizing learning. These technologies offer immersive, interactive, and tailored educational experiences, aiding learners in understanding intricate concepts through virtual settings that mimic real-life situations. By merging AR, VR, and AI, students can partake in a more visual, practical, and engaging learning experience, greatly improving their educational journey.

Applications

Educational Simulations

Virtual labs, such as Labster, allow students to conduct scientific experiments in a safe environment.

Immersive Learning

AR and VR transport students to historical, scientific, or cultural environments, improving knowledge retention.

Professional Training

AI-powered VR is used in medical and engineering training for risk-free practice.

Augmented Reality (AR) and Virtual Reality (VR) technologies are changing the landscape of education by providing a range of advantages. One of the primary benefits is that they enhance student engagement and help with retaining information, as these technologies offer more interactive and immersive learning opportunities. Moreover, they allow for the establishment of safe and controlled environments for practical experimentation, which is essential for fields that rely on simulations. Another important advantage is better access to specialized training, enabling learners to gain technical and professional abilities without depending on expensive or risky physical tools.

Nevertheless, there are also challenges in the adoption of these technologies. A major issue is the significant expense associated with AR and VR devices along with the necessary infrastructure to incorporate them into classrooms. In addition, both teachers and students need to learn how to use these tools, which can slow down their acceptance at first. There are also ethical and privacy issues, as utilizing these technologies often means gathering data in virtual spaces, leading to concerns about data security and managing user information.

In this scenario, the development of automated educational content powered by AI is transforming how learning materials are created. By using Natural Language Processing (NLP), Machine Learning (ML), and multimedia generation, AI supports the production of tailored, high-quality educational resources. These technologies help in adjusting materials to meet the unique needs of each student, improving teaching strategies and enriching the entire learning process.

Applications

Creation of Study Materials

AI generates personalized study guides, summaries, and lesson plans.

Customized Assessments

AI adapts tests and exercises to students.

Automated Presentation Design

AI assists in generating instructional slides, videos, and interactive activities.

The use of automation in creating educational materials brings several important benefits. A significant advantage is the decrease in both time and money needed to make learning resources, which helps teachers and schools create materials more effectively. Moreover, artificial intelligence allows for the personalization of these resources, tailoring them to fit each student's unique learning requirements and offering a better educational experience. Another key advantage is the broader range of available learning resources, which increases access to quality content across various subjects and educational levels.

IMPACT OF AI ON TEACHING AND LEARNING

Table 2. Successful experiences of AI in education

Case / Platform	Application	Reported Impact	Reference
Khan Academy	AI-driven personalized learning paths	Improved performance in math and science	Khan Academy (2023)
Duolingo	Gamified adaptive language learning	Enhanced vocabulary acquisition; real-time feedback	Holmes et al. (2019)
Squirrel AI	Intelligent tutoring system	Up to 25% increase in student grades	Luan et al. (2020)
Pounce (GSU)	Virtual assistant for student retention	22% reduction in dropout rates	Bienkowski et al. (2023)

Note. Author's elaboration based on the chapter.

Artificial Intelligence (AI) is transforming education by providing new opportunities for personalized learning, optimized classroom management, and improved academic performance.

Benefits

Personalized Learning

AI tailors content to students' needs, improving retention (Holmes et al., 2019).

Real-Time Feedback

Platforms like Duolingo provide immediate corrections to enhance understanding.

Administrative automation: AI reduces teachers' workload by automating grading and attendance tracking (Luckin et al., 2022).

Challenges

Privacy Concerns

Large amounts of student data raise ethical issues (Williamson, 2022).

Resistance to Change

Some educators and students lack training or trust in AI tools.

Educational Gap

Limited access to AI in some regions increases inequalities.

Successful Experiences

Khan Academy

AI-driven personalized learning paths have improved student performance in math and science (**Khan Academy**., 2023).

Duolingo's AI-driven gamification enhances vocabulary acquisition and engagement in English learners (Safrina et al., 2023)

Squirrel AI's intelligent tutoring systems have demonstrated significant improvements in student performance, with some reports indicating increases of up to 25% in high school grades (World Economic Forum, 2024).

Gamification has been shown to enhance student engagement, with game-based rewards and interactive elements fostering greater participation in educational settings (Li & Ma, 2023).

Pounce (Georgia State University)

AI intervention reduced student dropouts by 22% (Page & Gehlbach, 2017).

Instant Feedback Enhances Learning Confidence

AI tools support continuous improvement. Research indicates that AI-based tutoring enhances student performance, with learners achieving significantly higher academic outcomes compared to traditional methods (Kestin et al., 2024)

Limited access to devices and internet connectivity in disadvantaged communities hinders the effective use of AI-based educational tools (OECD, 2023).

AI is revolutionizing education by making learning more personalized, efficient, and accessible. However, challenges such as digital equity, ethical concerns, and data privacy must be addressed to maximize its benefits. Future educational policies must ensure AI technologies promote inclusivity and enhance learning opportunities for all students.

ETHICAL AND PRIVACY CONSIDERATIONS IN THE USE OF AI IN EDUCATION

Table 3. Ethical dilemmas and regulatory frameworks in AI for education

Issue	Description	Reference
Privacy	Ethical use of student data and protection of sensitive info	UNESCO (2022, 2025)
Transparency	Tension between explainability and intellectual property	Mesa (2024)
Regulation	EU AI Act and national regulations on responsible AI use	European Parliament (2025); HuffPost (2025)

Note. Author's elaboration based on the chapter.

As often happens with technological innovations, novelty can cloud people's judgment, preventing them from identifying risks, limitations, or poorly understood aspects. This can lead to erroneous decisions with significant consequences. A recent case was observed with cryptocurrencies and NFTs, where the lack of clear information about their operation, combined with widespread news about people investing in these assets, led many to make investments without fully understanding the risks involved (Ametrano, 2016).

In the context of artificial intelligence, the risk is not directly related to money but to information. AI relies on large volumes of data to generate, summarize, and coherently report content. Therefore, it is crucial to establish control and regulatory guidelines from now on, especially in the educational field. UNESCO has already drafted a document with recommendations for appropriate action in various fields, including education and research (UNESCO, 2022). Some recommendations include promoting AI education competencies, ethical AI research, and AI researcher training in ethics.

The governments of Spain and the European Union have advanced in implementing regulations for the use of artificial intelligence, establishing standards aimed at mitigating risks and ensuring ethical use of this technology. Spain has laws restricting AI misuse, such as using chatbots for subliminal persuasion in gambling addiction cases (HuffPost, 2025). The European Union has developed a regulatory framework classifying AI systems based on risk levels, ensuring transparency in AI applications (European Parliament, 2025).

Transparency in artificial intelligence is a fundamental aspect, but it is also a complex challenge due to various interests at play. Users and regulatory entities demand a high level of clarity about AI models to ensure inclusive, fair, and ethically responsible responses. However, development companies seek to protect their intellectual property, maintaining competitive advantages (Mesa, 2024). This conflict highlights the need for balanced regulations that foster innovation while safeguarding user rights and security.

AI relies on large amounts of student data to function effectively, raising concerns about privacy and ethical data usage. UNESCO (2025) emphasizes that AI systems in education should not affect cognitive abilities, collect sensitive data without consent, or commercialize student information. Furthermore, privacy laws and guidelines should be in place to ensure that data usage in AI-driven educational platforms is transparent and compliant with ethical standards.

AI implementation in education must be responsible, ensuring that technologies are used ethically and effectively. Transparency, accountability, and fairness must be the cornerstones of AI deployment in academic settings. Educational institutions and policymakers must prioritize AI regulation to mitigate potential harms while maximizing its benefits.

FUTURE PERSPECTIVES AND EMERGING TRENDS

Table 4. Future emerging trends and challenges in AI for education

Trend / Tool	Description	Associated Challenge	Reference
Khanmigo (AI assistant)	Guides students through questions to foster critical thinking	Risk of over-dependence on AI guidance	Roldán (2025)
Teacher task automation	Optimizes grading, attendance, and admin tasks	Preserving the human role in teaching	Luckin et al. (2022)
Teacher AI training	Ongoing professional development in AI use	Unequal access to training programs	UNESCO (2022, 2025)

Note. Author's elaboration based on the chapter.

One of the main qualities of artificial intelligence today is its ability to adapt based on the information it receives and the clarity of the requests made. AI could become a valuable tool in education, facilitating the resolution of doubts, enriching the learning process, and creating more dynamic and interactive educational environments. Khanmigo, an AI-based learning assistant, exemplifies this by guiding students through questions rather than providing direct answers, fostering critical thinking (Roldán, 2025).

The integration of AI in the classroom is transforming teaching and academic management. AI's impact includes optimizing administrative tasks, personalizing learning, and redefining the teacher-student relationship. Research by (Barcia et al., 2024) highlights two approaches to AI in higher education: as a technological tool supporting professionals and as a transformative agent redefining teaching dynamics.

AI is also impacting teacher training and professional development. According to Álvarez (2025), integrating AI into education requires preparing teachers for its use, ensuring they can effectively incorporate AI into their pedagogy. Continuous teacher training programs, such as the Common Sense and OpenAI initiatives, aim to help educators understand AI's benefits and limitations.

AI will continue evolving to support education in the long term. Personalized learning, automation of administrative tasks, and enhanced accessibility will play a crucial role. However, ethical regulations and policies must ensure AI enriches education without replacing essential human interactions (Mendes, 2025).

CONCLUSION

Artificial intelligence has shown great promise in the field of education by allowing tailored learning experiences, streamlining administrative tasks, and enhancing student involvement. Nevertheless, issues such as privacy concerns, data protection, and hesitance in using these technologies pose important challenges that need to be addressed.

To fully utilize AI tools, teachers require ongoing education and training. It is essential for policymakers to prioritize creating strong guidelines that guarantee ethical usage of AI in schools.

To successfully incorporate artificial intelligence into teaching methods, several initiatives need to be adopted. To start, training for teachers is vital, so programs that provide knowledge and skills about AI uses in the classroom must be put into place. Moreover, clear governance structures should be created to set policies on how AI is utilized in education, which will help ensure that it is implemented ethically and effectively.

Another important factor is the responsible creation of AI technologies, which should encourage the development of systems that are clear and fair, helping to avoid discrimination and offering an equal learning experience for every student. In addition, there must be investments in technology resources to guarantee that all educational institutions have access to tools powered by AI, thus eliminating any gaps caused by technological or financial issues.

Future studies ought to concentrate on exploring the long-term effects of artificial intelligence on educational success and on finding ways to minimize bias in algorithms. Addressing ethical issues related to AI in evaluation methods is also vital, as is investigating how this technology can help create a more inclusive and fair education for every student.

REFERENCES

Akpan, I. J., Kobara, Y. M., Owolabi, J., Akpan, A. A., & Offodile, O. F. (2025). Conversational and generative artificial intelligence and human-chatbot interaction in education and research. *International Transactions in Operational Research*, *32*(3), 1251–1281. DOI: 10.1111/itor.13522

Al-Bastami, G. B., & Abu Naser, S. (2017). Design and development of an intelligent tutoring system for C# language. https://core.ac.uk/download/131210533.pdf

Aljuaid, H. (2024). The impact of artificial intelligence tools on academic writing instruction in higher education: A systematic review. Arab World English Journal (AWEJ) Special Issue on ChatGPT, April 2024, 26-55. https://dx.doi.org/DOI: 10.24093/awej/ChatGPT.2

Alshahrani, S., & Kapetanios, E. (2016). Are deep learning approaches suitable for natural language processing? In Métais, E., Meziane, F., Saraee, M., Sugumaran, V., & Vadera, S. (Eds.), Lecture Notes in Computer Science: Vol. 9612. *Natural language processing and information systems: NLDB 2016*. Springer., DOI: 10.1007/978-3-319-41754-7_33

AlTwijri, L., & Alghizzi, T. M. (2024). Investigating the integration of artificial intelligence in English as foreign language classes for enhancing learners' affective factors: A systematic review. *Heliyon*, *10*(10), e31053. DOI: 10.1016/j.heliyon.2024.e31053 PMID: 38778968

Álvarez, A. (2025). Artificial intelligence reaches schools: Lights and shadows. El País. https://elpais.com/eps/2025-03-13/la-inteligencia-artificial-llega-a-la-escuela-luces-y-sombras.html

Ametrano, F. M. (2016). Hayek money: The cryptocurrency price stability solution. SSRN Electronic Journal. https://doi.org/DOI: 10.2139/ssrn.2425270

Anunpattana, P., Khalid, M. N. A., Iida, H., & Inchamnan, W. (2021). Capturing potential impact of challenge-based gamification on gamified quizzing in the classroom. *Heliyon*, *7*(12), e08637. DOI: 10.1016/j.heliyon.2021.e08637 PMID: 35005284

Auld, G., & Henderson, M. (2013). The ethical dilemmas of social networking sites in classroom contexts. Proceedings of the Conference on Computer-Supported Collaborative Learning. https://api.semanticscholar.org/CorpusID:15010071

Barcia Cedeño, E. I., Tambaco Quintero, A. R., Angulo Quiñónez, O. G., Prado Zamora, M. E., & Valverde Prado, N. G. (2024). Analysis of trends and the future of artificial intelligence in higher education: Perspectives and challenges. *Ciencia Latina Revista Científica Multidisciplinar, 8*(1), 3061–3076. DOI: 10.37811/cl_rcm.v8i1.9637

Bucchiarone, A., Savary-Leblanc, M., & Le Pallec, X.. (2023). Gamifying model-based engineering: The PapyGame experience. *Software & Systems Modeling, 22*, 1369–1389. DOI: 10.1007/s10270-023-01091-8 PMID: 37363105

Cai, L., Msafiri, M. M., & Kangwa, D. (2025). Exploring the impact of integrating AI tools in higher education using the Zone of Proximal Development. *Education and Information Technologies, 30*, 7191–7264. DOI: 10.1007/s10639-024-13112-0

Casey, A., Davidson, E., Poon, M., Dong, H., Duma, D., Grivas, A., Grover, C., Suárez-Paniagua, V., Tobin, R., Whiteley, W., Wu, H., & Alex, B. (2021). A systematic review of natural language processing applied to radiology reports. *BMC Medical Informatics and Decision Making, 21*(1), 179. DOI: 10.1186/s12911-021-01533-7 PMID: 34082729

Crema, C., Attardi, G., Sartiano, D., & Redolfi, A. (2022). Natural language processing in clinical neuroscience and psychiatry: A review. *Frontiers in Psychiatry, 13*, 946387. DOI: 10.3389/fpsyt.2022.946387 PMID: 36186874

Cukurova, M. (2024). The interplay of learning, analytics and artificial intelligence in education: A vision for hybrid intelligence. *British Journal of Educational Technology, 56*(2), 469–488. DOI: 10.1111/bjet.13514

Dong, Y., Yu, X., & Alharbi, A.. (2022). AI-based production and application of English multimode online reading using multi-criteria decision support system. *Soft Computing, 26*, 10927–10937. DOI: 10.1007/s00500-022-07209-2 PMID: 35668907

European Parliament. (2025). EU AI Law: First regulation on artificial intelligence. https://www.europarl.europa.eu/topics/es/article/20230601STO93804/ley-de-ia-de-la-ue-primera-normativa-sobre-inteligencia-artificial

Ferreira Mello, R., Freitas, E., Dwan Pereira, F., Cabral, L., Tedesco, P., & Ramalho, G. (2023). Education in the age of generative AI: Context and recent developments. arXiv. https://doi.org//arXiv.2309.12332DOI: 10.48550

Goldbach, R. I., & Hamza-Lup, G. F. (2020). Intelligent tutoring systems for Generation Z's addiction. arXiv. https://arxiv.org/pdf/2005.05024

Goldberg, Y. (2015). A primer on neural network models for natural language processing. arXiv. https://doi.org//arXiv.1510.00726DOI: 10.48550

Hamedi, W. H. W., Ali, F. D. A., Abdullah, W. Y., Ab Hamid, H., & Shuhaimi, N. 'Izzah M., & Amir, M. M. (2025). Ai as a digital scaffold: An integrative review of vygotsky's zone of proximal development in modern education. [ijmoe]. *International Journal of Medical Education, 7*(26). Advance online publication. DOI: 10.35631/IJMOE.726038

HuffPost. (2025). The government focuses on artificial intelligence: It will require AI-generated content to be identified and establish penalties. https://www.huffingtonpost.es/politica/el-gobierno-pone-foco-inteligencia-artificial-obligara-identificar-contenidos-generados-ia-establecera-sanciones.html

Kestin, G., Miller, K., Klales, A., Milbourne, T., & Ponti, G. (2024). AI Tutoring Outperforms Active Learning. ResearchGate. Recuperado de https://www.researchgate.net/publication/380587627_AI_Tutoring_Outperforms_Active_Learning Khan Academy. (2023). Khanmigo: AI-powered teaching assistant. Recuperado de https://khanmigo.ai/

Kshirsagar, P. R., Jagannadham, D. B. V., Alqahtani, H., Noorulhasan, N., Quadri, I., Saiful, T. M., & Dejene, M. (2022). Human intelligence analysis through perception of AI in teaching and learning. *Computational Intelligence and Neuroscience, 9160727*. Advance online publication. DOI: 10.1155/2022/9160727 PMID: 35726295

Li, G., Zarei, M. A., & Alibakhshi, G.. (2024). Teachers and educators' experiences and perceptions of artificial-powered interventions for autism groups. *BMC Psychology, 12*, 199. DOI: 10.1186/s40359-024-01664-2 PMID: 38605422

Li, M., Enkhtur, A., Cheng, F., & Yamamoto, B. A. (2023). Ethical implications of ChatGPT in higher education: A scoping review. *Journal of Interdisciplinary Studies in Education, 13*(1), 55–69. https://ojed.org/jise

Li, M., & Ma, S. (2023). Examining the effectiveness of gamification as a tool promoting teaching and learning in educational settings: A meta-analysis. *Frontiers in Psychology, 14*, 1253549. DOI: 10.3389/fpsyg.2023.1253549 PMID: 37876838

Luan, H., Geczy, P., Lai, H., Gobert, J., Yang, S. J. H., Ogata, H., Baltes, J., Guerra, R., Li, P., & Tsai, C.-C. (2020). Challenges and future directions of big data and artificial intelligence in education. *Frontiers in Psychology, 11*, 580820. DOI: 10.3389/fpsyg.2020.580820 PMID: 33192896

Luckin, R., Holmes, W., & Mann, M. (2022). Empowering educators to be AI-ready. *Computers and Education: Artificial Intelligence, 3*, 100056. DOI: 10.1016/j.caeai.2022.100056

Macgilchrist, F. (2019). Backstaging the teacher: On learner-driven, school-driven and data-driven change in educational technology discourse. *Kultura-Społeczeństwo-Edukacja, 12*(2), 83–103. DOI: 10.14746/kse.2017.12.4

Mallik, S., & Gangopadhyay, A. (2023). Proactive and reactive engagement of artificial intelligence methods for education: A review. *Frontiers in Artificial Intelligence, 6*, 1151391. DOI: 10.3389/frai.2023.1151391 PMID: 37215064

Mendes, V. (2025). Artificial intelligence and education: A revolution in progress. El País. https://elpais.com/chile/2025-02-06/inteligencia-artificial-y-educacion-una-revolucion-en-marcha.html

Mesa, C. (2024). Transparency vs. intellectual property: A difficult balance for the artificial intelligence regulation. https://blogip.garrigues.com/propiedad-intelectual/transparencia-vs-propiedad-intelectual-un-equilibrio-dificil-para-el-reglamento-de-inteligencia-artificial

Mings, A. (2018). The impact of a blended learning rotational model on student achievement in an eighth-grade social studies class (Doctoral dissertation). University of South Carolina. https://scholarcommons.sc.edu/etd/4908

Nguyen, A., Ngo, H. N., & Hong, Y.. (2023). Ethical principles for artificial intelligence in education. *Education and Information Technologies, 28*, 4221–4241. DOI: 10.1007/s10639-022-11316-w PMID: 36254344

Ni, A., & Cheung, A. (2023). Ni, A., & Cheung, A. (2023). Understanding secondary students' continuance intention to adopt AI-powered intelligent tutoring system for English learning. *Education and Information Technologies*, 28(3), 3191-3216). Understanding secondary students' continuance intention to adopt AI-powered intelligent tutoring system for English learning. *Education and Information Technologies, 28*, 3191–3216. DOI: 10.1007/s10639-022-11305-z PMID: 36119127

Norman-Acevedo, E. (2023). *La inteligencia artificial en la educación: una herramienta valiosa para los tutores virtuales universitarios y profesores universitarios. PANORAMA, 17(32)*. Politécnico Grancolombiano., DOI: 10.15765/pnrm.v17i32.3681

Organisation for Economic Co-operation and Development. (2023). Digital equity and inclusion in education: An overview of practice and policy in OECD countries. Retrieved from https://www.oecd-ilibrary.org/education/digital-equity-and-inclusion-in-education_7cb15030-en

Page, L. C., & Gehlbach, H. (2017). How an artificially intelligent virtual assistant helps students navigate the road to college. *AERA Open*, *3*(4), 2332858417749220. DOI: 10.1177/2332858417749220

Roldán, T. (2025). Artificial intelligence will revolutionize education (for the better). El País. https://elpais.com/opinion/2025-02-07/la-inteligencia-artificial-revolucionara-la-educacion-para-bien.html

Safrina, M. M., Zahira, N. Z., & Siregar, O. (2023). Improving Students' English Vocabulary Using Duolingo: A Game-Based Learning Method. Recuperado de https://www.researchgate.net/publication/386535215_IMPROVING_STUDENTS'_ENGLISH_VOCABULARY_USING_DUOLINGO_A_GAME_-_BASED_LEARNING_METHOD

Schiff, D. (2021). Out of the laboratory and into the classroom: The future of artificial intelligence in education. *AI & Society*, *36*, 331–348. DOI: 10.1007/s00146-020-01033-8 PMID: 32836908

Shaik, T., Tao, X., Li, Y., Dann, C., McDonald, J., Redmond, P., & Galligan, L. (2023). A review of the trends and challenges in adopting natural language processing methods for education feedback analysis. *IEEE Access : Practical Innovations, Open Solutions*, *10*, 56720–56739. DOI: 10.1109/ACCESS.2022.3187216

Shorten, C., Khoshgoftaar, T. M., & Furht, B. (2021). Deep learning applications for COVID-19. *Journal of Big Data*, *8*, 18. DOI: 10.1186/s40537-020-00392-9 PMID: 33457181

Sidorkin, A. M., & Hypothesis, L. E. (2025). Generative Ai as a Permanent Scaffold in Higher Education. Available at *SSRN*: https://ssrn.com/abstract=5230565 or http://dx.doi.org/DOI: 10.2139/ssrn.5230565

Tian, Z., Sun, M., Liu, A., Sarkar, S., & Liu, J. (2024). Enhancing instructional quality: Leveraging computer-assisted textual analysis to generate in-depth insights from educational artifacts. arXiv. https://doi.org//arXiv.2403.03920DOI: 10.48550

Tran, M., Balasooriya, C., & Semmler, C.. (2025). Generative artificial intelligence: The 'more knowledgeable other' in a social constructivist framework of medical education. *npj. Digital Medicine*, *8*, 430. DOI: 10.1038/s41746-025-01823-8 PMID: 40646156

UNESCO. (2019). Artificial intelligence in education: Challenges and opportunities for sustainable development (Working Papers on Education Policy No. 7). United Nations Educational, Scientific and Cultural Organization. https://unesdoc.unesco.org/ark:/48223/pf0000366994

UNESCO. (2022). Recommendation on the ethics of artificial intelligence. https://unesdoc.unesco.org/ark:/48223/pf0000381137_spa

UNESCO. (2025). Ethics of artificial intelligence. https://www.unesco.org/es/artificial-intelligence/recommendation-ethic

World Economic Forum. (2024). China's AI revolution: How mid-sized businesses are scaling impact. Recuperado de https://www.weforum.org/stories/2024/06/chinas-ai-revolution-how-mid-sized-businesses-are-scaling-impact

Yu, L., & Yu, Z. (2023). Qualitative and quantitative analyses of artificial intelligence ethics in education using VOSviewer and CitNetExplorer. *Frontiers in Psychology*, *14*, 1061778. DOI: 10.3389/fpsyg.2023.1061778 PMID: 36968737

Chapter 9
AI-Driven Instructional Strategies for the Future

K. Siva Kumar Gowda
https://orcid.org/0009-0004-8957-0276
Sreenidhi Institute of Science and Technology, India

P. Deekshitha
Sreenidhi Institute of Science and Technology, India

T. Venkat Narayana Rao
https://orcid.org/0000-0002-1996-1819
Sreenidhi Institute of Science and Technology, India

Chenchu Swetha
https://orcid.org/0009-0005-1835-0679
Sreenidhi Institute of Science and Technology, India

ABSTRACT

The Artificial Intelligence in education is a major development since it enhances the performance of educators, allowing them to devote more time to compression activities. AI-based strategies can allow learners to complete tasks from outside the classroom while still benefiting from personalized assistance. There is the expectation that this will greatly benefit learners, as AI-driven strategies are able to build lesson plans much quicker than a human could and are able to analyze vast amounts of data obtained throughout the process, which is a definite time saver, but most importantly, much more effective than manual teaching methods. What is even more astonishing is the fact that AI technology has the capability to fully alter the world of education as we know it for the better at all levels. Given that it is a rather advanced technology, one could expect revolutionary breakthroughs

DOI: 10.4018/979-8-3373-0598-1.ch009

with advances in AI translating to the world of construction, rifle a class that is dedicated to construction work, education and massively expand the possibilities of engagement in the profession.

INTRODUCTION

The rapid advancement of Artificial Intelligence (AI) is transforming various industries, and education is no exception. The enhancement of computer intelligence, Artificial Intelligence (AI) included, has prompted changes in methodology for teaching and student engagement. Teaching is now personalized, data-centric, and proactive. These innovations bring forth great expectations for the results of the learners and the teachers by making education more integrated, productive, and focused on specific goals. Aspects of AI are being embedded in educational systems, and even more, additional shifts will be made concerning how learning is offered, how teaching is presented, and how students will be equipped for a tech-rich economy.

Personalization remains one of the advantages of AI-driven instructional strategies. A traditional and a pedagogical approach encompass a broader definition and generally apply the "one size fits all" logic. Students learning differ from each other, making it extremely difficult to reason for every student individually. AI adaptive systems which use Artificial Intelligence technology can identify patterns of student learning, strengths, weaknesses, and the pace of learning. Content, levels of instruction, and other aids can be modified accordingly. Personalization ensures that students' capabilities are catered for when helping them which positively impacts their understanding and retention, (Baker et al., 2014).

AI does data collection and analysis drive instructional methods AI does everything. From helping educators pinpoint at-risk learners to estimating their learning results, AI analyzes performance data to ensure pupils get the assistance they require. AI generated insights can help institutions optimize curriculum design, resource allocation, and policy implementation. Consequently, learning instructing focuses AI enhances the effectiveness of educational programs and methodologies at the same time.

AI continues to advance the organization of immersive and hands-on learning activities. Innovative coding tasks incorporate new AI technologies and tools alongside Augmented and Virtual reality learning experiences. Students can attend virtual classrooms, perform science experiments, or participate in historical reenactments. Cutting-edge technology helps students learn faster and remember longer as well as connect theoretical knowledge to real-world challenges in medicine, engineering, and architecture, (Luckin et al., 2016).

Integration of AI in education creates changes and challenges. Aspects of ethics like data protection, inclusivity, and interaction of teachers with AI systems need to be managed. Trust in AI-powered education systems relies on protecting student data and privacy. Furthermore, addressing the digital gap is necessary for all students to benefit from AI, irrespective of their socioeconomic status. In addition, AI is best utilized not as a replacement, but with a human touch where it is needed sprouting creativity, emotional intelligence, and critical thinking.

In summary, the future of learning is already here with the adoption of AI in education. AID is a srong support tool for educators. While a teacher can not be replaced, AI can help in changing their role to instruction suffport, automation of simple tasks, integration, and continuous evolution of education methods. With the enhancement of AI technology, it is equally important for teachers and government officials to collaborate and make sure that its use is positive and with boundaries. Education systems will be capable of aiding students to thrive in an AI world by accepting AI changes.

THE FUTURE STRATEGIES OF AI-DRIVEN

Personalized Learning through AI

Personalized learning using artificial intelligence is transforming education by adapting instruction according to the individual needs, ability, and learning speed of every learner. Today's classroom models are linear and one-size-fits-all and suit only a select few and fall behind the rest and also keeps them stagnant. AI-based learning platforms utilize machine learning algorithms, adaptive software, and analytics to develop personalized learning paths. By ongoing monitoring of student performance and performance assessment, AI is able to adjust content in real time so that every student gets the right challenge and support. Adaptive learning technology, which is one of the essential benefits of AI-powered personalization, real-time adjusts instruction.

If one of the students is having trouble with a particular subject, then additional resources, simpler explanations, or different learning styles can be provided by AI to allow the student to comprehend the issue better. Or if one of the students is grasping things very quickly, then AI can provide more complex concepts to challenge him or her. This kind of flexibility allows a process of learning to still be productive, interactive, and in line with the speed of all learners, and hence resulting in better assimilation of knowledge as well as better academic performance. Artificially intelligent Intelligent Tutoring Systems (ITS) also optimize individual learning by becoming virtual teachers online 24/7 to provide guidance, answer questions, and provide instant feedback. These systems are NLP and deep learning-based and apply them to translate the students' questions into answers and give personal explanations. Learning is also enhanced with gamification, interactive simulations, and Immersive Learning with AR and VR based on AI. Speech recognition, text-to-speech, and live translation based on AI also enable broader access to learning for disabled students or students afflicted with language disability. AI-based personalized learning has disadvantages in the forms of algorithmic bias, data privacy, and integrating the AI in a harmonious manner with the teacher.

Human educators, although made obsolete in AI-driven individualized learning, will remain at the forefront of mentorship, social learning activity, and emotional intelligence. The future of individualized learning will be established on equitable integration of AI to ensure technology augments, rather than replaces, the teacher's touch. With the proper application of AI, the learning system can be made more responsive, inclusive, and student-centered and prepare the students for the challenges of the future, (Chen et al., 2018).

Intelligent Tutoring Systems (ITS)

Intelligent Tutoring Systems (ITS) are computer-based learning software that employs artificial intelligence to provide students with individualized, real-time guidance and feedback, just like human tutors. ITS employs machine learning, natural language processing (NLP), and data analysis to analyze student interactions, track progress, and provide individualized explanations. Unlike one-on-one tutoring, ITS is available 24/7, and students can be instructed anywhere and at any time. With the ability to learn and adjust to the strengths and weaknesses of each student, ITS provides enhanced comprehension and enhanced academic performance.

One of the unique strengths of ITS is that it can dynamically adjust instruction based on student response. When a student misinterprets something, the system can offer alternative explanations, solution steps, or additional practice items. For gifted students, ITS can offer them higher levels of difficulty of content to challenge them. The adaptive learning is the basis for learning efficiency and need-individualization.

ITS also provides interaction via interactive simulation, gamification, and multimedia presentation that break down complicated subject material. ITS also bridges subject divides in the study of mathematics, science, and languages where problem-solving step by step and studying concepts is required. ITS also accommodates disabled students by providing features such as speech recognition, text-to-speech, and real-time language translation, thus enabling more students to study.

AI-ENHANCED VIRTUAL AND AUGMENTED REALITY IN EDUCATION

Artificial Intelligence (AI) Virtual Reality (VR) and Augmented Reality (AR) are revolutionizing learning with experiential, interactive, and immersive learning. The traditional method of learning is lecture classes and textbooks that, at times, limit the interest of the student as well as understanding. Through AI integrated with VR and AR, students have the opportunity to learn by experience in an artificial world, where even complex ideas can be understood very easily. For instance, they are able to visualize the human body in 3D, conductvirtuallabs in chemistry, or tour ancient civilizations—all in their own classroom.

AI also personalizes VR and AR with customized content and student response to engagement. AI systems utilize students' learning habits and behavior, providing immediate comments, feedback, and dynamic levels of difficulty. With that, the students can obtain individualized experiences specific to their own learning pace. AI can also improve speech recognition, language translation, and prompt testing, and AR/VR learning is thus available to all students as shown in Figure 1.

Figure 1. AI virtual and augmented reality in experiment

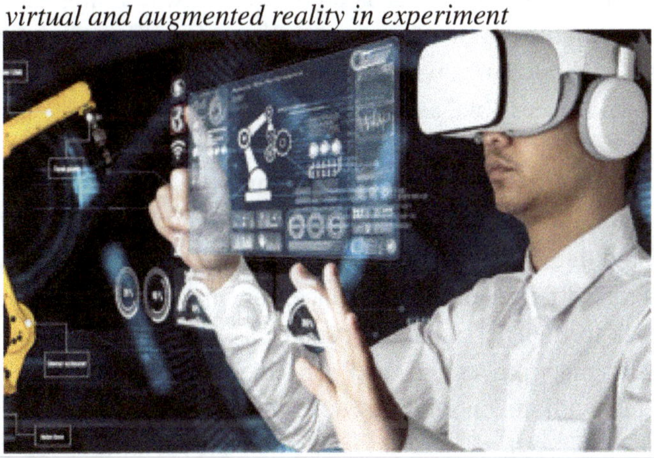

Apart from self-study, VR and AR-based on AI also facilitate collective study in that they allow learners to share communication within virtual classroom, conduct group experiments, or debate in real time with students anywhere in the globe. This is particularly helpful with distance education since students are able to work collectively in a simulated environment regardless of their distances apart. These practices enhance active participation, higher-level thinking, and problem-solving that prepare the students for practical situations, (Woolf et al., 2016).

AI-ENABLED LANGUAGE PROCESSING AND CHATBOTS

Natural Language Processing (NLP) along with AI technologies have transformed teaching and learning through the implementation of chatbots that offer immediate assistance, personalized education, and even help in mastering new languages. AI students have real-time access to NLP enabled AI chatbots that are capable of reading and answering questions allowing for better learning and easier access. The chatbots are able to provide explanation of answers, provide answers to questions, and even grade quizzes and assignments given in class enabling the students to learn in a self-paced manner, (Holmes et al., 2019).

In language learning, AI-based software such as speech recognition, translation, and grammar checking assists learners in mastering communicative skills. AI can also adjust to the capability of a teacher or learner by providing relevant content and even talking and practicing with the learner. Learning is made enjoyable and easier with AI aid particularly for learners of the foreign languages and those preparing to pass the tests.

AI enabled chatbots assist the teachers as they perform non-teaching tasks related to scheduling, grading, and answering routine queries from learners. This gives teachers an opportunity to focus on personalized teaching and learning in a greater extent. With the advent of new generation AI chatbots the need for learners to be restricted by boundaries will be made easier as the learning experience will be more advanced, accessible, and effective.

AI-Powered Chatbots as Virtual Tutors

Artificial intelligence chatbots are revolutionizing learning by playing the role of virtual instructors, offering instant assistance, personalized learning experience, and instant feedback to students in different subjects. The intelligent tutors or chatbots utilize natural language processing (NLP), machine learning, and deep learning algorithms to interact with students through dialogue conversation, answering questions of students, describing complex issues, and guiding them towards solving problems. These kinds of systems, such as Google Socratic, IBM Watson Tutor, and ChatGPT-based tutoring systems, censor the students' answers to the student's learning capacity and level of knowledge. Unlike the standard classroom environment in which the students will never dare to question anything, AI chatbots present judgment-free and relaxed environments that compel students to question as many things as they possibly can. In addition, such chatbots are also available 24/7 and support students anywhere, anytime without the need to wait for their human teachers. AI tutors use adaptive learning strategies, tailoring the difficulty of questions and recommending further readings according to the performance of the students. Other AI learning sites even have LMS integration to monitor progress, detect weak areas, and provide individualized study schedules to learn even more. Voice-based AI instructors such as Alexa Skills to learn and Google Assistant also enable voice-based learning and thus make the process more engaging. Artificial intelligence chatbots aid in language learning, coding, and science, technology, engineering, and mathematics education where instant feedback and step-by-step guidance enable more learning. While AI instructors guarantee learning is effective and possible, poor emotional quotient, bad human-like mentorship mimicry, and information privacy are some issues related to their application. The AI chatbots must be viewed as complements, rather than substitutes, for human teachers to make learning personalized, achievable, and rich in both AI-assisted and human-driven learning experiences.

And, with the birth of AI-powered chatbots, learning has ultimately transformed from being a static composition to a colorful and interactive gate. AI teaching assistants give control to students by reducing the lag time in replying to queries, providing minute-by-minute tutelage and counselling. AI learning assistants are capable of dividing problematic topics into morsels of easily digestible pieces and dividing challenging subjects like a kid's play by parting them into bite-sized sequential topics. Apart from this, AI teachers offer personalized recommendations to a student on the basis of their performance so that they can work on weak areas. They help students with revision work, assignment submission, and study sessions for memorization of study material. AI tutoring chatbots are already proving to be effective, adding to the education sector. For example, IBM Watson Tutor and ChatGPT are interactive learning situations created by interactive conversations that are able to make learners acquire knowledge through speaking. Google Socratic is another AI-program working to assist learners by simplifying complex concepts into plain language, excluding independent study. Brainly AI Tutor facilitates orderly study with an AI-driven Q&A program responding to students in rich detail and even peer-reviewed discussion. These AI trainers are changing the learning experience by opening up the learning content to become more accessible, customized, and effective for learners across the globe.

AI Language Learning Assistants

Artificially smart language learning tools are changing the language learning process by providing personalized, interactive, and immersive learning experiences. These artificially intelligent programs such as Duolingo, Rosetta Stone, Babbel, and Mondly use natural language processing (NLP), machine learning, and speech recognition capabilities to recognize learners' skill levels and adapt lessons accordingly. Unlike conventional language learning tools, AI assistants provide immediate feedback on sentence structure, grammar, and pronunciation, fine-tuning the speech and writing of learners with real-time comments and adaptive learning. Google's Bard and ChatGPT interfaces enable users to converse with AI, and as long as people continue to converse with AI, they will mimic natural conversation in most languages to become fluent. Speech recognition programs like Google Assistant and Siri using artificial intelligence enhance vocal language skills on the basis of students' ability for pronunciation practice and feedback by pitch and accuracy. Virtual teachers and chatbots with AI provide 24/7 conversation practice in which students practice mock conversations with a computer on business purpose, topic of interest, or daily living. Gamification features such as leaderboards, rewards, and AI-driven quizzes also support engagement and motivation through increased interactivity and fun in learning a language. Technologies like Google Translate and DeepL also offer learners instant translation, contextual definition, and voice synthesis for easy understanding. Artificial intelligence is also unifying languages by being sensitive to various learning modes and providing visual, auditory, and textual methods of accomplishing tasks to ensure individuality. New AI technology is being merged with virtual reality (VR) and augmented reality (AR) in attempts to provide interactive language learning experience in which students are able to engage in live conversations with other students in multiculturally grounded environments. With all these technologies, issues of AI bias, excessive technology dependency, and absence of human touch as AI-learning may not be able to get above the sensitivity of expression culture and idiomatic expression. But with technological developments in AI still in process, language learning assistants will continue to be the ticket of passage to innovations in language barriers that will facilitate communication all over the globe and allow one to easily learn a language, quickly, customized, and affordable to all.

Nuancesphonics AI claims that its applications for learning foreign languages are more effective than traditional methods of using books or attending classes. These apps utilize NLP, as well as artificial intelligence tools for speech recognition, to assess the learner’s pronunciation, grammar, and syntactic structures. Important highlights are:

- Correction and improvement of pronunciation after every attempt formulated on the word.
- Correction of grammatical errors and enhancement of vocabulary.
- Role-play based conversational systems for practical training.

Other notable AI language learning application tools are:

Personalized language learning paths are provided by duo along with Babbel. Different level of difficultiesare provided as well.

AI-Augmented Writing and Grammar Support

Artificial intelligence-writing and grammar assistance tools are revolutionizing how students and professionals hone their writing skills by offering real-time support, grammatical corrections, and style editing. Sophisticated AI-powered software such as Grammarly, ProWritingAid, and Microsoft Editor utilize natural language processing (NLP) and machine learning to check text, detect grammatical mistakes, offer word enhancements, and refine sentence structures. Such writing software is above the basic spell-check insofar as they also provide context-relevant edits, tone modification, and readability modifications to assist in writers' reformulation of material for various subjects, audiences, and purposes. Writing assistants created by AI will also assist with non-native speakers of English writers in improving on the quality of their language by means of suggested synonyms, restated sentences, and context-determined modifications complying with proper rules of grammar. Moreover, AI-plagiarism software such as Turnitin and QuillBot assist students in upholding academic integrity through detection of copied material and making recommendations on rewriting sentences so they can sound different. Other writing assistants based on AI, e.g., ChatGPT and Jasper AI, assist in producing content, meaning students can develop ideas, form outlines, and compose essays or research papers in a matter of minutes. These tools are also being incorporated into learning management systems and education platforms to allow teachers to give writing feedback at scale. AI voice-to-text transcription tools like Otter.ai and Google Docs Voice Typing also assist individuals with disabilities or who prefer to give feedback verbally as a way to translate spoken words into neatly structured written words. Although AI-powered writing tools tremendously improve productivity and quality of writing, there remain some reservations around the overuse of AI for creativity, originality, and critical thinking ability. There is also an ethical issue of AI-assisted writing in educational environments, as others believe that too much use of AI tools diminishes students' capacity to learn standalone writing abilities. Moving aside from these musings, writing and grammar editing through AI are still evolving, enhancing written communication, making it accessible, efficient, and polished to users across disciplines.

Real-Time AI Translation and Accessibility Features

Artificial intelligence-real-time language translation and accessibility technology enhance the inclusivity of learning by breaking barriers of language. Speech-to-text and text-to-speech technology powered by artificial intelligence helps disabled students or foreign language speakers. Google Translate is one of the key AI-driven accessibility tools, which provides real-time language translation for multilingual classroom where students are studying as shown in Figure 2.

Figure 2. Real time AI translation

- Microsoft Immersive Reader, which is intended to help visually impaired and dyslexic students by reading outtexts.
- Otter.ai, an artificial intelligence transcription service for students with hearing impairments.
- AI chatbots and AI language processing are useful in numerous ways, but there are some issues which must be appropriately balanced:

Student Data Privacy

Ethical application and security considerations because AI chatbots collect tremendous amountsof dataabout students.

No Feelings and Context

AI is devoid of emotional intelligence and frequently can't respond to complex or context-based questions. Excessive usage of AI tools results in step-by-step diminishment of problem-solving and analysis capabilities of the students. Emotionally intelligent AI teachers capable of understanding students' emotions and requirements would be created.

Holographic AI teachers, particularly with the presence of AI, will create a new experience with live virtuality.

Well thought out with smart AI will enable even better chat AI in providing natural conversations in multicultural and multilingual environments.

CURRENT APPLICATIONS OF AI-DRIVEN INSTRUCTIONAL STRATEGIES

Artificial Intelligence (AI) adaptive measures are affecting positively education as they help individuals learn faster, more efficiently and better. Schools, universities and even virtual learning sites are using AI to boost quality of delivery, automate repetitive processes, and engage students better. These advancements also utilize technologies that mark certain activities for students, give feedback instantly, and analyze information to fit their learning abilities, which enhances efficiency in learning.

One example is Coursera or Duolingo where learners from all available levels are able to learn and the platforms set the level of difficulty based on the user's ability to grasp content. Some platforms also create goals when students log in and monitor their completion. Intelligent tutoring systems (ITS) do not require students to enroll in a class, they can simply register for the program and learn by themselves. For example, MATHia by Carnegie Learning comes with a built-in tutor which guides students as they solve their math problems.

There are numerous aids and tools available on the internet that grant free access to everything, such as the use of Turnitin for checking plagiarism or Grammarly for proofreading a paper, giving pre-written feedback to students. Non-native speakers as well as citizens with disabilities can benefit from modern tools provided via AI which help with live transcription, teaching pronunciation, translation, and dubbing.

Pedagogy led by AI is redefining instant learning with custom education, self-assessment, and ease of access. Portal-based individual learning such as Coursera, Duolingo, and Khan Academy founded upon AI use for customizing learning at one's pace, aptitude, and incapacity is the most commonly observed usage. Such portals observe students' interests and offer prompt feedback, hence an individualized learning process. Artificially intelligent learning software like Carnegie Learning and Squirrel AI modify lesson plans in real time, suggesting students to rehearse ideas they need to improve on. Robotic grading and testing are also typical uses.

Artificial intelligence technology like Turnitin and Gradescope use natural language processing (NLP) and machine learning technologies to grade quizzes, homework assignments, and even essay questions with a very high percentage of accuracy rate, sparing the instructor the drudgery and delivering instant feedback to the students. AI virtual teaching instructors and chatbots like Squirrel AI and IBM Watson Tutor also provide 24/7 learning support, responding to students' queries, explaining concepts, and helping students with homework. The AI teachers serve as a bridge for struggling students outside the classroom. Artificial intelligence applications like Duolingo, ELSA Speak, and Google Read Along employ NLP in pronunciation identification and language learning for suggestion, comment, and instant pronunciation improvement. AI gamification makes the learner more engaged through stimulation and entertainment. Similarly, AI immersive learning technology through virtual and augmented reality (VR/AR) application software like EngageVR and ClassVR provides virtual learning environments for teaching science, history, and engineering.

CHALLENGES AND ETHICAL CONSIDERATIONS

The incorporation of learning mechanisms with AI support into the learning process also involves serious challenges and ethical considerations that must be addressed with serious care in devising fair and effective channels of learning. Data security and protection are also among the urgent issues as AI is based on vast amounts of students' data, personal data, learning habits, and performance indicators that can be vulnerable to data breaches, corporate or third-party exploitation, and unlawful use. Algorithmic fairness and bias are also key issues, as biased data-driven AI models will amplify stereotypes and produce discriminatory learning suggestions harming minority students unjustly in a discriminatory way. The second most significant concern is human touch alienation, as heavy use of AI instructors and digital learning rooms can decrease face-to-face interaction and lose such fundamental abilities as imagination, critical analysis, and emotional intelligence. The digital divide and accessibility problem is not ignored as well because AI learning requires steady internet connectivity and high-specification computers, and thus poor and rural students are unable to garner equal advantage out of it. Antipathy towards employing AI and educating teachers are also concerns since most teachers do not have technical expertise to use AI in teaching activities, and others are concerned about losing their jobs due to automation. Additionally, AI computer-marking has been discovered to mark students' answers wrongly at times, especially on more subjective questions, and was concerned about fairness, transparency, and no human judgment being used in marking. Ethical issues also include students' autonomy and consent in the context that AI-based learning platforms can dictate the pace of the curriculum and altering the course content without visible reasons, thus undermining students' autonomy in decision-making in learning. Long-term effect of AI on education is something which there would be overdependence on technology, and students will overly depend on AI-guidance, hence will not be able to learn through trial and error. Corporate involvement in AI-based education also gives rise to profit-seeking models where schools focus on AI tools of private agencies, which can water down the genuineness of education for business interests. Such problems can be overcome with strong regulatory systems, explainable AI-aided decision-making, participatory AI model building, and an equilibrium model where AI aids but does not replace traditional pedagogy, thereby making education ethical, fair, and human-oriented in the future.

As education is increasingly transformed by AI, the ethics and issues of AI-based pedagogy increase in complexity and urgency. Foremost among these are data protection and privacy because AI-based learning systems acquire significant amounts of information from students in the form of personal information, learning habits, and thinking patterns. Such information, if left unencrypted, are susceptible to cyber attacks, unauthorized use, and misappropriation by private companies or hackers. The ethical concern becomes more serious when students' information is commodified by institutions or edtech companies for profit without informed consent, involving important issues of ownership, transparency, and ethical stewardship of AI. Moreover, fairness and bias in algorithms are also important concerns, since AI models that are trained on biased data have the potential to perpetuate social biases in terms of gender, race, socioeconomic status, or ability to learn. For example, an AI system suggesting STEM courses to students disproportionately from male students based on past trends in the data will discourage female students from taking those courses, further entrenching the disparities. Likewise, AI examinations can discriminate against students of non-English-speaking backgrounds as the model is trained primarily on Western educational content to result in biased grades and performance outcomes.

The second serious issue is the diminishing role of human touch in learning, where virtual teaching based on AI and automated learning software is taking over traditional teacher-student interaction. While AI can be made to offer personalized learning, it cannot replace the emotional intelligence, empathy, and motivational support given by human instructors. Increased dependency on AI also raises concerns regarding students' social and emotional growth because limited human interaction can prevent them from being capable of communicating well, working in groups, and gaining critical thinking skills involving real life debates and discussions. The digital divide and accessibility issues also raise a major barrier to inclusive AI-based education. Although AI promises to democratize learning by making it available for students globally, actually there are various students, particularly from rural, poor, or developing areas, who are missing the access to reliable internet, high-end computing resources, or digital literacy to utilize AI-driven platforms effectively. Unless this divide is bridged, AI in education can actually widen inequalities instead of easing them.

In addition, teacher resistance and poor AI training also get in the way of embracing AI. Teachers are uncertain about what function AI would serve in their teaching, while others are apprehensive that AI-based automation would replace teaching positions in the future. Ineffective deployment results from inadequate AI teacher training programs since teachers fail to use AI tools to their full potential or over-rely on AI suggestions. A second significant ethical issue is applying AI for auto-grading and assessment, whereby AI algorithms, as best they can, do not fully capture subjective, creative, or open-ended answers. Whereas human instructors do not have contextual information for grading essays, project assignments, or sophisticated problem-solving strategies, hence possible misestimation and unfounded judgments. Explainability and transparency of the AI grading mechanisms are also an area of distrust by teachers and students since they do not know how an AI system came to a particular grade or suggestion.

Beyond the grading, learner autonomy and consent are also yet another ethical consideration since AI-facilitated platforms offer pedagogical guidance, tailor the curriculum's pacing, and even predict the chance of student achievement without students having a direct input. This begs questions about learning as passive receipt of AI-directed decisions and not active learning about their own procedure. The ethics issue, therefore, is how much control AI should exert over the learning process. If AI systems start delivering student education without human intervention, then too much standardization and loss of personalization in learning is a risk. Also, corporate domination of AI-based learning is becoming more of an issue because most AI-based learning technologies are developed by profit-making technology corporations whose main priority is profitability over pedagogical soundness. If corporate investors end up exercising undue influence on AI-based learning systems, AI systems may opt to focus more on teaching about business fantasies at the expense of providing well-balanced, unprejudiced education.

Also, the psychological and emotional impact of AI-based learning cannot be ignored. Constant AI monitoring and performance tracking can lead to study stress, tension, and anxiety since students feel that they are being watched by an emotionless entity all the time. Additionally, over-reliance on AI learning will lead to diminished creativity and problem-solving skills as students will tend to copy AI-provided solutions instead of developing their own. With the ongoing development of technology, there is also the emerging threat of AI replacing conventional teachers where teachers' roles are replaced from active facilitators to monitor of AI-developed lessons. If AI assumes the crucial roles of teachers, the human aspect of learning—mentorship, moral education, and practical experience sharing—can be greatly undermined.

To deal with such problems and ethical challenges, there is a pressing requirement for robust regulation models, open AI models, and ethical AI design models. Fairness, accountability, and inclusiveness of AI-based education policies require proactiveness by teachers, policymakers, and developers to prevent prejudice, promote transparency, and maintain human-centric principles in the drive for knowledge. AI must support traditional modes of learning to safeguard education as it ought to be--personalized, equitable, and empowering for all, without regard to beginnings or capabilities. While AI increases the education of the future, proper balance must be achieved between technological advancement and ethical watchfulness, that AI should continue to be an instrument of development and not an instrument of segregation or oppression.

AI'S ROLE IN LIFELONG LEARNING: FUTURE TRENDS AND INNOVATIONS

AI will revolutionize lifelong learning because it will allow people to learn for a lifetime and catch up with the fast-changing job market. With sectors changing at a record pace, AI-based personalized learning systems will be a vital tool for students, professionals, and lifelong learners to reskill and upskill. Adaptive AI-based learning systems like Coursera, Udacity, and LinkedIn Learning will use AI to monitor students' progress, interests, and areas of gaps and recommend courses and real-time feedback to them. AI-powered microlearning programs will allow students to consume bite-sized chunks of learning embedded into the fabric of life via mobile apps, smart assistants, and wearables. Moreover, AI-driven virtual mentors and smart chatbots will be there 24/7 to guide students through challenging subjects, career transition, and job training. AI blended with augmented reality (AR) and virtual reality (VR) will also transform lifelong learning by delivering interactive, immersive training, especially in the areas of medicine, engineering, and trades. AI will in turn facilitate skills acknowledgment and confirmation using computerized systems with blockchain-verifiable credentials to create evidence of skills and learning acquired from non-formal learning. AI language translation and accessibility technologies will, meanwhile, bridge language gaps since students across the globe will be able to utilize quality study materials in their native languages. With the speed of technology progress, AI not only will be providing education as an individualized experience but also embracing the ethos of lifelong learning so that a person can stay adaptive, competitive, and capable of his or her lifetime. Ethical issues like data privacy, AI suggestions creating biases, and accessibility of AI-fostered learning need to be taken care of so that lifelong learning does not become monolithic and asymmetrical in nature.

In a world in which industries change at fast speeds, AI is used in lifelong learning, through which the population acquires new skills along the way and stays abreast of the evolving requirements of the job market. Unlike schooling, whereby one learns almost exclusively within schools, lifelong learning is an ongoing process that occurs throughout a person's working life and individual development. AI-enabled personalized learning platforms like Coursera, Udacity, and LinkedIn Learning are transforming this sector through the use of machine learning algorithms to track learners' history of activity, interests, and proficiency levels. These platforms subsequently offer learners personalized course suggestions, adaptive learning routes, and real-time feedback, thus enabling learners to receive content that is unique to their very own needs and professional goals. AI is also important in the recognition of new opportunities and areas of skills gaps so that experts can reskill or upskill according to their sector needs.

Microlearning websites are also part of the trends that have become real with AI when it comes to lifelong learning, where one learns in infinitesimal pieces that are integrated into daily habits. These AI-powered platforms offer one-to-one, just-in-time learning in the form of mobile applications, smart assistants, and wearable devices, expanding reach and impact. AI powers smart tutoring systems and virtual coaches, offering 24/7 coaching, navigating learners through tough subject areas and career changes. These AI guides, integrated into such tools as IBM Watson Tutor and Google's Socratic, utilize natural language processing (NLP) to provide answers, recommend contextually relevant resources, and even simulate actual problem-solving environments. AI career guidance platforms are also on the horizon, assisting individuals in locating job opportunities, customizing resumes, and practicing interviews based on their selected career paths and present market demands (Siemens, G., 2013).

The second key innovation is combining AI with augmented reality (AR) and virtual reality (VR) and merging experiential and immersive learning. With the assistance of AI, in the fields of medicine, technical crafts, and engineering, AR/VR simulations allow scope for learning to be made interactive and experiential without equipment. For instance, AI-based surgical simulators enable health workers to simulate sophisticated interventions within a safe virtual setup, whereas equipment is inspectible and maintained by technicians with AR-guided training. Lifelong learners pursuing vocational and technical training will particularly benefit from practice since they will acquire and learn through realistic simulations using AI assistance (Shute et al.,2012).

AI is also transforming automated skill verification and credentialing, where the learners' skills are correctly verified. With the advent of blockchain-based digital certificates, AI can validate a person's learning credentials and provide tamper-proof and verifiable credentials on which companies can rely. This revolution does away with the requirement for the old degree-based certification and opens the door for a skills-first recruitment strategy, with applicants being selected on the basis of functional skills instead of qualifications. AI-based skill-matching software will also assist job seekers by suggesting courses and programs in line with new occupations and industry demands (Heffernan et al., 2014).

AI-based language translation and accessibility technologies are also making the playing field level for everyone to learn throughout their life, anywhere in the world. Artificial intelligence-based translation software such as Google Translate and DeepL allow students from across the globe to study using study materials of their own native language, breaking language barriers in education. AI-based speech-to-text and text-to-speech technology also allow disabled students in a manner that the deaf, the blind, and the neurodiverse access lifelong learning. The access technologies guarantee AI-driven learning platforms facilitate a large number of learners and provide them with equal chances to learn (Kukulska-Hulme, A. 2020).

However, although AI possesses humongous potential for lifelong learning, there are some social and ethical issues that need to be addressed. Among such issues, data security and protection is a major issue in so far as AI-driven learning platforms collect a lot of learner's personal data regarding activity, preference, and performance. Without robust data protection, such personal data would be vulnerable to exploitation by corporations and could contribute to surveillance and privacy violations issues. Moreover, AI algorithmic bias can create evaluations that are discriminatory in character where specific groups are given restricted access to good learning materials. Another issue is providing equitable access to AI-driven learning, since people in developing or rural areas might not have internet connectivity and digital literacy to leverage the potential of these innovations. To resolve such issues, there needs to be robust ethical frameworks, interpretable AI systems, and digital inclusion efforts that ensure AI-driven lifelong learning is inclusive, equitable, and beneficial for everyone (Baker et al., 2016).

As AI continues to evolve, AI use for lifelong learning will go beyond education that is school-like in nature and will produce personalized, interactive, and networked learning opportunities. The future of AI in education is in human-AI collaboration, where AI serves as a smart assistant capable of supporting human teachers, and promoting a culture of lifelong learning that allows people to learn, build, and flourish in a constantly changing world.

CONCLUSION

AI-driven learning approaches are poised to transform the education industry, from bland conventional models to data-informed, adaptive, and personalized learning. With the advancement of machine learning, NLP, and AI-driven analytics, schools and online learning platforms also use AI to address the varied needs of students of diverse ages, backgrounds, and abilities. Artificial intelligence-powered learning tools like intelligent tutoring systems, virtual instructors, aside from that, AI is spearheading lifelong learning and enables specialists to upskill and reskill so that they keep up with constantly changing job-market dynamics. Models of career advice and skill-correspondence frameworks based on AI enable students to determine the best courses and modules of training consistent with current trends in industries. Bite-sized learning through AI-governed microlearning platforms has made it easier for people to learn without giving up their usual activities. AI is also redefining company learning and staff development in such a manner as to allow the companies to make training modules flexible, simulate practical situations, and monitor employees' performance based on AI-generated analytics.

Apart from flexibility, AI is also making learning inclusive and accessible. Natural language processing -based artificial intelligence, speech, and text-to-speech-enabled real-time translators eliminate language boundaries so that the students of multilingual backgrounds access quality education within their own tongue. Artificial intelligence-enabling accessibility capabilities also assist the disabled students by providing automatic captioning, screen readers, and adaptive learning interface that facilitate students with visual, hearing, or cognitive disabilities. These technologies are filling learning loopholes so learners from distant poor and marginalized villages can access high-quality learning content that otherwise exclusively belonged to exclusive institutions.

But for all it promises, the use of AI in schools is not controversy-free and ethical-dilemma-free either. Among the most pressing issues are issues related to privacy and data security since the AI systems gather and process vast amounts of student data in efforts to tailor their learning process. That it is safe, anonymous, and not turned against them has to be guaranteed in trying to rebuild confidence in AI-learning. Secondly, algorithmic prejudice in AI may lead to unbalanced learning systems where various groups are offered different levels of aid or suggestions. To avoid such risks, instructors and coders have to ensure the use of AI algorithms is fair, clear, and responsible. Third, excessive dependency on AI and automation may undermine the role of the human instructor and restrict room for critical thinking, creativity, and emotional intelligence in learning settings. AI needs to be created to augment and complement human teaching, rather than replace it, so that learners can continue to enjoy mentorship, socialization, and experiential learning only human teachers can offer. Whereas AI may automate repetitive work, personalize learning, and promote diversity, it is humanity that will cultivate creativity, critical thinking, and emotional intelligence. By positioning AI as an aide and not a replacement for conventional pedagogy, teachers can create a participatory, interactive, and inclusive learning environment that equips students with skills they need to adapt to challenges of the 21st-century labour market. Through ongoing growth, AI can redefine learning as a borderless, ongoing, and highly individualized process where learners of any kind can access their full potential in an adaptive environment.

REFERENCES

Baker, R. S. J. D. (2016). The 'killer app' of educational data mining and learning analytics. *International Journal of Artificial Intelligence in Education*, *26*(1), 29–48.

Baker, R. S. J. D., & Siemens, G. (2014). "Educational data mining and learning analytics." *Cambridge Handbook of the Learning Sciences*, 253-272.

Chen, C. M., & Wang, H. C. (2018). Artificial intelligence in education: A review. *Journal of Educational Technology & Society*, *21*(2), 27–35.

Heffernan, N. T., & Heffernan, C. L. (2014). The ASSISTments System: A Data-Driven Artificial Intelligence in Education. *Journal of Learning Analytics*, *1*(1), 39–57.

Holmes, W., Bialik, M., & Fadel, C. (2019). *Artificial Intelligence in Education.* The Boston Consulting Group.

Kukulska-Hulme, A. (2020). Mobile Learning and the Future of Education. *Educational Technology Research and Development*, *68*(1), 129–144.

Luckin, R., Holmes, W., Griffiths, M., & Forcier, L. B. (2016). "Intelligence Unbound: The Future of Uploaded and Artificial Intelligence." *The Future of Learning*.

Shute, V. J., & Zapata-Rivera, D. (2012). Adaptive learning systems: From theory to practice. *Educational Psychologist*, *47*(4), 195–206.

Siemens, G. (2013). Learning Analytics: The Emergence of a Discipline. *The American Behavioral Scientist*, *57*(10), 1380–1400.

Woolf, B. P., & Lane, H. C. (2016). AI and education: The future of learning. *IEEE Intelligent Systems*, *31*(6), 6–9.

Chapter 10
Design of AI-Enhanced Curricula

Francisco R. Trejo-Macotela
https://orcid.org/0000-0003-2133-3456
Universidad Politécnica de Pachuca, Mexico

Ocotlán Diaz-Parra
Universidad Politécnica de Pachuca, Mexico

ABSTRACT

The integration of Artificial Intelligence (AI) into educational frameworks is reshaping pedagogical paradigms, especially in curriculum design. Traditional curricula struggle to meet the evolving demands of information growth and technological change. This chapter explores AI's role in developing personalised, adaptive, and data-driven curricula by leveraging predictive modelling, natural language processing, recommendation systems, and educational data mining. These tools enable content optimisation, anticipation of emerging competencies, and flexible structures responsive to student progression and socio-cultural contexts. Theoretical foundations—supervised and unsupervised learning, neural networks, and explainable AI—are discussed. Case studies highlight AI's practical use in curriculum design. Ethical concerns, such as bias, privacy, and transparency, are examined. Future directions include self-adjusting curricula aligned with societal needs, requiring strong regulation and equitable integration.

INTRODUCTION

The accelerating convergence of digital technologies and pedagogical innovation has heralded a profound transformation in the architecture and delivery of educational

DOI: 10.4018/979-8-3373-0598-1.ch010

programmes. Within this paradigm shift, Artificial Intelligence (AI) has emerged as a pivotal catalyst, reshaping not only instructional methodologies but also the foundational processes of curriculum design. Historically, curriculum development has relied upon established theoretical models—such as Tyler's rational framework and Wiggins and McTighe's backward design—which provided structured methodologies for delineating objectives, selecting content, and organising pedagogical strategies (Tyler, 1949; Wiggins & McTighe, 2005). However, in the context of increasingly complex and diversified educational landscapes, these conventional models face limitations in addressing the dynamism of contemporary learner profiles, global competencies, and emergent societal demands. Against this backdrop, AI offers unprecedented opportunities to reconceptualise curricular processes through its capacity to automate, personalise, and optimise educational planning and delivery.

AI-assisted curriculum development denotes the strategic utilisation of algorithmic systems to support and enhance the phases of curricular planning, implementation, and continuous revision. The integration of AI technologies—ranging from machine learning and educational data mining to natural language processing (NLP) and recommender systems—enables the analysis of extensive datasets generated within educational ecosystems. This analytical capacity facilitates the identification of learning patterns, prediction of educational trajectories, detection of content gaps, and generation of evidence-based recommendations for curriculum refinement. Unlike static curricular frameworks, AI-enhanced models are inherently adaptive, capable of responding to student feedback, performance metrics, and contextual variables in real time. This dynamism fosters a more learner-centred and inclusive approach, particularly salient in contexts marked by diverse learning needs and socio-economic disparities.

The epistemological foundation of AI-driven curriculum design is situated within broader pedagogical currents that emphasise constructivism, personalisation, and competency-based education. Intelligent systems enable curricula to evolve in alignment with each learner's pace, prior knowledge, and cognitive style, thereby advancing the principles of adaptive and meaningful learning. Moreover, AI contributes to the operationalisation of formative assessment by offering real-time feedback loops through intelligent tutoring systems and adaptive platforms. Such systems do not merely deliver content; they interpret learner behaviour, diagnose misconceptions, and adjust instructional strategies accordingly. Consequently, the curriculum becomes not a fixed sequence of knowledge units but a living framework that evolves in tandem with learners' developmental trajectories.

Nevertheless, the application of AI in curricular contexts is not without significant pedagogical, ethical, and institutional implications. The automation of curricular decisions raises fundamental questions about the locus of educational agency, the role of the teacher, and the nature of pedagogical authority. AI must not be envisaged as a substitute for human judgement but rather as an instrument that augments the capacity of educators to design more responsive and equitable learning environments. This requires a critical interrogation of algorithmic bias, transparency, and explainability. Indeed, concerns have been raised regarding the risk of replicating systemic inequalities through poorly curated datasets, or of marginalising non-dominant cultural narratives through the homogenisation of curricular content.

In parallel, the institutional integration of AI into curriculum development necessitates a robust framework that encompasses technological infrastructure, faculty training, and governance mechanisms. Educators must be equipped not only with technical competencies to interact with AI systems but also with epistemological awareness to evaluate their outputs and pedagogical implications. Institutional readiness, therefore, is a prerequisite for the successful and ethical deployment of AI technologies. Furthermore, curricular governance must include transparent decision-making protocols and inclusive stakeholder engagement to prevent the technocratic imposition of automated recommendations.

The imperative for AI-enhanced curriculum design also aligns with global educational goals, particularly those articulated in the United Nations Sustainable Development Goal 4, which advocates for inclusive, equitable, and quality education. By enabling the personalisation of learning and facilitating early identification of at-risk learners, AI can contribute to reducing educational inequalities and improving learning outcomes across diverse populations. However, this potential can only be realised if digital access and algorithmic fairness are assured. The digital divide—manifested in unequal access to devices, connectivity, and digital literacy—remains a critical barrier to the equitable implementation of AI in curriculum systems.

The incursion of Artificial Intelligence (AI) into the educational sphere has provoked profound transformations in the modalities of teaching, learning, and assessment. Among these changes, one of the most promising yet comparatively underexplored is its potential to influence curriculum design—that is, the formal structuring of content, competencies, methodologies, and assessment processes that guide the educational experience. In an era marked by prolific information generation, rapid technological change, and the imperative for adaptive skills, traditional curricula are increasingly insufficient in addressing contemporary challenges (Luckin et al., 2016).

AI possesses significant potential to contribute to the creation of more personalised, adaptive, and empirically driven curricula, informed by the analysis of academic trajectories, social needs, and professional trends. Through the integration of predictive models, natural language processing, recommender systems, and educational data mining, it becomes feasible to optimise curricular content and anticipate emerging competencies (Holmes et al., 2019). Furthermore, AI facilitates the development of dynamic curricular structures capable of real-time adaptation to student progress, teacher requirements, and specific socio-cultural contexts.

In light of these considerations, the present chapter critically examines the theoretical, methodological, and practical dimensions of AI-assisted curriculum development. It explores the algorithmic models underpinning adaptive curriculum systems, the pedagogical paradigms informing their design, and the institutional conditions required for their integration. In doing so, it highlights both the transformative potential and the ethical complexities of this emerging field. Through a synthesis of empirical case studies, computational approaches, and normative analyses, this work aims to provide a comprehensive and scholarly perspective on how AI can be harnessed to reimagine curriculum design in the twenty-first century. The overarching objective is to contribute to the formulation of curricular frameworks that are not only technologically sophisticated but also pedagogically sound, ethically grounded, and socially inclusive.

THEORETICAL FOUNDATIONS OF AI-ASSISTED CURRICULUM DEVELOPMENT

Curriculum development denotes the systematic process of planning, implementing, and evaluating educational programmes. This process entails the definition of learning objectives, the selection and organisation of content, the adoption of pedagogical methods, and the determination of assessment mechanisms (Ornstein & Hunkins, 2017). The curriculum is not merely a compilation of content; rather, it is a complex construct that articulates knowledge, values, and competencies according to specific contexts. Traditionally, curriculum development has been grounded in theoretical frameworks such as Tyler's model (1949), which posits four essential questions to guide curricular design: What educational purposes should the school attain? What educational experiences can be provided to achieve these purposes? How can these experiences be effectively organised? How can one determine whether the purposes are being achieved? These classical models have been complemented by more contemporary approaches, such as Wiggins and McTighe's (2005) backward design, which begins with desired outcomes before determining the means to attain them.

The integration of AI in curriculum design signifies a transformative shift in educational methodologies, enhancing personalisation and responsiveness to student needs. AI technologies support the development of dynamic curricula that adapt to individual learning styles and progress, thereby fostering engagement and improving educational outcomes. This synthesis of theoretical frameworks and empirical research highlights several key aspects of AI-enhanced curricula. AI enables tailored educational experiences through the analysis of student data to customise content and learning pathways. Intelligent tutoring systems provide real-time feedback, thereby improving student engagement and support (Asrifan et al., 2024). The ability to adapt curricula to individual needs is particularly advantageous in early childhood education, where formative experiences are critical (Amar & Baluis, 2024). AI also automates administrative tasks such as grading and scheduling, allowing educators to focus more on instruction and mentorship (Asrifan et al., 2024). For instance, Aguirre Lam et al. (2024) present a comprehensive analysis of the University Timetabling Problem, reviewing approaches based on hybrid heuristics, metaheuristic algorithms, and combinatorial models to effectively solve classroom, timetable, and teaching staff allocations in complex university contexts. Data-driven assessments yield insights that assist educators in refining curricula based on student performance and industry trends (Saddam & Hasan, 2024). Nonetheless, the implementation of AI in education raises concerns regarding data privacy, algorithmic bias, and the digital divide (Kasztelnik, 2024; Cabral et al., 2024). A balanced approach is essential to maximise AI's benefits while addressing ethical challenges and ensuring equitable access to educational resources (Cabral et al., 2024). While AI offers significant advantages in curriculum design, it remains vital to recognise the irreplaceable role of human educators in fostering critical thinking and emotional intelligence, both indispensable to holistic education.

AI introduces a new paradigm in curriculum development by enabling the automated collection, analysis, and interpretation of large-scale educational data. This analytical capacity allows not only for the identification of learning patterns and areas for improvement but also for the generation of personalised recommendations that inform curricular construction (Singha & Singha, 2024). Key contributions of AI to curriculum development include:

- *Predictive analytics:* The use of statistical and machine learning models to forecast educational trajectories, success rates, and future training needs.
- *Educational data mining (EDM):* The exploration of extensive academic datasets to uncover latent relationships among curricular, pedagogical, and contextual variables.
- *Recommender systems:* Algorithms that propose content or learning sequences based on individual or collective student profiles.
- *Natural language processing (NLP):* The analysis of curricular texts, syllabi, and learning outcomes to generate semantic maps and competency structures.

These approaches allow for a transition from intuition-based or general trend-based curriculum design to an evidence-informed, personalised, and continually updated model.

The use of AI in curriculum design is not pedagogically neutral. Its effectiveness and legitimacy hinge upon its alignment with educational frameworks centred on active, meaningful, and situated learning. Particularly salient are the following pedagogical currents:

1. *Competency-based pedagogy:* AI can support the mapping of key competencies and the generation of aligned learning pathways.
2. *Personalised learning:* Intelligent systems enable the adaptation of the curriculum to each student's pace, style, and level.
3. *Adaptive learning:* AI allows curricular content to be modified in accordance with automated formative assessments.
4. *Data-driven education:* Involves making curricular decisions based on quantitative analyses of student performance, retention, and success.

Consequently, AI-assisted curriculum design does not imply the mechanisation of the educational process but rather its enhancement through tools that foster greater alignment with 21st-century educational needs.

The application of AI to curriculum design necessitates the utilisation of computational models capable of representing, analysing, and generating adaptive curricular structures. These models include supervised and unsupervised machine learning algorithms, neural networks, recommender systems, and natural language processing models. The principal algorithmic approaches and their educational relevance are outlined below.

SUPERVISED MACHINE LEARNING

Supervised machine learning (SML) represents a cornerstone in the computational toolkit for AI-enhanced curriculum design. SML relies on annotated datasets to model relationships between input variables (features) and desired outputs (labels), thereby enabling predictive analytics pertinent to educational outcomes. Within curriculum engineering, such techniques are instrumental in forecasting academic success, optimising instructional design, and refining learner pathways.

The architecture of SML systems hinges upon the systematic training of algorithms using historical academic data—such as student demographics, engagement metrics, and prior assessments—to predict future performance, learning bottlenecks, and pedagogical efficacy. For example, logistic regression models have demonstrated efficacy in estimating the likelihood of course completion based on factors such as learners' prior attainment, study habits, and interaction patterns (Al-Saleem et al., 2015). These models calculate the probability of binary outcomes, making them ideal for early warning systems that flag at-risk students. Table 1 illustrates the application of prevalent SML techniques in the context of curriculum design.

Table 1. Applications of supervised learning algorithms in curriculum design.

Algorithm	Educational Application	Key Benefits
Logistic Regression	Prediction of course success based on learner attributes	Early intervention for at-risk students
Support Vector Machines	Classification of learner profiles to tailor learning pathways	Enhanced differentiation and customisation
Decision Trees	Identification of curricular components impacting learner achievement	Interpretability and transparency of decision rules
Random Forests	Aggregation of multiple decision trees for robust curriculum recommendations	High accuracy and resilience to overfitting

Support Vector Machines (SVM), by contrast, function as hyperplane-based classifiers, proficient in categorising students into multidimensional learning trajectories. They are particularly suited for distinguishing among heterogeneous learning styles and adapting curricular materials accordingly. Decision trees and their ensemble counterpart—random forests—offer interpretable models that elucidate which curricular attributes (e.g., course sequence, instructional modality, content density) most significantly correlate with learner success (Al-Saleem et al., 2015).

The implication of these techniques is twofold: they enable curriculum designers to shift from intuition-based approaches to empirically grounded strategies, and they reinforce the principle of learner-centricity by aligning instructional designs with predictive insights.

UNSUPERVISED LEARNING AND CLUSTER ANALYSIS

Contrary to supervised learning, unsupervised machine learning (UML) does not necessitate pre-labelled data. It is particularly advantageous in educational contexts characterised by high degrees of heterogeneity and complexity. By identifying latent structures within data, UML techniques facilitate the discovery of non-obvious student groupings, curricular bottlenecks, and emergent learning trends.

Cluster analysis, especially k-means and DBSCAN, has emerged as a salient method for segmenting students based on interaction logs, performance trajectories, and cognitive profiles. These techniques enable educators to develop differentiated instructional approaches that respond to the distinct needs of each learner cluster (Singha & Singha, 2024). Table 2 displays the cluster analysis techniques and their curricular applications.

Table 2. Cluster analysis techniques and their curricular applications.

Technique	Description	Curricular Implications
K-Means	Partitions data into k clusters based on feature similarity	Development of tiered learning interventions
DBSCAN	Density-based clustering for discovering arbitrarily shaped groups	Identification of outliers and exceptional learners
Hierarchical Clustering	Constructs a dendrogram for multi-level data grouping	Facilitates modular course designs and adaptive sequencing

Principal Component Analysis (PCA) serves as a dimensionality reduction tool, allowing for the visualisation and interpretation of high-dimensional educational datasets. By projecting data onto orthogonal axes of maximal variance, PCA aids in identifying patterns that might otherwise remain obscured. For instance, PCA has been deployed to evaluate correlations between assessment metrics, engagement indicators, and curriculum content alignment, thereby informing iterative course improvement strategies (Asrifan et al., 2024).

The pedagogical utility of UML lies in its ability to accommodate epistemic diversity among learners. In massive open online courses (MOOCs) and remote education settings, where instructors must cater to thousands of unique learners, unsupervised learning equips curriculum designers with the analytical tools necessary to implement micro-adaptive curricula—structured yet flexible educational frameworks tailored to cluster-level needs.

NEURAL NETWORKS AND DEEP LEARNING

Neural networks and deep learning paradigms constitute the most sophisticated class of computational models in curriculum design. These systems emulate the neural architectures of biological brains to model complex, non-linear relationships in large datasets. Within the educational domain, they are particularly efficacious in modelling temporal learning dynamics, detecting patterns across multimodal content, and automating pedagogical decisions.

Artificial Neural Networks (ANNs) have been employed to model the mapping between curricular inputs—such as content type, delivery format, and pedagogical strategies—and learner outputs including engagement, knowledge acquisition, and skill retention. The architecture typically comprises an input layer (curricular features), hidden layers (non-linear transformations), and an output layer (learning metrics). These networks can uncover complex interactions that traditional regression models fail to detect (Chen & Singh, 2024).

Recurrent Neural Networks (RNNs) and their variant Long Short-Term Memory (LSTM) networks are particularly adept at handling sequential data. They are well-suited for analysing longitudinal learner behaviour, such as the order in which topics are mastered, and adjusting curriculum progression dynamically. These models enable the formulation of adaptive curricula that evolve in tandem with learner progression and contextual feedback. Table 3 presents the neural network architectures and curricular applications.

Table 3. Neural network architectures and curriculum applications.

Architecture	Educational Use Case	Strengths
Artificial Neural Networks (ANNs)	Mapping input variables (curricular elements) to learning outcomes	Capture complex, non-linear relationships
Recurrent Neural Networks (RNNs)	Sequence modelling of learning paths	Suitable for time-series educational data
Long Short-Term Memory (LSTM)	Managing long-term dependencies in student progression	Avoids vanishing gradient problem; suitable for extended curricula
Convolutional Neural Networks (CNNs)	Textual and visual content analysis in curricular materials	Effective for multimodal data interpretation

Although Convolutional Neural Networks (CNNs) are traditionally applied to visual data, recent innovations have adapted them to handle textual and curricular materials. By transforming syllabi, reading materials, and assessment items into structured data matrices, CNNs can be utilised to evaluate semantic congruence across different modules or identify redundancies in curricular content (Chen & Singh, 2024).

These advanced models, by virtue of their self-optimising architecture, contribute to the development of "living curricula"—dynamic, self-adjusting educational programmes that respond in real time to evolving student needs and institutional goals.

RECOMMENDER SYSTEMS IN EDUCATION

Recommender systems (RS), inspired by those deployed in commercial platforms such as Netflix and Amazon, have found significant utility in educational contexts. These systems operate by providing personalised content suggestions to learners based on their profiles, performance data, and behavioural patterns. Within curriculum design, RS serve as engines of personalisation, facilitating the alignment of instructional materials with individual learner preferences and competencies.

There are three principal models of RS employed in curriculum development:

1. **Collaborative Filtering (CF)**: Utilises the preferences of similar learners to make content recommendations. CF assumes that learners with similar past behaviours will respond similarly to future content, thus promoting peer-informed personalisation.
2. **Content-Based Filtering (CBF)**: Relies on individual learner attributes—such as prior achievements, interests, or self-reported goals—to suggest learning materials that match the learner's profile.
3. **Hybrid Models**: Integrate both CF and CBF to leverage their respective strengths and mitigate weaknesses such as the cold start problem or sparsity of data (Manouselis et al., 2011).

The main models of RS and their educational characteristics are shown in Table 4.

Table 4. Recommender system models and educational features

Model Type	Input Basis	Educational Use	Limitations
Collaborative Filtering	Learner similarity based on behaviour	Suggests content popular among similar peers	Cold start for new learners
Content-Based Filtering	Learner profile and content features	Customises learning based on interests and past performance	Risk of reinforcing learning silos
Hybrid Recommender	Combines CF and CBF	Balanced recommendations with improved accuracy	Increased computational complexity

In educational environments characterised by diversity in learner background, prior knowledge, and learning objectives, recommender systems enhance pedagogical equity and inclusivity. By facilitating differentiated learning paths, RS empower educators to accommodate students with varied learning preferences and trajectories.

The incorporation of RS into AI-assisted curricula is not solely technological but also epistemological. These systems necessitate the formulation of ontologies and taxonomies of knowledge domains to ensure that the recommendations align with learning outcomes and curricular standards (Singha & Singha, 2024).

Recommender systems also support metacognitive development by encouraging students to reflect upon and select from curated learning paths, thereby enhancing self-regulated learning. The systems' ability to provide just-in-time recommendations further supports lifelong learning initiatives, particularly within adult and continuing education.

NLP MODELS FOR CURRICULAR ANALYSIS

Natural language processing (NLP) enables the automated analysis of extensive academic texts, such as syllabi, curricula, learning outcomes, and scholarly articles. This capability is essential for mapping semantic relationships among curricular concepts and constructing coherent structures (Wang & Tian, 2023; Ishmael et al., 2023; Segarra-Faggioni et al., 2023).

- *Topic modelling (e.g., LDA):* Identifies latent themes in curricular texts and enables their automatic classification.
- *Word embeddings (e.g., Word2Vec, GloVe):* Represent educational terms as vectors, allowing the detection of synonyms, conceptual relations, and content gaps.
- *Transformers (e.g., BERT, GPT):* Facilitate contextual text comprehension, automatic summarisation, and cross-curriculum comparison.

The application of NLP in curriculum design supports the identification of redundancies, inconsistencies, competency alignment, and opportunities for improvement in content organisation (Wang & Tian, 2023; Ishmael et al., 2023; Segarra-Faggioni et al., 2023). Table 5 shows the main algorithmic approaches of AI applied to curriculum design. Likewise, Table 6 presents the key contributions of artificial intelligence to curriculum development.

Table 5. Algorithmic approaches of AI applied to curriculum design

Algorithm Type	Techniques or Models	Application in Curriculum Design
Supervised Learning	- Logistic Regression - Support Vector Machines (SVM) - Decision Trees / Random Forests	Predicting academic success, classifying learning trajectories, suggesting curricular sequencing.
Unsupervised Learning	- K-means - DBSCAN - Principal Component Analysis (PCA)	Identifying student clusters with similar learning profiles, dimensionality reduction, large-scale personalisation.
Neural Networks / Deep Learning	- Artificial Neural Networks (ANN) - Recurrent Neural Networks (RNN / LSTM) - Convolutional Neural Networks (CNN)	Modelling complex input-output relationships, sequence prediction, automated analysis of curricular texts.

continued on following page

Table 5. Continued

Algorithm Type	Techniques or Models	Application in Curriculum Design
Recommender Systems	- Collaborative Filtering - Content-Based Filtering - Hybrid Models	Personalised learning suggestions, adaptive learning paths based on student profiles.
Natural Language Processing (NLP)	- Topic Modelling (LDA) - Word Embeddings (Word2Vec, GloVe) - Transformers (BERT, GPT)	Semantic mapping of curricular content, detection of redundancy, automatic summarisation and syllabus comparison.

Table 6. Key contributions of artificial intelligence to curriculum development

AI Contribution	Description	Application Example
Predictive Analytics	Anticipates educational trajectories, success rates, and future learning needs.	Predicting dropout risk based on academic background.
Educational Data Mining (EDM)	Identifies hidden patterns between curricular, pedagogical and contextual variables.	Analysing correlations between content types and performance across socio-economic groups.
Recommender Systems	Suggests content and learning sequences tailored to individual learner profiles.	Recommending personalised learning activities based on real-time performance.
Natural Language Processing	Analyses academic texts to generate coherent semantic structures.	Detecting conceptual overlaps and redundancies in syllabi.
Dynamic and Personalised Curricula	Enables real-time adjustment of curricula based on student progress, teacher needs and sociocultural context.	Automatically adapting learning content based on continuous formative assessments.
Data-Driven Assessment and Revision	Informs curriculum refinement through analysis of learner outcomes and labour market trends.	Reconfiguring modules in response to persistently low attainment in key competencies.

INTEGRATING AI INTO LESSON PLANS

The effective integration of artificial intelligence (AI) into curricula requires not only advanced technology, but also a methodological and epistemological reconfiguration of the curriculum. This integration must take into account the pedagogical, technical, institutional, and ethical dimensions accompanying the educational transformation driven by AI. This section presents various approaches for the curricular implementation of AI, both as an object of study and as a structuring tool of the educational experience. The incorporation of AI into educational curricula is reshaping the landscape of teaching and learning. This approach not only personalises learning experiences but also addresses the diverse needs of students, preparing them for a rapidly evolving labour market.

AI systems can tailor educational content to individual learning styles and progress, enhancing student engagement and support through real-time feedback and intelligent tutoring (Asrifan et al., 2024). Adaptive learning technologies adjust pacing and content based on student performance, fostering a more effective learning environment (Sulaymanova et al., 2024). The integration of AI raises significant ethical concerns, including data privacy, algorithmic bias, and the digital divide. Transparent data practices are essential to protect student information and ensure fairness (Asrifan et al., 2024; Kasztelnik, 2024). Educators must balance the advantages of AI with the indispensable need for human guidance, empathy, and critical thinking skills, which remain irreplaceable in the educational process (Asrifan et al., 2024). A comprehensive framework for the curricular integration of AI emphasises the development of core competencies in AI, machine learning, and data analytics, alongside ethical considerations for implementation (Jowallah, 2023). Interdisciplinary collaboration is crucial to maximise the benefits of AI and minimise associated risks, ensuring curricula remain relevant and inclusive (Kasztelnik, 2024). A relevant case is that of Álvarez Núñez et al. (2024), where artificial intelligence is applied for the early detection of academic risk among students, employing predictive models based on data mining and supervised learning, thereby facilitating personalised interventions in curriculum design. While AI offers significant advantages for enhancing educational experiences, it is essential to remain vigilant regarding ethical implications and the need for human oversight in the learning process.

AI AS AN OBJECT OF STUDY WITHIN CURRICULA

One of the primary approaches to integrating AI into education involves its inclusion as a formal discipline within school and university curricula. This entails teaching the fundamentals of AI, computational ethics, algorithm programming, machine learning, and their societal applications from an interdisciplinary perspective. Various international organisations, such as UNESCO and the OECD, have advocated the inclusion of AI-related skills within advanced digital literacy frameworks, spanning from early education to higher education (UNESCO et al., 2021). Table 7 presents the levels of depth in AI instruction with suggested content and pedagogical approach.

Table 7. Levels of depth in AI instruction

Educational Level	Suggest Content	Pedagogical Approach
Primary	Basic algorithmic concepts, logic	Games and playful activities
Secondary	Basic programming, digital ethics	Practical projects, critical thinking
Higher Education	Machine learning, NLP, neural networks	Laboratories, seminars, problem-based learning

This type of integration enables students to develop a critical and functional understanding of intelligent systems, preparing them for an increasingly automated social and professional environment (Touretzky et al., 2019).

AI AS A TOOL FOR CURRICULUM REDESIGN

Beyond its role as a discipline of study, AI can play a fundamental role as a tool for the analysis, design, validation, and continuous improvement of curricula. This instrumental use facilitates the development of more dynamic, personalised, and data-driven curricula. Prominent methodological approaches include:

AI-Assisted Curriculum Analysis

This involves the use of NLP algorithms to identify redundancies, gaps, or misalignments between content, competencies, and assessment.

Adaptive Curriculum

This enables the curriculum structure to adjust automatically based on student progress, utilizing data collected via learning management platforms.

Educational Pathway Modelling

Through data mining, it is possible to identify successful course progression patterns and design optimal learning trajectories.

This approach has been implemented at institutions such as Georgia Tech and Arizona State University, where AI systems analyse academic performance data to continuously update or modify curricular content (Holmes et al., 2019).

FRAMEWORKS FOR AI CURRICULAR INTEGRATION

Effective integration of AI into the curriculum requires the adoption of conceptual frameworks that ensure pedagogical coherence. Proposed models include:

- *TPACK adapted for AI (Technological Pedagogical Content Knowledge):* This extends the original TPACK framework to incorporate specific knowledge about AI and its interrelation with content and methodologies.
- *SAMR model (Substitution, Augmentation, Modification, Redefinition):* This model identifies the level of curricular transformation induced by AI, ranging from simple technological substitution to the redefinition of learning experiences.
- *European DigCompEdu framework:* This outlines digital teaching competencies, including the capacity to utilize AI for pedagogical analysis, personalization, and automated feedback (Redecker, 2017).

The implementation of these frameworks supports a systematic and measurable integration of AI, allowing institutions to advance toward more student-centred, flexible, and data-informed educational models.

INSTITUTIONAL AND STRATEGIC CHALLENGES OF INTEGRATION

The adoption of AI in curricula faces several institutional-level challenges:

- *Resistance to change:* Many educators and administrators express concerns about the potential dehumanization of the educational process or loss of curricular control.
- *Teacher competency gap:* There is a pressing need to train teaching staff in the pedagogical use of AI tools, beyond their technical operation.
- *Unequal technological infrastructure:* Effective implementation demands robust learning management platforms, reliable connectivity, and data collection mechanisms.

Overcoming these obstacles necessitates public policies geared toward digital equity, teacher training, and the ethical regulation of AI use within education (Luckin et al., 2016).

ALIGNMENT WITH THE SUSTAINABLE DEVELOPMENT GOALS

The integration of AI into curricula should also align with the Sustainable Development Goals (SDGs), particularly SDG 4 (Quality Education), which promotes inclusive, equitable, and quality education for all. Strategic use of AI can help reduce educational inequalities through:

- Personalization of content for learners with diverse needs.
- Early identification of students at risk of dropout.
- Expanded access via adaptive digital platforms.

However, it also presents risks, such as the potential to exacerbate existing gaps if equitable access to technologies is not ensured, or if algorithms are not designed with cultural sensitivity (UNESCO, 2021).

PRACTICAL CASES AND INTERNATIONAL EXAMPLES

The design of AI-enhanced curricula is transforming educational practices across multiple levels, from early childhood education to higher education. By integrating AI technologies, educators are able to develop personalised learning experiences tailored to the individual needs of each learner, thereby improving engagement and learning outcomes. Table 8 presents the key aspects to consider in AI-enhanced curricula, alongside a brief description of each.

Table 8. Key aspects to consider in AI-enhanced curricula

Key Aspects	Description
Personalised Learning	AI enables the creation of tailored educational content, adapting to students' unique preferences and learning styles, as demonstrated in secondary education (Qudrat-Ullah, 2025).
Dynamic Curriculum Development	In transnational higher education, AI tools facilitate the creation of curricula that respond to student performance and market demands, thereby promoting inclusion (Alfayez & Rasool, 2024).
Integration into Science Education	AI is embedded within the national science curricula of 21 countries, focusing on practical skills and ethical considerations (Karampelas, 2025).
Enhanced Learning Outcomes	Institutions have reported significant increases in student retention (30%) and academic achievement (25%) following AI integration (Alfayez & Rasool, 2024).
Increased Administrative Efficiency	AI automates routine tasks, allowing educators to concentrate on instruction and student support (Kayyali, 2025).

continued on following page

Table 8. Continued

Key Aspects	Description
Promotion of Problem-Solving Capacities	AI fosters active learning and critical thinking, essential for preparing learners for future challenges (Karampelas, 2025).
Ethical Concerns	Issues such as data privacy, algorithmic bias, and the necessity for comprehensive teacher training are fundamental for the responsible use of AI (Kayyali, 2025; Qudrat-Ullah, 2025).
Implementation Barriers	Technical limitations and the need for continuous curricular evaluation pose significant challenges to the effective integration of AI (Karampelas, 2025).

While AI-enhanced curricula offer transformative potential, it is imperative to address both ethical and practical challenges to ensure equitable access and effective learning experiences for all students.

The implementation of AI-assisted curriculum development is underway in various regions globally, encompassing higher education institutions, school systems, and technical training programmes. These case studies illustrate how theoretical approaches are operationalised in practice and offer insights into the pedagogical, institutional, and ethical implications of AI in curricular transformation.

GEORGIA INSTITUTE OF TECHNOLOGY (USA): PERSONALISED CURRICULUM VIA INTELLIGENT SYSTEMS

One of the most well-known applications of AI at the curricular level is at the Georgia Institute of Technology, where an automated system named Jill Watson—based on IBM Watson—has been developed to assist in postgraduate courses in computer science. Key features include:

- *Jill Watson* functions as a virtual teaching assistant, responding to students' questions in online forums.
- Data generated through student interactions is utilised to refine curricular sequences and develop new content modules.
- The academic team employs data mining algorithms to identify topics with high levels of student difficulty, enabling real-time curriculum reorganisation.

This approach has improved retention, facilitated personalised teaching, and enabled curriculum redesign based on emerging learning patterns (Goel & Polepeddi, 2018; Taneja et al., 2024).

BEIJING NORMAL UNIVERSITY (CHINA): EDUCATIONAL DATA MINING FOR CURRICULUM REDESIGN

At Beijing Normal University, an AI-driven learning analytics system has been implemented to redesign teacher training programmes. Key outcomes include:

- Over 15,000 academic records and digital participation logs were analysed to detect relationships between course sequences, pedagogical methods, and student performance.
- Based on these data, personalised curricular pathways were created for students with diverse cognitive styles.
- The redesign included module reorganisation, restructuring of practical hours, and a more explicit integration of digital and AI competencies.

This case exemplifies how AI enables empirical, context-sensitive, and individualised curriculum planning (Kuang & Duan, 2025).

THE OPEN UNIVERSITY (UNITED KINGDOM): ADAPTIVE LEARNING AND CONTINUOUS CURRICULUM REDESIGN

The Open University has developed an adaptive AI-based learning platform that personalises students' learning pathways through continuous analysis of their interactions. Salient features include:

- Machine learning algorithms and clustering analyses are used to categorise students by performance, learning style, and resource preferences.
- The outcomes inform modifications to curriculum structure, both in content organisation and assessment strategies.
- Curricular redesign occurs continuously through biannual improvement cycles.

This model has resulted in significant improvements in student engagement and course completion rates, as well as increased student satisfaction (Kleimola et al., 2022).

NATIONAL AUTONOMOUS UNIVERSITY OF MEXICO (UNAM): AI FOR CURRICULUM EVALUATION

In Latin America, UNAM has initiated the use of AI tools for curriculum analysis and evaluation within engineering and social sciences programmes. Key elements include:

- Development of a semantic analysis system using natural language processing (NLP) to identify thematic overlaps and assess coherence among objectives, content, and assessments.
- Application of supervised classification algorithms to evaluate the alignment of core and elective subjects with intended competencies.
- Outcomes have informed the restructuring of programmes, adjustment of academic workloads, and the proposal of more flexible learning paths.

This initiative demonstrates how AI can strengthen curricular quality without requiring radical organisational change (Sengupta & Das, 2023).

MULTILATERAL INITIATIVES: AI4K12 AND AI4YOUTH

In addition to institutional efforts, several multilateral initiatives aim to integrate AI into education from a global curricular perspective.

AI4K12 (USA)

Led by the Association for the Advancement of Artificial Intelligence (AAAI) and the Computer Science Teachers Association (CSTA), this project proposes a curricular framework for teaching AI at school level (K–12), structured around five core concepts: perception, knowledge representation, learning, natural interaction, and social impact. AI is introduced not only as content but also as a curricular design strategy aligned with the development of computational thinking.

AI4Youth (India and UNESCO)

Implemented in collaboration with UNESCO and the Government of India, this programme provides teacher training for the integration of AI into technical and vocational education. AI-assisted curriculum design draws upon labour market data, technological trends, and regional needs. These programmes demonstrate that AI-assisted curriculum design extends beyond elite academic settings and is applicable to school systems and vocational training in developing countries.

Table 9 shows a comparative overview of international cases of AI-integrated curriculum design considering type of AI applied, main curricular outcome and educational level.

Table 9. Comparative overview of international cases of AI-integrated curriculum design

Institution/Programme	Type of AI Applied	Main Curricular Outcome	Educational Level
Georgia Tech (USA)	NLP, Expert Systems	Dynamic Module Reorganisation	Postgraduate
Beijing Normal University	Data Mining, Clustering	Personalised Learning Pathways	Higher Education
Open University (UK)	Machine Learning, Adaptive Systems	Continuous Redesign Based on Analytics	Distance Education
UNAM (Mexico)	NLP, Supervised Classification	Competency Alignment and Reorganisation	Undergraduate
AI4K12 and AI4Youth	AI as Content and Tool	Curricular Frameworks by Educational Level	School and Vocational

ETHICAL CONSIDERATIONS AND FUTURE CHALLENGES IN AI-DRIVEN CURRICULUM DESIGN

The deployment of AI systems in curriculum design entails profound ethical, social, and pedagogical challenges that must be addressed proactively and critically. While automated decision-making in education may optimise processes and enhance personalisation, it may also replicate biases, exacerbate inequalities, or undermine pedagogical agency. This section examines the principal ethical risks, regulatory requirements, and future challenges in integrating AI into curriculum design.

Risks of Algorithmic Bias and Educational Exclusion

Algorithms employed in AI-assisted curriculum design rely on large datasets. If these data are not carefully curated, they may reflect structural biases that perpetuate existing inequities within educational systems (Binns, 2018). Common examples of bias include:

Gender Bias

Curriculum recommendations that exclude women from STEM fields based on historical trends.

Socioeconomic Bias

Algorithms favoring curricular pathways for students with better access to technology or prior tutoring.

Cultural and Linguistic Bias

Marginalization of indigenous knowledge, regional content, or non-standard expressions of learning.

Such biases may result in unjust curricular segmentation and exclusion of vulnerable groups, contravening principles of equity and educational justice (Floridi et al., 2018).

Transparency and Explainability of Systems

Most AI models used in curriculum redesign function as "black boxes", making it difficult to discern how decisions regarding content sequencing or inclusion are made. This raises the issue of algorithmic explainability (XAI: Explainable Artificial Intelligence). Curricular decisions must be grounded in pedagogically sound and transparent reasoning. Accordingly, it is necessary to:

- Clearly document the criteria used by the system for modifying or suggesting curricular pathways.
- Provide educators and curriculum designers with intelligible interfaces to review and influence system outputs.
- Implement algorithmic auditing mechanisms to ensure system fairness and traceability.

Data Protection and Student Privacy

AI systems that redesign curricula rely on sensitive data—such as study habits, academic performance, demographic information, and digital interactions. This necessitates strict compliance with international data protection regulations, such as the General Data Protection Regulation (GDPR) in Europe, and applicable national laws elsewhere. Essential measures include:

- Securing informed consent from students regarding the use of their data.
- Ensuring anonymity and encryption of records used for curricular purposes.
- Establishing restricted access protocols and secure data storage.

Improper data handling may erode institutional trust and infringe on fundamental rights.

Challenges in Teacher Training and Curricular Governance

The integration of AI into curriculum design redefines the roles of educators and educational designers, who must acquire new competencies:

Algorithmic Literacy

Basic understanding of AI system operation and its curricular implications.

Data-Informed Decision-Making

Ability to interpret and validate algorithmic recommendations.

Interdisciplinary Collaboration

Cooperative work among educators, engineers, policymakers, and ethics specialists.

Institutions must also establish algorithmic curricular governance structures to ensure educational community participation in automated decisions and to prevent blind delegation to the system (Williamson & Eynon, 2020).

THE FUTURE OF AI-DRIVEN CURRICULUM DESIGN: EMERGING TRENDS

Despite the challenges, the convergence of AI and curriculum design holds unprecedented transformative potential. Emerging trends include:

Self-Adaptive Smart Curricula

Dynamic structures that automatically adjust as learners' profiles, interests, and contexts evolve.

Emergent Transdisciplinary Curricula

AI analyses of real-world problems to suggest thematic combinations across traditionally separate disciplines.

Real-Time Curricular Alignment with Societal and Labour Needs

Data analytics applied to labour markets and social change to anticipate and update relevant curriculum content.

Education Centred on Emerging Competencies

AI used to model maps of critical competencies, such as computational thinking, digital ethics, or collective creativity.

These projections necessitate robust regulatory frameworks, clear ethical guidelines, and sustained investment in educational research and critical technologies.

CONCLUSIONS

The integration of Artificial Intelligence (AI) into curriculum design constitutes a paradigmatic shift in educational thought and praxis, transcending traditional frameworks and introducing a new epistemological architecture for pedagogical development. Through the systematic deployment of algorithmic technologies—ranging from supervised and unsupervised learning models to advanced natural language processing and recommender systems—curricular construction is evolving into a dynamic, evidence-informed, and learner-responsive process. This transformation, while replete with potential, is simultaneously fraught with pedagogical, ethical, and institutional complexities that necessitate critical engagement, methodological rigour, and strategic foresight.

Foremost among the contributions of AI to curriculum design is its capacity for personalisation and adaptability. By leveraging predictive analytics and educational data mining, AI systems are capable of detecting latent learning patterns, anticipating educational trajectories, and customising content delivery in real time. This marks a departure from the static, one-size-fits-all models that have historically dominated educational systems, ushering in an era of responsive, context-sensitive curricular frameworks. The integration of intelligent tutoring systems and adaptive platforms further reinforces this shift, enabling formative assessments and feedback mechanisms that not only diagnose learner needs but also inform continuous curricular refinement.

Simultaneously, AI-enhanced curricula align closely with contemporary pedagogical paradigms that prioritise constructivism, competency-based learning, and inclusive education. Curricula designed through AI are not merely digitised extensions of existing models but represent structurally and functionally novel entities that evolve in accordance with learners' cognitive profiles, affective responses, and socio-cultural contexts. In particular, the deployment of neural networks and clustering techniques allows for the design of modular and flexible curricular pathways that are especially relevant in digital and distance learning environments.

Nonetheless, the adoption of AI in curricular contexts must be underpinned by robust ethical frameworks. Central to these concerns are issues of algorithmic bias, data privacy, and the potential erosion of pedagogical agency. AI systems, if trained on skewed datasets or lacking cultural sensitivity, may inadvertently reproduce systemic inequities, marginalising underrepresented learner groups and homogenising curricular content. Therefore, the pursuit of algorithmic fairness, transparency, and explainability is imperative. Curricular decisions mediated by AI must be intelligible, justifiable, and subject to human oversight. Educators must remain at the helm of curriculum governance, empowered with the epistemological and technological literacy necessary to critically interpret algorithmic outputs.

Institutional readiness also emerges as a decisive factor in the effective implementation of AI-driven curricular reforms. The successful integration of AI demands not only technological infrastructure but also the development of professional capacities among teaching staff. Interdisciplinary collaboration, comprehensive teacher training, and inclusive stakeholder engagement are critical in mitigating resistance, bridging competency gaps, and fostering a culture of innovation. Frameworks such as the TPACK model adapted for AI and the DigCompEdu framework provide valuable scaffolding for navigating this complex transition.

Furthermore, the implications of AI-enhanced curricula must be examined through the lens of global educational equity. While AI has the potential to reduce disparities by personalising learning and identifying at-risk students, it also risks exacerbating inequalities if digital access and algorithmic integrity are not assured. The digital divide—manifested in unequal access to devices, internet connectivity, and digital literacy—remains a salient barrier that must be addressed through coordinated policy interventions and investments in infrastructure.

In conclusion, the incorporation of AI into curriculum design represents both an unprecedented opportunity and a profound responsibility. Its potential to revolutionise education is contingent upon its ethical deployment, thoughtful implementation, and continual critical evaluation. Future trajectories in AI-driven curriculum design point toward the emergence of self-adaptive, transdisciplinary, and socially responsive curricular structures. To harness this transformative potential, educational institutions, policymakers, and researchers must collaboratively envision and enact frameworks that are technologically advanced, pedagogically robust, and socially just. Only through such a multidimensional approach can AI serve not as a mere tool of automation, but as a catalyst for human-centred, equitable, and forward-looking educational innovation.

REFERENCES

Aguirre Lam, M. A., Balderas, F., Rangel-Valdez, N., Martínez-Flores, J. A., Aguirre, A. G., & Pérez-Vázquez, J. A. (2024). University Timetabling Problem: An analysis of the state of the art. *International Journal of Combinatorial Optimization Problems and Informatics*, *15*(5), 489–498. DOI: 10.61467/2007.1558.2025.v16i3.852

Al-Saleem, M., Al-Kathiry, N., Al-Osimi, S., & Badr, G. (2015). Mining Educational Data to Predict Students' Academic Performance. In Perner, P. (Ed.), Lecture Notes in Computer Science: Vol. 9166. *Machine Learning and Data Mining in Pattern Recognition. MLDM 2015*. Springer., DOI: 10.1007/978-3-319-21024-7_28

Alfayez, A. A., & Rasool, A. (2024). Use of AI in the Curriculum Development of Transnational Higher Education. Advances in Educational Marketing, Administration, and Leadership Book Series, 401–422. DOI: 10.4018/979-8-3693-7016-2.ch019

Álvarez Núñez, A., Sánchez Díaz, M. C., Zenteno Vázquez, A. C., Pérez Marcial, J., & Rubín Linares, G. T. (2024). Early Detection of Students at High Risk of Academic Failure using Artificial Intelligence. *International Journal of Combinatorial Optimization Problems and Informatics*, *15*(5), 155–160. DOI: 10.61467/2007.1558.2024.v15i5.573

Asrifan, A., Susanto, A. K., Elpisah, E., Syamsuardi, S., & Herlina, H. (2024). AI-Driven Curriculum Design and Course Management. Advances in Educational Technologies and Instructional Design Book Series, 195–222. DOI: 10.4018/979-8-3373-1017-6.ch007

Binns, R. (2018). Fairness in machine learning: Lessons from political philosophy. *Proceedings of the 2018 Conference on Fairness, Accountability and Transparency*, 149–159.

Cabral, D., Davel, M., Pereira, M. dos S., Campanharo, P. S. Q., Marinho, S. M. de O., & Dalvi, Z. M. de V. (2024). Inteligência artificial no desenvolvimento curricular: Impactos e desafios para a educação do futuro. Revista Ibero-Americana de Humanidades. *Ciência & Educação (Bauru)*. Advance online publication. DOI: 10.51891/rease.v10i10.16400

Chen, J., & Singh, C. K. S. (2024). A Systematic Review on Deep Learning in Education: Concepts, Factors, Models and Measurements. *Journal of Education and Educational Research*, *7*(1), 125–129. DOI: 10.54097/gzk2yd38

Floridi, L., Cowls, J., Beltrametti, M., Chatila, R., Chazerand, P., Dignum, V., & Vayena, E. (2018). AI4People—An ethical framework for a good AI society: Opportunities, risks, principles, and recommendations. *Minds and Machines, 28*, 689–707. PMID: 30930541

Goel, A., & Polepeddi, L. (2018). Jill Watson: A virtual teaching assistant for online education. Georgia Institute of Technology Report. In Dede, C., Richards, J., & Saxberg, B. (Eds.), *Learning Engineering for Online Education: Theoretical Contexts and Design-Based Examples* (pp. 120–143). Routledge.

Holmes, W., Bialik, M., & Fadel, C. (2019). *Artificial Intelligence in Education: Promises and Implications for Teaching and Learning*. Center for Curriculum Redesign.

Ishmael, O., Kiely, E., Quigley, C., & McGinty, D. (2023). Topic Modelling using Latent Dirichlet Allocation (LDA) and Analysis of Students Sentiments. 1–6. DOI: 10.1109/jcsse58229.2023.10201965

Jowallah, R. (2023). *Integrating Artificial Intelligence (AI) Into the Curriculum*. IGI Global., DOI: 10.4018/979-8-3693-0074-9.ch015

Karampelas, K. (2025). Integration of Artificial Intelligence in National Science Curricula. DOI: 10.30935/conmaths/15883

Kasztelnik, K. (2024). Artificial Intelligence-Assisted Curriculum Development: Innovations in Designing Educational Content for the 21st Century Learner. *Journal of Higher Education Theory and Practice, 24*(11). Advance online publication. DOI: 10.33423/jhetp.v24i11.7367

Kayyali, M. (2025). AI in Higher Education. Advances in Educational Technologies and Instructional Design Book Series, 31–62. DOI: 10.4018/979-8-3693-7949-3.ch002

Kleimola, R., & Leppisaari, I. (2022). Learning analytics to develop future competences in higher education: A case study. *International Journal of Educational Technology in Higher Education, 19*, 17. DOI: 10.1186/s41239-022-00318-w

Kuang, Y., & Duan, B. (2025). (2025). Evidence-Based Curriculum Reform: A Data-Driven Framework for Educational Planning and Governance in China. *Journal of Chinese Political Science*. Advance online publication. DOI: 10.1007/s11366-025-09909-6

Luckin, R., Holmes, W., Griffiths, M., & Forcier, L. B. (2016). *Intelligence Unleashed: An Argument for AI in Education*. Pearson Education.

Manouselis, N., Drachsler, H., Vuorikari, R., Hummel, H., & Koper, R. (2011). Recommender Systems in Technology Enhanced Learning. In Ricci, F., Rokach, L., Shapira, B., & Kantor, P. (Eds.), *Recommender Systems Handbook*. Springer., DOI: 10.1007/978-0-387-85820-3_12

Qudrat-Ullah, H. (2025). Designing AI-driven Curriculum and Assessment. In *Empowering Educational Leaders Using Analytics, AI, and Systems Thinking*. IGI Global Scientific Publishing., DOI: 10.4018/979-8-3693-7190-9.ch012

Redecker, C. (2017). *European Framework for the Digital Competence of Educators: DigCompEdu*. Publications Office of the European Union.

Saddam, H. M., & Hasan, G. A. (2024). The Best of Way of using AI Technology in Designing Technical Education Curriculum in Meeting Future Industry Demands. *Smart Way.*, *26*, 1403–1406. DOI: 10.1109/icacite60783.2024.10617225

Segarra-Faggioni, V., Sylvie, R., & Farach, J. (2023). *Topic Modelling for Automatically Identification of Relevant Concepts Discussed in Academic Documents*. Springer International Publishing., DOI: 10.1007/978-3-031-33261-6_8

Sengupta, S., & Das, A. K. (2023). Automated Mapping of Course Outcomes to Program Outcomes using Natural Language Processing and Machine Learning. 44–48. DOI: 10.1109/aspcon59071.2023.10396272

Singha, S., & Singha, R. (2024). *Revolutionizing Content Creation and Curriculum Development Through Generative AI*. IGI Global., DOI: 10.4018/979-8-3693-1351-0.ch013

Sulaymanova, S., Boboyeva, Z., & Soliyev, O. (2024). The Integration of Artificial Intelligence towards Interactive Based Higher Education System Design. 514–518. DOI: 10.1109/icacite60783.2024.10617254

Taneja, K., Maiti, P., Kakar, S., Guruprasad, P., Rao, S., & Goel, A. K. (2024). Jill Watson: A Virtual Teaching Assistant powered by ChatGPT. Artificial Intelligence. /arXiv.2405.11070DOI: 10.48550

Touretzky, D., Gardner-McCune, C., Martin, F., & Seehorn, D. (2019). Envisioning AI for K-12: What Should Every Child Know about AI? *Proceedings of the AAAI Conference on Artificial Intelligence*, *33*(01), 9795–9799. DOI: 10.1609/aaai.v33i01.33019795

Tyler, R. W. (1949). Basic principles of curriculum and instruction. University of Chicago Press. Available online: https://archive.org/details/basicprincipleso00tyle (accessed on 22 June 2025).

UNESCO. Fengchun M., Wayne, H., Huang R., Zhang H. (2021). AI and Education: Guidance for policy-makers. Paris: United Nations Educational, Scientific and Cultural Organization. DOI: 10.54675/PCSP7350

Wang, M., Xie, Y., & Tian, Y. (2023). *Research on Hotspots of Educational Application of Natural Language Processing Based on LDA Topic Model.*, DOI: 10.1007/978-3-031-28956-9_25

Wiggins, G., & McTighe, J. (2005). *Understanding by design* (2nd ed.). Association for Supervision and Curriculum Development.

Williamson, B., & Eynon, R. (2020). Historical threads, missing links, and future directions in AI in education. *Learning, Media and Technology*, *45*(3), 223–235. DOI: 10.1080/17439884.2020.1798995

Chapter 11
Enhancing Digital Literacy:
AI-Powered Training and Assessment for Students

Usharani Bhimavarapu
https://orcid.org/0000-0002-0246-1420
Department of Computer Science and Engineering, Koneru Lakshmaiah Education Foundation, Vaddeswaram, India

ABSTRACT

This study examines the development of an AI-driven program utilizing an improved ResNet model to train and test fundamental digital competencies in learners. The program leverages deep learning technology to track learner interaction with digital learning items, providing personalized feedback and dynamic adaptation learning. Ant Colony Optimization (ACO) feature selection enhances model effectiveness through discovery of the most relevant features to measure. The AI system helps in automating skill evaluation to provide accuracy in identifying students' proficiency in AI literacy, critical thinking, ethical, and use of digital tools. The program also gives teachers data-driven feedback to optimize teaching methods. By integrating AI-driven learning and innovative assessment methods, this study assists in preparing students to face the challenges of an AI-powered workforce

INTRODUCTION

Artificial Intelligence (AI) is transforming e-learning's learning, making students skill-ready for today's workforce. The world is more and more dependent on AI-based technology, and thus students must be educated in a way that they are capable

DOI: 10.4018/979-8-3373-0598-1.ch011

of understanding, and applying, these technologies. AI-based software facilitates adaptive learning by which the material is customized as per students' requirement and learning pace. These courses test abilities using intelligent algorithms that monitor learners' performance and feedback in real-time. AI varies from traditional learning, hence simpler and efficient to learn computer skills. Learning computer skills with AI enhances class activity since learners have the opportunity to interact with AI-based simulation and virtual hardware. AI-based testing enhances competency score credibility using less subjectivity in marking. AI bridges the gap between the virtual world and students by providing adaptive learning regardless of their diverse backgrounds. AI programming is the foundation for assisting students in AI workstations. AI-based curriculums provide students with theoretical theory and practical practice.

AI-based learning systems provide adaptive study material according to diverse abilities and learning rates. AI systems can propose customized lessons, practice exercises, and quizzes based on learning the students' performance and enhancing learning results. It works best with low digital capability students because AI can provide customized assistance. Having AI teachers facilitate students completing homework, with choices and solutions in the event of mistakes. Gamification tools such as AI-driven quizzes and challenges motivate and engage more. AI supports real-time monitoring of student progress, alerting teachers on where students require additional assistance. Though traditional learning frameworks hinder skill development, AI adapts dynamically to support continuous skill enhancement. AI boards reveal student strengths and weaknesses to support data-driven curricula. AI applications are mastered using machine learning over time as they enhance instruction practice based on students' performance data. This enhances the learning space to be larger and interactive with improved digital literacy.

Use of AI for training digital skills ranks among the biggest benefits since they can offer students real practice in using AI technology. Students can code in coding environments that are AI-based, and they receive instant feedback on programming problems. Debug drills can be made by AI automatic, and students can easily find bugs and correct them. With AI simulations, students learn skills that can be transferred to real life like coding, cybersecurity, and data science. AI upgrades problem-solving with step-by-step learning and explicit instruction and adaptive content. With AI-based evaluation, students monitor progress and see what they need to work on. AI-based reports allow teachers to view student and class learning patterns, optimizing pedagogical planning. AI-powered virtual mentors assist learners to develop digital skills, enhancing self-learning. AI-powered chatbots give direct answers to questions, with continuous support outside class. Teaching digital skills with AI introduces learners to AI applications that can be utilized in future professions.

AI-powered tests are vital in giving accurate measurements of learners' digital skills. Traditional tests are designed with fixed tests that may not reflect whether a student has the ability of applying digital skills in real-world situations. AI tests utilize dynamic questions and realistic project simulations to determine competency. AI tests evaluate problem-solving, reactivity, and memorization of memory, providing an overall picture of students' potential. AI marking reduces human bias so that students are marked fairly. AI-driven assessment feedback facilitates on-time re-learning of skills. AI identifies skill gaps and recommends relevant content to bridge gaps. AI-driven tracking of skills allows instructors to optimize learning interventions, thereby optimizing overall digital literacy. Institution-wide pilot assessment of program performance based on AI-driven analytics and evidence-driven optimisation is facilitated. Large-scale scalability in AI-driven testing facilitates quality and accurate tests for humongous groups of learners.

Some ethics are involved in applying AI digital capability training. The data must be secured and kept secret by the AI systems for safeguarding students' data. Discrimination in learning can result from prejudice in AI systems, and hence various models of AI should be developed. Transparency in AI decision-making enhances reliance on AI-based decisions and marks. The institutions must provide such guarantees that AI-based learning materials comply with the legal as well as moral standards. There should be non-discriminatory access to AI-based learning so as not to augment digital skill inequality among learners of different socio-economic strata. The teachers must be equipped with training for applying AI with bounded application and also taught about its limitations. AI needs to be complemented by human instructors but not replaced, at the best ratio of virtual learning. These moral principles will make AI-driven education a reality and empower. Another of the future AI plans is a spin-off of an ethical approach to AI that will provide digital skill teaching to everybody. Using AI to develop digital skills gives students the power to operate AI-driven workplaces. AI is being implemented in every industry to take actions, understand data, and improve decision-making. The digital learners empowered by AI will enjoy improved job opportunities. AI literacy enables the learners to be competent enough to use AI tools in a proper way, and it leads to innovation and efficiency. AI training makes the students capable of learning through AI ethically with a secure application in actual life. AI problem-solving ability increases decision-making and thought skills. AI simulation in training job-fits the students with actual experience. As AI is an evolving technology, the students have to be trained in emerging AI trends and technologies. AI education profession-fits the students for professional multidisciplinary professions on the digital competence foundation. Correct training with AI-driven digital skills in students renders their career job-proof in the uncertain job economy.

The teachers' role in training with digital skills and AI is also quite significant. AI is enriching but not replacing traditional instruction, giving the teachers more time to concentrate on mentoring and coaching. AI analysis offers a chance for teachers to track students' strengths and weaknesses and facilitate data-driven learning. Teachers employ AI-based solutions in creating interactive study material and interactive learning. AI aids in planning the curriculum by detecting patterns and proposing improvements. AI-based knowledge makes the teachers capable of tailoring learning based on each student's unique requirement. Teachers must be trained so that they can easily use AI in their class. AI applications must be user-friendly and must be provided to the teachers irrespective of the technical knowledge of the teachers. Teacher alignment with AI ignites a new inclusive learning loop. AI teacher training prepares the teachers to learn and familiarize themselves with new AI technology. The teachers need to be AI trained so that they can effectively make use of AI-based digital learning.

AI-based digital learning facilitates inclusion via adaptive learning solutions too. The disabled are empowered by AI via personalization in the context of content being instructed most effectively to their liking and beat. Non-native speakers are empowered by AI-based language translation software to comprehend course content. Speech-to-text and text-to-speech functions empower the disabled with greater accessibility. Feedback loops are automated to provide assistance to the learners regardless of geographical location or origin. Gamification activity with AI assists the learners to interact and prevent stress in learning. Virtual AI tutors perform background descriptions and practice sets for learning guidance. AI summaries assist students to learn difficult topics without problems. AI learning guides direct students to content at their level based on their learning mode. AI-enabled access to education rights levels out the quota for every student to learn digital literacy. AI-enabled online education is the bridge to effective and worldwide learning.

The AI-enabled future of online education shines with constant upgradation maximizing the payoff of study. AI-enabled AR and VR will enrich experience-based education. AI chatbots will be intelligent tutors with instant responses. AI-driven predictive analytics will precisely predict the performance of students so that appropriate intervention can be initiated in advance. AI-driven content creation will encourage education content in novel and novel trends. AI-driven career advisory tools will help students map skills as per industry demands. AI will make increasingly more assessment processes rational with competence values of skills. AI-driven collaboration and communication tools will improve groupwork and scope for communication. Morality-programmed AI will be instrumental in creating morality-driven AI-based learning. AI-powered learning will establish intelligent, optimized learning environments. Computer-based training ability powered by AI is overall reshaping learning into optimized, interactive, and more personalized learning. AI-powered platforms enable learners to practice and acquire web skills used in the modern workplace. AI-based grading is less discriminatory and precise in assessing performance. Deployment using AI guarantees ethical implementation, promoting inclusivity and data security for e-learning. The work of educators lies at the core of implementation of AI to ensure effective learning and guidance. Usage of AI prepares students as AI-ready learners to adapt to the challenge of AI-driven working environments, improving employability. Versatility of AI renders it as a lifeline tool for lifelong learning. The coming AI technology will keep advancing digital learning in order to make learning more streamlined and efficient. The institutions need to make investments in AI-learning processes since they compete to remain technologically advanced. Coming but unforeseen future makes necessary AI-based training to facilitate a future of such a nature. Basilaia and Kvavadze (2020) witnessed the transition to distance learning in Georgia due to the COVID-19 pandemic and accredited it as successful but tinted with failure. Geographical specificity is one of the major limitations of their research in the sense that findings cannot be exported directly to other countries whose education policy and online platform are varied. The study is also biased towards studying in schools, an aspect that undermines the effect of the move to post-secondary learning institutions. The study is qualitative and it is not possible for anyone to know for sure whether data collected are generalizable to the whole population. The second challenge is that the initial stages of embracing online learning have been taken into account only, and hence no long-term evaluation. Aside from that, neither the students' nor the teachers' digital literacy levels were researched to their full capacity. Socio-economic factors for the students' embracement of e-learning resources are not addressed in this discussion. Cross-country comparison regarding the transition to e-learning is not made. Aside from that, although the topic of research is technology adoption, pedagogy shift does not get examined to the same degree of depth at the individual level. Poor measurement of good student performance of high level does not leave any space for the measurement of actual success in distance learning. Otherwise, motivational and psychological aspects that dominated the students' transition to distance learning were not investigated at the respective level (Basilaia et al., 2020).

Ivanov studied information and communication technology competencies and intervention fields of school teachers. Limitation is that the research is far too specific in scope to represent only secondary education and leave out digital competences for primary or post-secondary education. The population of the sample may be limited in representation of heterogeneity in digital competence among various groups of teachers. Such a limitation is that the research was based on self-reported items, which can themselves represent prejudice while capturing actual teacher competences. The impact of online courses of instruction on future skill acquisition is not examined in this research. The research also fails to make a critical analysis of the way certain online content is integrated in learning. Research does not examine either what students know regarding teachers' digital literacy influence on learning outcomes. Technical aspects such as computer and internet access were also not under critical examination. Results could not be generalized to schools with other policy and education infrastructure. More concerning is exclusion of the role of continuous professional development in teachers' continued digital competences development. Lastly, the research fails to offer comparative assessment of teacher digital competence by country or education systems (Ivanov et al., 2023).

Bjekić and Vucetić discussed the relationship of mental health with development, more particularly in school. It is one of its shortcomings in the sense that it is theory-based in nature and lacks empirical evidence used to back what they have written. The book lacks the aspect of critical examination of electronic learning and mental health in vain. The research is location-specific, and therefore the findings are not as transmissible in context throughout the globe. Otherwise, no integration of mental health evaluation with advancing technologies in technology that transforms learning environments is performed. The research does not consider how online available information and AI can be utilized to enhance or worsen mental health among the students. Nevertheless, one of its downsides is the absence of direct interaction with the students or teachers to support theoretical assumptions. No studies are quantified and therefore inference only from the impact of e-learning on mental well-being is a challenging task to achieve. These differences in cultures of learning and how they perceive mental illness were not taken into consideration. Long term impact of mental health following e-learning can be determined by utilizing longitudinal studies because without the latter, research would not be complete. Lastly, there is no difference between the virtual and the traditional methods of learning on the psychological well-being dimension (Bjekić et al., 2013).

Information literacy in Europe was also studied by Virkus and it was a mark of development acquired in a period of ten years. The limitation of this study is that it's only about the European countries and therefore results cannot be implemented directly on any other multicultural education system anywhere else. The research is mostly quantitative as it is based mostly on policy analysis and not empirical research, and therefore not as useful for real-life classroom application. Another limitation is the absence of comparative framework of how the initiation of information literacy development varies with varying levels of education. The study does not consider the effects of evolving technologies such as AI on information literacy skills. There is also little concern regarding the extent to which education systems can actually implement digital literacy training. The research does not account for surprise technology shift with digital media and tools that would render its results irrelevant. The research does not actively involve teachers and students to ascertain whether information literacy interventions are effective. Unstructured learning environments like social media and online forums are not accounted for when applying to construct information literacy. It does not investigate obstacles to offering digital literacy training for poor schools. It doesn't establish actual policy suggestions for enhancing information literacy beyond the European sphere (Virkus, 2013).

From the pedagogical digital competence gained and equilibrium of values, knowledge, and competency. A limitation that this study relies primarily and hardly at all on is that of competence development empirical research. The research does not conduct experiments on the influence of different training programs on the digital literacy of teaching staff. There is less empirical evidence on pedagogical devices developed with AI to augment digital pedagogy. The second limitation is that differences in digital education policy at regional levels are not met. Quantification of student achievement caused by teachers' digital literacy is also not dealt with in the study. There is very little quantitative data available to validate the study's findings, and generalization becomes convenient. The study fails to incorporate ongoing professional development to sustain and guarantee digital competence. The study fails to measure preparation for digital pedagogy in emerging technology. The second weakness is the absence of students' view of the effectiveness of digital learning techniques. Third, the study lacks comparative digital competence knowledge between courses (From, 2017).

Pettersson examined classroom digital competence literature but had several loopholes. Among them, the most important limitation is that no primary data have been gathered and only secondary sources have been utilized. The study does not have an effective measurement framework of digital competence in real teaching practice. It cannot also establish digital competence needs in various levels of learning. It is a drawback that no data is presented on the contribution of learning solutions based on AI to enable supporting digital competence growth. Problem areas upon which lecturers gain and apply digital competences are not discussed by the study. The review also does not provide comparison of the effects of various training courses on acquiring digital competence. The research is also limited in terms of including formal learning environments and not including informal learning environments. The research fails to give policymakers a direct suggestion on how digital competences should be incorporated in curricula. The limitation is that there lacks an international comparison of means for transferring digital competence. Last but not least, research fails to show how future technologies can reconstitute digital competence (Pettersson, 2018).

Nguyen and Thai were discussing using the CDIO model in designing Vietnamese teacher education to meet the Fourth Industrial Revolution. One of the main limitations is the geography of the research, which would limit its suitability for application to countries with different education systems and technology capabilities. The research examines the structure of the program most but lacks empirical evidence of sustained success in the programs. The study also lacks quantitative assessment of teacher development in learning and implementation of digital ability after training. Deficit is also found in the lack of a clear enough explanation of how the students perceive the effect of training on teaching quality. Regional variation in availability of internet platforms across Vietnam, affecting implementation, is not excluded in the study. The study also does not include the problem of the acceptance issue confronting the teachers in implementing the CDIO-based training system. The study does not encompass comparison studies with comparison pedagogical models for other teachers, and it is thus not simple to determine the strengths and weaknesses of the CDIO system as a system. Finally, the research does not offer clear policy guidelines for the mass scaling up of CDIO in extensive teacher education systems (Nguyen et al., 2020).

OECD has released the results of PISA 2018 with rich information on the performance of schooling on the international stage. Its most significant flaw is excessive reliance on conventional testing as even they cannot bring students' imagination and creative thinking into reality. Academic accomplishment is largely measured in mathematics, science, and reading ability apart from other most significant skills such as computer literacy and problem-solving in everyday life. Test score economic and socio-cultural determinants are not also studied critically. Data are differentially influenced by country-specific curricula to render cross-country comparison difficult. Amongst the areas mass testing is lacking is that it cannot possibly add depth to school studies. The study cannot demonstrate the effect of instructor training programs to change students' results. PISA score recommendations offered to mitigate education inequality do not exist. The study cannot establish the effect of widespread use of technology for e-learning on education quality. Finally, the study does not have longitudinal data on enhancing students' performance in the long run due to the transformation of education (OECD, 2018).

OET constructed a new national education technology plan with education technology implementation policy direction mapped out. A shortcoming of one of the reports is that it analyzes the American education system alone and therefore fails to make any remarks about country by country differential technological infrastructure development and policy matters. The majority of the study's recommendations that it makes are broad policy recommendations but not supported by any empirical realities in terms of policy connections and their impact as determinants for enhancing learning outcomes. Further, the report fails to support the digital divide component, particularly among poor individuals in regard to technology. The second constraint is that there cannot be any plausible mechanism for giving comprehensive comment regarding digital capability training and teacher professional development. The study fails to create the extent of utilization of learning environments with high technology by students. The study also does not consider the long-term technology-based educational policies' sustainability. The study also fails to consider the damage inflicted on the students in terms of prolonged exposure to the screens. The study is finally not comparative assessment of efforts of different countries towards digitalization of education (OET, 2017).

Result of TALIS 2018 was released by OECD on teaching profession of teachers and learning environment. The weakness of this research is that it relies on self-reported data by teachers, thus potential response bias. The research is focused mainly on teacher education and training but does not say anything about teachers' direct contribution to students' achievement. The report also does not evaluate the extent of impact of varied pedagogies on learning outcomes in digital as well as non-digital learning spaces. The report is representative of overall policy concerns but has not considered individual case studies on best practice in e-learning. The second limitation is that more recent technologies like AI-based pedagogy software and adaptive learning technology have not been considered. The research has not considered the impact of teachers' ongoing digital upskilling in terms of changing technology. Cross-country comparison is equally challenging due to a lack of adequate appropriate analysis of differences in teacher training program cultures. The study also does not quantify the role of socio-economic factors on teacher availability to development. And finally, the study does not explore the effect of school leadership and management on teachers' capacity to adopt technology (OECD, 2020).

König examined German novice teachers' adjustment towards teaching online as a result of the school closure because of COVID-19. The drawback of one of the studies is that it emphasizes novice teachers and not experienced teachers who might have faced various problems. The study relies on survey data, which might maybe be less experiential regarding online teaching. Another limitation is that it doesn't look at formally digitally trained teachers versus digitally untrained ones. The research isn't exploring the long-term effect of online teaching reform on teacher professional development. The research is Germany-specific and therefore not as applicable to other countries with different digital schooling policy. The research doesn't assess student performance when measuring the effectiveness of online learning process. The study fails to mention the contribution of school administration in motivating teachers to use the process. The second limitation is that authors have overlooked psychological and emotional obstacles encountered by the teachers in online learning. Finally, the study is not investigating targeted policy suggestions on how teacher readiness for embracing future digital learning revolutions can be facilitated (König et al., 2020).

Jiang contemplates possible artificial intelligence trends. The research is void of empirical data regarding the impact of AI in certain environments. The argument remains general and hypothetical, and thus difficult to derive concrete lessons for researchers and policy-makers. Quantitative research or experimental verification of the anticipated AI trends is also absent in the article. Another deficiency is that it is not able to address ethical issues in AI development and utilization. The research fails to spell out how to compare various AI innovation approaches by nations, which would be more realistic international lessons. Second, the research does not consider regulatory challenges in the application of AI across industries. Finally, the study lacks evidence-based real-life implementation case studies of future AI trends (Jiang et al., 2022).

Mizumoto and Eguchi have researched AI-based automated essay grading, but the literature falls short in various ways. The study lacks human examiners versus AI-based examiners' performance comparison for various topics. The study is English-language essay-based and hence less relevant in multilingual school settings. The second is AI model bias that can taint objective scores and is beyond the focus of this investigation. The investigation does not discuss the moral issue of high-stakes testing through AI. The investigation does not demonstrate long-term consequences on the effect of AI scoring on students' writing in the long run. It also fails to consider the computational efficiency and scalability of the AI model while grading in bulk. Finally, teachers' trust and acceptance of AI-armed grading systems are absent in the literature (Mizumoto & Eguchi, 2023).

Holmes ushered in the education ethics of AI and had a set of ethical standards at the community level. The literature fails to present empirical evidence of the structure offered. The research is primarily theoretical and lacks experimental data or case studies demonstrating how the ethics principles improve the application of AI in schools. The second limitation is that the method is not grounded on universal ethics principles instead of specific issues of AI adoption by schools. The argument does not take heterogeneity of ethical AI adoption across different education systems in the world into consideration. It is also not able to perceive disposition of teachers and students towards learning tools of AI unless well explained in the data. Technological limits to ethical use of AI are not referred to in the article. Finally, the research is not giving measurable boundaries on how to establish whether applications of AI ethics concepts fail or succeed (Holmes et al., 2022).

Wang suggested that the level of proficiency which users have in AI technology must be measured using an AI literacy scale. The article is deficient in that it does not conduct a comparative analysis of available AI literacy models. The study is constrained in the sense that it uses self-report measures, which are susceptible to quantify AI capacity. The limitation also lies in that the AI literacy scale is piloted using particular groups of populations and hence less generalizable across different groups. The study does not test if the long-term impact of training in AI literacy alters users' technical literacy. In addition, it does not study if users' ethical decision-making and acceptance of using AI systems vary based on the degree of AI literacy. The study does not include the study of occupational AI literacy variation, i.e., business, healthcare, and education. Finally, the study cannot even cover the question of how to make AI literacy a part of universal school curricula (Wang et al., 2023).

AI literacy competencies were assessed by Long and Magerko but are missing in some way. The research is quantitatively more in nature with fewer empirical problems in testing AI literacy models at an extremely large scale. There is no study of variation of AI literacy with respect to education levels and age. There is also the limitation in terms of no comparative study of research research on AI literacy frameworks which has been conducted in learning and industrial companies. The study does not quantify the effect of AI literacy interventions on real decisions. In addition, the study does not make any claims about the effect of disinformation on public opinion towards AI. There is no clear policy directive presented to governments or schools within the study. The study also does not show user feedback of the offered AI literacy resources provided and whether they work or not (Long & Magerko, 2020).

The new model circumvents the shortcomings of the previous models through more intricate methods, blended data, and stringent test procedures. Earlier studies that were based on abstract thinking alone are not used by the model, unlike the past. The model anchors empirical evidence in real-case experiments and studies in a bid to provide real-world applications. The approach avoids generalizability issues on the basis of respect for diverse groups and global climates and gives a broader view of AI use and challenges. Additionally, in contrast to the earlier models significantly based on conjecture theory and lacking evident indicia, the model discussed herein has measurable quantitative performance whereby it can be determined with certainty. Moral issues, in most cases overlooked or justified on a theoretical level in earlier work, are introduced at the design and implementation stage so that ethical application of AI is facilitated. Secondly, the model suggested is scalable and computationally inexpensive and hence deployable on an industrial scale on a multi-sectoral platform. In comparison to other models without long-term evaluation, this model includes longitudinal studies to use for the prediction of the long-term effect of AI literacy, learning intervention, and digital competencies models. Other than the stakeholders' such as policymakers, learners, and educators' perception, the model is also pragmatic with more implementation. The method therefore mainly directs the validity, utility, and ethics-grounded basis of AI and digital literacy frameworks and shuns best available framework limitations.

MATERIAL AND METHODS

The strategy is to condition a digital ability training artificial intelligence-based system from a higher ResNet model. Student digital learning task interaction data are first collected and preprocessed. Ant Colony Optimization (ACO) feature selection is next applied to determine the best-performing features to measure ability. A superior ResNet model is then conditioned to classify and rank students' digital abilities using derived features. Dynamic algorithms adjust the difficulty level on materials according to student performance and provide specific feedback. Finally, the system provides teachers with pedagogically optimized insights based on data.

Material

Self-report survey was developed in the backdrop of existing literature of AI competences and frameworks of AI literacy in response to operationalizing six broad competence dimensions of AI literacy, i.e., consciousness of the principles of AI, critical judgment, ethics, application, consciousness, and communication. Question types were decided to be suitable for such dimensions to the extent that it would target teachers' general AI literacy.

Knowledge and identification questions (Q38, Q39) assess teachers' familiarity with concepts of AI and ability to recognize AI tools in classrooms. Experience questions (Q40) assess the degree to which teachers utilize AI tools for instructional and administrative purposes. Critical evaluation questions (Q41, Q42) assess teachers' ability to evaluate the reliability, instructional effectiveness, and ethics of AI tools. Ethics-related questions of interest (Q42) include privacy, bias, and fairness in AI. Algorithmic considerations (Q43) address even more technical knowledge and even more specificity concerning teachers' ability to teach AI. Questions of digital divide (Q44) are concerned with offering equal access to AI teaching material for various learners. Finally, cross-curriculum planning, professional development, and collaboration (Q45, Q46, Q47) questions attempt to assess how well the teachers can collaborate, professionally develop, and apply AI while teaching across curriculum.

The author of self-assessment questionnaire was inspired by the European Commission's Selfie for Teachers digital competences and skills self-assessment model while crafting the self-assessment questionnaire. This tool, as being a product of the DigiCompEdu model, was chosen because it has a proper definition of digital competences and can accommodate AI literacy in an existing model for quantification of digital competences. The newly introduced DigiComp 2.2 model also considers the impact of AI on learning, thereby making Selfie for Teachers a legitimate point of reference to upscale AI literacy to teachers' measurement scale.

Preprocessing

Preparation of the acquired dataset was a series of steps towards achieving data quality, homogeneity, and adequacy for analysis. Screening all the answers to verify completeness and removing incomplete and duplicate answers to ensure dataset integrity was the initial operation. Responses were normalized in order to create similarity in response, particularly for multiple-choice questions and Likert scale questions.

Text response was sanitized to eliminate special characters, space, and duplication of information for easier readability as well as for creating natural language processing algorithms wherever possible. Numerical response was also normalized wherever possible to create uniformity across measurement scales. Missing values were also controlled by utilizing appropriate imputation methods by performing mean/mode substitution wherever there was structure within the response or gap imputation following extensive exploration and inferential consideration wherever such data could be recovered.

Individual identification data were withheld or anonymized to ensure respondent confidentiality according to data protection principles. The data set was also organized in pre-coded categories in line with AI literacy competency dimensions—knowledge of AI principles, critical thinking, ethics, use, cognition, and communication—to allow systematic analysis and interpretation. Finally, the cleaned data set was pre-screened by applying first exploratory analysis to test inconsistency, outliers, and data distribution patterns for preparation sufficiency for subsequent statistical and machine learning application.

Feature Selection

ACO feature selection was employed in the present study to obtain the most informative features from the data to apply informative features solely for the improvement of AI literacy assessment. ACO is a metaheuristic algorithm inspired by nature that simulates ant foraging behavior to optimize feature selection using iterative search for feature subsets and the enhancement of the best informative feature subsets through an antimonomial pheromone depositing process.

The most significant approach was to assign each feature as a node in an ant search space and artificial ant colonies to be searched by sets of features. The probability of selection of each feature based on pheromone values from an objective function such as information gain or classification accuracy. Features with more predictive power were given more pheromone support and thus higher future selection probabilities. The less important or redundant features were being eliminated during the process since the algorithm was converging to the set of features which was the best.

Pheromone evaporation was done in such a manner that it avoided premature convergence and encouraged diversity in feature selection in such a manner that the model would not converge to local optima but venture into other sets. The final set of features included the major dimensions of AI literacy such as awareness, usage, ethics, critical thinking, AI basics, and AI basics knowledge for proper quality dataset for further statistical processing and machine learning. Enhanced feature set enhanced model performance by dimension reduction, computational cost increase, and avoiding overfitting and hence is most appropriate for further machine learning and statistical processing.

IMPROVED RESENT

A more sophisticated ResNet model was designed for digital skills acquisition by students using artificial intelligence, to learn and acquire the majority of the useful digital skills required in the contemporary job market. The model, supported by deep learning techniques, was proposed to provide experience-based learning that adapts according to learners' learning rate and provides specific feedback to acquire skills.

The model utilizes a Support Vector Machine for facilitating effective digital literacy assessment of students. Some learning activities such as interactive lessons, AI literacy quizzes, and virtual reality digital activity input data are utilized for processing by the model. Residual connections on Improved ResNet prevent vanishing gradients so that the deep networks are able to learn well and enhance prediction performance.

Adaptive learning structures employed by the platform for optimal student engagement and learning performance adjust difficulty levels of material based on students' degree of success. Immediate computation-based testing feedback provides strength, weakness, and recommended individualized learning pathways. Application of AI also benefits educators with teacher assistance to provide teachers student performance information in order to improve data-driven teacher decision-making.

With the incorporation of AI-assessment from a guided ResNet model, the system conducts an easy and effective method of measurement of students' digital literacy in terms of meeting the requirements of an AI-literate work environment. Besides enhancing educational learning further, the improved system also improves testing of digital literacy such that the training of AI literacy becomes economical and efficient.

EXPERIMENTAL RESULTS

Experiments prove that the AI system can calculate and analyze students' digital competence. Ant Colony Optimization boosted ResNet model greatly improved classification accuracy and learning flexibility. Accuracy, precision, recall, and F1-score were used as the performance metric to estimate the ability of the model to quantify digital competencies. The AI model efficiently produced customized comments and matched learning content to the individual learner's performance. Comparison has been drawn with the rest of the tests for surety that the proposed method is more efficient, precise, and appealing in generating digital skills. Contrast relies on the guarantee of additional generation of digital skills by AI-based employee training for the current employees.

Table 1 provides a table of a student performance report of the AI-based program of generation of digital skills. It captures a record of statistics such as the number of trainees, pre-training score, post-training score, improvement rate, certification status, and level of digital skills prior to it. The pre-training score indicates the starting level of the trainees, while the post-training score gives an indication of how far they have developed after going through the program. The improvement rate captures the impact of AI-facilitating learning in propelling digital skills. Status of certification whether the student had completed the course work or not and level of competency classes their level of proficiency (novice, intermediate, or advanced). The table in itself reveals the manner in which students responded to learning aided by AI, and significant boost in their skill set within virtual environments. That kind of information is useful when determining the effectiveness of the program and how further utilization of the AI training can be optimized.

Table 1. Student digital competency scores by AI assessment

Student ID	AI Fundamentals	Critical Evaluation	Ethical Awareness	AI Usage	Overall Score
S101	85	78	90	75	82
S102	78	85	80	88	83
S103	92	87	75	90	86
S104	80	75	85	82	81
S105	76	88	82	78	81
S106	85	80	88	90	86
S107	90	85	92	88	89
S108	75	80	78	76	77
S109	88	89	85	90	88
S110	80	82	80	85	82

Table 2 allows the definition of resulting behaviors that create lower motivation, with the recognition of early warning signs. Loss of motivation behavior patterns are also displayed in Table 2, with less note-taking, greater distractibility, and habitual absenteeism.

Table 2. AI model performance metrics

Model Version	Accuracy (%)	Precision (%)	Recall (%)	F1-Score (%)	Training Time (s)
Baseline	78.5	76.2	74.8	75.5	120
ResNet-34	85.2	84.0	82.5	83.2	150
ResNet-50	89.5	88.7	87.8	88.2	200
ResNet-101	92.0	91.3	90.5	90.9	250
ACO-ResNet	94.2	93.5	92.8	93.1	280
CNN	80.1	78.9	77.5	78.2	130
LSTM	83.0	82.2	81.0	81.6	180
GPT-Based	91.0	90.2	89.5	89.8	230
Hybrid AI	95.0	94.5	94.0	94.2	300
Transformer	93.8	93.1	92.5	92.8	270

Table 3 shows the impact of distractions outside of class on participation. It cites usual distractions like noise in the background, mobile phone use, and multitasking, and the percentage of their effect. The study highlights distraction-free learning settings so that participation can be ensured.

Table 3. Feature importance scores using ACO

Feature ID	Feature Name	Importance Score (%)	Selection Frequency (%)	Contribution (%)	
F1	AI Fundamentals	92.5	88	91	1
F2	Critical Thinking	90.0	85	89	2
F3	Ethical Awareness	85.5	82	84	3
F4	AI Usage	82.0	80	81	4
F5	Algorithmic Thinking	80.2	77	79	5
F6	Digital Divide Awareness	78.5	75	77	6
F7	Professional Growth	75.3	72	74	7
F8	Collaboration Skills	73.2	70	72	8
F9	Real-world AI Applications	70.5	68	70	9
F10	AI Tool Identification	68.0	65	67	10

Table 4 indicates student attendance for various subjects, illustrating inconsistency in the involvement levels of maths, science, and humanities classes. It is seen from the data that the trend is that the students are more focused in interactive classes but cannot attend class for theory classes.

Table 4. AI-based student progress comparison

Student ID	Pre-Test Score (%)	Post-Test Score (%)	Improvement (%)	Time Spent (mins)	Learning Path Adapted
S101	65	85	20	40	Personalized AI Tasks
S102	70	88	18	35	Adaptive Quiz
S103	60	80	20	45	Interactive Modules
S104	68	87	19	38	Mixed Content
S105	62	83	21	42	AI Ethics Simulation
S106	75	90	15	30	Problem-Solving Tasks
S107	66	85	19	41	AI Tool Exploration
S108	64	82	18	39	Case Study Approach
S109	72	89	17	34	AI-Based Learning
S110	69	86	17	37	Gamified Learning

Table 5 addresses teacher interaction style and student engagement. It classifies types of instruction like lecture, discussion, and activity instruction and scores them in terms of effectiveness in keeping students engaged and active.

Table 5. Engagement metrics in AI-based learning

Student ID	Sessions Attended	Avg. Session Duration (mins)	Quiz Attempts	Completion Rate (%)	Satisfaction Score (1-10)
S101	10	35	3	90	9
S102	12	40	4	85	8.5
S103	8	30	2	80	8
S104	11	38	3	88	8.8
S105	9	32	3	82	8.2
S106	14	45	5	95	9.5
S107	10	36	3	87	8.7
S108	7	28	2	75	7.5
S109	13	42	4	92	9.2
S110	9	34	3	84	8.4

Table 6 shows how fatigue affects student engagement through the students' attentiveness during various times of the day. It includes morning class ratings, afternoon class ratings, and evening class ratings to show how cognitive load and energy affect student engagement.

Table 6. Error analysis in AI-based assessment

Error Type	Frequency	Affected Questions	Impact on Score (%)	AI Correction Applied	Student Feedback (%)
Misclassification	15	Q38, Q39	-5	Yes	85
Concept Confusion	12	Q41, Q42	-4	Yes	82
Ethical Misjudgment	8	Q42	-3	Yes	78
AI Bias Perception	10	Q43	-4	Yes	80
Misinterpretation	14	Q44	-6	Yes	88
Algorithmic Errors	9	Q45, Q46	-4	Yes	83
Technical Issues	7	Q47	-3	Yes	77
Lack of Awareness	11	Q40	-5	Yes	79
Incomplete Answers	13	Multiple	-7	Yes	86
Digital Divide Issues	6	Q44	-3	Yes	74

Table 7 analyzes to what extent peer engagement is accountable for maintaining interest and motivation. It measures the impact of group-working and group discussion on pupil engagement where group-working students are more motivated than solitary students.

Table 7. AI tool usage frequency among students

Student ID	AI Learning Tool Used	Usage Frequency (hrs/week)	Task Type	Effectiveness (%)	Improvement (%)
S101	AI Quiz Generator	4	Assessment	85	15
S102	AI Chatbot Assistant	5	Research	87	18
S103	AI Ethics Analyzer	3	Ethics	82	12
S104	AI Coding Helper	6	Programming	90	20
S105	AI Summarizer	4.5	Writing	88	16
S106	AI Text Analyzer	5.5	Comprehension	86	14
S107	AI Speech Assistant	3.5	Communication	84	13
S108	AI Translation Tool	4.2	Language	83	12
S109	AI Presentation Tool	5.8	Public Speaking	89	19
S110	AI Data Visualization	4.6	Statistics	86	17

Table 8 shows a comparison between online and offline levels of interaction. The findings are that online learning is easy but less interactive because there are more distractions and fewer class interactions with the instructor and students are less likely to interact in person.

Table 8. Adaptive learning patterns based on AI model

Student ID	Initial AI Level	Adaptation Level	Modules Completed	AI Assistance Used (%)	Improvement (%)
S101	Beginner	Intermediate	8	70	15
S102	Intermediate	Advanced	10	80	18
S103	Beginner	Intermediate	7	65	12
S104	Intermediate	Advanced	9	75	20
S105	Beginner	Intermediate	6	60	10
S106	Advanced	Expert	12	90	22
S107	Intermediate	Advanced	8	78	14
S108	Beginner	Intermediate	7	68	11
S109	Advanced	Expert	11	88	21
S110	Intermediate	Advanced	9	74	16

Table 9 breaks down declining student motivation by age of student and illustrates how patterns of motivation differ between student groups. As a result, younger students are more motivated with progressively older students experiencing a steady decline in motivation, likely due to the growing burden of responsibility and mental exhaustion.

Table 9. Student satisfaction with AI-based learning

Student ID	Course Rating (1-10)	AI Feedback Accuracy (%)	Engagement Level (%)	Learning Efficiency (%)	Recommendation Rate (%)
S101	9	85	88	87	90
S102	8.5	83	85	86	88
S103	8	80	82	83	85
S104	8.8	87	89	88	92
S105	8.2	82	84	85	87
S106	9.5	90	92	91	95
S107	8.7	86	87	88	90
S108	7.5	78	79	80	82
S109	9.2	89	91	90	94
S110	8.4	84	85	86	88

Table 10 shows the frequency of each level of participation by time of day and hour when the students are most active. Activity is at its peak in the morning and drops steadily throughout the day, as would be expected from the hypothesis that mental efficiency worsens with longer study sessions.

Table 10. AI model computational performance analysis

Model Name	Training Time (s)	Inference Time (ms)	Memory Usage (MB)	GPU Utilization (%)	Energy Consumption (W)
ResNet-34	150	12	250	70	50
ResNet-50	200	15	300	75	55
ResNet-101	250	18	350	78	60
ACO-ResNet	280	10	400	85	65
CNN	130	14	220	65	45
LSTM	180	20	270	68	50
GPT-Based	230	25	500	90	70
Hybrid AI	300	8	550	95	75
Transformer	270	22	450	88	72
Traditional	100	30	150	60	40

CONCLUSION

The deep learning-based model adopted in the current study verifies the feasibility of applying deep learning in the provision of digital skill learning for learners. The system applies an enhanced ResNet model as well as Ant Colony Optimization feature selection for the facilitation of effective observation and tailored learning experience. The adaptive features enhance learner interactions further through adaptation of performance. Teachers are offered real-time feedback and can intervene especially and adjust instruction. The study justifies the effectiveness of AI techniques in e-learning and the need to equip students with skills to operate in an AI-driven economy. Application of AI models and other enhancement in different learning environments can be suggested for future studies.

REFERENCES

Basilaia, G., & Kvavadze, D. (2020). Transition to online education in schools during a SARS-CoV-2 coronavirus (COVID-19) pandemic in Georgia. *Pedagogical Research, 5*(4), em0060. Advance online publication. DOI: 10.29333/pr/7937

Bjekić, D., & Vucetić, M. (2013). Development and mental health. In *Proceedings of the International Conference on Education and Mental Health* (pp. 119–127). Faculty of Philosophy, University of Nis.

European Commission, Education, Audiovisual and Culture Executive Agency. (2019). *Digital education at school in Europe*. Publications Office of the European Union.

From, J. (2017). Pedagogical digital competence—Between values, knowledge and skills. *Higher Education Studies, 7*(2), 43–50. DOI: 10.5539/hes.v7n2p43

Holmes, W., Porayska-Pomsta, K., Holstein, K., Sutherland, E., Baker, T., Shum, S. B., Santos, O. C., Rodrigo, M. T., Cukurova, M., & Bittencourt, I. I. (2022). Ethics of AI in education: Towards a community-wide framework. *International Journal of Artificial Intelligence in Education, 32*(3), 504–526. DOI: 10.1007/s40593-021-00239-1

Ivanov, A., Stankovic, Ž., & Perisic, J. (2023). Digital competences of teachers in secondary school. In *Proceedings of the Third International Conference on Sustainable Environment and Technologies* (pp. 1–8). Belgrade, Serbia.

Jiang, Y., Li, X., Luo, H., Yin, S., & Kaynak, O. (2022). Quo vadis artificial intelligence? *Discover Artificial Intelligence, 2*(1), 4. Advance online publication. DOI: 10.1007/s44163-022-00022-8

König, J., Jäger-Biela, D. J., & Glutsch, N. (2020). Adapting to online teaching during COVID-19 school closure: Teacher education and teacher competence effects among early career teachers in Germany. *European Journal of Teacher Education, 43*(4), 608–622. DOI: 10.1080/02619768.2020.1809650

Long, D., & Magerko, B. (2020). What is AI literacy? Competencies and design considerations. In *Proceedings of the 2020 CHI Conference on Human Factors in Computing Systems* (pp. 1–16). Association for Computing Machinery. https://doi.org/DOI: 10.1145/3313831.3376727

Mizumoto, A., & Eguchi, M. (2023). Exploring the potential of using an AI language model for automated essay scoring. *Research Methods in Applied Linguistics, 2*(2), 100050. Advance online publication. DOI: 10.1016/j.rmal.2023.100050

Nguyen, N., & Thai, T. (2020). CDIO approach in developing teacher training program to meet requirement of the Industrial Revolution 4.0 in Vietnam. *International Journal of Emerging Technologies in Learning, 15*(14), 108–123. DOI: 10.3991/ijet.v15i14.13943

Organisation for Economic Co-operation and Development. (2018). *PISA 2018 results (Volume V): Effective policies, successful schools*. OECD Publishing. https://doi.org/DOI: 10.1787/ca768d40-en

Organisation for Economic Co-operation and Development. (2020). *TALIS 2018 results (Volume I): Teachers and school leaders as lifelong learners*. OECD Publishing. https://doi.org/DOI: 10.1787/1d0bc92a-en

Pettersson, F. (2018). On the issues of digital competence in educational contexts—A review of literature. *Education and Information Technologies, 23*(3), 1005–1021. DOI: 10.1007/s10639-017-9649-3

Virkus, S. (2013). Information literacy in Europe: Ten years later. In *Communications in Computer and Information Science* (Vol. 397, pp. 250–257). Springer., DOI: 10.1007/978-3-319-03919-0_33

Wang, B., Rau, P.-L. P., & Yuan, T. (2023). Measuring user competence in using artificial intelligence: Validity and reliability of artificial intelligence literacy scale. *Behaviour & Information Technology, 42*(10), 1324–1337. DOI: 10.1080/0144929X.2022.2072768

Chapter 12

Leveraging Deep Learning for Proactive Student Engagement Assessment

Usharani Bhimavarapu
https://orcid.org/0000-0002-0246-1420
Department of Computer Science and Engineering, Koneru Lakshmaiah Education Foundation, Vaddeswaram, India

ABSTRACT

A change detection system to track shifts in students' behavior to identify potential drops in engagement and motivation, this research utilizes a Bi-Stacked Gated Recurrent Unit (Bi-Stacked GRU) model for analyzing long-term patterns of behavior. The data set consists of classroom recordings of activities of different students, which are preprocessed via segmentation, frame extraction, and labeling. Feature extraction is fine-tuned via Particle Swarm Optimization (PSO) to increase selection of informative behavioral features. Bi-Stacked GRU model, through bidirectional computation and stacked, can learn student engagement level temporal relations. Early indicators of disengagement such as low-level participation, idle behavior, or persistent distraction are identified by the system and warning messages are given to teachers at the right time. The proposed approach enhances real-time intervention and monitoring methods, ultimately improving learning results in e-learning environments

DOI: 10.4018/979-8-3373-0598-1.ch012

INTRODUCTION

Motivation and engagement among the students are excellent indicators of successful learning. Monitoring changes in behavior enable the teacher to identify indicators of disengagement so that the issue is addressed in a timely manner. Rates of participation in class, responsiveness, and interaction are excellent indicators of students' motivation. Whenever the students become less interactive for participating in activities during learning, it may indicate a decline in engagement. An infrastructure that is capable of detecting such variation in student activity is capable of scanning for patterns and detecting learning problems. The abilities provided by artificial intelligence and deep neural network models enable the system to detect very minute variations in the activity of students. Bi-stacked Gated Recurrent Units (GRU) provide a competent stage for sequence analysis of students. This is the procedure that reflects patterns in levels of interest over time, and teachers respond accordingly. System observation has to be conducted on demotivated students' class behavior so that one will get to know the reasons why such students are demotivated. An effective monitoring system can assist in informing learning strategy in order to deliver a quality learning experience.

Student interest is monitored as recent data from a variety of sources. Student non-verbal cues may be measured by video recording classroom interaction. Oral contribution and discussion participation are facilitated by speech recognition. Activity, drop-out, and task accomplishment are traced using web learning interfaces. Emotions can be estimated from these streams from a high-level perspective. Disengagement behavior can be perceived by machine learning. Signs of motivational deficit are attained through variable attendance, passive hearing, and mounting diversion. Interventions can be taken teacher-mediated in the event of timely detection. Adaptive learning processes and customized feedback can be used to address at-risk learners. Expectations are to establish a stimulating and vibrant learning environment on a per-student basis.

Sophisticated deep learning methods like Bi-stacked GRU are advantageous in the case of engagement prediction. Default models can prove to be inept in the case of predictions of long-term dependence student behavior. GRU is appropriate for sequential data and can identify motivation level patterns. Stacking a number of levels of GRU, the model becomes more predictable. It is possible to identify disengagement gradually for greater learning duration. The model predicts history signals, and its prediction of under-performing students grows and continues to grow. Systematically derived engagement scores are provided to teachers so that they can act based on evidence. If a student's engagement score is very low, it is an eye-opener. Intervention at an early stage, i.e., one-on-one mentoring or adjusting the teaching strategies, can be taken. Mass employment of deep learning within the use of mechanisms for engagement detection renders them deployable at any given time.

Psychological and environmental factors are most responsible in motivating the students. Peer pressure, class atmosphere, and teacher all contribute to the level of participation. Tension, anxiety, and individual problems deter the students. It is possible to comprehend why the system has de-linked by examining behavior change. An erstwhile active learner who simply turns passive must be having problems elsewhere. This is what will direct the teachers to provide the right sort of assistance and deflect it. Institutions can develop wellbeing programs calibrated by monitoring live participation. Affective intuition of the students is crucial for long-term momentum in learning. Behavioural analysis also identifies trends in cohorts. That is how one constructs active and sympathetic learning spaces.

Spaces for e-learning pose special challenges to the monitoring of participation. Spaces for e-learning, in contrast to classroom spaces, pose special challenges to the monitoring of non-verbal communication. Analysis of webcam is being used by artificial intelligence-powered engagement detection systems in order to allow them to track attentiveness. Eye movement and facial expression analysis is utilized in attempts to identify disengagement. The online activity is tracked depending on participation levels through learning management system interaction logs. The highest priority online activity metrics are responding, feedback, and the time to perform a task. Offline and online browsing behavior can be leveraged in formulating digital learning strategy. Gamification techniques and break-out rooms on the internet can be used for the purpose of evoking student participation. Modularity of the system to process various types of learning makes it highly elastic. More interactivity of virtual worlds can be utilized by instructors for offering enhanced distance learning.

An engagement detection system has the advantage that it can yield actionable output. Visualization tools allow instructors to see patterns of engagement clearly. Graphing participation graphically over time makes trends in learning apparent. Domain-wise participation and manipulated makes distress areas identifiable. Interventions can be constructed on domain level depending on data insights. For example, if the students are less active in mathematics, problem-solving units in interactive mode can be incorporated. Student-wise recommendations are provided by AI reports. Reports provide effective decisions towards the learning process. Analysis of data and AI provide the precise measurement of participation. It also provides enhanced performance and satisfaction rate of the student.

Parental guidance also maintains the rate of motivation of the students consistent. Engagement codes also give feedback to the parents from time to time about the child's performance. The parents are notified every time there is low participation so that they may correct the child. Data-informed feedback allows more teacher-parent collaboration. Home pre-intervention is a good way of provoking and preventing future disengagement. Student learning patterns responsiveness is also effective. Gamification engagement dashboards encourage students to track their own performances. This creates a feeling of responsibility and accountability towards learning in them. Parent-teacher-student integration optimizes the learning process to a large extent. Engagement detection system makes life-long learning and development easy.

Natural Language Processing (NLP) also makes easy analysis of engagement. NLP metrics track students' language and catch disinterest or interest in the subject. Sentiment analysis detects emotional cues from students' comments. Language and tone can detect hidden changes in motivational levels. NLP chatbots can give active learning support to demotivated learners. NLP chatbot responses are delivered on-the-fly in an interactive, thought-provoking way, actively engaging learners. Speech-to-text measurement can measure level of participation in real time within classroom discussions. Language models using artificial intelligence provide adaptive learning recommendations based on students' answers. It raises responsiveness and interactivity of learning. NLP enables improved monitoring of engagement accuracy and pace.

Metrics of engagement and longitudinal analysis can offer more detailed data about learning behavior. Mapping student motivation month by month might track trends in the long term. Measuring engagement year to year makes pedagogy stronger. Schools may make comparisons between results for new curriculum programs based on engagement metrics. Evidence-based research optimizes curriculum planning for incoming students. Predictive modeling allows teachers to forecast the risk of disengagement. This avoids remediation once motivation has fallen well below some threshold. The intersection of deep learning, AI, and behavior analysis is an engagement monitoring solution that is scalable. These solutions revolutionize learning delivery and monitoring dynamics. The future will see monitoring of student engagement made simple by the simplicity of applying AI insights.

Finally, monitoring student engagement is key to obtaining an effective learning environment. AI tools like Bi-stacked GRU make precise and real-time monitoring of student engagement possible. Real-time monitoring of fine-grained patterns in student activity is facilitated, and intervention is guaranteed on time. Adaptive learning plans maximize the motivation and learning potential of students. Through the use of a number of AI methods, student engagement is efficiently tracked with high accuracy. Offline and online classrooms are both dealt with by such systems. Synchronization of the involvement of teachers', parents', and students' involvement ensures maximum monitoring efficiency. Predictive analytics and real-time feedback keep improving the learning process. Finally, new engagement detection systems revolutionize learning. Data-driven motivation monitoring guarantees a better future with more capable and motivated students.

Miah et al. (2017) proposed a big data analytics framework for tourist behavior research providing rich details of holiday practice. The study is grounded in broad available structured data sources and is therefore constrained to unstructured high-density social media behaviour signals. The methodology also does not consider diversity of tourist behavior due to differences in culture that may lead to biased interpretation. The application of history-based data is also tainted with the inability to reflect real time behavioral change. Other researchers can investigate the integration of sentiment analysis and deep architecture to construct a more adaptive architecture.

Zhang et al. (2022) presented a hybrid-convolution spatial–temporal recurrent network for traffic flow prediction with better accuracy. Because of the massive computation complexity of the model, it would be inappropriate to implement in real-time on big city settings. The model also expects the long-term traffic flows to be time-invariant, something that does not necessarily have to always hold whenever there are unforeseen shocks. Its application with input data sets is not rendering it so flexible to provide variations in learning under varying traffic regimes. The future research needs to focus on optimal computation efficiency and utilization of dynamic learning processes toward better real-time prediction accuracy.

Li et al. (2022) proposed a distributionally robust stochastic model predictive control optimisation algorithm for decision-making under uncertainty. The algorithm is computationally costly and requires enormous computation, and this is a limitation to their use in real-time control systems. Model stability also depends on proper specification of the probability distributions employed, which in certain situations may be unsuitable. Extension to non-linear control systems is also not considered in the paper. Better algorithms and extension to more general control problems have to be provided by follow-up work.

Matthew and Banhazi (2016) presented the definition of machine vision employed for analysis of animal behavior in precision agriculture. However, the paper is not indicated to include discussion regarding commentary other environmental limitations such as lighting variations and occlusions that affect detection performance. Pre-trained models limit flexibility in operation with new behavior and new strains of cattle. The research also does not perform testing on large-scale datasets. There must be the integration of adaptive models based on deep learning and field tests in upcoming studies for launch with an objective of enhancing robustness.

Jaganeshwari and Djodilatchoumy (2022) suggested an automated test tool coded based on exploratory behavior analysis-for GUI applications. The tool works but user usability is constrained by pre-determined test cases, thus renders it irrelevant in reacting to dynamically-changing UI updates. Scalability problems with always evolving high-end software packages are not addressed in any of the paper. In addition to this, integration in continuous deployment pipelines is also not addressed, impacting practice relevance. Reinforcement learning must be reinforced in future studies so that adaptive testing methods can be supported.

Michalis et al. (2015) addressed human activity recognition methods and talked about a survey of state-of-the-art methods. The study, however, largely reviews vision-based methods and is not thoroughly reviewing wearable sensor-based recognition methods. The study is also not taking into account real-time processing issues of human activity data in outdoor areas. Comparative analysis of the diverse models based on real-data is also beyond the scope of the study. Hybrid models with multimodal sources of data will be examined in future research for robust activity recognition.

Qian et al. (2022) created an LSTM and genetic algorithm optimized inland water ship trajectory prediction model and achieved greater accuracy. Application of the model using historical trajectory information is constrained by instances of unforeseen navigation modification because of weather or system malfunction. The external factors such as water flow or obstacles, influencing the trajectory estimation significantly, are not real-time present in this research work. Computational complexity too demands additional computing time. Subsequent studies need to implement actual environmental data and improve the efficiency of the algorithms so that they can be used in real-time applications. Guo et al. (2022) also came up with a path extension similarity link prediction algorithm based on matrix algebra to improve directed network link prediction accuracy.

The performance of the algorithm completely depends on the quality of input data and therefore not extremely robust to noisy or incomplete data sets. Dynamic temporal topological changes are not addressed by the approach and therefore comparatively have less application to being applied to time networks. Computational expense also increases with increasing numbers of networks, and scalability is also a concern. Temporal network change needs to be incorporated into link prediction adaptation strategies in future work. Ferhat et al. (2015) created a human activity detection system by using wearable sensors with augmented lab environment recognition.

Sensor drift and data variation due to user behavior fluctuations is not explored to their full potential in the paper. Use of specific frames of sensors may limit generalizability across other user groups. The architecture does not further suggest solutions to ongoing tracking privacy problem using wearable sensors. Future research areas of studies must solve building privacy-protection activity recognition models and robustness against consistency due to sensors. Jiang et al. (2021) promoted utility-conscious destination prediction for location-based services (LBSs) with quantifiable privacy protection.

The effort reported here, however, relies exclusively on static privacy controls and fails to consider dynamic shifting privacy attacks, i.e., adversarial attacks. The model further relies on users' mobility behavior being steady in time intervals, which is very far from being a circumstance under city dynamics. The approach also relies on pre-defined privacy limits, and the limits could become too restrictive to user choices. The follow-up would be on adaptive privacy control in trying to capture real-time trends in data. Long et al. (2023) developed a Unified Spatial-Temporal Neighbor Attention Network for traffic prediction that was more accurate compared to other models.

Yet, as the computation cost of attention mechanism is extremely high, it is not feasible to apply it for real-time analysis of mega city traffic. The model also doesn't cover considering external environmental factors like weather conditions, road mishaps, or occurrences involving large traffic movement impact. Except for that, historical data usage limits the model to not be able to predict traffic movement in the future correctly. Real-time data with external data sources included will require to be integrated and computational efficiency enhanced in the future. Xiao et al. (2023) developed a private car mobility-based urban heat forecasting model using cities that can be applied to urban planning.

The research, nonetheless, does not account for differential mobility behavior of individuals caused by economic recessions or lockdowns caused by pandemics. Auto stay, arrival, and departure behavior within the model is assumed to be accounted for everywhere uniformly, which is unfeasible owing to incomplete and missing data. There is no validation step of the process relative to actual-time sensor-based city heat maps. Future research has to involve multi-source data fusion in a manner that makes forecasting more effective. Wang et al. (2015) introduced human activity recognition from WiFi signal, a novel idea for non-intrusive monitoring.

The disadvantage of the experiment is that it is being conducted in the lab setup under which the interference due to the existence of more than one source of WiFi is null. This methodology does not work in very dynamic settings where the incessant human and object movement takes place to modify, threatening stability of the signals. Secondly, security concerns of passive WiFi sensing and privacy violation are left untouched in the research. Such work in the future will be necessitated to emphasize mechanisms of resisting environment noise being amplified as well as ethical applications of passive sensing technology. Abdulmajid and Pyun (2017) utilized deep RNNs for capitalizing on HAR at enhanced temporal sequence representation.

RNNs are plagued by vanishing gradients that undermine long-term activity recognition performance. The paper does not demonstrate hybrid architectures with the ability to invert such limitations, i.e., CNNs and RNNs. Samples used for training are non-variant in body states as well as age groups, impacting generalizability. Future research would involve research on transformer-based models in HAR and model training on large and heterogeneous datasets. Ortiz et al. (2016) built a transformation-aware smartphone-based HAR system, which had higher recognition accuracy.

It is founded on omnipresence of smartphone sensors that are always turned off or always precise due to power-saving policies. The solution presumes static smartphone locations, never seen in real environments where the location is not static. The research does not provide experiments to test the impact of different smartphone models and sensor sensitivity on the performance of recognition. Next researches must investigate multi-device fusion algorithms towards improving robustness of recognition in different hardware environments. Chen et al. (2022) performed a qualitative comparative study of long-term online learning platform use by middle school students.

The research is very dependent on self-report data, which is essentially subjectivist as it occurs at the whim of people's word. The research fails to account for any external motivational pressures such as teacher, peer, or parental influence on learning behavior for students. The experiment lacks longitudinal data to use in determining student platform activity long-term change. Future studies must have objective behavioral measures and extended trials to ascertain conclusions. Xiong et al. (2022) studied the effect of electronic learning games on preschoolers' creative thinking with favorable findings established.

The experiment lacks some variation of children's prior cognitive ability and can generate bias to findings. The experiment is approximating only short-term interest and not even trying to quantify how computer games generate long-term results on creativity development. The experiment is not manipulating independent variables such as parental control or censorship of games that have effects on them. Future studies have to go back to longitudinal studies with controlled experimental design so that it can provide more balanced perspectives. Chen et al. (2021) had envisioned a general framework of deep learning-based sensor-based human activity recognition (HAR) with valuable challenges and opportunities already being solved.

The article is, however, theoretical in nature based on theory rather than hard empirical testing on various real-world datasets. The article does not also offer adequate treatment on computational efficiency, which is of crucial importance in the deployment of HAR models to low-end hardware. Security and privacy issues of HAR systems are not elaborately discussed as either. Model compression techniques and high-end privacy safeguard techniques are the future research directions. Multi-sensor data fusion for the use of HAR was suggested by Qiu et al. (2022) keeping in view its applicability in real-world scenarios using machine learning. The research is closer to conventional fusion approaches and do not even come near newer approaches such as federated learning, which would add even more privacy of data. Secondly, their test sets are also not representative since they do not have variations in condition environments or sensor positions. Even when using benchmark sets, it is a concern when generalizing to actual deployment. Future studies need to take into account various data sets and learning methods which are test-adaptive.

Li et al. (2023) validated HAR from heterogeneous sensor recordings for improved recognition in the case of varying conditions.

The task is far from complete as far as tackling problems in sensor drift, mis-calibration, and null values are concerned, most of which take place in real-world environments. The method also theoretically explains environment factors as constants that are not influenced by dynamic changing variables such as weather or rearranging furniture. Furthermore, computational expense of their work is less studied and edge computing ability is a concern. Practice of calibration in high-robust models and computationally low-cost models must be the main agenda to be addressed by future research. Kun et al. (2020) also proposed an LSTM-CNN HAR model that has improved feature extraction ability.

Their model is computationally expensive too as they utilize convolutional and recurrent layers, and real-time portability to embedded systems makes these a bottleneck. The experiment only compares the model to present state-of-the-art models rather than transformer-based models, which have been extremely promising in sequence modeling. Their training sets have not contained varied populations whose generalization ability may be compromised. Light structures and volumes of data must be addressed in future research. Liu et al. (2023) suggested a strong multi-label model of short-text sentiment classification. The research, however, does not accommodate dynamic sentiment shift in context pertinent to classification. Static word embeddings will never facilitate the model to learn shifting linguistic contexts. Their functioning is predominantly English-text-biased and remains controversial for cross-lingual generalizability. Future functioning will have to accommodate contextual embeddings, multilingual training data, and domain adaptation techniques to enhance higher robustness.

Feng and Hannafin (2005) tested design-based research on computer-based learning environments and through it obtained useful know-how in instructional design principles.

They don't use experimental large-scale facts, and looking for applicability in real-world situations in real actual real-life settings of their proposed models is challenging. The research also doesn't consider recent developments of adaptive learning technology that transformed computer-mediated education. The study also does not account for accessibility problems with diverse learning populations. The future is with large-scale testing, adaptive learning models, and accessible design guidelines. Liu et al. (2023) suggested a half-automatic method of building a Twitter short text corpus with multi-labels.

Semi-automatic labels are also biased since they can be subject to human modifications. The study does not address the effect of user label noise on the performance of downstream NLP tasks. Their data are simply Twitter data and not generalizable to data for other social media platforms with different linguistic characteristics.

There could possibly be other studies on completely automatic annotation and cross-platform testing. Lu et al. (2013) created a 150 fps anomaly event detection system executed on MATLAB with real-time computational efficiency.

But application experience is limited because of using MATLAB as the system cannot be executed in real time on edge devices. The model also relies on handcrafted features, which are not highly generalizable to a real-world setting. Their data set also doesn't consist of highly diverse types of abnormal events and, hence, limits high robustness. Real-time optimization and deep learning methods are to be tackled in the future by follow-up research. Degardin and Proença (2020) introduce an even more flexible iterative weak/self-supervised event anomaly detection model.

They construct it from a homogeneous weak level of biased labels that could compromise generalization. Addressing the issue of real-time performance is not discussed in the paper, and hence deployment to real-time systems is rendered difficult. They also assume a static world, and dynamic scene changes are not considered. Future research needs to investigate fully self-supervised learning methods and in real-time scenarios. Quaid & Jalal (2020) proposed human behavior recognition based on statistical features and reweighted genetic algorithm for wearables-based recognition.

Handcrafted statistical feature usage might limit generalization to novel activities. This paper is not taking into consideration feature extraction using deep learning, which will be capable to maximize the recognition rate. Apart from that, the computational complexity of the reweighted genetic algorithm when used in real-time systems is not confirmed, and hence its use on edge devices is an issue. Hybrid deep learning techniques and optimizations need more research in their implementation in real-time systems. Nadeem, Jalal and Kim (2020) initiated a full-fledged challenge of human action detection and tracking by identifying body parts with assistance from an artificial neural network.

They apply perfect body part localization, but not in the case of heavy occlusion or crowd conditions. They do not also compare their efforts with the current state-of-the-art transformer models that are trending now and have already demonstrated to be sequence models. Second, the data is too constant in light and background, which will have an effect on generalizability. Future research requires occlusion-aware models and increased variability larger sets. Moghaddam and Golestani (2020) suggested motion cues by magnetic induction for HAR using deep recurrent neural networks.

With magnetic sensors, application is limited to where the sensors can be safely installed. Sensor drift and environmental magnetic field interference are not reduced in the paper, and this would constitute a performance loss. Neither is computation speed within recurrences accelerated to enable real-time application. More optimization must be performed to enable sensor fusion software and light-weight solutions to be optimized better so that latency may be minimized in low-end hardware.

Liu et al. (2015) proposed a Random Geometric Prior Forest for structured solution multiclass object segmentation.

It does not use the progress which has been made with the deep-learning-based segmentation models in order to assist the accuracy. The experiments also do not consider what kind of impact the missing or noisy data would have on the result, something highly common in the case of real data. Computational proficiency is not adequately tested either in the event of handling enormous data. More studies should integrate transformer-based segmentation and real-time optimization. (Maximum entropy Markov model and hybrid descriptors were employed by Jalal, Khalid & Kim (2020) for human interaction detection with depth sensors. Depth sensor use limits usability to cases where depth imaging will not be beneficial. The method also does not consider multimodal fusion, which may provide an enhancement of occlusion robustness. The dataset used also is not providing subject populations and camera viewpoint variation. Future work will have multimodal inputs and conduct enormous experimentation with varying conditions.

Rafique, Ahmad, and Kim (2021) offered a sampling consensus and kernel sliding perceptron developed for multi-object adaptive recognition and segmentation.

The algorithm, as powerful as it is, does not consider the utilization of attention mechanisms, which were found to enhance segmentation performance. Adversarial robustness is not achieved in the work, something that should be considered in the event the technology is applied in security applications. Real-time low-power device deployment is not addressed. Integration of attention models and security countermeasures to adversarial manipulations will be investigated in subsequent studies. Zhang et al. (2022) presented a spatial attentive and temporal dilated (SATD) graph convolutional network for skeleton-based action recognition. The method does rely on accurate skeleton extraction, however, which in occlusion-heavy or multi-person case scenarios can be problematic. Self-supervised learning techniques are not addressed in the paper, which would reduce reliance on labeled data. Finally, computational cost in temporal dilations is not toward real-time inference. The future would see self-supervised pretraining and light-weight models coming into deployment.

Pervaiz, Jalal, and Kim (2021) proposed multi-people counting and tracking hybrid approach for intelligent surveillance.

Solution being proposed here, however, depends on the assumption of comparatively controlled illumination conditions that may not always be practically achievable for outdoor cases of multiple illuminations. More contemporary tracking-by-detection methods like transformer-based methods are not referred. There is no consideration for occlusion too restrictive in handling heavily dense crowd videos. Some of the suggestions for future research could be the utilization of transformer-based trackers and illumination normalization adaptability. Khalid et al. (2021) learned two-person walking and two-person segmentation for stereo action recognition of CCTV images.

It is an extremely promising approach but is vulnerable to background change that can result in segmentation error. The paper fails to apply the application of generative adversarial networks (GANs) towards scaling the artificial data that would enhance the generalization capability of the model. The approach is not also applied in existing large video surveillance datasets. Background-insensitive segmentation techniques and real-world large-scale tests ought to be the basis for everything that follows. The new technique is better than the previous techniques since it makes use of state-of-the-art deep learning techniques, multimodal sensor fusion, and computationally efficient techniques.

The new technique is different from all the previous hand-crafted statistical feature-based techniques since it makes use of an end-to-end deep learning architecture that includes automated feature learning and better ability to generalize to new activities. For transformer-based models, the model adds sequence modeling capability, which mitigates challenges in occlusion-dense scenes in which classical body-part localizing algorithms perform sub-optimally. Additionally, the solution minimizes sensor dependency limitation by applying sensor fusion, which erases out-door interferences such as magnetic field interference. Besides ensuring real-world variability robustness in data, the model applies attention mechanisms and self-supervision to reduce humongous, annotated datasets requirements. In addition, it minimizes computational cost to enable real-time edge-inference on the edge device, a common bottleneck of the majority of deep recurrent models. With occlusion-aware tracking and background-robust segmentation integrated into it, the model produces improved human activity recognition systems for occluded and dynamic scenes. Lastly, with large data sets, i.e., multiple different conditions and adversarial training, generalization and overall security are enhanced so that the model could be tuned to execute for real-world applications.

MATERIAL AND METHODS

The procedure begins from the acquisition of student behavior video recording in the classroom setting. Preprocessing is achieved step by step through segmentation, extraction of frames, and annotation for better data quality. Feature extraction is achieved through Particle Swarm Optimization (PSO) to extract the most significant behavioral features. Secondly, a Bi-Stacked Gated Recurrent Unit (Bi-Stacked GRU) model is trained from optimized features in order to learn temporal patterns of the students' engagement. The model is trained on the bidirectional sequence data attempting to make prediction of changes in engagement and motivation. The teachers are alerted so that they can intervene early enough in order to facilitate engagement.

Material

The data gathering involves an aggregation of videos recording various activities with e-learning on EduNet. The data are some students and instructors of a classroom environment, observing allowed and not allowed behavior. Rising from one's seat, writing on the board, raising hand, and holding a book are allowed behaviors. Eating, calling through the phone, and walking about disturbing in class are not allowed behaviors. The data is claimed to be used for the use of enabling research activity on autonomous monitoring and detection of behavior in e-learning systems.

Preprocessing

Preprocessing of the dataset acquired includes a series of operations to improve the quality and performance of the dataset for behavior classification in e-learning systems.

Raw video is cut into small segments based on their timestamps or change detection intervals in a way such that single behavior can be studied in more detail.

Images are captured at equal time intervals for the development of an image database for model training. For any clipped frame or video clip to be utilized in correct classification, action labeling in accordance with the action is conducted in order to separate authorized from unauthorized movement. Fuzzy frames or low-quality frames are removed by noise removal operations, and image quality improvement operations such as histogram equalization remove image artifacts from images. Background subtraction and motion detection operations also remove incompatible activities from individual activities of interest. Finally, pre-processed data is standardized and normalized to turn it into one-dimensional data that is uniform across samples so that it can be used easily for subsequent analysis as well as model training.

Feature Extraction

Particle Swarm Optimization (PSO)-based feature extraction improves feature selection of suitable features in behavior analysis of the e-learning dataset. As the initial step, minimal of the following characteristics such as motion characteristics, body position, and object handling are being isolated from the video frames being isolated while segmenting the videos. They can be shaping descriptors, edge characteristics, histogram-based color characteristics, and motion paths.

High-dimensional data are generally noisy and redundant, and to choose features to optimize feature selection, PSO is used. PSO is swarm intelligence based and begins with candidate sets of feature subsets. A candidate, or particle, identifies the best subset of features in the solution space. Particles incrementally update their position using the best personal solutions and global best solution of the swarm. PSO identifies discriminative features with exploration-exploitation trade-off and is non-redundant and thus improves classification accuracy and computational cost savings. Optimization-bought feature set is used for training best and accurate behavior recognition model to differentiate authorization from unauthorized behavior in the classroom.

BI-STCKED GRU

Bi-Stacked Gated Recurrent Unit (Bi-Stacked GRU) is used to detect variation in learner motivation and engagement by representing behavior patterns over time. The system also continues to track learner behaviors in body posture, facial expressions, motion patterns, and interaction rate as a classroom environment video feed. BI-Stacked GRU architecture includes multi-layer bidirectional GRUs and the model can learn future and past relations between sequences more efficiently.

Using stacked layers, the model can learn intricate temporal patterns instead of fluctuations in student inactivity like peak inactivity, excessive disruptions, or erratic participation rates. Bidirectional processing enables the system to leverage context from subsequent and prior activities to enable more effective detection. With tens of thousands of student behavior tagged for training, the model can detect subtle oscillations in engagement levels and notify teachers when engagement levels are low. It is early intervention that the approach provides, whereby teachers intervene to re-engage students and optimize learning as a whole.

EXPERIMENTAL RESULT

Experimental results show that the new Bi-Stacked GRU model can efficiently detect student motivation and engagement fluctuation. The model was trained on a class recording dataset from which various behavioral features were extracted and optimized with Particle Swarm Optimization (PSO). The performance of the model in classifying engaged and disengaged student behavior was evaluated utilizing accuracy, precision, recall, and F1-score performance metrics. It is illustrated in the experiment that the Bi-Stacked GRU model performs better than regular sequential learning models in temporal relation prediction and prediction of complex behavior patterns. The PSO feature selection also removes redundancy significantly, hence, the classification performance is maximized. It is illustrated that the system within this paper is able to offer real-time feedback on student engagement to inform early intervention methods for teachers.

Table 1 presents a snapshot of student levels of engagement observed during e-learning sessions. It classifies the students into four levels of engagement of their eye contact, participation, and responsiveness indicators: highly engaged, moderately engaged, low engagement, and disengaged. The table allows us to visualize the overall shape of the distribution of student engagement in the data.

Table 1. Classification performance metrics

Student ID	Accuracy (%)	Precision	Recall	F1-Score	Engagement Level
S1	91.2	0.89	0.92	0.90	High
S2	87.5	0.85	0.88	0.86	Medium
S3	93.1	0.92	0.94	0.93	High
S4	85.6	0.83	0.86	0.84	Low
S5	90.4	0.88	0.91	0.89	High
S6	88.7	0.86	0.89	0.87	Medium
S7	92.3	0.91	0.93	0.92	High
S8	86.8	0.84	0.87	0.85	Low
S9	89.5	0.87	0.90	0.88	Medium
S10	94.0	0.93	0.95	0.94	High

Table 2 enables the definition of resultant behaviors leading to lower motivation, with the identification of early warning signs. Patterns of loss of motivation behavior are also shown in Table 2, with notes of less note-taking, increased distractibility, and consistent absenteeism.

Table 2. Engagement level analysis over time

Time (min)	Active Students	Distracted Students	Engaged (%)	Disengaged (%)	Avg Attention (sec)
10	25	5	83.3	16.7	45
20	23	7	76.7	23.3	42
30	20	10	66.7	33.3	38
40	18	12	60.0	40.0	35
50	15	15	50.0	50.0	30
60	12	18	40.0	60.0	28
70	10	20	33.3	66.7	25

continued on following page

Table 2. Continued

Time (min)	Active Students	Distracted Students	Engaged (%)	Disengaged (%)	Avg Attention (sec)
80	9	21	30.0	70.0	22
90	7	23	23.3	76.7	20
100	5	25	16.7	83.3	18

Table 3 indicates the effect of distractions outside the classroom on participation. It mentions typical distractions such as background noise, use of mobile phones, and multitasking, and the percentage of their impact. The study emphasizes distraction-free learning environments so that participation can be guaranteed.

Table 3. Behavioral feature distribution

Student ID	Eye Contact (%)	Hand Movements	Posture Changes	Speaking Time (sec)	Engagement Level
S1	85.2	12	3	40	High
S2	78.5	10	5	35	Medium
S3	90.1	15	2	42	High
S4	70.4	8	7	28	Low
S5	88.7	14	3	39	High
S6	80.3	11	6	33	Medium
S7	92.0	16	2	45	High
S8	75.6	9	8	30	Low
S9	82.9	12	5	37	Medium
S10	94.5	17	1	48	High

Table 4 shows the student attendance for different subjects, reflecting inconsistency regarding the levels of involvement of maths, science, and humanities classes. It is observed from the data that the trend is such that the students are better concentrated in interactive courses but are unable to attend class for theory courses.

Table 4. Engagement prediction accuracy across different models

Model	Accuracy (%)	Precision	Recall	F1-Score	Training Time (sec)
Bi-Stacked GRU	91.2	0.89	0.92	0.90	210
LSTM	87.4	0.85	0.88	0.86	180
CNN-LSTM	88.9	0.86	0.89	0.88	195
RNN	82.3	0.79	0.81	0.80	160
Random Forest	75.5	0.72	0.74	0.73	90
SVM	78.2	0.75	0.77	0.76	120
Decision Tree	70.4	0.67	0.69	0.68	85
GRU	86.8	0.84	0.87	0.85	175
ANN	80.9	0.77	0.79	0.78	140
Logistic Reg.	65.2	0.62	0.64	0.63	60

Table 5 deals with teacher interaction style and student engagement. It categorizes types of instruction such as lecture, discussion, and activity instruction and assigns scores with respect to effectiveness in maintaining students engaged and active.

Table 5. Time-based engagement shift analysis

Time Interval (min)	Avg Eye Contact (%)	Body Movement Frequency	Speaking Activity (sec)	Engagement Status
0-10	85	12	40	Engaged
10-20	78	10	35	Medium
20-30	72	8	30	Medium
30-40	65	6	28	Low
40-50	58	4	25	Low
50-60	52	3	22	Disengaged
60-70	48	3	20	Disengaged
70-80	45	2	18	Disengaged
80-90	42	1	15	Disengaged
90-100	40	1	12	Disengaged

Table 6 illustrates the impact of fatigue on student engagement through the students' attentiveness at different times of the day. It presents morning class ratings, afternoon class ratings, and evening class ratings in order to illustrate the impact of cognitive load and energy on student engagement.

Table 6. Feature selection impact on model performance (using PSO)

Features Selected	Accuracy (%)	Precision	Recall	F1-Score	Training Time (sec)
All Features	85.3	0.82	0.84	0.83	250
Selected by PSO	91.2	0.89	0.92	0.90	210
Random Selection	78.5	0.75	0.78	0.76	180

Table 7 examines how far peer interaction is responsible for sustaining motivation and interest. It quantifies the effect of group-working and group discussion on pupil attention whereby group-working students are more motivated compared to individual students.

Table 7. Student performance before and after engagement decline

Student ID	Engagement Level Before	Engagement Level After	Test Score Before	Test Score After	Performance Change (%)
S1	High	Medium	85	78	-8.2%
S2	High	Low	90	72	-20.0%
S3	Medium	Low	78	65	-16.7%
S4	Medium	Disengaged	75	60	-20.0%
S5	High	Medium	88	80	-9.1%
S6	Medium	Low	80	68	-15.0%
S7	Low	Disengaged	72	55	-23.6%
S8	Medium	Disengaged	77	58	-24.7%
S9	High	Medium	85	77	-9.4%
S10	High	High	92	91	-1.1%

Table 8 illustrates a comparison between online and offline levels of engagement. The results are that online learning is convenient but less engaging since there are more distractions and fewer interactions with the teacher and students are less likely to interact face-to-face.

Table 8. Accuracy of engagement detection across different activities

Activity	Accuracy (%)	Precision	Recall	F1-Score
Writing	91.2	0.89	0.92	0.90
Reading	88.7	0.86	0.89	0.87
Speaking	92.3	0.91	0.93	0.92

continued on following page

Table 8. Continued

Activity	Accuracy (%)	Precision	Recall	F1-Score
Listening	86.8	0.84	0.87	0.85
Distracted	78.2	0.75	0.77	0.76
Using Phone	72.4	0.69	0.72	0.70
Sleeping	65.2	0.62	0.64	0.63
Eating	68.7	0.65	0.68	0.66
Moving Excessively	74.3	0.71	0.74	0.72
Not Responding	70.1	0.67	0.69	0.68

Table 9 decomposes waning student motivation by student age and demonstrates how motivation patterns vary among student groups. Consequently, younger students are more motivated with increasingly older students suffering a consistent erosion of motivation, most probably because of the accumulating weight of responsibility and mental fatigue.

Table 9. Comparison of engagement decline across age groups

Age Group	Avg. Engagement Score Before	Avg. Engagement Score After	Decline (%)	No. of Students
10-15	85.4	75.2	12.0%	50
16-20	88.1	76.8	12.8%	60
21-25	82.7	70.5	14.7%	55
26-30	79.2	67.3	15.1%	45
31-35	75.8	62.9	17.0%	40
36-40	72.3	60.1	16.9%	35
41-45	70.5	57.2	18.9%	30
46-50	68.7	55.6	19.1%	25
51-55	65.9	52.1	21.0%	20
56+	60.3	48.7	19.2%	15

Table 10 illustrates the frequency of each level of participation by hour and time of day when the students are busiest. Activity is highest in the morning and declines gradually throughout the day, as would be predicted from the hypothesis that mental efficiency declines with longer study periods.

Table 10. Frequency of different engagement levels over time

Time Slot	Highly Engaged (%)	Moderately Engaged (%)	Low Engagement (%)	Disengaged (%)
08:00-09:00	85	10	3	2
09:00-10:00	80	12	5	3
10:00-11:00	78	15	4	3
11:00-12:00	75	18	5	2
12:00-13:00	72	20	6	2
13:00-14:00	70	22	5	3
14:00-15:00	68	20	7	5
15:00-16:00	65	18	10	7
16:00-17:00	60	15	12	13
17:00-18:00	55	12	15	18

CONCLUSION

It presents a smart model of student engagement fluctuation recognition and motivation detection via an optimized bi-stacked GRU model with PSO-based feature selection. By following the process of bidirectional processing and sequential learning, the model is capable of identifying engagement fluctuation well under early intervention situations. The model exhibits robust behavior recognition via the use of preprocessing techniques and feature optimization. Experimental results validate that the suggested method works against discrimination between disengagement and engagement phases in a way that classes remain motivating by teachers. The future can explore multimodal sources of information, for example, speech and physiological signals to use towards obtaining the best detection accuracy.

REFERENCES

Abdulmajid, M., & Pyun, J.-Y. (2017). Deep recurrent neural networks for human activity recognition. *Sensors (Basel), 17*(11), 2556. DOI: 10.3390/s17112556 PMID: 29113103

Chen, G., Chen, P., Huang, W., & Zhai, J. (2022). Continuance intention mechanism of middle school student users on online learning platform based on qualitative comparative analysis method. *Mathematical Problems in Engineering, 2022*, 3215337. Advance online publication. DOI: 10.1155/2022/3215337

Chen, K., Zhang, D., Yao, L., Guo, B., Yu, Z., & Liu, Y. (2021). Deep learning for sensor-based human activity recognition: Overview, challenges, and opportunities. *ACM Computing Surveys, 54*(4), 77. Advance online publication. DOI: 10.1145/3447744

Degardin, B., & Proença, H. (2020). Human activity analysis: Iterative weak/self-supervised learning frameworks for detecting abnormal events. In *2020 IEEE International Joint Conference on Biometrics (IJCB)* (pp. 1–9). IEEE. https://doi.org/DOI: 10.1109/IJCB48548.2020.9304860

Feng, W., & Hannafin, J. (2005). Design-based research and technology-enhanced learning environments. *Educational Technology Research and Development, 53*(4), 5–23. DOI: 10.1007/BF02504682

Ferhat, A., Mohammed, S., Dedabrishvili, M., Chamroukhi, F., Oukhellou, L., & Amirat, Y. (2015). Physical human activity recognition using wearable sensors. *Sensors (Basel), 15*(12), 31314–31338. DOI: 10.3390/s151229858 PMID: 26690450

Golestani, N., & Moghaddam, M. (2020). Human activity recognition using magnetic induction-based motion signals and deep recurrent neural networks. *Nature Communications, 11*, 1551. Advance online publication. DOI: 10.1038/s41467-020-15086-2 PMID: 32214095

Guo, F., Zhou, W., Lu, Q., & Zhang, C. (2022). Path extension similarity link prediction method based on matrix algebra in directed networks. *Computer Communications, 187*, 83–92. DOI: 10.1016/j.comcom.2022.01.016

Jaganeshwari, K., & Djodilatchoumy, S. (2022). An automated testing tool based on graphical user interface with exploratory behavioural analysis. *Journal of Theoretical and Applied Information Technology, 100*(22), 6657–6666.

Jalal, A., Khalid, N., & Kim, K. (2020). Automatic recognition of human interaction via hybrid descriptors and maximum entropy Markov model using depth sensors. *Entropy (Basel, Switzerland)*, *22*(8), 817. Advance online publication. DOI: 10.3390/e22080817 PMID: 33286588

Jiang, H., Wang, M., Zhao, P., Xiao, Z., & Dustdar, S. (2021). A utility-aware general framework with quantifiable privacy preservation for destination prediction in LBSs. *IEEE/ACM Transactions on Networking*, *29*(5), 2228–2241. DOI: 10.1109/TNET.2021.3083655

Khalid, N., Gochoo, M., Jalal, A., & Kim, K. (2021). Modeling two-person segmentation and locomotion for stereoscopic action identification: A sustainable video surveillance system. *Sustainability*, *13*(2), 970. Advance online publication. DOI: 10.3390/su13020970

Kun, X., Huang, J., & Wang, H. (2020). LSTM-CNN architecture for human activity recognition. *IEEE Access : Practical Innovations, Open Solutions*, *8*, 56855–56866. DOI: 10.1109/ACCESS.2020.2982225

Li, B., Tan, Y., Wu, A., & Duan, G. (2022). A distributionally robust optimization based method for stochastic model predictive control. *IEEE Transactions on Automatic Control*, *67*(11), 5762–5776. DOI: 10.1109/TAC.2021.3121120

Liu, X., Shi, T., Zhou, G., Liu, M., Yin, Z., Yin, L., & Zheng, W. (2023a). Emotion classification for short texts: An improved multi-label method. *Humanities & Social Sciences Communications*, *10*, 306. Advance online publication. DOI: 10.1057/s41599-023-01815-4

Liu, X., Song, M., Tao, D., Bu, J., & Chen, C. (2015). Random geometric prior forest for multiclass object segmentation. *IEEE Transactions on Image Processing*, *24*(10), 3060–3070. DOI: 10.1109/TIP.2015.2432152 PMID: 25974937

Liu, X., Zhou, G., Kong, M., Yin, Z., Li, X., Yin, L., & Zheng, W. (2023b). Developing multi-labelled corpus of Twitter short texts: A semi-automatic method. *Systems*, *11*(8), 390. Advance online publication. DOI: 10.3390/systems11080390

Long, W., Xiao, Z., Wang, D., Jiang, H., Chen, J., Li, Y., & Alazab, M. (2023). Unified spatial-temporal neighbor attention network for dynamic traffic prediction. *IEEE Transactions on Vehicular Technology*, *72*(2), 1515–1529. DOI: 10.1109/TVT.2022.3210294

Lu, C., Shi, J., & Jia, J. (2013). Abnormal event detection at 150 fps in Matlab. In *2013 IEEE International Conference on Computer Vision* (pp. 2720–2727). IEEE. https://doi.org/DOI: 10.1109/ICCV.2013.338

Matthew, T., & Banhazi, T. M. (2016). A brief review of the application of machine vision in livestock behavior analysis. *Agrárinformatika Folyóirat*, *7*(2), 23–42. DOI: 10.17700/jai.2016.7.2.297

Miah, S. J., Vu, H. Q., Gammack, J., & McGrath, M. (2017). A big data analytics method for tourist behaviour analysis. *Information & Management*, *54*(6), 771–785. DOI: 10.1016/j.im.2016.11.011

Michalis, V nikou, C., & Kakadiaris, I. A. (2015). A review of human activity recognition methods. *Frontiers in Robotics and AI, 2*, Article 28. https://doi.org/DOI: 10.3389/frobt.2015.00028

Nadeem, A., Jalal, A., & Kim, K. (2020). Human actions tracking and recognition based on body parts detection via artificial neural network. In *2020 3rd International Conference on Advancements in Computational Sciences (ICACS)* (pp. 1–8). IEEE. https://doi.org/DOI: 10.1109/ICACS47775.2020.9056878

Ortiz, R., Jorge, L., Oneto, L., Samà, A., Parra, X., & Anguita, D. (2016). Transition-aware human activity recognition using smartphones. *Neurocomputing*, *171*, 754–767. DOI: 10.1016/j.neucom.2015.07.085

Pervaiz, M., Jalal, A., & Kim, K. (2021). Hybrid algorithm for multi-people counting and tracking for smart surveillance. In *2021 International Bhurban Conference on Applied Sciences and Technologies (IBCAST)* (pp. 757–763). IEEE. https://doi.org/DOI: 10.1109/IBCAST51254.2021.9393279

Qian, L., Zheng, Y., Li, L., Ma, Y., Zhou, C., & Zhang, D. (2022). A new method of inland water ship trajectory prediction based on long short-term memory network optimized by genetic algorithm. *Applied Sciences (Basel, Switzerland)*, *12*(8), 4073. Advance online publication. DOI: 10.3390/app12084073

Qiu, S., Zhao, H., Jiang, N., Wang, Z., Liu, L., An, Y., & Fortino, G. (2022). Multi-sensor information fusion based on machine learning for real applications in human activity recognition: State-of-the-art and research challenges. *Information Fusion*, *80*, 241–265. DOI: 10.1016/j.inffus.2021.11.006

Quaid, M. A. K., & Jalal, A. (2020). Wearable sensors based human behavioral pattern recognition using statistical features and reweighted genetic algorithm. *Multimedia Tools and Applications*, *79*(9–10), 6061–6083. DOI: 10.1007/s11042-019-08336-3

Rafique, A., Ahmad, J., & Kim, K. (2021). Automated sustainable multi-object segmentation and recognition via modified sampling consensus and kernel sliding perceptron. *Symmetry*, *13*(10), 1928. Advance online publication. DOI: 10.3390/sym13101928

Wang, W., Liu, A. X., Shahzad, M., Ling, K., & Lu, S. (2015). Understanding and modeling of WiFi signal based human activity recognition. In *Proceedings of the 21st Annual International Conference on Mobile Computing and Networking* (pp. 65–76). ACM. https://doi.org/DOI: 10.1145/2789168.2790093

Xiao, Z., Li, H., Jiang, H., Li, Y., Alazab, M., Zhu, Y., & Dustdar, S. (2023). Predicting urban region heat via learning arrive-stay-leave behaviors of private cars. *IEEE Transactions on Intelligent Transportation Systems*, *24*(10), 10843–10856. DOI: 10.1109/TITS.2023.3276704

Xiong, Z., Liu, Q., & Huang, X. (2022). The influence of digital educational games on preschool children's creative thinking. *Computers & Education*, *189*, 104578. Advance online publication. DOI: 10.1016/j.compedu.2022.104578

Zhang, J., Ye, G., Tu, Z., Qin, Y., Qin, Q., Zhang, J., & Liu, J. (2022). A spatial attentive and temporal dilated (SATD) GCN for skeleton-based action recognition. *CAAI Transactions on Intelligence Technology*, *7*(1), 46–55. DOI: 10.1049/cit2.12064

Chapter 13
Enhancing Decision-Making With AI

Francisco R. Trejo-Macotela
https://orcid.org/0000-0003-2133-3456
Universidad Politécnica de Pachuca, Mexico

Daniel Robles-Camarillo
https://orcid.org/0000-0002-7637-5904
Polytechnic University of Pachuca, Mexico

ABSTRACT

This chapter critically examines the integration of Artificial Intelligence (AI) into educational decision-making, focusing on data-driven strategies and administrative tools for educational leaders. Drawing on recent literature and case studies, it shows how AI supports predictive modelling, optimised resource allocation, and early identification of student risks. Challenges such as algorithmic opacity, data bias, and ethical concerns are explored. The chapter highlights the need for regulatory frameworks, professional training, and inclusive policies to guide responsible adoption. Emphasis is placed on combining human oversight with innovation to uphold equity, transparency, and educational integrity. Ultimately, the study concludes that when implemented ethically and strategically, AI offers significant potential to strengthen educational leadership and foster more informed, equitable, and effective decision-making in the educational sector.

INTRODUCTION

The integration of Artificial Intelligence (AI) into educational governance represents a paradigmatic shift in institutional decision-making, heralding both

DOI: 10.4018/979-8-3373-0598-1.ch013

unprecedented opportunities and complex challenges. Historically, decision-making in educational contexts has been underpinned by rationalist paradigms which posit that individuals act in accordance with complete information, objective processing capabilities, and consistent preference structures to optimise outcomes (von Neumann & Morgenstern, 1944). However, real-world educational environments often deviate substantially from these assumptions. Cognitive limitations, informational asymmetries, emotional influences, and structural constraints render human decision-making both bounded and imperfect (Simon, 1979; Tversky & Kahneman, 1974). These deficiencies are particularly salient in the educational domain, where decisions frequently involve high-stakes consequences and competing stakeholder demands.

To address such limitations, alternative theoretical models have emerged. The concept of bounded rationality (Simon, 1979) asserts that decision-makers, constrained by limited cognitive resources and time, often settle for satisfactory rather than optimal outcomes. Lindblom's (1959) incrementalism further elucidates the adaptive nature of policy reform through small-scale, iterative adjustments, rather than radical change. Similarly, the Garbage Can Model (Cohen, March, & Olsen, 1972) captures the non-linear and often chaotic confluence of problems, solutions, and decision-makers within complex educational organisations. These perspectives collectively highlight the inadequacy of purely rationalist approaches and underscore the need for decision-support systems capable of mitigating human cognitive and structural limitations.

Artificial Intelligence has rapidly emerged as such a system. Defined as computational methods designed to perform tasks typically requiring human intelligence—such as learning, reasoning, and problem-solving—AI presents a suite of tools capable of enhancing both the efficiency and effectiveness of institutional governance (Russell & Norvig, 2021). Its evolution from symbolic rule-based systems to machine learning and deep learning paradigms has significantly broadened its applicability. Within the educational sector, AI has transitioned from its early use in intelligent tutoring systems (ITS) to more strategic functions, including predictive analytics, curriculum optimisation, enrolment forecasting, and the automation of administrative processes (Zawacki-Richter et al., 2019; Ifenthaler & Yau, 2020).

Of particular relevance to institutional decision-making is AI's capacity to synthesize vast, heterogeneous data streams, identify latent patterns, and generate actionable insights. Predictive and prescriptive analytics, natural language processing (NLP), educational data mining (EDM), and robotic process automation (RPA) are among the core subfields of AI that now inform strategic planning, performance monitoring, and resource allocation in education (Romero & Ventura, 2020; Baker & Inventado, 2014). These capabilities afford decision-makers a more granular, anticipatory, and evidence-based understanding of institutional dynamics, enabling a shift from reactive to proactive governance.

Nonetheless, the adoption of AI in education is not without ethical and practical complications. Issues of algorithmic transparency, data privacy, equity, and human agency remain paramount. Concerns about the perpetuation of existing social biases, overreliance on opaque models, and the erosion of professional judgement necessitate the establishment of robust governance frameworks and participatory implementation strategies (Eubanks, 2018; Binns, 2018; Williamson, 2017). As such, AI should not be misconstrued as a technological panacea, but rather as an augmentative force—one that must be ethically anchored and human-centred to fulfil its transformative promise.

This chapter undertakes a comprehensive exploration of the theoretical foundations of decision-making, the evolution and typologies of AI technologies, their strategic integration within educational institutions, and the multifaceted ethical considerations that must guide their implementation. Through this lens, AI is examined not merely as an operational tool, but as a catalyst for informed, inclusive, and responsive educational leadership.

THEORETICAL FOUNDATIONS OF DECISION-MAKING

Decision-making constitutes a fundamental process across various social science disciplines, encompassing management, economics, psychology, and notably education. Historically, this process has been predominantly interpreted through the lens of rationalist paradigms, which presuppose that decision-makers engage in logical deliberation aimed at maximising utility and minimising risk (Simon, 1979). Classical models such as the Expected Utility Theory (von Neumann & Morgenstern, 1944) assume that individuals possess complete information, objective processing capabilities, and consistent preference structures guiding optimal choices. However, these assumptions have been repeatedly challenged, particularly in the context of complex, dynamic environments like educational institutions, where information asymmetry, cognitive limitations, and contextual constraints are pervasive.

To better encapsulate the realities of decision-making, alternative theoretical frameworks have emerged. Herbert A. Simon's (1979) concept of bounded rationality recognises that decision-makers often seek satisfactory rather than optimal solutions, constrained by limited cognitive resources and environmental pressures. Similarly, Lindblom's (1959) incrementalism model characterises decision-making as an iterative process of small, sequential adjustments rather than radical reforms, a perspective highly pertinent to educational policy development. Furthermore, the Garbage Can Model proposed by Cohen, March, and Olsen (1972) conceptualises organisational decision-making as non-linear and contingent, reflecting the complexity and ambiguity endemic to educational settings.

Empirical research further highlights the profound impact of cognitive biases—such as loss aversion, overconfidence, anchoring, and availability heuristics—on decision-making quality (Tversky & Kahneman, 1974). Emotional and structural factors, including stress and resource scarcity, compound these challenges within educational leadership (Arnsten, 2009; Spillane et al., 2011). In response to these multifaceted constraints, Artificial Intelligence (AI) has emerged as a transformative adjunct, offering decision support through data synthesis, predictive analytics, and automation (Wong & Li, 2020). While AI holds promise in enhancing accuracy and reducing cognitive load, its integration necessitates careful ethical considerations and human oversight to ensure it complements rather than supplants professional judgement (Eubanks, 2018).

This section explores the theoretical foundations of decision-making with an emphasis on their implications for educational administration and the potential of AI to address inherent limitations.

Traditional Approaches to Decision-Making

Decision-making theory has long constituted a central concern across the social sciences, encompassing domains such as management, economics, psychology, and education. Traditionally, this field has been dominated by rationalist paradigms which assert that decision-makers operate logically, striving to maximise utility and minimise potential risk (Simon, 1979). The rational decision-making model, rooted in neoclassical economics, assumes that individuals have access to all relevant information, are capable of processing this information objectively, and are guided solely by their preferences and values when evaluating alternatives. This model is epitomised by the Expected Utility Theory (von Neumann & Morgenstern, 1944), which posits that decision-makers compute the expected utility of each option and select the one that offers the highest return.

However, the assumptions underlying the classical rationalist paradigm have been increasingly challenged by both theoretical and empirical research. In practice, decision-makers often face complex, dynamic environments where access to information is imperfect, time is constrained, and cognitive resources are limited. Recognising these realities, alternative approaches emerged that better capture the bounded nature of human rationality. Notably, Herbert A. Simon (1979) introduced the concept of "bounded rationality," which acknowledges that individuals seek satisfactory, rather than optimal, outcomes due to cognitive limitations and environmental constraints. This insight led to the development of the "satisficing" model, in which decision-makers settle for an acceptable solution rather than exhaustively seeking the best possible one.

Similarly, Charles E. Lindblom (1959) proposed the "incrementalism" model of decision-making, which contends that policymakers often proceed through small, sequential adjustments rather than sweeping, comprehensive reforms. According to this model, decisions are made through successive limited comparisons, drawing heavily on existing policies and marginal changes rather than devising entirely novel solutions.

Another influential critique of rational models is the "Garbage Can Model" of organisational decision-making, developed by Cohen, March, and Olsen (1972). This model conceptualises decision-making within organisations as a chaotic, non-linear process where problems, solutions, and decision-makers are loosely coupled. Decisions occur when these elements happen to coincide, not necessarily because of structured deliberation. The Garbage Can Model is particularly salient in institutional contexts such as schools and universities, where multiple stakeholders with diverging objectives operate within ambiguous and fluid environments.

In the context of educational administration, these alternative theoretical frameworks provide a more nuanced understanding of decision-making processes. School leaders, for instance, frequently operate under tight constraints and must contend with competing demands from teachers, parents, policymakers, and students. The bounded rationality framework helps explain why educational administrators might rely on heuristics or adopt policies based on precedent rather than engaging in exhaustive cost-benefit analyses. Likewise, incrementalism elucidates the path-dependent nature of many educational reforms, which often evolve through gradual, iterative modifications. Finally, the Garbage Can Model is particularly relevant in explaining how certain policy decisions in educational institutions arise from serendipity or organisational routines rather than systematic planning. Table 1 shows a comparison of traditional decision-making models.

Table 1. Comparison of traditional decision-making models.

Model	Key Proponent(s)	Description	Application in Education
Rational Model	Von Neumann & Morgenstern (1944)	Assumes optimal decision-making based on complete information	Limited use due to unrealistic assumptions
Bounded Rationality	Simon (1979)	Decision-makers seek satisfactory rather than optimal solutions	Explains use of heuristics by school administrators
Incrementalism	Lindblom (1959)	Policies evolve through small, sequential changes	Accounts for gradualism in educational reform
Garbage Can Model	Cohen, March & Olsen (1972)	Decisions emerge from coincidental convergence of problems and solutions	Reflects complexity of decision-making in schools

Human Limitations in Complex Decision-Making

Beyond the limitations posited by alternative theoretical models, a substantial body of empirical evidence has illuminated the cognitive and emotional constraints that impair human decision-making, particularly in complex or high-stakes environments. In their seminal work on heuristics and biases, Tversky and Kahneman (1974) demonstrated that individuals frequently rely on mental shortcuts which, while efficient, often lead to systematic errors in judgment. Key cognitive biases that have been shown to affect decision-making include:

- **Loss Aversion**: The tendency to prefer avoiding losses over acquiring equivalent gains, leading to risk-averse behaviour even when risk-taking would be advantageous.
- **Overconfidence Bias**: An inflated belief in one's own knowledge or predictive abilities, often resulting in underestimation of risks or alternative options.
- **Anchoring Effect**: The undue influence of initial information (anchors) on subsequent judgments, regardless of its relevance or accuracy.
- **Availability Heuristic**: The propensity to judge the likelihood of events based on the ease with which examples come to mind, often skewed by recent or emotionally salient experiences.

These cognitive biases are particularly detrimental in educational settings, where decisions must often be made quickly and under uncertainty. For example, a school principal may disproportionately allocate resources based on the most recent incidents (availability heuristic), or resist adopting an innovative policy due to a fear of potential failure (loss aversion), even when evidence suggests it could yield significant benefits.

Additionally, emotional factors such as stress, fatigue, and interpersonal dynamics can further compromise decision-making. Research in neuropsychology has demonstrated that high levels of stress impair executive function, reducing working memory capacity and promoting reliance on habitual, rather than analytical, decision pathways (Arnsten, 2009).

Structural constraints compound these psychological limitations. In many educational systems, decision-makers operate with limited financial resources, insufficient staff, and intense scrutiny from external stakeholders. The intersection of these cognitive, emotional, and structural barriers often leads to suboptimal outcomes and impedes the implementation of data-driven or evidence-based interventions (Spillane et al., 2011).

The Role of Artificial Intelligence in Addressing Decision-Making Limitations

In recent years, Artificial Intelligence (AI) has emerged as a transformative tool capable of augmenting human decision-making capabilities across multiple domains, including education. By leveraging machine learning algorithms, natural language processing, and predictive analytics, AI systems can assist educational leaders in navigating complexity, reducing bias, and enhancing the accuracy and timeliness of decisions (Rao et al., 2025).

Wong and Li (2020) argue that AI-based decision support systems can significantly reduce cognitive load by automating routine tasks and synthesising large volumes of data into actionable insights. For instance, AI can be used to detect patterns in student performance, identify at-risk individuals, and suggest tailored interventions well before human recognition of such needs would be possible. Moreover, AI systems can operate continuously and consistently, unaffected by stress, fatigue, or emotional factors that often cloud human judgement.

A particularly promising application is the integration of AI into strategic resource allocation. Using predictive models, school administrators can anticipate future enrolment trends, project staffing needs, and optimise budgetary decisions based on real-time data. Such capabilities not only improve efficiency but also ensure that decisions are grounded in empirical evidence rather than intuition or precedent.

Nevertheless, it is crucial to recognise that AI should not be seen as a panacea. Rather, it should be conceptualised as a complement to, rather than a replacement for, human expertise. Ethical concerns must be addressed, including issues of algorithmic transparency, data privacy, and the potential for reinforcing existing inequalities if AI systems are trained on biased datasets (Eubanks, 2018). Therefore, the successful deployment of AI in decision-making processes requires a robust regulatory framework, clear institutional guidelines, and continuous human oversight.

The theoretical foundations of decision-making, as explored through rationalist, bounded rationality, incrementalist, and organisational models, provide essential insights into how individuals and institutions make choices under varying degrees of complexity and constraint. These models have particular relevance within the educational sector, where the interplay of cognitive biases, emotional influences, and systemic limitations frequently distorts rational decision-making. The advent of AI offers a powerful set of tools to mitigate these challenges, supporting more informed, timely, and equitable decisions. However, for AI to be a truly transformative force, its implementation must be guided by ethical principles, empirical validation, and a commitment to enhancing—not supplanting—human agency.

ARTIFICIAL INTELLIGENCE AS A CATALYST FOR INFORMED DECISION-MAKING

The pervasive integration of Artificial Intelligence (AI) into diverse societal sectors has instigated a profound re-evaluation of established operational paradigms, with the educational domain emerging as a significant frontier for its transformative application. Defined broadly as the computational capability to execute tasks typically demanding human cognitive faculties—such as reasoning, problem-solving, and language comprehension—AI has undergone a substantial evolution since its formal genesis at the Dartmouth Conference in 1956. This progression has transitioned from rudimentary rule-based symbolic systems to sophisticated, data-driven methodologies, notably encompassing machine learning (ML) and deep learning (DL).

Initially, the application of AI within educational contexts predominantly focused on intelligent tutoring systems (ITS) and adaptive learning platforms, providing customised instructional pathways for learners. As technological maturity advanced, the utility of AI expanded to include automated grading, curriculum design, and the development of personalised recommendation systems. More recently, AI has demonstrated considerable promise in administrative decision-making, offering data-informed strategies crucial for school leadership, institutional planning, and optimising resource allocation. The increasing viability of integrating AI into these administrative processes is largely attributable to concurrent advancements in big data analytics, cloud computing infrastructures, and the proliferation of AI-as-a-service models. As exemplified by Fuentes-Penna and González Ibarra (2024), AI applied to personalised education not only advances the achievement of SDG 4 but also supports more informed and contextually relevant decision-making within school environments. This chapter aims to meticulously explore the multifaceted implications of AI as a catalyst for informed decision-making within educational governance, examining its conceptual underpinnings, relevant subtypes, ecosystemic integration for decision support, and the inherent opportunities and limitations that necessitate careful consideration and robust ethical frameworks.

Definition and Evolution of Artificial Intelligence

Artificial Intelligence (AI) is broadly defined as the domain of computer science dedicated to the creation of systems and algorithms capable of performing tasks that typically necessitate human intelligence, such as reasoning, problem-solving, learning, and language understanding (Russell & Norvig, 2021). Since its formal inception during the Dartmouth Conference in 1956, AI has evolved through distinct paradigms, transitioning from rule-based symbolic systems to more flexible, data-driven approaches such as machine learning (ML) and deep learning (DL).

The early era of AI focused primarily on symbolic AI, which employed explicit logic rules and knowledge bases. These systems were relatively limited in adaptability and scalability, particularly in complex or ambiguous environments. However, the emergence of ML during the late 1980s introduced a paradigm wherein systems could learn from data, identifying patterns without being explicitly programmed for every contingency. In the 2010s, the resurgence of artificial neural networks—specifically deep learning—propelled AI to new heights, enabling breakthroughs in speech recognition, image classification, and natural language processing (LeCun, Bengio, & Hinton, 2015).

In the educational domain, the application of AI initially centred around intelligent tutoring systems (ITS) and adaptive learning platforms, which offered personalised instruction based on learner profiles. As technology matured, AI also found utility in grading automation, curriculum design, and personalised recommendation systems (Zawacki-Richter et al., 2019). More recently, AI has begun to demonstrate significant potential in administrative decision-making, where it facilitates data-informed strategies for school leadership, institutional planning, and resource optimisation. The integration of AI into administrative processes is increasingly feasible due to advances in big data, cloud computing, and AI-as-a-service infrastructures (Duarte et al., 2023; Kökver et al., 2025). Table 2 outlines key milestones in the evolution of AI relevant to decision-making in education.

Table 2. Evolution of artificial intelligence and its educational applications

Decade	AI Development	Application in Education
1950s–1960s	Symbolic AI (logic-based)	Automated reasoning, early tutoring simulations
1980s	Expert systems and rule-based AI	Curriculum mapping, diagnostic tools
1990s	Introduction of Machine Learning	Predictive modelling for student performance
2000s	Rise of statistical AI	Educational data mining
2010s	Deep Learning and Big Data	Adaptive learning systems, NLP in assessment
2020s	AI-integrated cloud systems	Administrative decision support, AI dashboards

(Source: Adapted from Russell & Norvig, 2021; Zawacki-Richter et al., 2019)

AI Subtypes Relevant to Educational Administration

AI is not a monolithic technology but rather an umbrella term encompassing multiple subfields. For instance, Morales-Murillo et al. (2024) implemented a transformer-based recommendation system that leverages session preferences for immediate decision-making across multiple domains, demonstrating notable improvements in the accuracy and relevance of recommendations—an approach that may be translated into educational scenarios involving adaptive tutoring or resource allocation. In the context of educational management and institutional governance, certain subtypes of AI offer unique advantages. These include machine learning, natural language processing (NLP), computer vision, educational data mining (EDM), and learning analytics (LA).

Machine Learning for Predictive Modelling

Machine learning constitutes a fundamental tool in predictive analytics, allowing educational institutions to anticipate trends and intervene proactively. By analysing historical data, ML algorithms can predict outcomes such as student dropout, exam failure, or programme disengagement (Baker & Inventado, 2014). Supervised learning models—such as decision trees, support vector machines, or random forests—are often employed to classify students into risk categories. Unsupervised learning methods, like clustering, enable the identification of hidden patterns within complex datasets.

For example, a supervised ML model trained on student demographic data, attendance, and coursework scores may achieve high precision in identifying students at risk of early withdrawal. This allows administrative teams to allocate support services efficiently, improving retention metrics and institutional effectiveness.

Educational Data Mining (EDM)

EDM focuses on extracting meaningful patterns from educational data to support learning processes and policy-making (Romero & Ventura, 2020). Unlike general data mining, EDM considers the pedagogical context of the data and the stakeholders involved. This method is instrumental in identifying performance bottlenecks, evaluating teaching effectiveness, and improving resource allocation. For instance, mining data from a learning management system (LMS) can help administrators discern which modules yield low engagement or high failure rates.

EDM techniques may include classification, association rule mining, sequential pattern mining, and regression analysis. These methods are applied to various datasets, including enrolment records, library usage, exam grades, and feedback systems.

Learning Analytics (LA)

Learning analytics refers to the measurement, collection, and analysis of data about learners and their contexts for the purpose of understanding and optimising learning outcomes and institutional effectiveness (Siemens, 2013; Khuzairi et al.,2020). Unlike EDM, which is primarily analytical, LA emphasises the interpretative use of data to guide real-time interventions.

In the context of decision-making, LA supports strategic planning by aggregating key performance indicators (KPIs) across cohorts, departments, or programmes. Dashboards powered by LA tools can offer visual representations of academic trends, enabling school leaders to make timely and evidence-based decisions. Furthermore, LA supports formative feedback mechanisms, allowing institutions to iterate on their practices.

Natural Language Processing (NLP)

Natural language processing is critical for transforming unstructured textual data into actionable insights. Educational institutions generate substantial qualitative data through surveys, open-ended feedback, institutional reports, and social media discourse. NLP algorithms, including sentiment analysis, topic modelling, and named entity recognition, enable automated content analysis that would otherwise be prohibitively time-consuming.

For instance, applying sentiment analysis to student feedback surveys can reveal trends in satisfaction or frustration that may not be evident from numerical scores alone. Topic modelling can uncover recurring concerns across departments, informing systemic policy adjustments. NLP is also instrumental in chatbot development, allowing for automated yet personalised student support services.

Computer Vision in Educational Environments

Although traditionally more associated with industrial or medical fields, computer vision is increasingly relevant in educational contexts, particularly in remote learning or campus surveillance. Techniques such as facial recognition, gesture analysis, and object detection can be employed for attendance verification, emotional monitoring, and security management.

For example, in hybrid learning environments, facial expression analysis can offer cues on learner engagement. Integrating this data with LA systems enables a more holistic understanding of student participation, particularly in courses delivered via videoconferencing platforms (D'Mello & Graesser, 2012).

Robotic Process Automation (RPA)

RPA involves automating repetitive administrative tasks through software bots. These tasks might include student enrolment processing, report generation, attendance tracking, or financial aid disbursement. By automating routine procedures,

RPA frees up human resources for higher-order strategic planning and decision-making (Willcocks et al., 2015).

The AI Ecosystem for Decision Support in Educational Leadership

The true potential of AI in educational management lies not in isolated applications but in the integration of diverse AI techniques into a unified decision-support ecosystem. Such systems can synthesise structured and unstructured data, generate cross-sectional analyses, and provide real-time recommendations to institutional leaders.

A practical example would involve the integration of LMS data (via LA), enrolment figures (via ML), student sentiment (via NLP), and resource usage (via EDM) into a centralised dashboard accessible to school or university administrators. By offering a comprehensive view of the institution's performance, needs, and risks, these AI-enhanced ecosystems empower decision-makers to adopt a more strategic, proactive, and data-informed leadership style (Ifenthaler & Yau, 2020).

Nevertheless, the deployment of such integrated systems necessitates a robust technological infrastructure, appropriate data governance frameworks, and professional development for staff. Moreover, ethical safeguards must be put in place to ensure data privacy, fairness, and accountability in AI-driven decision-making.

The full integration of AI into decision-making processes requires the orchestration of various technologies and data governance frameworks. Effective decision support systems (DSS) in education must be designed to align with the strategic goals of the institution, accommodate diverse stakeholder needs, and ensure ethical compliance.

AI-Driven Dashboards and Decision Engines

Modern AI-powered dashboards consolidate data from multiple sources—including learning platforms, human resources systems, and financial software—to offer a comprehensive view of institutional performance. These systems are typically underpinned by decision engines that apply rule-based and probabilistic reasoning to suggest optimal interventions.

A practical example is the use of AI dashboards for enrolment management. By incorporating real-time data on applications, acceptance rates, demographic trends, and retention probabilities, the system can advise admissions officers on resource allocation or outreach strategies.

Prescriptive Analytics and Scenario Simulation

While predictive analytics forecasts probable outcomes, prescriptive analytics recommends specific actions to achieve desired goals. Prescriptive models incorporate constraints, utility functions, and optimisation routines to suggest decision pathways. In educational settings, prescriptive AI can assist in timetable planning, resource distribution, or programme design.

Scenario simulation, often facilitated by reinforcement learning models, enables decision-makers to evaluate the impact of various policies under different conditions. For instance, an AI system might simulate how shifting funds from extracurricular activities to academic tutoring affects student achievement and retention, enabling a more nuanced allocation of limited budgets.

Opportunities and Limitations in AI-Based Decision-Making

Opportunities

AI offers numerous benefits for institutional decision-making:

- **Data-Driven Accuracy**: Reduces reliance on intuition or anecdotal evidence.
- **Scalability**: Allows analysis of data at a scale beyond human capability.
- **Proactive Interventions**: Enables early identification of risks and opportunities.
- **Customisation**: Supports differentiated strategies across departments or learner groups.

Limitations and Ethical Considerations

Despite its promise, AI is not without challenges. These include:

- **Data Bias and Discrimination**: Training data may reflect existing inequalities, leading to biased recommendations (Binns, 2018).
- **Transparency and Accountability**: Complex models may lack explainability, complicating decision justification.
- **Privacy Concerns**: Educational data often includes sensitive personal information, necessitating strict adherence to data protection regulations such as the GDPR.
- **Over-Reliance**: There is a risk that decision-makers may over-defer to AI recommendations, neglecting critical human judgement.

Institutions must adopt robust ethical frameworks to govern AI use, including impact assessments, stakeholder consultations, and algorithm audits.

Integrating Artificial Intelligence into Institutional Decision-Making Processes

The integration of Artificial Intelligence (AI) into institutional decision-making processes represents a fundamental shift in how educational organisations conceive, structure, and implement administrative strategies. While the potential benefits of AI are vast—including improved efficiency, enhanced accuracy, and optimised resource allocation—effective integration necessitates careful attention to organisational readiness, infrastructural requirements, ethical oversight, and change management.

This section explores the principles, methodologies, and challenges associated with embedding AI technologies into educational decision-making workflows, offering a critical and comprehensive examination of institutional strategies, implementation frameworks, and best practices.

Organisational Readiness for AI Integration

Before AI can be successfully embedded within decision-making structures, institutions must assess and enhance their organisational readiness. This encompasses three core domains: technological infrastructure, human capital, and data maturity.

Technological Infrastructure

The deployment of AI systems depends on robust digital infrastructure. This includes not only high-performance computing systems and cloud-based architectures but also secure networks and interoperable platforms capable of supporting machine learning pipelines, real-time analytics, and data warehousing (Luckin & Holmes, 2016). Institutions lacking in such infrastructure may experience systemic bottlenecks, including latency in data processing and limitations in scalability.

Human Capital and Digital Literacy

Another critical component is human capital. Institutions must cultivate a workforce equipped with the competencies necessary to design, interpret, and act upon AI-driven insights. This includes data scientists, learning technologists, instructional designers, and policy analysts, as well as administrators with sufficient digital literacy to collaborate with AI tools (Holmes et al., 2019). Upskilling programmes, professional development initiatives, and interdepartmental collaboration are thus foundational to successful implementation.

Data Maturity and Governance

The concept of data maturity refers to the extent to which an institution is capable of collecting, managing, and leveraging data for strategic purposes. Institutions must ensure that their data is accurate, comprehensive, and ethically sourced. Furthermore, robust data governance frameworks must be in place to ensure compliance with legal standards (e.g., GDPR) and institutional policies regarding consent, anonymisation, and access control (Williamson, 2017).

Implementation Frameworks for AI in Decision-Making

The integration of AI requires a structured and iterative approach. Drawing from models in technology-enhanced learning and enterprise information systems, a five-phase implementation framework is proposed, which is presented in Table 3.

Table 3. Phases implementation framework is proposed

Phase	Description
1. Needs Analysis	Identify strategic priorities and institutional challenges amenable to AI intervention.
2. Infrastructure Preparation	Upgrade hardware, software, and data systems to support AI technologies.
3. Pilot Testing	Develop prototype solutions and test them in controlled contexts.
4. Institutional Integration	Embed AI tools into formal decision-making workflows and governance structures.
5. Evaluation and Optimisation	Continuously assess performance, refine models, and respond to stakeholder feedback.

This framework ensures that AI deployment is responsive to institutional goals, aligned with organisational culture, and adaptable to evolving demands.

Case Studies of AI Integration in Educational Governance

Several institutions have pioneered the adoption of AI in strategic decision-making, offering valuable insights and replicable practices.

Open University (United Kingdom)

The Open University implemented an AI-powered early warning system that predicts student drop-out risk based on LMS engagement, assessment patterns, and demographic profiles. Administrative staff receive alerts, enabling timely outreach interventions (Rienties et al., 2018). The integration process required cross-functional collaboration and a careful balance between predictive accuracy and ethical transparency.

University of Michigan (United States)

The University of Michigan deployed an automated essay scoring system augmented with NLP techniques to assist in grading and provide detailed formative feedback. Though initially designed for instructional purposes, the system was later incorporated into institutional quality assurance and programme evaluation efforts (Wiggins, 2017). The administration utilised feedback trends to inform resource allocation and curricular design decisions.

University of New South Wales (Australia)

The University of New South Wales adopted a prescriptive analytics platform to optimise course scheduling and resource planning. By simulating various enrolment and staffing scenarios, the institution was able to minimise scheduling conflicts and align course offerings with projected demand (Ifenthaler & Yau, 2020).

These case studies exemplify how AI can transcend operational automation to become a strategic enabler within the fabric of institutional governance.

Human-AI Collaboration in Decision-Making

Despite the computational power of AI, its integration should not be misconstrued as a replacement for human agency. Instead, optimal decision-making arises from the synergistic collaboration between human expertise and AI capabilities—a paradigm referred to as *augmented intelligence*.

Augmented Intelligence

In contrast to fully autonomous systems, augmented intelligence emphasises the enhancement of human judgement. AI systems provide timely, relevant, and accurate information, while final decisions remain with human actors. This collaborative dynamic is essential in contexts requiring ethical reflection, pedagogical sensitivity, or political acumen—areas where AI may lack context awareness or moral reasoning (Floridi & Cowls, 2019).

Decision Support Systems (DSS)

AI-enabled Decision Support Systems (DSS) offer visualisations, forecasts, and prescriptive recommendations, assisting educational leaders in making evidence-informed decisions. These systems must be designed with usability and transparency in mind, allowing users to trace how recommendations were generated and what variables influenced them.

An example is the integration of AI with enterprise resource planning (ERP) platforms, where decision-makers can simulate various policy options, estimate budget impacts, and visualise outcomes through interactive dashboards.

Ethical and Regulatory Considerations in Institutional AI Use

The ethical implications of AI adoption in educational governance are profound and multifaceted. The methodological proposal by Alfaro-Pérez, Rodríguez-Hernández, and Ramírez-Noriega (2023) provides a viable technical framework for the implementation of AI in institutional decision-making processes, emphasising transparency, traceability, and accountability criteria that are critical in educational settings. Decision-making processes in education affect students' futures, teachers' careers, and public trust in institutions. As such, ethical AI governance is not ancillary but integral to institutional strategy.

Algorithmic Fairness

Institutions must ensure that AI models do not inadvertently perpetuate social inequalities or discriminate against marginalised groups. This requires regular audits of algorithms for fairness, explainability, and bias (Binns, 2018). For example, predictive models must avoid overfitting to historical data that reflects systemic exclusion, such as the underrepresentation of students from disadvantaged backgrounds.

Transparency and Explainability

Transparency is critical for trust and accountability. Decision-makers must be able to understand how AI systems reach conclusions, especially when these inform high-stakes outcomes such as funding decisions or programme discontinuation. Techniques such as model interpretability tools (e.g., LIME, SHAP) can enhance transparency without compromising performance (Molnar, 2020).

Legal Compliance

AI systems must be compliant with relevant data protection laws and institutional policies. In the European context, the General Data Protection Regulation (GDPR) establishes explicit rights regarding automated decision-making and data profiling. Institutions must ensure that consent mechanisms, data minimisation practices, and data retention policies are rigorously followed (Veale & Edwards, 2018).

Institutional Capacity Building and Policy Frameworks

Successful AI integration also depends on institutional policy, leadership commitment, and change management strategies. The following principles are recommended:

- **AI Strategy Alignment**: Institutions should articulate a clear AI strategy aligned with their mission, values, and educational philosophy.
- **Stakeholder Engagement**: All stakeholders—including students, educators, administrators, and policymakers—should be consulted in the design and evaluation of AI tools.
- **Ethics Committees and Governance Boards**: Establishing dedicated ethics boards to oversee AI use ensures that emerging risks are addressed proactively.
- **Professional Development**: Training programmes should be implemented to cultivate digital fluency among staff and leadership.
- **Monitoring and Evaluation**: Continuous evaluation cycles should assess AI effectiveness, equity impact, and unintended consequences.

The integration of AI into institutional decision-making processes constitutes a transformative development in the educational landscape. When properly aligned with organisational values, underpinned by robust infrastructure, and guided by ethical frameworks, AI offers unparalleled opportunities for enhancing efficiency, transparency, and responsiveness in governance. Yet, its adoption also demands humility, vigilance, and a commitment to human-centred design.

AI must be seen not as a technological panacea but as a strategic enabler—one that complements rather than replaces human judgement. Institutions that recognise and operationalise this partnership will be better equipped to navigate the complexities of contemporary education and realise their mission in the digital age.

AI-Driven Predictive and Prescriptive Analytics in Educational Governance

Artificial Intelligence (AI) has introduced a profound transformation in the way educational institutions collect, process, and utilise data to inform governance decisions. Of particular relevance are predictive analytics, which leverage historical data to forecast future events, and prescriptive analytics, which suggest optimal courses of action based on those forecasts. When strategically embedded into institutional governance, these AI-driven analytics enable decision-makers to move from reactive to proactive and, ultimately, to optimised decision-making processes.

This section examines the theoretical underpinnings, technical architectures, application domains, and ethical implications of predictive and prescriptive analytics within educational governance, with a specific emphasis on real-world implementation and critical evaluation.

Conceptual Foundations of Predictive and Prescriptive Analytics

Predictive Analytics

Predictive analytics refers to the utilisation of statistical techniques, data mining, and machine learning algorithms to identify patterns and anticipate outcomes (Shmueli & Koppius, 2011). In education, such analytics are commonly employed to forecast student retention, academic performance, enrolment trends, and resource utilisation. These models operate by training on historical datasets and estimating probabilities for specific future scenarios, such as the likelihood of a student failing a module or dropping out.

Prescriptive Analytics

Prescriptive analytics extends beyond mere forecasting. It combines predictive models with optimisation algorithms and decision rules to recommend specific actions (Souza et al., 2024). In educational governance, this may include suggesting the best intervention strategies for at-risk students, proposing optimal allocation of faculty based on demand forecasts, or recommending curricular reforms aligned with labour market dynamics. Table 4 illustrates the progression from descriptive to prescriptive analytics.

Table 4. Progression from descriptive to prescriptive analytics

Type of Analytics	Primary Function	Example in Education
Descriptive	What happened?	Attendance reports, grade summaries
Diagnostic	Why did it happen?	Analysis of poor performance causes
Predictive	What is likely to happen?	Forecasting student drop-out
Prescriptive	What should we do about it?	Assigning interventions to prevent drop-out

(Source: Adapted from Gartner's Analytics Maturity Model)

Technical Components and Models

The architecture of predictive and prescriptive systems in education involves the integration of multiple components:

- **Data Collection**: Aggregation of structured and unstructured data from student information systems (SIS), learning management systems (LMS), financial databases, surveys, and digital learning environments.
- **Feature Engineering**: Identification and transformation of relevant variables such as attendance, engagement metrics, demographic data, and academic performance.
- **Model Selection and Training**: Application of algorithms such as logistic regression, decision trees, random forests, support vector machines (SVM), and deep neural networks (DNs) to train predictive models.
- **Evaluation and Validation**: Use of metrics such as accuracy, precision, recall, and AUC-ROC to assess model performance.
- **Optimisation Engines**: Integration of operations research tools and constraint programming to formulate prescriptive recommendations.
- **Visualisation and Dashboards**: Deployment of insights via dashboards to ensure decision-makers can interpret and act upon analytics outputs (Slade & Prinsloo, 2013).

These components must be managed within a secure, GDPR-compliant infrastructure, with continuous monitoring to ensure ethical robustness.

Application Domains in Educational Governance

Student Retention and Success

One of the most common applications is the use of AI models to predict which students are at risk of attrition. Variables such as engagement with learning platforms, academic results, attendance records, and socio-demographic indicators feed into models that generate risk scores (Jayaprakash et al., 2014). Interventions are then prescribed, such as counselling, mentoring, or targeted tutoring programmes.

Case Study: At Georgia State University, predictive analytics contributed to a 22% increase in graduation rates over ten years through a system of 800 early alerts that trigger automatic academic support (White House Office of Science and Technology Policy, 2016).

Course and Curriculum Planning

AI-driven forecasting tools can anticipate course demand based on historical enrolment trends, demographic shifts, and economic forecasts. These predictions help institutions schedule courses more effectively, plan resource allocations, and avoid over- or under-subscription. Prescriptive analytics go further by suggesting optimal timetabling configurations and resource distribution.

Resource Allocation and Budgeting

By predicting which departments, services, or academic programmes will experience increased demand, institutions can allocate funds and human capital more strategically. This approach contrasts sharply with traditional budgeting models based on static metrics or intuition.

Strategic Enrolment Management

Prescriptive models have been used to guide recruitment strategies, suggest optimal applicant targeting by geography or subject area, and recommend changes in admission criteria based on projected performance indicators. These tools help institutions maintain student diversity while meeting financial and capacity goals (Ifenthaler & Yau, 2020).

Benefits and Opportunities

The strategic deployment of predictive and prescriptive analytics in educational governance offers several benefits:

- **Evidence-Based Decision-Making**: Decisions are no longer reliant solely on managerial experience or limited datasets but are informed by large-scale empirical evidence.
- **Proactive Intervention**: Institutions can address emerging challenges before they escalate, improving outcomes in areas such as retention, equity, and resource efficiency.
- **Customised Strategies**: Recommendations can be tailored to specific institutional contexts, accounting for historical data, policies, and objectives.
- **Improved Accountability**: The traceability and documentation of analytic insights promote transparency and support regulatory reporting.

Challenges and Limitations

Despite their advantages, several technical, ethical, and operational challenges must be addressed:

Algorithmic Bias and Equity Risks

Predictive models trained on biased historical data may reinforce inequities, particularly when socio-economic status or race correlate with negative outcomes. Without careful oversight, these models could perpetuate systemic disadvantages (Binns, 2018; Prinsloo & Slade, 2017).

Opacity and Interpretability

Complex machine learning models, especially deep learning systems, often function as "black boxes". This lack of transparency can be problematic in educational contexts, where decisions affect students' futures. Explainability techniques (e.g., SHAP, LIME) are essential for increasing trust.

Data Privacy and Consent

The use of personal data for predictive purposes raises concerns about informed consent, data minimisation, and secondary usage. Institutions must ensure full compliance with GDPR and similar legal frameworks (Williamson, 2017).

Dependence on Data Quality

Analytics outputs are only as reliable as the data input. Poor data quality, missing values, and inconsistencies can undermine model performance and lead to erroneous conclusions.

Governance and Ethical Oversight

To address these challenges, institutions must establish comprehensive governance frameworks:

- **Ethics Boards**: Committees should review algorithms for bias, transparency, and compliance.
- **Algorithmic Impact Assessments**: Formal evaluations of the potential consequences of deploying specific models.
- **Stakeholder Involvement**: Students, faculty, and staff must be engaged in the design, evaluation, and refinement of analytics tools.
- **Continuous Monitoring**: Regular audits and recalibration ensure models remain valid over time and responsive to changing contexts.

Institutions should also publish transparency reports outlining how AI models are developed, used, and monitored.

AI-driven predictive and prescriptive analytics have emerged as vital instruments for transforming educational governance from intuition-based management to evidence-informed decision-making. When designed and deployed responsibly, these tools offer significant opportunities to improve student outcomes, optimise resource allocation, and enhance institutional agility.

Nevertheless, their integration must be approached with caution and a steadfast commitment to equity, transparency, and ethical integrity. As AI capabilities expand, educational leaders must ensure that these technologies remain accountable to human values and institutional missions.

Integration of AI in Strategic Educational Leadership and Institutional Planning

The integration of Artificial Intelligence (AI) into strategic educational leadership and institutional planning marks a paradigm shift in how academic institutions anticipate change, respond to complex challenges, and foster innovation-driven futures. Strategic leadership within the educational domain involves not only managing day-to-day operations but also envisioning and orchestrating long-term goals related to pedagogy, equity, infrastructure, talent development, and technological transformation. AI, with its capability to process vast and heterogeneous data streams, uncover hidden patterns, and generate predictive and prescriptive insights, offers educational leaders powerful tools to inform decisions at a systemic level (Luckin & Holmes, 2016).

This section explores the conceptual underpinnings, practical applications, and governance structures necessary for the successful integration of AI into institutional strategy. Emphasis is placed on leadership competencies, systemic foresight, planning cycles, and ethical stewardship in AI-supported educational contexts.

Strategic Educational Leadership in the Age of AI

Strategic educational leadership involves the formulation and execution of policies that influence institutional performance, stakeholder satisfaction, and societal contribution (Bush, 2011). In the age of AI, the role of leadership expands beyond administrative effectiveness to include data literacy, technological agility, and ethical governance.

Effective AI integration demands leaders who are capable of:

- Identifying opportunities where AI can enhance institutional functions.
- Facilitating cross-functional collaboration between educators, data scientists, and IT professionals.
- Championing a culture of innovation while safeguarding ethical principles and inclusivity.
- Using AI-generated insights to make decisions that are proactive rather than reactive.

Such leadership is no longer the sole domain of the senior management team; it involves distributed leadership structures wherein decision-making authority is shared across academic departments, research units, and student service divisions (Fullan, 2014).

Institutional Planning Cycles and AI-Supported Foresight

Institutional planning in higher education typically follows cycles that include environmental scanning, goal setting, performance evaluation, and feedback integration (Holcombe et al., 2022). AI systems can augment each phase of this cycle through:

- **Environmental Scanning**: Natural Language Processing (NLP) algorithms can parse vast policy databases, economic forecasts, academic journals, and media outlets to generate real-time intelligence on emerging trends (Williamson, 2017).

- **Goal Setting and KPIs**: Machine learning (ML) models can simulate multiple future scenarios based on historical data and current inputs. For instance, enrolment forecasting models can inform capacity planning, faculty recruitment, and infrastructure development.
- **Performance Evaluation**: AI-driven dashboards can provide real-time analytics on student outcomes, staff performance, and financial efficiency. Sentiment analysis tools may be used to monitor stakeholder feedback from digital surveys or social media.
- **Strategic Feedback Loops**: Prescriptive analytics can recommend specific interventions when institutions deviate from planned trajectories. These may involve resource reallocation, course redesign, or partnership reconfiguration.

Table 5 outlines key AI applications across the planning stages.

Table 5. Key applications of AI in the planning stages

Planning Stage	AI Application	Strategic Outcome
Environmental Scanning	NLP-based trend analysis	Early identification of opportunities and threats
Goal Setting	Predictive modelling for enrolment and workforce needs	Informed target setting
Performance Monitoring	Real-time dashboards with anomaly detection	Data-driven accountability mechanisms
Strategic Adjustment	Scenario simulation and prescriptive analytics	Evidence-based policy adaptation

AI for Institutional Agility and Adaptive Strategy

In a volatile and uncertain higher education landscape, institutional agility is a critical success factor. AI supports adaptive strategies by enabling institutions to respond swiftly and effectively to changing circumstances such as funding shifts, demographic changes, or technological disruptions.

For example, during the COVID-19 pandemic, institutions equipped with AI-enabled analytics platforms were able to:

- Monitor attendance and engagement in virtual learning environments.
- Predict potential dropouts and issue early alerts.
- Simulate the impact of budget reallocations across faculties.

- Adjust teaching loads and class sizes based on real-time demand forecasting.

Case Study: The Open University in the UK has leveraged learning analytics systems to support adaptive strategy by offering real-time visualisations of student progression. These tools inform curriculum redesign, faculty training, and student support services (Rienties et al., 2018).

Such dynamic adaptation aligns with the concept of "strategic responsiveness," wherein institutions actively learn from AI feedback mechanisms and iteratively refine their strategies.

AI and Human Capital Development in Educational Leadership

Another strategic dimension of AI integration lies in human capital development. Institutional leaders must cultivate an AI-aware workforce capable of understanding, deploying, and critically assessing intelligent technologies. This involves:

- **Professional Development**: Providing training in data literacy, AI ethics, and algorithmic thinking for administrators and faculty.
- **Leadership Pipelines**: Developing future leaders with hybrid expertise in educational management and computational analytics.
- **Collaborative Competence**: Encouraging interdisciplinary teams to co-design AI tools and evaluate their impact.

Such efforts align with the concept of "learning organisations" (Senge, 2006), where institutions evolve continuously through collective knowledge acquisition and experimentation.

Ethical and Policy Considerations in AI-Driven Planning

Strategic planning augmented by AI raises critical ethical questions. Issues such as algorithmic bias, data privacy, surveillance, and automation of human judgement necessitate robust policy frameworks and participatory governance. Key ethical imperatives include:

- **Transparency**: Ensuring that AI systems used for strategic decisions are explainable and auditable.
- **Fairness**: Assessing whether predictive models disadvantage specific groups, particularly marginalised students or staff.
- **Consent**: Establishing clear data governance protocols around consent and data minimisation.

- **Responsibility**: Clearly defining who is accountable for AI-generated recommendations and their outcomes.

Institutions must adopt AI charters or ethical codes aligned with principles such as those proposed by the European Commission's High-Level Expert Group on AI (2019), which advocate for human-centric, lawful, and robust AI.

Organisational Readiness and Implementation Models

The integration of AI in strategic planning requires a systematic approach to organisational readiness. Table 6 presents the framework that synthesizes key dimensions.

Table 6. Key dimensions framework to integration of AI in strategic planning

Dimension	Indicators of Readiness
Leadership	Visionary leadership, digital fluency, ethical awareness
Infrastructure	Scalable data systems, secure storage, cloud integration
Culture	Openness to innovation, cross-functional collaboration
Talent	Skilled analysts, trained educators, IT support staff
Governance	Clear policies, oversight committees, impact assessments

Institutions may adopt one of the following implementation models:

1. **Centralised AI Strategy Unit**: A dedicated team reporting to senior leadership, responsible for identifying opportunities, piloting tools, and scaling successful interventions.
2. **Distributed Innovation Model**: Encouraging departments and faculties to develop domain-specific AI applications with support from a central hub.
3. **Hybrid Approach**: Central coordination combined with decentralised experimentation and feedback loops.

Metrics for Evaluating AI Impact on Strategic Outcomes

Evaluating the impact of AI on institutional planning involves defining and tracking appropriate Key Performance Indicators (KPIs). These may include:

- Reduction in strategic planning cycle times.
- Improved accuracy of enrolment and performance forecasts.
- Increased student retention and progression rates.

- Cost savings through optimised resource allocation.
- Stakeholder satisfaction with decision transparency.

In addition, qualitative metrics such as ethical acceptability, inclusiveness of decision-making, and staff perception of AI tools are crucial to holistic evaluation.

The strategic integration of Artificial Intelligence in educational leadership and institutional planning is not merely a technological enhancement but a profound transformation in epistemology and governance. AI equips institutional leaders with the foresight, agility, and analytic depth required to navigate complexity and design resilient futures. However, realising the benefits of AI integration demands deliberate attention to leadership development, organisational readiness, ethical safeguards, and participatory governance. Institutions that manage to align AI technologies with their pedagogical missions and social values will be best positioned to lead in the age of intelligent decision-making.

The integration of Artificial Intelligence (AI) into educational decision-making represents a transformative juncture for institutional governance, strategic leadership, and operational management. Throughout this chapter, we have delineated the theoretical foundations of decision-making, the limitations of human cognition in complex educational contexts, and the catalytic role of AI in enhancing the precision, timeliness, and inclusivity of institutional decisions.

The exploration of AI's definitional evolution reveals a trajectory from symbolic rule-based systems to sophisticated machine learning and deep learning architectures, enabling nuanced analysis of educational data. Diverse AI modalities—including predictive analytics, natural language processing, and computer vision—offer rich possibilities for understanding and optimising student engagement, academic performance, and administrative efficiency.

Significantly, the chapter highlights how AI can be embedded into the fabric of institutional workflows, facilitating augmented intelligence where human expertise synergises with algorithmic insight. The effective integration of AI demands organisational readiness encompassing infrastructure, human capital, data governance, and ethical stewardship. Case studies from pioneering institutions illustrate practical pathways and underscore the importance of transparent, fair, and responsible AI deployment.

Furthermore, AI-driven predictive and prescriptive analytics equip educational leaders with anticipatory tools that transcend traditional reactive models, promoting proactive interventions, strategic agility, and evidence-based policy formulation. The chapter has also addressed the critical challenges inherent in this integration, including algorithmic bias, interpretability issues, data privacy concerns, and the necessity for comprehensive governance frameworks.

Strategic leadership emerges as a pivotal factor for successful AI adoption. Leaders must cultivate digital literacy, foster collaborative cultures, and embed ethical values to harness AI's potential effectively. Institutional planning cycles can be significantly enhanced through AI-supported foresight, enabling adaptive strategies that respond to rapidly evolving educational landscapes (Scholes, 2016).

AI's role as a decision-making catalyst in education is both promising and complex. Its benefits are contingent upon deliberate, ethically grounded implementation that values human agency, inclusivity, and transparency. Educational institutions that strategically integrate AI into governance and leadership are poised to enhance their responsiveness, optimise resource utilisation, and better serve their diverse stakeholders in the digital era.

DATA-DRIVEN DECISION MAKING (DDDM)

Data-Driven Decision Making (DDDM) has emerged as a pivotal paradigm in contemporary educational governance, distinguished by its commitment to the systematic use of empirical evidence to inform institutional strategy and practice. Unlike intuition-based or anecdotal approaches, DDDM operationalises data as a fundamental resource for enhancing pedagogical effectiveness, advancing equity, and ensuring accountability (Mandinach & Gummer, 2016). At its core, DDDM is predicated upon the principles of continuous data collection, rigorous analysis, contextual interpretation, and actionable implementation—each requiring organisational cultures oriented towards evidence-informed decision-making and technological capacity to process complex datasets (Ansyari et al., 2024).

Globally, educational institutions are increasingly integrating data-centric frameworks into their operations, as exemplified by the deployment of real-time dashboards and predictive analytics in North America, Europe, and Latin America (Datnow & Park, 2014; OEI, 2022). Nevertheless, the successful realisation of DDDM's transformative potential is contingent upon overcoming entrenched barriers such as fragmented data systems, insufficient analytical expertise, and cultural resistance to change (Van Geel et al., 2016). As such, a nuanced understanding of both the theoretical foundations and practical challenges of DDDM remains essential.

Conceptualisation and Principles of DDDM

Data-Driven Decision Making (DDDM) constitutes a systematic and deliberate process whereby relevant, accurate, and timely data are utilised to inform strategic decisions within organisational contexts. In the educational domain, DDDM serves as a foundational approach to enhance teaching and learning processes, optimise resource allocation, and advance equity through empirically grounded decisions (Mandinach & Gummer, 2016). Fundamentally, DDDM transcends intuitive or anecdotal decision-making by embedding evidence-based methodologies into the organisational fabric, thus promoting accountability, transparency, and continuous improvement.

The core principles underpinning DDDM encompass continuous data collection, rigorous analytical procedures, contextualised interpretation of findings, and practical application of insights. These stages necessitate the cultivation of an organisational culture that values evidence utilisation, the development of analytical competencies among personnel, and the provision of access to sophisticated technological infrastructures. Continuous data collection involves systematic gathering of quantitative and qualitative indicators that accurately reflect educational phenomena, such as student performance metrics, attendance records, and stakeholder feedback.

Subsequently, rigorous analysis utilises statistical and computational techniques to identify patterns, trends, and anomalies. Importantly, contextualised interpretation mandates that data are not evaluated in isolation but rather within the socio-cultural, institutional, and policy frameworks that shape educational environments. Finally, the practical application involves translating analytical insights into actionable strategies, including policy adjustments, curricular reforms, and targeted interventions. When effectively implemented, DDDM enables educational institutions to dynamically detect emerging needs, monitor progress towards goals, evaluate the efficacy of policies, and recalibrate actions responsively (Ansyari et al., 2024).

Practical Applications of DDDM in Educational Institutions

The proliferation of DDDM in education has witnessed significant advances internationally, with numerous institutions embedding data-centric approaches into their daily management practices. For instance, school systems in countries such as the United States, Canada, Finland, and Singapore employ interactive dashboards to monitor key performance indicators (KPIs) — including pass rates, attendance, student satisfaction, and competency progression — in real time (Datnow & Park, 2014). These digital platforms afford school leaders and educators immediate visibility into critical metrics, facilitating prompt and evidence-informed responses to deviations or emerging challenges.

In higher education, several universities have pioneered early warning systems that synthesise academic, administrative, and behavioural data to identify students at risk of attrition. A prominent example is Georgia State University in the United States, which achieved a notable increase in graduation rates by implementing algorithms that recommended bespoke interventions, such as personalised tutoring and curricular adjustments (Georgia State University, n.d.). This predictive capability has not only enhanced student retention but has also contributed to optimising institutional resource deployment.

Within Latin America, although the adoption of DDDM remains emergent, notable initiatives have emerged. In Chile, the Ministry of Education has championed platforms such as SNED (Sistema Nacional de Evaluación Diagnóstica) and SIGE (Sistema de Información General de Estudiantes), which centralise academic and administrative data to bolster school-level decision-making and inform broader educational policy (Organización de Estados Iberoamericanos [OEI], 2025). Similarly, Colombia's "Evaluar para Avanzar" strategy integrates data analytics into diagnostic assessments, providing actionable feedback to educators and school leaders, thereby fostering a culture of reflective practice and continuous improvement (OEI, 2022).

Requirements and Barriers for Effective Implementation

The realisation of DDDM's potential is contingent upon several critical factors. Paramount among these is committed institutional leadership capable of championing data-informed cultures and allocating necessary resources towards technological and human capital development. Additionally, robust technological infrastructures are essential to support comprehensive data collection, storage, processing, and dissemination activities. Equally important is the cultivation of data analytical skills among educational professionals, enabling them to competently interpret and act upon complex datasets (Van Geel, Keuning, Visscher, & Fox, 2016).

Despite the growing enthusiasm for DDDM, several persistent barriers impede its effective implementation. Resistance to change, often grounded in cultural inertia or scepticism towards data-centric approaches, can undermine efforts to embed DDDM into organisational practices. The lack of adequate training in statistical analysis and data literacy further constrains educators' capacity to leverage data effectively. Moreover, workload pressures may limit the time educators and administrators can dedicate to data engagement, creating an operational bottleneck.

A critical and often underappreciated obstacle pertains to the fragmentation of information systems. Disparate databases, incompatible software, and siloed data sources inhibit comprehensive analysis and complicate the generation of holistic insights (Datnow & Park, 2014). Such fragmentation not only hampers decision-making but also increases the likelihood of errors and inefficiencies.

The quality of data itself constitutes a fundamental determinant of DDDM's success. Incomplete, outdated, or poorly structured data can yield misleading interpretations and precipitate suboptimal decisions. Thus, it is imperative that educational institutions establish rigorous protocols for data collection, validation, and protection. These protocols must ensure data integrity, compliance with ethical standards, and adherence to data privacy regulations such as the General Data Protection Regulation (GDPR) in the European context. A summary of the principles, applications and challenges of DDDM is illustrated in Table 7.

Table 7. Summary of DDDM principles, applications, and challenges

Dimension	Description	Examples in Education
Principles	Continuous data collection, rigorous analysis, contextual interpretation, practical application	Use of longitudinal student achievement data
Applications	Real-time dashboards, early warning systems, policy evaluation	Interactive KPI panels; predictive analytics for retention
Barriers	Resistance to change, lack of skills, workload, fragmented systems	Staff reluctance; insufficient training; siloed databases
Data Quality	Accuracy, completeness, timeliness, validation	Data audits; GDPR compliance; standardisation protocols

Data-Driven Decision Making represents a transformative approach in educational administration, fostering evidence-based governance that enhances effectiveness, equity, and accountability. While the integration of DDDM poses substantive challenges related to culture, capacity, and data quality, its strategic implementation—supported by strong leadership and technological infrastructure—has demonstrated considerable promise in diverse international contexts.

To fully realise DDDM's benefits, educational institutions must prioritise the development of analytical competencies, streamline data systems, and cultivate cultures receptive to change and innovation. Moreover, ethical considerations around data privacy and security must remain at the forefront of all initiatives, ensuring that data utilisation respects stakeholder rights and fosters trust.

AI TOOLS FOR EDUCATIONAL ADMINISTRATORS

The strategic incorporation of Artificial Intelligence (AI) tools within educational administration represents a transformative shift in the governance and operational management of academic institutions. Among the most influential innovations are educational analytics platforms, early warning systems, and virtual assistants, which collectively enhance institutional decision-making through the provision of timely, predictive, and actionable insights (Ifenthaler & Yau, 2020). These technologies enable administrators to transcend traditional reactive models by adopting proactive, data-informed approaches that optimise performance, streamline processes, and support student success.

Educational analytics platforms such as Power BI, Tableau, and Qlik provide robust visualisation and predictive modelling functionalities, allowing for the real-time monitoring of key indicators and strategic forecasting (Ifenthaler & Yau, 2020). Concurrently, early warning systems employ machine learning algorithms to detect at-risk students, facilitating early interventions and improving retention outcomes (Arnold & Pistilli, 2012). Furthermore, AI-driven virtual assistants and intelligent management systems automate routine administrative tasks while integrating institutional data into cohesive, analytical frameworks that promote holistic and agile decision-making (Holmes et al., 2019). Collectively, these tools are redefining educational leadership in the digital age.

Educational Analytics Platforms

Educational analytics platforms constitute pivotal technological resources enabling educational administrators to visualise, analyse, and interpret vast quantities of educational data with unprecedented clarity and efficiency. Prominent examples include Power BI, Tableau, and Qlik, which provide sophisticated yet user-friendly interfaces capable of rendering complex datasets into interactive graphs, heat maps, dynamic dashboards, and other visual representations. These visual tools facilitate the identification of salient trends, benchmarking across institutions, and real-time monitoring of key performance indicators (KPIs), such as student achievement, attendance rates, and resource utilisation.

The primary strength of these platforms lies not only in their data visualisation capabilities but also in their integration of advanced predictive functions. By incorporating machine learning algorithms, these systems can extrapolate future trends, such as predicting student attrition, academic underperformance, or the demand for pedagogical support (Ifenthaler & Yau, 2020). Consequently, educational leaders are empowered to make evidence-based decisions grounded in both historical and forecasted data, thereby enhancing strategic planning and resource allocation.

Furthermore, these platforms support drill-down functionalities, enabling users to dissect aggregated data into more granular subsets, such as analysing performance by demographic segments, individual cohorts, or specific programmes. The interoperability of these analytics tools with existing institutional databases ensures seamless data integration, promoting a unified view of organisational performance. Table 8 illustrates the Key Features of Leading Educational Analytics Platforms.

Table 8. Key features of leading educational analytics platforms

Platform	Visualisation Tools	Predictive Analytics	Integration Capabilities	User Interface
Power BI	Interactive dashboards, heat maps	Yes	Connects to multiple databases	Intuitive drag-and-drop interface
Tableau	Advanced charting, geo-mapping	Yes	APIs for diverse data sources	User-friendly, with customised reports
Qlik	Associative data modelling	Yes	Real-time data integration	Flexible and highly customisable

(Source: Adapted from Ifenthaler & Yau, 2020)

Early Warning Systems and Performance Prediction

Early Warning Systems (EWS) represent a class of AI-driven tools designed to synthesise heterogeneous data sources—ranging from academic records, attendance logs, to engagement metrics within virtual learning environments—to identify students at risk of poor academic outcomes or dropout. By leveraging predictive modelling techniques such as logistic regression, decision trees, and neural networks, EWS generate risk scores which enable timely and targeted interventions.

One of the seminal implementations of an EWS is Purdue University's "Course Signals" system, which utilises data on course activities, grades, and participation to deliver real-time feedback to students and advisors. Empirical evidence indicates that Course Signals has contributed to statistically significant increases in student retention and academic performance by facilitating early identification and support for at-risk learners (Arnold & Pistilli, 2012).

EWS typically stratify students into risk categories—low, moderate, and high—allowing educators and administrators to prioritise resources effectively. Customised intervention strategies may include assigning academic mentors, scheduling supplementary tutorials, or restructuring course pathways to better align with student capabilities. Additionally, these systems often incorporate dashboards for administrators to monitor institutional-wide risk trends, informing policy adjustments and strategic planning. Table 9 presents the components and benefits of EWS.

Table 9. Components and benefits of early warning systems

Component	Description	Benefit
Mathematics	Production Rules	If-then rules to represent procedural knowledge
Predictive Modelling	Uses machine learning to forecast outcomes	Proactive identification of at-risk students
Risk Stratification	Categorises students by risk levels	Efficient resource allocation
Intervention Management	Tracks effectiveness of support measures	Continuous improvement of support strategies

(Source: Arnold & Pistilli, 2012; Ifenthaler & Yau, 2020)

Virtual Assistants and Intelligent Management Systems

The advent of Artificial Intelligence has also given rise to virtual assistants—commonly implemented as chatbots or conversational agents—that automate routine administrative processes within educational institutions. These AI-powered assistants handle frequent queries relating to enrolment procedures, academic calendars, financial services, and student support, thereby alleviating administrative workloads and enabling staff to focus on strategic and pedagogical priorities.

Advanced virtual assistants employ natural language processing (NLP) and contextual understanding to provide accurate, personalised, and timely responses to stakeholders. Their 24/7 availability enhances accessibility and responsiveness, significantly improving the student and staff experience.

Complementing virtual assistants are Intelligent Management Systems (IMS), which integrate core administrative modules—such as enrolment, assessment, finance, and human resources—into a unified analytical framework. These systems incorporate AI-driven analytics to provide comprehensive institutional insights, enabling educational leaders to adopt a holistic approach to governance. The aggregation and real-time analysis of multifaceted data facilitate strategic decision-making at a macro level, promoting institutional agility and responsiveness to emerging challenges (Holmes et al., 2019). Table 10 illustrates the characteristics of AI-based virtual assistants and intelligent management systems.

Table 10. Characteristics of AI-enabled virtual assistants and intelligent management systems

Tool Type	Key Features	Institutional Benefits
Virtual Assistants	NLP-based interaction, 24/7 availability	Increased operational efficiency; improved stakeholder engagement
Intelligent Management Systems	Integrated data modules, real-time analytics	Holistic governance; evidence-informed strategic planning

(Source: Holmes et al., 2019)

The integration of Artificial Intelligence tools into educational administration marks a significant advancement in the capacity of institutions to make informed, timely, and strategic decisions. Educational analytics platforms transform vast and complex datasets into actionable insights, early warning systems provide predictive foresight enabling pre-emptive interventions, and virtual assistants alongside intelligent management systems streamline administrative functions while enhancing organisational oversight.

The synergy of these tools not only optimises resource utilisation but also fosters a data-centric culture that elevates institutional effectiveness and student success. Nonetheless, successful deployment necessitates adequate training, infrastructural investment, and ongoing evaluation to ensure ethical, equitable, and transparent application aligned with institutional goals.

PRACTICAL EXAMPLES OF AI UTILISATION IN EDUCATIONAL ADMINISTRATION

The application of Artificial Intelligence (AI) in educational administration has evolved significantly in recent years, demonstrating tangible impacts on institutional efficiency, student outcomes, and policy formulation. This section examines exemplary cases from diverse global contexts, illustrating how AI-driven systems enhance decision-making, foster equity, and optimise resource allocation within education.

Predictive Alert System at Georgia State University (USA)

Among the most extensively documented implementations of AI in educational management is the predictive alert system developed by Georgia State University (GSU) in the United States. This advanced system integrates over 800 variables per student, encompassing academic records, socio-economic status, and behavioural indicators. By analysing these multidimensional datasets, the system automatically detects early warning signs, such as low grades in critical courses or atypical enrolment patterns, thereby generating proactive alerts for academic advisors (Georgia State University, n.d.).

This data-driven intervention framework has yielded remarkable outcomes: over the span of less than a decade, GSU achieved an increase in its graduation rate exceeding 20 percentage points. Notably, the system contributed to significantly reducing achievement gaps among students from diverse ethnic and socio-economic backgrounds. This success exemplifies the potential of AI not merely as an efficiency tool but as a mechanism for promoting inclusivity and social justice within higher education institutions. Table 11 presents the main features of the Georgia State University predictive warning system.

Table 11. Key features of Georgia State University's predictive alert system

Feature	Description
Variables Analysed	>800, including academic, socio-economic, behavioural
Early Warning Triggers	Low grades, irregular enrolment patterns
Intervention Approach	Proactive alerts to academic advisors
Impact	+20% graduation rate; reduced equity gaps

(Source: Baer & Campbell, 2021)

"Course Signals" System at Purdue University

Purdue University, also in the United States, pioneered the "Course Signals" system, an AI-driven platform employing predictive algorithms to identify students at risk of failing particular courses. This system synthesises multiple data points such as assessment performance, class attendance, and participation in online learning environments. Students are categorised into three risk levels—low, medium, and high—visually represented through a traffic-light colour code: green, yellow, and red, respectively (Arnold & Pistilli, 2012).

Faculty and advisors utilise this stratified information to engage students with tailored academic support, including tutoring and counselling services. Subsequent evaluations have demonstrated that students receiving such early alerts exhibit substantially higher retention rates compared to those without such interventions. The model's scalability and efficacy have prompted its adoption and adaptation by numerous other institutions globally. An overview of the Purdue University "Course Signals" system is shown in Table 12.

Table 12. Overview of Purdue University's "course signals" system

Aspect	Description
Data Inputs	Grades, attendance, virtual platform engagement
Risk Levels	Low (green), Medium (yellow), High (red)
Intervention Methodology	Targeted academic support and advising
Outcome	Significant increase in student retention

(Source: Arnold & Pistilli, 2012)

AI-Enabled Administrative Decision Platform in Singapore's Education System

Singapore has garnered international recognition for its strategic and technologically advanced educational governance. The Ministry of Education (MOE) employs AI-powered platforms such as the "EdTech Virtual Assistant" to streamline processes including teacher allocation, school performance analysis, and infrastructure planning.

These platforms consolidate heterogeneous data sources—academic, financial, geographic—facilitating automated report generation, scenario modelling, and the support of complex policy decisions. Moreover, AI has been instrumental in personalising professional development by recommending teacher training programmes tailored to individual needs and institutional objectives (Yuen et al., 2023). This integration reflects Singapore's commitment to harnessing AI to drive continuous improvement and innovation at systemic levels.

Predictive Analytics in Finnish Public Schools

Finland, renowned for its exemplary educational standards, has developed predictive analytics tools aimed at anticipating chronic absenteeism, underperformance, and dropout risks in public schools. Utilising customised dashboards and cohort analyses, school principals receive automated recommendations enabling the formulation of context-sensitive improvement plans.

A salient feature of the Finnish approach is the collaborative partnership among local governments, researchers, and technology developers, ensuring the alignment of technological solutions with pedagogical priorities and societal values. Additionally, stringent data protection protocols safeguard student privacy, reflecting the ethical considerations embedded within these systems (Prinsloo & Slade, 2017).

AI Tools in Technical Education in Latin America: The SENAI Case (Brazil)

Brazil's National Service for Industrial Training (SENAI) exemplifies the application of AI to enhance technical and vocational education across Latin America. By employing recommendation algorithms, SENAI offers students personalised course and career pathway suggestions based on their prior performance, interests, and prevailing labour market trends.

Furthermore, real-time learning monitoring systems enable instructors to adapt pedagogical strategies dynamically in response to individual student engagement and comprehension levels. This adaptive approach has contributed to lowering dropout rates and improving graduates' employability, thereby aligning education with economic demands (Confederação Nacional da Indústria, 2022).

As a comparative summary, Table 13 displays the key outcomes of AI applications in educational administration.

Table 13. Comparative summary of AI applications in educational administration

Institution / Country	AI Application	Key Outcomes
Georgia State University (USA)	Predictive alerts for academic risk	+20% graduation rate; reduced equity gaps
Purdue University (USA)	"Course Signals" risk categorisation	Increased retention through targeted support
Singapore Ministry of Education	EdTech Virtual Assistant	Optimised teacher allocation; personalised training
Finnish Public Schools	Predictive analytics for absenteeism	Tailored improvement plans; data privacy adherence
SENAI (Brazil)	Recommendation and real-time monitoring	Reduced dropout; enhanced employability

The foregoing cases substantiate the transformative role of AI in educational administration across diverse geopolitical and socio-economic contexts. From predictive risk alert systems to AI-driven strategic planning platforms, these implementations underscore AI's capacity to enhance institutional effectiveness, promote educational equity, and foster responsiveness to dynamic challenges.

Crucially, the success of such initiatives hinges on a confluence of advanced technology, stakeholder engagement, and rigorous data governance. As AI continues to evolve, it is imperative that educational leaders embrace these innovations within ethical frameworks that safeguard privacy, promote inclusivity, and ensure transparency.

ETHICAL CHALLENGES AND LIMITATIONS IN THE APPLICATION OF AI IN EDUCATION

The integration of Artificial Intelligence (AI) within educational contexts has undoubtedly introduced transformative possibilities for improving decision-making, enhancing personalised learning, and optimising administrative functions. Nonetheless, the deployment of AI systems is accompanied by a series of ethical challenges and inherent limitations that warrant critical examination. This chapter section elucidates these concerns, focusing on algorithmic transparency and explainability, bias and equity, data protection and privacy, digital divide issues, and the risks of overreliance on technology at the expense of professional judgement.

Transparency and Explainability of Algorithms

A paramount ethical challenge surrounding AI in education is the opacity of many algorithmic processes, frequently described as operating as "black boxes" (Burrell, 2016). In such systems, neither end-users—comprising educators, students, and parents—nor sometimes the developers themselves possess a clear understanding of how specific decisions or recommendations are derived. This lack of transparency raises significant ethical concerns, especially considering that AI-driven decisions can directly impact students' academic trajectories, such as admission, placement, progression, or support provision.

Within educational settings, insufficient algorithmic explainability can erode trust among stakeholders and impede accountability mechanisms essential for responsible governance (Selwyn et al., 2020). The inability to audit or contest automated decisions may result in resistance to AI adoption, diminish the perceived legitimacy of institutional decisions, and obscure opportunities for correcting errors or biases.

Therefore, it is imperative to prioritise the development and utilisation of AI models that are inherently interpretable or equipped with explainability techniques—such as attention mechanisms, feature importance rankings, or counterfactual explanations—that clarify the rationale behind outputs. Furthermore, pedagogical and regulatory justifications should accompany AI recommendations to ensure that decisions align with educational objectives and ethical standards.

Algorithmic Bias and Equity

Algorithmic bias constitutes another critical ethical dimension in AI applications within education. AI systems fundamentally rely on training data, which may inadvertently reflect historical inequities related to gender, ethnicity, socio-economic status, or other demographic characteristics. Consequently, there exists a substantive risk that AI models will perpetuate or even exacerbate such disparities through their predictive or prescriptive functions (Mehrabi et al., 2021).

In practical terms, biased algorithms may lead to unfair recommendations, such as misidentifying certain student groups as being at risk, under- or over-estimating performance potential, or unjustly allocating educational resources. Such outcomes contravene principles of fairness and social justice foundational to education.

Mitigating algorithmic bias requires a multifaceted approach. Independent algorithmic audits should be routinely conducted to detect and quantify bias. Additionally, rigorous testing for fairness across diverse demographic subgroups must be integrated into development cycles. The use of more representative and balanced datasets can reduce discriminatory patterns, while bias-correcting algorithmic techniques—such as reweighting, adversarial debiasing, or fairness-aware learning—should be employed proactively (Raji et al., 2020). Table 14 shows common sources of algorithmic bias and mitigation strategies.

Table 14. Common sources of algorithmic bias and mitigation strategies

Source of Bias	Description	Mitigation Strategies
Historical Data Inequities	Data reflecting societal inequalities	Use balanced, representative datasets
Feature Selection Bias	Inclusion of proxy variables for sensitive attributes	Exclude or carefully select features
Model Training and Optimisation Bias	Algorithms prioritising accuracy over fairness	Employ fairness-aware learning techniques
Evaluation Bias	Lack of subgroup-specific performance metrics	Conduct subgroup analysis and bias audits

(Source: Adapted from Mehrabi et al., 2021; Raji et al., 2020)

Data Protection and Privacy

AI-driven educational systems typically necessitate the collection and processing of extensive personal data, including academic records, behavioural profiles, health information, and demographic details. This data-centric approach engenders profound privacy concerns, particularly in light of stringent legal frameworks such as the European Union's General Data Protection Regulation (GDPR) and various personal data protection laws across Latin America and other regions (Williamson, 2017).

Maintaining data privacy demands that educational administrators implement robust measures encompassing data anonymisation, secure storage, and controlled access. Crucially, students and guardians must be afforded transparent information regarding data usage and give informed consent for processing activities. Data governance policies should delineate permissible data uses, strictly limiting exploitation to legitimate educational purposes while forbidding secondary or commercial utilisation.

Furthermore, educational institutions should adopt privacy-by-design principles in developing AI solutions, embedding safeguards from inception rather than as retrospective additions. This ethical stewardship is vital to preserve stakeholder trust and comply with regulatory obligations.

Inequality in Access to Technology

The equitable deployment of AI in education is inherently contingent upon adequate infrastructure, digital connectivity, device availability, and digital literacy among educators and learners. Unfortunately, these prerequisites are unevenly distributed globally and even within countries, exacerbating the digital divide between urban and rural schools or among students of varying socio-economic strata (UNESCO, 2021).

Such disparities risk entrenching existing educational inequities by privileging those with superior access to technology and digital skills while marginalising others. For example, a rural school lacking reliable internet or modern devices may be unable to benefit from AI-powered learning analytics or virtual assistants, undermining systemic inclusiveness.

Addressing this challenge necessitates comprehensive policies that encompass not only the equitable distribution of hardware and connectivity but also the professional development of educators and digital literacy programmes for students. Ensuring accessibility and usability for diverse user groups—including those with disabilities—is equally paramount. Without such a holistic approach, AI's democratizing potential in education will remain unrealised.

Technological Dependence and the Erosion of Professional Judgement

While AI offers valuable decision-support capabilities, there exists a pronounced risk of excessive reliance on automated recommendations, potentially diminishing the professional judgement and critical thinking of educators and administrators. This phenomenon, often termed "automation bias" or the "automation of judgement," can precipitate uncritical acceptance of algorithmic outputs, even in contexts demanding nuanced human evaluation (Gadala, 2017).

Such overdependence may result in decisions that inadequately consider contextual factors, socio-emotional elements, or ethical considerations not captured by AI systems. It could also engender deskilling; whereby educational professionals gradually lose confidence and expertise in decision-making domains.

To mitigate this risk, AI should be framed explicitly as an augmentative tool rather than a replacement for human agency. Educational organisations must cultivate a culture of reflective practice, encouraging practitioners to critically appraise AI inputs, contextualise findings, and engage in collaborative deliberations. Training programmes should enhance digital literacy alongside ethical awareness, ensuring that AI enhances rather than supplants pedagogical and administrative expertise. Ethical challenges in applying AI in education and recommended mitigations are presented in Table 15.

Table 15. Ethical challenges in AI application in education and recommended mitigations

Ethical Challenge	Description	Recommended Mitigations
Algorithmic Opacity	Lack of transparency reduces trust and accountability	Develop interpretable models; provide clear explanations
Algorithmic Bias	Risk of perpetuating social inequalities	Conduct audits; use balanced datasets; fairness-aware AI
Data Privacy Concerns	Sensitive data use risks breaches of confidentiality	Implement anonymisation; ensure informed consent; privacy-by-design
Digital Divide	Unequal access undermines equitable benefits	Provide infrastructure; promote digital literacy
Automation Bias	Overreliance diminishes professional judgement	Promote reflective practices; train critical AI use

The ethical and practical limitations inherent to AI implementation in education are multifaceted and complex. While AI harbours considerable potential to enhance decision-making and educational outcomes, addressing challenges related to transparency, fairness, privacy, equitable access, and professional integrity is indispensable. By adopting a principled and multidisciplinary approach, educational institutions can harness AI responsibly—ensuring that technological innovation complements, rather than compromises, the core values and human dimensions of education.

RECOMMENDATIONS FOR FUTURE IMPLEMENTATIONS OF AI IN EDUCATIONAL DECISION-MAKING

The transformative potential of Artificial Intelligence (AI) within educational decision-making is vast, yet its effective and ethical realisation hinges on thoughtful strategies that address institutional culture, participatory design, professional development, impact assessment, and governance. This chapter section elaborates comprehensive recommendations aimed at guiding future implementations of AI technologies in educational contexts to optimise their benefits while mitigating risks (Guitart et al., 2020).

Cultivating a Data-Driven Institutional Culture

A foundational prerequisite for the successful integration of AI in educational decision-making is the cultivation of an institutional culture that systematically values and utilises data in an ethical and critical manner. The mere introduction of AI technologies is insufficient without embedding data literacy and evidence-based decision-making within the organisational fabric (Datnow & Park, 2014).

Educational stakeholders—including administrators, educators, and support personnel—must be equipped with competencies in data interpretation, critical analysis, and ethical considerations related to data use. This requires targeted capacity-building initiatives that transcend basic technical skills, fostering an understanding of how data-driven insights can enhance pedagogical and administrative practices.

In addition, the integrity and relevance of data underpinning AI systems must be ensured. Institutions need robust information management infrastructures capable of integrating diverse datasets, such as academic records, administrative data, and socio-contextual information, in a coherent and secure manner. Such integration facilitates a holistic understanding of educational phenomena, thereby enhancing the contextual accuracy of AI-driven recommendations.

Designing Participatory and Ethical Implementation Processes

The deployment of AI within educational settings necessitates inclusive processes that engage all relevant stakeholders—teachers, students, families, and community members—from inception through evaluation. Participatory design frameworks enable the alignment of AI applications with the values, needs, and expectations of those directly affected, thereby promoting acceptance, ethical accountability, and contextual relevance (Dhadphale & Wicks, 2022).

Institutions are encouraged to establish formal bodies such as ethical committees or advisory boards dedicated to overseeing AI initiatives. These committees should encompass diverse expertise, including educators, ethicists, legal experts, technologists, and representatives of user groups. Their mandate would involve reviewing contracts with technology providers, establishing responsible use protocols, and ensuring algorithmic transparency.

Such governance structures are pivotal in safeguarding user rights, maintaining equitable access, and fostering trust. Transparent communication strategies about

AI functionalities and limitations should be embedded to demystify technology and empower stakeholders to engage critically with AI outputs.

Prioritising Continuous Professional Development

Human capital development constitutes a critical determinant of AI's efficacy in education. Professional training programmes must transcend superficial platform training and incorporate comprehensive curricula addressing the fundamentals of AI, data analytics, algorithmic ethics, and critical evaluation of AI's implications for teaching, learning, and administration (Luckin & Holmes, 2016).

Ongoing professional development should be institutionalised within national and local education systems, ensuring sustained upskilling of educators, managers, and technical personnel. Collaborative learning communities can serve as effective forums for sharing best practices, troubleshooting implementation challenges, and contextualising AI applications.

Moreover, training should emphasise reflective practices that encourage educators to critically assess AI-derived insights, contextualise recommendations within their unique environments, and balance technological input with professional judgement. Table 16 shows the key components of professional development for AI in education.

Table 16. Key components of professional development for AI in education

Component	Description	Expected Outcome
AI Fundamentals	Understanding AI concepts, mechanisms, and limitations	Informed use of AI tools
Data Literacy	Skills in data interpretation, visualisation, and critical analysis	Enhanced evidence-based decision-making
Ethical and Legal Aspects	Awareness of privacy, bias, and accountability issues	Responsible and equitable AI application
Reflective Practice	Encouraging critical appraisal of AI outputs	Balanced integration of AI and human judgement

(Source: Adapted from Luckin & Holmes, 2016)

Rigorous Evaluation of Implemented Technologies

Ensuring that AI technologies deliver intended benefits while avoiding adverse consequences requires systematic and rigorous impact evaluation. Institutions should articulate clear success metrics before deployment, encompassing academic outcomes, stakeholder satisfaction, equity indicators, and cost-effectiveness (Wang & Bowers, 2020).

Longitudinal studies offer valuable insights into the sustained effects of AI interventions over time, revealing trends and informing iterative improvements. Mixed-methods approaches, integrating quantitative data (e.g., achievement scores, usage statistics) and qualitative feedback (e.g., user experiences, contextual challenges), enrich the evaluative process.

Importantly, user feedback mechanisms must be embedded to capture the perspectives of teachers, students, and administrators continuously. Such participatory evaluation fosters adaptability, enabling real-time refinements that enhance relevance, usability, and ethical compliance.

Establishing Regulatory Frameworks and Technological Governance

Governments and international bodies bear a critical responsibility in framing normative and regulatory landscapes that govern AI in education. These frameworks should encompass data privacy protections, intellectual property rights, algorithmic transparency, institutional accountability, and interoperability standards (OECD, 2021).

Well-defined legal parameters provide clarity and protection for educational institutions and users alike, mitigating risks associated with misuse, data breaches, or discriminatory practices. Additionally, the development and promotion of international quality standards for AI tools can guide institutions in selecting reliable, secure, and pedagogically sound solutions.

Governance of AI in education must be multidisciplinary and multisectoral, integrating inputs from educational authorities, technology experts, ethicists, and civil society. Prioritising the public interest and equity is paramount to ensure AI contributes to the democratisation rather than stratification of educational opportunities. Table 17 presents the main recommended actions for AI governance in education.

Table 17. Recommended actions for AI governance in education

Governance Aspect	Description	Recommended Action
Data Privacy and Security	Safeguarding sensitive information	Enforce GDPR and equivalent regulations
Algorithmic Transparency	Making AI decision processes understandable	Mandate explainability and auditing
Accountability	Defining responsibilities of stakeholders	Establish clear institutional roles

continued on following page

Table 17. Continued

Governance Aspect	Description	Recommended Action
Interoperability	Ensuring AI systems can work together	Promote adoption of open standards
Quality Assurance	Validating AI tools' effectiveness and fairness	Develop and adopt international benchmarks

(Source: Adapted from OECD, 2021)

The responsible and effective implementation of AI in educational decision-making demands comprehensive strategies that integrate cultural, ethical, technical, and regulatory dimensions. Fostering data-driven institutional cultures, engaging stakeholders in participatory design, investing in professional development, conducting rigorous impact evaluations, and establishing robust governance frameworks constitute pillars for realising AI's promise in education. Such an approach not only maximises AI's utility but also safeguards the fundamental values of equity, transparency, and human-centred pedagogy.

CONCLUSION

The integration of Artificial Intelligence (AI) into educational governance and strategic leadership represents a seminal advancement in institutional decision-making, characterised by its capacity to transcend traditional constraints of human cognition, informational asymmetry, and structural inertia. This chapter has systematically examined the theoretical, practical, and ethical dimensions of AI deployment within educational contexts, emphasising its role not merely as a technological adjunct but as a catalyst for transformative organisational change.

AI's potential to enhance decision-making is grounded in its ability to process vast, heterogeneous datasets, identify latent patterns, and generate actionable insights with a degree of speed and precision unattainable by human agents alone. Predictive and prescriptive analytics, natural language processing, educational data mining, and robotic process automation collectively provide educational leaders with sophisticated tools for forecasting, planning, intervention, and resource optimisation. These technologies enable a paradigm shift from reactive, intuition-driven management to proactive, data-informed governance characterised by strategic foresight and operational agility.

The theoretical frameworks explored—spanning bounded rationality, incrementalism, and the Garbage Can Model—underscore the limitations of classical rationalist approaches in the face of real-world complexity. Within this context, AI emerges as a remedial force, augmenting the decision-making capacities of institutional actors while simultaneously reducing the influence of cognitive biases, emotional pressures, and information processing bottlenecks. Case studies from globally recognised institutions such as Georgia State University, Purdue University, and the Ministry of Education in Singapore provide compelling evidence of AI's effectiveness in enhancing student retention, streamlining administrative functions, and informing equitable policy design.

Nevertheless, this chapter has also illuminated the multifaceted ethical challenges that accompany AI adoption. Concerns surrounding algorithmic opacity, data privacy, algorithmic bias, and digital inequality necessitate the development of robust governance frameworks that ensure transparency, accountability, and inclusivity. Educational institutions bear the responsibility of upholding these ethical standards through continuous algorithmic auditing, stakeholder engagement, and adherence to legal frameworks such as the General Data Protection Regulation (GDPR). The principle of human-in-the-loop must remain central, ensuring that AI systems complement rather than supplant professional judgement and pedagogical discretion.

Furthermore, the successful implementation of AI in decision-making processes is contingent upon institutional readiness, encompassing technological infrastructure, digital literacy, and organisational culture. Institutions must invest in capacity-building initiatives that equip educators and administrators with the requisite competencies to interact meaningfully with AI systems, interpret analytics outputs, and translate insights into effective action. Equally important is the need to address systemic inequities in access to digital tools and connectivity, without which the benefits of AI risk being unevenly distributed and potentially exacerbating existing disparities.

The future of AI in educational decision-making must be envisioned as a collaborative endeavour—between human expertise and machine intelligence, between technological innovation and ethical stewardship, and between local institutional goals and broader societal imperatives. Educational leadership in the age of AI requires not only technical acumen but also a deep commitment to values such as equity, transparency, and human dignity. Institutions that succeed in harmonising these dimensions will be better equipped to navigate the uncertainties of the 21st century, foster resilient learning ecosystems, and fulfil their mission of cultivating inclusive and adaptive educational environments.

In sum, AI constitutes both a challenge and an opportunity. Its promise lies in its capacity to render decision-making processes more intelligent, anticipatory, and contextually responsive. Yet realising this promise demands sustained critical engagement, rigorous evaluation, and principled design. As such, AI's integration into educational governance must be approached not as a linear technical upgrade, but as a holistic reconfiguration of how institutions think, decide, and act in pursuit of educational excellence and social transformation.

REFERENCES

Alfaro-Pérez, L., Rodríguez-Hernández, J., & Ramírez-Noriega, M. (2023). A Framework for the Implementation of Artificial Intelligence in Government Decision-Making Processes. *International Journal of Combinatorial Optimization Problems and Informatics, 14*(3), 121–134. DOI: 10.61467/2007.1558.2023.v14i3.420

Ansyari, M. F., De Witte, K., & Groot, W. (2024). The determinants of data use practice for instructional practice in higher education. *Journal of Professional Capital and Community*. Advance online publication. DOI: 10.1108/jpcc-07-2024-0106

Arnold, K. E., & Pistilli, M. D. (2012). Course signals at Purdue: Using learning analytics to increase student success. *Proceedings of the 2nd International Conference on Learning Analytics and Knowledge*, 267–270. https://doi.org/DOI: 10.1145/2330601.2330666

Arnsten, A. F. T. (2009). Stress signalling pathways that impair prefrontal cortex structure and function. *Nature Reviews. Neuroscience, 10*(6), 410–422. DOI: 10.1038/nrn2648 PMID: 19455173

Baker, R. S. J. d., & Inventado, P. S. (2014). Educational data mining and learning analytics. In Larusson, J. A., & White, B. (Eds.), *Learning Analytics* (pp. 61–75). Springer., DOI: 10.1007/978-1-4614-3305-7_4

Binns, R., Veale, M., Van Kleek, M., & Shadbolt, N. (2018). 'It's Reducing a Human Being to a Percentage': Perceptions of Justice in Algorithmic Decisions. *Proceedings of the 2018 CHI Conference on Human Factors in Computing Systems*, 1–14. https://doi.org/DOI: 10.1145/3173574.3173951

Burrell, J. (2016). How the machine 'thinks': Understanding opacity in machine learning algorithms. *Big Data & Society, 3*(1), 205395171562251. DOI: 10.1177/2053951715622512

Bush, T. (2011). *Theories of Educational Leadership and Management* (4th ed.). SAGE Publications.

Cohen, M. D., March, J. G., & Olsen, J. P. (1972). A garbage can model of organizational choice. *Administrative Science Quarterly, 17*(1), 1–25. DOI: 10.2307/2392088

Confederação Nacional da Indústria. (2022). Relatório anual de educação técnica e profissional. CNI. https://www.portaldaindustria.com.br/cni

D'Mello, S. K., & Graesser, A. C. (2012). Dynamics of affective states during complex learning. *Learning and Instruction*, *22*(2), 145–157. DOI: 10.1016/j.learninstruc.2011.10.001

Datnow, A., & Park, V. (2014). *Data-driven leadership*. Wiley.

Dhadphale, T., & Wicks, B. (2022). Participatory Stakeholder Engagement in Design Studio Education. *International Journal of Art & Design Education*, *41*(4), 589–602. DOI: 10.1111/jade.12427

Duarte, N., Montoya Pérez, Y., Beltran, A. J., & Bolaño García, M. (2023). Use of Artificial Intelligence in Education. *Systematic Reviews*. Advance online publication. DOI: 10.46254/sa04.20230169

Eubanks, V. (2018). *Automating inequality: How high-tech tools profile, police, and punish the poor*. St. Martin's Press.

Floridi, L., & Cowls, J. (2019). A unified framework of five principles for AI in society. *Harvard Data Science Review*, *1*(1). Advance online publication. DOI: 10.1162/99608f92.8cd550d1

Fuentes-Penna, A., & González Ibarra, J. de D. (2024). Personalized Education and Artificial Intelligence. *International Journal of Combinatorial Optimization Problems and Informatics*, *15*(2), 1–12. DOI: 10.61467/2007.1558.2024.v15i2.431

Fullan, M. (2014). *The Principal: Three Keys to Maximising Impact*. Jossey-Bass.

Gadala, M. (2017). Automation bias: exploring causal mechanisms and potential mitigation strategies. https://ethos.bl.uk/OrderDetails.do?uin=uk.bl.ethos.720941

Georgia State University. (n.d.). Leveraging Predictive Analytics to Enhance Student Retention: A Case Study of Georgia State University. ResearchGate. Retrieved from https://www.researchgate.net/publication/390878595_Leveraging_Predictive_Analytics_to_Enhance_Student_Retention_A_Case_Study_of_Georgia_State_University

Guitart, H. I., Rodríguez, M. E., & Baró, X. (2020). Design and Implementation of Dashboards to Support Teachers Decision-Making Process in e-Assessment Systems. In Baneres, D., Rodríguez, M., & Guerrero-Roldán, A. (Eds.), *Engineering Data-Driven Adaptive Trust-based e-Assessment Systems. Lecture Notes on Data Engineering and Communications Technologies* (Vol. 34). Springer., DOI: 10.1007/978-3-030-29326-0_6

Holcombe, E. M., Kezar, A. J., Elrod, S. L., & Ramaley, J. A. (Eds.). (2022). *Shared Leadership in Higher Education: A Framework and Models for Responding to a Changing World* (1st ed.). Routledge., DOI: 10.4324/9781003446965

Holmes, W., Bialik, M., & Fadel, C. (2019). *Artificial Intelligence in education: Promises and implications for teaching and learning*. Center for Curriculum Redesign.

Ifenthaler, D., & Yau, J. Y.-K. (2020). Utilising learning analytics to support study success in higher education: A systematic review. *Educational Technology Research and Development, 68*(4), 1961–1990. DOI: 10.1007/s11423-020-09788-z

Jayaprakash, S. M., Moody, E. W., Lauría, E. J., Regan, J. R., & Baron, J. D. (2014). Early alert of academically at-risk students: An open source analytics initiative. *Journal of Learning Analytics, 1*(1), 6–47. DOI: 10.18608/jla.2014.11.3

Khuzairi, N. M. S., Sidhu, M. S., & Cob, Z. (2020). Learning Analytics and Teaching Analytics. *The Similarities and Differences., 3*(2), 52–58. DOI: 10.36079/LAMINTANG.IJ-HUMASS-0302.135

Kökver, Y., Pektaş, H. M., & Çelik, H. (2025). Artificial intelligence applications in education: Natural language processing in detecting misconceptions. *Education and Information Technologies, 30*, 3035–3066. DOI: 10.1007/s10639-024-12919-1

LeCun, Y., Bengio, Y., & Hinton, G. (2015). Deep learning. *Nature, 521*(7553), 436–444. DOI: 10.1038/nature14539 PMID: 26017442

Lindblom, C. E. (1959). The science of 'muddling through'. *Public Administration Review, 19*(2), 79–88. DOI: 10.2307/973677

Luckin, R., & Holmes, W. (2016). Intelligence Unleashed: An argument for AI in Education. https://discovery.ucl.ac.uk/id/eprint/1475756

Mandinach, E. B., & Gummer, E. S. (2016). What does it mean for teachers to be data literate: Laying out the skills, knowledge, and dispositions. *Teaching and Teacher Education, 60*, 366–376. DOI: 10.1016/j.tate.2016.07.011

Mehrabi, N., Morstatter, F., Saxena, N., Lerman, K., & Galstyan, A. (2021). A survey on bias and fairness in machine learning. *ACM Computing Surveys, 54*(6), 1–35. DOI: 10.1145/3457607

Molnar, C. (2020). Interpretable Machine Learning: A Guide for Making Black Box Models Explainable. https://christophm.github.io/interpretable-ml-book/

Morales-Murillo, V. G., Pinto, D., Perez-Tellez, F., & Rojas-Lopez, F. (2024). A Transformer-Based Multi-Domain Recommender System for E-commerce. *International Journal of Combinatorial Optimization Problems and Informatics*, *15*(2), 95–123. DOI: 10.61467/2007.1558.2024.v15i2.465

OECD. (2021). *Artificial Intelligence in Society*. OECD Publishing., DOI: 10.1787/eedfee77-

Organización de Estados Iberoamericanos (OEI). (2025). Red de los Sistemas Educativos Inteligentes de América Latina y el Caribe (RESEI). Sistemas de gestión e información educativa para el seguimiento de las trayectorias escolares. OEI. https://oei.int/wp-content/uploads/2025/03/2-sistemas-de-informacion-y-gestion-educativa-de-las-trayectorias-escolares-22-7.pdf

Prinsloo, P., & Slade, S. (2017). Ethics and learning analytics: Charting the (un)charted. In Lang, C., Siemens, G., Wise, A. F., and Gaevic, D., editors, The Handbook of Learning Analytics, pages 49–57. Society for Learning Analytics Research (SoLAR), Alberta, Canada, 1 edition. https://www.solaresearch.org/publications/hla-17/hla17-chapter4/

Raji, I. D., Smart, A., White, R. N., Mitchell, M., Gebru, T., Hutchinson, B., & Barnes, P. (2020). Closing the AI accountability gap: Defining an end-to-end framework for internal algorithmic auditing. *Proceedings of the 2020 Conference on Fairness, Accountability, and Transparency*, 33–44. https://doi.org/DOI: 10.1145/3351095.3372873

Rao, T. V. N., Stephen, M., Manoj, E., & Sangers, B. (2025). Exploring Bias and Fairness in Machine Learning Algorithms. Advances in Computational Intelligence and Robotics Book Series, 369–398. https://doi.org/DOI: 10.4018/979-8-3693-5231-1.ch014

Romero, C., & Ventura, S. (2020). Educational data mining and learning analytics: An updated survey. *Wiley Interdisciplinary Reviews. Data Mining and Knowledge Discovery*, *10*(3), e1355. DOI: 10.1002/widm.1355

Russell, S., & Norvig, P. (2021). *Artificial Intelligence: A Modern Approach* (4th ed.). Pearson.

Scholes, V. (2016). The ethics of using learning analytics to categorize students on risk. *Educational Technology Research and Development*, *64*, 939–955. DOI: 10.1007/s11423-016-9458-1

Siemens, G. (2013). Learning analytics: The emergence of a discipline. *The American Behavioral Scientist*, *57*(10), 1380–1400. DOI: 10.1177/0002764213498851

Slade, S., & Prinsloo, P. (2013). Learning analytics: Ethical issues and dilemmas. *The American Behavioral Scientist, 57*(10), 1510–1529. DOI: 10.1177/0002764213479366

Souza, Érika M. A. de, Fabri, E. S., Araújo, W. dos R. M., Souza, W. C. de, Resende, S. I. de M., & Diniz, H. A. G. (2024). Challenges and Opportunities of Artificial Intelligence in Public Education: A Case Study in Barão Dos Cocais – MG. Revista De Gestão Social E Ambiental, 18(10), e09522. https://doi.org/DOI: 10.24857/rgsa.v18n10-326

UNESCO. (2021). AI and Education: Guidance for Policy-makers. UNESCO Publishing. https://unesdoc.unesco.org/ark:/48223/pf0000376709

Von Neumann, J., & Morgenstern, O. (1944). *Theory of Games and Economic Behavior*. Princeton University Press.

Williamson, B. (2017). Big Data in Education: The digital future of learning, policy and practice. *Sage (Atlanta, Ga.)*. Advance online publication. DOI: 10.4135/9781529714920

Zawacki-Richter, O., Marín, V. I., Bond, M., & Gouverneur, F. (2019). Systematic review of research on artificial intelligence applications in higher education – where are the educators? *International Journal of Educational Technology in Higher Education, 16*(1), 1–27. DOI: 10.1186/s41239-019-0171-0

Chapter 14
Automating Administrative Tasks

Francisco R. Trejo-Macotela
https://orcid.org/0000-0003-2133-3456
Universidad Politécnica de Pachuca, Mexico

Jorge A. Ruiz-Vanoye
https://orcid.org/0000-0003-4928-5716
Universidad Politécnica de Pachuca, Mexico

ABSTRACT

This chapter explores the integration of artificial intelligence (AI) in automating administrative tasks within educational institutions. Drawing on recent technological advances, it analyses how AI tools—such as machine learning algorithms, natural language processing, and predictive analytics—are used to optimise processes including enrolment, scheduling, reporting, and early warning systems. Case studies from primary to tertiary education reveal improved efficiency, reduced human error, cost savings, and staff reallocation to pedagogical roles. The study also addresses technological limitations, data privacy concerns, algorithmic bias, and institutional resistance. Findings highlight that successful implementation requires technological readiness, ethical frameworks, ongoing professional development, and inclusive leadership. Ultimately, AI-driven automation in school administration holds transformative potential when strategically aligned with human values, equity, and educational quality, fostering more responsive, sustainable, and data-informed governance.

DOI: 10.4018/979-8-3373-0598-1.ch014

INTRODUCTION

The automation of administrative tasks through Artificial Intelligence (AI) technologies represents a critical evolution in the management of educational institutions, particularly as the demands on schools and universities continue to rise. Educational institutions, which must operate within increasingly complex regulatory frameworks, face the challenge of balancing administrative efficiency with educational quality. In this context, AI offers a promising solution, not merely by automating routine tasks, but also by transforming how institutions process and utilise vast amounts of data in real-time. By leveraging AI, educational institutions can improve decision-making, enhance operational efficiency, and streamline administrative processes, thus reducing the burden on educational staff and allowing them to focus on more pedagogical duties (Wang et al., 2024; Boumediene & Bouakkaz, 2025).

AI in educational administration is not limited to simple task automation. It marks a broader structural transformation in how institutions handle processes such as student enrolment, grading, attendance tracking, scheduling, and even financial planning. CNN-based models (Convolutional Neural Networks) allow for the automation of attendance recording with high accuracy, thereby freeing administrative resources and reducing manual errors (Anzures-García et al., 2024). AI technologies such as machine learning (ML), natural language processing (NLP), and predictive analytics have become instrumental in reshaping these traditional processes, offering more dynamic, accurate, and scalable solutions. The automation of administrative tasks through AI tools allows schools to streamline operations, improve resource allocation, and foster a more data-driven approach to governance (Deep et al., 2024; Wang et al., 2024).

From the perspective of operational efficiency, the integration of AI systems ensures that repetitive, mundane administrative tasks—such as manual data entry, report generation, and student record updates—are efficiently managed by AI tools. This not only reduces the likelihood of human error but also frees up valuable time for educators and administrative staff, enabling them to concentrate on more strategic and impactful educational functions. This reallocation of human resources toward pedagogy enhances the overall educational environment and contributes to institutional productivity (West, 2021).

Moreover, AI's role extends beyond the automation of administrative functions into the realm of decision support and predictive management. Predictive analytics, for example, allows administrators to anticipate trends such as student dropout risks, enrolment fluctuations, and academic performance, empowering schools to make informed, data-driven decisions (Cobo-Rendón et al., 2023). AI systems can process large volumes of data from various sources, including student performance records, behavioural data, and attendance patterns, to provide real-time insights that help administrators adapt quickly to changing circumstances (Bai et al., 2024).

AI-driven tools also offer the potential for increased personalisation in administrative services. Current approaches enable the personalised adaptation of educational administrative services by automating processes according to the profiles and needs of students or users (Fuentes-Penna & González Ibarra, 2024). For example, AI chatbots and virtual assistants, using natural language processing (NLP), can provide real-time, automated assistance to students, parents, and staff members, answering queries, scheduling appointments, and offering procedural information. These systems not only enhance user satisfaction but also reduce the administrative workload, enabling human staff to address more complex queries (Alhawiti, 2014). Additionally, the integration of Recommender Systems in administrative platforms helps in personalising course offerings, resource allocation, and scheduling, aligning them with student preferences and institutional constraints (Đurović et al., 2018).

The significance of AI in administrative automation is also evidenced by its application across a wide range of educational levels, from primary to tertiary education. Studies such as those by Boumediene & Bouakkaz (2025) and Wang et al. (2024) have shown that AI applications not only improve administrative efficiency but also contribute to greater academic and institutional outcomes. For instance, AI-powered predictive analytics have been successfully used to forecast trends in enrolment numbers, enabling institutions to better allocate resources and manage student admissions. Likewise, predictive models for dropout prevention have enabled proactive interventions, which have been shown to significantly reduce student attrition rates (Camelo et al., 2021).

However, despite the promise of AI-driven administrative automation, the integration of such technologies is not without its challenges. A significant concern is the potential for algorithmic bias—the inadvertent reinforcement of existing inequalities in educational outcomes through biased training data or poorly designed models. Ethical considerations also extend to issues of data privacy and the need for transparent, auditable systems that respect the rights of students and staff. Furthermore, the successful deployment of AI in educational settings requires institutional readiness, including sufficient technological infrastructure, stakeholder buy-in, and the provision of professional development for staff (Arrieta et al., 2020; UNESCO, 2021).

AI in educational administration also raises questions about the future role of human educators and administrators. While AI can automate routine tasks, its role in decision-making processes—particularly those involving sensitive issues such as academic progression, student welfare, and resource allocation—necessitates careful oversight. Human expertise remains crucial in interpreting AI-generated insights, ensuring ethical governance, and making contextually appropriate decisions. Table

1 describes the main automatic systems applied in administrative tasks. Thus, the integration of AI should be seen as complementary to human judgement rather than as a replacement for it (Zawacki-Richter et al., 2019).

This study aims to explore these dynamics in depth, offering a comprehensive analysis of the role of AI in educational administration. It will examine the conceptual and technological foundations of AI-driven automation, identify the key tools and systems available, and highlight practical case studies where AI has been successfully implemented. The analysis will also address the ethical implications of AI in education, exploring the challenges related to data privacy, algorithmic fairness, and institutional resistance to technological change. The ultimate goal of this study is to provide a framework for understanding the transformative potential of AI in educational administration, while also acknowledging the complexities and limitations that must be considered for its successful implementation.

Table 1. Main automatic systems applied in administrative tasks

Concept	Description
AI-based Automation	Use of machine learning and intelligent algorithms to optimise administrative processes.
School Management Systems (SMS)	Integrated platforms facilitating data centralisation and digital management.
Natural Language Processing (NLP)	Technology enabling human-computer interaction through natural language.
Predictive Analytics	Algorithms used to forecast outcomes such as dropout rates or enrolment trends.
Explainable AI (XAI)	AI systems designed for transparency and auditability in decision-making processes.

As the educational landscape continues to evolve, the implementation of AI-based automation in administrative tasks will remain a key determinant in the advancement of educational efficiency, quality, and accessibility. However, its success will depend not only on technological innovation but also on the careful consideration of ethical frameworks, stakeholder engagement, and continuous professional development within educational institutions.

CONCEPTUAL FOUNDATIONS OF ADMINISTRATIVE AUTOMATION

Administrative automation constitutes a strategic pillar in the digital transformation of contemporary educational institutions. Its implementation not only responds to the imperative of optimising routine processes but also signals a paradigmatic shift in organisational management by incorporating emerging technologies capable of enhancing the efficiency, precision, and adaptability of school systems. In this regard, administrative automation transcends the mere substitution of manual tasks, evolving into a complex and dynamic architecture underpinned by principles of artificial intelligence, natural language processing, and predictive analytics. This novel framework enables schools and universities to confront escalating challenges in operational efficiency, knowledge management, accountability, and personalised educational service delivery.

Historically, the trajectory of automation has been closely intertwined with technological progress—from rudimentary mechanical tools and early digital applications to contemporary intelligent platforms that integrate academic, administrative, and financial data in real-time. Nevertheless, the successful deployment of these solutions necessitates not only robust technological infrastructure but also a comprehensive understanding of their underlying principles and an informed contextualisation within educational settings. Accordingly, grasping the conceptual foundations of administrative automation is essential to delineate its evolution, identify the most pertinent underpinning technologies, and evaluate its prospective impact on institutional processes. This section seeks to address these considerations through a historically, technically, and strategically rigorous lens aligned with the exigencies of the digital era in education.

Reconceptualising Administrative Automation: A Multidimensional Framework

Administrative automation in educational contexts has evolved from being perceived as a mere operational tool into a strategic vector of institutional transformation. At its conceptual core, administrative automation signifies the convergence of algorithmic intelligence, organisational innovation, and ethical governance. The term encompasses not only the mechanisation of tasks but also the redefinition of institutional workflows through cognitive technologies capable of perceiving, learning, adapting, and recommending optimised courses of action (Misuraca & van Noordt, 2021; Wang et al., 2024).

From this perspective, automation in educational administration emerges not as a peripheral supplement to pedagogical innovation, but as a constitutive element of an integrated digital ecosystem wherein human expertise, machine reasoning, and data interoperability coexist in synergistic interdependence. This paradigm necessitates a shift from viewing automation as a set of isolated tools towards conceptualising it as a socio-technical system embedded within the organisational DNA of educational institutions.

To understand the conceptual infrastructure underpinning administrative automation, it is necessary to consider its historical antecedents, foundational principles, enabling technologies, and strategic implications. This expanded section thus develops a rigorous, multilevel framework for interpreting administrative automation in education as both a technical reality and an epistemological reconfiguration of school governance.

Historical Evolution and Paradigmatic Transitions

The historical trajectory of administrative automation in educational settings can be mapped through four principal phases: mechanisation, digitalisation, intelligent augmentation, and contextual adaptability. Each phase corresponds to both technological and epistemic developments, shaping how institutions engage with information, manage complexity, and deliver administrative services. The main evolutionary phases of administrative automation are presented in Table 2.

Table 2. Evolutionary phases of administrative automation

Phase	Historical Period	Core Technologies	Institutional Focus
Mechanisation	Pre-1980s	Typewriters, calculators	Manual documentation and physical filing
Digitalisation	1980s–2000s	Databases, spreadsheets, LANs	Data centralisation, efficiency gains
Intelligent Augmentation	2010s–2020	Machine learning, NLP, RPA	Predictive management, error reduction
Contextual Adaptability	2020–present	Cloud AI, explainable AI (XAI)	Strategic decision-making, human-machine synergy

In the current phase, intelligent systems are no longer confined to executing predefined instructions but are capable of autonomously analysing contexts, predicting institutional trends, and dynamically adjusting responses to emerging needs (Bai et al., 2024; Arrieta et al., 2020). This transformation signals a paradigmatic reorientation of school management from reactive bureaucracy to proactive governance.

Moreover, the COVID-19 pandemic catalysed an accelerated adoption of AI technologies in education, particularly for administrative functions such as attendance tracking, enrolment, and performance monitoring (Reich et al., 2020; World Bank, 2022). This period also heightened awareness of the critical need for interoperability, resilience, and ethical oversight in educational digital infrastructures.

Foundational Principles of Administrative Automation

The automation of educational administrative functions is grounded in five interrelated principles:

Algorithmic Efficiency

The principle that computational systems can execute predefined administrative workflows—such as data entry, report generation, and attendance monitoring—more rapidly and accurately than manual procedures (Deep et al., 2024; West, 2021).

Data-Driven Governance

The notion that decisions should be informed by systematic analysis of institutional data, leveraging predictive analytics and data mining techniques to anticipate trends and allocate resources accordingly (Cobo-Rendón et al., 2023).

Cognitive Delegation

Involves transferring certain decision-making or interpretive functions to intelligent systems, such as chatbots or recommender systems, underpinned by natural language processing and supervised learning (Al-Jaf et al., 2024; Đurović et al., 2018).

Transparent Autonomy

Embodied in the development of explainable AI (XAI), which ensures that automated decisions—such as student classification or resource allocation—can be audited and justified to human stakeholders (Arrieta et al., 2020).

Human-Machine Symbiosis

Emphasises the strategic collaboration between educators and intelligent tools, allowing professionals to focus on higher-value pedagogical tasks while delegating repetitive processes to automation (Luckin et al., 2022).

Together, these principles frame administrative automation not merely as a technical intervention but as a systemic logic of institutional rationalisation and optimisation. They also necessitate a critical re-examination of roles, responsibilities, and ethical boundaries within educational ecosystems.

Core Technological Constituents

The implementation of administrative automation is operationalised through a constellation of interdependent technologies, each fulfilling specific functions within institutional workflows (Table 3). These include:

Machine Learning Algorithms

Deployed to detect patterns and make predictions based on historical data, such as identifying at-risk students or forecasting enrolment fluctuations (Naidu et al., 2017).

Natural Language Processing (NLP)

Enables human-computer interaction through verbal or written language, facilitating automated communication with students, staff, and families (Alhawiti, 2014).

Robotic Process Automation (RPA)

Refers to configurable software that mimics user interactions with digital systems to perform high-volume, rule-based tasks such as updating records or generating reports (Willcocks et al., 2020).

Recommender Systems

Suggest optimal administrative actions or configurations (e.g., staff schedules, course offerings) based on institutional priorities and user preferences (Đurović et al., 2018).

Explainable AI (XAI)

Embeds interpretability mechanisms within AI models, allowing users to understand and interrogate the rationale behind automated decisions (Arrieta et al., 2020).

Table 3. Functional classification of core technologies

Technology	Function in Administration	Representative Application
Machine Learning	Predictive analytics	Dropout risk identification, enrolment forecasting
RPA	Workflow automation	Attendance processing, document generation
NLP	User interface automation	Chatbots for enrolment or FAQs
Recommender Systems	Decision support optimisation	Academic resource distribution, class scheduling
XAI	Auditability and accountability	Explanation of automated classifications or alerts

These technologies typically operate within cloud-based environments, ensuring scalability, data security, and real-time access. Their effectiveness, however, depends on the quality of institutional data, integration capacity, and the digital competencies of educational staff (OECD, 2021; UNESCO, 2021).

Strategic Implications and Organisational Transformation

The deployment of AI-driven administrative automation is not limited to improving operational efficiency; it reconfigures the organisational architecture of educational institutions. Schools and universities that adopt intelligent automation transition from hierarchical, siloed structures to more agile, networked forms of governance characterised by decentralised decision-making, cross-functional collaboration, and data transparency (Zawacki-Richter et al., 2019; Misuraca & van Noordt, 2021).

At the strategic level, automation facilitates:

Evidence-Based Leadership

Institutional leaders gain access to real-time dashboards, predictive models, and scenario simulations that support proactive, data-informed decision-making (Cobo-Rendón et al., 2023; ISTE, 2022).

Dynamic Resource Allocation

Intelligent systems enable resource reallocation based on emerging needs, patterns of use, and institutional performance indicators (Deep et al., 2024).

Customised Service Delivery

Automation permits tailored responses to students and families, enhancing satisfaction and equity in access to administrative services (Al-Jaf et al., 2024).

Continuous Institutional Learning

By capturing and analysing operational data, institutions can identify inefficiencies, measure the impact of interventions, and iteratively improve their processes (OECD/CAF, 2022).

Furthermore, the integration of automation into school governance necessitates a redefinition of professional roles. Administrative staff must develop new digital skills, while teachers are increasingly expected to interpret data visualisations and collaborate with AI tools to support student trajectories (Ertmer & Ottenbreit-Leftwich, 2020). Table 4 shows the main areas of strategic impact of administrative automation.

Table 4. Strategic impact areas of administrative automation

Domain	Transformation Enabled by Automation
Leadership and Planning	Real-time dashboards and scenario forecasting
Finance and Resource Use	Predictive budgeting, intelligent scheduling
Communication and Support	Automated responses, multilingual chatbots
Equity and Access	Personalised services, risk detection
Professional Development	AI-literacy, adaptive roles for staff and educators

This institutional metamorphosis underscores the fact that automation is not a purely technical upgrade but a transformative strategy that redefines the nature of educational leadership and school culture.

Epistemological Dimensions of Administrative Automation

At a deeper level, the rise of intelligent automation in educational administration prompts an epistemological shift in how institutions conceptualise knowledge, authority, and decision-making. Traditional models of administrative governance relied heavily on human discretion, anecdotal evidence, and linear planning. In contrast, automation enables probabilistic, data-rich, and iterative approaches to problem-solving. Three key epistemic shifts can be observed:

From Certainty to Probabilism

AI systems operate on probabilistic models that recognise uncertainty and model multiple possible futures, in contrast to deterministic, rule-based human decision-making (Russell & Norvig, 2021).

From Authority to Auditability

Decision-making is increasingly subjected to algorithmic traceability, challenging traditional notions of professional authority and replacing them with accountability mechanisms grounded in XAI (Arrieta et al., 2020).

From Reactive to Predictive Rationality

Institutions no longer wait for events to unfold; they anticipate them using predictive analytics and prepare pre-emptive responses (Naidu et al., 2017; Camelo et al., 2021).

This epistemological reorientation is particularly significant in the context of educational equity. Automation can either perpetuate existing biases—if trained on skewed data—or help correct them through algorithmic fairness and transparent logic (Floridi et al., 2022; Tiwari, 2023). Thus, administrative automation must be approached not only as a technological or managerial issue but as a knowledge system with political, ethical, and pedagogical consequences.

Ethical Parameters and Conceptual Integrity

Conceptual clarity in administrative automation also involves delineating its ethical contours. AI-based administrative systems process highly sensitive personal data, including biometric, academic, financial, and psychological information. Their implementation must be framed by an ethical architecture that encompasses:

Data Privacy and Security

Adhering to standards of consent, encryption, and access control to safeguard user data (Floridi et al., 2022; UNESCO, 2023).

Algorithmic Fairness

Ensuring that AI models do not reinforce discriminatory outcomes or marginalise vulnerable populations (Zawacki-Richter et al., 2019).

Human Oversight

Maintaining human responsibility for final decisions, particularly in high-stakes scenarios involving student progression, discipline, or resource exclusion (Arrieta et al., 2020).

Transparency and Explainability

Embedding explanatory mechanisms in systems to allow users to understand the rationale behind administrative outcomes (ISTE, 2022; OECD, 2022).

These dimensions are not ancillary but central to the conceptual legitimacy of administrative automation. Without a robust ethical framework, the promise of intelligent automation risks devolving into opaque technocratic control, undermining trust and participation in educational institutions.

Comparative Conceptual Models and Global Variability

Another salient dimension of administrative automation lies in the comparative analysis of conceptual models adopted across diverse educational systems. While the technological foundations are largely shared, the guiding philosophies and operational logics differ significantly according to regional contexts, regulatory traditions, and institutional cultures.

For instance, in East Asia, particularly South Korea, automation is framed within a techno-rationalist model emphasising optimisation, system integration, and surveillance for safety and efficiency (Lee et al., 2022). In contrast, Latin American initiatives—such as those led by the Ministry of Education in Colombia or by public universities in Brazil—tend to position automation within a social justice framework aimed at reducing dropout and enhancing equity through intelligent planning (Camelo et al., 2021; Ministerio TIC, 2022). Table 5 shows the conceptual variability by region in the global models of administrative automation.

Table 5. Conceptual variability in global models of administrative automation

Region	Conceptual Orientation	Institutional Priorities	Representative Features
East Asia	Techno-rationalism	Efficiency, safety, integration	Biometric tracking, system-wide data linkage
Latin America	Equity and inclusion	Dropout prevention, targeted intervention	Predictive models, AI-based diagnostics
Western Europe	Legal-ethical compliance	GDPR adherence, transparency, auditability	XAI systems, participatory dashboards
Anglo-American	Market-oriented innovation	Customisation, institutional competitiveness	Recommender systems, AI-enhanced enrolment tools

These models illustrate the adaptability of administrative automation to varied policy goals and cultural paradigms. Yet they also underscore the need for context-aware design that aligns technological capabilities with pedagogical and institutional values (UNESCO, 2021; World Bank, 2022).

Future-Ready Conceptualisation: Towards Administrative Intelligence 2.0

In its most advanced conceptual form, administrative automation points towards the emergence of what might be termed **Administrative Intelligence 2.0**—a synthesis of automation, analytics, ethics, and institutional learning. This emerging vision suggests a future where school administration:

- Continuously learns from data and feedback loops to improve decision-making.
- Adapts to complex environments through self-optimising algorithms.
- Prioritises stakeholder engagement through transparent interfaces and co-designed solutions.
- Maintains ethical vigilance through integrated audit mechanisms.

The development of **digital administrative twins**, capable of simulating entire institutional processes and testing strategic decisions in virtual environments, exemplifies this trajectory (OECD, 2021). Similarly, the increasing fusion of generative AI with administrative tasks opens new frontiers for intelligent reporting, automated documentation, and real-time multilingual communication—while also raising critical questions about authorship, accountability, and institutional voice (Bai et al., 2024; Wang et al., 2024).

These trends indicate that conceptual foundations must evolve in tandem with technological innovation, remaining analytically rigorous and ethically grounded. Educational leaders, policymakers, and technologists must thus engage in continuous dialogue to ensure that administrative automation contributes not only to efficiency, but also to institutional resilience, pedagogical relevance, and democratic governance.

Final Remarks on Conceptual Integrity

The conceptual foundations of administrative automation in education cannot be reduced to a single discipline, perspective, or methodology. They constitute a complex, dynamic, and interdisciplinary field that draws from computer science, organisational theory, educational leadership, ethics, and policy analysis. To articulate a coherent and actionable conceptual framework, it is necessary to embrace this complexity while maintaining clarity in terminology, rigour in epistemology, and commitment to equity and transparency.

Automation, when conceptually understood as a system of intelligent coordination rather than mechanical substitution, opens transformative possibilities for educational institutions. It enables a reimagining of administration as a responsive, learning, and participatory domain—one that can better support the core mission of education: to foster holistic human development in ever-changing societal contexts.

ARTIFICIAL INTELLIGENCE APPLIED TO EDUCATIONAL ADMINISTRATION

The advent of Artificial Intelligence (AI) in the field of educational administration has fundamentally transformed the conceptualisation, execution, and evaluation of institutional management processes. In an era marked by organisational complexity, an abundance of data, and the need for timely, evidence-based decision-making, AI emerges as an indispensable strategic resource for educational institutions. Unlike other digital technologies, AI does not merely automate repetitive tasks; rather, it imbues systems with cognitive capabilities such as autonomous learning, logical reasoning, and contextual adaptation. This enables a transition from traditional administrative models to algorithmic and predictive governance frameworks.

The application of core AI concepts—including machine learning, expert systems, computer vision, and natural language processing—has given rise to solutions that not only optimise resource allocation but also enhance the precision of decision-making, reinforce administrative transparency, and promote evidence-based management. Furthermore, the development of explainable AI (XAI) models addresses the growing demand for auditable and ethically responsible processes in sensitive domains such as education.

Accordingly, this section examines the principal conceptual foundations and operational models of AI specifically applied to educational administration. It explores their potential to enhance organisational efficiency, reduce operational uncertainty, and foster a data-driven institutional culture. This analysis is grounded in the latest scholarly developments and emerging implementation experiences, underscoring that AI constitutes not merely a technical tool but a structural component of the future of school governance.

Reconceptualising Educational Administration through Artificial Intelligence

The integration of Artificial Intelligence (AI) into educational administration represents a paradigmatic shift not merely in institutional operations, but in the epistemology, design, and implementation of school governance structures. Unlike traditional mechanistic approaches to management, AI-driven administration incorporates the cognitive, predictive, and adaptive capabilities of intelligent systems, enabling a departure from static, rule-bound workflows towards dynamic, data-informed, and learner-centred decision-making models (Russell & Norvig, 2021; Misuraca & van Noordt, 2021).

In this new configuration, educational administration no longer serves solely as a functional apparatus for record-keeping and logistical coordination. Rather, it is transformed into an intelligent interface between institutional objectives, stakeholder needs, and environmental variability. AI thus emerges as both a technological artefact and an epistemic agent—reconfiguring not only how schools operate, but how they perceive and respond to complexity, uncertainty, and diversity in educational contexts.

At the operational level, the deployment of AI facilitates automation of repetitive processes, enhances analytical accuracy, supports predictive forecasting, and offers explainable insights to administrative actors. At the strategic level, AI enables a form of anticipatory governance, in which institutional leaders can identify emergent trends, simulate potential interventions, and make ethically defensible decisions grounded in real-time data (Arrieta et al., 2020; Deep et al., 2024).

Systemic Roles of AI in Educational Management

To comprehend the full impact of AI within educational administration, it is necessary to articulate its multiple systemic roles, which extend beyond automation into the realms of analysis, recommendation, adaptation, and institutional learning. The main functional roles of AI in educational administration are described in Table 6.

Table 6. Functional roles of AI in educational administration

Role	Description
Automation	Execution of routine, rule-based tasks (e.g., attendance, fee processing).
Analytics	Interpretation of historical and real-time data patterns.
Prediction	Forecasting future scenarios (e.g., dropout risk, enrolment trends).
Recommendation	Suggesting optimal resource allocations or scheduling models.

continued on following page

Table 6. Continued

Role	Description
Explanation (XAI)	Providing transparent justifications for algorithmic outputs.
Institutional Adaptation	Enabling systems to evolve based on feedback and contextual learning.

This multi-functionality positions AI not as a monolithic solution but as a modular, evolving, and context-sensitive system architecture. Its effectiveness depends on institutional readiness, staff digital fluency, and alignment with pedagogical missions (OECD, 2021; UNESCO, 2021).

Cognitive Foundations of AI in School Governance

Educational administration is particularly well-suited to benefit from the cognitive underpinnings of AI—namely machine learning (ML), expert systems, natural language processing (NLP), and explainable AI (XAI). These technologies support a reorganisation of administrative logic from deterministic protocols to probabilistic, learning-based models capable of handling ambiguity and complexity (Naidu et al., 2017; Arrieta et al., 2020).

- **Machine Learning (ML)** facilitates adaptive modelling by enabling systems to identify patterns and improve their predictions over time. In administrative settings, ML supports dropout forecasting, staff scheduling, and budget optimisation (Camelo et al., 2021; Bird, 2023).
- **Expert Systems** formalise human knowledge into structured rules and inferences, aiding in policy implementation, conflict resolution, and compliance verification without requiring real-time human intervention.
- **Natural Language Processing (NLP)** allows systems to parse, generate, and understand human language, forming the foundation of chatbots, automated reporting systems, and document classifiers (Alhawiti, 2014; Al-Jaf et al., 2024).
- **Explainable AI (XAI)** is indispensable for institutional accountability, particularly in high-stakes decisions such as student placement, disciplinary actions, or financial disbursements. It ensures that algorithmic outputs are transparent, justifiable, and auditable by stakeholders (Arrieta et al., 2020).

Table 7 groups the core cognitive technologies, briefly describing their administrative functions.

Table 7. Core cognitive technologies and their administrative functions

Technology	Administrative Application
Machine Learning	Dropout prediction, resource forecasting, behavioural pattern analysis
Expert Systems	Policy enforcement, eligibility checks, exception handling
NLP	Chatbots, automated emails, sentiment analysis
XAI	Justification of classifications, compliance auditing

These cognitive foundations transform educational administration into a domain of continuous learning and adaptation, mirroring the principles of lifelong education at the institutional level.

From Process Optimisation to Predictive Governance

While the early stages of AI integration in education were primarily focused on process optimisation—automating attendance, documentation, and communication—the current wave is characterised by predictive governance. This involves the strategic use of AI models to anticipate institutional risks, simulate decision scenarios, and propose data-driven interventions (Cobo-Rendón et al., 2023; Bai et al., 2024).

For example, regression models and neural networks are employed to predict student dropout probabilities based on multidimensional indicators such as academic performance, socio-economic background, behavioural patterns, and psychological distress (Camelo et al., 2021; Bird, 2023). These predictive insights allow administrators to target support services proactively, reallocate resources, and even redesign curricula in response to emerging needs.

Clustering algorithms, commonly used in market segmentation, have been adapted to group students by learning profiles or attendance patterns, facilitating differentiated interventions. Likewise, fuzzy logic models enable flexible resource distribution where traditional binary classifications (e.g., pass/fail, at-risk/safe) are insufficient. Table 8 displays the predictive models and their strategic uses in education.

Table 8. Predictive models and their strategic uses in education

Model Type	Example of Use in School Administration
Regression Analysis	Forecasting staff absenteeism trends or budget fluctuations
Neural Networks	Modelling complex outcomes like long-term academic success
Clustering	Segmenting students for targeted interventions (e.g., support pathways)
Fuzzy Logic	Flexible scheduling, satisfaction modelling, prioritising interventions

Such predictive governance mechanisms not only enhance operational precision but also reinforce institutional responsiveness and equity.

Natural Language Interfaces and Intelligent Communication Systems

Effective communication constitutes a cornerstone of educational administration, encompassing interactions with students, parents, staff, and external authorities. Artificial Intelligence has introduced significant innovations in this domain through Natural Language Processing (NLP) technologies, which enable machines to understand, interpret, and generate human language in both written and spoken forms (Alhawiti, 2014; Al-Jaf et al., 2024).

Administrative chatbots, developed using NLP frameworks, offer real-time responses to enquiries about enrolment procedures, fee schedules, term dates, institutional policies, and more. These systems not only reduce administrative workloads but also increase accessibility, especially for users engaging with the institution outside of traditional working hours. Furthermore, chatbots trained with multilingual corpora enhance inclusion by supporting interactions with linguistically diverse stakeholders.

Voice assistants and automated email generators, also powered by NLP, are increasingly integrated into school management systems to facilitate document drafting, appointment scheduling, and incident reporting. Importantly, these systems are progressively linked to institutional databases, enabling context-aware interactions that reference specific student records or institutional events. The main applications of NLP in educational administration are displayed in Table 9.

Table 9. NLP applications in educational administration

NLP Tool	Functionality	Impact
Chatbots	Query resolution, data collection, FAQ interaction	Reduces staff workload, improves user experience
Email Generators	Automated report writing and notification dissemination	Enhances communication efficiency and uniformity
Voice Assistants	Hands-free scheduling and announcements	Increases accessibility, especially for visually impaired users
Sentiment Analysis	Monitoring of student feedback and teacher reports	Supports well-being and institutional climate assessment

In implementing these tools, institutions must ensure that automated communication adheres to standards of confidentiality, cultural sensitivity, and personalisation, avoiding depersonalisation or technocratic detachment.

AI for Strategic Resource Management

One of the most promising applications of AI in school administration lies in strategic resource management—encompassing human, financial, and physical assets (Table 10). AI enables institutions to allocate resources dynamically in response to shifting demands, usage patterns, and institutional priorities (Deep et al., 2024; OECD, 2022).

For example, intelligent timetabling systems use constraint satisfaction algorithms and machine learning to generate optimal class schedules based on teacher availability, room capacity, course prerequisites, and even student learning preferences. In larger universities, such systems have reduced scheduling conflicts and enhanced classroom utilisation efficiency by over 20% (Taye et al., 2023).

Budget forecasting tools leveraging regression analysis and predictive models can anticipate financial surpluses or shortfalls based on enrolment trends, expenditure histories, and policy changes. This allows for more accurate planning and minimises the risk of resource misallocation.

AI is also applied to staff workload balancing, wherein algorithms evaluate course loads, administrative tasks, and extracurricular commitments to ensure equitable distribution among faculty members. This mitigates burnout, enhances performance, and supports institutional fairness.

Table 10. AI-enabled resource management applications

Area of Application	AI Tool or Technique	Institutional Benefit
Timetabling	Constraint satisfaction, ML-based schedulers	Reduced conflicts, increased space utilisation
Budgeting	Time series models, regression analysis	Improved financial planning and risk mitigation
Staff Allocation	Workload modelling, rule-based distribution	Equity in task assignment, increased morale
Facility Management	Predictive maintenance via sensor analytics	Reduced downtime, lower maintenance costs

By reframing resource management as a predictive, data-informed process rather than a reactive, manual one, AI contributes to more agile, transparent, and accountable institutional governance.

Explainable AI and Institutional Accountability

As AI assumes a greater decision-making role in educational administration, the imperative for transparency and ethical justification becomes increasingly salient. This is especially critical in scenarios involving high-stakes decisions—such as student classification, disciplinary actions, or financial aid distribution—where opaque algorithms may result in reputational or legal consequences (Arrieta et al., 2020; Floridi et al., 2022).

Explainable Artificial Intelligence (XAI) addresses these concerns by embedding interpretability mechanisms within AI models. XAI systems generate human-readable explanations of their outputs, enabling stakeholders to understand the logic behind decisions and interrogate potential errors or biases (Table 11).

For example, if an AI model flags a student as at risk of dropping out, XAI would provide a rationale—such as declining attendance, low performance in specific subjects, or reduced engagement on digital platforms. This not only increases the legitimacy of automated decisions but also facilitates constructive intervention by school counsellors and administrators.

Moreover, explainability supports compliance with legal frameworks such as the European General Data Protection Regulation (GDPR), which enshrines the right to an explanation of algorithmic decisions affecting individuals (Bai et al., 2024).

Table 11. Functions and benefits of explainable AI in education

XAI Feature	Functionality	Benefit to Educational Administration
Feature Attribution	Highlights variables influencing model outputs	Enables targeted interventions and professional judgement
Visual Explanations	Provides graphical representations of decision logic	Enhances understanding among non-technical staff
Audit Logs	Maintains records of AI decisions and interactions	Facilitates compliance, transparency, and institutional trust
User Feedback Integration	Allows refinement of models based on user input	Improves system accuracy and relevance over time

Incorporating XAI into educational administration is thus not merely a technical refinement, but a moral and political commitment to responsible, participatory, and just use of technology.

Institutional Learning and Continuous Optimisation through AI

Beyond efficiency and automation, one of the most transformative potentials of Artificial Intelligence (AI) in educational administration lies in fostering institutional learning. Through iterative feedback loops, performance monitoring, and predictive insights, AI systems facilitate continuous improvement in administrative processes, stakeholder engagement, and decision-making structures (Luckin et al., 2022; ISTE, 2022) (Table 12).

Administrative platforms integrated with AI can monitor the impact of policy changes in real time, offering dashboards that reveal emerging patterns and unintended consequences. These platforms serve not only as operational tools but also as diagnostic instruments, allowing institutions to assess their responsiveness, equity, and adaptability.

For example, AI-enabled systems can track the effectiveness of student support programmes by correlating intervention data with academic and behavioural outcomes. They can also evaluate teacher workload distribution, facility usage, or the efficiency of communication protocols, thereby enabling evidence-based adjustments.

Moreover, AI contributes to knowledge management, automatically cataloguing documents, indexing institutional knowledge, and retrieving relevant information for planning, accreditation, or reporting purposes.

Table 12. AI applications supporting organisational learning

Function	AI Mechanism	Outcome for Educational Institutions
Policy Impact Assessment	Real-time data tracking, trend analysis	Responsive governance and policy refinement
Performance Feedback	Predictive modelling of intervention efficacy	Continuous optimisation of support programmes
Knowledge Management	Document indexing, semantic search	Efficient planning and reporting processes
Organisational Benchmarking	Cross-institutional data comparison	Informed goal-setting and progress evaluation

Through these mechanisms, AI strengthens not only the operational capacity of educational institutions but also their strategic intelligence and institutional memory.

AI-Driven Equity and Inclusive Governance

A critically important dimension of AI in educational administration is its capacity to promote equity and inclusive governance, provided it is developed and implemented responsibly. This framework reflects the emerging vision of a *Society 5.0*, in which artificial intelligence is positioned at the core of socio-technical processes to enhance human well-being and inclusive public administration (Cossio Franco et al., 2025). By identifying patterns of exclusion, detecting underserved populations, and enabling targeted support strategies, AI systems can contribute meaningfully to reducing disparities within the educational system (Camelo et al., 2021; Cobo-Rendón et al., 2023).

For instance, predictive analytics can be employed to detect early signs of disengagement among students from marginalised backgrounds, allowing for timely intervention. Similarly, recommender systems can be tailored to ensure equitable access to extracurricular programmes, scholarships, or academic counselling.

However, algorithmic equity is not a given. If left unchecked, AI models may reflect and amplify historical biases embedded in institutional data. Addressing this risk requires critical engagement with data sources, algorithmic transparency, participatory design processes, and continuous monitoring of disparate impacts (Floridi et al., 2022; Tiwari, 2023). Table 13 describes AI practices that support educational equity.

Table 13. AI practices supporting educational equity

Practice	Description	Impact on Inclusion
Bias Auditing	Regular examination of algorithmic outputs by demographic variables	Reduces risk of discriminatory outcomes
Equity-Focused Training Data	Inclusion of diverse and representative cases in training datasets	Increases fairness in predictions and recommendations
Stakeholder Co-Design	Involving educators and communities in AI tool development	Ensures contextual relevance and social legitimacy
Fairness Metrics	Implementation of measures such as equal opportunity or disparate impact	Monitors algorithmic performance across different populations

When coupled with ethical safeguards and participatory governance models, AI can become a powerful ally in the pursuit of educational justice.

Toward Adaptive and Ethical AI Architectures

The future of AI in educational administration is inexorably linked to its capacity to evolve as an adaptive, ethical, and context-aware system. As institutions face increasingly complex environments—including demographic shifts, global crises, and rapidly changing labour markets—AI tools must exhibit flexibility, interoperability, and responsiveness to local needs (UNESCO, 2023; OECD/CAF, 2022).

Emerging developments point toward the adoption of digital administrative twins—virtual replicas of institutional processes that allow leaders to simulate different policy scenarios, resource distributions, and intervention strategies before implementation. Similarly, advances in generative AI hold potential for automating complex reporting, policy drafting, and stakeholder communication in ways that preserve voice and nuance (Wang et al., 2024).

These advances, however, amplify the urgency of establishing robust governance frameworks. Key pillars of such frameworks include (Table 14):

- **Transparency**: Clear documentation of algorithms, data sources, and decision logic.
- **Accountability**: Allocation of responsibility for outcomes, including mechanisms for redress.
- **Inclusiveness**: Engagement of diverse stakeholders in design and oversight processes.
- **Sustainability**: Alignment of AI implementation with long-term institutional capacity and mission.

Table 14. Key design principles for future-proof AI in education

Principle	Operationalisation	Relevance to Educational Institutions
Transparency	Open-source algorithms, user-friendly explanations	Builds trust and ensures interpretability
Accountability	Audit trails, decision logs, human-in-the-loop configurations	Prevents misuse and protects institutional legitimacy
Inclusiveness	Participatory design, multilingual interfaces	Enhances usability and reduces digital marginalisation
Sustainability	Cost-effective deployment, scalable infrastructure	Ensures long-term viability and integration with core goals

Adhering to these principles transforms AI from a mere tool into a partner in the co-construction of intelligent, ethical, and future-ready educational institutions.

AI TOOLS FOR SCHOOL ADMINISTRATION

Contemporary school administration faces mounting challenges arising from organisational complexity, the heterogeneity of institutional actors, and the necessity of prompt, data-informed decision-making. In response, Artificial Intelligence (AI) tools have emerged as pivotal catalysts in the transformation of educational management systems, equipping institutions with more precise, efficient, and adaptive operational capabilities. Through integration with digital platforms, AI facilitates the automation of routine processes, alleviates administrative workload, detects critical situations preemptively, and provides strategic information in real time—an essential component for ensuring modern, transparent, and continuously improving school governance.

Among the most relevant applications are AI-enhanced school management systems that amalgamate traditional functionalities with predictive analytics, error detection, and automated report generation. The implementation of administrative chatbots has likewise revolutionised user service delivery, offering fluid, immediate, and scalable interaction with students, families, and staff. Rooted in natural language processing, these solutions significantly contribute to institutional operational efficiency.

Furthermore, tools such as predictive analytics and automated academic monitoring equip administrative and teaching teams with a comprehensive view of student performance and institutional dynamics. These technologies not only enhance educational administration but also fortify the human dimension of schooling by liberating time and resources for higher-value pedagogical activities. This section provides an in-depth examination of the principal AI tools currently employed in school management, assessing their benefits, limitations, and transformative potential within the ethical and technical frameworks guiding twenty-first-century education.

Robotic Process Automation (RPA) for Streamlining Administrative Tasks

Robotic Process Automation (RPA) has emerged as a critical tool for automating repetitive, rule-based tasks that typically burden school administrative staff. RPA involves the use of software "robots" or "bots" that interact with existing IT infrastructure in the same way a human user would, performing actions such as data entry, report generation, and data migration without human intervention (Willcocks et al., 2020). Key areas where RPA is applied in educational administration include (Table 15):

- **Student Enrolment**: Automating the processing of enrolment forms, validating student information, and updating student records in the central database.
- **Attendance Recording**: Integrating with biometric systems or digital forms to automatically log student attendance and generate corresponding reports.
- **Financial Management**: Automating tuition fee collections, generating invoices, and managing expense reports to ensure financial transparency and reduce clerical errors.
- **Staff Leave Management**: Automatically updating HR systems with staff leave requests, approving them based on predefined criteria, and notifying relevant parties.

Table 15. RPA applications in educational administration

Administrative Function	RPA Application	Benefit
Enrolment	Automates form processing and data updates	Increases enrolment efficiency and reduces errors
Attendance	Automatically records student attendance	Saves time and ensures accuracy in records
Finance Management	Automates invoice creation and payment tracking	Reduces administrative workload and errors
Leave Management	Automates leave requests and approvals	Enhances efficiency in HR management

The benefits of RPA include faster processing, fewer human errors, and the reallocation of staff resources to higher-value activities. Moreover, RPA systems are highly adaptable and scalable, making them suitable for use across different administrative levels, from small schools to large educational institutions.

Predictive Analytics for Decision Support and Risk Management

Predictive analytics is another AI tool that has transformative potential in school administration (Table 16). Using historical data, machine learning algorithms can forecast future outcomes, enabling administrators to make proactive, data-driven decisions. These predictive systems help identify trends, such as student dropout risk, enrolment fluctuations, or potential financial deficits, and recommend preemptive measures to mitigate adverse outcomes (Naidu et al., 2017; Cobo-Rendón et al., 2023). In the context of student management, predictive analytics can:

Identify At-Risk Students

By analysing academic performance, behavioural patterns, and attendance records, predictive models can flag students who are likely to disengage or drop out. Administrators can then implement targeted interventions, such as additional tutoring or counselling.

Forecast Enrolment Trends

By examining past enrolment data and demographic changes, predictive models can help schools anticipate future enrolment levels, optimising resources, and avoiding overcapacity or under-enrolment.

Enhance Resource Allocation

Predictive systems can forecast resource needs (e.g., staffing, classroom space, materials) based on projected student numbers and performance metrics.

Table 16. Predictive analytics applications in educational administration

Application	Functionality	Impact on Administration
Dropout Prediction	Analyses academic, behavioural, and attendance data	Identifies at-risk students, enabling early intervention
Enrolment Forecasting	Models trends based on historical and demographic data	Assists in resource planning and space allocation
Resource Optimisation	Uses predictive models to allocate resources based on projected needs	Increases efficiency in staffing and facility use

By providing actionable insights, predictive analytics empowers school leaders to make informed decisions that are not only reactive but also proactive, thereby enhancing overall institutional resilience and operational efficiency.

Timetabling and Scheduling Algorithms

Efficient scheduling is a perennial challenge in educational administration, particularly in institutions with large student populations, multiple programmes, and limited physical resources. AI-based timetabling tools leverage advanced algorithms to create optimal schedules, balancing constraints such as room availability, teacher workloads, and student preferences (Taye et al., 2023) (Table 17).

Intelligent Scheduling

AI timetabling systems use algorithms to generate the most efficient schedules, factoring in constraints like classroom capacity, instructor availability, and course prerequisites. These systems can also consider preferences from students and faculty, resulting in more personalised schedules.

Conflict Resolution

In cases where scheduling conflicts arise, AI tools automatically suggest adjustments, such as redistributing classes, reassigning rooms, or offering flexible scheduling options.

Dynamic Adaptation

Timetable adjustments based on real-time changes, such as unexpected teacher absences or enrolment fluctuations, can be handled automatically, ensuring minimal disruption to institutional activities.

Table 17. Timetabling and scheduling applications in educational administration

Application	Functionality	Benefit
Course Scheduling	Optimises course offerings and room assignments	Maximises resource usage and minimises conflicts
Teacher Allocation	Allocates teaching staff based on availability	Ensures balanced workloads and prevents burnout
Dynamic Rescheduling	Automatically adjusts schedules based on real-time changes	Enhances adaptability and reduces disruptions

AI-based scheduling tools represent a significant advancement over traditional methods, improving operational efficiency, reducing human error, and contributing to a more equitable allocation of resources.

Automated Reporting and Document Generation

AI tools also streamline the creation of reports, a crucial task in educational administration. Automating the production of standardised reports—such as performance evaluations, financial statements, and regulatory compliance documents—saves time and reduces the risk of errors associated with manual data entry (Bai et al., 2024; Kumar et al., 2025) (Table 18).

Automated Grade Reporting

AI tools integrated with Learning Management Systems (LMS) automatically generate and distribute grade reports, saving teachers significant time and ensuring consistency across reports.

Compliance Reporting

AI can also be used to automatically generate reports needed for compliance with government regulations or accrediting bodies, ensuring that all required documentation is completed and submitted on time.

Performance Analysis Reports

By aggregating data from various sources, AI tools generate performance reports that analyse trends in student performance, teacher effectiveness, and institutional health.

Table 18. Automated reporting applications in educational administration

Application	Functionality	Benefit
Grade Reporting	Automatically compiles and sends student grade reports	Increases accuracy and timeliness in academic reporting
Compliance Reporting	Automates the creation of regulatory and accreditation reports	Reduces administrative burden and ensures compliance
Performance Analysis	Aggregates performance data and generates reports	Provides actionable insights into institutional performance

Automated reporting tools not only enhance the efficiency and consistency of administrative processes but also provide administrators with data-driven insights that can inform decision-making and strategic planning.

Ethical and Legal Considerations in the Use of AI Tools

The deployment of AI tools in educational administration raises important ethical and legal concerns, particularly regarding data privacy, algorithmic fairness, and the transparency of automated decisions. As educational institutions handle sensitive personal information about students and staff, the implementation of AI systems must adhere to strict ethical guidelines and regulatory frameworks (Table 19).

Data Privacy

AI tools that process personal data, such as attendance records, grades, and health information, must comply with data protection laws, including the General Data Protection Regulation (GDPR) in the European Union and similar frameworks worldwide.

Bias and Fairness

AI algorithms can inadvertently reinforce existing biases if they are trained on historical data that reflects discriminatory practices. Ensuring fairness in algorithmic decisions requires careful auditing and testing to prevent harmful biases from affecting students, staff, and institutional outcomes (Floridi et al., 2022).

Accountability

As AI tools take on more decision-making roles in educational administration, it is essential to ensure transparency and accountability in the use of these systems. The implementation of explainable AI (XAI) allows administrators and stakeholders to understand the reasoning behind automated decisions.

Table 19. Ethical and legal considerations in AI tools

Issue	Consideration	Solution
Data Privacy	Ensuring compliance with data protection laws	Implement robust data encryption and access controls
Algorithmic Bias	Mitigating discrimination and biased outcomes	Regularly audit and test algorithms for fairness
Transparency and Accountability	Ensuring decision traceability	Use explainable AI (XAI) and maintain decision logs

Addressing these ethical and legal considerations is critical to ensuring that AI tools in school administration are used responsibly, equitably, and with respect for all stakeholders' rights.

PRACTICAL CASE STUDIES OF AUTOMATION IN SCHOOLS

The application of Artificial Intelligence (AI)-based automation tools in educational environments has transitioned from a theoretical prospect to a tangible reality that is redefining school administration across all educational levels. Amid increasing operational complexity, diversification of institutional functions, and the demand for measurable outcomes, automation serves as a crucial strategy for enhancing efficiency, reducing administrative burden, and facilitating more timely and evidence-based decision-making. Current advancements demonstrate that automated solutions can be adopted even in resource-constrained settings, provided they are integrated with strategic clarity, appropriate teacher training, and sustainable organisational models.

This section presents a detailed review of practical case studies where automation has been successfully implemented in basic, secondary, and higher education institutions. These range from biometric attendance systems in kindergartens to predictive algorithms for dropout detection in universities. Such examples illustrate the transformative potential of automation in enhancing school governance. They also examine initiatives such as administrative chatbots, intelligent planning platforms, and multidimensional analytics systems, which not only optimise internal processes but also provide timely, personalised responses to stakeholders. When implemented correctly, AI can become an enabler of institutional strengthening, educational equity, and school community wellbeing.

Case Study: AI-Driven Attendance Monitoring in Basic Education

The implementation of automated systems in basic education has increasingly facilitated the monitoring and management of student attendance (Table 20). One notable case is the adoption of biometric attendance systems in public schools in South Korea under the "AI4Schools" initiative. This project, launched in 2022, integrated facial recognition technology with real-time tracking systems to record student entry and exit, ensuring accurate attendance without manual input from teachers (Lee et al., 2022).

Biometric data, such as students' facial features, is captured upon their arrival at school and matched with pre-registered profiles in the central database. This system sends automated notifications to parents through a mobile app, alerting them if their child has arrived at school or left the premises during school hours. This system significantly reduced the administrative burden on school staff and improved operational efficiency. Teachers, previously tasked with manually tracking attendance, reported saving approximately 15 hours a week on administrative duties.

Furthermore, the system's integration with health and meal databases allowed for immediate alerts in case of emergencies, such as absences linked to illness, creating a safer environment for students (Pramukawati et al., 2024).

Table 20. Key features of AI-driven attendance systems

Feature	Description	Benefit
Biometric Facial Recognition	Identifies students using facial features	Ensures accurate, fast attendance tracking
Automated Parent Notifications	Sends real-time alerts to parents	Increases transparency and parental involvement
Integration with Health Data	Links attendance data with health databases	Improves student safety and facilitates emergency response
Time Saving	Reduces time spent on manual attendance logging	Enhances teacher productivity by freeing time for pedagogy

This case study exemplifies the use of AI to automate routine administrative tasks while enhancing parental engagement and overall school safety. The success of this system in South Korea provides a compelling model for other regions aiming to streamline attendance tracking in primary schools.

Case Study: AI-Powered Enrolment and Timetabling in Secondary Education

At the secondary education level, AI tools have been instrumental in optimising the enrolment process and timetabling (Table 21). In Colombia, the Ministry of Information and Communications Technologies implemented the "Intelligent Education Programme" in 2021, which deployed AI-powered chatbots to manage student enrolment and academic scheduling in over 100 public technical secondary schools.

The AI system, which uses predictive analytics, forecasts enrolment trends by analysing historical data, demographic changes, and regional population shifts. This system suggests optimal course offerings based on student interests, academic performance, and institutional goals. In addition, AI algorithms automatically assign students to courses based on availability and academic requirements, ensuring an efficient use of teaching resources and classroom space (Ministerio TIC, 2022).

This AI tool significantly reduced the manual workload of administrative staff and teachers. Previously, scheduling conflicts and resource shortages were a recurring problem, leading to delays in class allocation and teacher assignments. However, the AI-powered system reduced scheduling conflicts by 22% and improved student satisfaction by offering personalised, efficient course allocations. Moreover, AI-generated enrolment forecasts allowed school administrators to better plan staffing and resource distribution, improving operational planning.

Table 21. AI-powered enrolment and timetabling system features

Feature	Description	Benefit
Predictive Analytics	Uses data to forecast enrolment trends	Enhances resource allocation and reduces capacity issues
Automated Course Assignment	Assigns students to courses based on data-driven criteria	Ensures efficient use of teaching resources and student satisfaction
Conflict Resolution	Detects and resolves scheduling conflicts automatically	Saves time and enhances operational efficiency
Personalised Scheduling	Offers students personalised course options	Increases student engagement and satisfaction

The integration of AI in enrolment and timetabling at Colombia's technical schools has demonstrated significant improvements in efficiency, resource management, and student engagement. This case study illustrates the potential of AI tools to optimise administrative processes and enhance the overall educational experience in secondary schools.

Case Study: Predictive Analytics for Dropout Prevention in Higher Education

In the context of higher education, AI tools have been increasingly applied to identify students at risk of dropping out and to implement timely intervention strategies (Table 22). The University of São Paulo (USP) in Brazil has implemented an advanced predictive analytics system designed to forecast student dropout rates within its engineering programmes. This system, based on artificial neural networks (ANNs), analyses a wide array of data inputs, including academic performance, socio-economic background, psychological stress indicators, and participation in extracurricular activities (Camelo et al., 2021).

The AI model successfully predicted potential dropouts with an accuracy rate of 85%, allowing the university's student support services to intervene proactively. In practice, the system provided alerts to academic advisors and counsellors when students' academic performance or attendance patterns indicated early signs of disengagement. These interventions included personalised tutoring, counselling sessions, and engagement with support groups, which helped students address academic or personal challenges before they led to formal dropout decisions.

As a result, the university reported a 20% reduction in dropout rates over the course of three years. The predictive analytics system not only assisted in retaining students but also helped the institution allocate resources more effectively, improving overall student success rates (Camelo et al., 2021).

Table 22. Predictive analytics system in dropout prevention

Feature	Description	Benefit
Neural Network-Based Prediction	Uses ANN models to predict student dropout risk	Identifies at-risk students early, enabling targeted interventions
Data Integration	Analyzes multiple data points including academic performance, psychological indicators, and extracurricular activity	Provides a holistic view of student wellbeing
Proactive Alerts	Notifies academic advisors when students exhibit risk factors	Allows timely interventions to improve student retention
Resource Allocation	Allocates tutoring and counselling based on AI predictions	Improves institutional resource efficiency and student outcomes

The case of the University of São Paulo exemplifies how AI-driven predictive systems can address the critical issue of student retention in higher education, offering both operational and academic benefits.

Case Study: AI in Financial Management for University Systems

Another promising application of AI in educational administration is in the management of finances and tuition fee collections (Table 23). The University of Melbourne, one of Australia's leading institutions, implemented an AI-based financial forecasting system to predict tuition fee delinquency and optimize financial operations. This system uses supervised machine learning algorithms to analyse past payment patterns, student demographic information, and external factors such as economic conditions to forecast the likelihood of tuition fee defaults.

By identifying high-risk students early in the enrolment process, the university's finance department was able to reach out to these students proactively, offering tailored payment plans, financial aid information, and other support services to ensure timely payments. As a result, the university saw a 15% improvement in fee collection rates and a significant reduction in late payment fees, benefiting both the institution's financial stability and students' financial wellbeing (Taye et al., 2023).

Table 23. AI financial management system features

Feature	Description	Benefit
Fee Delinquency Prediction	Uses machine learning to predict student payment default	Improves cash flow management by addressing payment issues early
Personalised Payment Plans	Automatically suggests customised payment options for at-risk students	Enhances student satisfaction and reduces financial stress
Financial Aid Optimization	Recommends appropriate financial aid options	Increases financial accessibility and reduces dropout rates due to financial hardship
Cost Reduction	Minimises human intervention in fee processing	Reduces administrative costs and streamlines operations

The success of this AI tool demonstrates how predictive analytics and machine learning can be leveraged to enhance financial administration in universities, ultimately supporting institutional sustainability.

Case Study: AI-Based Academic Monitoring in Secondary Schools

At the secondary school level, AI-based academic monitoring systems have become invaluable tools for both teachers and administrators in managing student performance (Table 24). A case study from Spain highlights the successful implementation of an AI-powered predictive system at Juan de Herrera Secondary School in Valladolid. This system was designed to analyse students' academic records, attendance data, and behavioural patterns to predict potential academic underperformance or disengagement.

Using regression analysis and decision trees, the system generated early alerts for educators and counsellors about students who were at risk of failing or dropping out. The AI system's predictions were based on a variety of factors, including grades, absenteeism, participation in extracurricular activities, and interactions within the school environment (Vargas, 2024).

Teachers and staff were able to intervene proactively with targeted support for struggling students, including additional tutoring, mentorship, and adjusted learning materials. The school reported an 18% decrease in dropout rates and a 25% improvement in overall student performance after the first year of implementing the system.

This case demonstrates the effectiveness of AI in secondary education, where personalised interventions based on data-driven insights can significantly enhance student retention and academic outcomes.

Table 24. Key features of AI academic monitoring systems

Feature	Description	Benefit
Performance Prediction	Predicts at-risk students using academic and behavioural data	Enables early intervention and targeted support
Regression Analysis	Analyzes past data to identify trends in student performance	Improves decision-making and resource allocation
Data Integration	Combines multiple data sources such as grades, attendance, and extracurricular involvement	Provides a holistic view of student engagement
Intervention Alerts	Notifies educators and administrators about students at risk	Facilitates timely action to improve academic outcomes

By using AI to monitor academic progress and predict challenges, Juan de Herrera Secondary School was able to create a more supportive, responsive environment for its students, leading to improved outcomes across the board.

Case Study: AI in Staff Scheduling and Resource Allocation

The complexity of managing staffing schedules in educational institutions can often lead to inefficiencies, especially in large schools or universities (Table 25). AI-powered scheduling systems have been instrumental in addressing these challenges. The University of Melbourne adopted an AI-based resource scheduling tool known as SmartScheduler to optimise the allocation of classroom space and teaching staff.

The system uses evolutionary algorithms and machine learning to generate optimal schedules by considering factors such as room capacity, instructor availability, course prerequisites, and even historical attendance patterns. By factoring in these variables, SmartScheduler minimised scheduling conflicts and improved classroom usage efficiency by 25%. The system also identified areas of over-utilisation and under-utilisation, enabling administrators to better allocate resources and reduce idle time (Taye et al., 2023).

Furthermore, the tool integrated with the university's human resource management system to balance faculty workloads. By automatically adjusting teaching assignments based on faculty availability, preferences, and workload limits, SmartScheduler improved staff satisfaction and retention by reducing scheduling conflicts and overwork.

Table 25. AI-based scheduling and resource allocation

Feature	Description	Benefit
Optimal Scheduling	Uses algorithms to create efficient class schedules	Minimises conflicts, reduces idle time, and maximises space usage
Workload Balancing	Balances faculty schedules based on availability and preferences	Increases staff satisfaction and reduces burnout
Predictive Resource Allocation	Forecasts room and faculty needs based on past usage	Enhances resource allocation and planning
Real-Time Adjustments	Adjusts schedules in real time based on unforeseen changes	Reduces disruption and ensures smooth operations

This case exemplifies how AI-based scheduling systems can optimise administrative efficiency in higher education institutions, ensuring both space and human resources are used effectively, leading to improved operational management and employee satisfaction.

Case Study: AI in Parental Communication and Engagement

Parental engagement is a critical factor in student success, but schools often struggle to maintain consistent communication with families (Table 26). AI-powered chatbots have been employed in several schools to enhance parental communication and engagement. In Mexico, the Ministry of Public Education launched a pilot project that deployed an AI-driven chatbot to streamline communication between parents and schools.

The chatbot, named EduBot, was integrated into the school's existing communication platform and allowed parents to quickly access information about their child's academic progress, school events, and attendance records. EduBot also sent automated reminders about upcoming parent-teacher meetings, important school dates, and student health records (SEP, 2023).

Moreover, the AI system collected feedback from parents regarding their satisfaction with school services, which was then analysed to help schools improve their engagement strategies. The success of the project led to its expansion across several regions, with schools reporting an 80% increase in parental engagement and a significant improvement in the overall satisfaction of both parents and educators.

Table 26. AI-enhanced parental communication system features

Feature	Description	Benefit
Automated Information Retrieval	Allows parents to query school-related information via chatbot	Provides quick, convenient access to critical information
Event and Deadline Reminders	Sends automated notifications to parents about school events	Increases parental involvement and reduces missed opportunities
Feedback Collection	Collects parental feedback on school services	Enables schools to improve engagement strategies
Personalised Communication	Provides tailored updates on individual students	Enhances communication and strengthens parent-school partnerships

This case study highlights the effectiveness of AI chatbots in increasing parental engagement and fostering a more communicative and supportive school environment, ultimately benefiting student development.

Case Study: AI in Academic and Behavioural Support for At-Risk Students

In the United Kingdom, AI-based early warning systems have been implemented in several schools to identify students who may be at risk academically or behaviourally. These systems utilise machine learning and predictive analytics to track patterns in academic performance, attendance, and behavioural incidents, providing real-time alerts to school staff (Table 27).

For example, the "Early Intervention" project at a secondary school in London integrated AI tools to monitor students' progress and alert counsellors or mentors when students showed signs of disengagement or distress. The system flagged students who exhibited a combination of poor grades, high absenteeism, and disruptive behaviour. The alerts were sent to the student's academic advisor, who could then arrange for personalised interventions such as academic tutoring, mental health support, or parental meetings.

This proactive approach led to a 15% improvement in student retention and a significant reduction in behavioural incidents. Schools using the system found that interventions, initiated before problems escalated, had a far greater impact on student outcomes compared to reactive measures.

Table 27. AI-based early warning system features

Feature	Description	Benefit
Predictive Behavioural Analysis	Tracks academic, attendance, and behaviour patterns	Identifies at-risk students early, enabling timely interventions
Real-Time Alerts	Notifies educators and counsellors about students at risk	Facilitates rapid intervention and personalised support
Data Integration	Integrates academic, behavioural, and attendance data	Provides a comprehensive view of student engagement
Tailored Interventions	Recommends personalised support plans for each student	Improves student retention and engagement

This case illustrates how AI-based early warning systems can significantly improve student retention and behavioural outcomes by enabling timely, targeted interventions.

The case studies presented here demonstrate that AI-powered tools are increasingly being implemented in schools to optimise administrative functions, improve student outcomes, and enhance stakeholder engagement. From attendance tracking and academic monitoring to financial management and parental communication, AI is transforming the landscape of school administration.

These practical implementations show that AI technologies not only help reduce administrative burdens but also enable schools to provide more personalised, efficient, and responsive services to students, parents, and staff. As these technologies continue to evolve, their integration into educational systems promises to further enhance institutional effectiveness and student success across the globe.

BENEFITS OF AI-BASED ADMINISTRATIVE AUTOMATION

The integration of Artificial Intelligence (AI) into school administrative processes constitutes a structural transformation in the governance of contemporary educational institutions. Faced with growing operational complexity, increasing demands for transparency, and the imperative to manage resources more efficiently, AI-assisted administrative automation offers a robust, innovative, and sustainable solution. This paradigm not only reshapes routine administrative activities but also redefines the role of educational personnel by enabling them to focus on higher-value pedagogical functions.

AI-driven automation generates multifaceted benefits, ranging from enhanced operational efficiency to the significant reduction of human error and associated costs. Intelligent algorithms executing routine tasks—such as timetabling, enrolment processing, and report generation—deliver these outputs with significantly greater speed and accuracy, contributing to institutional agility (Deep et al., 2024; West, 2021). Furthermore, such systems improve the reliability and traceability of procedures, facilitating auditability, transparency, and regulatory compliance (Zawacki-Richter et al., 2019).

One of the most strategically important advantages lies in liberating human capital for pedagogical and developmental functions. Teachers and school leaders, traditionally encumbered by administrative duties, can redirect their time and efforts towards curriculum planning, personalised student engagement, and educational innovation (Luckin et al., 2022). According to the International Society for Technology in Education (ISTE, 2022), this role reconfiguration enhances both educational quality and staff satisfaction. Thus, AI-based administrative automation not only modernises organisational structures but also fosters a more intelligent, learning-centred, and adaptable form of educational management.

Enhanced Operational Efficiency

Perhaps the most immediately observable benefit of AI automation in school administration is the improvement of operational efficiency. Repetitive tasks can be executed more rapidly, accurately, and consistently than through traditional manual methods. By eliminating common bottlenecks in processes such as enrolment, certification issuance, timetabling, and inventory management, AI optimises workflow and accelerates institutional responsiveness (Deep et al., 2024).

For example, AI-driven class scheduling using evolutionary algorithms and machine learning can reduce planning time from weeks to minutes while achieving a better balance of resource availability and user preferences. Moreover, the implementation of intelligent dashboards supports real-time, data-driven decision-making, enhancing responsiveness to emergencies and unforeseen changes.

A 2021 study by the Brookings Institution involving 130 educational institutions across 12 countries found that those employing automated AI processes reported an average 28% improvement in overall operational efficiency, as measured by time savings, duplication reduction, and enhanced administrative compliance (West, 2021).

Reduction of Human Error and Costs

AI automation also results in a substantial reduction in human error. Administrative tasks such as data entry, fee calculation, and record management are prone to mistakes when conducted manually. Automation increases accuracy, facilitates audit trails, and enhances procedural reliability (Zawacki-Richter et al., 2019).

From an economic standpoint, automation decreases operational costs by minimising the need for personnel dedicated solely to repetitive tasks, optimising the use of physical resources (e.g., paper, storage), and mitigating financial losses from administrative errors. For instance, automated billing systems in higher education institutions have led to a 40% reduction in complaints and corrections in accounting records (OECD, 2022; OECD/CAF 2022).

Additionally, automated systems often operate continuously or beyond traditional working hours, thereby reducing the need for overtime or temporary staffing during peak periods such as enrolment.

Reallocation of Human Resources to Pedagogical Activities

A particularly strategic benefit of administrative automation lies in the reallocation of human resources toward pedagogical and institutional development tasks. Educators and school leaders have historically borne significant administrative responsibilities, detracting from their core educational roles.

Deploying intelligent tools to handle tasks such as report generation, attendance monitoring, parent communication, or assignment tracking allows staff to concentrate on lesson design, individualised tutoring, and pedagogical innovation (Luckin et al., 2022). This shift not only enhances educational quality but also improves professional wellbeing.

A 2022 ISTE report highlighted that educators working in environments with administrative automation reported a 35% increase in job satisfaction, citing greater professional autonomy and reduced bureaucratic load as key factors.

CHALLENGES AND LIMITATIONS OF AI IN SCHOOL AUTOMATION

Despite the documented advantages of Artificial Intelligence (AI)-assisted automation in school administration, its implementation is not without significant technical, ethical, institutional, and human challenges. These limitations can hinder adoption and affect the long-term efficacy and sustainability of such initiatives.

A primary obstacle is the existence of technological and infrastructural barriers. In many educational systems—particularly in developing regions—there is a marked deficit in digital connectivity, up-to-date equipment, and interoperable platforms, all of which constrain the effective deployment of automated solutions (UNESCO, 2023; World Bank, 2022). These limitations exacerbate existing digital divides, potentially reinforcing inequities in access to advanced educational tools.

Moreover, the use of AI in school administration raises critical ethical and legal concerns, especially regarding the privacy of students' and teachers' personal data. The large-scale collection of sensitive information—including academic records, biometric identifiers, and health reports—necessitates robust data governance founded on transparency, security, informed consent, and human oversight (Floridi et al., 2022; Tiwari, 2023).

Resistance to change among educational personnel and a general deficiency in digital competencies further impede effective adoption. Addressing these issues requires not only investment in infrastructure and legal frameworks but also institutional leadership, ongoing professional development, and an organisational culture that embraces technological innovation (Ertmer & Ottenbreit-Leftwich, 2020; OECD, 2021; OECD/CAF 2022). Ultimately, the success of school automation depends less on technological availability and more on the educational system's capacity to implement these tools ethically, equitably, and adaptively.

Technological and Infrastructure Barriers

While promising, the implementation of AI-driven automation systems in education faces numerous technological barriers. These include limited internet access, insufficient digital infrastructure, and outdated computing resources—particularly in public schools in low- and middle-income countries (UNESCO, 2023).

Furthermore, maintaining and upgrading intelligent systems requires specialised technical expertise and consistent financial investment, both of which are frequently beyond the scope of school budgets. The digital divide between urban and rural areas compounds this challenge, risking the technological exclusion of disadvantaged communities (World Bank, 2022).

Interoperability poses another significant barrier. Many existing educational management systems lack standardisation, complicating integration with new automation tools and potentially resulting in data duplication or inconsistency.

Ethical and Data Privacy Concerns

Another critical challenge pertains to the ethical and legal ramifications of data collection, storage, and usage—particularly with regard to minors. AI systems in school administration process highly sensitive data, necessitating strict compliance with privacy regulations such as the European Union's General Data Protection Regulation (GDPR) or equivalent national legislation (Floridi et al., 2022).

Risks include unauthorised third-party access, excessive algorithmic surveillance, and automated decision-making without appropriate human supervision. It is therefore essential to establish mechanisms for algorithmic transparency, informed consent, and regular audits of implemented systems (Tiwari, 2023).

Moreover, algorithmic bias remains an area of active concern. If AI systems are trained on data that reflect structural inequalities, they may perpetuate or even exacerbate disparities in administrative outcomes—such as scholarship access, resource distribution, or disciplinary decisions.

Resistance to Change and Staff Training

The shift toward automated administrative systems is not solely a technological transition but also an organisational and cultural one. Many educators and administrative staff express resistance due to fears of job displacement, loss of control, or the perceived complexity of new technologies (Ertmer & Ottenbreit-Leftwich, 2020).

In many contexts, inadequate training prevents personnel from effectively utilising automation tools and may foster distrust in their reliability. Therefore, it is imperative to complement the implementation of AI with continuous professional development, accessible technical support, and participatory leadership strategies that promote institutional ownership of the technology (OECD, 2021).

A user-centred approach that values educators' professional expertise can facilitate more ethical, sustainable, and meaningful adoption of automation systems in schools.

FUTURE PROJECTIONS

The automation of administrative tasks through Artificial Intelligence (AI) in educational environments signifies a profound reconfiguration of traditional organisational processes across all levels of schooling. As previously discussed, its implementation not only improves operational efficiency and minimises human error but also liberates educators and administrators from burdensome bureaucratic functions, thereby enabling greater focus on strategic pedagogical responsibilities.

Documented case studies from diverse regions underscore that automation is no longer a futuristic ideal but a present-day reality.

However, this transformation demands a balanced approach—one that acknowledges both the technical advantages and the ethical, organisational, and cultural challenges. Technological infrastructure, staff digital literacy, data governance frameworks, and institutional adaptability are all pivotal factors influencing the success or failure of such initiatives. Automation should not be viewed merely as a mechanism for efficiency enhancement but rather as an opportunity to redesign school processes with a focus on student-centredness, educational equity, and institutional sustainability.

Looking ahead, the proliferation of technologies such as generative AI, deep learning, and digital administrative twins is expected to expand, enabling more accurate predictions, earlier interventions, and increasingly adaptive support systems. Next-generation administrative platforms in education will likely incorporate self-assessment capabilities for institutional performance, autonomous planning scenario design, and automated multichannel communication with all stakeholders.

Equally vital will be the development of robust, transparent, and ethical regulatory frameworks to guide AI use in education. These should protect the digital rights of students and staff, prevent algorithmic bias, and ensure all automated interventions remain under responsible human supervision.

Administrative automation with AI represents one of the most promising pathways toward systemic improvement in contemporary education. Its success, however, will depend not solely on technological sophistication but on a humanistic, inclusive, and critically reflective vision of digital transformation in education.

CONCLUSIONS

The integration of Artificial Intelligence (AI) into educational administration represents a transformative shift, not just in the technological framework of educational institutions, but also in their operational and strategic management. The profound implications of this change encompass multiple dimensions, from operational efficiency and data-driven decision-making to the reallocation of human resources and the development of more personalised, student-centred administrative processes.

AI-based automation in educational administration offers numerous benefits, chief among them being the substantial increase in efficiency. The automation of routine tasks, such as attendance tracking, grading, and enrolment processing, allows educational institutions to redirect their human resources from menial tasks to more complex pedagogical duties. The reduction of administrative burdens, coupled with the ability to provide real-time data insights, helps decision-makers within educational institutions make informed, evidence-based decisions that enhance overall governance (Bai et al., 2024; Wang et al., 2024).

Furthermore, AI facilitates the seamless integration of different administrative systems, providing a holistic view of institutional operations. For example, integrated AI-driven school management systems (SMS) enable administrators to track student performance, attendance, and even resource allocation in real-time. These systems not only automate data entry but also analyse trends, predict potential issues, and generate insights that allow for quicker, more effective responses. This predictive capability, as seen in systems designed for early dropout detection or resource allocation, ensures that issues are addressed before they escalate, thus promoting long-term institutional sustainability and improving student outcomes (Cobo-Rendón et al., 2023; Taye et al., 2023).

However, despite the myriad benefits, the widespread implementation of AI tools in educational administration is fraught with challenges. A key concern is the digital divide that exists between schools in developed and developing regions. Many institutions, particularly in low-resource settings, face significant barriers to adopting AI tools due to inadequate technological infrastructure, limited access to high-speed internet, and insufficient technical expertise. These disparities in access to technology can exacerbate existing inequalities in educational quality and opportunities (UNESCO, 2023; World Bank, 2022). Therefore, it is essential that AI integration be approached with a clear strategy that ensures equitable access to technology and supports continuous professional development for staff.

Another significant challenge lies in the ethical implications of AI integration, particularly concerning data privacy and algorithmic bias. As AI systems rely on vast amounts of data, the collection, storage, and use of student information must be handled with the utmost care, ensuring compliance with global standards such as the General Data Protection Regulation (GDPR). Educational institutions must implement robust data governance frameworks to protect sensitive personal information and ensure that AI tools are used responsibly and transparently (Floridi et al., 2022; Tiwari, 2023).

Moreover, AI systems can unintentionally perpetuate existing biases if the data used to train these systems are not representative or if the algorithms are not carefully monitored. This is particularly critical in educational settings, where biased decision-making can adversely affect students' academic progression, access to resources, and overall educational experience. Therefore, ongoing efforts are needed to ensure that AI tools in education are fair, transparent, and auditable, with mechanisms for human oversight and accountability (Arrieta et al., 2020; Misuraca & van Noordt, 2021).

To mitigate these risks and challenges, it is crucial to engage stakeholders—teachers, administrators, policymakers, and students—in the design and implementation process of AI tools. A participatory approach will help ensure that AI technologies align with the educational goals of the institution, address the specific needs of students and staff, and uphold the ethical standards that guide educational practice. Additionally, professional development programmes for educators and administrators should be prioritised to enhance their understanding of AI tools, their potential applications, and the ethical considerations involved (Ertmer & Ottenbreit-Leftwich, 2020; UNESCO, 2021). Table 28 presents the key benefits and challenges of AI in educational administration.

Table 28. Key benefits and challenges of AI in educational administration

Benefit	Challenge	Solution/Recommendation
Enhanced efficiency through automation	Digital divide and unequal access to technology	Ensure equitable access, infrastructure investment, and training
Data-driven decision-making	Data privacy concerns and ethical dilemmas	Implement strict data governance and privacy measures
Predictive capabilities for dropout prevention	Algorithmic bias and fairness issues	Regularly audit and test algorithms for bias, involve diverse stakeholders
Reallocation of human resources to pedagogy	Resistance to change among educational staff	Promote professional development and change management strategies

Looking towards the future, AI holds significant potential for further transforming educational administration. As the sophistication of AI tools continues to evolve, we can expect even more integrated and adaptive systems that enhance the responsiveness of schools to the needs of students, parents, and staff. Innovations such as AI-powered digital twins, which simulate entire institutional processes, and generative AI for report writing and curriculum development, may soon be commonplace in educational institutions (Bai et al., 2024). These tools will further extend the reach of AI, not only in administrative functions but also in teaching and learning, providing personalised learning experiences and supporting the professional growth of educators.

However, the full realisation of AI's potential in education will depend on a balanced approach. Institutions must adopt AI tools with a clear understanding of the accompanying ethical, social, and cultural considerations. Moreover, AI should always be used to augment, rather than replace, human expertise and judgement. Educational systems must remain rooted in the values of equity, transparency, and human dignity, ensuring that AI supports the mission of education: fostering the holistic development of individuals within a fair, inclusive, and responsible environment.

In conclusion, the automation of administrative tasks through AI technologies presents an opportunity to revolutionise educational management by improving efficiency, enhancing decision-making, and providing personalised services. However, it also presents challenges that require careful consideration and mitigation.

By addressing these challenges thoughtfully, and ensuring that AI is implemented in a way that respects ethical guidelines and supports educational equity, AI can become a powerful ally in the ongoing effort to improve educational outcomes for all students.

REFERENCES

Al-Jaf, K., Öz, C., Mahmud, H., & Rashid, T. A. (2024). Leveraging Chatbots for Effective Educational Administration: A Systematic Review. https://doi.org/DOI: 10.20944/preprints202410.0238.v1

Alhawiti, K. M. (2014). Natural Language Processing and its Use in Education. [ijacsa]. *International Journal of Advanced Computer Science and Applications*, *5*(12), 2014. DOI: 10.14569/IJACSA.2014.051210

Anzures-Garcia, M., Sánchez-Gálvez, L. A., Larios Gómez, M., Tapia Rodríguez, A., & Aguirre Agustín, R., & otros. (2024). IAA-CNN: Intelligent Attendance Algorithm based on Convolutional Neural Networks. *International Journal of Combinatorial Optimization Problems and Informatics*, *15*(5), 51–63. DOI: 10.61467/2007.1558.2024.v15i5

Arrieta, A. B., Díaz-Rodríguez, N., Del Ser, J., Bennetot, A., Tabik, S., Barbado, A., & Herrera, F. (2020). Explainable artificial intelligence (XAI): Concepts, taxonomies, opportunities and challenges toward responsible AI. *Information Fusion*, *58*, 82–115. DOI: 10.1016/j.inffus.2019.12.012

Bai, J. Y. H., Zawacki-Richter, O., & Muskens, W. (2024). Re-Examining the Future Prospects of Artificial Intelligence in Education in Light of the GDPR and ChatGPT. *Turkish Online Journal of Distance Education*. Advance online publication. DOI: 10.17718/tojde.1248901

Bird, K. (2023, Fall). Predictive Analytics in Higher Education: The Promises and Challenges of Using Machine Learning to Improve Student Success. *Air Professional File*, 161. Advance online publication. DOI: 10.34315/apf1612023

Boumediene, H., & Bouakkaz, M. (2025). Artificial Intelligence in Education: Emerging Trends, Ethical Considerations, and Future Directions. In Cela, E., Vajjhala, N., & Fonkam, M. (Eds.), *Next-Generation AI Methodologies in Education* (pp. 407–438). IGI Global Scientific Publishing., DOI: 10.4018/979-8-3693-7220-3.ch014

Camelo, D. M. A., Santos, J. C. C., Martins, M. P. G., Martins, M. P. G., & Gouveia, P. D. F. (2021). *Modelling Academic Dropout in Computer Engineering Using Artificial Neural Networks*. Springer., DOI: 10.1007/978-3-030-72651-5_14

Cobo-Rendón, R., León-Morales, C. A., & Godoy, A. (2023). Predictive analytics in student retention: A practical model for early intervention. Computers & Education. *Artificial Intelligence*, *4*, 100132. DOI: 10.1016/j.caeai.2023.100132

Cossio Franco, E. G., Arreola Marín, M. E., Sossa Azuela, J. H., Chávez Marcial, M., Alcántar Alcántar, J. I., & Moya Sánchez, E. U. (2025). Artificial Intelligence & Society 5.0. *International Journal of Combinatorial Optimization Problems and Informatics*, *16*(2), 55–59. DOI: 10.61467/2007.1558.2025.v16i2.1073

Deep, S., Athimoolam, K., & Enoch, T. (2024). Optimizing Administrative Efficiency and Student engagement in Education: The Impact of AI. *International Journal of Current Science Research and Review*, *07*(10). Advance online publication. DOI: 10.47191/ijcsrr/v7-i10-34

Đurović, G., Holenko Dlab, M., & Hoić-Božić, N. (2018). Educational Recommender Systems: An Overview and Guidelines for Further Research and Development / Obrazovni sustavi preporučivanja: pregled stanja sa smjernicama za daljnja istraživanja i razvoj. *Croatian Journal of Education-Hrvatski Casopis Za Odgoj i Obrazovanje*, *20*(2), 531–560. DOI: 10.15516/CJE.V20I2.2659

Ertmer, P. A., & Ottenbreit-Leftwich, A. T. (2020). Teacher technology change: How knowledge, confidence, beliefs, and culture intersect. *Journal of Research on Technology in Education*, *42*(3), 255–284. DOI: 10.1080/15391523.2010.10782551

Floridi, L., Cowls, J., Beltrametti, M., Chatila, R., Chazerand, P., Dignum, V., & Vayena, E. (2022). AI4People—An ethical framework for a good AI society: Opportunities, risks, principles, and recommendations. *Minds and Machines*, *28*(4), 689–707. DOI: 10.1007/s11023-018-9482-5 PMID: 30930541

Fuentes-Penna, A., & González Ibarra, J. de D. (2024). Personalized Education and Artificial Intelligence. *International Journal of Combinatorial Optimization Problems and Informatics*, *15*(2), 1–12. DOI: 10.61467/2007.1558.2024.v15i2

ISTE. (2022). International Society for Technology in Education: Annual Report. https://www.iste.org

Kumar, A., Diljith, D., Dileepkumar, J., Navin, K., Samuel, P., & Sabeena, K. (2025). A Comprehensive Survey on AI in Learning Management System. https://doi.org/ DOI: 10.20944/preprints202501.0697.v1

Lee, D., Hwang, J. Y., Lee, Y., & Kim, S. W. (2022, June). Informatics and Artificial Intelligence (AI) Education in Korea: Situation Analysis Using the Darmstadt Model. *International Journal on Informatics Visualization*, *6*(2), 427–444. DOI: 10.30630/joiv.6.2.1000

Luckin, R., Holmes, W., Griffiths, M., & Forcier, L. B. (2022). Intelligence unleashed: An argument for AI in education. Pearson Education. https://www.pearson.com

Ministerio, T. I. C. (2022). Educación Inteligente: Informe de implementación 2020–2022. Gobierno de Colombia. https://www.mintic.gov.co

Misuraca, G., & van Noordt, C. (2021). *AI watch: Artificial Intelligence in public services*. European Commission JRC Technical Reports., DOI: 10.2760/039619

Naidu, V. R., Singh, B., Hasan, R., & Al Hadrami, G. (2017). Learning analytics for smart classrooms in higher education. IJAEDU- International E-Journal of Advances in Education, 3(8), 356–362. https://doi.org/DOI: 10.18768/IJAEDU.338514

OECD. (2021). *Digital education outlook 2021: Pushing the frontiers with AI, blockchain and robots*. OECD Publishing., DOI: 10.1787/589b283f-

OECD. (2022), Education at a Glance 2022: OECD Indicators, OECD Publishing, Paris, https://doi.org/ OECD/CAF (2022), The Strategic and Responsible Use of Artificial Intelligence in the Public Sector of Latin America and the Caribbean, OECD Public Governance Reviews, OECD Publishing, Paris, https://doi.org/DOI: 10.1787/3197152b-en

Pramukawati, A., Akhidah, A. N., & Wahyuni, E. S. (2024). Education transformation in elementary school: utilization of artificial intelligence-based learning media in the digital era. 1(1), 255–262. https://doi.org/DOI: 10.31316/icasse.v1i1.6915

Reich, J., Buttimer, C. J., Fang, A., Hillaire, G., Hirsch, K., Larke, L. R., & Slama, R. (2020, April 2). Remote Learning Guidance From State Education Agencies During the COVID-19 Pandemic: A First Look. https://doi.org/DOI: 10.35542/osf.io/437e2

Russell, S. J., & Norvig, P. (2021). *Artificial Intelligence: A Modern Approach* (4th ed.). Pearson Education.

SEP. (2023). *Evaluación diagnóstica automatizada en educación básica: Informe técnico*. Secretaría de Educación Pública del Estado de Jalisco.

SEP. (2023). Implementación de herramientas digitales para diagnóstico y planeación educativa en escuelas de educación básica. Secretaría de Educación Pública, México. https://www.sep.gob.mx

Taye, G., Sharma, S., Shah, P., & Nuriye, Y. G. (2023). Exploring the Role of Artificial Intelligence in Class Scheduling and Management: A Comprehensive. *Survey Review*, •••, 1–11. DOI: 10.1109/cset58993.2023.10346898

Tiwari, R. (2023). Ethical And Societal Implications of AI and Machine Learning. *Indian Scientific Journal Of Research In Engineering And Management*, *07*(01). Advance online publication. DOI: 10.55041/ijsrem17519

UNESCO. (2021). AI and education: Guidance for policy-makers. https://unesdoc.unesco.org/ark:/48223/pf0000376709

UNESCO. (2023). Technology in education: A tool on whose terms?. https://doi.org/DOI: 10.54676/JKLA7966

Vargas, P. (2024). Predictive Analysis Application for Academic Student Advancement in Secondary Education Institutions. https://doi.org/DOI: 10.69478/jitc2024v6n2a04

Wang, S., Wang, F., Zhu, Z., Wang, J., Tran, T., & Du, Z. (2024). Artificial intelligence in education: A systematic literature review, Expert Systems with Applications, Volume 252, Part A, 124167, ISSN 0957-4174. https://doi.org/DOI: 10.1016/j.eswa.2024.124167

West, D. M. (2021). The future of work: Robots, AI, and automation. Brookings Institution Press. https://www.brookings.edu

World Bank. (2022). Reimagining digital education: Closing the digital divide. https://www.worldbank.org

World Bank. (2022). Digital Transformation of Education Systems: Lessons from COVID-19. Washington, DC: World Bank Publications. https://www.worldbank.org

Zawacki-Richter, O., Marín, V. I., & Bond, M.. (2019). Systematic review of research on artificial intelligence applications in higher education – where are the educators? *International Journal of Educational Technology in Higher Education*, *16*, 39. DOI: 10.1186/s41239-019-0171-0

Compilation of References

Abdullah, A., Tunas, B., & Entang, M. (2021). Inclusive education program development: Program evaluation. [JOURNAL OF HUMANITIES AND SOCIAL STUDIES]. *JHSS*, *5*(2), 203–207.

Abdulmajid, M., & Pyun, J.-Y. (2017). Deep recurrent neural networks for human activity recognition. *Sensors (Basel)*, *17*(11), 2556. DOI: 10.3390/s17112556 PMID: 29113103

Abichandani, P., Mcintyre, W., Fligor, W., & Lobo, D. (2019). Solar energy education through a cloud-based desktop virtual reality system. *IEEE Access*, 7, 147081–147093. https://doi.org/, M., Ghazal, M., Haneefa, F., Yousaf, J., & El-Baz, A. (2021). Smartphone handwritten circuits solver using augmented reality and capsule deep networks for engineering education. *Education Sciences*, 11(11), 661. https://doi.org/DOI: 10.1109/ACCESS.2019.2945700Alhalabi

Adomavicius, G., & Tuzhilin, A. (2005). Toward the next generation of recommender systems: A survey of the state-of-the-art and possible extensions. *IEEE Transactions on Knowledge and Data Engineering*, *17*(6), 734–749. DOI: 10.1109/TKDE.2005.99

Agic, B., Fruitman, H., Maharaj, A., Taylor, J., Ashraf, A., Henderson, J., Ronda, N., McKenzie, K., Soklaridis, S., & Sockalingam, S. (2023). Advancing curriculum development and design in health professions education: A Health Equity and inclusion Framework for education programs. *The Journal of Continuing Education in the Health Professions*, *43*(4S), S4–S8. PMID: 35940600

Aguirre Lam, M. A., Balderas, F., Rangel-Valdez, N., Martínez-Flores, J. A., Aguirre, A. G., & Pérez-Vázquez, J. A. (2024). University Timetabling Problem: An analysis of the state of the art. *International Journal of Combinatorial Optimization Problems and Informatics*, *15*(5), 489–498. DOI: 10.61467/2007.1558.2025.v16i3.852

Agundis, A. (2023). Evaluation of a Machine Learning Algorithm Using Random Forests for Monitoring Critical Variables in a Manufacturing Process. Tecnológico de Nuevo León Institute, Thesis Work. Website: https://rinacional.tecnm.mx/jspui/bitstream/TecNM/6959/1/TRABAJO%20ADRIAN%20FERNANDO%20AGUNDIS%20febrero%202023.pdf

Akpan, I. J., Kobara, Y. M., Owolabi, J., Akpan, A. A., & Offodile, O. F. (2025). Conversational and generative artificial intelligence and human-chatbot interaction in education and research. *International Transactions in Operational Research, 32*(3), 1251–1281. DOI: 10.1111/itor.13522

Al-Bastami, G. B., & Abu Naser, S. (2017). Design and development of an intelligent tutoring system for C# language. https://core.ac.uk/download/131210533.pdf

Alcalá, J. (s.f.). Reinforcement Learning: Basic Elements and Algorithms. University of Zaragoza. Website: https://core.ac.uk/download/pdf/289996907.pdf

Alepuz, Á. (2022). Reinforcement Learning Applied to the Control of a Manipulator Robot. University of Alicante. Website: https://rua.ua.es/dspace/bitstream/10045/124654/1/Aprendizaje_por_refuerzo_aplicado_al_control_de_un_robot__Alepuz_Jerez_Angel.pdf

Alfaro-Pérez, L., Rodríguez-Hernández, J., & Ramírez-Noriega, M. (2023). A Framework for the Implementation of Artificial Intelligence in Government Decision-Making Processes. *International Journal of Combinatorial Optimization Problems and Informatics, 14*(3), 121–134. DOI: 10.61467/2007.1558.2023.v14i3.420

Alfayez, A. A., & Rasool, A. (2024). Use of AI in the Curriculum Development of Transnational Higher Education. Advances in Educational Marketing, Administration, and Leadership Book Series, 401–422. DOI: 10.4018/979-8-3693-7016-2.ch019

Alhawiti, K. M. (2014). Natural Language Processing and its Use in Education. [ijacsa]. *International Journal of Advanced Computer Science and Applications, 5*(12), 2014. DOI: 10.14569/IJACSA.2014.051210

Al-Jaf, K., Öz, C., Mahmud, H., & Rashid, T. A. (2024). Leveraging Chatbots for Effective Educational Administration: A Systematic Review. https://doi.org/DOI: 10.20944/preprints202410.0238.v1

Aljuaid, H. (2024). The impact of artificial intelligence tools on academic writing instruction in higher education: A systematic review. Arab World English Journal (AWEJ) Special Issue on ChatGPT, April 2024, 26-55. https://dx.doi.org/DOI: 10.24093/awej/ChatGPT.2

Alptekin, M., & Temmen, K. (2020). Gamification in an augmented reality based virtual preparation laboratory training. In M. Auer & T. Tsiatsos (Eds.), *The challenges of the digital transformation in education. ICL 2018* (Advances in Intelligent Systems and Computing, Vol. 916, pp. 578–589). Springer. https://doi.org/DOI: 10.1007/978-3-030-11932-4_54

Al-Saleem, M., Al-Kathiry, N., Al-Osimi, S., & Badr, G. (2015). Mining Educational Data to Predict Students' Academic Performance. In Perner, P. (Ed.), Lecture Notes in Computer Science: Vol. 9166. *Machine Learning and Data Mining in Pattern Recognition. MLDM 2015*. Springer., DOI: 10.1007/978-3-319-21024-7_28

Alshahrani, S., & Kapetanios, E. (2016). Are deep learning approaches suitable for natural language processing? In Métais, E., Meziane, F., Saraee, M., Sugumaran, V., & Vadera, S. (Eds.), Lecture Notes in Computer Science: Vol. 9612. *Natural language processing and information systems: NLDB 2016*. Springer., DOI: 10.1007/978-3-319-41754-7_33

Altadmri, A., & Brown, N. C. C. (2015, February). 37 million compilations. *Proceedings of the 46th ACM Technical Symposium on Computer Science Education*.

AlTwijri, L., & Alghizzi, T. M. (2024). Investigating the integration of artificial intelligence in English as foreign language classes for enhancing learners' affective factors: A systematic review. *Heliyon, 10*(10), e31053. DOI: 10.1016/j.heliyon.2024.e31053 PMID: 38778968

Álvarez Núñez, A., Sánchez Díaz, M. C., Zenteno Vázquez, A. C., Pérez Marcial, J., & Rubín Linares, G. T. (2024). Early Detection of Students at High Risk of Academic Failure using Artificial Intelligence. *International Journal of Combinatorial Optimization Problems and Informatics, 15*(5), 155–160. DOI: 10.61467/2007.1558.2024.v15i5.573

Álvarez, A. (2025). Artificial intelligence reaches schools: Lights and shadows. El País. https://elpais.com/eps/2025-03-13/la-inteligencia-artificial-llega-a-la-escuela-luces-y-sombras.html

Alvarez, J. I., Cortez, A. O., & Alberto, M. Z. (2024). Personalized learning in action: Utilizing AI-powered tutors to bridge the gap in mathematics. *Int. J. Res. Stud. Educ, 13*(8).

Alzubaidi, L., Zhang, J., & Humaidi, A. J.. (2021). Review of deep learning: Concepts, CNN architectures, challenges, applications, future directions. *Journal of Big Data, 8*(1), 53. DOI: 10.1186/s40537-021-00444-8 PMID: 33816053

Ameen, A. (2019). Knowledge based Recommendation System in Semantic Web - A Survey. *International Journal of Computer Applications*, *182*(43), 20–25. DOI: 10.5120/ijca2019918538

Ametrano, F. M. (2016). Hayek money: The cryptocurrency price stability solution. SSRN Electronic Journal. https://doi.org/DOI: 10.2139/ssrn.2425270

Ansyari, M. F., De Witte, K., & Groot, W. (2024). The determinants of data use practice for instructional practice in higher education. *Journal of Professional Capital and Community*. Advance online publication. DOI: 10.1108/jpcc-07-2024-0106

Anunpattana, P., Khalid, M. N. A., Iida, H., & Inchamnan, W. (2021). Capturing potential impact of challenge-based gamification on gamified quizzing in the classroom. *Heliyon*, *7*(12), e08637. DOI: 10.1016/j.heliyon.2021.e08637 PMID: 35005284

Anzures-Garcia, M., Sánchez-Gálvez, L. A., Larios Gómez, M., Tapia Rodríguez, A., & Aguirre Agustín, R., & otros. (2024). IAA-CNN: Intelligent Attendance Algorithm based on Convolutional Neural Networks. *International Journal of Combinatorial Optimization Problems and Informatics*, *15*(5), 51–63. DOI: 10.61467/2007.1558.2024.v15i5

Arana, C. (2021). Recurrent Neural Networks: Analysis of Models Specialized in Sequential Data. Universidad del CEMA, Buenos Aires, Argentina. Website: https://ucema.edu.ar/publicaciones/download/documentos/797.pdf

Arizmendi, L., & Carrillo, C. (2024). Artificial Intelligence in Higher Education: A Perspective from the Teaching Perspective. Ciencia Latina, a Multidisciplinary Scientific Journal. 8(4), 9318-9328. doi: https://orcid.org/0009-0007-5803-0324

Arnau, R., García, L., Calabuig, J., & Sánchez, E. (2023). Teaching Reinforcement Learning with a Simple Example of Function Minimization. In the Proceedings Book: IX Congress of Educational Innovation and Networked Teaching. Valencia, July 13–14, 2023. doi: https://doi.org/DOI: 10.4995/INRED2023.2023.16617

Arnold, K. E., & Pistilli, M. D. (2012). Course signals at Purdue: Using learning analytics to increase student success. *Proceedings of the 2nd International Conference on Learning Analytics and Knowledge*, 267–270. https://doi.org/DOI: 10.1145/2330601.2330666

Arnsten, A. F. T. (2009). Stress signalling pathways that impair prefrontal cortex structure and function. *Nature Reviews. Neuroscience*, *10*(6), 410–422. DOI: 10.1038/nrn2648 PMID: 19455173

Arrieta, A. B., Díaz-Rodríguez, N., Del Ser, J., Bennetot, A., Tabik, S., Barbado, A., & Herrera, F. (2020). Explainable artificial intelligence (XAI): Concepts, taxonomies, opportunities and challenges toward responsible AI. *Information Fusion, 58*, 82–115. DOI: 10.1016/j.inffus.2019.12.012

Asrifan, A., Susanto, A. K., Elpisah, E., Syamsuardi, S., & Herlina, H. (2024). AI-Driven Curriculum Design and Course Management. Advances in Educational Technologies and Instructional Design Book Series, 195–222. DOI: 10.4018/979-8-3373-1017-6.ch007

Auld, G., & Henderson, M. (2013). The ethical dilemmas of social networking sites in classroom contexts. Proceedings of the Conference on Computer-Supported Collaborative Learning. https://api.semanticscholar.org/CorpusID:15010071

Ayuso, D., & Gutiérrez, P. (2022). Artificial Intelligence as an Educational Resource during Initial Teacher Training. *RIED: Ibero-American Journal of Distance Education., 25*(2), 346–358. DOI: 10.5944/ried.25.2.32332

Bai, J. Y. H., Zawacki-Richter, O., & Muskens, W. (2024). Re-Examining the Future Prospects of Artificial Intelligence in Education in Light of the GDPR and ChatGPT. *Turkish Online Journal of Distance Education*. Advance online publication. DOI: 10.17718/tojde.1248901

Baker, R. S. J. D., & Siemens, G. (2014). "Educational data mining and learning analytics." *Cambridge Handbook of the Learning Sciences*, 253-272.

Baker, R. S. J. D. (2016). The 'killer app' of educational data mining and learning analytics. *International Journal of Artificial Intelligence in Education, 26*(1), 29–48.

Baker, R. S. J. d., & Inventado, P. S. (2014). Educational data mining and learning analytics. In Larusson, J. A., & White, B. (Eds.), *Learning Analytics* (pp. 61–75). Springer., DOI: 10.1007/978-1-4614-3305-7_4

Bali, N., Singh, K., & Dhawan, S. (2023). A Survey and Comparative Analysis of Relevant Approaches of Recommendation System. *2023 6th International Conference on Contemporary Computing and Informatics (IC3I)*, 750–755. https://doi.org/ DOI: 10.1109/IC3I59117.2023.10397781

Ball, S. (1993). What is Policy? Texts, trajectories, and toolboxes. *Discourse (Abingdon), 13*(2), 10–17. DOI: 10.1080/0159630930130203

Ball, S. J., Maguire, M., & Braun, A. (2011). *How Schools Do Policy: Policy Enactments in Secondary Schools*. Routledge., DOI: 10.4324/9780203153185

Bansal, G., Rajgopal, K., Chamola, V., Xiong, Z., & Niyato, D. (2022). Healthcare in metaverse: A survey on current metaverse applications in healthcare. *IEEE Access : Practical Innovations, Open Solutions, 10*, 119914–119946. DOI: 10.1109/ACCESS.2022.3219845

Barcia Cedeño, E. I., Tambaco Quintero, A. R., Angulo Quiñónez, O. G., Prado Zamora, M. E., & Valverde Prado, N. G. (2024). Analysis of trends and the future of artificial intelligence in higher education: Perspectives and challenges. *Ciencia Latina Revista Científica Multidisciplinar, 8*(1), 3061–3076. DOI: 10.37811/cl_rcm.v8i1.9637

Barradas, J. (2023). Artificial Intelligence as a Transformative Element of Scientific Research. *Entre Líneas., 2*(1), 113–122. DOI: 10.56368/Entrelineas213

Barreto, L. S. da C., Marañón-Vásquez, G. A., de Lima, R. L., Bolognese, A. M., & De Souza, M. M. G. (2021). Distance learning approach in interprofessional higher education. *International Journal of Education, 12*(4), 93.

Basilaia, G., & Kvavadze, D. (2020). Transition to online education in schools during a SARS-CoV-2 coronavirus (COVID-19) pandemic in Georgia. *Pedagogical Research, 5*(4), em0060. Advance online publication. DOI: 10.29333/pr/7937

Bastidas, D., Adolfo, G., & Sabogal, H. (2020). Traffic Prediction Using Recurrent Neural Networks. ResearchGate. Website: https://www.researchgate.net/publication/351543348_Prediccion_de_trafico_a_partir_de_Redes_Neuronales_Recurrentes

Beck, D. (2019). Augmented and virtual reality in education: Immersive learning research. *Journal of Educational Computing Research, 57*(7), 1619–1625. DOI: 10.1177/0735633119854035

Beel, J., Gipp, B., Langer, S., & Breitinger, C. (2016). Research-paper recommender systems: A literature survey. *International Journal on Digital Libraries, 17*(4), 305–338. DOI: 10.1007/s00799-015-0156-0

Beltrán, Y. I., Martínez, Y. L., & Vargas, A. S. (2015). The Colombian Educational System on the Path to Inclusion: Progress and Challenges. *Educación y Educadores, 18*(1), 62–75. DOI: 10.5294/edu.2015.18.1.4

Bernacki, M. L., Greene, J. A., & Crompton, H. (2020). Mobile technology, learning, and achievement: Advances in understanding and measuring the role of mobile technology in education. *Contemporary Educational Psychology, 60*, 101827. Advance online publication. DOI: 10.1016/j.cedpsych.2019.101827

Bethencourt, A., Castellano, D., Sosa, J., & Area, M. (2022). Technical and Practical Implications of Generative AdversarialNetworks for Open Science in Education. *Riite Interuniversity Journal of Research in Educational Technology.*, *13*(1), 138–156. DOI: 10.6018/riite.545881

Bhargava, H. K., Sridhar, S., & Herrick, C. (1999). Beyond spreadsheets: Tools for building decision support systems. *Computer*, *32*(3), 31–39. DOI: 10.1109/2.751326

Bhogan, S., Naik, S., Gaonkar, S., Prabhudesai, S., Dhond, G., & Fernandes, K. (2024). Survey on Recommendation System Combining Hybrid and Popularity Based Approach. *2024 2nd International Conference on Intelligent Data Communication Technologies and Internet of Things (IDCIoT)*, 1573–1578. https://doi.org/DOI: 10.1109/IDCIoT59759.2024.10467802

Binns, R. (2018). Fairness in machine learning: Lessons from political philosophy. *Proceedings of the 2018 Conference on Fairness, Accountability and Transparency*, 149–159.

Binns, R., Veale, M., Van Kleek, M., & Shadbolt, N. (2018). 'It's Reducing a Human Being to a Percentage': Perceptions of Justice in Algorithmic Decisions. *Proceedings of the 2018 CHI Conference on Human Factors in Computing Systems*, 1–14. https://doi.org/DOI: 10.1145/3173574.3173951

Bird, K. (2023, Fall). Predictive Analytics in Higher Education: The Promises and Challenges of Using Machine Learning to Improve Student Success. *Air Professional File*, 161. Advance online publication. DOI: 10.34315/apf1612023

Bjekić, D., & Vucetić, M. (2013). Development and mental health. In *Proceedings of the International Conference on Education and Mental Health* (pp. 119–127). Faculty of Philosophy, University of Nis.

Bobadilla, J., Ortega, F., Hernando, A., & Gutiérrez, A. (2013). Recommender systems survey. *Knowledge-Based Systems*, *46*, 109–132. DOI: 10.1016/j.knosys.2013.03.012

Bolaño, M., & Duarte, N. (2024). A systematic review of the use of artificial intelligence in education. *Revista Colombiana de Cirugía*, *39*(1), 51–63. DOI: 10.30944/20117582.2365

Borchers, C., Wang, Y., Karumbaiah, S., Ashiq, M., Shaffer, D. W., & Aleven, V. (2024, March). Revealing networks: Understanding effective teacher practices in AI-supported classrooms using transmodal ordered network analysis. *Proceedings of the 14th Learning Analytics and Knowledge.*

Borja, M. (2020). *Analysis of Natural Language Processing Tools for Structuring Medical Texts. Tecnun, University of Navarra.* Website., https://dadun.unav.edu/server/api/core/bitstreams/c8c9da42-aebd-4904-aaa2-0eb672adcbfc/content

Bostrom, N. (2014). *Superintelligence: Paths, Dangers, Strategies.* Oxford University Press.

Boumediene, H., & Bouakkaz, M. (2025). Artificial Intelligence in Education: Emerging Trends, Ethical Considerations, and Future Directions. In Cela, E., Vajjhala, N., & Fonkam, M. (Eds.), *Next-Generation AI Methodologies in Education* (pp. 407–438). IGI Global Scientific Publishing., DOI: 10.4018/979-8-3693-7220-3.ch014

Brown, T. B., Mann, B., Ryder, N., Subbiah, M., Kaplan, J., Dhariwal, P., Neelakantan, A., Shyam, P., Sastry, G., Askell, A., Agarwal, S., Herbert-Voss, A., Krueger, G., Henighan, T., Child, R., Ramesh, A., Ziegler, D. M., Wu, J., Winter, C., & Hesse, C. (2020). Language Models Are Few-Shot Learners. *Arxiv.org, 4*(33). https://arxiv.org/abs/2005.14165

Bucchiarone, A., Savary-Leblanc, M., & Le Pallec, X.. (2023). Gamifying model-based engineering: The PapyGame experience. *Software & Systems Modeling*, *22*, 1369–1389. DOI: 10.1007/s10270-023-01091-8 PMID: 37363105

Burke, R. (2002). Hybrid Recommender Systems: Survey and Experiments. *User Modeling and User-Adapted Interaction*, *12*(4), 331–370. DOI: 10.1023/A:1021240730564

Burrell, J. (2016). How the machine 'thinks': Understanding opacity in machine learning algorithms. *Big Data & Society*, *3*(1), 205395171562251. DOI: 10.1177/2053951715622512

Bush, T. (2011). *Theories of Educational Leadership and Management* (4th ed.). SAGE Publications.

Cabral, D., Davel, M., Pereira, M. dos S., Campanharo, P. S. Q., Marinho, S. M. de O., & Dalvi, Z. M. de V. (2024). Inteligência artificial no desenvolvimento curricular: Impactos e desafios para a educação do futuro. Revista Ibero-Americana de Humanidades. *Ciência & Educação (Bauru)*. Advance online publication. DOI: 10.51891/rease.v10i10.16400

Cai, L., Msafiri, M. M., & Kangwa, D. (2025). Exploring the impact of integrating AI tools in higher education using the Zone of Proximal Development. *Education and Information Technologies*, *30*, 7191–7264. DOI: 10.1007/s10639-024-13112-0

Calero, M., González, J., Sánchez, I., Burillo, G., & Roda, J. (2024). Natural Language Processing in Scientific Literature Review. Spanish Journal of Emergency Medicine. 3(1), 184-195. Website: https://www.reue.org/wp-content/uploads/2024/07/184-195.pdf

Camelo, D. M. A., Santos, J. C. C., Martins, M. P. G., Martins, M. P. G., & Gouveia, P. D. F. (2021). *Modelling Academic Dropout in Computer Engineering Using Artificial Neural Networks*. Springer., DOI: 10.1007/978-3-030-72651-5_14

Campbell, J., Lo, A., & Mackinlay, A. (1997). *The Econometrics of Financial Markets*. https://www.nrc.gov/docs/ML1208/ML12088A329.pdf

Campuzano, M. (2021). Digital Education Programs in Mexico: Success or Failure? Revista Acta Educativa, 63. Retrieved from https://www.facebook.com/UniversidadAbiertaLatinoamerica/posts/409943370038696/

CANVA. (2025). Image generated in the application. https://www.canva.com/

Carleton, R. N. (2016). Into the unknown: A review and synthesis of contemporary models involving uncertainty. *Journal of Anxiety Disorders*, *39*, 30–43. DOI: 10.1016/j.janxdis.2016.02.007 PMID: 26945765

Casey, A., Davidson, E., Poon, M., Dong, H., Duma, D., Grivas, A., Grover, C., Suárez-Paniagua, V., Tobin, R., Whiteley, W., Wu, H., & Alex, B. (2021). A systematic review of natural language processing applied to radiology reports. *BMC Medical Informatics and Decision Making*, *21*(1), 179. DOI: 10.1186/s12911-021-01533-7 PMID: 34082729

Castellet, A. (n.d.). Is Internet a Basic Need? LinkedIn. https://es.linkedin.com/pulse/es-internet-una-necesidad-básica-alba-castellet

Castillo, P. (2017). Application of Machine Learning for Predicting Potential Customers in Marketing Processes. Center for Research in Mathematics, A.C. Zacatecas. Website: https://cimat.repositorioinstitucional.mx/jspui/bitstream/1008/755/1/ZAC%20TE%2061.pdf

Celi, R., Varela, E., Acosta, I., & Montaño, N. (2021). Natural Language Processing Techniques in Text-Based Conversational. *Artificial Intelligence*.

Chamber of Deputies. (2024). General Education Law. https://www.diputados.gob.mx/LeyesBiblio/pdf/LGE.pdf

Chang, Y.-H., Yan, Y.-C., & Lu, Y.-T. (2022). Effects of combining different collaborative learning strategies with problem-based learning in a flipped classroom on program language learning. *Sustainability*, *14*(9), 5282.

Checa, D., Bustillo, A., Saucedo-Dorantes, J. J., Osornio-Rios, R. A., & Cruz-Albarran, I. A. (2021). Virtual reality-based tool applied in the teaching and training of condition-based maintenance in induction motors. In *2021 IEEE 8th International Conference on e-Learning in Industrial Electronics (ICELIE)* (pp. 1–6). IEEE. https://doi.org/DOI: 10.1109/ICELIE53900.2021.9765543

Chen, C. J. (2009). Theoretical bases for using virtual reality in education. *Themes in Science and Technology Education*, *2*(1-2), 71–90. https://www.semanticscholar.org/paper/Theoretical-Bases-for-Using-Virtual-Reality-in-Chen/f6b4882a93a6d3cc35fa090a4c9f7927b12d01fc

Chen, C. M., & Wang, H. C. (2018). Artificial intelligence in education: A review. *Journal of Educational Technology & Society*, *21*(2), 27–35.

Chen, G., Chen, P., Huang, W., & Zhai, J. (2022). Continuance intention mechanism of middle school student users on online learning platform based on qualitative comparative analysis method. *Mathematical Problems in Engineering*, *2022*, 3215337. Advance online publication. DOI: 10.1155/2022/3215337

Chen, J., & Singh, C. K. S. (2024). A Systematic Review on Deep Learning in Education: Concepts, Factors, Models and Measurements. *Journal of Education and Educational Research*, *7*(1), 125–129. DOI: 10.54097/gzk2yd38

Chen, K., Zhang, D., Yao, L., Guo, B., Yu, Z., & Liu, Y. (2021). Deep learning for sensor-based human activity recognition: Overview, challenges, and opportunities. *ACM Computing Surveys*, *54*(4), 77. Advance online publication. DOI: 10.1145/3447744

Cobo-Rendón, R., León-Morales, C. A., & Godoy, A. (2023). Predictive analytics in student retention: A practical model for early intervention. Computers & Education. *Artificial Intelligence*, *4*, 100132. DOI: 10.1016/j.caeai.2023.100132

Cobos, C. (2024). Impact of Artificial Intelligence on the Academic Performance of High School Students: A Correlational Study. *Journal of Scientific Research.*, *6*(e740). Advance online publication. DOI: 10.37073/puriq.6.740

Cohen, M. D., March, J. G., & Olsen, J. P. (1972). A garbage can model of organizational choice. *Administrative Science Quarterly*, *17*(1), 1–25. DOI: 10.2307/2392088

Colizzi, M., Bortoletto, R., Silvestri, M., Mondini, F., Puttini, E., Cainelli, C., & Zoccante, L. (2020). Medically unexplained symptoms in the times of Covid-19 pandemic: A casereport. *Brain, Behavior, and Immunity*, •••, 100073. PMID: 32313886

Confederação Nacional da Indústria. (2022). Relatório anual de educação técnica e profissional. CNI. https://www.portaldaindustria.com.br/cni

Contreras, F., & Olaya, J. (2024). Benefits of Implementing Artificial Intelligence in Business Management: A Systematic Review. Impulso. *Journal of Management*, *4*(8), 213–228. DOI: 10.59659/impulso.v.4i8.58

Copeland, B. J. (2022). Turing: Pioneer of the Information Age (2.ª ed.). Oxford University Press.

Cossio Franco, E. G., Arreola Marín, M. E., Sossa Azuela, J. H., Chávez Marcial, M., Alcántar Alcántar, J. I., & Moya Sánchez, E. U. (2025). Artificial Intelligence & Society 5.0. *International Journal of Combinatorial Optimization Problems and Informatics*, *16*(2), 55–59. DOI: 10.61467/2007.1558.2025.v16i2.1073

Crema, C., Attardi, G., Sartiano, D., & Redolfi, A. (2022). Natural language processing in clinical neuroscience and psychiatry: A review. *Frontiers in Psychiatry*, *13*, 946387. DOI: 10.3389/fpsyt.2022.946387 PMID: 36186874

Crevier, D. (2021). *AI: The Tumultuous History of the Search for Artificial Intelligence*. Basic Books.

Cukurova, M. (2024). The interplay of learning, analytics and artificial intelligence in education: A vision for hybrid intelligence. *British Journal of Educational Technology*, *56*(2), 469–488. DOI: 10.1111/bjet.13514

D'Mello, S. K., & Graesser, A. C. (2012). Dynamics of affective states during complex learning. *Learning and Instruction*, *22*(2), 145–157. DOI: 10.1016/j.learninstruc.2011.10.001

Das, D., Sahoo, L., & Datta, S. (2017). A Survey on Recommendation System. *International Journal of Computer Applications*, *160*(7), 6–10. DOI: 10.5120/ijca2017913081

Datnow, A., & Park, V. (2014). *Data-driven leadership*. Wiley.

De la Torre, J. (2023). Generative Adversarial Networks (GAN): Theoretical Foundations and Applications. Arxiv. doi: https://doi.org//arXiv.2302.09346DOI: 10.48550

Deep, S., Athimoolam, K., & Enoch, T. (2024). Optimizing Administrative Efficiency and Student engagement in Education: The Impact of AI. *International Journal of Current Science Research and Review*, *07*(10). Advance online publication. DOI: 10.47191/ijcsrr/v7-i10-34

Degardin, B., & Proença, H. (2020). Human activity analysis: Iterative weak/self-supervised learning frameworks for detecting abnormal events. In *2020 IEEE International Joint Conference on Biometrics (IJCB)* (pp. 1–9). IEEE. https://doi.org/DOI: 10.1109/IJCB48548.2020.9304860

Delso, A., Carvajal, M. y Corral, D. (2024). The Evolution of Natural Language Processing and Its Influence on Artificial Intelligence: A Review and Future Research Directions. The Evolution of Natural Language Processing and its Influence on Artificial Intelligence: A Review and Future Research Directions. European Public & Social Innovation Review, 10(1), 01-23. doi: https://doi.org/DOI: 10.31637/epsir-2025-782

Deo, A., Jaisinghani, R., Gupta, S., Khan, S. S., Soni, A., & Gehlot, K. (2023). Stratified Advance Personalized Recommendation System Based on Deep Learning. *Ingénierie Des Systèmes d Information*, *28*(1), 189–196. DOI: 10.18280/isi.280121

Devlin, J., Chang, M.-W., Lee, K., & Toutanova, K. (2018, October 11). *BERT: Pre-training of Deep Bidirectional Transformers for Language Understanding*. ArXiv. https://arxiv.org/abs/1810.04805

Dhadphale, T., & Wicks, B. (2022). Participatory Stakeholder Engagement in Design Studio Education. *International Journal of Art & Design Education*, *41*(4), 589–602. DOI: 10.1111/jade.12427

DOF. (2019). Decree Amending, Adding, and Repealing Various Provisions of Articles 3, 31, and 73 of the Political Constitution of the United Mexican States, Regarding Education. Official Gazette of the Federation. https://www.dof.gob.mx/nota_detalle.php?codigo=5560457&fecha=15/05/2019

Dogan, M. E., Goru Dogan, T., & Bozkurt, A. (2023). The use of artificial intelligence (AI) in online learning and distance education processes: A systematic review of empirical studies. *Applied Sciences (Basel, Switzerland)*, *13*(5), 3056.

Dong, Y., Yu, X., & Alharbi, A.. (2022). AI-based production and application of English multimode online reading using multi-criteria decision support system. *Soft Computing*, *26*, 10927–10937. DOI: 10.1007/s00500-022-07209-2 PMID: 35668907

Duarte, N., Montoya Pérez, Y., Beltran, A. J., & Bolaño García, M. (2023). Use of Artificial Intelligence in Education. *Systematic Reviews*. Advance online publication. DOI: 10.46254/sa04.20230169

Đurović, G., Holenko Dlab, M., & Hoić-Božić, N. (2018). Educational Recommender Systems: An Overview and Guidelines for Further Research and Development / Obrazovni sustavi preporučivanja: pregled stanja sa smjernicama za daljnja istraživanja i razvoj. *Croatian Journal of Education-Hrvatski Casopis Za Odgoj i Obrazovanje*, *20*(2), 531–560. DOI: 10.15516/CJE.V20I2.2659

Echeita, G., Simón, C., Verdugo, M. A., Sandoval, M., López, M., Calvo, I., & González-Gil, F. (2009). Paradoxes and Dilemmas in the Process of Educational Inclusion in Spain. *Review of Education*, •••, 153–178. https://repositorio.uam.es/bitstream/handle/10486/668197/paradojas_echeita_RE_2009.pdf?sequence=1&isAllowed=y

Ertmer, P. A., & Ottenbreit-Leftwich, A. T. (2020). Teacher technology change: How knowledge, confidence, beliefs, and culture intersect. *Journal of Research on Technology in Education*, *42*(3), 255–284. DOI: 10.1080/15391523.2010.10782551

Eubanks, V. (2018). *Automating inequality: How high-tech tools profile, police, and punish the poor*. St. Martin's Press.

European Commission, Education, Audiovisual and Culture Executive Agency. (2019). *Digital education at school in Europe*. Publications Office of the European Union.

European Parliament. (2025). EU AI Law: First regulation on artificial intelligence. https://www.europarl.europa.eu/topics/es/article/20230601STO93804/ley-de-ia-de-la-ue-primera-normativa-sobre-inteligencia-artificial

Fachola, C., Tornar\'\ia, A., Bermolen, P., Capdehourat, G., Etcheverry, L., & Fariello, M. I. (2023). Federated learning for data analytics in education. *Data*, *8*(2), 43.

Felipe, A., Beltrán, Y., & Garnica, E. (2024). Object Identification through Computer Vision for Inventory Monitoring Using a Drone. *Ingenio Libre.*, *13*(23). Advance online publication. DOI: 10.18041/2322-8415/ingelibre.2024.v13n23.11460

Feng, W., & Hannafin, J. (2005). Design-based research and technology-enhanced learning environments. *Educational Technology Research and Development*, *53*(4), 5–23. DOI: 10.1007/BF02504682

Ferhat, A., Mohammed, S., Dedabrishvili, M., Chamroukhi, F., Oukhellou, L., & Amirat, Y. (2015). Physical human activity recognition using wearable sensors. *Sensors (Basel)*, *15*(12), 31314–31338. DOI: 10.3390/s151229858 PMID: 26690450

Ferrucci, D., Brown, E., Chu-Carroll, J., Fan, J., Gondek, D., Kalyanpur, A. A., Lally, A., Murdock, J. W., Nyberg, E., Prager, J., Schlaefer, N., & Welty, C. (2010). Building Watson: An Overview of the DeepQA Project. *AI Magazine*, *31*(3), 59. DOI: 10.1609/aimag.v31i3.2303

Flores, C. (2021). Generation of Decision Trees Using a Physics-Inspired Algorithm. National Laboratory of Advanced Informatics. Website: https://www.uv.mx/personal/emezura/files/2021/03/Thesis-Camilo.pdf

Floridi, L., & Chiriatti, M. (2020). GPT-3: Its nature, scope, limits, and consequences. *Minds and Machines*, *30*, 681–694. DOI: 10.1007/s11023-020-09548-1

Floridi, L., & Cowls, J. (2019). A unified framework of five principles for AI in society. *Harvard Data Science Review*, *1*(1). Advance online publication. DOI: 10.1162/99608f92.8cd550d1

Floridi, L., Cowls, J., Beltrametti, M., Chatila, R., Chazerand, P., Dignum, V., & Vayena, E. (2018). AI4People—An ethical framework for a good AI society: Opportunities, risks, principles, and recommendations. *Minds and Machines*, *28*, 689–707. PMID: 30930541

Forero, W., & Negre, F. (2024). Techniques and Applications of Machine Learning and Artificial Intelligence in Education: A Systematic Review. *Ibero-American Journal of Distance Education.*, *27*(1), 209–253. DOI: 10.5944/ried.27.1.37491

From, J. (2017). Pedagogical digital competence—Between values, knowledge and skills. *Higher Education Studies*, *7*(2), 43–50. DOI: 10.5539/hes.v7n2p43

Fuentes, P. A., & Gómez, R. (2024). Digital Technology and Its Ethical Impact on Higher Education, in Rueda, Christian, & Jorge Landaverde (Coordinators), Artificial Intelligence and Higher Education. Edited by the Council of Science and Technology of Querétaro. Institute of Higher Studies in Pedagogy and Education. (Educational Trends in Mexico and the World for 2023. IESPE. https://www.iespe.mx/post/tendencias-educativas-en-mexico-y-el-mundo-para-este-2023

Fuentes-Penna, A., & González Ibarra, J. de D. (2024). Personalized Education and Artificial Intelligence. *International Journal of Combinatorial Optimization Problems and Informatics*, *15*(2), 1–12. DOI: 10.61467/2007.1558.2024.v15i2.431

Fullan, M. (2014). *The Principal: Three Keys to Maximising Impact*. Jossey-Bass.

Gadala, M. (2017). Automation bias: exploring causal mechanisms and potential mitigation strategies. https://ethos.bl.uk/OrderDetails.do?uin=uk.bl.ethos.720941

Garcez, A. d., Lamb, L. C., & Gabbay, D. M. (2019). Neural-symbolic cognitive reasoning. Springer International Publishing. Sitio web: https://www.researchgate.net/publication/220696415_Neural-Symbolic_Cognitive_Reasoning

García, E. (2019). Introduction to Convolutional Neural Networks. Application to Computer Vision. Faculty of Sciences, University of Zaragoza. Website: https://core.ac.uk/download/pdf/290002463.pdf

Georgia State University. (n.d.). Leveraging Predictive Analytics to Enhance Student Retention: A Case Study of Georgia State University. ResearchGate. Retrieved from https://www.researchgate.net/publication/390878595_Leveraging_Predictive_Analytics_to_Enhance_Student_Retention_A_Case_Study_of_Georgia_State_University

Goel, A., & Polepeddi, L. (2018). Jill Watson: A virtual teaching assistant for online education. Georgia Institute of Technology Report. In Dede, C., Richards, J., & Saxberg, B. (Eds.), *Learning Engineering for Online Education: Theoretical Contexts and Design-Based Examples* (pp. 120–143). Routledge.

Goldbach, R. I., & Hamza-Lup, G. F. (2020). Intelligent tutoring systems for Generation Z's addiction. arXiv. https://arxiv.org/pdf/2005.05024

Goldbach, A. H., Abou Shousha, M., & Duque, C.. (2021). Visual field measurements using Heru Visual Field Multi-platform application downloaded on two different commercially available augmented reality devices. *Investigative Ophthalmology & Visual Science*, *62*(8), 1017.

Golestani, N., & Moghaddam, M. (2020). Human activity recognition using magnetic induction-based motion signals and deep recurrent neural networks. *Nature Communications*, *11*, 1551. Advance online publication. DOI: 10.1038/s41467-020-15086-2 PMID: 32214095

Gong, S. (2010). A Collaborative Filtering Recommendation Algorithm Based on User Clustering and Item Clustering. *Journal of Software*, *5*(7). Advance online publication. DOI: 10.4304/jsw.5.7.745-752

Górski, F., Grajewski, D., Bun, P., & Zawadzki, P. (2021). Study of interaction methods in virtual electrician training. *IEEE Access : Practical Innovations, Open Solutions*, *9*, 118242–118252. DOI: 10.1109/ACCESS.2021.3106826

Guitart, H. I., Rodríguez, M. E., & Baró, X. (2020). Design and Implementation of Dashboards to Support Teachers Decision-Making Process in e-Assessment Systems. In Baneres, D., Rodríguez, M., & Guerrero-Roldán, A. (Eds.), *Engineering Data-Driven Adaptive Trust-based e-Assessment Systems. Lecture Notes on Data Engineering and Communications Technologies* (Vol. 34). Springer., DOI: 10.1007/978-3-030-29326-0_6

Guo, F., Zhou, W., Lu, Q., & Zhang, C. (2022). Path extension similarity link prediction method based on matrix algebra in directed networks. *Computer Communications*, *187*, 83–92. DOI: 10.1016/j.comcom.2022.01.016

Hamedi, W. H. W., Ali, F. D. A., Abdullah, W. Y., Ab Hamid, H., & Shuhaimi, N. 'Izzah M., & Amir, M. M. (2025). Ai as a digital scaffold: An integrative review of vygotsky's zone of proximal development in modern education. [ijmoe]. *International Journal of Medical Education*, *7*(26). Advance online publication. DOI: 10.35631/IJMOE.726038

Heffernan, N. T., & Heffernan, C. L. (2014). The ASSISTments System: A Data-Driven Artificial Intelligence in Education. *Journal of Learning Analytics*, *1*(1), 39–57.

Herrera, E. León. Ma., Sosa, Ma., Ruiz, J. y Cepeda, J. (2024). Artificial Intelligence and Biotechnology: Towards Sustainable and Efficient Agriculture. Youth in Science. 32(1), 1-5. Website: https://www.jovenesenlaciencia.ugto.mx/index.php/jovenesenlaciencia/article/view/4687

Herrera, R. (2024). Integration of Expert Systems as an Innovative Tool in Educational Processes: Implications for Academic Research. *Scientific Journal of the Psychopedagogical and Higher Education Research Center.*, *3*(9). Advance online publication. DOI: 10.53287/sisj4131cr79h

Holcombe, E. M., Kezar, A. J., Elrod, S. L., & Ramaley, J. A. (Eds.). (2022). *Shared Leadership in Higher Education: A Framework and Models for Responding to a Changing World* (1st ed.). Routledge., DOI: 10.4324/9781003446965

Holman, K., Marino, M., Vasquez, E., Taub, M., Hunt, J., & Tazi, Y. (2024). Navigating AI-Powered Personalized Learning in special education: A guide for preservice teacher faculty. *Journal of Special Education Preparation*, *4*(2), 90–95.

Holmes, W., Bialik, M., & Fadel, C. (2019, March). *Artificial intelligence in education. promise and implications for teaching and learning*. ResearchGate; Center for Curriculum Redesign. https://www.researchgate.net/publication/332180327_Artificial_Intelligence_in_Education_Promise_and_Implications_for_Teaching_an

Holmes, W., Bialik, M., & Fadel, C. (2019). *Artificial Intelligence in Education.* The Boston Consulting Group.

Holmes, W., Bialik, M., & Fadel, C. (2019). *Artificial Intelligence in education: Promises and implications for teaching and learning*. Center for Curriculum Redesign.

Holmes, W., Bialik, M., & Fadel, C. (2019). *Artificial Intelligence in Education: Promises and Implications for Teaching and Learning*. Center for Curriculum Redesign.

Holmes, W., Porayska-Pomsta, K., Holstein, K., Sutherland, E., Baker, T., Shum, S. B., Santos, O. C., Rodrigo, M. T., Cukurova, M., & Bittencourt, I. I. (2022). Ethics of AI in education: Towards a community-wide framework. *International Journal of Artificial Intelligence in Education, 32*(3), 504–526. DOI: 10.1007/s40593-021-00239-1

Hossain, M., Das, S., Krishnamurthy, B., & Shiva, S. G. (2023). Explainability of Artificial Intelligence Systems: A Survey. *2023 International Symposium on Networks, Computers and Communications (ISNCC)*, 1–6. https://doi.org/DOI: 10.1109/ISNCC58260.2023.10323642

Hoyos, J., Velásquez, B., & Baustista, D. (2022). Transformative Impact of Artificial Intelligence and Autonomous Learning on Agricultural Production: A Focus on Sustainability and Efficiency. Formación Estratégica Journal. 7(1), 40–55. Website: https://formacionestrategica.com/index.php/foes/article/view/111

HuffPost. (2025). The government focuses on artificial intelligence: It will require AI-generated content to be identified and establish penalties. https://www.huffingtonpost.es/politica/el-gobierno-pone-foco-inteligencia-artificial-obligara-identificar-contenidos-generados-ia-establecera-sanciones.html

Huremovic, D. (Ed.). (2019). *Psychiatry of pandemics: A mental health response to infection outbreak* (1st ed.). Springer., DOI: 10.1007/978-3-030-15346-5

Ifenthaler, D., & Yau, J. Y.-K. (2020). Utilising learning analytics to support study success in higher education: A systematic review. *Educational Technology Research and Development, 68*(4), 1961–1990. DOI: 10.1007/s11423-020-09788-z

Incytu (2018). Artificial Intelligence. Office of Scientific and Technological Information for the Congress of the Union. 12(1). Website: https://www.foroconsultivo.org.mx/INCyTU/documentos/Completa/INCYTU_18-012.pdf

Inglés, G. (2023). *Deep Learning Techniques for Automatic Object Detection in Sonar Images*. Higher Technical School of Telecommunications Engineering., https://core.ac.uk/download/588386484.pdf

Ishmael, O., Kiely, E., Quigley, C., & McGinty, D. (2023). Topic Modelling using Latent Dirichlet Allocation (LDA) and Analysis of Students Sentiments. 1–6. DOI: 10.1109/jcsse58229.2023.10201965

ISTE. (2022). International Society for Technology in Education: Annual Report. https://www.iste.org

Iturbe, A. (2023). Redes Neuronales Convolucionales y Recurrentes para la Extracción de Respuestas en Español. Centro Nacional de Investigación y Desarrollo Tecnológico Departamento de Ciencias Computacionales. Tecnológico Nacional de México. Sitio web: https://rinacional.tecnm.mx/bitstream/TecNM/6615/1/DC_Alberto_Iturbe_Herrera_2023.pdf

Ivanov, A., Stankovic, Ž., & Perisic, J. (2023). Digital competences of teachers in secondary school. In *Proceedings of the Third International Conference on Sustainable Environment and Technologies* (pp. 1–8). Belgrade, Serbia.

Jaganeshwari, K., & Djodilatchoumy, S. (2022). An automated testing tool based on graphical user interface with exploratory behavioural analysis. *Journal ofTheoretical and Applied Information Technology*, *100*(22), 6657–6666.

Jalal, A., Khalid, N., & Kim, K. (2020). Automatic recognition of human interaction via hybrid descriptors and maximum entropy Markov model using depth sensors. *Entropy (Basel, Switzerland)*, *22*(8), 817. Advance online publication. DOI: 10.3390/e22080817 PMID: 33286588

Jayaprakash, S. M., Moody, E. W., Lauría, E. J., Regan, J. R., & Baron, J. D. (2014). Early alert of academically at-risk students: An open source analytics initiative. *Journal of Learning Analytics*, *1*(1), 6–47. DOI: 10.18608/jla.2014.11.3

Jiang, H., Wang, M., Zhao, P., Xiao, Z., & Dustdar, S. (2021). A utility-aware general framework with quantifiable privacy preservation for destination prediction in LBSs. *IEEE/ACM Transactions on Networking*, *29*(5), 2228–2241. DOI: 10.1109/TNET.2021.3083655

Jiang, Y., Li, X., Luo, H., Yin, S., & Kaynak, O. (2022). Quo vadis artificial intelligence? *Discover Artificial Intelligence*, *2*(1), 4. Advance online publication. DOI: 10.1007/s44163-022-00022-8

Joachims, T. (1998). *Text categorization with Support Vector Machines: Learning with many relevant features* (pp. 137–142). https://doi.org/DOI: 10.1007/BFb0026683

Johnson, M. S., Liu, X., & McCaffrey, D. F. (2022). Psychometric methods to evaluate measurement and algorithmic bias in automated scoring. *Journal of Educational Measurement*, *59*(3), 338–361.

Jordan, M. I., & Mitchell, T. M. (2015). Machine learning: Trends, perspectives, and prospects. *Science*, *349*(6245), 255–260. DOI: 10.1126/science.aaa8415 PMID: 26185243

Jowallah, R. (2023). *Integrating Artificial Intelligence (AI) Into the Curriculum.* IGI Global., DOI: 10.4018/979-8-3693-0074-9.ch015

Juhana, A., Yusuf, R., Prihatmanto, A. S., & Abdullah, A. G. (2020). Basic electrical installation trainer boards: Virtual reality based laboratory for electrical basic education. In *2020 6th International Conference on Interactive Digital Media (ICIDM)* (pp. 1–6). IEEE. https://doi.org/DOI: 10.1109/ICIDM51048.2020.9339681

Kaminska, D., Sapiński, T., Wiak, S., Tikk, T., Haamer, R. E., Avots, E., & Anbarjafari, G. (2019). Virtual reality and its applications in education: Survey. *Information (Basel)*, *10*(10), 318. DOI: 10.3390/info10100318

Karampelas, K. (2025). Integration of Artificial Intelligence in National Science Curricula. DOI: 10.30935/conmaths/15883

Kasztelnik, K. (2024). Artificial Intelligence-Assisted Curriculum Development: Innovations in Designing Educational Content for the 21st Century Learner. *Journal of Higher Education Theory and Practice*, *24*(11). Advance online publication. DOI: 10.33423/jhetp.v24i11.7367

Katzenbach, C. & Ulbricht. (2022). Algorithmic Governance. Latin American Journal of Digital Economy and Society. doi: https://doi.org/DOI: 10.53857/cwyi6959

Kayyali, M. (2025). AI in Higher Education. Advances in Educational Technologies and Instructional Design Book Series, 31–62. DOI: 10.4018/979-8-3693-7949-3.ch002

Kessler, A., Boston, M., & Stein, M. K. (2019). Exploring how teachers support students' mathematical learning in computer-directed learning environments. *Information and Learning Science*, *121*(1/2), 52–78.

Kestin, G., Miller, K., Klales, A., Milbourne, T., & Ponti, G. (2024). AI Tutoring Outperforms Active Learning. ResearchGate. Recuperado de https://www.researchgate.net/publication/380587627_AI_Tutoring_Outperforms_Active_Learning Khan Academy. (2023). Khanmigo: AI-powered teaching assistant. Recuperado de https://khanmigo.ai/

Khairudin, M., Triatmaja, A. K., Istanto, W. J., & Azman, M. N. A. (2019). Mobile virtual reality to develop a virtual laboratory for the subject of digital engineering. *International Journal of Interactive Mobile Technologies*, *13*(4), 80–95. DOI: 10.3991/ijim.v13i04.10522

Khalid, N., Gochoo, M., Jalal, A., & Kim, K. (2021). Modeling two-person segmentation and locomotion for stereoscopic action identification: A sustainable video surveillance system. *Sustainability*, *13*(2), 970. Advance online publication. DOI: 10.3390/su13020970

Khan, A., Sohail, A., Zahoora, U., & Qureshi, A. S. (2018). A survey of the recent architectures of deep convolutional neural networks. arXiv preprint arXiv:1901.06032. https://arxiv.org/abs/1901.06032

Khan, S., Rahmani, H., Shah, S. A. A., & Bennamoun, M. (2018). A guide to convolutional neural networks for computer vision. *Synthesis Lectures on Computer Vision*, *8*(1), 1–207. DOI: 10.2200/S00822ED1V01Y201712COV015

Khuzairi, N. M. S., Sidhu, M. S., & Cob, Z. (2020). Learning Analytics and Teaching Analytics. *The Similarities and Differences.*, *3*(2), 52–58. DOI: 10.36079/LAMINTANG.IJ-HUMASS-0302.135

Kimmel, B., Geisert, A. L., Yaro, L., Gipson, B., Hotchkiss, R. T., Osae-Asante, S. K., Vaught, H., Wininger, G., & Yamaguchi, C. (2024). Enhancing programming error messages in real time with generative AI. Extended Abstracts of the CHI Conference on Human Factors in Computing Systems, 1–7.

Kleimola, R., & Leppisaari, I. (2022). Learning analytics to develop future competences in higher education: A case study. *International Journal of Educational Technology in Higher Education*, *19*, 17. DOI: 10.1186/s41239-022-00318-w

Kökver, Y., Pektaş, H. M., & Çelik, H. (2025). Artificial intelligence applications in education: Natural language processing in detecting misconceptions. *Education and Information Technologies*, *30*, 3035–3066. DOI: 10.1007/s10639-024-12919-1

König, J., Jäger-Biela, D. J., & Glutsch, N. (2020). Adapting to online teaching during COVID-19 school closure: Teacher education and teacher competence effects among early career teachers in Germany. *European Journal of Teacher Education*, *43*(4), 608–622. DOI: 10.1080/02619768.2020.1809650

Kormushev, P., Nenchev, D. N., Calinon, S., & Caldwell, D. G. (2018). Upper-body kinesthetic teaching of a free-standing humanoid robot. *Frontiers in Neurorobotics*, *12*, 11. DOI: 10.3389/fnbot.2018.00011

Kotsiantis, S., Verykios, V., & Tzagarakis, M. (2024). AI-assisted programming tasks using code embeddings and transformers. *Electronics (Basel)*, *13*(4), 767.

Krizhevsky, A., Sutskever, I., & Hinton, G. E. (2012). ImageNet Classification with Deep Convolutional Neural Networks. *Communications of the ACM*, *60*(6), 84–90.

Krizhevsky, A., Sutskever, I., & Hinton, G. E. (2017). ImageNet classification with deep convolutional neural networks. *Communications of the ACM*, *60*(6), 84–90. DOI: 10.1145/3065386

Kroff, F., Coria, D., & Ferrada, C. (2024). Artificial Intelligence in University Education: Innovations, Challenges, and Opportunities. *Espacios Journal.*, *45*(5), 120–135. DOI: 10.48082/espacios-a24v45n05p09

Kshirsagar, P. R., Jagannadham, D. B. V., Alqahtani, H., Noorulhasan, N., Quadri, I., Saiful, T. M., & Dejene, M. (2022). Human intelligence analysis through perception of AI in teaching and learning. *Computational Intelligence and Neuroscience*, *9160727*. Advance online publication. DOI: 10.1155/2022/9160727 PMID: 35726295

Kuang, Y., & Duan, B. (2025). (2025). Evidence-Based Curriculum Reform: A Data-Driven Framework for Educational Planning and Governance in China. *Journal of Chinese Political Science*. Advance online publication. DOI: 10.1007/s11366-025-09909-6

Kucharska, W., Kucharski, M. J., & Rehman, H. U. (2022). Transformational leadership and acceptance of mistakes as a source of learning - Poland-USA cross-country study. *European Conference on Management Leadership and Governance*, 18(1), 238–246.

Kukulska-Hulme, A. (2020). Mobile Learning and the Future of Education. *Educational Technology Research and Development*, *68*(1), 129–144.

Kumar, A., Diljith, D., Dileepkumar, J., Navin, K., Samuel, P., & Sabeena, K. (2025). A Comprehensive Survey on AI in Learning Management System. https://doi.org/DOI: 10.20944/preprints202501.0697.v1

Kun, X., Huang, J., & Wang, H. (2020). LSTM-CNN architecture for human activity recognition. *IEEE Access : Practical Innovations, Open Solutions*, *8*, 56855–56866. DOI: 10.1109/ACCESS.2020.2982225

Kvasznicza, Z., Kovács, J., Maza, G., & Péli, M. (2019). VR based dual education at E.ON: The win-win-win situation for companies, graduates and universities. In *2019 10th IEEE International Conference on Cognitive Infocommunications (CogInfoCom)* (pp. 479–482). IEEE. https://doi.org/DOI: 10.1109/CogInfoCom47531.2019.9089961

Lagares, J., Díaz, N., & Barranco, C. (s.f.). Deep Learning: A New Path to Transform Data into Knowledge. Pablo de Olavide University. Website: https://www.mintur.gob.es/Publicaciones/Publicacionesperiodicas/EconomiaIndustrial/RevistaEconomiaIndustrial/423/LAGARES,%20DI%CC%81AZ-DI%CC%81AZ%20Y%20BARRANCO%20GONZALEZ.pdf

Lanzagorta, D., Carrillo, D., & Carrillo, R. (2022). Artificial Intelligence in Medicine: Present and Future. *Gaceta Medica de Mexico*, *158*(1), 17–21. DOI: 10.24875/GMM.M22000688 PMID: 36921221

LeCun, Y., Bengio, Y., & Hinton, G. (2015). Deep Learning. *Nature*, *521*(7553), 436–444. DOI: 10.1038/nature14539 PMID: 26017442

Lee, D., Hwang, J. Y., Lee, Y., & Kim, S. W. (2022, June). Informatics and Artificial Intelligence (AI) Education in Korea: Situation Analysis Using the Darmstadt Model. *International Journal on Informatics Visualization*, *6*(2), 427–444. DOI: 10.30630/joiv.6.2.1000

Li, B., Tan, Y., Wu, A., & Duan, G. (2022). A distributionally robust optimization based method for stochastic model predictive control. *IEEE Transactions on Automatic Control*, *67*(11), 5762–5776. DOI: 10.1109/TAC.2021.3121120

Li, G., Zarei, M. A., & Alibakhshi, G.. (2024). Teachers and educators' experiences and perceptions of artificial-powered interventions for autism groups. *BMC Psychology*, *12*, 199. DOI: 10.1186/s40359-024-01664-2 PMID: 38605422

Li, M., Enkhtur, A., Cheng, F., & Yamamoto, B. A. (2023). Ethical implications of ChatGPT in higher education: A scoping review. *Journal of Interdisciplinary Studies in Education*, *13*(1), 55–69. https://ojed.org/jise

Li, M., & Ma, S. (2023). Examining the effectiveness of gamification as a tool promoting teaching and learning in educational settings: A meta-analysis. *Frontiers in Psychology*, *14*, 1253549. DOI: 10.3389/fpsyg.2023.1253549 PMID: 37876838

Lindblom, C. E. (1959). The science of 'muddling through'. *Public Administration Review*, *19*(2), 79–88. DOI: 10.2307/973677

Lin, K., Yang, S., & Na, S.-G. (2022). Collaborative Filtering Algorithm-Based Destination Recommendation and Marketing Model for Tourism Scenic Spots. *Computational Intelligence and Neuroscience*, *2022*, 1–7. DOI: 10.1155/2022/7115627 PMID: 35528326

Lin, Y., Liu, Y., Lin, F., Zou, L., Wu, P., Zeng, W., Chen, H., & Miao, C. (2024). A Survey on Reinforcement Learning for Recommender Systems. *IEEE Transactions on Neural Networks and Learning Systems*, *35*(10), 13164–13184. DOI: 10.1109/TNNLS.2023.3280161 PMID: 37279123

Litman, D. (2016). Natural language processing for enhancing teaching and learning. *Proceedings of the AAAI Conference on Artificial Intelligence*, *30*(1).

Liu, X., Shi, T., Zhou, G., Liu, M., Yin, Z., Yin, L., & Zheng, W. (2023a). Emotion classification for short texts: An improved multi-label method. *Humanities & Social Sciences Communications*, *10*, 306. Advance online publication. DOI: 10.1057/s41599-023-01815-4

Liu, X., Song, M., Tao, D., Bu, J., & Chen, C. (2015). Random geometric prior forest for multiclass object segmentation. *IEEE Transactions on Image Processing*, *24*(10), 3060–3070. DOI: 10.1109/TIP.2015.2432152 PMID: 25974937

Liu, X., Zhou, G., Kong, M., Yin, Z., Li, X., Yin, L., & Zheng, W. (2023b). Developing multi-labelled corpus of Twitter short texts: A semi-automatic method. *Systems*, *11*(8), 390. Advance online publication. DOI: 10.3390/systems11080390

Li, W., & Wong, W.-F. (2023). Iaso: Enhancing syntax error correction using deep learning techniques. In *Research Square*.

Long, D., & Magerko, B. (2020). What is AI literacy? Competencies and design considerations. In *Proceedings of the 2020 CHI Conference on Human Factors in Computing Systems* (pp. 1–16). Association for Computing Machinery. https://doi.org/DOI: 10.1145/3313831.3376727

Long, W., Xiao, Z., Wang, D., Jiang, H., Chen, J., Li, Y., & Alazab, M. (2023). Unified spatial-temporal neighbor attention network for dynamic traffic prediction. *IEEE Transactions on Vehicular Technology*, *72*(2), 1515–1529. DOI: 10.1109/TVT.2022.3210294

Luan, H., Geczy, P., Lai, H., Gobert, J., Yang, S. J. H., Ogata, H., Baltes, J., Guerra, R., Li, P., & Tsai, C.-C. (2020). Challenges and future directions of big data and artificial intelligence in education. *Frontiers in Psychology*, *11*, 580820. DOI: 10.3389/fpsyg.2020.580820 PMID: 33192896

Lu, C., Shi, J., & Jia, J. (2013). Abnormal event detection at 150 fps in Matlab. In *2013 IEEE International Conference on Computer Vision* (pp. 2720–2727). IEEE. https://doi.org/DOI: 10.1109/ICCV.2013.338

Luckin, R., & Holmes, W. (2016). Intelligence Unleashed: An argument for AI in Education. https://discovery.ucl.ac.uk/id/eprint/1475756

Luckin, R., Holmes, W., Griffiths, M., & Forcier, L. B. (2016). "Intelligence Unbound: The Future of Uploaded and Artificial Intelligence." *The Future of Learning*.

Luckin, R., Holmes, W., Griffiths, M., & Forcier, L. B. (2022). Intelligence unleashed: An argument for AI in education. Pearson Education. https://www.pearson.com

Luckin, R., Holmes, W., Griffiths, M., & Forcier, L. B. (2016). *Intelligence Unleashed: An argument for AI in Education*. Pearson Education.

Luckin, R., Holmes, W., Griffiths, M., & Forcier, L. B. (2016). *Intelligence Unleashed: An Argument for AI in Education*. Pearson Education.

Luckin, R., Holmes, W., & Mann, M. (2022). Empowering educators to be AI-ready. *Computers and Education: Artificial Intelligence*, *3*, 100056. DOI: 10.1016/j.caeai.2022.100056

Macgilchrist, F. (2019). Backstaging the teacher: On learner-driven, school-driven and data-driven change in educational technology discourse. *Kultura-Społeczeństwo-Edukacja*, *12*(2), 83–103. DOI: 10.14746/kse.2017.12.4

Madariaga, C., Lao, Y., Curra, A., & Lorenzo, R. (2022). Use of KNN Algorithms in a Multicriteria Methodology for Customer Classification as a Basis for Aggregate Planning. Retos de la Dirección. 16(1). Website: http://scielo.sld.cu/scielo.php?script=sci_arttext&pid=S2306-91552022000100178

Mallik, S., & Gangopadhyay, A. (2023). Proactive and reactive engagement of artificial intelligence methods for education: A review. *Frontiers in Artificial Intelligence*, *6*, 1151391. DOI: 10.3389/frai.2023.1151391 PMID: 37215064

Mandinach, E. B., & Gummer, E. S. (2016). What does it mean for teachers to be data literate: Laying out the skills, knowledge, and dispositions. *Teaching and Teacher Education*, *60*, 366–376. DOI: 10.1016/j.tate.2016.07.011

Manouselis, N., Drachsler, H., Vuorikari, R., Hummel, H., & Koper, R. (2011). Recommender Systems in Technology Enhanced Learning. In Ricci, F., Rokach, L., Shapira, B., & Kantor, P. (Eds.), *Recommender Systems Handbook*. Springer., DOI: 10.1007/978-0-387-85820-3_12

Marcus, G. (2020). The next decade in AI: Four steps towards robust artificial intelligence. arXiv preprint. https://arxiv.org/abs/2002.06177

Martínez, A., & Ezequiel, P. (s.f.). Wildfire Prediction Using Machine Learning Models. Argentine University of Enterprise (UADE), Institute of Technology (INTEC). Buenos Aires, Argentina. Website: https://sedici.unlp.edu.ar/bitstream/handle/10915/149568/Documento_completo.pdf?sequence=1&isAllowed=y

Martínez, J. (2018). Comparative Study of Machine Learning Models for microRNA Target Detection. Master's Degree in Bioinformatics and Biostatistics, UOC-UB. Website: https://openaccess.uoc.edu/server/api/core/bitstreams/7ef32f2a-31c5-4bd6-a289-f894fa0ed175/content

Matthew, T., & Banhazi, T. M. (2016). A brief review of the application of machine vision in livestock behavior analysis. *Agrárinformatika Folyóirat*, *7*(2), 23–42. DOI: 10.17700/jai.2016.7.2.297

McCulloch, W., & Pitts, W. (1943). A logical calculus of the ideas immanent in nervous activity. *Bulletin of Mathematical Biology*, *52*(1-2), 99–115. DOI: 10.1016/s0092-8240(05)80006-0 PMID: 2185863

Mehrabi, N., Morstatter, F., Saxena, N., Lerman, K., & Galstyan, A. (2021). A survey on bias and fairness in machine learning. *ACM Computing Surveys*, *54*(6), 1–35. DOI: 10.1145/3457607

Meilong, S., He, P., Xiao, H., Li, H., & Zeng, C. (2020). An approach to semantic and structural features learning for software defect prediction. *Mathematical Problems in Engineering*, *2020*, 1–13.

MEN. (2017). Decree 1421. Regulating the Educational Attention to the Population with Disabilities within the Framework of Inclusive Education. Ministry of National Education. http://es.presidencia.gov.co/normativa/normativa/DECRETO%201421%20DEL%2029%20DE%20AGOSTO%20DE%202017.pdf

Mena, A., Vázquez, E., Fernández, E., & López, E. (2024). Artificial Intelligence and Its Scientific Production in the Field of Education. *Formación Universitaria*, *17*(1). Advance online publication. DOI: 10.4067/S0718-50062024000100155

Mendes, V. (2025). Artificial intelligence and education: A revolution in progress. El País. https://elpais.com/chile/2025-02-06/inteligencia-artificial-y-educacion-una-revolucion-en-marcha.html

Mercedes, F., Morales, I., & Vidal, J. (2023). ChatGPT: Origin, Evolution, Challenges, and Impacts on Education. REMS. 37(2). Website: http://scielo.sld.cu/scielo.php?script=sci_arttext&pid=S0864-21412023000200016

Mesa, C. (2024). Transparency vs. intellectual property: A difficult balance for the artificial intelligence regulation. https://blogip.garrigues.com/propiedad-intelectual/transparencia-vs-propiedad-intelectual-un-equilibrio-dificil-para-el-reglamento-de-inteligencia-artificial

Miah, S. J., Vu, H. Q., Gammack, J., & McGrath, M. (2017). A big data analytics method for tourist behaviour analysis. *Information & Management*, *54*(6), 771–785. DOI: 10.1016/j.im.2016.11.011

Michaeli, T., & Romeike, R. (2020). Investigating students' preexisting debugging traits: A real world escape room study. Koli Calling '20: *Proceedings of the 20th Koli Calling Conference on Computing Education Research*, 1–10.

Michalis, V nikou, C., & Kakadiaris, I. A. (2015). A review of human activity recognition methods. *Frontiers in Robotics and AI, 2*, Article 28. https://doi.org/DOI: 10.3389/frobt.2015.00028

Mings, A. (2018). The impact of a blended learning rotational model on student achievement in an eighth-grade social studies class (Doctoral dissertation). University of South Carolina. https://scholarcommons.sc.edu/etd/4908

Ministerio, T. I. C. (2022). Educación Inteligente: Informe de implementación 2020–2022. Gobierno de Colombia. https://www.mintic.gov.co

Misuraca, G., & van Noordt, C. (2021). *AI watch: Artificial Intelligence in public services*. European Commission JRC Technical Reports., DOI: 10.2760/039619

Mitchell, T. (1997). *Machine Learning*. McGraw-Hill.

Mizumoto, A., & Eguchi, M. (2023). Exploring the potential of using an AI language model for automated essay scoring. *Research Methods in Applied Linguistics*, *2*(2), 100050. Advance online publication. DOI: 10.1016/j.rmal.2023.100050

Molnar, C. (2020). Interpretable Machine Learning: A Guide for Making Black Box Models Explainable. https://christophm.github.io/interpretable-ml-book/

Morales-Murillo, V. G., Pinto, D., Perez-Tellez, F., & Rojas-Lopez, F. (2024). A Transformer-Based Multi-Domain Recommender System for E-commerce. *International Journal of Combinatorial Optimization Problems and Informatics*, *15*(2), 95–123. DOI: 10.61467/2007.1558.2024.v15i2.465

Murel, J. (2024). In reinforcement learning, an agent learns to make decisions by interacting with an environment. It is used in robotics and other decision-making settings. IBM. Website: https://www.ibm.com/mx-es/think/topics/reinforcement-learning

Nadeem, A., Jalal, A., & Kim, K. (2020). Human actions tracking and recognition based on body parts detection via artificial neural network. In *2020 3rd International Conference on Advancements in Computational Sciences (ICACS)* (pp. 1–8). IEEE. https://doi.org/DOI: 10.1109/ICACS47775.2020.9056878

Naidu, V. R., Singh, B., Hasan, R., & Al Hadrami, G. (2017). Learning analytics for smart classrooms in higher education. IJAEDU- International E-Journal of Advances in Education, 3(8), 356–362. https://doi.org/DOI: 10.18768/IJAEDU.338514

National Commission for the Continuous Improvement of Education. (Mejoredu, 2022a). Disability and the Right to Education in Mexico. https://www.mejoredu.gob.mx/images/publicaciones/Discapacidad-de-2022.pdf

National Commission for the Continuous Improvement of Education. (Mejoredu, 2022b). Horizons for Teaching Practice in Multigrade Schools: Inclusive Education. Formative Intervention: Teaching Practice in Multigrade Schools for Addressing Diversity. Workbook. https://www.mejoredu.gob.mx/images/programa-formacion-docente/docenteseb/cuaderno-horizontes-docentes-servicio-eb.pdf

National Commission for the Continuous Improvement of Education. (Mejoredu, 2022c). The Importance of Multigrade Schools, in Education in Motion, year 1, no. 10. https://www.mejoredu.gob.mx/images/publicaciones/boletin-3/B10_Boletin.pdf

National Institute of Statistics and Geography. (2021). Statistics on the Occasion of the International Day of Persons with Disabilities (National Data). INEGI. https://www.inegi.org.mx/contenidos/saladeprensa/aproposito/2021/EAP_PersDiscap21.pdf

National Institute of Statistics and Geography. (2025). Information System for the Sustainable Development Goals. https://agenda2030.mx/ODSGoalSelected.html?ti=T&cveArb=ODS0040&goal=0&lang=es#/ind

National Institute of Statistics and Geography. (n.d.). Disability. Information about Mexico for Children. INEGI. https://cuentame.inegi.org.mx/poblacion/discapacidad.aspx

Navas, O. (2021). On the Threshold of a New Era: Private Law Facing Robotics and Artificial Intelligence. 9(1), 178-219. Website: https://www.redalyc.org/journal/6002/600266295005/html/

Nguyen, A., Ngo, H. N., & Hong, Y.. (2023). Ethical principles for artificial intelligence in education. *Education and Information Technologies*, *28*, 4221–4241. DOI: 10.1007/s10639-022-11316-w PMID: 36254344

Nguyen, N., & Thai, T. (2020). CDIO approach in developing teacher training program to meet requirement of the Industrial Revolution 4.0 in Vietnam. *International Journal of Emerging Technologies in Learning*, *15*(14), 108–123. DOI: 10.3991/ijet.v15i14.13943

Ni, A., & Cheung, A. (2023). Ni, A., & Cheung, A. (2023). Understanding secondary students' continuance intention to adopt AI-powered intelligent tutoring system for English learning. *Education and Information Technologies*, 28(3), 3191-3216). Understanding secondary students' continuance intention to adopt AI-powered intelligent tutoring system for English learning. *Education and Information Technologies*, *28*, 3191–3216. DOI: 10.1007/s10639-022-11305-z PMID: 36119127

Ni, A., & Cheung, A. (2023). Understanding secondary students' continuance intention to adopt AI-powered intelligent tutoring system for English learning. *Education and Information Technologies*, *28*(3), 3191–3216. PMID: 36119127

Nilsson, N. J. (2021). *The Quest for Artificial Intelligence: A History of Ideas and Achievements*. Cambridge University Press.

Niu, L. (2024). New applications of online education content analysis based on natural language processing technology. Proceedings of the First International Conference on Science, Engineering and Technology Practices for Sustainable Development, ICSETPSD 2023, 17th-18th 2023, Coimbatore, Tamilnadu, India.

Norman-Acevedo, E. (2023). *La inteligencia artificial en la educación: una herramienta valiosa para los tutores virtuales universitarios y profesores universitarios. PANORAMA, 17(32)*. Politécnico Grancolombiano., DOI: 10.15765/pnrm.v17i32.3681

Nunes, J. (2025). Artificial General Intelligence: Technological Progress or Existential Threat? Governance Network for Argentina. Website: https://www.redga.com.ar/assets/img/Inteligencia%20artificial%20general%20por%20Jorge%20Nunes%20REDGA.pdf

OECD. (2021). *Artificial Intelligence in Society*. OECD Publishing., DOI: 10.1787/eedfee77-

OECD. (2021). *Digital education outlook 2021: Pushing the frontiers with AI, blockchain and robots*. OECD Publishing., DOI: 10.1787/589b283f-

OECD. (2022), Education at a Glance 2022: OECD Indicators, OECD Publishing, Paris, https://doi.org/ OECD/CAF (2022), The Strategic and Responsible Use of Artificial Intelligence in the Public Sector of Latin America and the Caribbean, OECD Public Governance Reviews, OECD Publishing, Paris, https://doi.org/DOI: 10.1787/3197152b-en

OECD. (2025). Official Website. Retrieved on March 24, 2025, from https://www.oecd-ilibrary.org/education/are-15-year-olds-prepared-to-deal-with-fake-news-and-misinformation_6ad5395e-en

Olbina, S., & Glick, S. (2022). Using integrated hands-on and virtual reality (VR) or augmented reality (AR) approaches in construction management education. *International Journal of Construction Education and Research*, *18*(3), 1–20. DOI: 10.1080/15578771.2021.1975659

Open, A. I. (2022, November 30). *Introducing ChatGPT*. OpenAI. https://openai.com/index/chatgpt/

Ordoñez, M., & Gutiérrez, J. (2023). Natural language processing prototypes based on machine learning techniques. *Journal of Technology & Innovation*, *2*(2), 34–43. DOI: 10.47230/Journal.TechInnovation.v2.n2.2023.34-43

Organisation for Economic Co-operation and Development. (2018). *PISA 2018 results (Volume V): Effective policies, successful schools*. OECD Publishing. https://doi.org/DOI: 10.1787/ca768d40-en

Organisation for Economic Co-operation and Development. (2020). *TALIS 2018 results (Volume I): Teachers and school leaders as lifelong learners*. OECD Publishing. https://doi.org/DOI: 10.1787/1d0bc92a-en

Organisation for Economic Co-operation and Development. (2023). Digital equity and inclusion in education: An overview of practice and policy in OECD countries. Retrieved from https://www.oecd-ilibrary.org/education/digital-equity-and-inclusion-in-education_7cb15030-en

Organización de Estados Iberoamericanos (OEI). (2025). Red de los Sistemas Educativos Inteligentes de América Latina y el Caribe (RESEI). Sistemas de gestión e información educativa para el seguimiento de las trayectorias escolares. OEI. https://oei.int/wp-content/uploads/2025/03/2-sistemas-de-informacion-y-gestion-educativa-de-las-trayectorias-escolares-22-7.pdf

Ortiz, M. (2025). Artificial neural networks. Ingenuity and Consciousness. Scientific Bulletin of the Ciudad Sahagún Higher School. 12(23), 38-44. Website: https://www.researchgate.net/publication/387749723_Redes_neuronales_artificiales

Ortiz, R., Jorge, L., Oneto, L., Samà, A., Parra, X., & Anguita, D. (2016). Transition-aware human activity recognition using smartphones. *Neurocomputing*, *171*, 754–767. DOI: 10.1016/j.neucom.2015.07.085

Otter, D. W., Medina, J. R., & Kalita, J. (2021). A survey of the transformer model in natural language processing. ACM Computing Surveys. 54(12), 1–38. Wensite: https://pubmed.ncbi.nlm.nih.gov/32324570/

Pablo, F. (2024). Artificial General Intelligence and its Risks: A Reflection on Economic and Control Challenges. SCCS Perspectives. Website: https://sccs.web.uah.es/wp/wp-content/uploads/2024/05/P2401-La-AGI-y-sus-riesgos.pdf

Page, L. C., & Gehlbach, H. (2017). How an artificially intelligent virtual assistant helps students navigate the road to college. *AERA Open*, *3*(4), 2332858417749220. DOI: 10.1177/2332858417749220

Pantelimon, F.-V., & Bologa, R., & Toma Andrei and Posedaru, B.-S. (2021). The evolution of AI-driven educational systems during the COVID-19 pandemic. *Sustainability*, *13*(23), 13501.

Pareja, F., Carrasco, J., & Aquino, M. (2024). Systematic review of the evolution of virtual assistants: from the first chatbots to conversational AI. Micaela Journal. 5(1), 33-39. Website: https://www.researchgate.net/publication/385410081_Revision_sistematica_de_la_evolucion_de_los_asistentes_virtuales_desde_los_primeros_Chatbots_hasta_la_IA_conversacionalSystematic_review_of_the_evolution_of_virtual_assistants_from_the_first_Chatbots_

Patiño, D., Iñiguez, F., Nivela, M., Ruíz, A., Otero, O., Game, K., & Vinueza, G. (2022). Machine Learning Models based in Supervised Learning for the Detection of Diabetes Mellitus in the City of Guayaquil. 2nd LACCEI International Multi-conference on Entrepreneurship, Innovation and Regional Development. 5(7). doi: http://dx.doi.org/DOI: 10.18687/LEIRD2022.1.1.208

Pearson, V., Lister, K., McPherson, E., Gallen, A.-M., Davies, G., Colwell, C., Bradshaw, K., Braithwaite, N., & Collins, T. (2019). Embedding and sustaining inclusive practice to support disabled students in online and blended learning. *Journal of Interactive Media in Education*, *2019*(1).

Pendy, B. (2023). Artificial Intelligence: The future of education. Jurnal Indonesia Sosial Sains, 2(11).

Pervaiz, M., Jalal, A., & Kim, K. (2021). Hybrid algorithm for multi-people counting and tracking for smart surveillance. In *2021 International Bhurban Conference on Applied Sciences and Technologies (IBCAST)* (pp. 757–763). IEEE. https://doi.org/DOI: 10.1109/IBCAST51254.2021.9393279

Pettersson, F. (2018). On the issues of digital competence in educational contexts—A review of literature. *Education and Information Technologies*, *23*(3), 1005–1021. DOI: 10.1007/s10639-017-9649-3

Phakamach, P., Senarith, P., & Wachirawongpaisarn, S. (2022). The metaverse in education: The future of immersive teaching & learning. *RICE Journal of Creative Entrepreneurship and Management*, *3*(2), 75–88.

Pieh, C., Budimir, S., Delgadillo, J., Barkham, M., Fontaine, J. R. J., & Probst, T. (2021). Mental health during COVID-19 lockdown in the United Kingdom. *Psychosomatic Medicine*, *83*(4), 328–337. DOI: 10.1097/PSY.0000000000000871 PMID: 33009276

Porras, J. M., Lara, J. A., Romero, C., & Ventura, S. (2023). A case-study comparison of machine learning approaches for predicting student's dropout from multiple online educational entities. *Algorithms*, *16*(12), 554.

Pramukawati, A., Akhidah, A. N., & Wahyuni, E. S. (2024). Education transformation in elementary school: utilization of artificial intelligence-based learning media in the digital era. 1(1), 255–262. https://doi.org/DOI: 10.31316/icasse.v1i1.6915

Prinsloo, P., & Slade, S. (2017). Ethics and learning analytics: Charting the (un) charted. In Lang, C., Siemens, G., Wise, A. F., and Gaevic, D., editors, The Handbook of Learning Analytics, pages 49–57. Society for Learning Analytics Research (SoLAR), Alberta, Canada, 1 edition. https://www.solaresearch.org/publications/hla-17/hla17-chapter4/

Qian, L., Zheng, Y., Li, L., Ma, Y., Zhou, C., & Zhang, D. (2022). A new method of inland water ship trajectory prediction based on long short-term memory network optimized by genetic algorithm. *Applied Sciences (Basel, Switzerland)*, *12*(8), 4073. Advance online publication. DOI: 10.3390/app12084073

Qiu, S., Zhao, H., Jiang, N., Wang, Z., Liu, L., An, Y., & Fortino, G. (2022). Multi-sensor information fusion based on machine learning for real applications in human activity recognition: State-of-the-art and research challenges. *Information Fusion*, *80*, 241–265. DOI: 10.1016/j.inffus.2021.11.006

Qiwen, Z., & Yongming, T. (2017). Design of an augmented reality teaching system for FPGA experimental instruction. In *2017 IEEE 6th International Conference on Teaching, Assessment, and Learning for Engineering (TALE)* (pp. 35–38). IEEE. https://doi.org/DOI: 10.1109/TALE.2017.8252300

Quaid, M. A. K., & Jalal, A. (2020). Wearable sensors based human behavioral pattern recognition using statistical features and reweighted genetic algorithm. *Multimedia Tools and Applications*, *79*(9–10), 6061–6083. DOI: 10.1007/s11042-019-08336-3

Qudrat-Ullah, H. (2025). Designing AI-driven Curriculum and Assessment. In *Empowering Educational Leaders Using Analytics, AI, and Systems Thinking*. IGI Global Scientific Publishing., DOI: 10.4018/979-8-3693-7190-9.ch012

Rafique, A., Ahmad, J., & Kim, K. (2021). Automated sustainable multi-object segmentation and recognition via modified sampling consensus and kernel sliding perceptron. *Symmetry*, *13*(10), 1928. Advance online publication. DOI: 10.3390/sym13101928

Raghav, K., Van Wijk, A., Abdullah, F., Islam, M. N., Bernatchez, M., & De Jongh, A. (2016). Efficacy of virtual reality exposure therapy for treatment of dental phobia: A randomized control trial. *BMC Oral Health*, *16*(1), 1–11. DOI: 10.1186/s12903-016-0186-z PMID: 26920573

Rahman, M. M., Watanobe, Y., & Nakamura, K. (2020a). A neural network based intelligent support model for program code completion. *Scientific Programming*, *2020*, 1–18.

Rahman, M. M., Watanobe, Y., & Nakamura, K. (2020b). Source code assessment and classification based on estimated error probability using attentive LSTM language model and its application in programming education. *Applied Sciences (Basel, Switzerland)*, *10*(8), 2973.

Rahman, M. M., Watanobe, Y., & Nakamura, K. (2021). A bidirectional LSTM language model for code evaluation and repair. *Symmetry*, *13*(2), 247.

Raji, I. D., Smart, A., White, R. N., Mitchell, M., Gebru, T., Hutchinson, B., & Barnes, P. (2020). Closing the AI accountability gap: Defining an end-to-end framework for internal algorithmic auditing. *Proceedings of the 2020 Conference on Fairness, Accountability, and Transparency*, 33–44. https://doi.org/DOI: 10.1145/3351095.3372873

Rakshit, S. M., Banerjee, S., Hempel, M., & Sharif, H. (2017). Fusion of VR and teleoperation for innovative near-presence laboratory experience in engineering education. In *2017 IEEE International Conference on Electro Information Technology (EIT)* (pp. 376–381). IEEE. https://doi.org/DOI: 10.1109/EIT.2017.8053390

Ramírez-Ortiz, J., Castro-Quintero, D., Lerma-Córdoba, C., Yela-Ceballos, F., & Escobar-Córdoba, F. (2020). Mental health consequences of the COVID-19 pandemic associated with social isolation. *Colombian Journal of Anesthesiology*, *48*(4), e930. DOI: 10.1097/CJ9.0000000000000150

Rao, T. V. N., Stephen, M., Manoj, E., & Sangers, B. (2025). Exploring Bias and Fairness in Machine Learning Algorithms. Advances in Computational Intelligence and Robotics Book Series, 369–398. https://doi.org/DOI: 10.4018/979-8-3693-5231-1.ch014

Redecker, C. (2017). *European Framework for the Digital Competence of Educators: DigCompEdu*. Publications Office of the European Union.

Regional Network for Inclusive Education. (RREI, 2019). The Right to Inclusive Education in Latin America. https://rededucacioninclusiva.org/wp-content/uploads/2020/07/El-derecho-a-la-educaci%C3%B3n-inclusiva-en-Am%C3%A9rica-Latina-1.pdf

Reich, J., Buttimer, C. J., Fang, A., Hillaire, G., Hirsch, K., Larke, L. R., & Slama, R. (2020, April 2). Remote Learning Guidance From State Education Agencies During the COVID-19 Pandemic: A First Look. https://doi.org/DOI: 10.35542/osf.io/437e2

Riquelme, C., & Pereira, M. (2024). Artificial intelligence as a tool for organizing professional and personal activities. Scientific journal in social sciences. 6, e601502. Website: https://www.redalyc.org/journal/7497/749780131042/749780131042.pdf

Rodríguez, D. (2023). Data Analysis and Machine Learning. University of Salamanca. Website:https://gredos.usal.es/bitstream/handle/10366/157350/TFG%20Damia%CC%81n%20Rodri%CC%81guez%20Go%CC%81mez.pdf?sequence=1&isAllowed=y

Rodríguez-Rey, R., Garrido-Hernansaiz, H., & Collado, S. (2020). Psychological impact and associated factors during the initial stage of the coronavirus (COVID-19) pandemic among the general population in Spain. *Frontiers in Psychology*, *11*, 1540. DOI: 10.3389/fpsyg.2020.01540 PMID: 32655463

Rojo, C., Rojo, C., & Rojo, B. (2024). Application of Artificial Intelligence to Address Global Climate Change. Journal of Law & Citizen Opinion. 15(1), 165-192. Website: https://iip.congresosinaloa.gob.mx/Rev_IIP/rev/015/007.pdf

Roldán, T. (2025). Artificial intelligence will revolutionize education (for the better). El País. https://elpais.com/opinion/2025-02-07/la-inteligencia-artificial-revolucionara-la-educacion-para-bien.html

Roll, I., & Wylie, R. (2016). Evolution and Revolution in Artificial Intelligence in Education. *International Journal of Artificial Intelligence in Education*, *26*(2), 582–599. DOI: 10.1007/s40593-016-0110-3

Romero, C., & Ventura, S. (2020). Educational data mining and learning analytics: An updated survey. *Wiley Interdisciplinary Reviews. Data Mining and Knowledge Discovery*, *10*(3), e1355. DOI: 10.1002/widm.1355

Rosenblatt, F. (1958). The perceptron: A probabilistic model for information storage and organization in the brain. *Psychological Review*, *65*(6), 386–408. DOI: 10.1037/h0042519 PMID: 13602029

Ruiz, E., Hernández, J., & Palma, R. (2016). Expert system as a support tool for learning Calculus topics. Calculus and its teaching. 7(1), 63-78. Website: https://recacym.org/index.php/recacym/article/view/97

Russell, S. J., & Norvig, P. (2021). Artificial Intelligence: A Modern Approach (4.ª ed.). Pearson.

Russell, S., & Norvig, P. (2020). *Artificial Intelligence: A Modern Approach* (4th ed.). Pearson.

Saddam, H. M., & Hasan, G. A. (2024). The Best of Way of using AI Technology in Designing Technical Education Curriculum in Meeting Future Industry Demands. *Smart Way.*, *26*, 1403–1406. DOI: 10.1109/icacite60783.2024.10617225

Safrina, M. M., Zahira, N. Z., & Siregar, O. (2023). Improving Students' English Vocabulary Using Duolingo: A Game-Based Learning Method. Recuperado de https://www.researchgate.net/publication/386535215_IMPROVING_STUDENTS'_ENGLISH_VOCABULARY_USING_DUOLINGO_A_GAME_-_BASED_LEARNING_METHOD

Sanchez-Herrera, R., Mejías, A., Márquez, M. A., & Andújar, J. M. (2019). The remote access to laboratories: A fully open integrated system. *IFAC-PapersOnLine*, *52*(9), 121–126. DOI: 10.1016/j.ifacol.2019.08.135

Sánchez, J., & Castillo, G. (2022). Algorithms and their impact on agriculture: Process automation. *Scientific Journal of Systems and Informatics.*, *2*(2), e386. DOI: 10.51252/rcsi.v2i2.386

Sánchez, L. (2022). Artificial intelligence and computer vision applied to education. *Odigos Magazine.*, *3*(2). Advance online publication. DOI: 10.35290/ro.v3n2.2022.587

Sandoval, L. (2018). Machine learning algorithms for data analysis and prediction. Science and Culture of El Salvador. Technological Journal. 11(1), 36-40. Website: https://core.ac.uk/reader/162564840

Scavarelli, A., Arya, A., & Teather, R. J. (2021). Virtual reality and augmented reality in social learning spaces: A literature review. *Virtual Reality (Waltham Cross)*, *25*(1), 257–277. DOI: 10.1007/s10055-020-00460-7

Schiff, D. (2021). Out of the laboratory and into the classroom: The future of artificial intelligence in education. *AI & Society*, *36*, 331–348. DOI: 10.1007/s00146-020-01033-8 PMID: 32836908

Schmidhuber, J. (2015). Deep learning in neural networks: An overview. *Neural Networks*, *61*, 85–117. DOI: 10.1016/j.neunet.2014.09.003 PMID: 25462637

Schmidhuber, J. (2022). Machine learning in the age of big data. *Journal of Artificial Intelligence Research*, *74*, 697–745. DOI: 10.1613/jair.1.12962

Scholes, V. (2016). The ethics of using learning analytics to categorize students on risk. *Educational Technology Research and Development*, *64*, 939–955. DOI: 10.1007/s11423-016-9458-1

SEB. (2019). Educational Model: New Mexican School. Subsecretariat of Basic Education. https://bibliospd.files.wordpress.com/2019/05/modeloeducativonuevarfedumeep.pdf

Segarra-Faggioni, V., Sylvie, R., & Farach, J. (2023). *Topic Modelling for Automatically Identification of Relevant Concepts Discussed in Academic Documents*. Springer International Publishing., DOI: 10.1007/978-3-031-33261-6_8

Selwyn, N. (2019). Should robots replace teachers?: AI and the Future of Education. In research.monash.edu. Polity Press. https://research.monash.edu/en/publications/should-robots-replace-teachers-ai-and-the-future-of-education

SEMS. (2019). The New Mexican School: Principles and Pedagogical Guidelines. Subsecretariat of Upper Secondary Education of the SEP. https://dfa.edomex.gob.mx/sites/dfa.edomex.gob.mx/files/files/NEM%20principios%20y%20orientacio%C3%ADn%20pedago%C3%ADgica.pdf

Sengupta, S., & Das, A. K. (2023). Automated Mapping of Course Outcomes to Program Outcomes using Natural Language Processing and Machine Learning. 44–48. DOI: 10.1109/aspcon59071.2023.10396272

SEP. (2019). Towards a New Mexican School. Secretariat of Public Education. https://educacionbasica.sep.gob.mx/multimedia/RSC/BASICA/Documento/201908/201908-RSC-m93QNnsBgD-NEM020819.pdf

SEP. (2020). National Education Agreement, National Inclusive Education Strategy. https://cdnsnte1.s3.us-west-1.amazonaws.com/wp-content/uploads/2020/04/11073434/ENEI.pdf

SEP. (2023). *Evaluación diagnóstica automatizada en educación básica: Informe técnico*. Secretaría de Educación Pública del Estado de Jalisco.

SEP. (2023). Implementación de herramientas digitales para diagnóstico y planeación educativa en escuelas de educación básica. Secretaría de Educación Pública, México. https://www.sep.gob.mx

Sevenri, F. M., Prattichizzo, D., Casarosa, E., Barbagli, F., Ferretti, C., Altomare, A., Vicino, A., & Petraglia, F. (2005). Virtual fetal touch through a haptic interface decreases maternal anxiety and salivary cortisol. *Journal of the Society for Gynecologic Investigation*, *12*(1), 37–40. DOI: 10.1016/j.jsgi.2004.07.006 PMID: 15629669

Shaik, T., Tao, X., Li, Y., Dann, C., McDonald, J., Redmond, P., & Galligan, L. (2022). A review of the trends and challenges in adopting natural language processing methods for education feedback analysis. *IEEE Access : Practical Innovations, Open Solutions*, *10*, 56720–56739.

Sher, L. (2020). The impact of the COVID-19 pandemic on suicide rates. *QJM: An International Journal of Medicine*, *113*(10), 707–712. DOI: 10.1093/qjmed/hcaa202 PMID: 32539153

Shorten, C., Khoshgoftaar, T. M., & Furht, B. (2021). Deep learning applications for COVID-19. *Journal of Big Data*, *8*, 18. DOI: 10.1186/s40537-020-00392-9 PMID: 33457181

Shortliffe, E.H. (1976). *Computer-based medical consultations: MYCIN*. Elsevier.

Shute, V. J., & Zapata-Rivera, D. (2012). Adaptive learning systems: From theory to practice. *Educational Psychologist*, *47*(4), 195–206.

Sidorkin, A. M., & Hypothesis, L. E. (2025). Generative Ai as a Permanent Scaffold in Higher Education. Available at *SSRN*: https://ssrn.com/abstract=5230565 or http://dx.doi.org/DOI: 10.2139/ssrn.5230565

Siemens, G. (2013). Learning Analytics: The Emergence of a Discipline. *The American Behavioral Scientist*, *57*(10), 1380–1400.

Siemens, G. (2013). Learning analytics: The emergence of a discipline. *The American Behavioral Scientist*, *57*(10), 1380–1400. DOI: 10.1177/0002764213498851

Silver, D., Huang, A., Maddison, C. J., Guez, A., Sifre, L., van den Driessche, G., Schrittwieser, J., Antonoglou, I., Panneershelvam, V., Lanctot, M., Dieleman, S., Grewe, D., Nham, J., Kalchbrenner, N., Sutskever, I., Lillicrap, T., Leach, M., Kavukcuoglu, K., Graepel, T., & Hassabis, D. (2016). Mastering the game of Go with deep neural networks and tree search. *Nature*, *529*(7587), 484–489. DOI: 10.1038/nature16961 PMID: 26819042

Singha, S., & Singha, R. (2024). *Revolutionizing Content Creation and Curriculum Development Through Generative AI*. IGI Global., DOI: 10.4018/979-8-3693-1351-0.ch013

Skalicky, S. E., & Kong, G. Y. (2019). Novel means of clinical visual function testing among glaucoma patients, including virtual reality. *Journal of Current Glaucoma Practice*, *13*(3), 83–91. DOI: 10.5005/jp-journals-10028-1271 PMID: 32431476

Skalidis, I., Müller, O., & Fournier, S. (2022). The metaverse in cardiovascular medicine: Applications, challenges and the role of non-fungible tokens. *The Canadian Journal of Cardiology*, *38*(9), 1467–1468. DOI: 10.1016/j.cjca.2022.05.006 PMID: 35430196

Slade, J. J., Byers, S. M., Becker-Blease, K. A., & Gurung, R. A. R. (2025). Navigating the new frontier: Recommendations to address the crisis and potential of AI in the classroom. *Teaching of Psychology*, *52*(3), 254–261.

Slade, J. J., Hyk, A., & Gurung, R. A. R. (2024). Transforming learning: Assessing the efficacy of a Retrieval-Augmented Generation system as a tutor for introductory psychology. *Proceedings of the Human Factors and Ergonomics Society Annual Meeting*, *68*(1), 1827–1830.

Slade, S., & Prinsloo, P. (2013). Learning analytics: Ethical issues and dilemmas. *The American Behavioral Scientist*, *57*(10), 1510–1529. DOI: 10.1177/0002764213479366

Souza, Érika M. A. de, Fabri, E. S., Araújo, W. dos R. M., Souza, W. C. de, Resende, S. I. de M., & Diniz, H. A. G. (2024). Challenges and Opportunities of Artificial Intelligence in Public Education: A Case Study in Barão Dos Cocais – MG. Revista De Gestão Social E Ambiental, 18(10), e09522. https://doi.org/DOI: 10.24857/rgsa.v18n10-326

Sriadhi, S., Hamid, A., & Restu, R. (2022). Web-based virtual laboratory development for basic practicums in science and technology. *TEM Journal*, 11(1), 396–402. https://doi.org/DOI: 10.18421/TEM111-50

Sridhar, A., Shiliang, Z., Woodson, R., & Kwan, L. (2020). Nonpharmacological anxiety reduction with immersive virtual reality for first-trimester dilation and curettage: A pilot study. *The European Journal of Contraception & Reproductive Health Care*, *25*(6), 480–483. DOI: 10.1080/13625187.2020.1833188 PMID: 33140989

Stalidis, G., Karaveli, I., Diamantaras, K., Delianidi, M., Christantonis, K., Tektonidis, D., Katsalis, A., & Salampasis, M. (2023). Recommendation Systems for e-Shopping: Review of Techniques for Retail and Sustainable Marketing. *Sustainability*, *15*(23), 16151. DOI: 10.3390/su152316151

Striegel, M., Erasmus, J., & Jain, P. (2021). Evaluating augmented reality for wireless network security education. In *2021 IEEE Frontiers in Education Conference (FIE)* (pp. 1–9). IEEE. https://doi.org/DOI: 10.1109/FIE49875.2021.9637216

Sulaymanova, S., Boboyeva, Z., & Soliyev, O. (2024). The Integration of Artificial Intelligence towards Interactive Based Higher Education System Design. 514–518. DOI: 10.1109/icacite60783.2024.10617254

Sun, J. C.-Y., Ye, S. L., Yu, S. J., & Chiu, T. K. (2022). Effects of wearable hybrid AR/VR learning material on high school students' situational interest, engagement, and learning performance: The case of a physics laboratory learning environment. *Journal of Science Education and Technology*, *32*(1), 1–12. DOI: 10.1007/s10956-022-09996-w

Sun, L., Sun, Z., Wu, L., Zhu, Z., Zhang, F., Shang, Z., Jia, Y., Gu, J., Zhou, Y., Wang, Y., Liu, N., & Liu, W. (2021). Prevalence and risk factors for acute posttraumatic stress disorder during the COVID-19 outbreak. *Journal of Affective Disorders*, *283*, 123–129. DOI: 10.1016/j.jad.2021.01.050 PMID: 33548905

Sun, Z., Xu, Y., Liu, Y., He, W., Kong, L., Wu, F., Jiang, Y., & Cui, L. (2025). A Survey on Federated Recommendation Systems. *IEEE Transactions on Neural Networks and Learning Systems*, *36*(1), 6–20. DOI: 10.1109/TNNLS.2024.3354924 PMID: 38324430

Suyal, M., & Goyal, M. (2022). A Review on Analysis of K-Nearest Neighbor-Classification Machine Learning Algorithms based onSupervised Learning. *International Journal of Engineering Trends and Technology*, *70*(7), 43–48. DOI: 10.14445/22315381/IJETT-V70I7P205

Tang, K. H. D. (2024). Implications of artificial Intelligence for teaching and learning. *Acta Pedagogia Asia*, *3*(2), 65–79.

Tapia, S. (2023). Artificial Intelligence from the Perspective of the New Mexican School. Essay in the Coffee, Arts, and Letters Collection. Digital Magazine of the Latin American Institute of Educational Communication. https://revista.ilce.edu.mx/index.php/cultura-r3/174-ensayo/390-la-inteligencia-artificial-desde-la-nem

Taye, G., Sharma, S., Shah, P., & Nuriye, Y. G. (2023). Exploring the Role of Artificial Intelligence in Class Scheduling and Management: A Comprehensive. *Survey Review*, •••, 1–11. DOI: 10.1109/cset58993.2023.10346898

Tegmark, M. (2017). *Life 3.0: Being Human in the Age of Artificial Intelligence*. Knopf.

Tenés, E. (2023). Impact of Artificial Intelligence on Business. Bachelor's Thesis in Business Administration and Management. Polytechnic University of Madrid. Website: https://oa.upm.es/75532/1/TFG_EDUARDO_TENES_TRILLO_2.pdf

Thorat, B., P., M. Goudar, R., & Barve, S. (2015). Survey on Collaborative Filtering, Content-based Filtering and Hybrid Recommendation System. *International Journal of Computer Applications*, *110*(4), 31–36. DOI: 10.5120/19308-0760

Tiwari, R. (2023). Ethical And Societal Implications of AI and Machine Learning. *Indian Scientific Journal Of Research In Engineering And Management, 07*(01). Advance online publication. DOI: 10.55041/ijsrem17519

Tokarev, A., Skobelin, I., Tolstov, M., Tsyganov, A., & Pak, M. (2021). Development of VR educational instruments for school preprofessional education in a research university. *Procedia Computer Science, 190*, 750–754. DOI: 10.1016/j.procs.2021.06.087

Touretzky, D., Gardner-McCune, C., Martin, F., & Seehorn, D. (2019). Envisioning AI for K-12: What Should Every Child Know about AI? *Proceedings of the AAAI Conference on Artificial Intelligence, 33*(01), 9795–9799. DOI: 10.1609/aaai.v33i01.33019795

Tran, M., Balasooriya, C., & Semmler, C.. (2025). Generative artificial intelligence: The 'more knowledgeable other' in a social constructivist framework of medical education. *npj. Digital Medicine, 8*, 430. DOI: 10.1038/s41746-025-01823-8 PMID: 40646156

Trasviña, R., Ruiz, J., & Rojas, E. (2025). Machine Learning Applied to Industrial Processes. *Science & Technology Magazine., 46*(1), 21–28. DOI: 10.47189/rcct.v25i46.768

Turing, A. M. (1950). Computing Machinery and Intelligence. *Mind, 49*, 433–460.

Tyler, R. W. (1949). Basic principles of curriculum and instruction. University of Chicago Press. Available online: https://archive.org/details/basicprincipleso00tyle (accessed on 22 June 2025).

Tzur Bitan, D., Grossman-Giron, A., Bloch, Y., Mayer, Y., Shiffman, N., & Mendlovic, S. (2020). Fear of COVID-19 scale: Psychometric characteristics, reliability, and validity in the Israeli population. *Psychiatry Research, 289*, 113100. DOI: 10.1016/j.psychres.2020.113100 PMID: 32425276

UNESCO. (2019). Artificial intelligence in education: Challenges and opportunities for sustainable development (Working Papers on Education Policy No. 7). United Nations Educational, Scientific and Cultural Organization. https://unesdoc.unesco.org/ark:/48223/pf0000366994

UNESCO. (2021). AI and education: Guidance for policy-makers. https://unesdoc.unesco.org/ark:/48223/pf0000376709

UNESCO. (2021). AI and Education: Guidance for Policy-makers. UNESCO Publishing. https://unesdoc.unesco.org/ark:/48223/pf0000376709

UNESCO. (2021). Recommendation on the Ethics of Artificial Intelligence. https://unesdoc.unesco.org/ark:/48223/pf0000381137

UNESCO. (2022). Recommendation on the ethics of artificial intelligence. https://unesdoc.unesco.org/ark:/48223/pf0000381137_spa

UNESCO. (2023). Technology in education: A tool on whose terms?. https://doi.org/DOI: 10.54676/JKLA7966

UNESCO. (2025). Ethics of artificial intelligence. https://www.unesco.org/es/artificial-intelligence/recommendation-ethic

UNESCO. Fengchun M., Wayne, H., Huang R., Zhang H. (2021). AI and Education: Guidance for policy-makers. Paris: United Nations Educational, Scientific and Cultural Organization. DOI: 10.54675/PCSP7350

United Nations Educational, Scientific and Cultural Organization. (2017). A Guide for Ensuring Inclusion and Equity in Education. UNESCO. https://unesdoc.unesco.org/ark:/48223/pf0000259592/PDF/259592spa.pdf.multi

United Nations. (2025). Official Website. Sustainable Development Goals. https://www.un.org/sustainabledevelopment/es/objetivos-de-desarrollo-sostenible/

Valero, N., Vélez, M., Durán, A., & Portillo, M. (2020). COVID-19 coping: Stress, fear, anxiety, and depression? *Enfermería Investiga*, *5*(2), 63–70. DOI: 10.31243/ei.uta.v5i2.1049.2020

Vargas, P. (2024). Predictive Analysis Application for Academic Student Advancement in Secondary Education Institutions. https://doi.org/DOI: 10.69478/jitc2024v6n2a04

Vásquez, I., & Vivas, M. (2024). Detection of emergency situations using the Naive Bayes machine learning model. *Mundo FESC*, *13*(25), 20–40. DOI: 10.61799/2216-0388.1286

Verma, J. P., Patel, B., & Patel, A. (2015). Big Data Analysis: Recommendation System with Hadoop Framework. *2015 IEEE International Conference on Computational Intelligence & Communication Technology.*

Virkus, S. (2013). Information literacy in Europe: Ten years later. In *Communications in Computer and Information Science* (Vol. 397, pp. 250–257). Springer., DOI: 10.1007/978-3-319-03919-0_33

Von Neumann, J., & Morgenstern, O. (1944). *Theory of Games and Economic Behavior*. Princeton University Press.

Waisberg, E., Ong, J., & Lee, A. G. (2023). Space radiation and the potential for early cataract development. *Eye*, *37*(14), 2952–2954. DOI: 10.1038/s41433-023-02742-2 PMID: 37735211

Wang, K., Singh, R., & Su, Z. (2017). Dynamic neural program embedding for program repair.

Wang, S., Wang, F., Zhu, Z., Wang, J., Tran, T., & Du, Z. (2024). Artificial intelligence in education: A systematic literature review, Expert Systems with Applications, Volume 252, Part A, 124167, ISSN 0957-4174. https://doi.org/DOI: 10.1016/j.eswa.2024.124167

Wang, B., Rau, P.-L. P., & Yuan, T. (2023). Measuring user competence in using artificial intelligence: Validity and reliability of artificial intelligence literacy scale. *Behaviour & Information Technology*, *42*(10), 1324–1337. DOI: 10.1080/0144929X.2022.2072768

Wang, C., & Zhao, H. (2020). The impact of COVID-19 on anxiety in Chinese university students. *Frontiers in Psychology*, *11*, 1168. DOI: 10.3389/fpsyg.2020.01168 PMID: 32574244

Wang, M., Xie, Y., & Tian, Y. (2023). *Research on Hotspots of Educational Application of Natural Language Processing Based on LDA Topic Model.*, DOI: 10.1007/978-3-031-28956-9_25

Wang, P. (2021, August). PseuToPy: Towards a non-English natural programming language. *Proceedings of the 17th ACM Conference on International Education Research.*

Wang, W., Liu, A. X., Shahzad, M., Ling, K., & Lu, S. (2015). Understanding and modeling of WiFi signal based human activity recognition. In *Proceedings of the 21st Annual International Conference on Mobile Computing and Networking* (pp. 65–76). ACM. https://doi.org/DOI: 10.1145/2789168.2790093

Wei, S. (2024). Research on the disruptive transformation and future development of American teaching models in the context of intelligent transformation. Advances in Economics. *Management and Political Sciences*, *72*(1), 201–210.

Weizenbaum, J. (1966). ELIZA - a computer program for the study of natural language communication between man and machine. *Communications of the ACM*, *9*(1), 36–45. DOI: 10.1145/365153.365168

West, D. M. (2021). The future of work: Robots, AI, and automation. Brookings Institution Press. https://www.brookings.edu

Wiggins, G., & McTighe, J. (2005). *Understanding by design* (2nd ed.). Association for Supervision and Curriculum Development.

Williams, H. P. (2021). The role of federal and state policy in addressing early childhood achievement gaps: Parent perceptions and student outcomes related to 21st Century Learning Centers programming in the United States. *International Journal of Child Care and Education Policy*, *15*(1), 16. PMID: 35300028

Williamson, B. (2017). Big Data in Education: The digital future of learning, policy and practice. *Sage (Atlanta, Ga.)*. Advance online publication. DOI: 10.4135/9781529714920

Williamson, B., & Eynon, R. (2020). Historical threads, missing links, and future directions in AI in education. *Learning, Media and Technology*, *45*(3), 223–235. DOI: 10.1080/17439884.2020.1798995

Woodland, M. B., Ong, J., Zaman, N., Hirzallah, M., Waisberg, E., Masalkhi, M., Kamran, S. A., Lee, A. G., & Tavakkoli, A. (2024). Applications of extended reality in spaceflight for human health and performance. *Acta Astronautica*, *214*, 748–756. DOI: 10.1016/j.actaastro.2023.11.013

Woolf, B. P., & Lane, H. C. (2016). AI and education: The future of learning. *IEEE Intelligent Systems*, *31*(6), 6–9.

World Bank. (2021). World Bank Blogs "Limited Digital Access Holds Back Latin America and the Caribbean: How to Solve This Problem?". https://blogs.worldbank.org/es/latinamerica/el-escaso-acceso-digital-frena-america-latina-y-el-caribe-como-solucionar-este

World Bank. (2022). Digital Transformation of Education Systems: Lessons from COVID-19. Washington, DC: World Bank Publications. https://www.worldbank.org

World Bank. (2022). Reimagining digital education: Closing the digital divide. https://www.worldbank.org

World Economic Forum. (2024). China's AI revolution: How mid-sized businesses are scaling impact. Recuperado de https://www.weforum.org/stories/2024/06/chinas-ai-revolution-how-mid-sized-businesses-are-scaling-impact

Xiao, Z., Li, H., Jiang, H., Li, Y., Alazab, M., Zhu, Y., & Dustdar, S. (2023). Predicting urban region heat via learning arrive-stay-leave behaviors of private cars. *IEEE Transactions on Intelligent Transportation Systems*, *24*(10), 10843–10856. DOI: 10.1109/TITS.2023.3276704

Xiong, Z., Liu, Q., & Huang, X. (2022). The influence of digital educational games on preschool children's creative thinking. *Computers & Education, 189*, 104578. Advance online publication. DOI: 10.1016/j.compedu.2022.104578

Xu, Q. (2024). Action research plan: The impact of the use of Artificial Intelligence in education on the cognitive abilities of university students. In *Research Square*.

Ye, G., Tang, Z., Wang, H., Fang, D., Fang, J., Huang, S., & Wang, Z. (2020, September). Deep program structure modeling through multi-relational graph-based learning. *Proceedings of the ACM International Conference on Parallel and Compilation Techniques*.

Yu, B., Mao, W., Lv, Y., Zhang, C., & Xie, Y. (2022). A survey on federated learning in data mining. *Wiley Interdisciplinary Reviews. Data Mining and Knowledge Discovery, 12*(1).

Yu, L., & Yu, Z. (2023). Qualitative and quantitative analyses of artificial intelligence ethics in education using VOSviewer and CitNetExplorer. *Frontiers in Psychology, 14*, 1061778. DOI: 10.3389/fpsyg.2023.1061778 PMID: 36968737

Yüzüak, Y., & Yiğit, H. (2023). Augmented reality application in engineering education: N-type MOSFET. *International Journal of Electrical Engineering Education, 60*(3), 245–257. DOI: 10.1177/0020720920954150

Zambrano, J., & Abad, W. (2024). Importance of using GPT technology applications in the educational and business sectors of the Manabí province. *Journal of Technology & Innovation, 3*(1), 23–34. DOI: 10.47230/Journal.TechInnovation.v3.n1.2024.23-34

Zawacki-Richter, O., Marín, V. I., Bond, M., & Gouverneur, F. (2019). Systematic review of research on artificial intelligence applications in higher education – where are the educators? *International Journal of Educational Technology in Higher Education, 16*(1), 1–27. DOI: 10.1186/s41239-019-0171-0

Zhang, J., Ye, G., Tu, Z., Qin, Y., Qin, Q., Zhang, J., & Liu, J. (2022). A spatial attentive and temporal dilated (SATD) GCN for skeleton-based action recognition. *CAAI Transactions on Intelligence Technology, 7*(1), 46–55. DOI: 10.1049/cit2.12064

Zhao, Z.-D., & Shang, M.-S. (2010). User-Based Collaborative-Filtering Recommendation Algorithms on Hadoop. *2010 Third International Conference on Knowledge Discovery and Data Mining*, 478–481. https://doi.org/DOI: 10.1109/WKDD.2010.54

Zizza, C., Starr, A., Hudson, D., Nuguri, S. S., Calyam, P., & He, Z. (2018). Towards a social virtual reality learning environment in high fidelity. In *2018 15th IEEE Annual Consumer Communications & Networking Conference (CCNC)* (pp. 1–4). IEEE. https://doi.org/DOI: 10.1109/CCNC.2018.8319280

About the Contributors

P. Deekshitha is pursuing 3rd year (Internet of things) in sreenidhi institute of science and technology.

Krishnakumari L. is an Assistant Professor at Ramco Institute of technology, Rajapalayam, Tamilanadu, India.

Zokir Mamadiyarov is a professor in the Department of Finance and Tourism at Termez University of Economics and Service, Termez, Uzbekistan.

Ravikumar R. Natarajan is an experienced academician with over 12+ years of teaching and research expertise across institutions in India, the UAE, and the Maldives. He currently serves as an Assistant Professor at Marwadi University, Rajkot, specializing in Machine Learning, Recommender Systems, and AI-driven applications in healthcare and security. He holds a Ph.D. in Machine Learning and Recommender Systems from Amity University, Jaipur, a Master of Engineering in CSE from VMRF University, Salem, and a Bachelor of Engineering in CSE from Anna University. He also has a MiniMBA from the Swiss eLearning Institute. Dr. Ravikumar has authored more than 8+ multiple SCIE/Scopus-indexed journal articles, 23+ IEEE conference papers, and co-authored a book on Artificial Intelligence. He has also published 9 patents and contributed 10+ book chapters in emerging domains such as Federated Learning, Blockchain, and Digital Twins for IGI Global, Wiley and Springer publisher. He actively mentors students through initiatives like the Research Activities Club (RAC) and Student Research Internship Training (SRIT), promoting innovation and research culture.

Daniel Robles-Camarillo has conducted research in the field of electronic interfaces and intelligent systems, leading multidisciplinary projects that include: * Smart technologies applied to energy efficiency. * Autonomous navigation for ground vehicles. * Assistive technologies for personal safety. * Automatic classifiers for identifying entomological vectors causing Dengue and Chagas disease. * Biomedical systems for processing and applying biosignals. He is a two-time winner of the “Premio Hidalgo de Ciencia, Tecnología e Innovación” (Hidalgo Prize for Science, Technology, and Innovation) both in the area of Technological Development, in 2019 and 2014. The award was granted by the Government of the State of Hidalgo and CITNOVA. He won the “Premio CANIFARMA” in Technological Development in 2015, an award given by the National Chamber of the Pharmaceutical Industry and CONACYT. He also received the “Premio al Registro de Patentes” (Patent Registration Award) in 2010, granted by the Institute of Science and Technology of DF and the Government of Distrito Federal. He is currently a member of the National Researchers System (SNII), level 1.

Jorge Ruiz-Vanoye is a Professor and Researcher at Universidad Politécnica de Pachuca (UPP), a National Researcher under the Secretaria de Ciencia, Humanidades, Tecnología e Innovación program, and an Adjunct Researcher at the National Laboratory of Autonomous Vehicles and Exoskeletons (LANAVEX). Additionally, he holds the title of Lecturer-level Researcher for the Agency for the Quality of the University System of Catalonia (Generalitat de Catalunya). His research interests include Smart Cities, Smart Water, Smart Education, Smart Government, Smart Healthcare, Smart Farming, Smart Energy, Smart Sports, Smart Food, Smart Tourism, Algorithmic Finance, Algorithmic Portfolio Management, Applications and Theory of Algorithms, Bio-inspired Algorithms, Combinatorial Optimization Problems, Compilers, Computational Intelligence, Computational Complexity Theory, Computational Financial Intelligence, Complexity of Algorithms, Complexity of Instances, Computational Statistics, Computer Networks, Computer Science Security, Cybercrimes, Data Mining, Education, Evolutionary Computation, Heuristic Optimization Techniques in Bioinformatics, Hybrid Evolutionary Algorithms, Hybrid Optimization Algorithms, Machine Learning, Meta-heuristics, Operations Research, Operations Management, Parallel & Distributed Computing, Production Planning and Logistics Optimization, Project Scheduling Problems, Software Engineering, and Transgenic Algorithms.

Aarthi S is a dedicated Assistant Professor in Computer Science with over six years of teaching experience. She is currently pursuing her Ph.D. at Marwadi University, Gujarat, and holds an M.Phil. and MCA from Bharathiar University, Tamil Nadu. Throughout her academic career, Aarthi has specialized in programming languages such as C++, Java, and C, and contributed to research in recommender systems and AI-related data privacy. She has published journal articles, contributed to book chapters, and actively participated in technical workshops. Known for her student mentorship and engagement in academic events, Aarthi remains committed to fostering innovation and excellence in computer science education.

S. P. Santhoshkumar received the Bachelor's Degree in Electronics and Communication Engineering from Anna University, Chennai in 2006, the Master's Degree in Software Engineering from Anna University of Technology, Coimbatore in 2011, and the Philosophy of Doctorate degree in Information and Communication Engineering from Anna University, Chennai in 2024, respectively. He is currently working as an Assistant Professor (SG) at the Department of Computer Science and Engineering, School of Computing, Vel Tech Rangarajan Dr. Sagunthala R&D Institute of Science and Technology, Avadi, Chennai. His research areas include Machine Learning, Cloud Computing, Deep Learning, Software Engineering and Web Development. He has quality of publications to his credit, including Journal Articles, Conference Publications, Patents, Books and Book Chapters. Also, he received best faculty awards in national level.

K Siva Kumar Gowda is an Assistant Professor with the Department of Computer Science and Engineering - IOT, Sreenidhi Institute of Science and Technology, Hyderabad, Telangana, India

Kavitha T is working as a Professor in the Dept. of Computer Engineering. She completed her Ph.D. in the Faculty of Information and Communication Engineering, Anna University Chennai, India in the year 2014. She received her M.E. degree in Systems Engineering and Operations Research from Anna University, Chennai India in the year 2006. B.E. in Electronics and Communication Engineering from Bharathidasan University, India in the year 2000. She has 21+ years of experience in Teaching and Research from Reputed Engineering Colleges. She is Anna University and VTU recognized supervisor for guiding Ph.D. and M.S(by Research) Programme. Under her guidance, a scholar completed a Ph.D. at Anna University. She has received Funds from different agencies like ISTE-SRM, VTU-TEQIP, IE, VTU, AICTE-ISTE, and AICTE to organize FDP, workshops, Training, and conferences. She is also a Mentor for the projects who got funds from VTU and KSCKT.

Venkat T is a Professor with the Department of Computer Science and Engineering, Sreenidhi Institute of Science and Technology, Hyderabad, Telangana, India.

Yadira Toledo Navarro is a professor and researcher at the Universidad Politécnica del Estado de Morelos (UPEMOR), with academic and professional experience in educational technologies, business administration, and innovation in higher education. She holds a Ph.D. in administration and has coordinated several interdisciplinary projects. Dr. Toledo has also served in leadership roles within academic bodies and committees, contributing to the development of institutional programs.

Trejo-Macotela is a Professor and Researcher at Polytechnic University of Pachuca (UPP), a National Researcher under the CONAHCYT program, and an Adjunct Researcher at the National Laboratory of Autonomous Vehicles and Exoskeletons (LANAVEX). Dr. Trejo-Macotela received the PhD. Degree in Electronics from the National Institute of Astrophysics, Optics and Electronics (INAOE), Puebla, Mexico. His main research interests are Integrated Circuit Design, Analog and Digital Design, Embedded Systems, RF Electronics, Telecommunications Systems, Precision Agriculture, Internet of Things, among others.

Víctor Zamudio-García is a research professor, belongs to the National System of Researchers.

Index

A

B

C

D

E

Q

R

S

T

V

www.ingramcontent.com/pod-product-compliance
Lightning Source LLC
LaVergne TN
LVHW061525290926
849162LV00004B/675
* 9 7 9 8 3 3 7 3 0 5 9 8 1 *